Global Legal Insights
Fund Finance

2023, Seventh Edition
Contributing Editors: Wes Misson & Sam Hutchinson
Published by Global Legal Group

GLOBAL LEGAL INSIGHTS – FUND FINANCE
2023, SEVENTH EDITION

Contributing Editors
Wes Misson & Sam Hutchinson, Cadwalader, Wickersham & Taft LLP

Publisher
James Strode

Production Editor
Megan Hylton

Head of Production
Suzie Levy

Chief Media Officer
Fraser Allan

CEO
Jason Byles

We are extremely grateful for all contributions to this edition.
Special thanks are reserved for Wes Misson and Sam Hutchinson for all of their assistance.

Published by Global Legal Group Ltd.
59 Tanner Street, London SE1 3PL, United Kingdom
Tel: +44 207 367 0720 / URL: www.glgroup.co.uk

Copyright © 2023
Global Legal Group Ltd. All rights reserved
No photocopying

ISBN 978-1-83918-240-2
ISSN 2399-1887

This publication is for general information purposes only. It does not purport to provide comprehensive full legal or other advice. Global Legal Group Ltd. and the contributors accept no responsibility for losses that may arise from reliance upon information contained in this publication. This publication is intended to give an indication of legal issues upon which you may need advice. Full legal advice should be taken from a qualified professional when dealing with specific situations. The information contained herein is accurate as of the date of publication.

Printed and bound by TJ Books Limited
Trecerus Industrial Estate, Padstow, Cornwall, PL28 8RW
January 2023

CONTENTS

Introduction	Wes Misson & Sam Hutchinson, *Cadwalader, Wickersham & Taft LLP*	
Expert analysis chapters	*NAV and hybrid fund finance facilities* Leon Stephenson, *Reed Smith LLP*	1
	Collateral damage: What not to overlook in subscription line and management fee line facility diligence Anthony Pirraglia, Peter Beardsley & Richard Facundo, *Loeb & Loeb LLP*	15
	Derivatives at fund level Jonathan Gilmour, Peter Hughes & Joseph Wren, *Travers Smith LLP*	27
	Subscription facilities: Through the Looking Glass and into Wonderland Jan Sysel, Jons Lehmann & Kathryn Cecil, *Fried, Frank, Harris, Shriver & Jacobson LLP*	39
	A fund borrower's guide to NAV and Hybrid Facilities: Considerations for a "bankable" partnership agreement for fund-level leverage beyond the sub line Julia Kohen, Ashley Belton Gold & Jakarri Hamlin, *Simpson Thacher & Bartlett LLP*	50
	Sharpest tool in the shed: A primer on asset-backed leverage facilities Patricia Lynch, Patricia Teixeira & Douglas Hollins, *Ropes & Gray LLP*	58
	Enforcement: Analysis of lender remedies under U.S. law in subscription-secured credit facilities Ellen G. McGinnis & Richard D. Anigian, *Haynes and Boone, LLP*	68
	The rise of Hybrid Facilities and increasing use of capital commitments in NAV Facilities Meyer C. Dworkin & Kwesi Larbi-Siaw, *Davis Polk & Wardwell LLP*	90
	Assessing and mitigating "bad acts" risk in NAV loans Angie Batterson, Brian Foster & Patrick Calves, *Cadwalader, Wickersham & Taft LLP*	96
	Comparing the European, U.S. and Asian fund finance markets Emma Russell & Emily Fuller, *Haynes and Boone, LLP*	104
	Umbrella facilities: Pros and cons for a sponsor Richard Fletcher & Yagmur Yarar, *Macfarlanes LLP*	114
	Side letters: Pitfalls and perils for a financing Thomas Smith, Margaret O'Neill & John W. Rife III, *Debevoise & Plimpton LLP*	124
	Fund finance lending: A practical checklist James Heinicke, David Nelson & Daniel Richards, *Ogier*	134
	Assessing lender risk in fund finance markets Robin Smith, Alistair Russell & Holly Brown, *Carey Olsen Jersey LLP*	146

Expert analysis chapters cont'd	*Fund finance meets securitisation* Richard Day & Julia Tsybina, *Clifford Chance LLP*	158
	Fund finance in Ireland and Luxembourg: A comparative analysis Jad Nader, *Ogier, Luxembourg* Phil Cody, *Arthur Cox LLP, Ireland*	166
	Fund finance facilities: A cradle to grave timeline Bronwen Jones, Kevin-Paul Deveau & Brendan Gallen, *Reed Smith LLP*	178
	Newer liquidity solutions for alternative asset fund managers – increasingly core Jamie Parish, Danny Peel & Katie McMenamin, *Travers Smith LLP*	188
	The rise of ESG and green fund finance Briony Holcombe, Robert Andrews & Lorraine Johnston, *Ashurst LLP*	196
	Robust liquidity solutions for complex Cayman Islands fund structures Agnes Molnar, Richard Mansi & Catharina von Finckenhagen, *Travers Thorp Alberga*	205
	More than a decade of global fund finance transactions Michael Mbayi, *Pinsent Masons Luxembourg*	217
	NAVs meet margin loans: The rise in single asset financings Sherri Snelson & Juliesa Edwards, *White & Case LLP*	224
	Regime change but business as usual – updates to sanctions and restructuring regimes in the Cayman Islands Alexandra Woodcock & Danielle Roman, *Mourant*	235
	VC vs PE: Comparing the venture capital and private equity fund financing markets Cindy Lovering & Corinne Musa, *Cooley LLP*	245
	Subscription facilities: Key considerations for borrowers – a global experience Jean-Louis Frognet, Caroline M. Lee & Eng-Lye Ong, *Dechert LLP*	251
	Innovative rated note structures spur insurance investments in private equity Pierre Maugüé, Ramya Tiller & Christine Gilleland, *Debevoise & Plimpton LLP*	261
	Financing secondary fund acquisitions Ron D. Franklin, Jinyoung Joo & Allison F. Saltstein, *Proskauer*	269

Jurisdiction chapters

Australia	Tom Highnam, Rita Pang & Jialu Xu, *Allens*	278
Bermuda	Matthew Ebbs-Brewer & Arielle DeSilva, *Appleby*	290
British Virgin Islands	Andrew Jowett & Johanna Murphy, *Appleby*	298
Canada	Michael Henriques, Alexandra North & Kenneth D. Kraft, *Dentons Canada LLP*	307
Cayman Islands	Simon Raftopoulos & Georgina Pullinger, *Appleby*	314

England & Wales	Sam Hutchinson & Nathan Parker, *Cadwalader, Wickersham & Taft LLP*	324
France	Philippe Max & Meryll Aloro, *Dentons Europe, AARPI*	331
Guernsey	Jeremy Berchem, *Appleby*	338
Hong Kong	James Ford, Patrick Wong & Charlotte Robins, *Allen & Overy*	346
Ireland	Kevin Lynch, Ian Dillon & Ben Rayner, *Arthur Cox LLP*	359
Italy	Alessandro Fosco Fagotto, Edoardo Galeotti & Valerio Lemma, *Dentons Europe Studio Legale Tributario*	374
Jersey	James Gaudin, Paul Worsnop & Daniel Healy, *Appleby (Jersey) LLP*	384
Luxembourg	Vassiliyan Zanev, Marc Meyers & Maude Royer, *Loyens & Loeff Luxembourg SARL*	389
Mauritius	Malcolm Moller, *Appleby*	400
Netherlands	Gianluca Kreuze, Michaël Maters & Ruben den Hollander, *Loyens & Loeff N.V.*	407
Norway	Snorre Nordmo, Ole Andenæs & Karoline Angell, *Wikborg Rein Advokatfirma AS*	415
Singapore	Jean Woo, Danny Tan & Cara Stevens, *Ashurst LLP*	422
Spain	Jabier Badiola Bergara, *Dentons Europe Abogados, S.L. (Sociedad Unipersonal)*	431
USA	Jan Sysel, Flora Go & Duncan McKay, *Fried, Frank, Harris, Shriver & Jacobson LLP*	439

INTRODUCTION

Fund finance: Past, present and future

And there we stood. Amongst nearly 900 people, all jammed into the circular lobby bar of a South Beach resort. Everyone with a new-found level of energy catching up over cocktails with old friends and networking new relationships that were born over the prior two years – a span that seemed much closer to a decade in many regards. It was a surreal moment. We had been here before, but the world was much different then. COVID took its toll on everyone. It pushed us all to our limits at times and made us adapt both our personal lives and our businesses.

Much like the 2022 conference in Miami felt different (almost like old times), our market felt forever changed. We had been through the Great Recession but life continued much the same with our day-to-day routines. Our market flourished and it was the start of an incredible run of growth that perhaps no finance segment had ever seen over a relatively short span. Certainly not in our lifetime.

The COVID era brought both new challenges and new opportunities. Activity compacted, and some pumped the breaks for a minute while others grew. We all became overworked and even more thankful for our teams and their sacrifice. We became a more appreciative and empathetic bunch. As the months rolled on, new norms developed and the business of fund finance soared to new heights many thought unimaginable in March of 2020.

Today's challenges, on the heels of the pandemic's multiple ups and downs, are different. We are faced with unprecedented inflation, geopolitical risks and regulatory scrutiny – the likes of which our market has never seen (certainly not all at once). Where we go from here will define us for the next decade plus.

The past: Remarkable growth

Fund finance origination volume in the U.S., as of late 2022, was on course to plateau after years of remarkable growth. Exhibit 1 summarizes this expansion using Cadwalader's U.S. representations as lender's counsel as a proxy for the overall market. This leveling off comes in the context of an annual increase of nearly 50% in lender commitments for each of the last three years, 2018–2021.

Exhibit 1: Charting the growth in fund finance

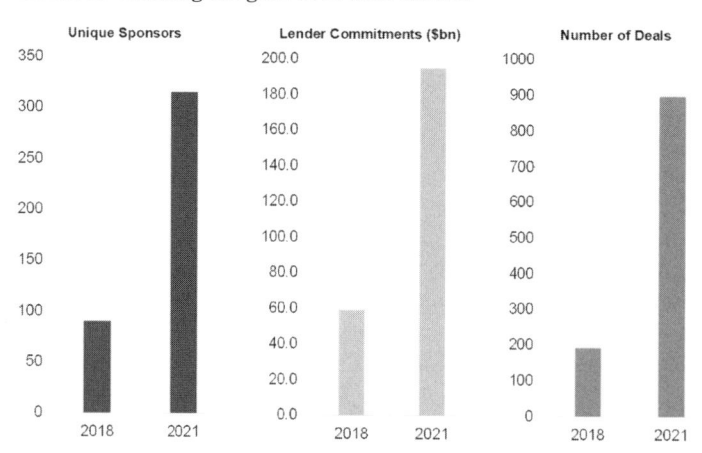

Note: Data limited to Cadwalader advised transactions including new originations plus increase and extension amendments; 2022 origination volume represents an annualized estimate based on data through Q3.
Source: Cadwalader, Wickersham & Taft LLP.

Fund finance growth in recent years can be attributed to a number of factors: rising private market assets under management drove demand for fund financing higher; lender segmentation resulted in products and processes tailored to serve a wide range of funds; bank lenders were positioned to expand credit availability; and low short-term interest rates meant floating-rate credit facilities provided a compelling low cost of capital.

Based on Cadwalader's most recent full-year data, 80 lenders were involved in lending to 315 distinct sponsors in 2021. The number of sponsors represents a more than three-fold increase over the course of three years. More widespread adoption of fund finance generally, and subscription facilities in particular, among funds explains most of the increase in sponsors, since the number of funds raised per year held relatively flat from 2018 to 2021.

Lenders' ability to adapt to the market environment has been key. In 2022, such adaptability came into play in providing financing to some of the largest funds ever raised. Fundraising for the flagship funds of large sponsors proved more resilient during the year than the broader private market. For the fund finance market, that meant the origination of several multi-billion-dollar facilities enlisting a large syndicate of lender groups. The effect was significant enough to lead the average newly originated subscription credit facility size meaningfully higher from prior years.

Exhibit 2: Loans to large funds led the average new facility size higher

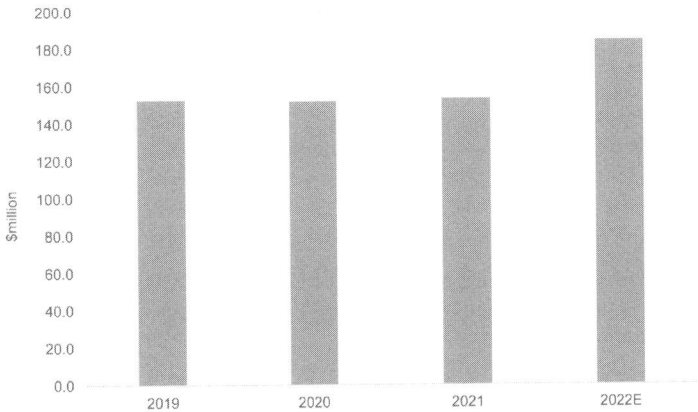

Note: Cadwalader advised transactions including only new originations.
Source: Cadwalader, Wickersham & Taft LLP.

The present: Change is in the air

As is clear from our most recent origination data, 2022 will finish on a changed tone. In the broader market, the Federal Reserve made an about-face from adding to its securities holdings late into the spring to then executing a 4.25% increase in the Fed Funds rate over the course of seven meetings. Credit markets spent much of the year calibrating to the new direction and pace of monetary policy with volatility taking a toll on origination volumes across markets.

Exhibit 3: Fund finance origination growth set to moderate in 2022

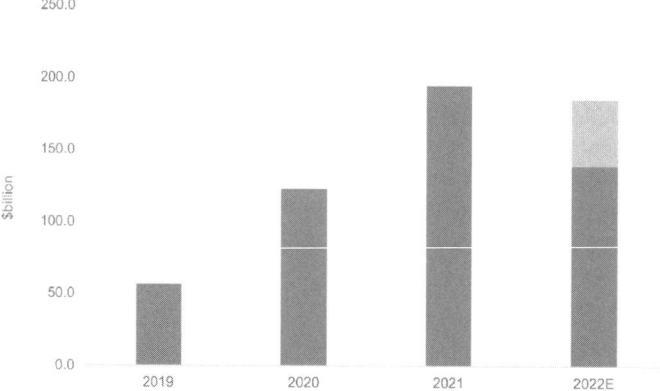

Note: Data limited to Cadwalader advised transactions including new originations plus increase and extension amendments; 2022 origination volume represents an annualized estimate based on data through Q3.
Source: Cadwalader, Wickersham & Taft LLP.

We saw several themes play out in fund finance during the year. For lenders, portfolio growth took a back seat to return on capital measures amid rising forward cost of capital assumptions, with the result showing up in facility pricing. Margins widened and lenders revisited stayed norms for commitment and unused fees. Lenders also became more selective, consistent with credit standards tightening across asset classes. On the fund side, the pace of fundraising slowed, although a pre-existing pipeline will mean year-end totals likely land in line with the five-year average.

The future: A forecast

A transition started in 2022 that is likely to carry over into 2023. While this period may be marked by a moderation in fundraising and fund finance originations, we believe it is a waypoint along the journey to the next chapter for the fund finance market.

During this transition phase, private market fundraising appears likely to slow further as investors work with reduced proceeds from public and private investments to recycle back into private market allocations. Buyout deal exits is one market barometer of capital returns to investors, and the trend here points to a further slowdown. Longer term, however, investor surveys continue to point to sustained demand for alternative assets supported by realized returns and investors' diversification objectives.

For lenders, balance sheet capacity is likely to be more carefully rationed, with a continued focus on all facets of transaction economics. Ancillary revenue streams, deposits, and fee income are likely to continue to weigh heavily in the decision-making process. Facility advance rates could also potentially be throttled lower to limit facility sizes consistent with limited balance sheet capacity.

Exhibit 4: Loans as a share of total bank assets have room to recover

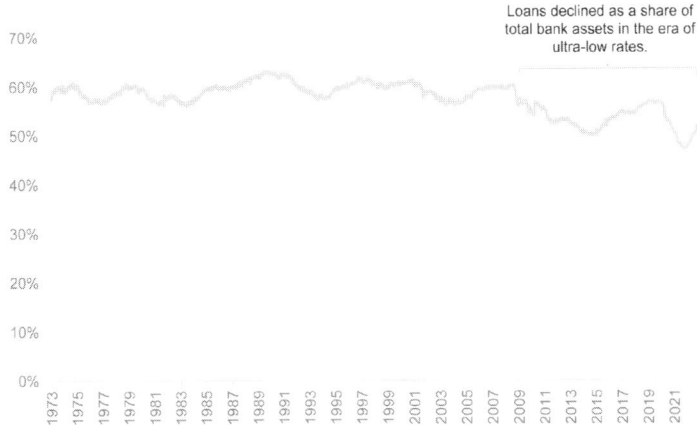

Source: Federal Reserve H.8 Summary of Assets and Liabilities of Commercial Banks.

On the lender side, these trends, while challenging, are not the ultimate destination. Risk processes are likely to remain tighter as performance among investors and among funds diverge and all-in return on capital metrics likely to continue to stay in focus, but we expect the market to adapt. In fact, a number of fund finance lenders are likely to further grow originations meaningfully in 2023.

As shown in Exhibit 4, loans have occupied a diminished share of bank balance sheets in the post-GFC era, and 2021 data indicate that normalization so far is happening primarily through loan growth (as opposed to declining asset balances). Consistent with this, in an October 2022 survey of fund finance group heads at banks, 64% of respondents reported an expectation of growth in fund finance commitments at their institution in 2023.

Longer term, we believe the transition that is already in process will enable the market to consider a wider range of capital sources, including non-bank loan participants along with possible term funded capital markets solutions.

Conclusion

The evolution of this market, and where it is heading despite the noise on the macro-level and new headwinds, is just remarkable. It is a true testament to the pioneers, the new participants and the next generation of the industry's players. A mature market faces challenges and we have never been better poised to face them. The fund finance community has always been committed to the solution. We all enter 2023 with optimism. And it is with this optimism that we are pleased to present the seventh edition of *Global Legal Insights – Fund Finance* (a.k.a. the Pink Book). Cadwalader, Wickersham & Taft LLP is once again honored to serve as the contributing editor of this market-leading legal resource. As with its predecessor editions, this book commences with 27 product- and market-oriented chapters. The context in many cases will take a fresh spin on or deeper dive into material from prior years. We then proudly present 19 jurisdiction-specific update chapters. We have endeavored to provide the reader with a comprehensive global update that is valuable for your daily practice.

We are grateful to all of the esteemed contributors for their market-leading insights. We think this may be the best edition yet. Our final thanks to Global Legal Group Ltd. You all continue to be wonderful partners and great supporters of the industry. Until we meet again in a packed lobby bar at the Fontainebleau, we hope you all enjoy this seventh edition.

Wes Misson & Sam Hutchinson
Cadwalader, Wickersham & Taft LLP

NAV and hybrid fund finance facilities

Leon Stephenson
Reed Smith LLP

Overview

There has been substantial growth in the fund finance market over recent years, with more and more funds seeking subscription line or capital call facilities from lenders.

Capital call or subscription line facilities are debt facilities provided by lenders to funds where the recourse of the lender is to the uncalled investor commitments of the fund. The bank will generally provide a short-term facility to the fund to effectively bridge the commitments of the investors of the fund. Therefore, the bank's credit risk is on the investors of the fund and their obligations to provide monies to the fund when called upon to do so. This requires detailed credit analysis by the bank on the creditworthiness of the investors they are effectively lending against, usually carried out by assigning each investor a rating together with an advance rate against each investor. Many banks have been and are still entering this market.

With the rapid growth of these facilities, there have been substantial pressures on pricing as lenders compete between each other for this business. There continues to be a significant growth in the market for net asset value (NAV) or asset-backed facilities. These are fund finance facilities provided by lenders to the fund, or to a special purpose vehicle (SPV) owned by the fund, that are not secured against the undrawn investor commitments, but rather the underlying cashflow and distributions that flow up from the underlying portfolio investments.

Therefore, lenders under these facilities are "looking down" for recourse against the underlying investments rather than "looking up" to the investor commitments. The credit analysis that is required to be undertaken by the banks for these types of facilities is very different from that needed for subscription line facilities. For pure asset-backed and NAV facilities, the creditworthiness of the investors of the fund is much less important than the value of the underlying assets.

Nevertheless, these asset-backed facilities are still provided to the same fund managers who are also looking for subscription line facilities, and therefore this is an opportunity for lenders to widen the products they currently provide and to deepen the relationships they have with their fund clients. Providing asset-backed facilities can allow lenders to continue to provide liquidity lines to their clients, even when the investment period of a fund has terminated and there are no uncalled capital commitments remaining. Very often, the pricing a lender can obtain for these NAV facilities is higher than for subscription line facilities, so there is a tendency in the market for traditional lenders of subscription line facilities to move into more asset-backed facilities. Furthermore, there are a number of non-bank lenders increasingly focused on this space.

Types of fund utilising NAV and asset-backed fund finance facilities

Introduction

There is a wide range of different funds focusing on different types of investments that may benefit from utilising such facilities. Secondary funds that acquire and hold limited partnership and other equity interests in funds can borrow from banks secured against the limited partnership interests that the secondary fund holds or is about to acquire.

Direct lending funds, and credit funds that acquire and hold loans and other debt instruments, may enter into such facilities and provide security over the benefit of the underlying loan portfolio.

Private equity firms that have a more illiquid portfolio of assets (perhaps only 10–20 investments in the portfolio) may also borrow from lenders, secured against the shares of the various holding companies that hold each investment and/or bank accounts in which distributions of income or sale proceeds of underlying assets are transferred. This provides liquidity to such funds outside the ring fence of the investment itself that may have been provided as collateral for senior debt provided at the portfolio investment level.

There has also been a recent growth in NAV facilities being provided to real estate and infrastructure-focused funds. This usually involves teams at banks, who have traditionally been focused on financing against individual assets, now looking to provide financing against a portfolio of assets. In the real estate finance context, financing would take the form of a loan secured by a mortgage over the property and, in the infrastructure context, this would often be a project finance structure with security against the project cashflows and direct agreements in place at the asset level. If lenders already have a good understanding of the underlying assets, whether infrastructure or real estate, and can get their heads around lending higher up in the fund or corporate structure of the borrower, then there are real opportunities for these teams to provide portfolio-wide NAV financing against multiple real estate or infrastructure assets.

Although very different types of funds may utilise these facilities and for different purposes, the key characteristics of these facilities are that they are generally provided at the fund level or directly below the fund level, and the primary source of repayment will be from the underlying assets. The other difference between these NAV fund financing facilities and mezzanine or other holdco facilities is that the NAV fund finance facilities usually have recourse against the cashflows of all or a multitude of the underlying assets, whereas mezzanine facilities are often only provided to one underlying investment.

The type of security a lender will take will depend on the structure of the relevant fund and the nature of its underlying investments. However, unless a hybrid structure, it is unlikely that the principal security given will be over uncalled capital commitments. It is much more likely to be security that allows the lender to control the underlying assets or distributions paid on such assets.

Secondary funds

For secondary funds, it is important for a bank to ensure that it has direct rights to any distributions that are payable to the secondary fund from the limited partnership interest it holds. It may be commercially and legally difficult to get direct security over these limited partnership interests, so often security is just taken by the lender over the shares of an SPV entity that will be set up to hold all of the limited partnership interests the lender is lending against.

The typical structure would involve the secondary fund first establishing an SPV vehicle. If the limited partnership interests have not yet been acquired by the secondary fund, then this

SPV vehicle would directly acquire the various limited partnership interests. If the limited partnership interests are already held directly by the secondary fund, then the secondary fund will attempt to transfer all of the limited partnership interests to be financed into a new SPV vehicle. The lender will then lend directly to the SPV and take security over the shares of the SPV, and over any bank accounts of the SPV into which distributions from the underlying limited partnership interests are paid. On enforcement, the lender will take control of the SPV and enforce over the SPV's bank accounts so that it will be the sole beneficiary of any distributions that are paid up to the SPV.

Direct lending and credit funds

For direct lending funds and other credit funds, the lenders will usually take security over the benefit of the underlying loan portfolio (not too dissimilar to the security that may be granted to a lender under a collateralised loan obligation (CLO) warehousing facility). The lenders will analyse the underlying loan portfolio of the fund to establish what level of loan-to-value (LTV) ratio it can provide. There will be eligibility criteria that will need to be met for a particular loan to be included in the asset pool that the lender is lending against. The eligibility criteria may require that the underlying loan is senior-secured, not subject to any default, and is provided to an underlying borrower that has a minimum EBITDA located in a particular jurisdiction or geography.

Furthermore, there may be certain borrower concentration limits applied to the collateral assets, so that no group of loans with the same borrower (or affiliate of borrowers) can exceed a certain percentage of the whole portfolio of collateral assets. Often the lender will also want to limit the proportion of underlying borrowers of the loans that are in a particular industry. Some lenders structure these facilities as a loan facility; others as a note purchase facility not too dissimilar from a securitisation structure.

A lender may structure such facilities as a note purchase facility in order to facilitate its ability to sell down a portion of the debt to other noteholders who would like to participate. Certain lenders may not insist on security directly over the loans themselves, but rely on NAV covenants alone and blocked accounts into which the proceeds of such loans are paid. For these facilities, it is important to have strong undertakings on group entities to pay all proceeds into these accounts over which the lender has control. Other lenders will want direct asset security over the loans, which often is provided by way of a general floating charge or single security agreement over all of the assets.

Another important factor for LTV ratio is the diversification of the underlying loan portfolio. Typically, the more diversified the loan portfolio, the more favourable the LTV terms the borrower can expect to apply. Some lenders are able to provide facilities to a direct lending fund or one of its SPVs, secured against a single loan asset. In this instance, from an economic risk perspective, the credit fund is essentially sub-participating the relevant loan to the bank that is providing the fund finance. However, the LTV ratios in these instances are likely to be very low, and may be around the 5–15% range. A deeper due diligence analysis is normally required by the bank when lending against single loans, and the security package may need to be extensive to allow the bank to benefit directly from the security on the underlying loan if there is a default. This may require local security to be granted if there is security for the underlying loan, subject to different governing laws.

Most recently, there has been a significant number of special situation and dislocation credit funds set up that seek to capitalise on the low valuation of loan assets in the market and to provide capital to borrowers who have a more urgent need for it. We predict there will be an important increase in the demand for NAV facilities to these sorts of credit funds as such funds typically have a heavy leveraged strategy.

Private equity funds

The NAV facility to a private equity fund has seen rapid growth during the course of 2020 and 2021. The need for this type of facility was accentuated by the spread of the COVID-19 virus, the various "kickdowns" in different jurisdictions and the consequential increased need of private equity funds for additional liquidity at portfolio level. Furthermore, with less fundraising towards the end of 2022 and private equity funds holding on to assets longer due to investor cautiousness, NAV facilities are starting to provide an extremely useful source of liquidity. There have been a number of larger sponsors who have decided to take out such a facility for their more vintage funds that are heavily invested and have a large portfolio NAV. In these structures, the lenders often take security over the shares in the one or more holding companies of the private equity fund that directly or indirectly own the portfolio investments.

Usually, the lenders providing these facilities to private equity funds may be structurally subordinated to other lenders that have provided finance that is secured directly against the underlying portfolio companies. These facilities generally carry higher risk, as the portfolio of assets is not as diversified as the facilities provided to direct lending and credit funds with diversified and numerous assets. These types of facilities may also be known as "holdco" loans and essentially amount to mezzanine financing, albeit with recourse to cashflows from multiple rather than single investments. Providing financing to holdcos secured against the shares of the holdcos rather than the underlying assets of the portfolio companies means that the lender has less control over the assets of the portfolio, normally resulting in higher pricing of such loans. There is also a trend in the market for these facilities to be provided to an SPV finco of the fund. The basic structure would be a loan to the finco from the lenders and then the finco would on-lend the proceeds into the holding vehicles that sit underneath the fund. The advantage of this structure is that it may avoid issues such as change of control triggers in shareholders' agreements and leveraged finance facility agreements, or avoid the need to seek a regulatory consent in relation to regulated assets. The finco "on-lending" structure allows the lender and the fund to "cherry-pick" which assets the lenders have control over and therefore to only take "controlling" share pledges over holding vehicles where change of control issues do not exist. Another very recent development is for the SPV finco not to lend to a holding vehicle in the equity structure, but rather for such a holding vehicle to issue preference shares to the finco in return for the proceeds of the NAV facility. The lender to the finco would then take security over the preferred shares. This is a clever way of providing the private equity portfolio with capital without any debt actually being incurred by any entity within the private equity group.

With the typical private equity fund existing for a period of 10 years, many funds are set to see most of their life dominated by this market uncertainty. This presents a number of challenges, in particular, finding the right time to sell investments – and get the right price – which has become a real concern for fund managers; and if funds are not selling investments, they need cash available to support them. The fund finance market has evolved over this period to meet this demand.

When a private equity fund makes an investment, it commonly pays for the investment through a combination of borrowing from a lender and deploying its own capital. The pattern then repeats with the fund making its next investment and arranging separate borrowing for that second investment. As the fund continues to make investments, a misalignment of interest begins to occur, as the fund manager is managing the fund's portfolio of investments, but the fund's lenders are each solely focused on the individual investments that they are lending against.

The NAV facility to private equity funds as a financing structure aligns itself with the portfolio of investments the fund has, rather than looking at the investments individually, and in doing so, is able to recognise the NAV of the fund as a whole and allow the fund manager the flexibility to deploy this borrowing where it deems best for the fund. This, amongst other things, neatly resolves any liquidity issues for investments where the lender(s) to that investment may not want to provide more debt, or the cost of doing so is prohibitively expensive.

Currently, use of NAV facilities is in addition to, rather than instead of, the traditional investment-by-investment borrowing funds utilised, and is typically put in place once the fund has acquired most of its investments.

As always, careful consideration needs to be given to the extent to which any private equity fund borrows money, and whether it will ultimately benefit its investors. NAV facilities are deliberately structured so as to ensure benefits to the fund and its investors, through:

- the borrowing always being measured against the NAV of the fund (i.e. the value of the investments after the borrowing incurred on each individual investment has been accounted for);
- lenders only being prepared to lend at a conservative level (e.g. most NAV facilities are set at around 10–20% of the NAV of the fund);
- borrowing under a NAV facility will be caught by any borrowing restrictions imposed on the fund by its investors, so the fund manager cannot arrange borrowing above pre-agreed levels; and
- fund managers often discussing plans to enter into a NAV facility with investors to gauge their appetite for this kind of borrowing.

The last thing a fund manager wants to do is be forced to sell an investment when it would prefer not to. Investors do not want this either. This, combined with the continued market uncertainty, has generated another trend in the private equity market at the same time as NAV facilities: fund secondaries (where a number of investments in a fund's portfolio are grouped together and sold into another fund – a so-called "continuation fund"). Because a NAV facility is set up to look at a portfolio of investments, it is extremely well suited to finance secondaries transactions, and support value creation long term.

The key feature of NAV facilities to private equity funds is that they are flexible: flexible to recognise value where it exists in a fund's portfolio; flexible to allow the fund manager discretion to decide how best to deploy the borrowing; and flexible to enable the fund manager to sell investments at the correct time. Given such flexibility, the potential for use of NAV facilities is huge, and the very clear increase in funds implementing NAV facilities is only set to continue.

Structure and terms

Unlike subscription line and capital call facilities that typically take the form of a revolving credit facility, NAV finance facilities usually take the form of term loan facilities. If the facility is being provided to allow for a certain liquidity event or to bridge a particular exit of one of the investments, then the tenor may be quite short (e.g. six to 18 months). However, if the fund is entering into the facility shortly following fund-close as part of a leverage strategy, the facility will have a longer tenor, perhaps five years or more.

The key covenant in such facilities is the LTV covenant. This is the financial ratio of the amount of the financial indebtedness of the borrower against the NAV of the portfolio that will be securing the facility. For credit funds and secondary funds, LTV ratios range from 10% to as high as 60%, depending on the diversification of the underlying assets. Such facilities may contain an "LTV grid" which allows the borrower to benefit from higher LTV ratios, and therefore a higher facility amount provided by the lender in the event that more assets are placed into the portfolio. Likewise, the interest rate payable on the facility may decrease, the more diversified the portfolio.

The eligibility criteria of the portfolio (i.e. the list of conditions that need to apply to the underlying assets for them to be eligible for the purposes of lending against them) will often be listed in a schedule to the facility agreement. The lender may also require a veto right on the acquisition of the assets, although there is usually strong push-back from the fund on this. The fund will argue that it alone should decide which assets can be purchased and, as long as such assets comply with the eligibility criteria, the fund should be allowed to select which assets will serve as collateral assets. The existence of veto rights will be much more prevalent in NAV facilities to private equity funds where the number and concentration of investments is likely to be much higher than a credit fund. If there were a clear and precise set of eligibility criteria for a financing to a credit fund, the fund would not expect the lender to then have a separate veto right on whether each new asset can be treated as eligible collateral.

These term loans often have cash-sweep and amortisation features, so that all or a portion of any distributions that are paid up to the borrower from the underlying investments go first to repay outstanding utilisations under the facility. The amount of such cash-sweep may vary depending on the LTV that exists at the point in time that such distribution is paid. There may be a specific obligation to sweep all available cash, or the lender may just rely on the LTV covenant compliance, so that a prepayment would only be needed if failure to do so would cause an LTV covenant breach.

The security package is often negotiated quite hard between the lender and the borrower. It is likely that the underlying assets are located in or subject to different governing laws and jurisdictions. The lender will certainly need an overriding security document (often governed by English or New York/Delaware law) that seeks to take security over all of the underlying assets. The lender may then require local security to be granted and local perfection of security to be undertaken. There will be a cost-benefit analysis at the start of the transaction to determine whether a full security package can be provided, and also a discussion about whether there are any contractual or legal restrictions on providing such security.

As discussed previously, for NAV facilities to credit funds, it is quite usual for just one overriding single security document taking security over all of the loan portfolio (notwithstanding different governing laws of the underlying loan agreements) to be entered into. However, if there is a high proportion of the NAV allocated to loans in a particular jurisdiction, it is then worth the borrower and lender discussing whether separate asset security should be taken in that local jurisdiction as well, to ensure valid and locally perfected security.

For facilities provided to secondary funds against their limited partnership interests, taking security over the underlying limited partnership interests usually requires the general partner of the underlying fund to provide its consent. As discussed previously in this chapter, the lender and the borrower may need to devise structures to avoid seeking this consent, or to make it more likely that consent will be given by general partners of the underlying funds. Generally, when seeking consent from general partners for security to be given for NAV facilities to secondary funds, four consents are required:

- consent to transfer the limited partnership interests from the secondary fund (if held directly by the secondary fund) into a wholly owned SPV located under the secondary fund;

- consent to the secondary fund granting security to the lender over the shares/interest it has in the SPV;
- consent to the lender enforcing its security over the shares/interest it holds; and
- consent to the lender selling the shares it owns post-enforcement to a third party.

In our experience, some of these consents, if given by the general partners of the underlying funds, are likely to be conditional on items such as no adverse tax or regulatory consequences to the underlying fund, and also restrictions on the lender's ability to transfer its interest in the underlying fund to one of its competitors.

For facilities provided to direct lending and credit funds, the terms of the underlying loan agreements will need to be diligenced very carefully. The provisions relating to transfers and assignments of the loans (typically entitled "Changes to the Lenders") must be reviewed to see whether the underlying borrower has any consent or consultation rights prior to the fund transferring its loan to the lender on enforcement. In relation to facilities provided to private equity funds, if security has been granted over shares in a holding company that owns the underlying assets, it is important that no change-of-control provisions are triggered in senior facilities agreements or under material contracts entered into by the portfolio companies.

Even if the lender and borrower take the view that there are too many loan documents to be diligenced prior to entering into the facility, we would still strongly recommend that copies of all of the loan documents be made available to the lender prior to the putting in place of the NAV facility. If there is ever a default on the NAV facility in the future, the lender needs to be sure that it has the underlying documents, so that it knows where and how to enforce without breaching terms of the underlying loan agreements.

Furthermore, if the private equity fund does not own 100% of all of the assets but has joint venture arrangements with other third-party equity investors, then it is very important for the lenders to due diligence any joint venture or shareholders' agreements that have been entered into. There may be restrictions on the ability of the joint venture shareholders (i.e. the private equity fund or one of its holding companies) to transfer its shareholding in the joint venture entity. Sometimes this can be worked around by inserting a wholly owned topco above the joint venture shareholder, and giving security to the lender over the shares in the newly formed topco. In any event, the provisions of these shareholders' agreements need to be looked at very carefully.

There may also be confidentiality restrictions in the shareholders' agreements that prevent disclosure by the private equity fund to the lenders without the other joint venture parties' consent. If the private equity fund also has asset-level senior loan financing, then a NAV lender would also want to understand whether these senior loans contain change-of-control provisions that would require the underlying borrower to repay the senior facility in full. This is important because it may not be in the best interests of the NAV lender to enforce its share security and trigger a mandatory prepayment of any senior loan if the underlying portfolio company does not have available cash to repay it.

The lender will want to make sure there is tight security over the bank accounts into which the distributions from the underlying assets flow. More often than not, the lender will require a new account to be opened with it, and require the borrower to direct that all distributions be paid into this account. The lender needs to understand how distributions flow from the underlying operating companies up to the holding vehicles, and to ensure that cash is moved into an account secured in favour of the lender as soon as possible.

In some instances, lenders that are lending to an SPV owned by the fund will require a guarantee or other shareholder support to be provided by the fund to further enhance the security for the asset-backed facility. However, lenders need to be careful and ensure that if this is the proposed structure, no borrowing limits of the fund are exceeded. Furthermore, if the fund has a subscription line facility, the terms of the subscription line finance documents will need to be reviewed to ensure there are no restrictions on other financial indebtedness and that there are no negative pledges included.

If there are borrowing and guaranteeing limits at the fund level, it may be that an equity commitment letter (ECL) is provided to the NAV lender instead of a guarantee. An ECL is a letter that is addressed by the fund to the SPV borrower, pursuant to which the fund agrees that it will capitalise or provide funds to the SPV borrower as and when needed by the SPV borrower. Depending on the jurisdiction of the entities concerned and the way in which the ECL is drafted, this may not amount to a guarantee and so avoid breaching any guarantee limitations in the funds limited partnership agreement.

There has been a recent trend for some NAV lenders requiring second-ranking security/recourse to the undrawn commitments of investors. If the fund has, or is intending to also have, a subscription line lender provide financing to the fund, this can give rise to detailed discussions on intercreditor arrangements, with the subscription line provider and asset-backed lender negotiating to get the strongest position possible with respect to the fund's assets.

These intercreditor discussions focus on important issues, such as: cross-defaults between the NAV facility and the subscription line facility; restrictions on payments going to and from the fund when there is a default under the NAV facility or the subscription line facility; and standstill periods during which one lender must wait until the other lender has decided whether to enforce. A more detailed discussion about so-called "hybrid" facilities is provided towards the end of this chapter.

Information

There should be rigorous information requirements in the facility agreement so that the lender is made aware at any time of potential issues connected with the value of the underlying assets. The borrower may provide regular certificates confirming that financial covenants such as LTV ratios, leverage ratios and portfolio interest coverage ratios are met. There may be scheduled quarterly portfolio telephone calls between the borrower and the lender to discuss the performance of the collateral assets. Some lenders go further and require copies of management presentations, any rating agency reports delivered, and financial information provided to the borrower in relation to the underlying assets.

Valuations

These facilities typically have detailed provisions in relation to valuation of the underlying assets. An independent valuation agent may need to be appointed by the borrower (in agreement with the lender). The lender will usually want to make sure that the valuation agent owes a contractual duty to the lender (on a reliance basis) and this may be documented through a specific engagement letter with the valuation agent that is addressed to both the borrower and the lender, or through a separate reliance letter. The valuation agent will be required to provide periodic valuations (e.g. every quarter or, in some circumstances, every month) to the lender. There will also be times when the latest valuation will need to be used to determine a particular course of action under the facility agreement. For example, an LTV ratio may need to be determined prior to any acquisition or sale of an asset. Only if the LTV exceeds a given threshold will the relevant acquisition or sale of the collateral asset be permitted.

In addition, there will usually be provisions in the facility agreement that allow the lender to seek an alternative valuation if the lender does not agree with the valuation provided by the valuation agent or the fund. The amount of deviation needed between the lender's calculation of the value of the portfolio and that of the valuation agent may be negotiated between the borrower and the lender before the lender has the right to instruct a separate valuation. Sometimes the valuation methodology is set out in a schedule to the facility agreement so that the borrower and the lender agree the principles and terms on which the underlying assets are valued. There will be further discussions between the lender and the borrower about who should bear the cost of the valuation, and in what circumstances.

Some lenders do not wish for an independent valuation agent to be appointed, but instead prefer to value the assets themselves internally. If a lender has the experience and resources to do this, then it is clearly to the benefit of the lender. However, borrowers may have concerns about this and wish to provide for some objectivity on the lender's calculation. This may be resisted strongly by the lender, and lead to negotiations between the borrower and the lender to find a compromise position. The fund's starting point in relation to valuations will usually be that the lender should rely on the valuations that the fund provides to its investors. This may be fine for the lender, provided that it has a right to have the investments separately valued if it believes that the fund's valuation is inaccurate.

Hedge funds and funds holding highly liquid assets

NAV facilities to hedge funds are structured very differently from those asset-backed funds facilities provided to closed-ended funds such as secondary, direct lending and private equity funds. The hedge fund often segregates the investments it wishes to use as collateral into separate securities accounts with a bank. The securities intermediary that holds the investments becomes the legal owner of the investments by signing the relevant subscription agreements of the hedge fund. However, the hedge fund remains the beneficial owner of the investments.

The hedge fund then provides security over its entitlement or rights to the hedge fund investments, while the owner of the assets remains the same. This security can take the form of an account charge (if the account is in the UK) or a security agreement and control agreement (if the account is located in the US). This structure can avoid any restrictions on transfer that exist in respect of the underlying assets. If there is then a default under the facility agreement and the lender wants to be repaid, it can direct the account bank (as the case may be, in accordance with the control agreement or acknowledgment of the account charge signed by the account bank) to redeem the hedge fund interests, and for the proceeds once received to be paid over to the lender.

Some lenders are providing NAV facilities to debt funds that hold various debt instruments as portfolio assets. We have worked with lenders on structures that involve no direct security over the underlying assets but simply security over the bank account, into which income or disposal proceeds from the underlying debt instruments are paid. The borrower then has an obligation to post cash margin, depending on the level of the NAV of the existing portfolio, to make sure there is a minimum level of cash available in the account over which the lender has security. This NAV facility structure is particularly helpful to funds that are regularly trading their debt instruments.

Securitisation regime

The European Securitisation Regulation, Regulation 2017/2402/EU (ESR), came into force from 1 January 2019. The ESR sets out certain obligations with respect to transactions that amount to a securitisation. There is a risk that some NAV facilities that are provided by lenders against loan assets could amount to securitisation transactions and therefore have the ESR applied to them. An analysis should be undertaken by the lender's and borrower's lawyers when commencing a NAV loan-on-loan transaction to establish at the outset whether the ESR applies.

The ESR is only intended to apply to entities established in the European Union, so borrowers established in Luxembourg and Ireland (two of the most popular jurisdictions for credit funds) could fall within the regulation. Part of the analysis will be to determine whether the repayments to the NAV lender are reliant only on the underlying cashflows from the loan assets, or whether it has recourse to other cashflows/assets (such as undrawn commitments of a fund).

If it is determined that the transaction does amount to a securitisation, then the NAV lender needs to ensure that there is a 5% interest (risk retention) retained by an entity referred to as an "original lender", "originator" or "sponsor" for the life of the securitisation. Furthermore, there are certain disclosure requirements that the NAV borrower will need to fulfil to the NAV lender and the regulator, including the submission of a transaction summary prior to closing of the transaction and ongoing reporting using the applicable reporting templates. There are severe penalties on both the fund borrower and the NAV lender if they do not comply with the requirements of the ESR.

Key developments

There is an increasing number of new lenders entering this market, as the returns are generally higher than the returns available for subscription line and asset-backed facilities. These new entrants to the market are not only the existing banks that provide fund finance facilities, but also credit and special situations funds and insurance companies that are searching for sufficient yields.

A perfect example of where this product can prove highly desirable to a private equity fund is when there is some sort of urgent liquidity required at the fund level but there are no imminent distributions from portfolio investments foreseeable. A fund may need to make distributions to its investors to, for example, ensure such investors can make new investments into the fund managers' new fund. The lenders of these facilities (which are often established as funds themselves) may provide interesting financing structures that allow them to provide capital by obtaining preferred priority distribution rights in the waterfall set out in the limited partnership agreement of funds. This allows financing to be made available other than by way of debt at the fund level. Obtaining capital by way of preferred stock means that the finance provider effectively sits as preferred limited partner in the fund.

There has been some recent growth in the provision of these preferred share facilities, and as discussed previously in this chapter, facilities to a finco that takes a preferred share interest in the PE fund portfolio. They are most helpful at the end of the life of the fund, where borrowing limits in the partnership agreements prohibit additional debt at the fund level, and such facilities may be a tax-efficient way of getting additional capital to the end-of-life fund.

There have been a number of direct lending funds and other credit funds who themselves are focusing on providing NAV facilities to private equity funds rather than the traditional unitranche product. This is a further indication that the market for these facilities is likely to grow significantly over the coming year. These facilities may be provided against the fund's assets or to the manager or co-investment vehicle controlled by the employers/partners secured against the co-invest stake in the fund.

Therefore, having access to this liquidity can ensure fund managers continue to fundraise successfully. Alternatively, a follow-on expense or investment may need to be made by the fund. If its investor commitments are fully drawn, the fund may have an urgent and pressing need for short-term liquidity until distributions come up from the investment portfolio.

Traditionally, NAV facilities were put in place during the later stages of the life funds, as a sort of "after care" liquidity line. This is due to the fact that these facilities generally lend themselves more to funds that have been fully or nearly fully invested and have assets to lend against. However, we are seeing some funds looking to put in place NAV and asset-backed facilities at the start of the life of the fund, so that such facilities can be utilised as and when investments are brought into the portfolio. This trend is consistent with the general trend in the fund finance market for funds to be much more aware of the uses and benefits of fund finance facilities, and the desire to have the relevant financing structures in place from inception as part of the funds strategy.

On the direct lending side, it is important that leverage is applied to the fund by way of NAV or asset-backed facilities to ensure that the fund is producing the rates of return promised to its investors. The challenge then becomes making sure these facilities are provided at sufficiently low margins to ensure that they can enhance the internal rate of return (IRR) of the direct lending fund. The quality of the underlying loan assets and the security provided against such underlying loans is clearly an important factor in a financial institution, determining what sort of pricing is offered for a NAV or asset-backed facility. Diversification is also very important, and so competitive pricing appears to be more available to larger senior-secured direct lending and credit funds that have a large portfolio of loan assets.

There has also been some syndication of these NAV and asset-backed facilities. Pension funds and other non-bank investors, who would typically invest in a fund as a limited partner, are also considering providing capital by way of fixed income by participating in these facilities. Typically, a large investment bank would arrange the transaction, then go out to these non-bank lenders to sell down their participation in the loan. Investment banks are often keen on a distribution strategy that allows them to reduce their exposure, but at the same time continue to hold a majority portion of the loan and run the facility agency and security agency function. This allows the investment bank to continue to develop the relationship with the underlying fund while not being fully exposed to the facility. It may be that the investment bank arranging the NAV facility needs to rate the debt in order to facilitate distribution to these non-bank lenders. This can lead to a change in the structure of the NAV facility itself, so that it takes the form of a note.

There are other types of users of these facilities that seem to be active in the market, including large limited partner investors such as sovereign wealth funds, family offices and funds of funds. These investors have a diversified pool of assets they hold (usually limited partnership interests in other funds) that can be used as collateral to secure financings provided by lenders. This provides such borrowers with liquidity if they need it, without having to liquidate any of their underlying investments. Private wealth arms of investment banks, in particular, are looking to grow this business as it allows them to develop close relationships with key principals that are their current or potential clients.

Hybrid facilities

There has been a continued increase in the use of "hybrid" facilities. These are facilities provided by lenders that look down to the value of the underlying assets, but in almost all cases, there will be covenants that ensure there is sufficient headroom of undrawn investor commitments. These facilities are particularly useful to funds that are looking for long-term financing facilities that are available from the fund's first close until the end of the life of the fund, when all of its commitments have been fully drawn down and the fund is fully invested. A lot of banks have found it challenging to make such facilities available. This is mainly because different parts of banks will have expertise with respect to analysis of investor commitments and the value of the underlying assets, respectively. However, some banks have been very successful in having their CLO teams and fund finance/financial institutions teams collaborate closely together to allow this offering to be put forward to their fund clients.

A hybrid facility provided by one lender might be very different to that provided by another. Some banks refer to a hybrid facility when actually it is just a capital call or subscription line facility with a NAV covenant inserted and a looser financial covenant ratio of undrawn investor commitments to financial indebtedness. These facility agreements will be drafted as classic subscription line facilities but will have a NAV ratio that needs to be satisfied once the ratio of undrawn commitments to financial indebtedness reaches a certain level.

Other institutions have provided hybrid facilities when there is some sort of issue obtaining clean security over all of the relevant undrawn commitments of investors into the fund. For example, there are situations when a group of certain investors, for tax or other reasons, will invest in a fund through a separate feeder fund vehicle. In some instances, the manager of the fund has not set up this feeder fund vehicle, and so the fund is not able to provide security over the rights of the feeder fund to draw down from the ultimate investors. To mitigate this imperfect security structure, lenders may, in addition to taking security over the rights of the fund to draw down from the feeder fund, take security over any shares in holding companies of the fund that own the assets. The lender may also take security over any intercompany loans or other receivables owed by the holding companies to the fund. This ensures that the lender can have the first right over any distributions or cashflows coming up from the underlying assets if there is a default by the fund.

We have seen the growth of hybrid facilities that are put in place when the fund is heavily invested but there are still some undrawn investor commitments remaining. The bank will provide financing against the underlying assets of the fund by way of term debt, but the fund may also need a working capital facility to finance fund expenses and follow-on investment.

One of the structures we have put together involves a tranche A facility that is a revolving credit facility of a modest amount to finance the fund expenses, and a tranche B facility that is a term loan facility of longer duration. If the fund already has an existing subscription provider who provides a facility of a relatively small amount (due to a limited number of undrawn investor commitments remaining), then it may make sense to "take out" this subscription facility and replace it with the tranche A facility made available by a lender under the hybrid facility. This means that the fund only needs to deal with one fund finance provider, which may have cost and execution benefits to the fund. Many funds have the ability to recall capital distributed to the investors after the investment period. Some lenders are able to lend against this recallable capital and to treat it in the same way as undrawn commitments. In end-of-life hybrids, it is quite common for a lender to include this recallable capital in its borrowing base or LTV covenants.

There are lenders in the market who have the ability to execute both a subscription line facility and a separate asset-backed facility at the start of the life of the fund, but to only make available the commitments of the subscription line facility, so that no non-utilisation fee is payable on the asset-backed line. After a certain amount of time, the borrower can then give notice to the lender to "switch" the commitments from the subscription line facility to the asset-backed facility. This is a clever way of ensuring the fund has cradle to grave financing, without incurring additional fees for this.

Certain lenders are able to lend against a blended financial covenant that consists of a ratio of the total debt of the borrowers as against the aggregate value of: (i) the undrawn investor commitments; (ii) the NAV of the fund; and (iii) the total amount of cash held in accounts secured in favour of the lender. This provides a neat solution to a fund, which is able to utilise the facility at the start of the life of the fund when the investor commitments are large, but then continue to utilise it as investments are made and the NAV increases.

The year ahead

The range of these types of facilities will continue to grow as different funds with different strategies begin to realise the benefits of fund finance facilities that do not look just to the undrawn commitments of the funds. As we enter a global recession and the balance sheets of banks providing capital call facilities become more limited, bank and non-bank lenders should increase the amount of NAV facilities they provide. The increased use of NAV facilities at the end of the life of the fund, and the establishment of continuation funds, demonstrate that funds are prepared to hold on to assets longer to realise their true value.

NAV facilities secured against diversified loan portfolios are fast becoming another structural way of lenders providing financing against such portfolio, and then distributing risk to investors that would typically invest in securitisation structures. Provided that the NAV facility allows lenders to freely transfer their commitments, it could be an alternative to, and potentially simpler than, undertaking a full securitisation programme. However, care needs to be taken to ensure that the ESR is analysed and its obligations adhered to.

Hybrid facilities seem to be a perfect way for lenders to develop strong relationships with funds, and enable the lender to "stay with them" from the start until the end of the fund's life, increasing the chances of the lender picking up ancillary business. There are certainly more lenders providing hybrid facilities, and who are able to lend against undrawn commitments and the value of the underlying assets. This trend is set to continue and should provide funds with more certainty around their fund-level financing throughout the life of the fund.

It looks like fund finance will continue to grow notwithstanding the world entering a global recession. Portfolio businesses will require liquidity as fundraising becomes more limited and assets are held on to for longer. NAV and hybrid financings are a perfect solution to these liquidity demands.

Leon Stephenson
Tel: +44 20 3116 3594 / Email: lstephenson@reedsmith.com

Leon is co-head of the Reed Smith fund finance team, based in London. Leon and the team work with banks, other financial institutional lenders, managers, general partners and limited partners of funds on specialist fund financing transactions with private equity, secondaries, real estate, direct lending and infrastructure funds.

Leon has particular specialist knowledge of NAV/asset-backed and hybrid facilities, secondary funds facilities, capital call facilities, co-investment and GP/manager support facilities and other types of liquidity facilities provided to funds.

Leon is recognised as a Leading Individual in Fund Finance by *The Legal 500 UK* 2023 and the team was awarded Band 1 in Fund Finance by *The Legal 500 UK* 2023. Leon was recognised as "Partner of the Year for Banking" at the Client Choice Awards 2017. Leon represents a large proportion of lenders that provide fund financing as well as a number of private equity and other funds on complex fund finance transactions.

Reed Smith LLP

Broadgate Tower, 20 Primrose Street, London EC2A 2RS, United Kingdom
Tel: +44 20 3116 3594 / Fax: +44 20 3116 3999 / URL: www.reedsmith.com

Collateral damage: What not to overlook in subscription line and management fee line facility diligence

Anthony Pirraglia, Peter Beardsley & Richard Facundo
Loeb & Loeb LLP

Two of the more popular fund finance products are subscription line lending and management fee lines of credit. While they both provide liquidity to a sponsor and its private equity funds and managers, the facilities serve different purposes and are underpinned by substantially different collateral. An in-depth understanding of those differences and the correct focus of diligence efforts in respect to each type of facility is crucial. This chapter provides a framework for these diligence efforts to ensure a successful transaction.

Introduction to subscription line due diligence

The foundation of subscription line lending is the strength of the investors' capital funding commitments. Therefore, financial institutions engaging in subscription line lending must take a systematic approach to the due diligence required to underwrite and consummate a lending facility to a private equity fund. Such an approach will help determine the strengths and weaknesses of such investors' obligations.

A lender's due diligence should have two broad focuses: credit and legal. Lenders assess the credit quality of the mix of investors presented by the fund and counsel reviews the legal documents that make up the lender's collateral. If the investors' and fund's contracts do not provide sufficient confidence that the investors' obligations to the fund will be enforceable, then the credit quality of the investor pool is meaningless.

The due diligence review described below focuses on a standard U.S.-based subscription line facility. Many fund structures also include offshore (non-U.S.) entities. Consulting experienced counsel in each relevant jurisdiction is imperative, as offshore legal requirements may influence credit decisions. In the event that lenders and their fund customers are considering a hybrid or net asset value ("NAV") facility, the due diligence requirements will include those discussed below, but will also expand into additional areas that are beyond the scope of this chapter.

Step one of due diligence: Review organizational chart and organizational documents

Lenders and their counsel should start their review with the fund's organizational chart. It is crucial to understand the fund structure at the outset, since it will impact the remaining due diligence process and influence the drafting of loan documents. Attention should be paid to the relationship among the parties on the organizational chart, particularly regarding: entities that make investments and may need to become borrowers; entities that can call capital on limited partners to ensure that such entities are pledgers; and how monies and capital commitments will be down-streamed to ensure that there are no gaps in the collateral package. After reviewing the organizational chart, lenders should request the underlying documents for each key party on the chart.

The organizational and management documents of the various parties are among the most fundamental and important documents to review in connection with subscription line facilities. These documents include the limited partnership agreement or other operating agreement of each fund (referred to here as the "LPA"), the organizational documents of the general partner and other obligors, such as alternate investment vehicles and qualified borrowers (the "Obligor Organizational Documents"), and any management or investment agreements, usually between the fund and an affiliated investment manager (the "Management Agreements").

Generally, the LPA sets forth the relationship between the fund, the general partner and the investors. The Obligor Organizational Documents determine the authority and the ability of the general partner and the other obligors to enter into the facility. The Management Agreement governs the interaction between the management company and the fund.

Because many of the lenders' rights under a subscription line facility are derived from the LPA, lenders and their counsel should understand the provisions of the LPA in depth. While many recent LPAs include provisions that lenders and their counsel require for a subscription line credit facility, older LPAs may either be silent on some of those items or limit certain rights or remedies that lenders expect to have. Despite this recent progress, the Institutional Limited Partners Association recently published a model LPA that fails to include a number of provisions that are customary in the subscription facility market, much to lenders' chagrin. Ultimately, the interrelationship of the funds and the structure of the credit facility will determine which LPA provisions are particularly relevant.

While an exhaustive analysis of the relevant LPA provisions is not possible in this chapter, lenders and counsel (which should be engaged to review the relevant documents) should note the following in their review:

- *Separate LPAs.* Each type of fund will have its own LPA. In connection with the first closing of investors in a fund, the LPA is typically amended and restated to include specifics about the capital commitments, the capital call process, and the ability of the fund to enter into credit facilities and pledge fund assets, as well as specific provisions addressing investor concerns. It is important to note that the LPA is subject to amendments as circumstances change over the life of the fund. A credit agreement should require that any such amendments that may be material to the lenders is subject to the prior review and approval of the lenders, and that all such amendments are delivered to the lenders promptly after taking effect.

- *Borrowing.* The LPA should clearly permit the fund to borrow. An important consideration is determining whether the LPA expressly permits joint and several liabilities, cross-collateralization and the ability to guarantee the obligations of subsidiaries, to the extent relevant. The LPA may include limitations on borrowings (including on the amount a fund may borrow), the amount of time borrowings may remain outstanding under a credit facility, and the permissible use of borrowings. Upon reviewing these provisions, a determination should also be made as to whether the credit agreement should expressly reference these limitations.

- *Capital commitments; right to pledge.* The LPA should contain an irrevocable commitment by the investors to fund capital when called (subject to limitations that may be set forth in the LPA or other governing documents) and expressly allow the fund (or the related general partner) to: call capital to repay borrowings; pledge the unfunded capital commitments by the fund's investors and the accounts into which such related capital contributions will be remitted; assign the right to make capital calls; and enforce the obligations of the fund's investors to fund their capital commitments.

With respect to capital commitments, attention should be paid to how the unfunded capital commitments by the investors are impacted by actions such as the distributions of portfolio liquidations and the return of capital to the investors, the expiration of the investment or commitment period, and the transfer of investor commitments.

If the LPA does not expressly permit a pledge and assignment of the expected collateral, the fund should confirm to the lenders that the fund's counsel will give a clean legal opinion on these powers or, in the alternative, amend the LPA. If neither option is available, the investors (especially investors included in the borrowing base, if that is the intended loan structure) should be required to acknowledge and consent to the pledge and assignment in stand-alone investor letters in favor of the lender. However, if the LPA prohibits the assignment of the rights of the fund and the general partner, the LPA will require amending to eliminate such a prohibition.

- *Waiver of counterclaims, defenses and setoffs.* Lenders and their counsel should review the LPA for a waiver of counterclaims, defenses and setoffs by the investors. The inclusion of this provision in the LPA (or in the subscription agreement) gives additional comfort to the lender that an investor will not (or that a court will not permit an investor to) deduct amounts the investor believes it is owed by the fund from the investor's required capital contributions under the LPA and the subscription agreement.
- *Third-party beneficiary provisions.* LPAs typically contain a provision that expressly prohibits those not party to the LPA from having the benefit of the LPA's provisions. Lenders should seek to have the lenders and their agent under a credit facility carved out from that prohibition, so that they are third-party beneficiaries of the LPA. If the fund balks at such a broad carve-out, lenders should, at a minimum, seek modifications such that they are beneficiaries of the provisions governing the right to call capital, the right to enforce remedies against defaulting investors, and the right to pledge assets to secure borrowings of the fund. The lenders may enforce the provisions of the LPA independently, which would supplement the general partner's assignment to the lenders of its rights under the LPA. In the event that such language is missing from the LPA, the fund may still be financeable, but lenders should consult with experienced counsel to discuss the risks and whether there are other provisions in the LPA that provide enough confidence to lenders to enter into a credit facility with such fund.
- *Investment period.* Generally, LPAs contain an investment period, during which the fund and the general partner have the ability to call capital from the investors for certain purposes. The review of provisions governing the investment period should focus on when capital calls are permitted and for what purpose. A lender will want the right to call capital to repay fund indebtedness at all times, whether before or after the termination of the investment period. Some older LPAs do not expressly permit capital calls to repay fund indebtedness after the expiration of the investment period, but instead only permit capital calls after the expiration of the investment period for follow-on investments, payment of fund expenses, and for investments that have been committed to prior to the expiration of the investment period. It is important to confirm whether repayment of indebtedness is included as a permissible fund expense in such an instance. Otherwise, lenders should be careful to structure the maturity of the credit facility to be well inside of the investment period's expiration.
- *Investment period termination or suspension.* Lenders should review LPAs to determine in what circumstances their right to call capital, or the investment period, may be terminated or limited. One provision that may impact the investment period is

the so-called "key person" provision, which provides that the investment period may be terminated or suspended (subject to an investor vote in some cases) if certain named individuals are no longer involved in the day-to-day operations of the fund. Ideally, the LPA will include language permitting the fund to call capital after the occurrence of a key person event for the repayment of existing indebtedness. Lenders should determine whether the termination or suspension of the investment period should result in a default of the subscription line, a suspension of borrowing, or some other limitation on the credit facility.

- *Excuse or exclusion provisions.* LPAs usually contain excuse or exclusion provisions that permit investors to be excused or excluded from making capital contributions for certain investments or in other limited circumstances. Lenders should understand these excuse and exclusion provisions and account for them in the credit facility, including by ensuring that the capital commitments of the excused or excluded investors are not included in the relevant borrowing base.
- *Overcall provisions and percentage limitations.* Overcall provisions limit the ability of the fund to call capital from its investors to cover shortfalls created by other investors' failure to fund their capital commitments when called. LPAs (or investors) may also limit the percentage of a fund's aggregate capital commitments or capital contributions that a single investor's capital commitment or capital contributions may comprise. Overcall and concentration limits restrict the ability of lenders to seek capital on a fully joint and several basis among the investors, increasing the risk that an investor default may affect the lenders' ability to be fully repaid.
- *Remedies against investors.* LPAs should provide strong remedies against investors that have failed to satisfy capital calls in order to strongly deter investors from failing to fund capital. The remedies should also provide a mechanism for addressing investor defaults.
- *Manager.* LPAs often permit the general partner to engage an investment manager (usually an affiliate) to source and advise on potential investments. The role of an investment manager may be substantially broader, however. Under the Management Agreement, the investment manager may be delegated or assigned the right to call capital from investors, pledge the assets of the fund, and exercise remedies against defaulting investors. If an investment manager has been delegated or assigned the rights of the general partner under the LPA, the manager should be included as a party to the applicable security agreement and, potentially, the credit agreement in order to cover each entity or person that has rights in the collateral securing the subscription line facility.

Next step: Review investor subscription agreements and disclosures for material information about the investor and its investment in the fund

Subscription agreements are generally form agreements entered into by each investor in a fund. Typically, an investor will subscribe to a fund as a limited partner, although an investor may also subscribe as a member or other equity holder, depending on the type of entity. Nevertheless, the subscription agreement will provide key information regarding the investor, which a lender should confirm in its diligence review.

Additionally, investors typically complete an investor qualification statement or other investor questionnaire, and provide supplementary information and representations required by the sponsor. By executing a subscription agreement and providing investor disclosures, an investor is agreeing to its rights and obligations in a fund's LPA, and is making representations and warranties to the fund, including confirmation that it is qualified to invest in the fund. Lenders and counsel should review subscription agreements and investor disclosure documents for material information about the investor and its investment in the fund, including the following:

- *Legal name of the investor.* The legal name of the investor should be provided in the subscription agreement. Occasionally, investor lists provided by a fund manager include abbreviated names, which lenders should cross-check with the subscription agreement and confirm with the fund manager, to ensure that the list is consistent with the subscription agreements. While a discrepancy may be the result of a typo or abbreviation, it may reflect that the investor is a different party from the one expected by the lenders.
- *Capital commitment amounts.* The amount of capital committed by the investor is provided in the subscription agreement. The list of investors provided by the fund manager typically indicates the total commitment pledged by each investor. This amount should be compared to the investor's subscription agreement. Discrepancies between the subscription agreement and any investor list provided by the fund should be addressed by the fund manager.
- *Acceptance of subscription.* The general partner of the fund should expressly accept the capital commitment subscribed to by an investor, usually by countersignature to the subscription agreement. To that end, lenders and their counsel should ensure that they have copies of the fully executed and completed subscription agreements or risk raising questions about the subscription agreement's enforceability.
- *Parallel or feeder funds.* A fund may occasionally have parallel or feeder funds that are parties to the credit being extended by a lender. A subscription agreement should identify to which fund the investor made its capital commitment. Sometimes, an investor may have more than one subscription agreement if it is investing in multiple funds.

Notably, lenders and counsel should perform a general review of the subscription agreement, to ensure that it has no provisions that may be adverse to a lender, such as any limits to an investor's obligations to fund its commitment. While many of these limitations are more often found in side letters (discussed below), they may seep into subscription agreements.

In the wake of the highly publicized fraud case of JES Global Capital in 2021, lenders may wish to review their investor diligence processes. Such processes may include: the creation of a parallel investor database by the lender whereby inconsistencies in the name or contact information of a fund across facilities could be a red flag; access rights to the funding account and a requirement that the fund have successfully called capital prior to closing the subline facility so that the lender can see where the funds came from; or even requesting the ability to perform "spot checks" to call investors to confirm the existence of their capital commitment.

Remember to check for and review side letters

A side letter is an agreement between an investor and a fund that alters the general terms of the investor's investment in the fund by superseding some of the applicable terms in the LPA or subscription agreements. A side letter alternatively may add additional terms to the agreements and commitments between the fund and the investor. Certain investors require side letters because of regulatory or tax requirements that are specific to the investor. Other investors, particularly investors with large capital commitments, may request special economic or other benefits as a condition of their investment.

Due diligence review of side letter agreements should focus on terms that could adversely affect the lender's rights to payment under a credit facility with the fund or with respect to the collateral pledge. Terms in side letters that restrict an investor from funding, or that limit its obligations to fund its capital commitment, are of particular concern. The most commonly found provisions that could affect an investor's obligations to contribute its capital to a fund include:

- *Most-Favored Nation (MFN) provisions.* MFN provisions specify that the fund agrees to give the investor the most favorable terms it makes available to other investors. Lenders should review all side letters to determine which provide the most favorable terms and whether other side letters, as a result of their MFN provisions, automatically adopt the more favorable terms. Lenders should ask whether any investors have opted into any MFN provisions.
- *Investment policy exceptions.* Investors may have different policy considerations when committing capital to a fund and require side letters to memorialize these policy exceptions. Typically, but not exclusively, government pension funds will have state-specific restrictions on contributing capital to investments in companies that directly or indirectly do business with certain countries or certain industries that may be politically controversial. Other investors may have internal policies or other limitations regarding investments in which they may participate. These concerns can be addressed in the loan documentation by providing for the exclusion of such investor's capital commitment from the borrowing base calculation for loan requests that are based on investments in such excepted investments.
- *Transfers to affiliates.* Most side letters will allow an investor to transfer its interests to its affiliates. These transfers are typically subject to the satisfaction of the general partner of the fund and the general partner's subsequent consent to the transfer. Transfer provisions in the side letter may also accommodate circumstances in which state legislation triggers the transfer provisions of the LPA and, under such circumstances, deem the general partner to have consented to such transfer.
- *Sovereign immunity.* Government entities, such as public pensions and sovereign wealth funds, may have immunity from contract claims and other lawsuits unless they waive their immunity. Sovereign immunity provisions may provide for a waiver or may reserve the rights of such investors to waive their immunity. Some jurisdictions may not permit waivers of sovereign immunity except through legislation. Other jurisdictions waive sovereign immunity if an investor is engaging in "commercial acts." Lenders should be mindful of the sovereign immunity laws of different jurisdictions and how they may affect an investor's obligations to contribute capital to a fund.
- *Placement agent disclosures.* Funds sometimes use placement agents in their fundraising process. In response to corrupt practices connected with governmental investors, state legislatures and other regulatory agencies, certain investors request disclosures regarding the use of placement agents. Such disclosures typically take the form of questionnaires. To the extent that there are any material misrepresentations in the disclosures, investors may include in their side letters the right to cease making capital contributions.
- *Overcall and concentration limits.* Overcall provisions (discussed above in the context of LPAs) limit the amount an investor is obligated to fund to cure the shortfalls created by another investor's failure to fund its called capital commitment.
- *The Employee Retirement Income Security Act (ERISA).* ERISA regulations restrict how much of an interest an employee retirement pension plan can own in any class of equity interests in a fund before the fund is considered a "plan asset vehicle" under ERISA. Investors may have provisions in side letters that provide them with the right to exit a fund in the event that the fund is deemed a plan asset vehicle.

Additional due diligence: Review private placement memorandum, financial statements and SEC filings; conduct UCC and other searches

Lenders should consider reviewing other materials that can help assess a given fund's creditworthiness and enhance the credit and risk analysis of the underwriting process.

- *Offering or private placement memorandum.* The offering or private placement memorandum is not executed by any investor in the fund and is not a source of obligations or, generally, rights associated with an investor's investment in the fund. However, lenders will typically include a review of this memorandum as part of their initial due diligence because it provides a broad overview of the fund's business, objectives, strategies and material terms. The memorandum typically includes the past investment performance of the sponsor, a broader discussion of the fund's applicable market, the management structure of the fund, risk factors associated with an investment in the fund, and certain legal and tax considerations for investors considering investing in the fund.
- *Financial statements and communications.* If the fund is already operating, lenders should review available financial statements of the fund and request copies of communications sent to investors. Similarly, once they provide a fund with a subscription credit facility, lenders commonly require that they be provided copies of all financial reporting and other communication provided to investors by the fund, general partner, investment manager, or investment advisor.
- *SEC filings/other searches.* The Dodd-Frank Wall Street Reform and Consumer Protection Act obligates the manager or investment adviser of certain funds to make particular filings with the Securities and Exchange Commission (SEC), which are also a valuable source of information for lenders both before and during the term of a subscription facility. In particular, the SEC requires that fund managers register as investment advisers under the Investment Advisers Act, unless they are exempt from registration under either the private fund exemption or the venture capital fund exemption (both of which apply to domestic fund advisers). The private fund exemption is available to managers that manage only private funds (defined as having either 100 or fewer beneficial owners or beneficial owners who are all qualified purchasers) and have no more than $150 million under management in the United States. The venture capital fund exemption applies to funds that represent to their investors that they pursue a venture capital strategy and meet certain technical requirements.

Registered investment advisers, as well as private fund managers and venture fund managers, must file a Form ADV annually and are subject to SEC examination. The form includes extensive information about the adviser, its business, business practices, personnel and clients, and the people whom it controls and who control it. In addition, the form requires disclosure of the disciplinary history of the advisor and its personnel for the previous 10 years. A registered adviser must also file a Form ADV, Part 2, Brochure, which contains investor-directed information.

- *Uniform Commercial Code (UCC) searches.* At an absolute minimum, lenders should order UCC searches from the applicable governmental authority in each jurisdiction in which a pledgor of the subscription facility's collateral is organized. These searches will confirm that there are no intervening liens on their proposed collateral.
- *Other information searches.* Lenders often conduct searches of other public and governmental filings, databases and records, including non-UCC lien searches (i.e., tax and other liens), bankruptcy filings, judgment filings, litigation filings, PATRIOT Act filings, and certificates of status/standing and qualifications to do business. These searches are all part of a comprehensive risk and credit analysis.

Request standard loan-closing documents

In addition to reviewing the organizational documents of the fund and its agreements with its investors, lenders typically require that certain standard loan-closing documentation be delivered in connection with any closing of a subscription credit facility. Generally, these deliveries serve to confirm that the fund, and those of its affiliates that are party to the various loan documents, have the power and authority to enter into and perform under the documents, and that the documents have been duly authorized and executed. Typically, a lender will require:

- *a standard secretary's or closing certificate* by the fund and each applicable affiliate, which includes, among other things, resolutions and/or consents of the fund and the applicable affiliates, whereby the fund and its applicable affiliates are authorized to enter into the loan documents and perform thereunder;
- *copies of all the organizational documents of the fund* and the applicable affiliates, along with a representation and warranty that these organizational documents have not been modified or amended in any manner;
- *incumbency certificates* for each person who is authorized to execute the loan documents on behalf of the fund and its applicable affiliates;
- *opinions from counsel to the applicable funds*, general partners and other entities covered by the credit facility, that cover, among other things, due authorization, execution and delivery, and enforceability of the credit facility documents and perfected liens in the collateral securing the credit facility; and
- *certificates of good standing or status* from the applicable governmental authority in the fund's and applicable affiliates' respective jurisdictions of formation or organization.

Conclusion to subscription line due diligence

As these summaries of the various due diligence tasks illustrate, subscription lending is a document-intensive endeavor. Lenders and their counsel look to build a complete structure of legal agreements to give lenders a clear path to realization of the underlying basis of their credit – the unfunded capital commitments of the fund's investors.

Introduction to Management Line due diligence

Another important fund finance product that many lenders offer and many sponsors utilize is management fee credit facilities ("Management Lines"). Like subscription credit facilities, the collateral supporting the fund's obligations and the rights and remedies of the lender or agent are based on contractual rights that are being assigned as collateral. And, like subscription credit facilities, if those contractual rights are deficient or not properly understood, lenders may end up in a materially worse position than expected.

A Management Line is a revolving or term credit facility provided to the manager (or general partner) of a private equity fund or series of funds. While the collateral supporting the Management Line may include other assets, the primary collateral is the management fees payable to the manager and the account into which the management fees are paid.[1] These fees are typically paid by the private equity fund to the manager pursuant to the LPA of the private equity fund and a management or advisory agreement between the private equity fund and the manager. A private equity fund typically pays the management fees to the manager on a periodic basis as payment for, among other things, identifying and analyzing potential investment opportunities, overseeing the administration of the investment and otherwise managing the fund and to reimburse the manager for expenses it incurs in the satisfaction of its obligations. Management fees are typically calculated as a percentage of the fund's total committed capital during the fund's investment period and thereafter as a percentage of the fund's called capital and value of investments. Since management fees are paid periodically, Management Lines allow the management company to smooth cash flows and have liquidity to make strategic hires, make payments to equity and other stakeholders, and invest in the business.

Management Line due diligence

Since the right to receive management fees is contractual (set forth in the partnership agreement, the Management Agreements and any related documents), it is imperative to understand the provisions and limitation of those documents by asking questions including:

- Do the management company's organizational documents expressly permit the borrowing and pledging as contemplated under the Management Line? While the organizational documents of private equity fund borrowers have evolved to include express language regarding the ability to borrow (on a joint and several or several basis) and pledge collateral, management company organizational documents sometimes still lack these express provisions.
- Is there a limitation on the company's ability to pledge or transfer the rights under the partnership agreement and the Management Agreement? Since the collateral is contractual, the Management Agreement and partnership agreements may expressly prohibit the assignment of the Management Agreements and partnership agreements or the rights under them. While the UCC may invalidate some of these provisions, it is important to understand the transfer and assignment rights.
- Are the management fee payment obligations in the partnership agreement, Management Agreement or both? If both, do the provisions track one another? The collateral should cover each document (and the rights thereunder) under which the management fees are paid.
- Crucially, who are the express recipients of the management fees and who are the payors of those fees? Given the complexity of fund structures, management fees may be paid by multiple entities (including the private equity funds or portfolio companies) and be paid to multiple entities. It is imperative to review each of the Management Agreements and partnership agreements to confirm the payors and recipients.
- When are the management fees paid? How are they calculated? Management fees can be paid on a monthly, quarterly or other periodic basis. To understand the credit support provided by the management fees, the documents should be reviewed to confirm the calculation and payment of management fees.
- Are there offsets or limitations to the obligation to pay management fees? Related to the item above, there may be reductions or setoffs against the payment of management fees, including whether the fees payable by a private equity fund to a manager are reduced by the fees received by that manager by portfolio companies. Another consideration is whether the fees payable to a management company may be offset by the manager against the capital contributions the manager or the general partner may be required to make to the private equity fund.
- When are the Management Agreements permitted to be terminated? Management Agreements may provide for termination events, which should be understood and incorporated into the Management Line documentation.

These questions can be answered by a careful review of the documents and an understanding of the organizational structure of the private equity funds and the manager. While the partnership agreement and the Management Agreement will be the principal documents in which the answers are found, other documents may impact the payment and receipt of management fees. There may be side letters (either with investors or between the manager and the private equity fund) or agreements between portfolio companies and the manager (or another entity in the structure) that also govern the payment of fees (or setoffs against the payment of those fees). Each of these documents should also be reviewed.

Further, it is often useful to request a breakdown of the management fee payment streams. Similar to an investor list in a subscription facility context, the management fee schedule can help identify all payors and recipients of management fees and is a useful means of cross-checking the delivered management fee agreements to confirm that all documents have been received. This fee schedule can also be attached to the credit agreement and form a representation by the borrower of the management fee payors and expected management fees for the projected period.

Additionally, since management fees are typically paid with the proceeds of capital contributions by investors in the private equity fund, it is important to understand (and limit, if possible) the debt at the private equity fund level. In fact, whether a subscription facility exists at the private equity fund level is a particularly relevant question, since the Management Line is structurally subordinated to any debt at the private equity fund. In the event of a default of the subscription facility, the subscription lender may exercise its remedies and prevent capital contributions from being retained by the private equity fund to make the management fee payments. Often, a lender may need to request that the terms of the subscription facility be amended to permit the payment of management fees in order to have a viable Management Line.

Conclusion of Management Line due diligence

Management Lines serve an important role in fund finance, providing liquidity to private equity fund managers and another opportunity for lenders to solidify their relationship with sponsors. However, both parties need to understand the contractual provisions and limitations governing the receipt and payment of the management fees and structure the facility based on the diligence. Using this diligence process will ensure a credit facility that reflects the reality of the management fees and the alignment of the expectations of the lenders and the management company under the Management Line.

* * *

Endnote

1. Depending on various considerations, including the needs of the private equity funds and managers, the payment structure and the credit support required by the lender, Management Lines may be structured in a number of ways and may include additional borrowers, guarantors or pledgors, including the general partners of the private equity funds. While each variation in structure requires its own specific analysis, this portion of the chapter focuses on Management Lines where the manager is the sole borrower and pledgor.

Acknowledgment

The authors acknowledge with thanks the contribution to this chapter of:

David C. Fischer
Tel: +1 212 407 4827 / Email: dfischer@loeb.com

David Fischer is of counsel in Loeb & Loeb's New York office. He represents public and private companies in a diverse range of corporate and capital markets transactions. His broad experience includes public and private securities offerings, derivative securities transactions, corporate governance and public company compliance, mergers and acquisitions, and licensing agreements. Mr. Fischer also assists clients with research and development, cryptocurrency offerings, business and fund formations, executive employment agreements, and employee equity plans.

Anthony Pirraglia
Tel: +1 212 407 4146 / Email: apirraglia@loeb.com

Anthony Pirraglia, deputy chair of the firm's Finance department, focuses his commercial finance practice primarily on fund financing transactions, representing both lenders and borrowers in subscription line lending, management fee line facilities, co-investment facilities and net asset value facilities. He is a respected advisor to money center banks and other lenders in advising on structuring, diligence and other aspects of fund finance. He was also recently recognized in *IFLR1000*'s Leading Lawyers list in Finance.

Peter Beardsley
Tel: +1 212 407 4278 / Email: pbeardsley@loeb.com

Peter Beardsley is a partner in the New York office of Loeb & Loeb LLP. He focuses his practice in the area of commercial finance and private bank lending, representing both borrowers and lenders in cash flow credit facilities, fund finance (both capital call and management lines), private bank lending to high-net-worth individuals, asset-based loans and lender finance. Mr. Beardsley regularly represents lenders, private equity funds and other investors in their loans to, and investments in, companies. He also has substantial experience in loan workout negotiations, restructuring distressed credit facilities and representing DIP lenders.

Richard Facundo
Tel: +1 212 407 4178 / Email: rfacundo@loeb.com

Richard Facundo is senior counsel in the firm's Finance department and focuses his practice on the representation of banks and other financial institutions in private banking and commercial lending transactions, including secured and unsecured lending. Mr. Facundo's practice includes financings structured around hedge fund interests, private equity interests, margin lending and fine art. These transactions include representation of lenders and agent banks in syndicated and club deals. Richard also has experience assisting clients in financial restructurings and bankruptcy proceedings.

Loeb & Loeb LLP

345 Park Avenue, New York, NY 10154, USA
Tel: +1 212 407 4000 / Fax: +1 212 407 4990 / URL: www.loeb.com

Derivatives at fund level

Jonathan Gilmour, Peter Hughes & Joseph Wren
Travers Smith LLP

Overview

Against the backdrop of global macroeconomic uncertainty, as we see growth slowing, interest rates and inflation rates rising, and the potential for periods of rapid dislocation in the foreign exchange (forex/FX) markets, this chapter highlights some key structural and documentary legal issues that should be considered by a private capital manager thinking about entering into derivatives transactions at fund level.

This chapter does not provide detailed legal and regulatory analysis in relation to particular issues by reference to the laws of any particular jurisdiction. The observations made in this chapter are drawn from experience in the European fund finance and derivatives markets and are not tailored to any particular derivatives strategy. Any manager who intends to enter into derivatives transactions at fund level should obtain legal and regulatory advice under the laws applicable to the proposed parties to the transaction and to the transaction itself, which should be tailored to the particular characteristics of the parties, the fund's constitutional documents, and the circumstances of the transaction.

Introduction

There are a wide variety of reasons why a manager may consider entering into derivatives transactions, but derivatives use can generally be split between those of a speculative nature and hedging. At one end of the spectrum, funds can use derivatives to speculate in the active pursuit of investment return (for example, using total return swaps as a form of leverage to increase the funds' exposure to a particular asset) and, in so doing, may be expected to enter into a wide array of derivatives transactions.

At the other end of the spectrum, derivatives can be used purely to hedge against the economic impact of a particular risk. At the time of writing, interest rates continue to rise globally and there are significant movements in currencies; so, for many managers, eliminating or mitigating this risk through the use of hedging instruments will be a vital part of their strategy. Examples of risks that a manager may wish to mitigate with derivatives use are: FX exposure (for example, covering the currency exposure for a EUR fund that will be drawing EUR amounts from investors to fund a particular investment that is denominated in GBP); and interest rate exposure (for example, covering the risk of an adverse movement in interest rates increasing the amount required to be paid on borrowings made by the fund). Indeed, for many managers, FX and interest rate hedging will be all that the derivatives strategy needs to cover. This chapter will focus on the use of fund-level derivatives for pure hedging purposes.

Sometimes a fund's exposure to a particular risk is indirect, and it is more appropriate for the relevant derivatives to be entered into below fund level. A common example is interest rate hedging for an acquisition finance facility in the context of a private equity transaction. The buyer under the relevant acquisition will be a vehicle established by the fund to make the acquisition. It is this vehicle that would enter into any acquisition finance facility to assist in funding the acquisition. Consequently, it is this vehicle that is exposed directly to any interest rate fluctuations on that facility; the fund is only indirectly exposed through its ownership of the vehicle.

As such, it is most appropriate for the vehicle, not the fund, to hedge the interest exposure on the acquisition finance facility. The lenders under the acquisition finance facility may require that hedging be put in place, as an important part of their protections against a borrower payment default. If interest rates increase, the borrower will have the benefit of the derivatives to help fund the increased interest payments that it owes under the acquisition finance facility. In such a scenario, it is inappropriate for a derivatives transaction to be entered into at fund level.

Advantages and considerations entering into derivatives at fund level

Any manager deciding whether to enter into derivatives at fund level will need to consider its specific circumstances carefully. In addition to legal considerations, it will need to understand the accounting, regulatory and tax treatments of the derivatives. It will also want to consider the operational impact of the derivatives upon the fund.

Key advantages of entering into derivatives at fund level

The primary benefit of entering into derivatives at fund level is that the risk protection is at the level where risk is borne by the fund. Where a particular risk directly affects a fund, it may not be commercially possible to hedge that risk anywhere other than at the fund level.

The manager may also be able to obtain better pricing for the relevant derivatives by entering into them directly rather than via a fund-owned vehicle. The counterparty to the derivatives transaction may welcome the financial strength and risk profile of the fund, as well as the ability to enforce its rights directly against the fund.

The taxation treatment of the derivatives may be better if the derivatives are entered into at fund level rather than in an investment vehicle owned by the fund. This will depend upon the tax rules applicable to the structure.

Having an agreed derivatives platform (for example, having International Swaps and Derivatives Association (ISDA) Master Agreements and Schedules negotiated and signed with one or more counterparties) at fund level means that the manager can enter into multiple derivatives transactions using the same documents, rather than having the cost, complexity and delay of negotiating documentation on multiple occasions – as would be required if each new derivative was instead to be entered into, on a case-by-case basis, by separate investment vehicles owned by the fund. Netting can also be effected across multiple transactions under the same ISDA Master Agreement, helping to reduce exposure.

Key considerations of entering into derivatives at fund level

Although derivatives transactions of this kind are entered into with the intention of increasing performance or mitigating risk, there are some considerations that the manager must be aware of.

The fund must monitor any permissions required under its constitutional documents to ensure that its use of derivatives does not fall outside its powers. Permissions requirements are considered in more detail later in this chapter.

Additional operational burden may arise as a result of the regulation of derivatives – regimes such as the European Market Infrastructure Regulation (EMIR) (and its "onshored" UK equivalent) and the Dodd-Frank Wall Street Reform and Consumer Protection Act impose obligations on parties entering into derivatives transactions. These include to report on, and actively mitigate the risk of, their derivatives transactions. Specified classes of derivatives face more onerous regulatory obligations, including requirements to clear specified classes of derivatives through approved clearing houses (mainly interest rate derivatives), and to post cash as credit support (margin/collateral).

If, commercially or as a matter of regulation, the derivatives transaction involves an obligation to post margin, the manager must monitor and respond to margin requirements, which may be on a daily basis. Some managers will not have the in-house resources to manage such processes, nor ready access to liquidity (particularly those managers who would need to rely on calling unfunded commitments from their investors). Even for those managers that do have access to such liquidity, the deployment of cash as margin may have an adverse impact on fund returns.

Consequently, careful analysis of these regulatory obligations needs to be made by any manager who is considering entering into derivatives at fund level. For example, the definition of "Financial Counterparties" under EMIR/UK EMIR determines the types of entity that are in-scope for material obligations such as mandatory clearing or mandatory posting of variation margin. A range of funds potentially fall within this definition, so managers will need to consider whether their funds may fall within scope of those obligations. There are, however, some useful carve-outs and exemptions.

For most funds, being required to post collateral to counterparties under their derivatives transactions would be a suboptimal use of resources, resulting in a drag on performance. It is helpful for those funds that EMIR/UK EMIR provides for a carve-out from the obligation to post variation margin in respect of certain types of over-the-counter (OTC) derivative. The mandatory exchange of variation margin on physically settled FX forwards and physically settled FX swaps applies only to transactions between credit institutions and investment firms treated as credit institutions for prudential purposes, which are established in the EEA (in the case of EMIR) or the UK (in the case of UK EMIR) (or equivalent entities located in a third country), and so would not capture most funds. EMIR/UK EMIR also includes a "Small Financial Counterparty" classification, exempting certain financial counterparties from the requirement to clear their trades, so smaller funds that use interest rate derivatives (of a type that would otherwise need to be cleared) may be able to sidestep the clearing obligation.

When assessing how these rules might have an effect on a fund's hedging strategy, it is worth noting that regulatory impact can often be reduced by careful structuring of the derivatives or by using an appropriate vehicle to enter into the trades.

While, at the moment, obligations for funds under UK and EU EMIR are largely aligned, in future there may be further divergence between the UK and EU EMIR regimes. To give one example of a point of distinction between EMIR and UK EMIR, UK managers will need to ensure that details of their transactions are reported to a UK authorised trade repository, as they will no longer be able to report to an EU authorised trade repository for the purpose of UK EMIR. However, they may also need to report to an EU trade repository under EU EMIR on behalf of EU alternative investment funds (AIFs) under their management, leading to a potential double reporting requirement. The potential for drift between the regimes will possibly increase over time, so managers are advised to work with their legal counsel to stay abreast of potential implications for their funds.

The use of derivatives at fund level also adds a layer of complication in relation to other fund-level transactional documentation. As analysed in more detail later in this chapter, a manager will need to consider carefully the interaction between any credit agreement and derivatives documentation.

Some of these issues may be mitigated by entering into the trade via a dedicated treasury vehicle established by the manager. Whether particular legal or regulatory obligations then apply will depend upon the particular rule sets and facts involved. However, the use of a treasury vehicle itself can bring potential structural complications, particularly if the derivatives counterparty is not satisfied that the vehicle alone represents an adequate covenant and therefore requires some level of recourse against the fund itself (for example, by way of a guarantee by the fund of the treasury vehicle's obligations). The impact of any such recourse to the fund would need to be carefully considered.

A further consideration for funds subject to the Alternative Investment Fund Managers Directive (AIFMD) is whether the use of derivatives at fund level would create leverage within the fund, and the extent to which this may be undesirable. In December 2020, ESMA published final guidance for supervisors on limits on leverage in the AIF sector, supplementing the rules by which managers have to calculate leverage employed by their funds under AIFMD. Detailed consideration of these issues sits outside the focus of this chapter.

Constitutional considerations when entering into derivatives at fund level

A manager that is considering entering into derivatives at fund level will need to ensure that it has the power and authority under its constitutional documentation to do so (taking into account any limits on quantum/type of its derivatives exposure – which, in certain circumstances, may be contained in side letters with its investors).

Optimally, the question of whether, and in what circumstances, the fund is entitled to enter into derivatives transactions should be considered at the formation stage with any permission, together with any parameters around that permission, clearly addressed in the constitutional documentation when the fund is established.

Constitutional limitations in relation to entering into derivatives transactions

An express prohibition on entering into derivatives in the fund's constitutional documents is increasingly rare but, unless there are clear commercial justifications for seeking an alternative method of authorisation, such as an express investor consent, is potentially the end of the matter. In older funds, it is possible for constitutional documentation to be silent on derivatives use, which may create its own issues – particularly if the fund's legal counsel (who might not be retained to advise on any derivatives) is required to give a capacity opinion on the fund's ability to enter into derivatives transactions.

Examples of other restrictions that may appear in fund constitutional documents are:
(a) *Limitation on the level of financial indebtedness that the fund may incur.* If the constitutional documents contain limits upon the financial indebtedness that the fund is permitted to incur, then the fund will need to consider whether actual or contingent exposures under derivatives will constitute financial indebtedness and, if so, how the exposure under the derivatives will be valued for the purpose of complying with the relevant provisions.
(b) *Prohibition from entering into speculative derivatives.* Here, the manager will need to consider carefully the nature of the derivatives to be entered into by the fund and whether, on a correct construction of the limitation language, they could be caught. For example, a derivatives transaction entered into to hedge interest rate exposure on a fund-level loan may not be speculative, as it is hedging a genuine risk faced by the fund.

However, if the loan is repaid but the derivatives transaction remains outstanding (or if the nominal value hedged is not reduced in line with repayments of the loan), then have the derivatives become speculative? What if the facility under which the loan has been drawn and repaid is revolving (and therefore technically capable of being redrawn) but it is commercially unlikely that the facility will be redrawn? Similarly, if a derivatives transaction entered into at fund level is not hedging a risk to which the fund is directly exposed, but instead hedging a risk to which the fund is only indirectly exposed – for example, a risk to which an investee company is exposed – then would this alone cause the derivatives transaction to be categorised as speculative?

(c) *Limitation on wagering or gaming contracts.* This sort of limitation, sometimes seen in investor side letters, must be considered carefully on its terms. There could be an argument that derivatives transactions, particularly those that are not simply hedging a risk to which the fund is directly exposed, may be characterised as wagers or gaming contracts.

Constitutional limitations in relation to granting credit support for derivatives transactions

If, commercially or as a matter of regulation, the fund's derivatives transactions will need to be collateralised or supported by a fund guarantee (for example, if the derivatives are being entered into by a treasury vehicle), then the manager will need to ensure that giving that credit support is permitted under the fund's constitutional documentation:

(a) *Security.* Fund documentation will frequently circumscribe the fund's ability to grant security. This may be prohibited or limited by reference to either the value of collateral that may be posted or the assets over which security may be granted. There may also be limitations on giving security in respect of the liabilities of an investee company. The manager will need a clear understanding of how any such limitations operate and will need to ensure that the limitations are not breached.

Security under derivatives contracts may be effected in a number of ways, including by the creation of security interests over collateral (for example, under the ISDA 1995 Credit Support Deed (Security Interest – English law)) or by way of title transfer of collateral (for example, under the ISDA 1995 Credit Support Annex (Transfer – English law)). Where collateralisation is mandatory as a matter of regulation, parties will often use the ISDA 2016 Credit Support Annex for Variation Margin (VM) (Title Transfer – English law) and, in certain circumstances, the ISDA 2018 Credit Support Deed for Initial Margin (IM) (Security Interest – English law).

(b) *Guarantees.* The manager may be required by its counterparty to guarantee the obligations of a fund-owned or treasury vehicle that has entered into derivatives transactions for the benefit of the fund. In these circumstances, the manager will need to consider whether the fund's constitutional documents limit its ability to do so. A limitation could take the form of a direct limit on the giving of guarantees or it could be indirectly effected by including exposure under the relevant guarantee within another limitation (for example, a limitation on financial indebtedness).

If guarantees are so limited, then the manager will need to understand how the guarantee obligation is to be valued for the purpose of ensuring compliance with the limitation. For example, is the maximum contingent exposure used, or is the accounting value placed upon the guarantee used?

(c) *Indemnities.* Similar to guarantees, the manager will need to consider whether the fund's constitutional documents limit its ability to give indemnities in respect of derivatives and, if so, how the contingent liability under any such indemnity is to be valued for the purpose of the limitation. For example, the standard form 2002 ISDA Master Agreement contains an indemnity for certain costs and expenses.

Constitutional limitations on the ability to draw investor commitments to make payments in respect of derivatives transactions

The manager will also need to consider any ongoing requirements under the proposed derivatives transaction to make payments or to post collateral. The proposed source of any required liquidity will need to be identified. If the manager will use investors' uncalled commitments, then it will need to confirm that commitments can be drawn down for this purpose. If the fund has a subscription facility or other credit agreement where the available facility is calculated by reference to uncalled commitments, the manager will also need to factor into its use of such a facility the effect of payments funded from undrawn commitments.

Other contractual permissions required for the fund to enter into derivatives at fund level

In addition to restrictions under its constitutional documents, a manager will need to consider the impact of any existing contractual restrictions to which the fund is subject – in particular, any credit agreements.

The extent of any contractual restrictions will be a matter for the fund to determine by reference to the specific finance documents that it has in place. For mid-sized and smaller funds, the starting position would be to assume that any credit agreement on reasonably market-standard terms will restrict the fund's ability to incur debt, give guarantees and grant security – subject to a relatively narrow suite of permissions and a general permission "basket". This is considered below in more detail. For larger funds, any credit agreement may be less restrictive, but managers should nonetheless carefully consider whether any of the following apply.

Contractual limitations under credit agreements in relation to entering into derivatives transactions

Limitations commonly appear in credit agreements that directly address the ability of the fund to enter into derivatives transactions:

(a) *Restriction on entering into derivatives transactions.* The underlying credit agreement should be reviewed for a restriction on entry into derivatives transactions. Although a blanket ban is unlikely, other restrictions are more common, such as limits around speculative derivatives and around derivatives lasting beyond a maximum duration.

(b) *Restriction on incurring financial indebtedness.* Credit agreements will invariably restrict the fund's ability to incur financial indebtedness. The exposure of the fund under derivatives transactions will often be treated as financial indebtedness – whether it is, or is not, is a matter of interpretation of the particular finance document. If derivatives exposure must be treated as financial indebtedness, then the next question is how the exposure should be measured. The common measure is the mark-to-market value of the derivatives transactions from time to time, but again this is a question of interpretation of the contractual provision (other valuation measures may include mark-to-model or the notional value of the derivatives transactions). A manager may be able to mitigate this risk by negotiating a sufficiently large permitted "basket" in the limitation to allow for anticipated fluctuations in derivatives exposure. It may also be possible for the fund to protect against unexpected increases in exposure by implementing a strategy, or including express terms in the derivatives, that cap(s) the fund's maximum exposure under those derivatives.

Contractual limitations under credit agreements in relation to granting credit support for fund-level derivatives transactions

Credit agreements will also commonly contain provisions that limit the fund's ability to give credit support in relation to derivatives, so if the fund needs to post margin collateral or give any guarantee in respect of the proposed derivatives, those provisions will need to be considered:

(a) *Security*. Credit agreements will invariably include a negative pledge that limits the fund's ability to grant security. This restriction will invariably apply to security over the investors' uncalled commitments and any collateral or deposit account into which any investor commitments are paid when called, but it may apply to the creation of other security as well. The manager will need a clear understanding of how any such limitation operates.

A fund that may be required to enter into security arrangements in relation to derivatives should seek to include appropriate permissions in its fund finance documentation to allow this activity. Whilst a subscription lender, for example, is unlikely to accommodate a competing grant of bilateral security over uncalled commitments, it may be prepared to allow the fund to enter into an ISDA Credit Support Annex as credit support for exposure under any permitted derivatives activity. It may also consider allowing a derivatives counterparty to share in its security package where adjustments are made to the borrowing base, to reflect the fund's exposure to that derivatives counterparty. This is considered in more detail below. A net asset value (NAV) lender, on the other hand, is likely to be more resistant to such arrangements, as it usually looks to fund assets other than uncalled investor commitments – including cash that is upstreamed from portfolio companies – for repayment. Any such lender would generally expect cash distributions to be applied in repayment of its credit facility rather than being used to collateralise derivatives exposure.

(b) *Guarantees*. If a fund guarantee will be provided, then the manager will need to ascertain whether any finance documents limit its ability to do so. This could be by way of a direct limitation on the giving of guarantees, or an indirect limitation where another restriction is broad enough to apply to guarantees (such as guarantees being designated as financial indebtedness for the purposes of the limitation on financial indebtedness or for any leverage-style financial covenant). If so, the manager will need to understand how the guarantee will be valued for the purpose of the limitation, and the treatment of any such guarantee for the purposes of calculating the borrowing base (where the underlying credit agreement relates to a subscription or hybrid facility) will also need to be considered. Equally, to the extent that it is commercially agreed that a derivatives counterparty can share in a subscription lender's security package, the benefit of any guarantee given under the finance documents may extend to that derivatives counterparty. In each case, the specific terms of the relevant finance documents will need to be considered.

(c) *Indemnities*. As with guarantees, careful thought must be given as to whether indemnities are limited directly or indirectly through any other limitation (for example, on financial indebtedness) and if so, how the indemnity liability is to be valued for this purpose.

(d) *Priority arrangements*. As a precondition to the manager successfully negotiating permissions under its credit agreement for the fund to enter into derivatives (and any related security or guarantees), the credit agreement may require that the derivatives counterparty joins into a priority agreement that regulates the relative ranking of the rights of the lenders under their loans, and of the derivatives counterparty under the derivatives. Such priority arrangements are, however, rarely seen – probably because: (i) subscription lenders are prepared to rely on their security over the investors' uncalled commitments and general fund NAV; and (ii) other lenders at the fund level would satisfy themselves that any such exposure was limited by ensuring that any baskets permitting such activities were relatively low.

To the extent that a derivatives counterparty is permitted to share in a lender's security package, which is considered in more detail below, this can usually be dealt with by including some relatively simple intercreditor-style provisions in the credit agreement.

A shared security package between a fund's lenders and its hedge counterparties

Fund-level derivatives usage can broadly be divided into two categories: secured and unsecured. The term "secured" is primarily used to refer to a scenario where the derivatives counterparty is party to security arrangements given in favour of the fund's lenders (and often such derivatives counterparty is also a lender (or an affiliate of a lender) under the fund's facility). Somewhat unhelpfully, there is scope for confusion as to what is meant by "secured" derivatives because the adjective "secured" is sometimes used to indicate that the derivatives documentation requires the posting of collateral to cover exposures. In this chapter, "secured" is used in the former sense.

Where a fund is considering secured hedging and the facility lenders are amenable to sharing their security with the derivatives counterparties, the security package would be granted in favour of a security agent, which holds that security on trust for both the lenders and the derivatives counterparties. The benefit of any guarantee granted in favour of the lenders under the credit agreement and associated security documents would also be extended to the derivatives counterparties.

Typically, the credit agreement would contain a mechanic, which allows the manager to allocate a portion of the fund's borrowing base to secured hedging, being either: (i) any hedging transaction that is designated by the manager as a secured hedging transaction; or (ii) any hedging transaction entered into under a hedging agreement that is designated by the manager as a secured hedging agreement. As any secured hedging is documented under separate derivatives documentation – and does not therefore constitute a utilisation of the facility – lenders would expect the aggregate amount of the borrowing base that can be allocated to all secured hedging to be capped. Otherwise, the risk for the lenders is that a substantial proportion of the borrowing base is used for secured hedging, resulting in a significant reduction in the lenders' income from the facility and a poor use of capital as a result.

The onus is on the manager to allocate a sufficient portion of the borrowing base to the secured hedging. In determining how much to allocate, the manager will be required to balance the need for headroom (to take account of potential mark-to-market fluctuations in the derivatives transactions) with the fact that any headroom will (further) reduce the borrowing base for the purposes of the credit agreement.

If the fund's exposure under the secured hedging exceeds the amount of borrowing base allocated to that secured hedging, the manager would typically be required to: (i) increase the amount of borrowing base allocated to those hedging transactions; (ii) post collateral for the excess (on a bilateral basis in favour of the derivatives counterparty); or (iii) wholly or partially close out some derivatives transactions to eliminate the excess.

Option (i) assumes, of course, both that the fund has capacity within its borrowing base to do so, and that by doing so, it would not exceed the overall cap on the amount of its borrowing base that can be allocated to secured hedging. Option (ii) requires careful analysis of where the relevant collateral will be sourced, and the impact of applying that collateral for that purpose. Option (iii) would result in the partial loss of the hedge and, potentially, costs to the fund if the derivatives to be closed out are out of the money.

From the lenders' perspective, it is critical to ensure that any claims of a derivatives counterparty under secured hedging transactions that exceed the borrowing base allocated to those transactions rank behind the lenders' claims. The relevant derivatives counterparty should only rank *pari passu* with the lenders to the extent its claim is equal to or less than the borrowing base allocated to the derivatives.

Further issues to consider under credit agreements in relation to the fund entering into derivatives

There are a number of other potential points of interaction between a fund's credit agreement and its derivatives documents (and these considerations apply to both secured and unsecured hedging). These need to be considered by reference to the terms of the relevant documents, but common issues are:

(a) *Cross-default*. This is potentially very serious; for example, a minor breach of a technical nature under the fund's derivatives documentation, which is not a concern for the derivatives counterparty, might nevertheless trigger an event of default under the fund finance documents – potentially resulting in a default under the credit facility as well.

If the manager has to give a cross-default trigger under the fund's credit facility, the fund should seek to include language in the credit agreement to mitigate its effect – for example, by limiting cross-default triggers that can be tripped by derivatives documentation breaches to events such as one or more of: (i) material derivatives documentation breaches only (like a payment default); (ii) hedging documentation breaches in respect of exposure in excess of an agreed threshold amount; (iii) actual derivatives documentation events of default rather than just potential events of default; or (iv) derivatives documentation events of default in respect of which the derivatives counterparty actually takes enforcement action.

(b) *Financial covenants*. The manager will also need to consider the impact of any derivatives on the financial covenants (if any) contained in its credit agreements. Whilst a pure subscription facility is unlikely to look to anything other than uncalled commitments cover, NAV facilities (for example) are likely to contain a more comprehensive suite of covenants. When negotiating its credit agreements, the manager should seek to tailor the terms of any financial covenant definitions and ratios so that anticipated derivatives use does not erode headroom and, as the fund moves through its life cycle, the financial covenants do not inappropriately dictate the fund's derivatives strategy.

Derivatives use may impact upon a number of financial covenants:

(1) *Uncalled commitments cover*. This financial covenant measures the level of financial indebtedness incurred by the fund against the quantum of its uncalled commitments. As noted above, the manager will need to understand to what extent derivatives exposure (including any guarantee, where relevant) is included within financial indebtedness for the purpose of this covenant and how that exposure is measured.

(2) *Interest cover*. This financial covenant, often seen in NAV facilities, measures the level of finance charges that the fund must pay under its financial indebtedness against net cashflow generated by its portfolio of investments. The manager will need to determine to what extent payments and other charges on its derivatives will constitute finance charges for the purpose of assessing compliance with the covenant.

(3) *Loan to value*. This financial covenant, usually found in NAV or other "aftercare" facilities, compares the level of financial indebtedness to fund NAV. The manager will need to identify the extent to which the derivatives transactions will either need to be included in the financial indebtedness calculation or will impact upon the NAV figure for the purpose of this covenant. Impact on NAV is more likely in circumstances where the derivatives have been entered into below fund level.

(c) *Availability of subscription facility*. Derivatives transactions may impact upon the availability of a subscription facility (or other credit agreements, where the facility limit is dictated by the level of uncalled commitments). This is because the terms of the credit agreement may require that, when calculating the borrowing base, the uncalled commitments be reduced by the amount of any derivatives liabilities (and any guarantee given in relation to derivatives transactions).

More generally, if the manager proposes to use a subscription facility to fund payments, or to fund collateral in respect of its derivatives transactions, then the manager will need to ensure that the subscription facility allows such use, and that it can be drawn down quickly enough to meet the timing of the payment.

Issues to consider under the derivatives documentation

The manager will need to negotiate its derivatives documentation by reference to the fund's circumstances and needs. Among the matters that the manager should consider are:

(a) *Recourse*. The manager will need to ensure that its derivatives documents reflect the correct separation of liability and recourse across its fund structure (for example, if hedging is only for liabilities relating to some investors (say a USD sleeve of a fund that mainly raises capital in EUR and invests in EUR assets) or certain fund-owned vehicles but not others (such as friends and family or carry vehicles)).

(b) *Cross-default*. The manager should carefully consider the extent to which a default under any credit agreement could give rise to a termination right under its derivatives documents (for example, under paragraph 5(a)(vi) (Cross-Default) of the 2002 ISDA Master Agreement). The manager should seek to include language to mitigate the effect of any such trigger (but this is likely to prove difficult if the derivatives counterparty is a lender under the credit agreement).

(c) *Additional termination events*. Derivatives counterparties will usually seek to include additional termination events (ATEs) in their derivatives documents, unless the manager has a very strong negotiating position or embedded relationship with the derivatives counterparty. This can have serious repercussions for the fund:

(1) *Uncalled commitments cover*. This termination event is triggered if the financial indebtedness of the fund exceeds an agreed ratio of the fund's uncalled capital commitments. Borrowings under any fund-level facility will usually fall within the definition of financial indebtedness.

The problem with this ATE is that a reduction in the fund's uncalled capital commitments is not necessarily a sign that it is in financial difficulty. Indeed, managers will be actively seeking to draw down investor commitments in order to invest them. A focus on uncalled commitments makes sense in the context of a subscription facility, but careful consideration is required when such provisions appear in derivatives documentation (particularly because the duration of the average subscription facility will often be shorter than the duration of the derivatives transactions being entered into). For example, where commitments have been invested, it may be appropriate for a component of fund NAV to be counted in the test in place of the deployed commitments, similar to the mechanics used in hybrid fund finance facilities.

(2) *NAV floor*. This termination event is triggered if the fund NAV drops below a particular level. The problem with this ATE is that a successful fund expects to reduce its NAV as it realises assets and returns value to investors. Conversely, "zombie" funds that continue well beyond their scheduled termination date, or that

are not being actively managed, may not trigger this ATE. Any trigger based on a NAV floor means that the fund should not plan to have derivatives transactions outstanding with the relevant counterparty significantly beyond the point where it expects to enter into the realisation and distribution phase.

Whilst the need for derivatives may reduce as the fund's life cycle moves to the realisation and distribution phase, it often does not disappear entirely. If a particular counterparty refuses to agree to there being appropriate flexibility in the NAV floor trigger (for example, a step down following the realisation of assets in line with the fund's strategy), the manager would want to be able to trade with one or more alternative counterparties who do not insist on a NAV floor trigger that would prevent derivatives use towards the end of the fund's life cycle.

(3) *NAV movement*. This termination event is triggered if the fund's NAV decreases by more than prescribed amounts (or percentages) over particular periods. This trigger is difficult for a manager if the termination event has not been calibrated to deal with expected NAV movements – particularly where it is seeking to return cash to investors during the realisation and distribution phase, or where it wishes to "flip" an asset early in its investment period (which could trigger a dramatic decrease in NAV if it is the only, or one of a handful of, investment(s) made by the fund at that date). The manager should seek to mitigate any such trigger appropriately (for example: adjusting the trigger movement thresholds to reflect different stages of the fund's life; adding back distributions to investors that remain eligible for recall; or applying the trigger only to decreases that have a material adverse effect upon the fund's ability to perform its payment obligations under the relevant instrument). There are other ways for the manager to mitigate this point, such as agreeing that instead of a termination trigger, a decrease in NAV will increase the level of collateral required to be posted by the fund in respect of its hedging exposure (the lesser of the two evils).

(d) *Use of collateral*. In addition to the issues relating to collateral highlighted above, managers should note that, to the extent the fund is required by regulation to exchange margin collateral in respect of its derivatives, it may not be possible for the manager to control the amount and frequency of margin collateral by setting large transfer threshold amounts and minimum transfer amounts. The ability of funds to use such mechanisms is increasingly limited by derivatives regulation such as EMIR/UK EMIR (and its equivalents in other jurisdictions).

Conclusion

Looking ahead, the global economy is showing signs of significant stress, which is resulting in increased exposures for market participants as currency rates fluctuate, interest rates rise and asset values seesaw. Reduced returns on investments makes the need to mitigate unwanted risks more relevant. Consequently, the need for fund-level hedging to address economic risk shows no signs of abating and managers should be aware of the challenges that they may face in doing so, and in implementing strategies at an acceptable cost and in a workable timeframe. It is perhaps no surprise that hedging desks are, at the time of writing, busier than ever.

Jonathan Gilmour
Tel: +44 20 7295 3425 / **Email:** jonathan.gilmour@traverssmith.com

Jonathan is a partner in the finance department at Travers Smith, and head of its Derivatives & Structured Products Group. Specialising in derivatives and structured products from both a transactional and advisory standpoint, he is widely regarded by peers and clients as one of the leading specialists in his field, and as a champion of "buy-side" interests in the UK derivatives market. He counts among his clients some of the UK's largest and most sophisticated financial institutions, investment managers, alternative asset managers, challenger banks, fintechs and occupational pension schemes. Jonathan is rated as a "Leading Individual" by both *Chambers* and *The Legal 500*, and is "Highly Regarded" by the *IFLR*.

Peter Hughes
Tel: +44 20 7295 3377 / **Email:** peter.hughes@traverssmith.com

Peter is a partner in the finance department at Travers Smith, where he is part of the Derivatives & Structured Products Group. Peter regularly acts for funds (including private equity houses, investment funds and hedge funds), investment managers and other buy-side and sell-side market participants. He is named as a key lawyer in the latest edition of *The Legal 500*.

Peter also specialises in advising pension trustees in relation to derivatives, security arrangements and debt restructurings.

Joseph Wren
Tel: +44 20 7295 3401 / **Email:** joseph.wren@traverssmith.com

Joseph is a partner in the finance department at Travers Smith, where he is part of the Derivatives & Structured Products Group. He regularly acts for private equity and private credit funds, infrastructure and real estate funds, investment managers, asset managers, pension schemes and corporates. He also advises sell-side institutions such as banks and other financial institutions. Joseph is described by *The Legal 500* as "approachable, knowledgeable and commercial", and is ranked as an "Up and Coming Individual" by *Chambers* and also recognised as a "Next Generation Partner" by *The Legal 500*. Joseph has also co-authored articles on the subject of derivatives and associated regulation for the *Butterworths Journal of International Banking and Financial Law*, *IFLR* and *Private Equity News*, and co-authors the LexisNexis practice guides on the repo market and the securities lending market.

Travers Smith LLP

10 Snow Hill, London EC1A 2AL, United Kingdom
Tel: +44 20 7295 3000 / URL: www.traverssmith.com

Subscription facilities: Through the Looking Glass and into Wonderland

Jan Sysel, Jons Lehmann & Kathryn Cecil
Fried, Frank, Harris, Shriver & Jacobson LLP

Introduction

As is common wisdom, the subscription facility has evolved into a significant and global financing tool for investment funds seeking efficient access to capital. Borrowers utilise subscription facilities in a myriad of ways, ranging from short-term borrowings (used primarily to bridge liquidity needs *in lieu* of making frequent and/or irregular investor capital calls) to long-term leverage (which seeks to increase the overall fund size and serve as a permanent source of capital) as well as various combinations thereof.

Subscription facilities are the bedrock of the fund manager's arsenal to facilitate the effective management of a fund's liquidity needs. Used by a wide variety of funds, with different investment strategies, across the full range of asset classes in North America and around the globe, including Europe (in particular the UK) and Asia-Pacific, where the market has significantly expanded, the prevalence and importance of the subscription facility is unquestionable. As the use of debt financing by funds has become ubiquitous, investors are now accustomed to, and more educated about, the use of such facilities. In tandem, fund structures have evolved to offer investors a menu of levered and unlevered options and different investment currencies to choose from.

The number, size, variety and complexity of investment funds have grown over the years, and subscription facilities have adapted to the changing landscape. Fund sponsors and lenders continue to collaborate to develop financing solutions designed to address the evolving needs of borrowers and their investors. Indeed, a "cookie-cutter" subscription financing is a myth. The subscription facility market today is robust and sophisticated, continuously attracting new entrants on both the borrower and the lender side. Increasing demand and bespoke financing needs have resulted in the development of customised liquidity solutions to suit the particular profile of the underlying fund. While NAV facilities, GP financings and other products have risen further in prominence during the past year, subscription facilities have continued to dominate overall activity in the fund finance market through 2022. Investors and sponsors continue to highly value quick access to liquid capital and other related benefits in fund management and deployment. As the world slowly recovers from the longer-term effects of the global pandemic and faces the challenges of greater geopolitical uncertainty and more volatile economic conditions, the subscription facility is once again proving to be a versatile and flexible instrument. Even in an age where the structuring and negotiation of transactions is increasingly virtual, the benefits of subscription facilities are still very much tangible and real.

This chapter looks at the breadth of the types of subscription financings and trends currently in the marketplace by examining select aspects of facilities for various kinds of investment funds in the US and UK markets.

Once upon a time, long, long ago: Subscription facility fundamentals

Subscription facilities are effectively a form of "asset-based lending", where the ability to borrow is determined principally by reference to the value of certain eligible assets provided as collateral for such loan. Such assets also count towards the "borrowing base" against which a bank will advance. A subscription facility's collateral package is anchored by the commitments of the fund's investors that have not yet been funded.

These financings tend to be structured as revolving credit facilities, giving the borrower readily available access to liquidity for the purpose of making investments, without having to call equity capital and wait for the contributions to be received. The short period required to draw advances (typically one to three days) enables quick execution of underlying asset acquisitions or other investments. Such investments may include back-to-back funding arrangements in the case of debt funds, which increasingly look to offer similar products to underlying borrowers with the inherent short-term liquidity requirements. Subscription facilities also allow funds to improve cash management by avoiding inefficient holding of reserves for covering expenses, and often provide additional flexibilities, such as availability of alternative currencies and letters of credit.

Although the security package may vary depending on the fund structure and other factors, a typical security package for subscription facilities comprises security over: (i) the unfunded capital commitments of the fund's investors; (ii) the right to make capital calls from investors, and receive proceeds of such capital calls in the form of contributions; (iii) the bank accounts into which the capital contributions are funded; and (iv) certain rights related to the foregoing (including the right to enforce against such investors) pursuant to the documentation evidencing such rights (including subscription agreements of the investors and organisational documents of the fund).

Because the collateral for a subscription facility is intrinsically tied to the obligation of the investors to make capital contributions (rather than the fund's underlying assets), lenders closely scrutinise the investor base of the fund and the legal relationship between the investors and the fund. The types of investors and the life-cycle stage of the fund will influence and help determine the optimal approach for calculating the borrowing base against which the loan will be advanced.

Investors are generally considered eligible, and typically categorised as either an "included investor" (usually institutional investors with a specific rating and/or sufficient financial strength) or a "designated investor" (other investors meeting relevant criteria). Certain investors may be ineligible due to restrictions on their ability to fund in particular situations, for example, due to regulatory reasons, or those for whom a lender lacks sufficient financial information. It is important to note that the uncalled commitments of ineligible investors still form part of the collateral package granted to lenders, typically leading to some element of over-collateralisation. Further, an otherwise eligible investor may subsequently become ineligible and its commitments disregarded due to certain specified exclusion events, such as a decline in its financial condition (including bankruptcy).

After determining the basic composition of investors that will be included in the borrowing base of the subscription facility, the parties negotiate appropriate advance rates and any applicable concentration limits in respect of these investors. Advance rates are the basic measure of the amount of credit a lender will allow a borrower, and are generally expressed as a percentage of the included investors' (up to 90–95%) and designated investors' (up to 65–70%) uncalled capital commitments.

We now commonly see further bifurcation of advance rates, depending on additional criteria. For example, there may be a higher advance rate afforded from the moment in time at which capital commitments over a certain threshold (sometimes referred to as a "hurdle") have already been funded. This feature caters to the natural cycle of an investment fund because, as capital is drawn, the amount of credit support available for a subscription facility decreases. However, a higher advance rate may alleviate or even equalise these consequences. From a lender's perspective, the diminished uncalled capital is counterbalanced by the investors having more "skin in the game". Another similar feature is a fluctuation of the advance rate based on the value of assets in the fund, when, as the value of fund assets increases over time, so does the percentage applied to uncalled commitments.

There are other potential approaches to categorising investors – for example, a now common segment of the US market functions on the basis of a "simplified" borrowing base with a (typically somewhat lower) "flat" advance rate against an aggregate investor pool. In this structure, the borrowing base generally encompasses all of a fund's investors, regardless of eligibility criteria or exclusion triggers (which is similar to the "coverage ratio" principle traditionally used in subscription lines in the UK market).

Concentration limits present a further refinement of how the overall borrowing base credit is distributed among various classes of investors, and are generally determined based upon the makeup of a particular fund's investor pool. Lenders often look to reduce their risk exposure through diversification and thus aim to calibrate the classes of investors within the borrowing base. This is done in order to ensure that, from their perspective, a disproportionate amount is not advanced against the uncalled capital commitment of a particular class, either individually or in the aggregate for such class. Historically, there has been focus on limiting the amount of credit that is attributed to investor categories such as individuals (natural persons) and their tax and estate planning vehicles. However, we have seen an increase in lenders' willingness to lend against such investor commitments.

A variation of this principle that we have seen banks propose is that they seek to ensure that the largest investor (no matter what class or category it would have otherwise been in) does not constitute more than a certain percentage of the overall fund commitments. On the other hand, in order to increase flexibility, lenders may consider holidays or waivers in respect of concentration limits (e.g. not apply them during a "ramp up" period during the fundraising stage after the first, but before the final, fund closing, when the initial investor pool is less diverse than it ultimately will be) or the upward flexing of applicable percentages to relax such requirements for a specified period.

From a legal perspective, sponsors and lenders alike pay attention to the organisational documents of the fund, which (within the statutory framework applicable to the particular entity in question) set forth the contractual obligation of the investors to fund capital if and when called. In addition to the general powers of the fund, certain express provisions authorising the borrower (or its general partner, manager or other controlling person) to incur debt and grant liens (including, importantly, a pledge of the uncalled capital commitments) without further consent or action by the investors are expected. Also commonly included are a host of other ancillary acknowledgments and consents for the benefit of subscription lenders (often as express third-party beneficiaries), which can provide additional comfort.

As the sophistication of market participants grows, much more attention is paid to subtle nuances and technical drafting of the fund documentation (typically the limited partnership agreement). This is true particularly in respect of certain provisions that have come to be increasingly negotiated between the funds and investors. These include investment "excuse" provisions (allowing an investor not to participate in a particular investment due to regulatory, tax or other considerations specifically applicable to it) and other important elements with regard to the mechanics of funding, such as "overcall" provisions (which mitigate risk of another investor funding default) or any entitlement of the fund to "recycle" capital (such as to recall certain amounts previously distributed to the investors).

As a result of these developments, "investor letters" (i.e. separate bilateral arrangements between the lenders on the one hand, and the investors on the other hand, which would establish direct contractual privity between the lender and the investor) are now only rarely used. We will address certain situations in which obtaining such letters may be beneficial for structuring the subscription facility from both the borrower and lender perspective in more detail below.

The variations of fund structures and underlying investor pools can result in differing considerations, and typically require custom and complex loan documentation in each specific case. Below, we illustrate the need for bespoke tailoring in the context of: (i) funds of one and/or separately managed accounts (which may have only a single investor); (ii) complex commingled vehicles (which may have hundreds or more investors and utilise numerous entities that are part of one fund family); and (iii) by comparison, funds in the UK market.

Cinderella goes to the ball: The separately managed account

As discussed above, the investor composition of a fund is a key factor for lenders in establishing the borrowing base for a subscription facility. When there is only one investor, as is the case for "funds of one" or "separately managed accounts" (SMAs), certain unique considerations arise, including those stemming from an increased concentration risk. In our experience, the number of SMAs has continued to dramatically increase in recent years, as large institutional investors (including state and private pension funds, educational endowment funds, insurance companies and sovereign wealth funds) have been keen to put their capital to work faster than managers have raised a commingled fund. SMAs may also allow such investors to take advantage of customised structures, which can accommodate unique tax and/or regulatory requirements or investment objectives.

While, from a financing perspective, SMAs present some specific challenges, there are also certain advantages. Indeed, it appears that as the number of SMAs in the marketplace has increased, so too have subscription facilities available for these investment products, and lenders appear to be increasingly willing to extend credit to SMAs. Like any other fund, the terms of the organisational documents of an SMA must satisfy the general requirements of the subscription facility lender, but enhanced due diligence may often underpin a bank's SMA lending decision.

Many lenders view the facility as akin to making a loan to the underlying investor and so, as an alternative (or in addition) to incorporating certain provisions in the organisational documents, lenders may request that the investor in the SMA enters into an investor consent letter. The primary benefit of such letter is generally to establish a direct privity of contract between the investor and the lender. Such a letter might also address any other specific considerations that may arise in a particular context (for example, as many investors in SMAs are government pension plans, there may be sovereign immunity issues that lending against such investors might potentially present to banks). In the context of SMAs in particular, investor letters may be coupled with additional credit support documentation to the extent that an investor is utilising one or more intermediate entities through which it invests. This often takes the form of a "comfort letter" under which the ultimate creditworthy parent undertakes to keep the vehicle (which is the direct limited partner in the fund) sufficiently capitalised to meet capital calls.

Understandably, the treatment of such issues requires a highly individualised analysis that needs to be performed on a case-by-case basis. As compared to subscription facilities for multiple-investor funds, advance rates for the single-investor SMAs tend to be more customised and negotiated. While banks generally lend based on the creditworthiness of each investor, and would thus be expected to assign an advance rate for an investor in an SMA that is substantially equivalent to the advance rate such investor would receive if it were investing in a commingled fund, other factors may necessitate a different approach. For example, in an SMA scenario, lenders cannot rely upon a diversified investor base that, in the aggregate, reduces their exposure to an individual investor's funding failure. Further, as noted above, in many commingled fund facilities there are investors who do not qualify for inclusion in the borrowing base, but their uncalled capital commitments are still pledged as collateral and so effectively provide for "over-collateralisation".

There may be other terms in SMA subscription facilities for which lenders may seek a different regime, as compared to commingled fund subscription facilities. For example, certain exclusion events (i.e. events that, if they were to occur with respect to an investor, would trigger removal of such investor from the borrowing base) under a commingled fund subscription facility may be characterised as events of default (i.e. events that give the lender a right to accelerate the amounts outstanding under the facility and pursue remedies) under an SMA subscription facility.

Another approach to mitigating the increased risk profile of an SMA is that certain exclusion events that might otherwise be afforded a grace period, allowing the investor, the borrower and the lender to work out a potentially problematic situation, are either immediate breaches or the period is reduced. There is rationale for this approach; for instance, if the SMA investor defaults on its obligation to fund a capital call, the lack of any other investor commitments to fall back on makes it reasonable to characterise such an occurrence as an event of default. However, if the same failure to fund capital were to occur in a commingled fund, the typical subscription facility would simply no longer give credit for such investor's commitment in the borrowing base. Only if investors with material capital commitments (above agreed-upon thresholds) defaulted would an event of default be triggered under a commingled fund's facility, in most cases.

In a similar vein as the exclusion events, investor transfer restrictions may also be tightened in the credit documentation for an SMA.

Focusing on potential advantages, sponsors with multiple SMAs may be able to utilise the straightforward nature of the single-investor vehicle in order to achieve greater efficiency with respect to the facility documentation. Indeed, some sponsors have found that SMAs are generally well suited for employing the so-called "umbrella" technology, pursuant to which the same lender provides individual and separate loan commitments to multiple borrowers under one credit agreement.

Under these instruments, many of the terms are shared by all of the SMAs party to the loan document, but investor-specific terms (such as the pricing, the advance rate and the loan amount) can be different for each SMA. Importantly, each SMA remains severally (and not jointly) liable for its own borrowings and the distinct facilities are not cross-defaulted or cross-collateralised. This means that potential issues under one SMA's facility will not impact another SMA's facility, even if both are party to the same credit agreement. Umbrella facilities may allow sponsors to streamline negotiations into essentially a single set of documentation while putting multiple facilities in place.

The time and cost efficiencies of umbrella facilities has also prompted commingled funds to consider implementing such an approach, and the number of them employing this technology has increased. More and more managers are seeking to combine a number of subscription facilities for different funds (whether that be of different strategies or vintages) within one overarching framework. This promotes closer alignment of terms with the benefit that reporting and covenant regimes are kept consistent across a number of separate facilities, mitigating the monitoring and compliance burden that would result from diverging standards.

The town musicians of Bremen: Large commingled funds

At the other end of the spectrum, there are pooled investment fund vehicles with diverse investor bases, which may include a variety of institutional investors, as well as private wealth management clients (such as high-net-worth individuals and their family offices) and, at times, the sponsor's management and employees. Depending on the composition of the investor base, such funds often require, due to various tax, regulatory and other considerations, multiple entities through which the investors can access the underlying investments, resulting in structures that can be quite complex.

A frequently used technology is a multi-tiered structure, sometimes referred to as the "master-feeder" structure. This arrangement utilises two or more separate entities on top of each other; investors contribute capital through a "feeder" fund, which then passes on ("feeds") the capital to a "master" fund, which in turn makes investments, either directly or indirectly, through subsidiaries. In certain circumstances, there may be some investors who invest through the feeder fund, and other investors who invest into the master fund.

In other situations, a separate fund structure may be formed for different types of investors without there being an aggregating master fund, which is sometimes referred to as a "parallel fund" structure. For US-based sponsors, an initial fund is often formed as a Delaware or Cayman Islands limited partnership that is treated as a "pass-through entity" for US federal income tax purposes and typically includes taxable US investors. When the investor pool includes non-US investors and/or certain tax-exempt US investors, one or more separate "offshore" funds, which are treated as non-US corporations (or non-US limited partnerships) for US federal income tax purposes, are often formed in various jurisdictions (frequently the Cayman Islands, British Virgin Islands and Bermuda, and increasingly also European domiciles such as Luxembourg, Ireland and Scotland as well as the Channel Islands of Guernsey and Jersey).

The general trend appears to be that the complexity of fund structuring continues to evolve and increase as more investors are exploring different or new asset classes, and the regulatory and tax environment keeps developing. It is not unusual for a large fund with a widely diversified investor base to employ multiple parallel vehicles at the same time as they also utilise several layers of feeder funds. This often results in creating a complex web of dozens (or even hundreds) of entities, which requires a good understanding of the structure by both sponsors and lenders.

Regardless of jurisdiction and/or legal form, all of the entities in these types of structures are part of one fund family, and are managed by a common investment manager – such management can be accomplished in a variety of ways, including by utilising multiple affiliated entities and/or independent managers. Each of the various vehicles is typically a separate legal entity, though the exact characteristics may depend on how the relevant legal forms of the vehicles are treated in their applicable jurisdictions. In some cases, they may be statutorily required to act through another entity (for example, a Cayman Islands limited partnership acts through its general partner).

The considerations that determine the characteristics of each entity can contribute to the complexity of the structures in terms of which entities need to be party to the subscription facility documentation. Most multi-tiered funds need to ascertain at which level borrowings will be made (in other words, which entity will be the borrower under the subscription facility). This choice may be affected by any number of different factors, including tax and regulatory considerations, administrative ease and the operational requirements of the sponsor (for example, the ability to accommodate other creditors within the structure, whether that be for the provision of hedging, or structural leverage). To the extent that investor capital commitments are not made directly to the borrowing entity, consideration must be given as to how to mechanically ensure that a security interest in the collateral has been granted, directly or indirectly, for the lenders' benefit.

A "cascading pledge" structure is one potential method utilised to assure that lenders have an appropriate "path" to the ultimate source of capital commitments. In this scenario, the upper-tier feeder fund pledges the capital commitments of its investors to the lower-tier master fund, in order to secure such feeder fund's obligations to make capital contributions into the master fund. The lower-tier master fund then, in turn, pledges the capital commitments of its "investors" (i.e. the upper-tier feeder funds), and any rights under the pledge from the upper-tier feeder funds, to the lenders to secure such master fund's obligations as a borrower under the subscription facility.

Other possible alternatives include an arrangement where (if permissible from a regulatory and tax perspective) the feeder fund may become a party to the subscription facility agreement and/or security agreement with the lender. Under this approach, the feeder fund may become a co-borrower of the loans, become a guarantor of the indebtedness incurred by the master fund, or just provide a "naked" pledge of the investors' capital commitments directly to the lender.

There are situations where it may not be possible to have multiple parallel entities within a fund structure jointly and severally liable for repayment of the loans and, in some instances, the "onshore" and "offshore" entities may be required to enter into separate credit agreements. Another example is a dual "levered" and "unlevered" silo structure, where one fund silo does not incur debt at all, or only takes advantage of a subscription facility to manage cash-flows, but the other fund silo also obtains asset-based leverage.

If separate credit agreements are put in place, they may or may not be permitted to be cross-collateralised, whether for tax and/or regulatory reasons or because of an understanding with the investors in the separate vehicles. This effectively means that each of the parallel vehicles must rely on a borrowing base comprising only capital commitments of its own investors. As banks typically provide different advance rates and concentration limits for different investors based on their underwriting criteria, the borrowing capacity of one silo may be different from the borrowing capacity of the other silo(s). Since sponsors ordinarily aim to manage borrowings on a consistent level across the various vehicles in a fund family, the ability to borrow might then be dictated by the vehicle with the lowest borrowing capacity.

One potential solution may be (where this is acceptable from a commercial perspective and permitted under the applicable fund documents) to provide for a "limited" cross-collateralisation (by certain assets only), cross-guarantee and/or cross-default between the individual credit agreements. This might allow the borrowing base to be calculated on an aggregate basis for all the silos. Another approach may be to utilise "investor letters", which, by giving an increased level of comfort to the lenders, may allow for higher advance rates and/or concentration limits.

The golden goose: The European lands of magic

Over time, the internationalisation of the subscription finance market has influenced the documentation and transaction terms of subscription facilities in the European market. US-based sponsors have been expanding their investment activities across the Atlantic and continue to seek subscription facilities similar to what they have been accustomed to in the US. In addition, European and US-based lenders have increasingly offered subscription facility terms similar to those seen in the US market.

Nevertheless, despite a trend for convergence of the terms, broadly speaking, certain differences persist due to differing approaches to credit evaluation and local law requirements with respect to the creation and perfection of security interests in collateral.

The relatively recent trend for ESG-linked financings in the European finance market is also increasingly becoming a feature incorporated within subscription facilities in the US market, where a number of sponsors have sought to incorporate ESG-driven financing terms. While Europe may have adopted ESG principles earlier than the US and Asia, those considerations have very quickly picked up steam in those markets as well and are now becoming commonplace.

Subscription facilities in the UK market were historically almost exclusively the product of "relationship" deals, with lenders primarily focusing on the track record of the larger sponsor group and success of their earlier vintages when determining whether to offer a subscription facility to an individual fund. This difference in approach used to be reflected in some of the terms typical of subscription facilities in the UK market. For example, traditionally, subscription facilities in the UK market frequently used the "coverage ratio" to limit the amount that may be drawn under the facility at any given time.

The coverage ratio is the ratio of the uncalled capital commitments of the included investors to the aggregate indebtedness of the fund, and is typically set at no less than 1:1. Notably, the coverage ratio approach does not typically involve applying advance rates to the uncalled capital commitments of included investors, meaning that once an investor is deemed an "included investor", the borrower receives credit for 100% of that investor's uncalled capital commitment.

In recent years, the coverage ratio approach has become less common in the UK market and is frequently substituted by a US-style borrowing base model. Parallel to the development of the borrowing base methodology, investor exclusion events have also been refined. These events are typically narrower in scope for facilities that apply a borrowing base methodology, but are often tailored to particular investors and address a greater number of specific events that would result in a reduction of the borrowing base. Lenders are increasingly focused on the exclusion event definitions – a trend that goes hand in hand with the increased focus on, and diligence of, organisational and fund-related documents.

Irrespective of the internationalisation of the subscription finance market and the convergence of certain terms of subscription facilities in US and European markets, the granting of security interests in respect of a borrower's obligations under a subscription facility remains specific to the jurisdiction applicable to the relevant fund entity. Granting and perfecting security interests over the uncalled capital commitments of the funds' investors, the rights to call capital commitments, and the bank accounts into which any capital contributions are funded, represent the cornerstone on which the collateral base of the subscription facilities are built.

In the US market, to perfect the security interest and enforce the lender's rights against third parties, generally a UCC-1 financing statement should be filed (and a control agreement entered into with respect to pledged accounts). Under English law, however, the security interest of lenders in the rights to call capital is typically created pursuant to an assignment by way of security, which is perfected by notification to the investors in the fund. To manage and protect the relationship with their investors, borrowers often seek to negotiate the timing for the delivery of the notices to investors, and are also highly sensitive to the form of any such notifications. This process is balanced against the lenders' desire to obtain a perfected security interest reasonably promptly after the facility is made available.

A happy ever after? The story continues…

In a record 2021 for the fund financing market, we have again witnessed a sustained and steady increase in the volume and size of subscription facilities, and overall other fund financing transactions more broadly. A key driver behind the market's solid growth has been the willingness of sponsors and investors to work with lenders on devising and implementing customised solutions addressing all parties' needs and requirements. Thus, market participants have been successful in developing products flexible enough to adapt to evolving fund structures and prospective new investors as well as liquidity solutions for the "long run" that can cater to the different stages of the life of a fund.

This is evidenced by a growing number of combinations of subscription facilities and asset-based facilities (collateralised by the underlying fund investments). Such financing can take the form of hybrids (with a collateral package that consists of both uncalled capital commitments and underlying investment assets) or other bespoke instruments (for example, where a traditional subscription-based borrowing base is enhanced by a component based on the value of the underlying investment assets, but without a corresponding pledge). Indeed, by coupling the components of a subscription facility with those of asset-based financings, a solution can be tailored to support the fund's ongoing liquidity requirements beyond the termination of the investment period while balancing the different risk profile at that stage of the fund life. This trend is likely to continue and expand as fund products evolve further, in particular in the light of the increased interest in semi-liquid fund products and continuation funds.

Additional products, such as capital provided in the form of preferred equity, GP/management fee financing solutions, and employee loan programmes continue to be widely utilised and developed. Moreover, there has been a convergence of the fund financing market with the larger bond and capital markets where we are observing an increasing appetite for syndicated facilities that can take the form of rated notes and even incorporate features historically seen in securitisations. We believe that the future of these products and markets is intrinsically tied together and, for certain types of deals, they will eventually combine.

As ESG-compliant investments in general become more prevalent, the broader loan market is developing financing products that include ESG-linked criteria to reward positive performance of borrowers in the related key metrics. European regulatory requirements to classify funds under the Sustainable Finance Disclosure Regulation as either not investing in accordance with sustainability factors (article 6), promoting sustainability (article 8) or having sustainability as an investment objective (article 9) have led to an increase in funds identifying as sustainable. Legislation in this area, to be implemented in England and Wales next year, is likely to further shape the fund finance market. While, in the US, the regulation of ESG is in its nascent stages, the Securities and Exchange Commission (as one of the key regulators of the financial investment and advisory industry) has taken a keen interest in the top and published a voluminous proposal for future rulemaking.

In credit facilities in particular, a margin adjustment – either a discount if certain ESG-related performance criteria are met or a premium if the criteria are not met – may be used to incentivise the borrower to meet certain ESG-related thresholds. Likewise, in the fund finance market, there is a noticeable and accelerating trend towards ESG criteria, including facilities where the interest rate is determined by a ratchet mechanism based on agreed key performance indicators referencing the fund's portfolio companies (or, in the case of debt funds, the performance or percentage of their own loans with such criteria), or external third-party ratings, in each case tested on a periodic basis. The variety of ESG metrics is also developing and covers areas from renewable energy investments to gender and race equality on management boards of portfolio companies.

While a number of the foregoing investment strategies and debt products are as yet relatively new developments, we expect the market to evolve and align over time, gravitating towards increased consistency in principles and reporting standards.

We believe that the popularity of subscription facilities is driven in part by the strong performance these loans have demonstrated over extended periods of time, and the strength of the alternative asset sector, as well as the continued ability of sponsors and lenders to craft solutions that meet the growing needs and complexities of today's investment fund structures. Despite the broader markets encountering some tumultuous times in 2022, with significant geopolitical developments as well as unexpected economic challenges (with a sudden and significant increased global inflation), the fund financing space has remained largely stable and terms of the underlying financing documents generally consistent.

We remain optimistic about the outlook for the industry, which, due to the versatility of its products and adaptability of market participants, has shown its resilience to difficult conditions and the capacity to weather challenges so far.

* * *

Acknowledgment

Jacqueline Punjabi – Associate, Finance
Email: jacqueline.punjabi@friedfrank.com

The authors would particularly like to acknowledge the assistance and input provided by Jacqueline Punjabi in preparing this chapter. Jacqueline is a corporate finance associate in Fried Frank's London office and represents clients on a wide array of corporate matters including fund financings.

Jan Sysel
Tel: +1 212 859 8713 / Email: jan.sysel@friedfrank.com

Jan Sysel represents sponsors, borrowers, arrangers, and lenders across a range of industries on financing transactions, primarily in connection with fund formation. Clients highly regard Jan's extensive experience in structuring, negotiating, documenting, and executing complex financings, including syndicated senior facilities, mezzanine facilities, and private debt placements. Jan's work includes unsecured and secured first and second lien facilities, both cash-flow-based and asset-based, with a particular focus on fund subscription facilities and other types of investment fund leverage. Clients also seek Jan's advice in leveraged acquisitions, spinoffs, recapitalisations, and restructurings. A member of the Fund Finance Association (FFA) US Advisory Council, Jan speaks frequently at FFA and other industry conferences as a trusted voice in the space. Espousing a deep commitment to the community, he is also a mentor on the FFA's NextGen platform, supporting junior market participants.

Jons Lehmann
Tel: +44 20 7972 9149 / Email: jons.lehmann@friedfrank.com

Jons Lehmann is a corporate partner resident in Fried Frank's London office. He represents clients in domestic and cross-border finance transactions across all levels of the capital structure. Private equity sponsors, investment banks, direct lenders, hedge funds, and public and private companies benefit from Jons' broad experience, which includes in-depth expertise of subscription facilities, NAV/leverage facilities, preferred equity transactions, GP financings and hybrid facilities in the fund financing space.

The Legal 500 UK recognises Jons in Investment Funds: Fund Finance and Acquisition Finance, Bank Lending: Investment Grade Debt and Syndicated Loans. The publication quotes a client praising Jons for "offering practical advice" and bringing "innovative legal solutions and market experience to their work". Jons is also recognised by *IFLR1000* in the Banking category.

Kathryn Cecil
Tel: +44 20 7972 9624 / Email: kathryn.cecil@friedfrank.com

Kathryn Cecil is a partner in the Corporate Department and the Finance Practice, resident in Fried Frank's London office. She acts for funds, lenders, borrowers, and sponsors on a range of complex domestic and cross-border finance transactions focusing on leveraged finance and fund finance.

Clients benefit from Kathryn's pragmatic advice on subscription, asset-backed, and other fund financing arrangements, leveraged and acquisition financings, and financial restructurings.

The Legal 500 UK recognises Kathryn in Acquisition Finance, Bank Lending and Fund Finance where she wins praise from a client as having "excellent knowledge of the fund financing market". *Chambers UK* also recognises Kathryn in the Banking and Finance: Fund Finance category (Band 2).

Kathryn has been appointed to Fund Finance Association's (FFA) EMEA Executive Committee as Deputy Chair.

Fried, Frank, Harris, Shriver & Jacobson LLP

One New York Plaza, New York, NY 10004, USA
Tel: +1 212 859 8000 / Fax: +1 212 859 4000 / URL: www.friedfrank.com

A fund borrower's guide to NAV and Hybrid Facilities:
Considerations for a "bankable" partnership agreement for fund-level leverage beyond the sub line

Julia Kohen, Ashley Belton Gold & Jakarri Hamlin
Simpson Thacher & Bartlett LLP

Introduction

Over the past 15 years, fund sponsors (with the assistance of experienced fund finance counsel) have improved the form of their fund limited partnership agreements ("**LPAs**") to provide the flexibility necessary to enter into subscription credit facilities backed by the uncalled capital commitments of the fund's investors ("**Subscription Facilities**"). These LPA improvements include express language as to (i) the authority to incur debt, whether on a several, joint and several, guaranteed or cross-collateralised basis, (ii) the ability to pledge the fund's assets to secure such obligations, (iii) investor acknowledgments to fund capital contributions without defence, offset or counterclaim, and (iv) third-party beneficiary rights for lenders as to the foregoing provisions. These improvements help make the LPAs "bankable" and facilitate the streamlined execution of Subscription Facilities, often without the need to deliver investor consent letters, which can be expensive, burdensome and time-consuming.

A Subscription Facility is an essential tool in a fund's toolbox. Such a facility is often put in place soon after the initial investor closing, increased in size as additional investor commitments are added, supplemented with additional borrowers based on the fund's ongoing investment needs, and extended past the initial maturity date to support the fund through its investment period and beyond. An inherent limitation of a Subscription Facility, however, is the aggregate amount of uncalled capital commitments, which declines over time as capital is called and deployed to make investments.

Over the last several years, funds have sought additional liquidity in the form of (i) supplementing their Subscription Facilities by adding collateral relating to the investment value of the fund ("**Hybrid Facilities**"), or (ii) entering into new credit facilities backed by the net asset value of their investment portfolios ("**NAV Facilities**"). With a combination of Subscription Facilities, Hybrid Facilities and/or NAV Facilities, a fund can meet its financing needs from its inception (when uncalled capital is high and asset values are low), through its investment period (as uncalled capital declines and asset values increase), and after the end of its investment period (to support existing investments and return capital to investors when uncalled capital may be low). Historically, a NAV Facility was most commonly put in place later in a fund's life as a replacement for a Subscription Facility. However, recently, funds are showing interest in NAV Facilities earlier in their life cycles, when there is still a large pool of uncalled capital and the Subscription Facility is in active use.

Increased interest in NAV Facilities and Hybrid Facilities extends across fund strategies and types, including secondaries funds, infrastructure funds, open-ended funds and buy-out funds. While these funds often have fulsome provisions in their LPAs relating to Subscription Facilities, fund sponsors and their counsel may wish to evaluate their LPAs and related investor disclosures with a view toward ensuring that there is sufficient flexibility to enter into other financing arrangements (including NAV Facilities and Hybrid Facilities) that may be in the best interest of the fund and its investors. To this end, fund sponsors may consider updating their LPAs to include terms that will streamline the execution and implementation of NAV Facilities and Hybrid Facilities.

It is important to note that any analysis of a fund's LPA cannot be done in a vacuum. It is a fact-specific inquiry that is based on the totality of the circumstances, including the fund structure, the fund strategy and the nature of investments, the fund's desired debt capacity, investor expectations as to the use of leverage, investor sensitivities to fund-level debt (whether tax, ERISA or otherwise), and disclosures by the fund to its investors (including in the fund's private placement memorandum). There is no "one-size-fits-all" approach. Rather, the terms of a fund's LPA will reflect the negotiated arrangement between the fund and its investors as to permitted indebtedness.

This chapter aims to provide fund borrowers and their counsel with guideposts for reviewing and negotiating LPA provisions, all with the goal of maximising the fund's flexibility to incur and secure debt to support its investments and other activities throughout its life cycle.

NAV Facility basics: Comparisons and contrasts to Subscription Facilities

The primary distinction between a NAV Facility and a Subscription Facility is the nature of the assets that form the basis of the collateral and the borrowing base (or the amount of debt that the fund can incur). At the most basic level, a Subscription Facility "looks upward" to the investors' uncalled capital commitments and a NAV Facility "looks downward" to the fund's investment portfolio.

The borrowing base under a Subscription Facility is equal to the product of one or more advance rates, multiplied by the uncalled capital commitments of the investors. Investors may be divided into groups that receive varying advance rates, depending on their credit quality. Further, certain investors may be subject to concentration limits or hurdle conditions, while others may be excluded entirely from the borrowing base. In contrast, the borrowing base under many NAV Facilities is equal to the product of one or more advance rates, multiplied by the net asset value of the fund's investments. Investments may be divided into groups that receive different advance rates – these may be based on the jurisdiction or credit rating of the investments, or whether they are public or private investments. Similar to a Subscription Facility, certain types of investments may be subject to concentration limits or excluded entirely from the borrowing base. While there are obvious parallels between these two types of facilities, the calculations determining the amount of debt that a fund can incur are fundamentally different.

The collateral under a Subscription Facility typically comprises (i) the uncalled capital commitments of the fund's investors, (ii) the right of the fund and its general partner to issue capital calls to the fund's investors, (iii) the right of the fund to receive capital contributions from such investors, and (iv) the accounts into which the capital contributions are deposited. The scope of Subscription Facility collateral has become relatively standardised, although there may be complications based on the structure of the fund and the investors' capital commitments. In contrast, there is greater variation in the collateral provided under a NAV Facility, which can be tailored to suit a fund's particular circumstances and financing needs. This variation is largely driven by (a) the structure of the fund and how its investments are held (whether directly or through one or more holding companies), (b) the need of the particular fund to maintain other debt arrangements, whether at the fund or asset level, (c) the position of the NAV Facility borrower within the overall fund structure (whether at the fund level or at one or more special purpose vehicles), and (d) the commercial understanding between the lender and the fund sponsor.

Collateral and partnership agreement pledging provisions

The scope of the collateral package is a gating item when negotiating a NAV or Hybrid Facility. The most robust collateral package requested by lenders might include a lien on each borrower's (i) rights to receive proceeds and distributions in respect of its investments, (ii) accounts into which such amounts are deposited, and/or (iii) equity interests in its underlying investment vehicles. This type of package will require fund sponsors and their counsel to review the fund documents to confirm that they include appropriate authorisations, as well as the underlying investment documents to determine whether they include any applicable restrictions.

Juxtaposed against these arrangements are more borrower-friendly "collateral-lite" facilities, where the collateral comprises the bank accounts into which distributions and other proceeds are deposited. This pledge is then coupled with a covenant by the borrowers to deposit distributions and other proceeds into such accounts. In these cases, lenders may seek additional protection by requiring a negative pledge on certain assets (including equity interests) held by the borrowers. The benefits of these facilities from a fund sponsor perspective are:

- they are more cost-effective from a legal perspective to put in place in light of the narrower scope of security documentation;
- there is no ongoing collateral management, particularly as investments are purchased and sold during the life of the fund; and
- this approach may avoid potential legal, regulatory and contractual complications (as discussed further below).

As a threshold matter, a fund should determine whether its LPA and other fund documents permit the pledge of the required collateral. For a fund sponsor looking for maximum flexibility, the pledging provisions of the LPA will permit the fund to grant a security interest in each of (i) its investments (whether its entire portfolio or a subset thereof), (ii) any distributions or proceeds related to its investments (including the fund's rights to receive such amounts), and (iii) the bank accounts into which such amounts are deposited. Additionally, if the NAV or Hybrid Facility will be used to finance a single investment or a subset of investments, a fund sponsor should discuss with its funds and tax counsel, as well as accountants, to determine whether collateral relating to the non-financed investments may be used to support those borrowings.

Diligence considerations relating to NAV Facility collateral packages

Aside from analysing the fund documents in connection with a proposed collateral package, fund borrowers and their counsel then have to address any restrictions contained in asset-level documents, including relevant financing and acquisition agreements and governing documents. For example, an agreement with respect to an investment may prohibit any transfer or pledge (whether it be direct or indirect) of the fund's equity interest therein. These considerations are not only relevant in cases where the fund is pledging its equity interests in investments; they may also be applicable in cases where the fund agrees to (i) a negative pledge on such equity interests, or (ii) a pledge of (or negative pledge on) its economic rights in respect of such equity interests. Therefore, in most cases, there will necessarily be a certain amount of diligence to be completed with respect to the underlying documentation governing the investments.

This analysis will be largely dependent on the fund structure, including at what level within the structure the NAV Facility borrowings will be incurred (whether at the fund level or at one or more entities that sit below the fund). A fund sponsor may wish to position the debt below the fund for a number of reasons. If the fund already has a Subscription Facility in place, some NAV Facility lenders prefer that debt be incurred below the fund so that the Subscription Facility lenders are structurally subordinated to the NAV Facility. If this structuring is not envisioned when the fund is first established or the Subscription Facility is first entered into, a fund sponsor may try to "retro-fit" newly formed aggregators or special purpose vehicles into the existing fund structure. However, doing so could create additional complications, such as triggering third-party consent requirements or necessitating regulatory filings.

Below are some diligence questions to consider:
- Do any deal-level counterparties or the organisational documents with respect to the investment require notice and/or consents in order for the fund to pledge its direct or indirect equity interest in such investment? For example, are there transfer or change of control provisions that would be breached upon any foreclosure on the fund's equity interest in a default scenario? Or, if broadly worded, could a transfer or change of control provision be inadvertently triggered by the fund granting a lien or agreeing to a negative pledge on its equity interest or its rights to receive distributions in respect thereof?
- To the extent the collateral includes investments consisting of public securities, or the NAV Facility lenders request a negative pledge with respect to such investments, are there any securities law or other regulatory considerations (such as Regulation U) that need to be discussed with the fund's counsel?
- Are any notices required to, or consents required from, regulators in connection with the direct or indirect pledge of the fund's equity interest in any investment or right to receive proceeds therefrom? What is the process and timing necessary for such notices or consents?
- Are there any local law issues relating to the jurisdiction of the pledged investments?

Analysing these provisions may require coordinating with various local counsel, regulatory specialists and deal-level counsel who are most familiar with the fund's investments. As such, the diligence process may be cumbersome and expensive, particularly if (i) a large number of investments will be pledged, or (ii) the collateral package (including any negative pledge) is broad in scope. One of the key benefits to a "collateral-lite" facility (where the collateral comprises solely the bank accounts into which distribution and other investment proceeds are deposited) is the reduction of potential legal, regulatory and contractual issues.

Liability of borrowers

Negotiations regarding the extent of the collateral package will be influenced by the allocation of liability among the borrowers. As a condition to providing a single borrowing base calculated by reference to the net asset value of the fund's entire investment portfolio, NAV Facility lenders may require the borrowers (including any main fund, parallel fund or alternative investment vehicle ("**AIV**")) to provide credit support for each other's obligations. Such credit support may be in the form of joint and several liability, guarantees or cross-collateralisation. The level at which the NAV Facility debt is incurred (whether at or below the fund level) may inform a fund's analysis as to its preferred approach, but each of the below considerations may still apply. In any case, a fund may want to maximise its optionality by permitting each such arrangement in its fund documents in order to obtain the best possible financing terms.

Before diving into the merits and drawbacks of each approach, it is important to understand why the liability structuring for NAV Facilities differs from that of Subscription Facilities. Unlike NAV Facilities, many Subscription Facilities are carefully crafted to avoid any credit support being provided by a main fund for the benefit of any of its AIVs, or *vice versa*, whether in the form of joint and several liability, guarantees or cross-collateralisation. These entities all have access to the Subscription Facility collateral, as they each have the ability to call capital from the same pool of investors that subscribed to the main fund. Therefore, there is no compelling reason to have any credit support (let alone joint and several liability) provided among these entities in connection with a Subscription Facility. From a funds and tax perspective, avoiding linkage between a main fund and its related AIVs is ideal. AIVs may be set up to accommodate the preferences of investors with different tax profiles and objectives. Having an AIV provide credit support to its related main fund (or *vice versa*) may increase the risk that the separateness of these vehicles will not be respected for U.S. tax purposes. As a result, many Subscription Facilities are set up so that each AIV secures only its own obligations and not the obligations of its related main fund or other related AIVs. Similarly, the main fund secures its own obligations and not those of its related AIVs.

While AIVs have access to the same pool of investor commitments as their related main fund, these entities typically make different investments. Therefore, any collateral provided by a main fund and its related AIVs in connection with a NAV or Hybrid Facility may not be shared among such entities in the same manner as the shared pool of uncalled capital commitments that secure a Subscription Facility. As a result, NAV and Hybrid Facility lenders may expect some type of credit support to be provided for the benefit of all borrowers, including as between a main fund and its AIVs.

NAV and Hybrid Facility lenders may insist on the borrowers being jointly and severally liable for, or providing guarantees of, all obligations under the facility. With this approach, each borrower is liable for the full amount of loans outstanding under the facility, regardless of which borrower incurred the loans. During an event of default, the lender (or, in the case of a syndicated facility, the agent) can demand repayment of any loan from any or all of the borrowers and exercise remedies against any of the pledged collateral. However, there are some potential pitfalls with this approach. First, it may negatively impact the U.S. tax analysis, as described above. Further, some borrowers may have significantly less asset value than other borrowers, and that disparity could render a small borrower immediately insolvent (or in violation of applicable debt limits in its organisational documents) upon the incurrence of a loan by a larger borrower. Savings language that limits the liability of each borrower to the maximum that may be incurred without rendering such borrower insolvent (or in violation of its LPA) can mitigate this result.

Fund sponsors tend to prefer cross-collateralisation in their fund-level debt arrangements over both joint and several liability and guarantees, mainly as a result of the authorisations included in the fund documents, the investors' expectations and tax considerations. Each borrower may cross-collateralise each other borrower's obligations by granting a lien on its collateral to secure its own obligations as well as the obligations of each other borrower. With this approach, even though borrowings by the main fund, any parallel fund and any AIV are on a several basis, the obligations of each borrower are secured by the combined collateral. As it relates to the obligations owed by any borrower, lenders will have full recourse against the combined collateral (subject to any applicable savings limits); however, they will not otherwise have recourse to any other assets of the borrowers, except in the case of the borrower that initially incurred the loan.

Regardless of which approach is agreed upon, a fund sponsor may explore options with their fund, fund finance and tax counsel to help mitigate any fund- or tax-related concerns without disadvantaging lenders. For example, the borrowers may enter into a contribution and reimbursement agreement to ensure that each borrower is ultimately only liable for its applicable share of the facility obligations. In any case, funds and tax counsel should be consulted to determine whether the liability structure works under the fund documents or affects the U.S. tax analysis described above.

Impact of LPA debt limitations on NAV and Hybrid Facilities

When reviewing a fund's organisational documents, in addition to any collateral- or liability-related issues, attention should be given to any provisions governing incurrence of indebtedness. Of course, a fund's LPA has to permit the incurrence of debt, and many LPAs undoubtedly allow the incurrence of Subscription Facility debt. However, in the case of a NAV or Hybrid Facility, it is critical to analyse how the LPA limits the fund's ability to incur debt and whether any investor side letters further restrict a fund's debt capacity.

Some common issues that arise in connection with fund-level debt limits are as follows:

- As a fund calls and deploys capital, the amount of its uncalled capital reduces over time. Any debt limit that prohibits debt in excess of uncalled capital may inadvertently limit (or even prohibit) a NAV Facility or Hybrid Facility or any other indebtedness later in the life of the fund.
- Any debt limit tied to asset value (but which excludes uncalled capital) may inadvertently limit the ability of a fund to incur any indebtedness early in its life before it has made many investments.
- If a debt limit solely relates to (or excludes) debt incurred under a Subscription Facility, the fund will have to determine whether a Hybrid Facility (which is secured by typical Subscription Facility collateral, in addition to other collateral) should be similarly limited or excluded.
- Are there any side letters that place further restrictions (whether on amount, use of proceeds or tenor) on the fund's ability to incur debt?
- Does the calculation of uncalled capital require a reserve for, or reduction of, any outstanding debt and, if so, does that impact any of the agreed debt limits in the LPA?
- Is there sufficient disclosure to investors regarding how debt is calculated and reported, and the possible risks of leverage generally?
- Do the debt limitations in the fund-level LPA apply to debt incurred by any entities that sit below the fund in the structure (i.e., holding companies or other special purpose vehicles through which the fund makes its investments)?

Fund document limitations on use of NAV and Hybrid Facility loan proceeds

In terms of potential uses of loan proceeds, NAV and Hybrid Facilities may enable a fund sponsor to further leverage its investments, refinance asset-level debt, fund follow-on investments and accelerate distributions to investors in advance of exiting investments. Given this wide range of possible uses of proceeds, a fund should give thought to its expected use of such facilities when drafting its LPA and negotiating its other fund documents.

To the extent the fund would like to borrow to make distributions to investors, query whether it is permitted to do so under its LPA and side letters. Note that, regardless of whether such authorisations are included in the fund documents, some lenders may not be comfortable lending for the purpose of making distributions or may have internal policies restricting such use of proceeds.

Additionally, funds should consider any tenor limitations included in LPAs with respect to borrowings. For example, if Subscription Facility debt is intended only to bridge capital calls (and not for any longer-term purposes), shorter tenor limitations may not present any issues. However, in the case of a NAV or Hybrid Facility, longer-term leverage may be in the best interest of the fund. NAV Facility loans are intended to be repaid with investment proceeds, the timing of which are not fully within the fund's control. Likewise, Hybrid Facility loans may be repaid with investment proceeds. Therefore, to preserve optionality, a fund should consider incorporating flexibility in its fund documents to allow NAV and Hybrid Facility borrowings to be outstanding for longer durations.

Conclusion

NAV and Hybrid Facilities are bespoke in nature and need to be individually tailored to reflect a fund's structure, investment portfolio, investor expectations and liquidity needs. Given the increasing importance of these financing arrangements in providing liquidity to funds, a fund sponsor and its counsel should review the fund LPA in advance of any such financing (and ideally in advance of the execution of the LPA and other fund documentation) to ensure that it maximises flexibility for the fund's financing objectives and is "bankable" for any anticipated credit facility structure. Specifically, the fund sponsor and its counsel will want to consider the following in their LPA and fund documentation review:

- Collateral that will be permitted to secure the facility.
- Liability structure of the borrowers under the facility.
- Debt limitations that may impact borrowing capacity.
- Use of loan proceeds provisions that may affect expected facility usage.

The foregoing is also a helpful list of items to bear in mind in any LPA and other fund document discussions with investors regarding the fund's anticipated use of leverage to support its investments and other activities. Front-loading this LPA analysis will help the fund streamline execution of its credit facilities and achieve best-of-market terms for the financing structure selected.

* * *

Acknowledgments

The authors wish to thank Mary Touchstone and Jennifer Levitt of Simpson Thacher & Bartlett LLP for their assistance in the preparation of this chapter.

Julia Kohen
Tel: +1 212 455 2375 / **Email:** jkohen@stblaw.com

Julia Kohen is a Partner at Simpson Thacher & Bartlett LLP, where she is a member of the Firm's pre-eminent Banking and Credit and Fund Finance Practices. Julia represents financial sponsors in connection with subscription credit facilities and NAV financings for their private equity, real estate, energy, infrastructure, secondaries, credit and other investment funds, as well as management lines and co-investment loan programmes. She has extensive experience structuring complicated financing arrangements designed to provide fund-level leverage to facilitate and support investment activities of funds and their related vehicles.

Julia received her B.A., *cum laude* and Phi Beta Kappa, and M.A. from the University of Delaware in 2003. She received her J.D. from Duke University School of Law in 2007, where she served as the Article Editor for the *Duke Journal of Gender Law & Policy*.

Ashley Belton Gold
Tel: +1 212 455 3499 / **Email:** ashley.beltongold@stblaw.com

Ashley Belton Gold is a Partner in Simpson Thacher & Bartlett LLP's Banking and Credit and Fund Finance Practices. Her practice focuses on crafting tailored financing solutions for investment funds with complex structures across a variety of asset classes, including private equity, real estate, credit, secondaries and infrastructure. She regularly advises financial sponsors on a wide range of fund-level financings, such as subscription facilities, NAV-based facilities and employee loan programmes, among other bespoke arrangements.

Ashley received her B.A. *magna cum laude*, with distinction, from the University of Pennsylvania in 2010 and her J.D., *cum laude*, from New York University School of Law in 2013, as a Robert McKay Scholar.

Jakarri Hamlin
Tel: +1 310 407 7545 / **Email:** jakarri.hamlin@stblaw.com

Jakarri Hamlin is an Associate in Simpson Thacher & Bartlett LLP's Banking and Credit Practice. His practice focuses on matters related to financing transactions, including leveraged and acquisition financings, liquidity lines, NAV facilities, subscription facilities, hybrid facilities, margin loans and repurchase, securities lending and prime brokerage facilities. He advises on a range of financing transactions for lenders and borrowers in the energy, real estate, infrastructure, technology and entertainment industries.

Jakarri also advises clients on the structuring and trading of complex derivatives and structured financial products.

Jakarri received his B.A. from Colgate University in 2012 where he was a Cleon O. Morgan Award Recipient, and his J.D. from New York University School of Law in 2016.

Simpson Thacher & Bartlett LLP

425 Lexington Avenue, New York NY 10017, USA
Tel: +1 212 455 2000 / URL: www.stblaw.com

Sharpest tool in the shed: A primer on asset-backed leverage facilities

Patricia Lynch, Patricia Teixeira & Douglas Hollins
Ropes & Gray LLP

Introduction

Over the past few years, Ropes & Gray has seen an increased demand for asset-backed leverage facilities from our private credit fund clients, who recognise these facilities as a powerful tool to enhance returns to their investors. An asset-backed leverage facility, (relatively) simply put, is a medium-term revolving or term loan credit facility backed by a defined pool of a credit fund's portfolio assets that have been isolated in a bankruptcy-remote special purpose vehicle (SPV) in a manner similar to the structure found in many securitisations. In effect, an asset-backed leverage facility is a "mini-securitisation" designed to provide capital to a credit fund more cheaply and over a longer timeframe than other, more widespread types of credit. For a credit fund, a leverage facility can be a sharp tool: powerful in impact, narrow in focus, but with accompanying rough edges; as with many traditional securitisations, the advantages of this type of financing are accompanied by certain legal and regulatory challenges. Navigating the structural idiosyncrasies of an asset-backed leverage facility is therefore critical for supporting credit fund clients as they implement this increasingly popular technology.

This chapter aims to begin to demystify fund leverage facilities, first by briefly discussing the major reasons for implementing them, then by describing the structure and collateral pool of a typical facility, and finally by highlighting several of the major distinguishing features and key considerations facing legal advisors to credit fund clients who seek to put these facilities in place.

Right tool for the job: Why asset-backed leverage facilities?

As with any specialised tool, an asset-backed leverage facility may be called for in a specific set of circumstances; so, before examining the structure of a leverage facility in detail, it is worth considering why a credit fund would consider having such a facility in the first place. An asset-backed leverage facility can complement a fund's existing credit facilities in a number of ways: in particular, (a) it is secured by a discrete pool of assets, and (b) it has a longer term than a traditional subscription facility. In contrast to a subscription facility, a leverage facility is secured not by the commitments of a fund's investors to contribute capital to the fund, but by the assets that the fund has acquired (whether with capital contributions, with borrowings under the fund's subscription facility or with the proceeds of advances under the leverage facility). This type of collateral is quite conducive to leverage, even more so once isolated in an SPV, shielding the lender from any ancillary risks faced by the fund itself. Moreover, unlike a subscription facility, which may mature initially only a year or two after effectiveness, a leverage facility can have an initial term of up to five years. Taken together, these factors result in a greatly reduced cost of capital for the fund.

Of course, as with any credit facility, a leverage facility can be adapted to suit the needs of a given fund. Certain of a fund's investors may have less of an appetite for leverage, so funds will typically create levered and unlevered sleeves in order to provide levered returns only to those investors that desire it. Some investors might invest in both the levered and unlevered sleeves in percentages that achieve a desired risk/return profile. A single fund could even set up multiple SPVs for the purpose of entering into multiple leverage facilities, further enhancing its returns.

To illustrate the potential of a leverage facility, consider a hypothetical Fund A, which has a $150 million leverage facility, and a hypothetical Fund B, which does not. Each of Fund A and Fund B has $100 million of capital with which to make debt investments, earning a blended return of 7%. However, Fund A's leverage facility, with an assumed interest rate of 5.75%, allows Fund A to invest in (and earn a 7% return on) $150 million of additional assets. Thus, despite having an equal amount of committed capital as Fund B, Fund A earns a net return of 8.875%. In both instances, the gross return on investment would be reduced by any management fees and distributions to general partners, further reducing Fund B's return relative to that of Fund A. Still, even accounting for such fees, the impact of a leverage facility on a fund's performance is clear.

Some assembly required: A typical structure

Whether structured as a revolving credit facility, a term loan credit facility, or a delayed draw facility, a typical leverage facility follows a basic framework. A borrower is created as a subsidiary of a fund,[1] typically as a Delaware limited liability company (LLC).[2] At the closing of the facility, the parties will implement certain mechanics designed to make the borrower "bankruptcy remote" from the fund. As in a traditional securitisation, the concept of "bankruptcy remoteness" refers to an entity being sufficiently isolated from the rest of its corporate structure that a bankruptcy court would be unlikely to use its equitable powers to (a) consolidate the entity with the rest of the corporate structure, or (b) void any transfers of assets to the entity. In the context of a leverage facility, a consolidation of the borrower with the fund would be burdensome to the lenders, which expect to be over-collateralised and to be the only creditors of the borrower. Alternatively, if a bankruptcy court were to recharacterise any sales or contributions of portfolio assets to the borrower as loans from the borrower to the fund, secured by assets owned by the fund, the lenders' ability to realise on their collateral would be severely diminished, as they might have to compete with the fund's other creditors for access to those assets.

With the borrower mechanics in place, the collateral pool can be created. The fund will sell or contribute portfolio assets to the borrower under a separate purchase agreement, either at closing or from time to time thereafter (or often both).[3] For efficiency's sake, the fund may also participate loans to the borrower (which participations will be elevated to full assignments at a later date, often within 60 days); these participations are typically acknowledged in the credit agreement and governed by a master participation agreement entered into at closing. As in any asset-based facility, lenders will not advance 100% of the value of the collateral, so the borrower will pay for a portion of the value of each portfolio asset sold by the fund through debt incurred under the facility, and the remainder will be contributed by the fund.[4] At closing, the borrower will pledge all of its assets (i.e., the portfolio assets) as collateral. The fund also frequently pledges the equity of the borrower as collateral.

As part of the bankruptcy remoteness structure, it is important that these sales or contributions of portfolio assets constitute "true sales" or "true contributions".[5] A true sale analysis is not exact, but a major factor is whether the relevant transaction shifts the risks and benefits of ownership effectively. It is thus critical that, under the purchase agreement, the fund does not remain liable for any debt (or receive any surplus) in respect of any transferred portfolio asset and does not guarantee the collectability of any portfolio asset or accept any risk of loss.[6]

Several characteristics about the borrower itself also support the bankruptcy remoteness analysis. First, the borrower's operating agreement (and often the credit agreement itself) will contain a number of separateness covenants designed to ensure that the borrower is viewed by third parties as a separate entity from the fund. These customarily include obligations to (a) observe proper LLC/limited partnership formalities, (b) hold itself out to the public as separate and distinct from any other entity and conduct business solely in its own name, including by maintaining separate books and records and even its own stationery, (c) pay its expenses from its own funds, (d) not be consolidated with another entity (other than for tax and accounting purposes), (e) not commingle assets with another entity, and (f) not guarantee the debt of another entity. Second, the borrower's management will include an independent director or manager (customarily employed by a third-party service provider) whose consent will be required for any material actions, including any mergers or asset sales by the borrower, any insolvency filings involving the borrower, and any dissolution of the borrower. Finally, the transaction documents should include non-petition provisions that prevent a third party from dragging the borrower into a bankruptcy proceeding before the end of the applicable preference period.

Several other parties are involved in the operation of a leverage facility. The portfolio manager or servicer, which is typically either the fund or the investment advisor to the fund, is responsible for making decisions with respect to the buying and selling of the portfolio assets by the borrower and other management of the collateral pool throughout the life of the facility, for servicing the portfolio assets held by the borrower, and for certain reporting obligations. The borrower may pay the portfolio manager a fee, or, if the portfolio manager is the investment advisor to the fund, the fee may be subsumed in the investment advisory fee that the fund pays. The administrative agent and the collateral agent fulfil their traditional responsibilities under the facility. And the collateral custodian, which is sometimes the same party as the agents, is responsible for holding and verifying the required documentation for each of the portfolio assets.

The lifecycle of a leverage facility customarily follows three phases. Often, a facility will include a ramp-up period, during which the borrower is allowed to borrow funds and acquire portfolio assets subject to a lower commitment fee (or even no commitment fee at all). During this period, the eligibility criteria and concentration limitations (both discussed below) with respect to the portfolio assets may also be relaxed. During the reinvestment period, the mechanics of the facility will operate normally, and the borrower may invest the proceeds of the facility, and reinvest returns from its portfolio, in additional portfolio assets or in certain pre-approved categories of assets (e.g., U.S. government debt securities and highly rated short-term bank deposit products, money market funds, and commercial paper). Finally, there is usually a wind-down period,[7] during which the borrower will no longer be able to borrow money or reinvest proceeds and will be expected to pay down the facility and sell any remaining portfolio assets.

Defining the collateral pool

The upshot of the carefully planned bankruptcy-remote structure discussed above is that a leverage facility is anchored by a borrower that is effectively an empty vessel holding a collateral pool that provides the lenders' entire recourse. The valuation of the assets in the collateral pool is critical and heavily negotiated, as is the proportion of the collateral pool against which the lenders will advance.

Worth every penny: The art of collateral valuation

The lenders set very specific and heavily negotiated criteria on the assets that the borrower can acquire. In some facilities, the administrative agent will have approval rights over any assets purchased by the borrower. Other facilities allow the borrower to freely add assets to the portfolio as long as such assets meet certain pre-established eligibility criteria. Customary criteria include (a) basic requirements that mirror standard borrower representations and warranties and include the borrower having good and marketable title to an asset, (b) type of asset (e.g., loan, bond, structured finance obligation, letter of credit, equity security), (c) whether an asset is secured, (d) payment currency, (e) frequency of interest and principal payments, including any required cash or payment-in-kind spread, (f) term to maturity, (g) credit rating, (h) minimum purchase price, and (i) size of the total facility or issuance. Typically, the loan documentation underlying a portfolio asset must satisfy certain basic requirements, and often the loan transfer documentation is required to be on LSTA standard forms. Other, more bespoke criteria with respect to a portfolio asset can include (1) the lack of any significant risk of declining in credit quality or market price, (2) the lack of any material non-credit-related risk, (3) the lack of any required future advances to the underlying obligor, (4) the required number of available bid-side price quotations (the "bid depth"), and (5) the asset not being subject to partial or non-cash offers or redemptions. There may also be criteria related to relevant tax and regulatory concerns.

As with any asset-based credit facility, the collateral pool is generally also subject to certain concentration limitations designed to ensure the diversity of the portfolio assets. These limitations can be based on any of the eligibility criteria listed above but also frequently include restrictions on the proportion of the pool that can be occupied by loans to the largest individual obligors or groups of obligors. Some facilities also include restrictions on loans to obligors within certain S&P or Moody's industry classifications; indeed, recently, some facilities have included restrictions with respect to certain industries particularly impacted by the COVID-19 pandemic. Other possible concentration limits relate to the proportion of obligors affiliated with the fund, the proportion of distressed loans or the borrower's unfunded exposure amount (i.e., the amount still potentially to be paid to the obligor under, for example, a delayed draw loan).

With the range of potential portfolio assets sorted, how are those assets to be valued once they are part of the collateral pool? Terminology varies widely among lenders with respect to valuation mechanics, but generally, valuation follows a common framework. Typically, when a portfolio asset is acquired by the borrower, the administrative agent will value the asset at its purchase price (assuming it was not acquired above market value, in which case it would be valued at par); any *de minimis* original issue discount (often 3% or less) will be disregarded in this calculation. In certain cases, the administrative agent may revalue each portfolio asset, usually as the product of its market value (as a percentage of par) and its outstanding principal balance, either at its discretion or on certain prescribed dates throughout the life of the facility. These dates generally include the measurement dates for any monthly collateral reports, the dates of any borrowings or repayments, the dates of any reinvestments of portfolio asset principal collections, and the dates of any sales or substitutions of portfolio assets by the borrower.

But how exactly is the market value of a portfolio asset determined? If an asset is sufficiently liquid, its market value will usually be determined by reference to the bid prices published by certain reputable independent valuation firms (e.g., LoanX/Markit or Loan Pricing Corporation) or, in the absence of published quotations from those firms, other nationally recognised competitors (either alone or averaged). If an asset is not sufficiently liquid or if quotations are not available from any independent valuation firms, the administrative agent will generally determine the value of an asset itself. In these circumstances, administrative agents are generally required to act in good faith and with commercially reasonable discretion. The borrower should also have a right to challenge a valuation by the agent with which it disagrees, usually by reference to observable market prices, by submitting bids or by obtaining a valuation from one or more independent valuation firms, in each case within a certain window of time after receipt of the agent's valuation.

Certain facilities do not permit the administrative agent to revalue the portfolio assets in the ordinary course. Importantly, however, these facilities permit a portfolio asset to be revalued upon the occurrence of certain adverse events (often called "value adjustment events" or "market trigger events"). These revaluation triggers typically include payment defaults or insolvency events with respect to the obligor, after which an asset will often be given a $0 value. Other potential value adjustment events include (a) a portfolio asset being on non-accrual status or not being collectible, (b) defaults in the obligor's financial covenants, (c) an obligor's failure to deliver its periodic financial statements, and (d) material modifications to the underlying loan documentation,[8] including (i) waivers or modifications of any principal or interest payments or capitalisation of any interest, (ii) reductions in interest rate, (iii) structural or contractual subordination of payments or liens, (iv) modification of the maturity date or any prepayment date, (v) changes to any *pro rata* sharing, payment, or distribution mechanics, (vi) the release of a material guarantor, (vii) substitutions, alterations, or releases of liens on a material portion of the underlying collateral, and (viii) amendments to the obligor's financial covenants. Facilities with periodic valuation mechanisms typically also permit revaluation in these circumstances.

The penny drops: Calculating loan availability

As with other types of asset-based credit facilities, the borrowing capacity under a leverage facility is less than the full value of the collateral pool. Loan availability is generally implemented through a borrowing base mechanic.[9] A percentage (the "advance rate") of each potential type of collateral will be specified, and the value of the collateral pool multiplied by the applicable advance rates (the "borrowing base") provides the current borrowing limit. The borrowing limit is deal-specific, but, importantly, because of the revaluation mechanics in a leverage facility, that limit can fluctuate more than it would in a subscription facility.

If the value of the borrowing base falls below the outstanding amount of the loan at any time (a "borrowing base deficiency" or "borrowing base shortfall"), the consequences for the borrower often vary depending on the size of the deficiency. In the case of a small deficiency, the only consequence for the borrower may be the temporary suspension of its ability to borrow under the facility and/or to make distributions to the fund. If the borrowing base deficiency is larger, however, the borrower will be required to "cure" the deficiency – i.e., to bring the borrowing base into line with the outstanding loan amount – using one or more of the following options:[10] (a) contributing cash or additional portfolio assets to the collateral pool; (b) selling or substituting one or more portfolio assets; or (c) prepaying one or more of the outstanding advances under the facility. Generally, a borrowing base deficiency that is not cured within a certain period using one of these methods will become an event of default.

Rough edges: Unique features

As is likely apparent from the discussion thus far, the power and complexity of a leverage facility – the sharpness of this specialised tool – brings with it a number of complexities and idiosyncrasies for legal advisors to consider when guiding clients – rough edges that must be refined or at least looked out for. While many of the standard provisions that appear in any traditional credit facility also feature in asset-backed leverage facility documentation, the bespoke structure that gives a leverage facility its strength also leaves lenders requesting certain additional protections.

<u>Allocating proceeds</u>

The bankruptcy-remote structure involved in a leverage facility results in two features that distinguish it from a subscription facility. Because the borrower's only assets are the collateral pool securing the facility, similar to a more traditional securitisation, a leverage facility will include a payment waterfall to carefully control the use of the proceeds of the portfolio assets and to avoid leakage of the collateral from the borrower to the fund before the secured parties have been paid. Principal and interest payments on the portfolio assets are required to be paid to a collection account that is pledged to the secured parties, and the borrower is typically required to run those collections, as well as proceeds of any other permitted investments, through the waterfall on a monthly or quarterly basis. The funds will then be applied to (a) any fees or costs and expenses due to the agents, the custodian, the lenders, or the portfolio manager, (b) certain other administrative expenses due to third parties, (c) any interest or margin due to the lenders, and (d) any required amortisation payments. The borrower will also be required to pay down any outstanding advances as necessary to cure any borrowing base deficiency. During the reinvestment period, any excess interest proceeds are generally permitted to be distributed to the fund so long as no event of default exists, while any excess principal proceeds may be reinvested in additional assets, subject to the satisfaction of any concentration limits.[11] After the reinvestment period, all excess proceeds are generally required to be applied to pay down the loan.

Because the borrower is permitted to distribute and/or reinvest its cash during the reinvestment period, subject to the waterfall, rather than keeping it on hand, lenders will customarily require the borrower to maintain a reserve account in which is deposited a sufficient amount of cash (in the eyes of the lenders) to cover any lending obligations under any portfolio assets comprising revolving or delayed draw debt. Often the borrower will be required to periodically replenish the reserve account (including as part of its waterfall payments) if it contains insufficient funds, and the borrower is usually required to top up the account at the end of the reinvestment period so that there is sufficient cash to meet any funding needs under the portfolio loans as the leverage facility is paid down.

<u>Getting to know your product: Representations, warranties, and covenants</u>

Because of the bespoke nature of the collateral pool in a leverage facility, lenders typically ask for fairly extensive collateral reporting. Generally, the borrower or the portfolio manager will be required to submit to the secured parties monthly reports on the collateral pool, including information on the eligibility, type, value, and status of each portfolio asset, certain financial metrics, and information as to any modifications to any portfolio asset. Some facilities also require these reports to calculate compliance with any financial covenants and to detail any contributions to and distributions by the borrower. Reports with respect to months during which waterfall payments are due customarily also include certain information related to those payments, such as outstanding principal and interest proceeds and amounts on deposit in any reserve accounts. Furthermore, the lenders may require a firm of nationally recognised independent public accountants to perform certain agreed-upon procedures with respect to the monthly reports and the portfolio manager's servicing of the collateral on an annual basis.

Additionally, the borrower will generally be required to submit to the administrative agent one or more of the following documents with respect to portfolio assets held by the borrower: (a) any financial reporting packages delivered by the obligors, including any financial statements; (b) any management discussion and analysis provided by the obligors; (c) copies of any material modifications or waivers of loan documentation; (d) notice of any credit event or material litigation; and (e) in certain cases, portfolio monitoring reports. The collateral agent may also request monitoring access to any collateral or custodial accounts in order to view balances in real time.

Apart from the reporting requirements, a typical leverage facility will usually contain certain covenants restricting the activities of the borrower due to its bankruptcy remoteness. Generally, the borrower will be permitted to engage solely in those activities contemplated under the facility or necessary to carry out the borrower's obligations thereunder. As such, the borrower will customarily be prohibited from engaging in other transactions or incurring other indebtedness outside the scope of the facility.

<ins>In case of emergency: Events of default</ins>

In addition to customary events of default, leverage facilities have a few notable events of default that underline the importance lenders place on the bankruptcy-remote structure of the borrower and a healthy collateral pool. A failure to maintain the bankruptcy remoteness of the borrower can often directly trigger an event of default. A failure to maintain a perfected lien on the collateral or to properly maintain any collateral accounts can also trigger an event of default (with minimal opportunity to cure). There are also usually defaults specific to the portfolio manager that can include a key person event or change of control with respect to the portfolio manager.

Remedies for events of default include those customary for any other credit facility, but the nature of the collateral pool means the administrative agent generally has some additional rights. The borrower will be prohibited from purchasing further portfolio assets or investing any funds on hand. The administrative agent will be permitted to seize and distribute any cash in any collateral accounts according to a default waterfall described in the credit agreement and to direct the portfolio manager in the servicing and sale of any portfolio assets in order to prepay any outstanding advances under the facility. In addition to these remedies, a portfolio manager default usually triggers the administrative agent's ability to terminate the portfolio manager and appoint a successor. To forestall these remedies, a fund can sometimes negotiate the right to contribute assets to the borrower or sell assets. A borrower can also sometimes require the lenders to seek bids for any portfolio assets being sold in order to avoid a fire sale. Finally, a fund may request a right to match the highest offer for portfolio assets being sold or to have a last look at those assets.

<ins>Second opinions: True sale and non-consolidation</ins>

The final consequence of the bankruptcy-remote structure is some additional opinion requirements beyond those found in a traditional credit facility. Borrower's counsel will customarily deliver a true sale and contribution opinion with respect to the assets transferred from the fund to the borrower, stating that a bankruptcy court would likely not claw any portfolio assets back into the bankruptcy estate of the fund in the event of an insolvency, and a non-consolidation opinion, stating that a bankruptcy court would likely not substantively consolidate the assets and liabilities of the borrower and the fund in the event of an insolvency. Because the U.S. bankruptcy courts have considerable discretion in making such determinations, these opinions are reasoned and fact-intensive and often require a healthy amount of time to prepare.

Conclusion

Despite a unique and complex structure, leverage facilities are a powerful "sharp tool" in a private credit fund's toolbox, able to enhance the fund's returns to its investors relatively cheaply and over a longer timeframe than other types of financing. However, as with any specialised tool, a leverage facility is suited for certain circumstances; for example, a fund manager should consider whether such a facility would place material constraints on the fund's ability to manage its credit portfolios during times of market uncertainty. In addition, a fund and its counsel will need to navigate the "rough edges" of a leverage facility's bankruptcy-remote structure, collateral pool valuation mechanics, and ongoing obligations if the facility is to successfully integrate with the fund's other projects. Thoughtfully addressing these and other considerations is key to helping the fund accomplish its objectives.

* * *

Endnotes

1. Usually, the borrower is created prior to closing using basic organisational documents, allowing for tax forms to be completed and collateral accounts to be opened. The organisational documents are then amended and restated at closing.
2. The borrowers under certain leverage facilities are Delaware limited partnerships with general partners that are Delaware limited liability companies. In such a structure, the bankruptcy-remote mechanics discussed should be put in place at the level of the general partner.
3. Some facilities also allow the borrower to purchase portfolio assets on the open market, upon advice from the portfolio manager. This mechanic can also be used to warehouse assets for a future collateralised loan obligation offering.
4. The contributed value also accounts for any original issue discount or other market discounts.
5. The fund and the borrower generally expressly state their intention that any transfer of assets constitutes a true sale or true contribution; nevertheless, out of an abundance of caution, the fund will also grant a "back-up" security interest in the relevant assets to the borrower (which security interest will be perfected at closing through a UCC filing) in case any transfer is recharacterised.
6. Some purchase agreements require the fund to repurchase or otherwise substitute portfolio assets in the case of breaches of certain limited representations and warranties that are given by the fund at the time that the relevant asset is transferred to the borrower, but this mechanic should not interfere with the true sale analysis as long as the relevant representations do not relate to the credit quality of the asset or otherwise guarantee collectability.
7. In some facilities, the reinvestment period lasts until the final maturity date.

8. The negative covenants in leverage facilities may also place certain limits on the borrower's ability to modify the documentation for its asset portfolio, in order to avoid negative effects on the quality of the collateral pool.
9. Some lenders prefer to calculate availability through a loan-to-value ratio mechanic, which has the same practical effect.
10. Some facilities allow even greater flexibility than is described here.
11. Certain facilities permit the distribution of excess principal proceeds during the reinvestment period as well.

Patricia Lynch
Tel: +1 617 951 7940 / Email: patricia.lynch@ropesgray.com

Patricia Lynch co-leads the firm's U.S. fund finance team, representing asset managers on subscription facilities, credit fund leverage facilities and loans to management companies. In addition, Patricia leads the firm's U.S. securitisation practice and advises on a wide range of structured finance transactions, including loan securitisations, receivables-backed variable funding note facilities, and whole-business securitisations.

Patricia Teixeira
Tel: +1 212 596 9043 / Email: patricia.teixeira@ropesgray.com

Patricia Teixeira is counsel in the finance group and regularly advises fund clients and lenders on a variety of fund-level financings, including bilateral and syndicated subscription facilities, NAV facilities, leverage facilities for credit funds, management company lines to investment advisors, and employee co-investment loan programmes.

Douglas Hollins
Tel: +1 617 951 7343 / Email: douglas.hollins@ropesgray.com

Douglas Hollins is an associate in the finance group and focuses on fund finance and structured finance transactions. He regularly represents registered and unregistered fund clients in a variety of financings, including bilateral and syndicated subscription lines, leverage facilities, and NAV facilities, and also represents operating companies in connection with loan securitisations.

Ropes & Gray LLP

Prudential Tower, 800 Boylston Street, Boston, MA 02199-3600, USA
Tel: +1 617 951 7000 / Fax: +1 617 951 7050 / URL: www.ropesgray.com

Enforcement: Analysis of lender remedies under U.S. law in subscription-secured credit facilities

Ellen G. McGinnis & Richard D. Anigian
Haynes and Boone, LLP

Lenders must have a sound understanding of their legal rights in regard to, and the process of, enforcing remedies against a borrower and its limited partners[1] under a subscription-secured credit facility in order to assess risk, price the risk, and properly document the facility. Lenders who adequately plan for an event of default and exercise of remedies are more likely to prevail against the borrower and its investors when enforcing rights. Lenders must be prepared to execute every step of their enforcement strategy, beginning with the occurrence of an event of default, through the decision to accelerate the obligations, to the exercise of remedies, and, finally, to recovery of payment.

Establishing an event of default: Issues of jurisdiction and service of process

Before a lender can exercise its remedies, there must first be a legally undisputed event of default under the facility documents. In many cases, the occurrence and continuation of an event of default will be clear (*e.g.*, failure to make payment or failure to timely act under the terms of the facility documents). However, if a borrower contests the existence of a default, the lender should consider immediately filing a declaratory judgment action in an appropriate court to establish that an event of default has occurred.[2] A declaratory judgment filing does not set forth a cause of action for damages, but instead seeks a declaration from the court establishing existing rights, status or other legal relationships under the terms of a contract. It provides a remedy to a party that is uncertain of its rights and wants an early adjudication without having to wait for its adversary to file suit.[3]

The court must have jurisdiction over the parties and the subject matter to issue a declaratory judgment. Typically, the borrower agrees to submit to jurisdiction in a particular forum in the facility documents, which establishes personal jurisdiction over the borrower.[4] Subject-matter jurisdiction is the court's jurisdiction over the nature of the case and the type of relief sought. A U.S. federal court has the power to hear a declaratory judgment action under 28 U.S.C. § 2201(a)[5] if the case is within its subject-matter jurisdiction and involves an actual controversy.[6] A lender seeking a declaratory judgment has the burden of establishing, by a preponderance of the evidence, that there is an actual controversy.[7] Similarly, under most state laws, a declaratory judgment is only proper when there is an actual controversy and the existence of the controversy is not "contingent upon the happening of future events which may never occur."[8]

In federal court, service of process on domestic entities is governed by the Federal Rules of Civil Procedure. *Rule 4* provides that a corporation, partnership, or other type of business association may be served by delivering the summons and complaint to an officer, managing or general agent, or an agent authorized by appointment or law to receive service.[9] New York and Delaware courts have similar service of process rules.[10] If the borrower agrees in the facility documents that service of process may be effected by registered or certified mail sent to a specific address, the state or federal court will recognize such service as effective.[11]

Several additional issues must be considered when the defaulting borrower is a non-U.S. ("*foreign*") entity. First, lenders must decide whether to pursue the foreign entity in the United States or in its home country.[12] A number of factors favor suit in the United States. First, a judgment from any American court, state or federal, is relatively easy to register and enforce throughout the United States. Second, a U.S. court will be more familiar with the contractual obligations at issue. Finally, depending upon the applicable foreign jurisdiction, there may be considerable local bias in the foreign jurisdiction in favor of the foreign defendant that must be overcome.

Establishing personal and subject-matter jurisdiction over a foreign entity requires the same analysis.[13] Once jurisdiction has been established, the lender must effectively serve process on the foreign entity. If a foreign borrower has agreed in the facility documents to accept service of process by certified or registered mail, this manner of service will be enforceable unless the borrower demonstrates that such service is precluded by foreign laws.[14]

If the manner of service in the facility documents fails, is impractical, or is deemed unenforceable, the Hague Convention on the Service Abroad of Judicial and Extrajudicial Documents (the "*Hague Convention*") provides an additional method of service on a defendant residing in any nation that is a signatory to the Hague Convention,[15] such as the United States,[16] the United Kingdom, or the Cayman Islands.[17] Therefore, knowledge of the Hague Convention procedure for service of process is useful as it provides the most foolproof manner of service in applicable jurisdictions.

The Hague Convention provides for formal service through the foreign defendant's government's designated "*Central Authority*," where the process is sent to the Central Authority with instructions to forward it to the defendant.[18] Alternatively, in *Article 10(a)*, the Hague Convention states that, unless the foreign government has lodged an official objection, service by international registered mail directly to the defendant in the foreign nation is adequate.[19]

As a practical matter, lenders should seek the advice of local counsel in the applicable jurisdiction to confirm the best methods to effect service. The outcome may be simultaneous service by different methods. Full compliance with the formal Central Authority process under the Hague Convention may be slow and cumbersome, but it should yield nearly unimpeachable service. At the same time, service by registered mail should be attempted, as it does not add any significant cost and there is always the chance that the defendant will respond to it and appear in the lawsuit.

Once jurisdiction has been established and the foreign entity has been properly served, the lawsuit may proceed just as any other and a declaratory judgment may be obtained. Under U.S. law, a declaratory judgment issued by a court has the force and effect of a final judgment or decree.[20]

Recovery from borrower and investors

Once an event of default is established, lenders may either direct the borrower to make a capital call on the investors for repayment of the obligations or issue a capital call directly on the investors.[21] If the borrower files for bankruptcy, a motion to lift the stay will be required prior to the lender taking action. In well-documented, subscription-secured facilities, the obligations of the borrower and the rights of lenders *vis-à-vis* the investors should be so well defined that even if the borrower challenges the lender's right to call capital, the fundamental obligation of the borrower to repay the obligations, and the lender's rights to call capital, are likely to be resolved in summary judgment. By contrast, more complicated issues regarding recovery arise with respect to enforcement against the investors. Under most subscription-secured facilities, each investor enters into agreements or makes acknowledgments that run to the lender, either in an "***Investor Letter***" or in the partnership agreement, wherein the investor expressly acknowledges and confirms, *inter alia*, its obligation to make capital contributions without defense, setoff or counterclaim when called to repay the facility.[22] These agreements, together with the nature of the collateral securing subscription-secured facilities, constitute the foundation for recovery from the investors.

Legal theories of recovery against investors

If, after an event of default has occurred and has been legally established, any investor fails to pay a required capital contribution in response to a capital call, resulting in a payment deficiency, the lender's recourse is to file a lawsuit against the defaulting investors to enforce remedies. The lender should consider its rights under statutory law, the facility documents, any Investor Letter, and the borrower's partnership agreement (collectively, the "***Relevant Documents***").

Depending on the language of the Relevant Documents and the factual circumstances, the lender should be able to establish liability against the investors for the capital contributions through claims of reliance, breach of contract, unjust enrichment or promissory estoppel.

Reliance claims arise out of statutory principles contained in the Revised Uniform Limited Partnership Act ("***RULPA***"), as applied in each state, and are based on the lender's actions taken (*e.g.*, to advance loans) in reliance upon any of the Relevant Documents.

Breach of contract claims may be based on:
- enforcement of lender's rights under the collateral documents, by which the rights of the partnership to demand capital contributions from investors were pledged to the lenders, and perfected in accordance with the Uniform Commercial Code (the "***UCC***");
- the agreements and acknowledgments made by investors in the partnership agreement or Investor Letters, in particular the agreement to fund capital contributions for the purpose of repaying the facility without defense, setoff or counterclaim; and
- the lender's status as a third-party beneficiary of the partnership agreement.

If there is no express contract between the lender and the investors,[23] or if a contract between them is unenforceable or unproven,[24] the lender may be able to assert a claim for unjust enrichment on the equitable principle that the investors should not be permitted to enjoy the benefit of the lender's extension of credit if the lender is provided no remedy for an investor's subsequent default. The lender may also be able to assert a promissory estoppel claim based on the investors' capital commitment promise.[25,26]

Creditor enforcement under limited partnership law based on reliance

Rights of lenders

In Delaware, the Delaware Revised Uniform Limited Partnership Act ("***DRULPA***") provides a statutory basis for asserting a reliance claim for the benefit of a lender.[27] Under DRULPA, unless otherwise provided in the partnership agreement, the obligation of investors to make contributions may be "compromised" only by the consent of all investors.[28]

The practical effect of DRULPA is to confer the benefit of the obligations of investors to a borrower on a lender who reasonably relied upon the capital call rights contained in the partnership agreement (*i.e.*, the lender would not have extended credit to the fund but for the fund's right to call capital from its investors). There is limited guidance as to what constitutes reasonable reliance; however, some courts have found reliance simply by virtue of the fact that the capital contribution obligations were contained in a publicly filed certificate of limited partnership.[29] It has also been suggested that evidence of reliance may include:

- references in the lenders' credit files to the capital contribution obligations as a source of repayment of the loan;
- references to the capital contribution obligations in the facility documents or solicitation materials;
- communications with the general partner and limited partners regarding the basis on which the loan will be repaid;
- review of the partnership's books and records, such as capital accounts and financial statements; and
- execution of an undertaking pursuant to which the general partner agrees to issue, and/or the limited partners agree to make, capital contributions to repay the debt.[30]

In *In re LJM2 Co-Investment, L.P. Ltd. Partners Litig.*, 866 A.2d 762 (Del. Ch. 2004), the Delaware Court of Chancery held that the bankruptcy trustee of the limited partnership adequately demonstrated that the bank creditors reasonably relied, for purposes of DRULPA, on the limited partners' representations that they would honor their capital commitments, which allowed the creditors to enforce the capital commitments.[31]

Specifically, the trustee alleged that the bank creditors reasonably relied on *Section 3.1* of the partnership agreement to extend credit to LJM2 because: (i) under that section, the limited partners were obligated to contribute their commitments only when called for by the general partner; and (ii) the bank creditors removed this solitary condition by creating interrelated agreements compelling the general partner to make capital calls if LJM2 defaulted (through the combination of the Credit Agreement and the General Partner Undertaking to the effect that, if LJM2 defaulted on the Credit Agreement, the [general partner] would be bound to issue Drawdown Notices to the limited partners to the extent necessary to cure such payment default).[32]

Defenses

Generally, if a limited partner's obligation to make capital contributions is not subject to conditions in the certificate of limited partnership (or in Delaware, the partnership agreement),[33] the circumstances in which payment will be excused are few and narrow because third parties and other limited partners have a right to rely on receipt of such capital contributions.[34] However, limited partners *may* be able to raise one or more of the following defenses.

First, under Delaware law, a limited partner's obligation to make capital contributions to a limited partnership may not be enforced unless the conditions to funding obligations have been satisfied or waived.[35]

Second, one court applying a state analog of *Section 502* of DRULPA has suggested that contribution obligations may be excused – even as to partnership creditors – where there has been a "profound failure of consideration such as repudiation of, or fraud incident to, the essentials of the venture to which the [partnership] was made."[36] The court provided two examples: (i) the general partner had absconded with the limited partners' initial contributions, without putting any money into the construction of a proposed apartment project; and (ii) a failure by the general partner to take any steps at all in furtherance of the apartment complex venture.[37]

However, a "material breach of the limited partnership agreement – including mismanagement, negligence, diversion of some assets, or unauthorized acts of the general partners, or disappointed expectations, or failure to perform certain elements of the agreement – would not excuse a limited partner's commitment to contribute additional capital" and thus would not constitute a valid defense to a *Section 502* claim.[38] One court held that proof of the general partner's fraudulent activities did not excuse the limited partners' capital contribution obligations and did not provide adequate defense to a creditor's claim under *Section 502* because the fraud had not resulted in a total failure of consideration.[39]

Third, another court has suggested that when loan proceeds are not used for partnership purposes, lenders may not be able to recover from those limited partners that lacked knowledge of such use.[40]

Finally, a limited partner may deny that it had the authority to execute a subscription agreement, partnership agreement, or Investor Letter as a defense to payment. However, the evidence of authority (in the form of an opinion of counsel or a secretary's certificate) that typically accompanies Investor Letters may estop the investor from asserting such a defense in transactions with Investor Letters.

Creditor enforcement based on breach of contract under a *security agreement*

Under typical facility documents, lenders may "step into the shoes" of the general partner to enforce rights under the partnership agreement.

Application of the UCC and right of recovery against investors

Because the investors are obligated to make capital contributions under the partnership agreement, and the collateral pledged to the lenders constitutes general intangibles, investors are considered "*account debtors*" under the UCC.[41] Under UCC § 9-406, after a lender delivers notice to investors that the amount due or to become due has been assigned *and* that payment is to be made to the assignee,[42] the investors may discharge their obligations to make capital contributions only by paying the lender. If the investors fail to fund their capital contributions, the lender may assert a breach of contract claim against the investors as an assignee under the security agreement.[43]

While no particular form of notice is mandated under UCC § 9-406, other than that the notice must be authenticated,[44] notice will be effective so long as the lender's chosen method of notifying the investor is sufficiently specific and direct.[45] Conversely, if the notice of the assignment does not reasonably identify the rights assigned, then it will be deemed ineffective.[46]

The courts uniformly hold that, if the notice simply informed the investors that the right to payment has been assigned to the lender – without also informing the investors that future payments are to be made to the lender – then the investors, by paying the borrower, are discharged and need not pay the lender as well.[47] It is not clear whether the notice requirement is satisfied by delivery of notice to investors at the closing of a facility, which notice would presumably disclose that payments would be required to be made to the lender upon an event of default and issuance of a capital call notice by the lender, both of which are conditions subsequent that may never occur. Thus, the prudent lender will deliver a notice, upon an event of default, that the right to payment has been assigned and that future payments must be made to the lender, so that any payment by the investors to the borrower will not discharge any liability to the lender – investors must pay the lender directly.[48]

After sending notice, the lender may exercise remedies under the partnership agreement *in lieu* of the general partner.[49] Under UCC § 9-404(a), this means that, unless the investors have agreed to fund capital contributions without defense, the lender's rights are subject to any claims or defenses the investors have against the borrower. This principle is an "application of the elementary ancient law that an assignee never stands in any better position than his assignor. An assignee is subject to all the equities and burdens which attach to the property assigned because he receives no more … than his assignor."[50]

"Waiver of defenses"

The key provision in any Investor Letter or partnership agreement addressing a subscription-secured facility is the agreement by investors to fund capital contributions to repay the facility without defense, setoff or counterclaim. This agreement is often referred to, in shorthand, as a "waiver of defenses," but it is, in most cases, simply an agreement to fund capital contributions to repay the obligations under a subscription-secured facility, without raising, against the lender, any defenses that may exist as between the investor and the borrower, while retaining rights to make claims against the borrower and the other investors.

Creditor enforcement based on breach of contract under an *Investor Letter*

In a facility with Investor Letters, the lender should also assert a breach of contract claim as a party to the Investor Letter.

In its Investor Letter, each investor will acknowledge and confirm that the lender, by extending the credit facility to the partnership, is relying on the obligation of the investor to make capital contributions to the partnership. Facility documents typically permit the lender to issue capital calls directly to the investors, and the investors will have agreed to fund capital contributions without defense, setoff or counterclaim. If any investor fails to fund its capital contribution when called by the lender, it will have breached the terms of its Investor Letter, and the lender may bring a breach of contract claim. After discovery, the lender may be able to move for summary judgment, since proof of the executed Investor Letter and its terms and provisions will likely eliminate many issues of fact that may otherwise prevent the lender from obtaining summary judgment against such investor. Even short of an actual agreement, if an investor, by execution of an Investor Letter, *acknowledges and confirms* its obligations under the partnership agreement, such acknowledgment and confirmation may constitute an enforceable contract.[51]

Creditor enforcement based on breach of contract under a *partnership agreement*

If the partnership agreement expressly grants the lender the right to directly demand payment of capital contributions from the investors, the lender will be an intended third-party beneficiary of the agreement; partnership agreements often make the third-party beneficiary status of the lenders explicit. The lender should then be able to enforce the investors' capital call obligations for its benefit. In *Chase Manhattan Bank v. Iridium Africa*, the limited liability company agreement (the "**LLC Agreement**") at issue gave the lender the right to directly demand payment of the members' capital call obligations.[52] In that case, the court granted the lender's summary judgment request on its breach of contract claim (as a third-party beneficiary of the LLC Agreement) based on the members' refusal to comply with the lender's demand for payment under the LLC Agreement.[53] However, it appears that the court granted summary judgment based solely on the relevant provisions of the LLC Agreement (which gave the lenders the right to directly demand capital contributions from the members), without reviewing the lender's rights under the security agreement.[54]

Relevance of "waiver of defenses"

Good litigation strategy often dictates that a lender should assert as many legitimate claims as possible against an obligor – in this case, the investors. Initial pleading requirements are, in most U.S. jurisdictions, liberal, and a lender is not limited to pursuing only its best claim. Any such strategy should also take into account, however, potential affirmative defenses that may be asserted by investors, in the context of the "waiver of defenses" discussed above.

Although lenders may have the right to require investors to make capital contributions through the security agreement, partnership agreement or *Section 502* of RULPA (as enacted in Delaware and many other states), the investors may have defenses at their disposal.[55] However, if the partnership agreement, the subscription agreements or the Investor Letter contain the customary waiver of defenses language,[56] the investors should be estopped from raising those defenses and the lenders may be able to obtain summary judgment against the investors.[57]

Enforceability of waiver of defenses under general contract law

Parties to a contract may contractually agree to waive certain rights. A party may waive a defense to a contract,[58] and courts have enforced such waivers if the waiver language is manifested in some unequivocal manner.[59]

For example, in *Relational Funding Corp. v. TCIM Services, Inc.*, the Delaware District Court dismissed a lessee's counterclaims due to the following waiver in the lease agreement: "Lessee's obligation under the Lease with respect to Assignee shall be absolute and unconditional and not subject to any abatement, reduction, recoupment, defense, offset or counterclaim[.]"[60] The court held that this provision was enforceable based on the degree and specificity to which it explicitly waived the defendant's rights.[61]

As to whether fraud (especially, fraud in the inducement) as a defense is waivable, the Third Circuit in *MBIA Ins. Corp. v. Royal Indemnity Co.* noted that "we predict that when sophisticated parties have inserted clear anti-reliance language[62] in their negotiated agreement, and when that language, though broad, *unambiguously* covers the fraud that actually occurs, Delaware's highest court will enforce it to bar a subsequent fraud claim."[63] However, the same court also pointed out that the standards for effective waiver would be stricter, if waiver is possible at all, if fraud in the factum was raised as a defense.[64]

In 2007, the Sixth Circuit endorsed and adopted the *MBIA* court's analysis regarding waivers of defenses.[65] In *Commercial Money Center, Inc. v. Illinois Union Insurance Co.*, the Court of Appeals for the Sixth Circuit, applying California law, enforced a contractual provision waiving an insurance company's right to assert the defense of fraud.[66] In doing so, the court noted that the parties had negotiated for and "sculpted" provisions containing anti-reliance language and explicitly waiving the right to assert defenses relating to "all issues of fraud."[67]

An exception to the enforceability of a waiver of defenses may exist when public policy concerns arise. Principally, some courts have refused to enforce a waiver of defenses provision when the defendant was fraudulently induced to enter into the agreement.[68] Other courts have permitted waiver when sophisticated parties agree to clear any unambiguous waiver language covering the fraud that occurred.[69] Generally, courts will not permit waiver under any circumstances when a contract is procured by fraud in the factum, such that the waiving party does not even know the "true nature" of what it is signing.[70] If investors have not agreed to an enforceable waiver of defenses, then the lender's breach of contract claim will be subject to any valid affirmative defenses that the investors can assert.

Enforceability of waiver of defenses under the UCC

If a lender is enforcing its rights under a security agreement, UCC § 9-403 provides guidance as to: (i) the enforceability of the investor's waiver of defenses; and (ii) what types of defenses may be waived, and what types of defenses may not be waived.[71]

Under UCC § 9-403, a waiver by an account party, in favor of an assignee, of defenses that such account party may otherwise have against the assignor is enforceable.[72] If a waiver of defense clause in favor of an assignee is recognized as enforceable under UCC § 9-403, the assignee will be subject to only those defenses that could be asserted against a holder in due course (which are not waivable under the UCC),[73] which may include defenses (among others less relevant) based on:

- duress, lack of legal capacity, or illegality of the transaction, which, under other law, nullifies the obligation of the obligor;
- fraud in the factum (*i.e.*, fraud that induced the obligor to sign the instrument[74] with neither knowledge nor reasonable opportunity to learn of its character or its essential terms);[75] or
- discharge of the obligor in insolvency proceedings.[76]

On the other hand, the assignee will *not* be subject to the defense of:

- failure of consideration;[77]
- non-delivery of goods;
- fraud in the inducement;[78]
- breach of warranty; or
- the lack of a meeting of the minds between the parties and, accordingly, no valid contract.[79]

Lack of waiver of defenses

In the event that no waiver of defenses has been entered into, the circumstances under which an investor's capital call obligation will be excused should still be few and narrow. Courts are reluctant to excuse capital call obligations because third parties and other investors generally rely upon them.[80]

Sovereign immunity concerns with certain investors

An additional category of defenses that may be relevant in the case of state or municipal investors (such as public pension funds or sovereign wealth funds) is that of sovereign or governmental immunity. This longstanding doctrine protects governmental entities to varying degrees, from liability generally to being sued in court, or both.[81] Some states have, either by statute, constitutional provision, or case law, waived or eliminated such immunity for governmental entities that enter into contracts.[82] Other states have not implemented such waivers or have limited them to specific circumstances.[83] Any analysis of sovereign immunity must begin with a review of the particular protections that apply by constitution, common law, or statute to the specific governmental entity investor at issue.

Separate from any waiver by statute or constitution, an Investor Letter by a state or municipal pension fund often contains a waiver of immunity that such state or municipal pension fund may otherwise be entitled to claim. (The partnership agreement and such partner's subscription agreement usually do not contain such a waiver.) An explicit waiver of sovereign immunity defenses in an Investor Letter is obviously preferable from the lender's standpoint. Without such a waiver, the general partner's (and, upon a pledge to the lenders of the collateral, the lender's) ability to enforce capital commitment obligations of a state or municipal pension fund or sovereign wealth fund may be limited.

Still, even in circumstances when the governmental entity investor retains immunity from suit and is unwilling to provide a waiver, lenders are not entirely without tools to encourage compliance. For instance, if the basis for the sovereign investor's refusal to fund a capital contribution is a dispute over whether an event of default has occurred, it should be possible for a lender to seek judicial resolution of this question through a declaratory judgment action against the fund without naming the sovereign entity as a defendant, thereby avoiding any immunity defenses. And if the fund has other limited partners that are not governmental entities, a judicial finding that these private entities are obligated to make contributions could help induce compliance by the governmental investor (or even provide an opening for legislative action to permit suit against the investor).[84] Finally, lenders may reasonably hope that governmental entity investors will remain sufficiently concerned about their own credit and market reputation that they will not often use sovereign immunity as a shield against otherwise clear and material contractual obligations.

Enforcing judgments

The last step in the litigation process, after a judgment is obtained, is to enforce the judgment against the investors' assets. This process can be time-consuming and difficult; however, *Federal Rule of Civil Procedure 69* provides for very broad post-judgment discovery of a judgment debtor's assets.[85] All of the discovery tools under the Federal Rules of Civil Procedure are available to locate a debtor's assets, including requests for documents, interrogatories, and depositions.[86] Federal courts have broad authority to sanction judgment debtors that refuse to comply with post-judgment discovery.[87] Once a judgment debtor's assets have been located, *Federal Rule of Civil Procedure 69* provides that execution of those assets proceeds in the manner of the state where the federal court is located. Depending on the jurisdiction, common judgment enforcement mechanisms include garnishments,[88] attachments, turnovers, and execution on property.[89]

Moreover, transferring an American judgment from one U.S. jurisdiction to another so that it may be locally enforced is a relatively simple matter. Federal law provides for the registering of a federal judgment in a different federal district simply by filing a certified copy of the judgment.[90] In state courts, the Uniform Enforcement of Foreign Judgments Act (the "***UEFJA***") has been adopted by every state except Vermont and California (which have adopted a similar procedure).[91] The UEFJA allows enforcement of a judgment from another state upon the simple filing of the judgment with the clerk of court.[92]

Registering a U.S. judgment abroad against foreign investors

Unlike many countries, the United States has no treaty or agreement with any other country respecting the enforcement of judgments.[93] Therefore, a country-by-country analysis is required to determine how to enforce a U.S. judgment against assets of an investor outside of the United States, or against a non-U.S. investor. Common criteria to consider include the following:
- whether the court of origin had jurisdiction over the judgment debtor;
- whether the judgment debtor was properly served in the original action;
- whether enforcement of the judgment would violate local public policy; and
- whether the judgment is "final."[94]

As a practical matter, registration and enforcement of a judgment outside of the United States will involve collaboration with local counsel, who will be able to advise on strategies specific to each applicable jurisdiction.

Conclusion

Although material borrower defaults in the subscription lending universe have been rare, the few that have occurred are instructive. In each known case, a facility default has resulted in the borrower's full repayment of the facility, usually from proceeds of a capital call on the investors. In the *Chase Manhattan Bank v. Iridium Africa*[95] case, the lenders recovered from investors as well. However, the rarity of defaults means that there is little guidance from case law that confirms the legal analysis relating to enforcement and recovery. Thus, it is critical to a lender's adequate risk-management strategy and credit analysis to understand the issues and anticipate a strategy for enforcement of remedies against a borrower and its investors, should the need arise.

* * *

Endnotes

1. We will refer to funds as "limited partnerships," and make corresponding reference to limited partners, partnership agreements and partnership-related terms, which may be read to also refer to limited liability companies, their members and corresponding organizational documents, or to other types of entities that may be borrowers under subscription-secured credit facilities. In addition, as to analysis of the application of Delaware law, the Delaware Limited Liability Company Act is generally similar to the Delaware Revised Limited Partnership Act.
2. The decision on whether to file in state *versus* federal court will depend on several factors, including the citizenship of the parties and the amount in controversy. One other consideration is the relative speed in which a judgment can be obtained. In some jurisdictions it is possible to obtain a quicker resolution in state court rather than federal court.
3. See *Wilton v. Seven Falls Co.*, 515 U.S. 277, 288 (1995).
4. See *In re Gantt*, 70 N.Y.S.2d 55 (N.Y. Sup. Ct. 1947) ("[t]he parties to a contract may confer jurisdiction by consent" (citation omitted)); *see also Cambridge Nutrition A.G. v. Fotheringham*, 840 F. Supp. 299, 303 (S.D.N.Y. 1994).
5. Also known as "The Declaratory Judgment Act."
6. For an actual case or controversy to exist, the dispute must be definite and concrete (not hypothetical) between parties who have adverse legal interests of sufficient immediacy and reality. See *MedImmune, Inc. v. Genentech, Inc.*, 549 U.S. 118, 126–27 (2007); *Aetna Life Ins. Co. v. Haworth*, 300 U.S. 227, 240–41 (1937).
7. See *Shell Oil Co. v. Amoco Corp.*, 970 F.2d 885, 887 (Fed. Cir. 1992).
8. *Town of Coeymans v. City of Albany*, 237 A.D.2d 856, 858 (N.Y. App. Div. 1997); *see* N.Y. C.P.L.R. § 3001 (2009) (stating that the court may issue a declaratory judgment "as to the rights and other legal relations of the parties to a justiciable controversy") (New York law); *Burris v. Cross*, 583 A.2d 1364, 1371 (Del. 1990) (holding that an action under the Delaware Declaratory Judgment Act must meet the threshold requirements of an actual controversy) (Delaware law).
9. Fed. R. Civ. P. 4(h). The general test is that service on an organization should be to someone at the organization who stands in a position of authority so it would be reasonable to assume that person would know what to do with the papers. *See* 4A Charles Alan Wright & Arthur R. Miller, Federal Practice and Procedure § 1101 (4th ed. 2017); *see also Direct Mail Specialists, Inc. v. Eclat Computerized Techs., Inc.*, 840 F.2d 685, 688 (9th Cir. 1988). In practice, domestic organizations are required to maintain a registered agent for service of process, and service on this agent would be effective. *See, e.g.*, 8 Del. C. § 132 (2017) (providing that every corporation shall maintain a registered agent that shall "[a]ccept service of process and other communications directed to the corporations for which it serves as registered agent and forward same to the corporation to which the

service or communication is directed …"). Note, however, that the lender may also obtain a waiver of formal service requirements from the defendant under the Federal Rules. Fed. R. Civ. P. 4(d). The Federal Rules provide an incentive for a defendant to waive formal service in the form of 60 days to answer the complaint as opposed to 20. Fed. R. Civ. P. 12(a)(1). The option to seek a waiver is in the lender's discretion, however, and the lender may not wish to give the defendant more time to answer.

10. *See, e.g.*, N.Y. C.P.L.R. § 311 (2016) (service on a corporation may be made by delivering the summons to an officer or managing or general agent or other agent authorized by law to receive service); N.Y. C.P.L.R. § 310-a(a) (2016) (service on a limited partnership may be made by delivering the summons to any managing or general agent or general partner of the limited partnership). 8 Del. C. § 321(a) (2017) "[s]ervice of legal process upon any corporation of this State shall be made by delivering a copy personally to any officer or director of the corporation in this State, or the registered agent of the corporation in this State, or by leaving it at the dwelling house or usual place of abode in this State of any officer, director or registered agent (if the registered agent be an individual), or at the registered office or other place of business of the corporation in this State").

11. *See Nat'l Equip. Rental, Ltd. v. Szukhent*, 375 U.S. 311, 315-16 (1964) ("[I]t is settled … that parties to a contract may agree in advance to submit to the jurisdiction of a given court, to permit notice to be served by the opposing party, or even to waive notice altogether" (citations omitted)); *Comprehensive Merch. Catalogs, Inc. v. Madison Sales Corp.*, 521 F.2d 1210, 1212 (7th Cir. 1975) (applying New York law) ("[i]t is well-settled that parties to a contract may agree to submit to the jurisdiction of a particular court and may also agree as to the manner and method of service"); *Greystone CDE, LLC v. Santa Fe Pointe L.P.*, No. 07 CV. 8377(RPP), 2007 WL 4230770 at *3 (S.D.N.Y. Nov. 30, 2007) ("[t]he parties in this case agreed as to the methods by which service of process is valid and effective. Such agreements are permissible and upheld by courts in the event of litigation … . The parties' contractual language, and not the Federal Rules of Civil Procedure, governs what constitutes proper service in this case" (citations omitted)).

12. Note that this will likely necessitate retaining local foreign counsel.

13. The analysis will be the same as with a domestic entity. *See supra* notes 4–7 and accompanying text.

14. *See, e.g., Mastec Latin America v. Inepar S/A Industrias E Construcoes*, No. 03 Civ. 9892(GBD), 2004 WL 1574732 at *2 (S.D.N.Y. July 13, 2004) (Brazilian defendant specifically agreed by contract to service of process upon its designated agent in New York. Because New York law permitted such an agreement on service of process, the court held that the method of service was valid absent a showing by the defendant that such an agreement was precluded by Brazilian law). It is interesting to note that New York courts hold that a New York plaintiff is not required to comply with foreign service of process requirements absent a treaty. *See Morgenthau v. Avion Res. Ltd.*, 898 N.E. 2d 929, 11 N.Y.3d 383, 391 (N.Y. 2008). *See also infra* note 16.

15. *See* HCCH Members, https://www.hcch.net/en/states/hcch-members (last visited Nov. 3, 2022).

16. *See* Fed. R. Civ. P. 4(f)(1) (providing that service of process abroad is proper under the Hague Convention). Note that if the defendant or an agent (*i.e.*, subsidiary) of the defendant can be found in New York, service under New York law may be effective against the defendant itself, with no need to resort to the Hague Convention. *See Volkswagenwerk Aktiengesellschaft v. Schlunk*, 486 U.S. 694, 707 (1988) ("[w]here service on a domestic agent is valid and complete under both state law and the Due Process Clause, our inquiry ends and the Convention has no further implications").

17. The Cayman Islands is a British Overseas Possession, and as such is not an independent nation. However, it will be considered separately because certain financial privacy legislation presents special difficulties with enforcing a judgment there. *See* Cayman to Welcome Third Party Rights Rules, Appleby Legal Updates, available at https://www.mondaq.com/caymanislands/offshore-financial-centres/309882/cayman-to-welcome-third-party-rights-rules (last visited Nov. 2, 2022). *See also* Exempted Limited Partnership Act 2021 § 32(11) (Cayman Islands).
18. *See* 1965 Convention Outline, https://www.hcch.net/en/publications-and-studies/details4/?pid=2728&dtid=3 (last visited Nov. 3, 2022) for a practical outline of service of process under the Hague Convention. Each participating government designates its own "Central Authority." For example, the United States' Central Authority is the Office of International Judicial Assistance, a part of the Justice Department. *See* U.S. Dep't of State, http://travel.state.gov/content/travel/en/legal-considerations/judicial/service-of-process.html (last visited Nov. 3, 2022). England's Central Authority is the Senior Master of the Royal Courts of Justice in London. *See* Central Authority, https://www.hcch.net/en/states/authorities/details3/?aid=278 (last visited Nov. 3, 2022).
19. Hague Convention *Article 10(a)*, Nov. 15, 1965, 20 U.S.T 361, 658 U.N.T.S 163. Note that the United Kingdom and the Cayman Islands have made no objection to service by mail. *See McCarron v. British Telecom*, No. Civ. A. 00-CV-6123, 2001 WL 632927, at *1-2 (E.D. Pa. June 6, 2001) (holding that mailing documents via certified mail to the defendant's business address in London, England was sufficient under the Hague Convention).
20. *See* 28 U.S.C. § 2201(a) (2010).
21. In some facilities, borrowers negotiate a short standstill period to permit time for the borrower to make a capital call before the lender may act. Lenders sometimes agree to this provision under the theory that the investors may be more inclined, as a practical matter, to respond to an "ordinary course of business" capital call than one issued by a lender. However, in most subscription-secured facilities, lenders have an immediate right to make capital calls upon a payment default or acceleration of the debt following an event of default.
22. Note that investors typically agree to fund capital contributions for the repayment of the facility without defense, setoff or counterclaim, whether called by borrower or the lender. Strictly speaking they do not waive defenses against the fund, but this mechanism keeps the risk of mistake, fraud or bad investments between the investors and the fund.
23. Many states and the District of Columbia preclude recovery for unjust enrichment if there is an express contract between the parties. *See, e.g., Nemec v. Shrader*, Nos 3878-CC, 3934-CC, 2009 WL 1204346, at *6 (Del. Ch. Apr. 30, 2009) ("Delaware courts, however, have consistently refused to permit a claim for unjust enrichment when the alleged wrong arises from a relationship governed by contract"); *Schiff v. American Ass'n of Retired Persons*, 697 A.2d 1193 (D.C. 1997) (no claim for unjust enrichment when an express contract exists between the parties); *Marshall Contractors, Inc. v. Brown University*, 692 A.2d 665 (R.I. 1997) (same); *W&W Oil Co. v. Capps*, 784 S.W.2d 536 (Tex. App.—Tyler 1990) (same). Note that if there is only an express contract between the investors and the fund (such as the partnership agreement), this may not bar a claim for unjust enrichment between the investors and the lender. *See Leasepartners Corp. v. Robert L. Brooks Trust Dated November 12, 1975*, 942 P.2d 182 (Nev. 1997) (permitting claim for unjust enrichment by leaseholder against owner because the only express written contract was between the owner and tenant).

24. *See, e.g., Shapiro v. Solomon*, 126 A.2d 654 (N.J. Super. Ct. App. Div. 1956) (New Jersey law) (permitting quasi-contractual recovery after action was brought on an unenforceable express contract); *Kennedy v. Polar-BEK & Baker Wildwood Partnership*, 682 So. 2d 443 (Ala. 1996) (noting the law may recognize an implied contract for the purposes of unjust enrichment when the existence of an express contract on same subject matter is not proven).

25. A common law promissory estoppel claim in most states is subject to the same requirement that there is no express or enforceable contract. *See, e.g., Tripoli Management, LLC v. Waste Connections of Kansas, Inc.*, No. 10-1062-SAC, 2011 WL 2897334, at *13 (D. Kan. July 18, 2011) (opining that "it is hornbook law that quasi-contractual remedies, such as unjust enrichment and promissory estoppel, are unavailable when an enforceable express contract regulates the relations of the parties with respect to the disputed issue").

26. Lenders may also consider recovery against limited partners pursuant to the so-called "control rule," which provides that limited partners can be liable for partnership obligations if they "participate in the control" of the business of the partnership. *Id.* Although the control rule was eliminated in the most-recent amendments to the Uniform Limited Partnership Act, it remains the law in many states, including the State of Delaware. *See* 6 Del. C. § 17-303 (2017). However, limited partners typically do not act in a management role, and participation in control may be difficult to prove.

    Limited partnership law also sometimes recognizes lenders' rights to sue the limited partners to recover distributions that were made to such limited partners when the partnership was insolvent or in the zone of insolvency, or to recover returned capital contributions to the extent necessary to satisfy partnership obligations. Thomas J. Hall and Janice A. Payne, *The Liability of Limited Partners for the Defaulted Loans of Their Limited Partnerships*, 122 Banking L.J. 687 (2005). In jurisdictions that recognize this right, an action to recover such distributions or returned capital contributions may be asserted by the lenders themselves, obviating the need for the lenders to rely on the partnership to pursue such claims. *Id.*

27. DRULPA is based on the 1985 version of the Revised Uniform Limited Partnership Act ("*RULPA*"), which was adopted in most states. Because the financial provisions of most limited liability company statutes have been modeled on RULPA, lenders should also generally have the right to enforce contribution obligations against member investors. *See* 1 Ribstein and Keatinge on Ltd. Liab. Cos. § 5:7, 5:9 (2008).

    Hierarchically speaking, the court will first look to the unambiguous language of the contracts at issue to determine the parties' respective rights, before resorting to statutory law to fill in any gaps. As explained by the Delaware Court of Chancery:

    > "Consistent with the underlying policy of freedom of contract espoused by the Delaware Legislature, limited partnership agreements are to be construed in accordance with their literal terms. 'The operative document is the limited partnership agreement and the statute merely provides the 'fall-back' or default provisions where the partnership agreement is silent.' Only 'if the partners have not expressly made provisions in their partnership agreement or if the agreement is inconsistent with mandatory statutory provisions, … will [a court] look for guidance from the statutory default rules, traditional notions of fiduciary duties, or other extrinsic evidence.' In other words, unless the partnership agreement is silent or ambiguous, a court will not look for extrinsic guidance elsewhere, so as to 'give maximum effect to the principle of freedom of contract' and maintain the preeminence of the intent of the parties to the contract."

Twin Bridges Ltd. Partnership v. Draper, No. Civ. A. 2351-VCP, 2007 WL 2744609 at *12 (Del. Ch. Sept. 14, 2007) (internal citations omitted).
28. 6 Del. C. § 17-502(b)(1) (1995). The same holds true for creditors of limited liability companies. *See also* Ribstein and Keatinge, *supra* note 27 at § 5:8 ("[t]he [LLC] statutes also generally provide that creditors who rely on the original contribution may enforce original contribution obligations notwithstanding an intervening compromise" (citing, *inter alia*, 6 Del. C. § 18-502(b) (1995), which says: "Notwithstanding the compromise, a creditor of a limited liability company who extends credit, after the entering into of a limited liability company agreement or an amendment thereto which, in either case, reflects the obligation, and before the amendment thereof to reflect the compromise, may enforce the original obligation to the extent that, in extending credit, the creditor reasonably relied on the obligation of a member to make a contribution or return")).
29. Hall & Payne, *supra* note 26 (citing *P'ship Equities, Inc. v. Marten*, 443 N.E.2d 134, 136 (Mass. App. Ct. 1982)). To the extent that there is an Investor Letter, the acknowledgment/agreement contained therein should substantiate the lender's reasonable reliance claim against the investors under 6. Del. C. § 17-502 (1995).
30. Hall & Payne, *supra* note 26.
31. 866 A.2d 762.
32. *Id*. at 781. *Section 3.1*, as part of the partnership agreement, was attached to the Confidential Information Memorandum given to the bank creditors. *Id.* It provided, *inter alia*, that:
    - each limited partner made an initial capital contribution of 15% of its overall Commitment;
    - the Commitment means "the aggregate amount of cash agreed to be contributed as capital to the Partnership by such limited partner as specified in such limited partner's Subscription Agreement …;"
    - the limited partners need to make additional capital contributions to the Partnership "at such times as the General Partner shall specify in written notices (each, a 'Drawdown Notice');"
    - each partner's funding obligation would expire upon the "termination of the Commitment Period" but, nevertheless, required contributions thereafter "to pay or provide for payment of Partnership Expenses, including Partnership funded indebtedness;" and
    - there is no obligation by the limited partners directly to creditors, as follows: [T]he provisions of this Agreement (including this Article III) are intended solely to benefit the Partners and, to the fullest extent permitted by applicable law, shall not be construed as conferring any benefit upon any creditor of the Partnership (and no such creditor shall be a third-party beneficiary of this Agreement), and no limited partner shall have any duty or obligation to any creditor of the Partnership to make any Capital Contributions or to cause the General Partner to make a call for Capital Contributions.
    Id.
33. *Id.* at 762 ("[t]o the extent a partnership agreement requires a partner to make a contribution, the partner is obligated, except to the extent such obligation is modified by the terms of the partnership agreement, to make such contribution to a limited partnership"); *see also* 6 Del. C. § 17-502(b)(1)(1995).
34. *P'ship Equities, Inc. v. Marten*, 443 N.E.2d 134, 136 (Mass. App. Ct. 1982); *see also* 59A Am. Jur. 2d Partnership § 871 (2003).

35. Conditional obligations include contributions payable upon a discretionary call of a limited partnership or general partner prior to the time such call occurs. *See* 6 Del. C. § 17-502(b)(2) (1995). *See also supra* notes 31–32 and accompanying text.
36. *P'ship Equities, Inc.*, 443 N.E.2d at 136.
37. *Id.* at 138–139.
38. *Id. See also Stobaugh v. Twin City Bank*, 771 S.W.2d 282 (Ark. 1989); 59A Am. Jur. 2d Partnership § 871 (2003).
39. *In re Securities Group 1980*, 74 F.3d at 1108–09 (11th Cir. 1996) (holding that any fraud on part of Chapter 11 debtor-limited partnerships and their general partners based upon general partners' convictions for income tax fraud arising out of activities related to limited partnerships, including use of "rigged straddles" and "rigged repurchase agreements" to create fraudulent income tax losses, which were then passed through to investors such as limited partners and subsequently disallowed by IRS, was not sufficient to permit limited partners to avoid their liability, under New York partnership law, to make additional capital contributions to partnerships upon capital call by Chapter 11 trustee, given strong statutory purpose of New York partnership law to favor creditors over limited partners).
40. Liability for contribution obligations – Liability to partnership creditors for unpaid contributions, *see* J. William Callison and Maureen Sullivan, Partnership Law & Practice § 24:4 (2006) (citing *Northwestern Nat. Bank of Minneapolis v. Swenson*, 414 N.W.2d 543 (Minn. Ct. App. 1987) (holding that evidence supported trial court's finding that limited partner had no knowledge that his notes, which were given for his investment in limited partnership, would be used as collateral for loans to general partner, which were then used by general partner for nonpartnership purposes, and, therefore, limited partner was not estopped from asserting defense that proceeds of loans were used for nonpartnership purposes)).
41. *See* UCC § 9-102(a)(3) (AM. LAW INST. & UNIF. LAW COMM'N 2010) ("account debtor" means a person obligated on an account, chattel paper, or general intangible).
42. Because the notice must recite that payment is to be made to the assignee, it is prudent to provide notice upon an event of default, which is the time after which a lender has the right to receive payment of the capital contributions, even if prior notice has been delivered or if Investors Letters are in the transaction.
43. *See, e.g., IIG Capital LLC v. Archipelago, L.L.C.*, 36 A.D.3d 401, 404–05 (N.Y. Sup. Ct. 2007) (holding assignee properly asserted a breach of contract cause of action against account debtors under New York's version of UCC § 9-406).
44. This requirement normally can be satisfied by the lender sending notification on its letterhead or on a form on which its name appears. *See also* UCC § 9-102(a)(7) (AM. LAW INST. & UNIF. LAW COMM'N 2010) (defining "authenticate" to mean "with present intent to adopt or accept a record, to attach to or logically associate with the record an electronic sound, symbol, or process").
45. *See, e.g., Banque Arabe et Internationale D'Investissement v. Bulk Oil (USA) Inc.*, 726 F. Supp. 1411 (S.D.N.Y. 1989) (holding notice of an assignment is effective when the debtor receives notice that the funds have been assigned and that payment is to be made to the assignee); *General Motors Acceptance Corp. v. Albany Water Bd.*, 187 A.D.2d 894 (N.Y. App. Div. 1992) (no particular form of notice is necessary in order to require payment to the assignee; it is sufficient if information known to the debtor either apprises it of the assignment or serves to put it on inquiry).
46. *See* UCC § 9-406(b)(1) (AM. LAW INST. & UNIF. LAW COMM'N 2010); *Warrington v. Dawson*, 798 F.2d 1533, 1536 (5th Cir. 1986).

47. *See* 29 Williston on Contracts § 74:61 (4th ed. 2008). In this scenario, the lender would likely have alternative cause of action against the fund for unjust enrichment and/or *quantum meruit*. The existence of a valid and enforceable contract typically precludes recovery in quasi-contract for events arising out of the same subject matter, but if there is a *bona fide* dispute as to the existence of a contract or if the contract does not cover the dispute in issue, then the plaintiff may be able to proceed on an alternative theory such as unjust enrichment or *quantum meruit*. *See IIG Capital*, 36 A.D.3d at 404–05 (citations omitted).
48. *See IIG Capital*, 36 A.D.3d at 402–03.
49. It is important to note that "[n]otification is for the benefit of the assignee, who would otherwise have no recourse against the account debtor if the assignor failed to forward payment that the account debtor made directly to the assignor." *Novartis Animal Health US, Inc. v. Earle Palmer Brown, LLC*, 424 F. Supp. 2d 1358, 1364 (N.D. Ga. 2006).
50. *GMAC Commercial Credit LLC v. Springs Industries, Inc.*, 171 F. Supp. 2d 209, 214 (S.D.N.Y. 2001) (quoting *Septembertide Publishing, B.V. v. Stein and Day, Inc.*, 884 F.2d 675, 682 (2d Cir. 1989)).
51. *See, e.g., C.H.I. Inc. v. Marcus Bros. Textile, Inc.*, 930 F.2d 762, 763 (9th Cir. 1991) (enforcing terms of contract confirmation form that was sufficiently specific and provided for mutuality of remedy).
52. (*Iridium I*), 307 F. Supp. 2d 608, 612 (D. Del. 2004); *see also Blair v. Anderson*, 325 A.2d 94, 96–97 (Del. 1974) (holding that a federal prisoner could enforce a contract between the United States and Delaware involving care for prisoners, and stating: "It is established Delaware law that a third-party beneficiary of a contract may sue on it"); *John Julian Constr. Co. v. Monarch Builders*, 306 A.2d 29 (Del. Super. Ct. 1973) (creditor of liquidated corporation could enforce the assumption of liabilities contract against the defendants as a third-party beneficiary). Note that the analysis provided in these cases should apply equally to the investors in a limited partnership.
53. *Iridium I* at 612.
54. "Accordingly, the Court will grant Chase summary judgment on its first claim for relief, breach of contract." *Id.* "It is undisputed that Iridium LLC defaulted on the Chase Loan and that Chase called the Members' RCC obligations pursuant to Section 4.02 of the amended LLC Agreement. The Members refused to comply with Chase's demand for payment in contravention of the amended LLC Agreement, thus compelling the Court to grant Chase summary judgment on its breach of contract claim." *Id.* at 612 n.1. *See also Chase Manhattan Bank v. Iridium Africa* (*Iridium II*), 474 F. Supp.2d 613 (D. Del. 2007). "Based on the Court's conclusion that the Members may not deny the validity of the Certificate's representation that the amended LLC Agreement is "true and correct," the Court will not discuss the Magistrate Judge's Report and Recommendation on the issues of … 2) whether Chase is entitled to summary judgment on its first claim for relief due to the Security Agreement." *Iridium I* at 612 n.2.
55. For a highly publicized example, *see Wibbert Investment Co. v. New Silk Route PE Asia Fund LP*, case number 650437/2013, in the Supreme Court of the State of New York. Wibbert Investment Co., the investor, declined to fund a capital call after allegations of the general partner's gross negligence and/or willful malfeasance and the conviction of a related person for insider trading. Wibbert alleged that the Fund had threatened to implement default remedies. The parties ultimately stipulated that the action would be discontinued and all associated orders and rulings would be vacated. *See* Stipulation of Discontinuance with Prejudice, *Wibbert Inv. Co.*, No. 650437/2013, (N.Y. Sup. Ct.

2017) (No. 326). Although the arrangement between the parties – if any – is not public, the years-long litigation is a reminder of the importance of strong waivers of defenses.
56. When the partnership agreement and subscription agreements do not contain waiver of defenses, the Investor Letters usually contain such language.
57. *See Iridium I* at 612–13 (where the LLC Agreement provided that each Member agreed that its duty to perform under the Reserve Capital Call ("***RCC***") obligation was "absolute and unconditional" and each Member waived "any defense it may have or acquire with respect to its obligations under the [RCC]").
58. *See* 17B C.J.S. Contracts § 868 Waiver of Defenses (2008).
59. *See Wells Fargo Bank Minnesota Nat. Ass'n v. Nassau Broadcasting Partners, L.P.*, No. 01 Civ. 11255(HB) 2002 WL 31050850, at *2 (S.D.N.Y. Sept. 13, 2002) ("[t]he hell or highwater provisions at issue, especially in light of the degree in which they explicitly waive [defendant's] right to assert setoffs, defenses or counterclaims, are generally enforceable") (citations omitted).
60. No. Civ. A. 01-821-SLR, 2003 WL 360255, at *2-3 (D. Del. Feb. 14, 2003).
61. *Id.* at *3, n.1.
62. It appears by "anti-reliance language," the court refers to broad waiver of defense language that is clearly inconsistent with reasonable reliance on extracontractual representations (and therefore the defense of fraud in the inducement). In particular, the court refers as "anti-reliance language" the following language (emphasis added):

> "The right of the beneficiary to receive payment for losses under this policy shall be absolute, continuing, irrevocable and unconditional irrespective of … (c) *any other rights or defenses that may be available to the insurer to avoid payment of its obligation under this policy (all of which rights and defenses are hereby expressly waived by the insurer)* . . . ."

MBIA Ins. Corp. v. Royal Indemnity Co., 426 F.3d 204, 210 (3d Cir. 2005) (emphasis added) (Wells Fargo (and others) as beneficiaries under credit risk insurance policies insuring payment of principal and interest in the event of defaults on underlying student loans brought action against Royal Indemnity Company ("***Royal***"), as insurer, to recover under the policies. Royal defended on the ground that the lender of the underlying student loans fraudulently induced it to issue the policies and that this fraud in the inducement entitled it to rescission. The court held that Royal's policies unambiguously and effectively waived defenses to its obligations even if induced by fraud).
The court pointed out that, to establish fraudulent inducement, the defendant insurer must show *reasonable and detrimental reliance* on a misrepresentation intentionally or recklessly made to induce action or inaction. *Id.* at 211. The court thought it was unfathomable that an insurer that intended to rely on extracontractual representations would agree that its obligations are "absolute, continuing, irrevocable and unconditional irrespective of … any other rights or defenses that may be available to the insurer … (all of which rights and defenses are hereby expressly waived by the insurer)." *Id.* at 212. Thus, according to the court, the defendant insurer could not possibly claim that its reliance on those representations was reasonable when it waived all defenses based on reasonable reliance. *Id.* Thus, an agreement may foreclose a fraud defense not only by waiving "fraud" but also by setting forth terms clearly inconsistent with reasonable reliance on extracontractual representations. *Id.* at 213.
63. *Id.* at 218 (emphasis added). The court acknowledged that some cases, in particular a line of New York cases, had referred to "*specificity*" (of the waiver language) as a test for the enforceability of waiver of defense language. However, the court then rejected

such test and predicted that the Delaware Supreme Court would adopt the "*clarity*" (of the waiver language) test.
64. *Id.* at 217. Fraud in the factum is "the sort of fraud that procures a party's signature to an instrument without knowledge of its true nature or contents" and the party does not even know the "true nature" of what it is signing. *Id.*; *see also supra* note 62 and accompanying text.
65. *Commercial Money Ctr., Inc. v. Illinois Union Ins. Co.*, 508 F.3d 327 (6th Cir. 2007).
66. *Id.* Commercial Money Center, Inc. ("***CMC***") was an equipment leasing business allegedly engaged in a Ponzi-type scheme. When CMC collapsed, numerous creditors and insurance companies filed claims and counterclaims related to credit transactions to which CMC was a party. One such transaction was a surety agreement between CMC (principal), Illinois Union (surety) and JPMorgan Chase (creditor, as trustee of Citibank). Under the surety agreement, Illinois Union was obligated to "answer for the debt, default, or miscarriage" of CMC notes purchased by Citibank. When CMC filed for bankruptcy, Illinois Union sought rescission of the surety agreement, arguing, *inter alia*, that CMC fraudulently induced Illinois Union to provide surety coverage through various material misrepresentations. In discussing Illinois Union's waiver of the right to assert fraud as a defense under the surety agreement, the court explicitly followed the MBIA opinion, ultimately finding that the allegations against CMC did not rise to the level of fraud in the factum (which is discussed below).
67. *Id.* at 344.
68. *See Eureka Broadband Corp. v. Wentworth Leasing Corp.*, 400 F.3d 62, 69–70 (1st Cir. 2005); *Computer Sales Intern., Inc. v. Lycos, Inc.*, No. Civ. A. 05-10017 RWZ, 2005 WL 3307507 at *5 (D. Mass. Dec. 6, 2005) ("under Massachusetts law, it is well settled that clauses 'attempting to protect a party against the consequences of his own fraud are against public policy and void where fraud inducing the contract is shown'" (citations omitted)); *see also F.D.I.C. v. Borne*, 599 F. Supp. 891, 894 (E.D.N.Y. 1984) ("[a] waiver of the right to assert a setoff or counterclaim is not against public policy and has been enforced by this court. However, such a waiver will not be enforced so as to bar a viable setoff or counterclaim sounding in fraud" (internal citations omitted)).
69. *See MBIA Ins. Corp. v. Royal Indemnity Co.*, 426 F.3d 204, 210 (3d Cir. 2005). Wells Fargo (and others) as beneficiaries under credit risk insurance policies insuring payment of principal and interest in the event of defaults on underlying student loans brought action against Royal Indemnity Company ("***Royal***"), as insurer, to recover under the policies. Royal defended on the ground that the lender of the underlying student loans fraudulently induced it to issue the policies and that this fraud in the inducement entitled it to rescission. The court held that Royal's policies unambiguously and effectively waived defenses to its obligations even if induced by fraud. The court pointed out that, to establish fraudulent inducement, the defendant insurer must show *reasonable and detrimental reliance* on a misrepresentation intentionally or recklessly made to induce action or inaction. *Id.* at 212. The court thought it was unfathomable that an insurer that intended to rely on extracontractual representations would agree that its obligations are "absolute, continuing, irrevocable and unconditional irrespective of … any other rights or defenses that may be available to the insurer … (all of which rights and defenses are hereby expressly waived by the insurer)." *Id.* Thus, according to the court, the defendant insurer could not possibly claim that its reliance on those representations was reasonable when it waived all defenses based on reasonable reliance. *Id.* Therefore, an agreement may foreclose a fraud defense not only by waiving "fraud" but also by

setting forth terms clearly inconsistent with reasonable reliance on extracontractual representations. *Id.* at 213. *See also Manufacturers Hanover Trust Co. v. Yanakas*, 7 F.3d 310, 316–17 (2d Cir. 1993) (comparing New York state law waiver cases and concluding that "[w]here the fraud claim has been dismissed, the disclaimer has been sufficiently specific to match the alleged fraud[,]" but that "the mere general recitation that a guarantee is 'absolute and unconditional' is insufficient … to bar a defense of fraudulent inducement, and that the touchstone is specificity").

70. For further analysis of the distinction between fraud in the factum and fraud in the inducement, *see infra JPMorgan Chase Bank v. Liberty Mutual Insurance Co.*, in which the surety was asked to insure the delivery of a commodity when, in fact, it was guarantying a loan. 189 F. Supp. 2d 24, 28 (S.D.N.Y. 2002); *see also MBIA Ins. Corp.*, 426 F.3d at 217 (describing *JPMorgan Chase Bank* as an "unusual and extreme case" and questioning whether waiver would even be possible when a contract is procured through fraud in the factum).

71. In a capital commitment facility, the collateral granted by a limited partnership borrower to the lender falls under "general intangible" as defined in Article 9 of the UCC and the security agreement is governed by Article 9.

72. "Except as otherwise provided in this section, *an agreement between an account debtor and an assignor* not to assert against an assignee any *claim or defense that the account debtor may have against the assignor* is enforceable by an assignee that takes an assignment:
    (1) for value;
    (2) in good faith;
    (3) without notice of a claim of a property or possessory right to the property assigned; and
    (4) without notice of a defense or claim in recoupment of the type that may be asserted against a person entitled to enforce a negotiable instrument under UCC § 3-305(a)." UCC § 9-403(b) (AM. LAW INST. & UNIF. LAW COMM'N 2010) (emphasis added); *see also id.* at Comment 2 ("[h]owever, this section expands former Section 9-206 to apply to all account debtors; it is not limited to account debtors that have bought or leased goods").

73. *See* 68A Am. Jur. 2d Secured Transactions § 402 (2017).

74. Since UCC § 9-403's scope is not limited to waiver of defenses in negotiable instruments, it appears that when applying UCC § 9-403, one should read the word "instrument" in UCC § 3-305 as referring to whatever agreement or document that contains the waiver of defenses language in question. And presumably, it is regarding the same agreement or document the account debtor is raising a fraud in the factum defense. *See generally Chase Manhattan Bank, N. A. v. Finger Lakes Motors, Inc.*, 423 N.Y.S.2d 128 (N.Y. Sup. Ct. 1979); *MBIA Ins. Corp. v. Royal Indemnity Co.*, 426 F.3d at 217 ("Royal does not seriously question the nature of the transactions covered by its policies").

75. This defense is most frequently referred to by the courts as fraud in the factum, but is also sometimes denominated fraud in the essence or fraud in *esse contractus*, among other terms. *See* Milton Roberts, Annotation, Fraud in the Inducement and Fraud in the Factum as Defenses under UCC § 3-305 Against Holder in Due Course, 78 A.L.R.3d 1020 § 2 (1977); *see also supra* at notes 69–70 and accompanying text.

76. *See* UCC §§ 9-403, 3-305 (AM. LAW INST. & UNIF. LAW COMM'N 2010).

77. *Supra* note 73 (citing *Equico Lessors, Inc. v. Mines*, 148 Cal. Rptr. 554 (Cal. Ct. App. 1978) (lessees refused to pay rent to lessor's assignee; court rejected as a valid defense

against the assignee lessees' defense of failure of consideration – that the equipment had not been delivered); *Stenger Industries, Inc. v. Eaton Corp.*, 298 S.E.2d 628 (Ga. Ct. App. 1983) (lessee refused to pay rent to lessor's assignee; court rejected as a valid defense against the assignee lessee's defense – that machinery was defective); *Washington Bank & Trust Co. v. Landis Corp.*, 445 N.E.2d 430 (Ill. App. Ct. 1983) (lessee refused to pay rent to lessor's assignee; court rejected as a valid defense against the assignee lessee's defense – that the machine under the lease never worked and it was taken from lessee to make room for a replacement lessee never accepted)).

78. *See F.D.I.C. v. Kassel*, 421 N.Y.S.2d 609 (N.Y. App. Div. 1979) (lessee refused to pay rent to the successor in interest of the lessor's assignee; court rejected as a valid defense against the successor in interest of the lessor's assignee lessee's defense – that the lessee was fraudulently induced to enter into the lease arrangement); 68A Am. Jur. 2d Secured Transactions § 402 (citing C*hase Manhattan Bank, N. A. v. Finger Lakes Motors, Inc.*, 423 N.Y.S.2d 128 (N.Y. Sup. Ct. 1979) (lessees refused to pay rent to lessor's assignee; court rejected as a valid defense against the assignee lessees' defense – that the lessor entered into the contract for the express purpose of fleecing the lessees, assigning the paper to the assignee, taking the money and not performing)).

79. *Supra* note 73 (citing *Compton Co. v. Minolta Business Systems, Inc.*, 319 S.E.2d 107 (Ga. Ct. App. 1984) (lessees refused to pay rent to lessor's assignee; court rejected as a valid defense against the assignee lessees' defense – that there had been no meeting of the minds with respect to certain terms of the contract and thus no contract was formed between the lessor and lessee).

80. *See P'ship Equities, Inc. v. Marten*, 443 N.E.2d 134, 136 (Mass. App. Ct. 1982). However, one court has suggested a possible defense to a capital call contribution obligation where "a profound failure of consideration such as a repudiation of, or fraud incident to, the essentials of the venture to which subscription was made." *Id.* The example provided by the court of this possible defense was a general partner who absconded with all of the initial contributions and did nothing at all in furtherance of the partnership's goals. *Id.* Notably, a material breach of the partnership agreement, negligence, mismanagement, or disappointed expectations do not constitute defenses to capital call obligations. *Id.* at 138.

81. *See, e.g., Hans v. Louisiana*, 134 U.S. 1 (1890), holding that "[i]t is inherent in the nature of sovereignty not to be amenable to the suit of an individual without its consent." (Quoting The Federalist No. 81.)

82. *See, e.g.,* NY Ct of Claims Act § 8 (L. 1939, c 860) (waiving sovereign immunity for commercial contract claims); Cal. Gov. Code § 814 (same); *Commonwealth v. AMEC Civil, LLC*, 699 S.E.2d 499, 516 (Va. 2010) (waiving sovereign immunity for contract claims) (reaffirming *Wiecking v. Allied Medical Supply Corp.*, 391 S.E.2d 258, 261 (Va. 1990)).

83. *See, e.g., Emps.' Ret. Sys. of Tex. v. Putnam, LLC*, 294 S.W.3d 309, 324-27 (Tex. 2009) (holding that state pension's acceptance of benefits under a contract does not constitute waiver of sovereign immunity under Texas law).

84. For example, Texas law provides for a procedure whereby a party may seek specific legislative permission to sue a state governmental entity, upon passage of a concurrent resolution by the Texas Legislature. *See* Tex. Civ. Prac. & Rem. Code §§ 107.001-005. While such requests have been only infrequently successful, the odds of success may be somewhat greater when other similarly situated private investors have been found liable for the contribution, and the state entity lacks grounds for opposition aside from its sovereign status.

85. *See British Int'l Ins. Co. Ltd. v. Seguros La Republica, S.A.*, No. 90 Civ. 2370 (JFK) (FM), 2000 WL 713057, at *5 (S.D.N.Y. June 2, 2000).
86. *See Greyhound Exhibit Group, Inc. v. E.L.U.L. Realty Corp.*, No. 88 CV 3039 (ILG), 1993 WL 50528, at *1 (E.D.N.Y. Feb. 23, 1993).
87. *See Banco Central de Paraguay v. Paraguay Humanitarian Found.*, No. 01 Civ. 9649 (JFK), 2006 WL 3456521, at *11 (S.D.N.Y. Nov. 30, 2006).
88. *See, e.g.*, N.Y. C.P.L.R. § 5201 (2017).
89. *See, e.g.*, N.Y. C.P.L.R. § 5230 (2017).
90. 28 U.S.C. § 1963 (2017).
91. Uniform Law Commission, Enforcement of Foreign Judgments Act Legislative Fact Sheet, available at https://www.uniformlaws.org/committees/community-home?CommunityKey=e70884d0-db03-414d-b19a-f617bf3e25a3 (last visited Nov. 3, 2022). California has a similar statute in place that accomplishes the same basic objective. Cal. Civ. Proc. Code §§ 1710.10–1710.65 (1974, 1977, 1982, 1983, 1984, 1985, 2003).
92. UEFJA § 2 (UNIF. LAW COMM'N 1964). Recall that domestic state pension plans with Eleventh Amendment immunity must be sued in the courts of their own state, and that there will be statutory requirements particular to each state that must be followed. *See supra* notes 23–24 and 26 and accompanying discussion.
93. *Enforcement of Judgments*, U.S. Dep't of State, https://travel.state.gov/content/travel/en/legal/travel-legal-considerations/internl-judicial-asst/Enforcement-of-Judges.html (last visited Nov. 3, 2022).
94. Philip R. Weems, *Guidelines for Enforcing Money Judgments Abroad*, 21 Int'l Bus. Law. 509 (1993).
95. 307 F. Supp. 2d 608 (D. Del. 2004).

* * *

Acknowledgment

The authors would like to thank Wilson Miller, an associate in Haynes and Boone's Business Litigation Group, for his invaluable assistance with this chapter.

Ellen G. McGinnis
Tel: +1 202 654 4512 / Email: ellen.mcginnis@haynesboone.com
Ellen McGinnis co-leads Haynes and Boone's Fund Finance Practice Group, advising clients on subscription-secured credit facilities, a product she has worked on since its initial development in the late 1980s. Clients value Ellen's critical thinking and the innovative approach she takes to structuring and executing their financing transactions. Offering thoughtful, practical advice, Ellen serves as trusted counsel for U.S. and foreign commercial and investment banks as lenders to private equity funds. She works on many of the practice's hybrid collateral facilities and international and multi-currency transactions. Ellen serves on the firm's Executive Committee, Board of Directors and the HB REAL Diversity Oversight Committee, which serves as an advisory committee on diversity, equity, and inclusion and oversees the implementation of improvements to recruitment, retention, and promotion of diverse talent at the firm. Her current external focus is as a Council member of Women's Health Research at Yale, which advances health research for women across medical and psychosocial disciplines.

Richard D. Anigian
Tel: +1 214 651 5633 / Email: rick.anigian@haynesboone.com
Rick Anigian is a trial lawyer and former department chair of the firm's Litigation Practice Group. Rick has become a trusted business advisor by providing practical and efficient counseling and advice to implement clients' business strategies while solving their complex business disputes. Rick concentrates his practice on a wide variety of complex commercial disputes in federal and state courts, as well as arbitral proceedings. Rick has extensive experience in commercial and financial transactions litigation and real estate and oil and gas disputes, and has handled complex disputes among partners and business owners, as well as a wide range of business torts litigation. Rick has passed all sections of the examination to become a Certified Public Accountant. Rick is very active in the community in a wide range of activities including public education, the assistance of at-risk children and their families, and youth sports.

Haynes and Boone, LLP

800 17th Street, NW, Suite 500, Washington, D.C. 20006, USA
Tel: +1 202 654 4500 / Fax: +1 202 654 4501 / URL: www.haynesboone.com

The rise of Hybrid Facilities and increasing use of capital commitments in NAV Facilities

Meyer C. Dworkin & Kwesi Larbi-Siaw
Davis Polk & Wardwell LLP

Background

Credit facilities provided to private equity funds generally follow one of two primary forms: Subscription Facilities and NAV Facilities. Subscription Facilities – often referred to as "capital call" facilities – have become fundamental features of newly formed funds with dedicated investor capital commitments, in which the loans are secured by the fund's (and its general partner's) rights to call the capital commitments. Availability under a Subscription Facility is subject to a "borrowing base" determined as a percentage of the unfunded commitments of investors in the fund. Subscription Facilities were traditionally utilised to finance the fund's short-term working capital needs, primarily bridging the 10–15 business-day period between the issuance of capital calls by the general partner and the required timing for the investors to make the related capital contributions to the fund. Increasingly, private equity funds use Subscription Facilities for their medium- and longer-term financing needs, including financing multiple investments and providing letters of credit and alternative currency loans to portfolio companies, with the result that related capital calls are less frequent but larger.

Many private equity funds are unable or find it impractical to use a Subscription Facility as a source of long-term financing, either because the fund's organisational documents do not permit or materially limit such facilities or, in the case of a mature fund, the fund has already called a significant portion of its investor commitments. These private equity funds often seek to raise capital through an "asset-backed" or "net asset value" facility: a "NAV Facility". NAV Facilities are financings backed by the fund's investment portfolio. Unlike Subscription Facilities, which look "up" to the capital commitments of investors in the fund for the borrowing base and collateral, NAV Facilities look "down" to the underlying portfolio investments for credit support. For a traditional private equity buy-out fund, these investments will be the direct portfolio company interests purchased by the fund, and for a "fund of funds", the NAV Facility credit support will consist of equity interests in hedge funds and private equity funds purchased by the fund of funds borrower in the secondary market.

While lenders have historically offered Subscription Facilities and NAV Facilities as separate solutions to the particular financing needs of private equity funds, more recently, funds have sought, and lenders have increasingly been willing to provide, "hybrid" facilities that combine important structural features of both Subscription Facilities and NAV Facilities ("Hybrid Facilities"). In this chapter, we discuss the rise of Hybrid Facilities and increasing inclusion of capital commitments as support in otherwise traditional NAV Facilities.

What is a Hybrid Facility?

At its core, a Hybrid Facility is a hybrid – and contains certain of the defining features – of a Subscription Facility and a NAV Facility. In particular, these facilities both look "up" to the unfunded capital commitments of investors (the defining feature of a Subscription Facility) as well as look "down" to the fund's investment portfolio (the defining feature of a NAV Facility) for collateral and credit support. There are different forms of Hybrid Facilities, especially with respect to the formulation and types of credit support included in the borrowing base.[1] References to Hybrid Facilities in this chapter, however, will focus on financings that include both uncalled capital and underlying portfolio investments in a combined or blended borrowing base.

Hybrid Facilities are most useful to private equity funds looking for a single, permanent financing available throughout the fund's life cycle, from the fund's inception – when it has significant uncalled capital commitments, but few (if any) investments – through maturity – when capital commitments have been (nearly) fully utilised to acquire underlying portfolio investments. They may also appeal to more mature, later-stage private equity funds that lack sufficient available capital commitments – due to, e.g., concentration limitations or remaining investor mix – to support a traditional Subscription Facility.

Borrowing base

Borrowing capacity under a Hybrid Facility is typically subject to a combined borrowing base calculated by reference to both an "asset borrowing base" and a "UCC borrowing base". The asset borrowing base is equal to an agreed advance rate against the fair market value or "net asset value" of eligible portfolio investments satisfying specific investment criteria (e.g., the absence of certain material adverse investment events) and adjusted for single position, sponsor, industry and other concentration limits. The UCC borrowing base, in contrast, is equal to an agreed advance rate against the uncalled capital commitments of specified "included" (or, in certain cases, all) investors, with advance rates and inclusionary criteria typically dependent on the creditworthiness of each applicable investor. Once separately calculated, the asset borrowing base and UCC borrowing base are aggregated to determine a combined borrowing base upon which the lenders will advance loans. Lenders sometimes may also include a single advance rate measured against the sum of the net asset value of the eligible portfolio investments and the uncalled capital commitments, which functions as an override or cap on the borrowing base that is calculated using the separate advance rates. Where the inclusion of uncalled capital commitments in a Hybrid Facility is intended solely to bridge the natural investment "ramp up" of a fund, the borrowing base may be structured such that, following a pre-determined date or specified condition (e.g., more than 25% of capital commitments has been called from investors), the maximum advance rate is measured solely by reference to the asset borrowing base. Put differently, once the level of available uncalled capital commitments decreases below a specified threshold, the hybrid nature of the facility falls away and effectively converts to a traditional NAV Facility.

Structure of Hybrid Facilities

Hybrid Facilities may take the form of a revolving loan facility or may be structured as separate revolving loan and term loan facilities. A revolving loan generally provides the private equity fund with the most flexible and cost-effective solution to meet its financing needs, as the revolver may be drawn to meet both short-term liquidity needs, which provides a key benefit of a Subscription Facility, as well as to fund portfolio investments, thereby achieving a key feature of a NAV Facility. Revolving facilities may be less cost efficient, however, for funds with shorter investment cycles, as such funds will be required to continue to pay a commitment fee on the unused portion of the facility even after the fund no longer has a need for a revolving line of credit.[2] As an alternative, lenders may agree to structure the Hybrid Facility as two separate facilities, consisting of a revolving facility, based on the UCC borrowing base, with a shorter maturity date for working capital purposes, and a term facility utilising the asset borrowing base, with a longer maturity to be used to finance a pool of investments (often at or soon after closing). The facilities may or may not be cross-collateralised. As the fund matures and no longer has a need for the revolving component, the fund may seek to refinance the facilities to terminate the revolving component, resulting in a NAV Facility with an expanded collateral pool of portfolio investments and remaining uncalled capital commitments.

Collateral

The collateral package for Hybrid Facilities includes support that is typically included in both Subscription Facilities and NAV Facilities. The fund, as borrower, and the general partner of the fund grant, as applicable, have a security interest in favour of the lender in: (a) the unfunded capital commitments of the investors in the fund; (b) the right to make capital calls on such investors; (c) the deposit accounts into which the resulting capital contributions are funded; (d) the equity interests in the holding vehicle that holds the underlying portfolio investments (or, in situations where the borrower directly holds the underlying portfolio investments, a pledge of the equity interest in the borrower by its direct parent entity) (the "Equity Interest Collateral");[3] and (e) a pledge of the deposit and securities accounts into which distributions on and proceeds of underlying portfolio investments are paid. To perfect the lenders' security interest in such collateral, UCC financing statements are filed against the fund and general partner and the deposit and securities accounts of the fund are subject to control agreements, with the lenders' right to block such accounts most often springing upon an event of default or borrowing base deficiency.

Considerations for lenders

As lenders become increasingly accustomed to providing Hybrid Facilities, they face a number of challenges. First, lenders will need to perform more diligence than would typically be performed for traditional, standalone Subscription Facilities or NAV Facilities, which, depending on the structure of the lending institution, may involve different internal legal and commercial teams. Second, because Hybrid Facilities are intended to span the entire life cycle of the fund borrower, lenders need to contemplate and address potential issues, however remote, applicable to both early- and late-stage funds. A primary example is a rapid decline in the net asset value of portfolio investments during a period in which the Hybrid Facility is primarily functioning as a Subscription Facility, which may result in investors questioning whether to honour their remaining capital commitments. To address and seek to mitigate such concerns, lenders may (a) provide that the UCC borrowing base falls away at a certain minimum NAV threshold, or (b) include a maximum or overriding single advance rate.

Use of capital commitments in NAV Facilities

In order to incentivise lenders to provide NAV Facilities at lower interest rates or supported by more concentrated or otherwise illiquid portfolios of investments (or to address other challenging credit or structural concerns the lenders identify), funds may agree to include elements of Subscription Facilities (other than the UCC borrowing base) in NAV Facilities.

Enhanced credit support

As noted, NAV Facilities have historically been used by funds of funds to borrow against the value of limited partnership and other equity interests in private equity and hedge funds. Recently, however, a number of private equity funds have applied NAV Facility technology to borrow against the equity value of their investments in operating portfolio companies.[4] Given the illiquidity of these assets – even as compared to secondary fund interests – lenders may insist that these facilities be secured by a pledge of investors' capital commitments to the fund in addition to the underlying portfolio investment interests.

In another application of this concept, private equity sponsors are increasingly creating and utilising pooled investment vehicles ("Aggregator Vehicles") for the purpose of aggregating the investments of a number of their managed funds in a single pool of underlying portfolio investments. As in a traditional NAV Facility, the funds investing in an Aggregator Vehicle may seek to obtain financing based on their ownership interests in the Aggregator Vehicle (and, indirectly, their proportionate share of the underlying portfolio investments held by the Aggregator Vehicle). Where portfolio investments are owned by Aggregator Vehicles, the Equity Interest Collateral is limited to the borrower's equity interest in the Aggregator Vehicle. As these non-controlling interests provide lenders with less flexibility and optionality in a post-event of default enforcement scenario, lenders may, in such circumstances, seek to enhance the credit support of the loan by requiring the borrower (and its general partner, if applicable) to also pledge uncalled capital commitments from its direct investors.

The pledged capital commitments may come from true third parties (where the borrower or its direct parent are an "external-facing" fund) or internal feeder funds. Where the pledge is of commitments of an affiliated entity (especially where such entity is a pass-through vehicle that is not separately creditworthy), the affiliate's capital contribution obligations may be supported by a "bad boy" guaranty from the sponsor (or other creditworthy affiliate) of the borrower triggered upon a failure of the pledgor fund to satisfy required capital calls to the borrower.

The enhanced credit support provides NAV Facility lenders with the comfort that, following an event of default, they will have the right to not only exercise remedies with respect to the Equity Interest Collateral pursuant to a customary UCC public or private sale process, but also rely on the pledged capital commitments to satisfy any shortfall in the liquidation value of the portfolio assets.

<u>Liquidity covenants</u>

In NAV Facilities, lenders increasingly include covenants to address liquidity concerns that may impact a borrower's ability to repay its obligations. These covenants may include (a) a requirement that the borrower maintain a specified level of unfunded capital commitments to the extent the "loan-to-value ratio" of the NAV Facility exceeds a specified threshold, (b) a mandatory prepayment event upon the NAV Facility loans exceeding an agreed percentage of unfunded capital commitments, or (c) a requirement that the borrower maintain sufficient unfunded capital commitments to satisfy the sum of the NAV Facility loan amount and the capital commitment requirements of the portfolio investments.

Conclusion

As private equity funds continue to realise the benefits of using Hybrid Facilities, and lenders become more accustomed to providing such financings, we expect to see the types of funds using such facilities, as well as the purposes for which such facilities are used, continue to broaden. We further expect to see an expansion in the use of capital commitments in NAV Facilities as funds continue to expand the scope of portfolio investments for which they employ the use of NAV Facility technology.

Endnotes

1. In certain NAV Facilities, uncalled capital of intermediate fund entities is pledged to the lenders, but does not provide lenders with claims against the ultimate third-party investors in the fund.
2. Such facilities also typically include a commitment termination premium, such that the borrower will incur a material cost (often equal to the remaining commitment fee through maturity) upon early termination of the facility commitments.
3. A fund typically establishes two special purpose vehicles ("SPVs") under a NAV Facility. The first SPV, the borrower, is created for the sole purpose of obtaining the financing under the NAV Facility and holding the equity interests of the second SPV ("Holdco"), which directly (or, less frequently, indirectly) owns the portfolio investments included in the borrowing base. The borrower generally provides a pledge of 100% of the equity interests of Holdco.
4. Lenders providing these facilities to private equity funds are almost always structurally subordinated to lenders providing financing secured directly by the assets of the underlying portfolio companies.

Meyer C. Dworkin
Tel: +1 212 450 4382 / Email: meyer.dworkin@davispolk.com
Mr. Dworkin is a partner in Davis Polk's Corporate Department, practising in the Finance Group. He advises lenders and borrowers on a variety of finance transactions, including acquisition financings, asset-based financings, debtor-in-possession financings, bankruptcy exit financings and structured financings. In addition, Mr. Dworkin regularly represents hedge funds and corporations in negotiating prime brokerage agreements, ISDA and BMA-standard agreements and other trading and financing documentation and other complex structured financial products.

Kwesi Larbi-Siaw
Tel: +1 212 450 3803 / Email: kwesi.larbi-siaw@davispolk.com
Mr. Larbi-Siaw is counsel in Davis Polk's Corporate Department, practising in the Finance Group. He advises financial institutions and borrowers on a variety of fund financing transactions and structured financings, including NAV facilities, capital call facilities and back-leverage transactions.

Davis Polk & Wardwell LLP

450 Lexington Avenue, New York, NY 10017, USA
Tel: +1 212 450 4000 / Fax: +1 212 701 5800 / URL: www.davispolk.com

Assessing and mitigating "bad acts" risk in NAV loans

Angie Batterson, Brian Foster & Patrick Calves
Cadwalader, Wickersham & Taft LLP

Overview

One aspect of NAV loans that lenders often focus on is the risk of "bad acts" by a borrower. For our purposes, NAV loans are loans to alternative investment entities (e.g., private equity funds, secondaries funds, hedge funds, funds of hedge funds, pension funds and family office vehicles) that are underwritten, either on a secured or unsecured basis, by the value of the borrower's investments. By "bad acts" we mean the risk that a borrower takes actions that cause or result in the underwritten investments and other assets ceasing to be owned by the borrower, or becoming subject to the claims of other creditors, in each case in contravention of the terms of the NAV loan terms.

When entering into NAV loans, lenders assess the investments and other assets owned by a borrower at closing that are to be included in the collateral pool and then continue to monitor those investments and assets after closing for compliance with various financial covenants, NAV covenants, cash sweep tests and other requirements that have been negotiated and memorialised in the loan documents. For most NAV loans, the underwritten investments and assets are typically owned and controlled by the borrower, either directly or indirectly through one or more special purpose subsidiary holding vehicles. This is different from various, more common securities financing products (think prime brokerage, securities lending, repo, or typical bank margin loans), where a lender or a third-party custodian on behalf of the lender holds or controls the securities against which credit is being extended. In certain secured NAV loan facilities, the investments and assets themselves often are not directly pledged to the lenders by the borrower but are instead owned by special purpose subsidiary holding vehicles, the equity interests of which are pledged to the lenders as collateral for the loan (i.e., an "indirect pledge" of the underwritten investment and assets themselves). In these structures, the underlying investments and assets are not subject to the lenders' liens but instead are typically subject to a negative pledge and are therefore unencumbered.

Because borrowers in NAV facilities (directly or indirectly) typically maintain complete control over the investments and assets that the lenders are underwriting throughout the term of the facility, these structures involve a degree of "bad acts" risk. This is in addition to the "market risk" of the facility (i.e., the risk that the value of the borrower's investments and assets will decline). More specific examples of bad acts might include a borrower (i) transferring an investment or asset to an affiliate, (ii) selling an investment or asset at less than full value or for illiquid consideration, (iii) pledging an investment or asset to another creditor, (iv) directing proceeds of an investment or asset to an account other than the pledged account, or (v) commencing an insolvency proceeding as a means of obstructing or delaying creditors' exercise of remedies. Lenders will negotiate detailed covenants limiting such actions, but since the lenders do not control these assets, they are heavily reliant on the borrower to comply with such negotiated limits. While breach of the covenants may give rise to an event of default, such breach already may have impaired the value of the collateral pool (and the creditworthiness of the borrower) in a way that makes it less likely that the NAV loan will be repaid in full. In this chapter, we will first discuss factors that lenders analyse in evaluating the potential for these bad acts before turning to various tools that we see lenders employ to mitigate these risks.

Lenders analyse several factors in assessing the degree of "bad acts" risk of any potential NAV facility, which broadly include: (i) the profile of the borrower; (ii) the scope of the lenders' relationships with the borrower; and (iii) the nature of the investment portfolio on which the loan is underwritten.

Profile of the borrower

One of the key risk factors that lenders consider in evaluating bad act risks with respect to NAV loans is the market profile of the borrower, or more specifically, the borrower's sponsor. Lenders may evaluate factors such as:

- *Frequency of NAV financing*: Certain sponsors are serial users of NAV financing such that the use of these types of loans is an integral part of the sponsor's business model. An example would be a secondaries sponsor that consistently employs financing to acquire portfolios of private equity interests in the secondaries market. Lenders may take comfort from the fact that such a sponsor has a verifiable track record of responsible use of NAV loan financing. Further, lenders may view the sponsor's continued need for financing to operate its business as an effective incentive to avoid defaults under the sponsor's existing financings, particularly as a result of bad acts.
- *Breadth of the sponsor's "brand"*: Certain sponsors have brands that expand well beyond the fund involved in the particular financing. Such sponsors may be affiliated with larger financial institutions or may have extensive asset management platforms encompassing a broad range of investment strategies, products, and asset classes. Lenders may take comfort in the resources such platforms have dedicated to operational integrity and compliance. Sponsors with "brands" and business activity of this scope may be perceived by lenders to be more averse to the type of negative publicity and reputational harm to the sponsor's overall brand that would be associated with any intentional bad acts, while also having the wherewithal to put in place controls to ensure that unintentional bad acts are unlikely.
- *Sources of equity capital*: Lenders often take comfort from a sponsor's management of a significant amount of external money. External capital (and particularly institutional capital) can act as a check on certain types of opportunistic behaviour. Lenders may be concerned that investment entities with internal or proprietary sources of capital may evaluate potential consequences of a financing default solely in the context of a specific transaction and lender relationship, whereas sponsors beholden to large and sophisticated external investors may be forced to account for broader consequences of a financing default (e.g., the need to raise additional debt or equity capital for future fund launches).

Relationship between the lenders and the borrower

Another key factor that lenders consider in evaluating bad act risks with respect to NAV loans is the lender's overall relationship with any given borrower or sponsor. Financings are often entered into with alternative investment entities in the context of a much broader relationship between the lenders and the sponsors of such entities. NAV loans are not always viewed as profitable on a standalone basis. Instead, they are often part of a package of services offered by a financial institution to broaden or deepen engagement with a sponsor and their respective affiliates. Where a sponsor has extensive touch points with a lender and its affiliates, comfort may be taken that a financing transaction with such sponsor is less prone to bad acts given the extent of a lender's familiarity with a sponsor and its principals and the sponsor's reliance on the other services provided by the lender.

Characteristics of the investment portfolio

Finally, lenders may also consider the impact of the characteristics of a borrower's investment portfolio on the risk of any bad acts. While the characteristics of a borrower's investment portfolio might not make the likelihood of bad acts more or less likely, as with market risk, a concentrated portfolio raises the stakes to lenders in the event of any impairment of the portfolio, including any bad acts. As a result, the consequence of a bad act with respect to a single investment in a well-diversified portfolio is likely to have less dire consequences for a lender than a bad act relating to one crown jewel in the portfolio or the sole asset, as the case may be.

Notwithstanding the inherent risk of "bad acts" in certain NAV loan structures, there are still various tools that lenders can employ to mitigate these risks (some more onerous for borrowers than others). Unfortunately, there is no one-size-fits-all solution. Whether one or more of these approaches is appropriate for a given transaction will depend heavily on the facts and circumstances of the parties, the borrower's investment structure and the collateral. While market participants continue to innovate new approaches to address these issues, we have summarised below a number of the most common tools that we see employed to address the risk of bad acts.

Structural mitigants

There are several different ways that lenders can structure NAV facilities to mitigate and deter bad acts risk, including the following:

- *Custody arrangements.* Lenders can require that investments be transferred to a custodian and held in a custody account. Under this approach, the custodian becomes the registered owner of the investment and has the sole right to give instructions to the issuer of the investment. The custodian will be party to an account control agreement detailing the circumstances under which the custodian will take instructions from the borrower and the lenders in respect of the investments. Given that there is an independent third party in control of the investments, custody arrangements are the most effective approach to ensuring that bad acts do not occur; however, they are not a practical solution for some transactions. They impose additional costs on the borrower, and they require the borrower to interact with its underlying investments through the custodian. And not all investments can be held with a custodian. (For example, most custodians will not custody interests in private equity funds due to concerns around liability for unfunded capital commitments.) Further, custody arrangements may also have drawbacks from a lender perspective. Where an investment portfolio is held by a holding vehicle, the entire portfolio typically can be sold in foreclosure via a sale of the interests in such holding vehicle to the extent pledged as collateral for the NAV loan. However, a custody account cannot simply be transferred to a third party. Instead, a transfer of the custodied investments will often require the custodian to approach the issuer of each investment for consent to a transfer or to process a redemption (where applicable).
- *Direct pledge.* While secured NAV loans most commonly use indirect pledge structures, in certain instances lenders may insist on direct pledges of the underwritten

investments and assets. A direct pledge ensures that the lender can exercise rights in respect of each investment upon an event of default without pursuing legal remedies against or through other entities, which can be time-consuming and very expensive. Pledge consents from the issuers of the underlying investments may limit transfers of the investments without lender consent and as described more fully below, may provide for proceeds of the investments to be paid to a pledged collateral account controlled by the lender. Negotiating individual consents with the issuer of each investment can be time-consuming and difficult, so this approach is often limited to either: (i) financings of investment portfolios with a limited number of positions; or (ii) the most concentrated positions in larger, more diversified portfolios.

- *Payment direction.* It is common for NAV facilities to require the proceeds of the underwritten investments and assets to be paid into an account that is subject to the lenders' security interest and control. To ensure compliance with this requirement, where there is a direct pledge of the underwritten investments and assets, lenders may look to include a provision in the pledge consent from the issuer of the investment whereby the issuer agrees that it will only pay distributions to the specified collateral account. Additionally, if the investments are held indirectly by a special purpose subsidiary holding vehicle, the lender may require the subsidiary to send notifications and payment direction letters to the issuers of its underlying investments to make payments directly to a pledged collateral account of the borrower, thereby avoiding deposit of any monies into an account of the subsidiary and eliminating the chances of the borrower siphoning off the money before it can be used for repayment of the NAV loan. Alternatively, the lender may require that any monies deposited directly into the special purpose subsidiary holding vehicle's account be subject to a standing sweep order, so that any monies in those accounts that may be outside of the lender's control will be swept to a controlled account on a weekly or even daily basis.
- *Modification of constituent documents.* Protections against bad acts can be addressed in the constituent documents of the entity holding the underwritten investments (i.e., either the borrower or subsidiary holding vehicle, as applicable). One approach is to disclose the existence of the financing in the constituent documents of the relevant entity and to disclose that certain actions (such as a sale of an investment, incurrence of debt or a distribution of assets to equity holders) may only be taken with the consent of the lenders, or in accordance with other conditions specified in the loan documents. The goal of including such provisions is to condition the authority of the entity holding the investments to engage in certain transactions and activities that could be averse to the interests of the lenders, and to put potential creditors or counterparties on notice as to negotiated limitations in the loan documents. Going a step further, the constituent documents of the relevant entity may be revised to require an independent manager or director that will be responsible for protecting the interests of the lenders in certain instances, such as filing for bankruptcy. In these structures, the independent manager's or director's consent would be required for certain transactions or activities consistent with the terms of the NAV loan documents, giving the lenders some comfort that a non-affiliated third party is opining on major decisions that may impact the ability of the lenders to be repaid. Additionally, the lenders may require that the constituent documents contain special purpose language that requires the entity to remain "bankruptcy remote" and lessen the chances that the entity will be entangled in an affiliate's insolvency proceedings.

Additional credit support

Often, the borrower in a NAV loan is owned by a more creditworthy parent fund. The risk of a loss resulting from bad acts in respect of the underwritten investments can be mitigated where the lenders have recourse to the parent fund. This recourse typically comes in one of the following forms:

- *Formal credit support.* A parent fund may guarantee the obligations of the borrower under the facility or commit to fund capital to the borrower to enable it to pay its debts. Such capital commitments often arise under the constituent documents of the borrower (and the borrower may pledge those capital commitments or may merely covenant to maintain a minimum level of uncalled capital from its parent relevant to the amount of the loan). *In lieu* of a pledge of capital commitments, this additional credit support may arise in the context of an equity commitment letter, in which the parent fund provides a contractual commitment to the borrower or the lenders that it will contribute capital to the borrower to enable the borrower to repay its obligations pursuant to the NAV loan. In each case, the recourse to the parent fund mitigates the lenders' complete reliance on the underlying investment assets as the sole source of repayment. Such recourse also may incentivise the parent fund to ensure that the borrower does not engage in bad acts in respect of the underlying investments, since it will be on the hook for any deficiency that results in repayment of the loan.
- *Conditional/bad boy guaranty.* Where a parent fund is unwilling or unable to fully guarantee repayment of the loan, a contingent or "bad boy" guaranty may be appropriate. Under a contingent or "bad boy" guaranty, the obligation of the parent fund to repay the loan only arises upon the occurrence of specified bad acts. The specified acts may relate to a breach of negotiated representations or covenants (such as limitations on incurring indebtedness, granting liens, making distributions to investors, transferring assets, entering into affiliate transactions, or commencing insolvency or dissolution proceedings) or may relate to conceptual acts (such as actions that constitute bad faith, fraud, or wilful misconduct). These bad acts generally are within the control of the parent fund to prevent, and a contingent or "bad boy" guaranty is typically designed to protect the lender in instances where the fund intentionally acts to harm the lender. Given the contingent nature of the payment obligation, the parent fund may not have to record a debt liability as a result of providing such a guaranty.
- *Other assets held with the lender.* Where a lender provides credit products beyond NAV financing to a borrower such as FX or rate hedging, prime brokerage, custody, etc., lenders may take comfort that their recourse to additional assets of the borrower through these services provides a disincentive for borrowers to engage in bad acts under a NAV loan. However, lenders must be careful that the documentation under either the NAV facility or the other credit products is sufficiently broad to either permit the lender to set off obligations across the various products or use collateral securing one product to satisfy obligations under the other. Lenders should also be particularly careful when relying on these sorts of arrangements where the NAV financing and such other credit products are not being provided by the same entity, but rather affiliated institutions.

Due diligence and reporting

Lenders can also rely on various reporting and diligence measures to monitor for any potential bad acts. This has the benefit of both (i) deterring bad acts by ensuring that any such actions will ultimately be detected, and (ii) alerting lenders to any bad acts as soon as possible, so that appropriate remedies can be implemented. These measures can take on multiple forms, and below we discuss a few of these:

- *Audited financial statements.* Requiring borrowers to deliver audited financial statements on an annual and/or quarterly basis provides lenders with the comfort that an independent party has reviewed and confirmed the composition of the borrower's special purpose subsidiary holding vehicle's assets. Lenders can then use the audited financials to confirm a borrower's compliance/non-compliance with NAV loan covenants regarding dispositions of investments and the veracity of borrower-provided reporting regarding its investment portfolio. However, relying on audited financials as a third-party check on bad acts has one glaring shortcoming: timing. Audited financial statements take significant time and resources to prepare. As a result, they are often provided on a significant time lag for the period that they are covering (i.e., several months). Additionally, funds typically will only provide audited financial statements on an annual basis. So, while audited financial statements do provide an independently verified snapshot of a borrower's or special purpose subsidiary holding vehicle's assets, this comfort is typically only available on an annual basis and, even then, the information is typically stale by several months by the time of delivery.
- *Third-party valuations.* In certain NAV facilities, lenders retain the right to challenge a borrower's valuation of its underlying assets. If the lenders believe that the borrower is no longer adequately valuing or is artificially inflating the value of its underlying assets to maintain covenant compliance, the lenders can require that a separate valuation be provided, typically by an independent third-party appraiser. If there are discrepancies between the borrower's valuations and the third-party appraiser's valuation, the corresponding loan covenants will be tested based upon the third party's value. Such valuations can give the lenders an early insight into bad acts of the sponsor but are also expensive and time-consuming. As a result, many NAV loan facilities contain limitations on the number of times a lender may request a valuation and the number of times the borrower must be required to pay for such valuations.
- *NAV statements.* For NAV loans where the underwritten assets are third-party managed investments (e.g., secondaries funds, funds of hedge funds, REITS, third-party managed co-investments, etc.), lenders also may require NAV or capital account statements from the manager or issuer of the investments. As with audited financial statements, these third party-provided statements will similarly provide lenders with the comfort that an independent party is confirming the borrower's ownership of the relevant investment. While the independent party here will not be a regulated and reputable accounting firm (as with audited financial statements), NAV and capital account statements have the added benefit of typically being provided more frequently (e.g., on a quarterly basis) and with less of a time lag than audited financial statements.
- *Transfer agreements and law firm letters.* Another example of independent documentation that lenders can look to for verification of a borrower's ownership of its purported investments are copies of the transfer agreements or subscription documentation governing the relevant investment. These will typically be prepared or at least countersigned by the issuer, manager, general partner, etc. of the relevant investment. From time to time, we also see lenders require letters from law firms that worked on the borrower's acquisition of the relevant investments confirming that the relevant acquisition was successfully closed. In each of these cases, the lenders receive some form of independent comfort that the borrower did own the relevant investments at some point; however, the obvious limitation here is that these are not forms of ongoing/ periodic verification of the borrower's continued ownership of the relevant investments.

- *Bank account audits and access.* Certain NAV facilities may require that the borrower certify on an annual or quarterly basis that the borrower has not opened any new bank accounts that are not subject to control arrangements with the lender. Additionally, lenders can request that the borrower's account bank grant the lenders with online view only access to borrower's accounts so that the lender can monitor cash flows in and out of the accounts daily. In the event that the borrower begins to divert funds and deposit monies into accounts not subject to the lender's lien and/or control in contravention of the loan terms, the lender will be able to spot the bad act sooner rather than later and take appropriate remedial action.

Periodic portfolio audits/inspection

Lenders sometimes will also require borrowers to agree to periodic audits/inspections of a borrower's portfolio (whether in whole or in part) to verify ownership. This can either be structured as a right for the lenders or their agents to audit the borrower's portfolio or for a reputable independent firm to perform the audit. We most commonly see this agreed to by borrowers that may not otherwise prepare audited financial statements.

Conclusion

NAV financing and its myriad of different uses, types of borrowers, lenders and structures require market participants and their counsels to be nimble and understanding of the different incentives, concerns, and goals that they and their counterparts are facing on any given transaction and how they may employ one or more of the various tools in their proverbial toolbox to achieve a satisfying outcome for all involved. While the possibility of "bad acts" inherent in the most common NAV loan structures is something that lenders and borrowers alike must be mindful of when structuring and negotiating the terms for a transaction, as discussed, there are a multitude of different mechanisms that lenders and borrowers can employ to mitigate these risks. While this chapter seeks to summarise these tools, we continue to see market participants come up with novel approaches to address these concerns and ensure that lender and borrower interests are aligned.

Angie Batterson
Tel: +1 212 504 6539 / Email: angela.batterson@cwt.com

Angie Batterson has advised clients in complex leveraged financing transactions across a broad array of industries, including healthcare, telecommunications, media, manufacturing, and energy, for 20 years. She represents financial institutions, sponsors, issuers, and mezzanine providers in private debt financings, including in connection with secured and unsecured senior credit facilities, first lien/second lien credit facilities, unitranche facilities, and mezzanine financings. Angie also advises on intercreditor agreements and distressed debt financings, including debtor-in-possession (DIP) financings, fund to fund loans, and senior housing loans.

She is a frequent speaker and has recently covered topics such as unitranche, agreements among lenders in workouts, and the practical impact on recent revisions to Section 956 of the Internal Revenue Code.

Brian Foster
Tel: +1 212 504 6736 / Email: brian.foster@cwt.com

Brian Foster is a partner in Cadwalader's Finance Practice and a member of Cadwalader's market-leading fund finance team. Brian focuses on financing, derivatives and structured products transactions involving financial institutions and investment funds. His experience covers a broad range of derivatives (including OTC trades, structured notes, options, forwards and swaps, with particular focus on equity- and fund-linked derivatives) and financing arrangements (including secondaries financing, fund of hedge fund and single manager hedge fund leverage, management company loans, dividend recapitalisations, NAV facilities, subscription lines, hybrid transactions, preferred share issuances, collateralised fund obligations, margin loans, securities lending and repo facilities and prime brokerage arrangements).

Prior to joining Cadwalader, Brian worked at Lehman Brothers Holdings Inc. in connection with the unwinding of its derivatives book in bankruptcy.

Patrick Calves
Tel: +1 212 504 5557 / Email: patrick.calves@cwt.com

Patrick Calves is a special counsel in the firm's Finance Group. He counsels clients on a variety of bilateral and syndicated financing structures, including term loans, liquidity lines, NAV facilities, subscription facilities, hybrid facilities, margin loans and repurchase, securities lending and prime brokerage facilities. Patrick's practice includes work on structures involving a variety of non-standard collateral, such as hedge fund interests, private equity fund interests, capital contribution obligations and restricted stock positions.

Patrick also counsels both financial institutions and "buy-side" market participants on a variety of regulatory and compliance issues relating to securities and derivatives trading. This includes, *inter alia*, advice as to numerous aspects of swap regulatory issues arising under Title VII of the Dodd-Frank Act.

Cadwalader, Wickersham & Taft LLP

200 Liberty Street, New York, NY 10281, USA
Tel: +1 212 504 6000 / URL: www.cadwalader.com

Comparing the European, U.S. and Asian fund finance markets

Emma Russell & Emily Fuller
Haynes and Boone, LLP

Introduction

This chapter considers the differences between the European, U.S. and Asian approach to fund finance, both from a high-level market perspective and the contrasting nuances of transactions.

Market differences

Historically in Europe, the fund finance market originated with a few banks offering products on a bilateral basis to existing customers who required more liquidity, and the market was very much relationship-driven. Because of the existing relationship between bank and borrower, the banks would make an effort to structure the deals without the need for investor consents or amendments to the limited partnership agreements ("**LPAs**"), and often offered these facilities on an unsecured and/or uncommitted basis. The European banks carried out limited due diligence on the creditworthiness of, and potential enforceability against, investors.

However, over the last 10 years, the European lender landscape has become saturated by the emergence of U.S., Australian, Asian and new fund finance market entrant European banks competing with the long-standing European bank players already in this space, and it is estimated that there are now more than 40 lenders offering this product in the European market. This competition had led to pricing pressure for banks operating in the European market and familiarity with fund finance products, as well as cheaper financing. Recently there has also been an uptick in alternative non-bank lenders entering this space, and we will discuss this further later on in this chapter. This has resulted in larger facility sizes, necessitating more club deals and syndicated financings, given bank balance sheet restrictions and borrower appetite for a diverse lender base.

Although more recent, the Asian markets have also now begun to see increased competition resulting in similar effects. A similar trend of growth in the market and corresponding pressure to push down pricing were seen in the U.S. over a decade ago. In the U.S., the current market is more lender-friendly (as further explained in this chapter) and is mainly dominated by a few U.S. banks, although recently a number of European and Asian banks have started to build up their presence in the U.S. The majority of deals in the U.S. tend to be syndicated, as opposed to bilateral. For this reason, U.S. deals tend to be structured in a way that makes them easier to be rated by agencies.

Over the last few years, there has been a shift by certain banks in Europe to an approach more akin to that taken in the U.S. By comparison, the Asian market is still primarily relationship-driven, both by lender relationships with fund sponsors and, in many instances, with investors. This results in more bespoke covenant structures and deal terms. However, indicators such as increased Asian participation in the Fund Finance Association ("**FFA**"), and other cross-border contact between the markets, would suggest that the future of the Asian markets will be more heterogeneous. Furthermore, the component parts of the market are quite distinct: firstly, there are the large European and U.S. managers looking to raise funds in Asia; secondly, there are the Asian-based sponsors raising funds in Asia with Asian investors; and thirdly, there is what some would describe as the Australian sub-market.

Traditionally, fund sizes in Asia were smaller than some of the funds being raised in Europe and the U.S., and relationship facilities were provided by lenders on a bilateral basis. Like Europe, the Asian market is changing, in part in response to the increase in fund sizes and a corresponding increase in facility sizes, which pushes the need for these facilities to be syndicated. However, whilst fund closings have continued at a steady pace throughout 2022, fund closes have tended to be smaller than anticipated this year due to managers' eagerness to lock investors' commitments in during a time of uncertainty. Separately managed accounts ("**SMAs**") are also on the rise as large institutional investors seek to negotiate an investment structure designed specifically for them, and correspondingly more lenders are looking at how they can get comfortable with lending against such a concentrated pool. In general, the use of fund finance facilities, whilst not as prevalent as in the U.S. and Europe, is on the increase in Asia. The demand for NAV lines (facilities secured against the underlying assets of a fund) remains high as borrowers look to utilise any source of leverage available to them. The governing law for Asian deals varies in reflection of the market, often depending on the identity of lenders, funds and investors. In recent times, Asian facilities have been governed by U.S., English or Japanese law.

It is fair to say that the size of the fund finance market is largest in the U.S., followed by Europe and then Asia. The fund finance market has remained busy for the first three quarters of 2022, despite fundraising being down from 2021. According to Pitchbook's third quarter 2022 report on Global Private Market Fundraising, fundraising for private equity was down 26.2% from 2021, with private capital being down 31.6% and secondaries being down 40.2%. Although smaller in size, the European market remains more innovative with products such as NAV facilities, hybrids, general partner ("**GP**") lines, SMAs and secondary structures being more commonplace than in the U.S. 2020 and 2021 also saw a rise in non-bank lenders stepping into the shoes of traditional bank lenders as they offered an important source of funding during the COVID-19 pandemic whilst also offering stable returns for investors. Russia's invasion of Ukraine in early 2022 led to a global hike in energy prices, which in turn has seen inflation rise dramatically. In order to combat rising inflation, many central banks also raised interest rates as a response. This has inevitably led to higher costs of funding. As subscription line facilities are typically floating rate products, banks have needed to increase their pricing. The uncertainty caused by the global disruption earlier in the year caused many borrowers to maximise as many liquidity options as possible, causing a liquidity crunch. The rush for debt meant that many lenders had used up their balance sheet earlier in the year than they would have otherwise, leading to a quieter end of year than normal. This has also created an ideal space for non-bank lenders to operate in as they are not subject to the same capital adequacy regulations as bank lenders, and they do not face the same cost of funding issues. The landscape for 2023 looks similar to 2022 with fundraising remaining challenging across all of the U.S., EMEA and Asia and pockets of liquidity drying up. There is great opportunity for innovation and alternative markets to take a piece of this supply and demand imbalance.

Due diligence

As the U.S. and European markets have developed in different ways, the due diligence process similarly differs between U.S. and European lenders. In Asia, although deals are much more relationship-driven, influencing covenant structures and deal terms, the level of due diligence is mainly driven by the governing law. The choice of governing law not only affects the issues necessary to address in the due diligence phase, but also tends to dictate either a U.S. or European cultural approach.

Since the fund finance market emerged in Europe and Asia originally as a relationship-driven product, the level of due diligence conducted by European and Asian lenders has historically been less extensive than that required by U.S. lenders.

Traditionally, U.S. lenders will require significant diligence on all of a fund's constituent documents, including its LPA, subscription agreements and any side letters entered into between the fund or its GP and any investor. Additionally, U.S. lenders will closely analyse the creditworthiness of borrowing base-eligible investors, including by receiving financial information in respect of investors, as well as guarantees or other credit linkage documents demonstrating the connection between any special purpose vehicle ("**SPV**") investor and its credit provider.

In recent years, European and Asian lenders have likewise started to focus more energy on investor diligence; now, lenders in all three markets will review LPAs, side letters and subscription agreements, too (along with any other relevant fund documentation). In performing this diligence, lenders will look for comfort on a variety of issues. In addition to the obvious borrowing, guaranteeing and security checks, of particular concern to a lender will be any provisions that could potentially limit the amount that may be called from investors. In Asia, however, side letters containing sovereign immunity provisions are commonplace; this is due to the fact that cornerstone investors in Asian funds are often sovereign wealth funds. Some lenders in Asia are comfortable lending to such sovereign investors if they have a track record of advancing capital commitments, whilst other Asian lenders may require such investors to waive their immunity, as per the European and U.S. approach, if such investors are to be counted towards the borrowing base. This becomes even more important in an SMA deal where the sole investor is a sovereign wealth fund, and the majority of lenders will require these rights to be waived in an investor letter.

As investors increasingly look for geographic diversity and opportunity, lenders increasingly leverage internal institutional market intelligence from their branches around the globe in making credit decisions with respect to investors. Having a branch with useful credit information in a jurisdiction where a particular investor is located can provide a competitive edge in other jurisdictions where the lender is structuring a loan where the market is seeing the said investor for the first time.

In order to facilitate this due diligence review, U.S. lenders will often require completion of diligence checklists on all relevant fund documentation as part of their credit underwriting, which identifies the various issues of concern for the lender and addresses how such concerns are dealt with in the LPA and the credit facility documentation. In recent years, European and Asian lenders have also begun developing their own form of diligence checklists, though the level of granularity on issues that could affect enforcement and interpretation of the LPA and investor documentation differs between U.S., European and Asian jurisdictions.

Further to the foregoing, U.S. and European banks typically have different expectations as to what provisions are included in LPAs or other constituent documents. Customarily, U.S.

banks expect the borrower's LPA to include explicit language made for the benefit of the lender, including: (a) provisions authorising the credit facility and the pledge to the lender of the fund's and GP's rights to call for and receive capital contributions; and (b) language whereby the investors agree to fund capital calls made by the lender without defence, setoff or counterclaim.

To the extent that an LPA does not contain these lender-focused provisions, the lender will often require the investors to deliver investor letters including the desired language. Conversely, European lenders tend to get comfortable if the LPA permits security to be granted over the GP's/manager's right to issue call-down notices, without specific reference to the lender. A lender would then be able to rely on the contractual relationship created under any security document that, amongst other things, assigns the right to issue call-down notices to the lender (and the power of attorney included in the related security agreement to execute any notices on behalf of the GP/manager).

Often, English law-governed LPAs that relate to older vintages of fund do not include the "without defence, setoff or counterclaim" language, and typically they explicitly state that there is nothing in the LPA that confers any right on any person not a party to the LPA, and furthermore that any person not party has no right under the Contracts (Rights of Third Parties) Act 1999 to enforce any provision of the LPA. In contrast, many U.S. law-governed LPAs state that the lenders will be third-party beneficiaries under the LPA.

Anti-terrorism and sanctions due diligence is an ever-more prevalent part of all financial transactions, and the fund finance space is not immune. Asia, and Hong Kong in particular, has some of the most onerous regulatory requirements that can and do delay closings. The problem is more acute for U.S.-based funds that are not only unfamiliar with Asian procedures, but are often put in difficult positions by conflicting laws across jurisdictions. For instance, the Hong Kong requirement that copies of passports for responsible officers be certified as true and correct by a certified public accountant or lawyer is at odds with liability-mitigating rules applicable to U.S.-based certified public accountants or lawyers. Reconciling these, and many other similar issues, can be time-consuming and costly. The relatively small nature of the Asian markets, coupled with the more recent emergence of both the Asian markets and Asian anti-terrorism and sanctions regulations, means that mechanisms for addressing these issues are just now evolving; however, lenders and lawyers alike are diligently working to develop cost-effective and efficient solutions.

Security

As the European fund finance market developed out of existing relationships between banks and customers, European banks have previously been willing to provide these facilities on an unsecured basis. However, as this product became more popular in Europe, European banks adopted the same approach as their U.S. counterparts in terms of security packages, and nearly all European deals now require the fund and its GP to pledge collateral to support the fund's obligations. In Asia, these transactions were often unsecured; however, owing to the trend towards a more syndicated market requiring multiple lenders, the majority of deals are now being done on a secured basis. In general, the terms for Asian fund financings are beginning to converge with the terms in the U.S. and Europe; in particular, requiring robust security packages.

Whilst the actual assets a lender will look to secure are essentially the same in all three markets (i.e. the rights to call down from investors and any collateral account into which

investor calls are paid), the methods around granting security, perfection and enforcement vary across jurisdictions. A few of the dissimilarities to be aware of are as follows:
1. *Deposit account control agreements ("DACAs")* – Under the Uniform Commercial Code ("**UCC**"), the statutory authority governing secured transactions in the U.S., in order for a lender to perfect its security interest in a deposit account, it is required to maintain "control" (as defined in the UCC) over the deposit account. The most common method of maintaining control is by the execution and delivery of a DACA, which is an agreement between the account bank, the fund and the lender, whereby the account bank will agree to honour instructions issued by the lender with respect to the account without the further consent of the fund. The DACA is usually in a form generated by the account bank, and account banks will typically not accept many changes to their preferred form.
Though not required for control under the UCC, an account bank may insist on a DACA being in place in the U.S., even where the account bank and the secured party are the same entity, in order to set forth the relative rights and obligations of separate branches or divisions of the bank. This is most important in syndicated deals, where the lender syndicate has a vested interest in the agent bank clearly delineating its roles as agent and account bank. In England and Wales, and generally in Asia, it is usual for the terms of how any secured monies will be dealt with to be contained in the facility agreement and/or the account security agreement itself.
In terms of account security in England and Wales, perfection is achieved by the receipt of a notice by the account bank, putting the account bank on notice that the monies they hold in that account are subject to a security interest, and to make the account bank aware of the secured party's signing rights. It is market standard for account banks to request that their own form of notice and acknowledgment be used, or to countersign the notice by way of acknowledgment.
2. *Notices* – In England and Wales, any security over the right to call down from investors will be perfected by notice being duly served on, and received by, the investors. Depending on the method of delivery of notice, a secured party may accept read receipts if notices are delivered to investors via email, or evidence that the notices have been uploaded to an investor portal.
In the U.S., notices are not required in order to perfect security over call-down rights, and are rarely, if ever, delivered. Rather, under the UCC, the right to call capital on the investors is classified as a "general intangible" (as defined in the UCC). Therefore, in order to perfect the lender's security interest in the right to call capital, the lender is required to file a UCC-1 financing statement naming the fund and the GP as debtors and the lender as the secured party. The UCC-1 financing statement must be filed in the "location" of the debtor (as set forth in the UCC), and serves to put third-party creditors on notice of the lender's security interest.
3. *Collateral waterfalls* – Funds and investors that participate in U.S. law-governed fund finance facilities must also be mindful of certain regulatory and statutory regimes that could govern the relationship between the lender and the fund or the investors. For example, if an investor is a pension or retirement fund (an "**ERISA Investor**") that is subject to the Employee Retirement Income Security Act 1974, as amended ("**ERISA**") and if the credit facility is determined to create contractual privity between the lender and the investor, then this could result in a "prohibited transaction" under ERISA. Failure to comply with ERISA could expose the investor and the fund to significant liability, or trigger excuse rights that would permit the ERISA Investor to avoid funding capital contributions.

As further protection for ERISA Investors, funds will often require ERISA Investors to be limited partners in a feeder fund that will then feed into the main fund. In this instance, a "cascading collateral structure" is put in place whereby the feeder fund will pledge to the main fund its and its GP's rights to call capital on its investors, and the main fund will then on-pledge to the lender its rights under the security documents between the main fund and the feeder fund. This type of cascading collateral structure may also be utilised by funds that are sensitive to the tax implications or other legal or structural considerations that could be triggered by creating privity between the investors and the lender, or else by virtue of the loans provided under the credit facility. There are no similar instances where this type of security structuring is required in respect of English funds, as generally there is no issue with English entities contracting directly with a lender. However, given that many European financings involving other jurisdictions are project-managed out of England, alternative financing structures such as equity commitment letters and put and call options may be adopted, as opposed to typical financing and security structures, to accommodate any jurisdictional tax or regulatory concerns.

Additionally, choice of governing law remains an important consideration for investors and lenders for the credit facility and the LPA and other investor documents. Typically, transactions governed by the laws of a U.S. jurisdiction tend to see more Cayman or Delaware organised borrowers, as such jurisdictions offer preferable tax and corporate governance laws for a fund and its investors. Likewise, U.S. lenders are comfortable that the laws of such jurisdictions will enable enforcement by the fund or GP (or the lender, under the security documents) of the investor's obligations to fund their capital contributions. For similar reasons, in European deals, it is more common to see Luxembourg, Channel Island, Scottish, Irish, English, Nordic, Netherlands or Cayman structures, whereas in Asia, investors have historically favoured Cayman, British Virgin Island and Australian vehicles. Traditionally, Asian fund sponsors have used Cayman Island fund vehicles, typically formed as limited partnerships. Some sponsors have introduced Singapore and Hong Kong vehicles for local investors. The Asian fund finance market also sees Luxembourg, Delaware and Australian vehicles for larger funds.

In certain jurisdictions (particularly those in Europe that are subject to the Rome Convention), the governing law of where the borrower's assets are *situs* will dictate how security is taken in that jurisdiction; for example, if an LPA is governed by the laws of England and Wales, then the call-right security will be taken under the laws of England and Wales as the investors' obligation to meet a call-down notice is governed under an English law contract. Conversely, this is not strictly the case in non-EU jurisdictions, including New York, Delaware and the Cayman Islands, where the governing law of a security agreement might not necessarily be the same jurisdiction as where that asset is based.

The majority of U.S.-based fund finance facilities are governed by New York law, as lenders are comfortable that the laws of New York contain favourable provisions for the interpretation of the credit documents and enforcement of remedies against the fund. Therefore, the law governing the security agreement, and the creation and attachment of a security interest in the collateral, would be New York law. However, under the UCC, security filings are required under the law of the debtor's location (as defined in the UCC) to perfect the security interest in the collateral. Consequently, if a fund is organised under the laws of Delaware, the UCC would specify that Delaware is the "location" of the debtor, and perfection of the collateral would be made by the filing of a UCC-1 financing statement in Delaware. This would be the case regardless of what governing law is included under the LPA and investor documents (though such governing law typically corresponds to the fund's jurisdiction of organisation).

Covenants

Historically, U.S. deals have sought comfort from lending against a borrowing base (looking at each investor on an individual basis by applying individual advance rates, haircuts and concentration limits before aggregating results) and granular due diligence of fund documentation, including any side letters entered into by the fund or GP for the benefit of investors. By contrast, European deals have taken a more holistic view on the financial covenants (looking at the investor base as a whole and applying one advance rate), and sought comfort through covenants in the facilities agreement – for example, through a repeating representation that no side letter, or other agreement between an investor and the fund or GP, contains terms that are materially averse to the rights of a finance party under the finance documents or, if taken one step further, would affect the ability of the fund or GP to require investors to make capital contributions to the fund.

Historically, in Asia, deals were structured with a coverage ratio. Nowadays, facilities may be sized on a borrowing base calculation or coverage test.

The reporting obligations of the borrower tend to be more frequent, onerous and administratively burdensome in U.S. deals. U.S. lenders usually require more visibility regarding the amount and frequency of any distributions made to investors, financial information on the investor base and more-frequent monitoring of the borrowing base threshold.

Conditions precedent

As mentioned above, one of the key differences, when it comes to security conditions precedent, will be delivery and receipt of perfection notices (in England and Wales) and UCC-1 financing statements (in the U.S.).

Completion searches differ between jurisdictions, with lien searches under the applicable UCC and tax laws being carried out where a borrower is located under the UCC in the U.S., and in some cases in the U.S. jurisdiction where its chief executive officer is located. The purpose of a UCC lien search is to determine whether any other creditors hold existing liens against the collateral that would take priority over the liens to be created by the credit documents. Likewise, under U.S. law, any tax lien filed against the fund by a governmental authority would hold higher priority than the liens created by the security agreement.

Whilst similar security searches are carried out at the relevant Companies House in the UK for corporate entities and limited liability partnerships, there is no security searches register for limited partnerships, which is the typical private equity fund structure in the UK. Therefore, any security granted by a fund, in the form of a limited partnership, over its assets will not be noted at the registry (unless there is a corporate GP that is an English entity and party to the security, in which case the security can be registered against such entity), and so priority liens in respect of such a fund cannot be searched for. Depending on the type of security being granted, different filing obligations will also apply in the UK. Again, security filings can only be made in respect of security interests granted by corporate vehicles or limited liability partnerships over their assets, not limited partnerships.

Legal opinions are a requirement for lenders in all three markets. However, although the content and substance will be largely the same, the market expectation as to who provides which opinions differs greatly. In Europe, it is expected that lender's counsel will provide the enforceability of security opinion and that borrower's counsel will provide the capacity and authority opinions and any ranking opinion (if required). In the U.S., it is expected that borrower's counsel will provide all legal opinions, though the fund's main counsel might provide only the enforceability opinions and rely on local counsel that is licensed in the jurisdiction of the fund's organisation to deliver corporate opinions on capacity and authority. Many U.S. lenders will also accept an opinion of a borrower's in-house counsel as to capacity and authority to enter into the finance documents. With regard to cross-border transactions, it should be agreed between all parties, as soon as possible, who is providing which opinions, so as to have an accurate indicator of costs and to avoid last-minute delays.

Execution of documents/completion mechanics

The signing process in England and Wales is very strict in the wake of *R (on the application of Mercury Tax Group and another) v HMRC* [2008] EWHC 2721 ("**Mercury Case**"). Following the findings in the *Mercury Case*, English counsel follow best practice guidance when it comes to virtual signings and closings. Hong Kong practice is in large part following the same path. The method of signing will depend on whether or not the document in question is a deed, but in summary the best practice for execution of a deed virtually is as follows (and it is worth noting that the English market often follows this same approach for documents that are not deeds, albeit not strictly necessary):

1. the final version of the deed to be circulated to all parties;
2. the signatories to print the entire deed (or the signature page);
3. a scanned copy of the entire deed (or the signature page) to be sent back to the lawyer who circulated the deed, together with the final form deed; and
4. the signatories to confirm whether the deed is deemed to be delivered and/or when it is deemed to be delivered.

In respect of executing documents in England and Wales that are not deeds, the guidance following the *Mercury Case* is as follows:

1. the final version of the document to be circulated to all parties;
2. the signatories to print and sign the signature page; and
3. a scanned copy of the signature page to be sent back to the lawyer who circulated the document, together with written authority of the relevant signatory to attach that signature page to the final form document.

Where the document in question is not a real estate contract, the signature page may be circulated and signed whilst the document is still being negotiated. The signature page would then be held to order and released once the relevant signatories have confirmed that their signature page can be attached to the final form document.

Conversely, in the U.S. there is no requirement to circulate a final form of the document prior to execution of signature pages. Signature pages to documents that are still subject to negotiation can be circulated, signed and returned separately to the complete agreement. The parties will then each agree that their pre-signed signature pages can be attached to the final version of the document once it is in the agreed form.

Summary

Whilst there remain many differences between the U.S., European and Asian markets, it is expected that lenders in Europe will continue to be influenced by their U.S. counterparts, and lenders in Asia will continue to be influenced by their counterparts in the U.S. and Europe. However, there will always be inconsistencies at the transactional level that borrowers, lenders and their counsels should be aware of and appreciate.

Looking ahead, the disruption that the economy has felt in 2022 due to a legacy of lockdowns and the Ukraine crisis is likely to continue into 2023. The tough exit market for private equity and write-down in valuations have affected some asset classes more than others, with infrastructure and private debt remaining strong. As in any downturn there is also opportunity, and fund finance products can assist with a borrower's ability to manage its portfolio during tougher times; for example, NAV facilities can be used to facilitate "synthetic exists" by unlocking value in a fund's investments and making returns to investors if a full exit is not possible at that time due to market conditions. It is also likely that fundraising and deal closing will continue to take longer than it has in previous years, with the market hopeful that 2024 will see a marked improvement.

* * *

Acknowledgment

The authors would like to acknowledge with grateful thanks the significant contribution made to this chapter by colleagues in Haynes and Boone's U.S. and Asian offices, in particular by Deborah Low, partner in the New York office of Haynes and Boone.

Deborah's background is in representing foreign and domestic institutional lenders in various forms of secured and unsecured finance transactions including fund finance, commodities and energy finance, syndicated lending, corporate finance, project finance, acquisition finance and cross-border export financing loan agreements. Deborah was selected for inclusion in New York Super Lawyers Rising Stars, Thomson Reuters, for Securities and Corporate Finance, 2017.

http://www.haynesboone.com/people/l/low-deborah.

Tel: +1 212 918 8987 / Email: deborah.low@haynesboone.com

Emma Russell
Tel: +44 20 8734 2807 / Email: emma.russell@haynesboone.com

Emma Russell is a partner and head of the Finance Practice Group in the London office of Haynes and Boone. Emma is an experienced loan finance lawyer with extensive knowledge in global fund finance, real estate finance transactions, and structured and specialty finance, as well as more general experience in acquisition, leverage, and general corporate finance. Her practice focuses on the full range of fund-lending products across all fund sectors (including private equity, real estate, secondaries, SMAs, infrastructure, and hedge), from capital call facilities, hybrid/NAV facilities, to general partner support, co-invest facilities and portfolio acquisition facilities and assisting funds with structuring. Emma has significant experience advising credit funds and their lenders in relation to leverage facilities to CLOs/CDOs and securitisation vehicles. Emma has spent significant time working in-house with various financial institutions during her career.
http://www.haynesboone.com/people/r/russell-emma.

Emily Fuller
Tel: +44 20 8734 2831 / Email: emily.fuller@haynesboone.com

Emily Fuller is a counsel in the Finance Practice Group in the London office of Haynes and Boone. Emily acts on a full range of finance transactions, with a particular focus on fund finance, including syndicated and bilateral leveraged/NAV, hybrid and capital call facilities, speciality financings and real estate financings. Emily's practice focuses on acting for bank and non-bank lenders, sponsors and a variety of borrowers (including private equity, hedge, infrastructure, SMAs, real estate and credit funds, corporate entities and joint ventures) and has also gained valuable experience of both open-ended and closed-ended offshore fund and co-investment structures.
http://www.haynesboone.com/people/f/fuller-emily.

Haynes and Boone, LLP

1 New Fetter Lane, London EC4A 1AN, United Kingdom
Tel: +44 20 8734 2800 / Fax: +44 20 8734 2820 / URL: www.haynesboone.com

Umbrella facilities:
Pros and cons for a sponsor

Richard Fletcher & Yagmur Yarar
Macfarlanes LLP

Overview

In this chapter, we will discuss what constitutes "umbrella facilities" (including how they compare and contrast with more standard fund finance facilities) and explore the pros and cons of using these products from the perspective of a sponsor. We will also cover which types of funds tend to use umbrella facilities, and the outlook for the future of umbrella facilities in the market.

Description of umbrella facilities

A standard fund finance facility will involve a single fund (or several parallel funds, still referred to in this chapter as "a fund") as borrower, with the lender(s) providing a single revolving facility, or sometimes both a revolving facility and a term facility, on a committed basis under a single facility agreement. These facilities can be utilised by the fund for any permitted purpose in the usual way, with multiple drawdowns, repayments and redrawings (in the case of a revolving facility) depending on the needs of the fund. The usual security package for a standard fund finance facility includes security over the uncalled commitments of the fund's investors, and security over the bank account into which the proceeds from drawdowns of those commitments are paid.

In contrast, umbrella facilities have multiple borrowing bases, which can include multiple funds, or a single fund, and one or more of its subsidiary special purpose vehicles ("**SPVs**") as borrowers. Umbrella facilities can take several different forms, the most popular models of which are generally split into two main types as described below.

A brief history of umbrella facilities

The concept of an umbrella facility for fund financing first developed in the early 2010s. The idea for this type of facility was born out of a desire by fund borrowers to enter into new facilities speedily and in a cost-effective manner. The costs savings arise from both the lack of commitment fee (on the basis that umbrella facilities are provided on an uncommitted basis) and due to reduced administration time and legal fees being incurred for a succession of new facilities under the umbrella facility compared to legal fees for a succession of standalone facilities.

It is worth noting that a solid relationship between borrower and lender is key to a successful umbrella facility. We have experience of umbrella facilities working very well when the borrower is familiar with the lender's internal credit process and there is a strong relationship between the parties. Where the umbrella facility is uncommitted, lenders usually need to obtain credit approval quickly in order to meet a specific deal timetable set by the borrower. This process is expedited when the borrower knows exactly what to provide to the lender in terms of information or documentary evidence, and the lender's credit committee is familiar with the borrower's investors (in particular, their creditworthiness) and the borrower's investment activities.

The flexibility that is built into umbrella facility finance documents also helps lenders meet a borrower's needs in a timely fashion because there is (usually) no need to amend the existing facilities agreement to accommodate a specific deal structure; however, it is worth noting that more unusual deal structures can be discussed and implemented relatively quickly when using the master facilities agreement as an agreed starting point. The latter being said, any additional security or variation of term for a specific sub-facility would require negotiation at the time (as discussed below).

Types of umbrella facilities

One type of umbrella facility ("**Model A**") involves documenting the various facilities using an uncommitted "master facilities agreement". This provides an agreed framework under which a fund can request facilities from time to time from the lender(s), subject to an overarching master facilities limit agreed between the parties. The facilities that may be requested can include term, revolving and letter of credit facilities. Typically, SPVs can also accede as borrowers for specific facilities, or just a single facility, with their obligations being guaranteed by the fund (or by the fund entering into a binding commitment to provide funds to its subsidiary SPV, which is capable of being enforced by a lender).

Each time a borrower (whether the fund as original borrower or a new SPV borrower) requires a new facility, it submits a new facility request, typically using an agreed template, to the lender(s) detailing the type of facility it requires, the new facility amount and any other specific commercial terms relevant to that new facility (such as interest rates, currency and fees). The lender(s) will then approve (or not) that requested facility. Recourse for the lender(s), for both borrowings by the fund and guarantees by the fund of borrowings of the SPVs, is to the fund's investors and the bank account into which proceeds of investor commitments are paid, as for a standard fund finance facility.

Under a Model A umbrella facility, each new facility remains outstanding until its specific maturity, subject to an overall master facilities agreement long-stop maturity date, and the aggregate committed amount of all facilities cannot exceed the overarching master facilities limit. The purpose for borrowing each new facility may be for general fund purposes (such as working capital or payment of fees and expenses) or a particular purpose often related to the needs of the fund's specific investment strategy (such as real estate or private equity).

Another difference between a Model A umbrella facility and a standard fund finance facility is the different levels of events of default. Events of default that are relevant only to a single facility ("**Sub-Facility EoDs**") will usually only trigger an early repayment of that facility. Events of default that are relevant to the fund as borrower and guarantor (such as insolvency at fund level, or significant levels of investor default or non-payment) ("**Master Facility EoDs**") usually trigger early repayment of all facilities. Of course, a Sub-Facility EoD at a borrower SPV level that results in that facility being accelerated may lead to a call on the fund guarantee, and if the fund guarantee is not paid when due, this will trigger a Master Facility EoD, thereby potentially accelerating all the facilities outstanding under the master facilities agreement.

A further key difference between a Model A umbrella facility and a standard fund finance facility is that the Model A umbrella facility is provided on an uncommitted basis, one consequence of which is that commitment fees are not charged until an individual sub-facility is committed, and are then charged for that sub-facility only to the extent it is not utilised. This lowers the ongoing cost of Model A facilities compared to a standard fund finance facility, which we will discuss later in this chapter.

A second type of umbrella facility ("**Model B**") also involves a master facilities agreement but typically sees a different fund acceding as borrower for each new facility. The funds are managed by the same manager, and so are within the same fund group, but will usually have different, or slightly different, investors. Whilst the recourse position superficially appears the same as for a standard fund finance facility or for a Model A umbrella facility, with recourse to the uncalled commitments of the investors and the bank accounts into which proceeds of such commitments are paid, it is actually different. The lenders will only have recourse to the specific investors of the fund that is the borrower or guarantor of a particular sub-facility, and not to all investors of all the funds of that manager. There is no cross-guaranteeing by the borrower (or fund) of one sub-facility by the borrower (or fund) of another sub-facility. A Model B umbrella facility is particularly relevant when investors are providing their commitments for a specific investment purpose, which will also be the purpose for that sub-facility.

Tied to the preceding point, Model B umbrella facilities are also frequently used by managers with multiple investment strategies. For example, a manager that invests in credit for leveraged buyouts might also invest in real estate debt. Those two asset classes would ordinarily be part of separate investment strategies, and hence separate funds. On the basis that there is a common manager for each of the funds, banks frequently accept including those separate funds within the same umbrella (or Model B) facility and allow for each to become a borrower under separate sub-facilities. However, the ability of a manager to utilise a Model B umbrella facility structure is largely dependent on it having an established track record and, of course, on the strength of its investor base(s). Accordingly, Model B is suited to managers of funds with larger institutional investors with a correspondingly strong borrowing covenant. In a typical Model B umbrella financing, the lenders will already know all of the investors of that fund group and there will be no question regarding the solvency of these "top-class" investors. It is not uncommon for lenders and managers to have a pre-agreed list of such "top-class" pre-vetted investors that invest into different funds who then borrow a sub-facility for a specific investment. The lenders' awareness of such investors reduces the time taken to complete on-boarding checks for each borrower in a new sub-facility and increases the lenders' confidence in the investor base of that borrower.

In a Model B umbrella facility, once the manager and lenders have agreed acceptable forms of formation documents and structures for a borrower, the manager can establish each successive sub-facility borrower with formation documents in the same or similar form, giving them confidence that the lenders will be able to accept such documents and reducing the amount of time lenders require for credit approval.

Whilst the overarching framework of Model B is similar to that of Model A (i.e. a master facilities agreement under which sub-facilities are entered into on an as-needed basis), due to the existing familiarity of the relationship between the manager and the lender(s), the strength of the manager's investor base and the frequency of transacting between the parties, the lender(s) and the manager of the fund group will have an agreed framework in place that will be replicated again and again (for each new borrower).

A variant of Model B uses a common terms agreement (in conjunction with a short-form loan agreement for each borrower) rather than a master facilities agreement. The common terms agreement sets out the main body of borrowing terms that apply to each facility, whilst the short-form loan agreement entered into by individual fund borrowers incorporates the common terms by reference, and documents the agreed commercial terms and any other terms that are bespoke to that particular borrower and facility.

Recourse and security

The basic security package for an umbrella facility operates on the same basis as any other fund finance transaction. As mentioned above, the lenders' key recourse is to the uncalled commitments of the fund's investors, and the lenders will therefore require security over uncalled commitments and security over the bank account into which the proceeds of such commitments are paid when drawn down. If there are feeder funds between a borrower/guarantor fund and the investors to which the lenders are to have recourse, typically those feeder funds will give guarantees and security over the uncalled commitments of their investors. In this way, the lenders always have direct security over the commitments of each investor, whether that investor is a direct investor in the fund or an indirect investor through a feeder vehicle. Furthermore, whilst the primary recourse of the lenders is to the uncalled commitments of the investors in that fund and the bank account(s) into which the proceeds of drawdowns from investors are paid, those same fund bank accounts frequently receive distributions and proceeds from the underlying investments of the fund. Where the latter is the case, the lenders will also, in practice, have security over distribution proceeds.

In some circumstances, lenders may also require security over certain fund assets for a specific facility or facilities. For example, if a facility is borrowed by an SPV, the lenders might require security over the bank accounts of that SPV in addition to the bank accounts of the fund. Lenders might also require share security to be granted over the fund's shareholding in the SPV and, if the SPV owns shares in another company, potentially from the SPV over that other company. The latter will clearly need to accommodate any security granted to third-party lenders in respect of any financing for a fund's portfolio company, and is therefore not always obtainable.

This practice of taking additional security over the fund's or SPV's underlying assets is frequently required for a more mature fund where there are fewer uncalled investor commitments remaining. The positive benefit to the fund is therefore to extend the life of its financing, which might otherwise be unavailable due to that reduced level of investor commitments. This additional security can be combined with guarantees being provided by each of the fund's SPVs in respect of each other SPV and the fund's own obligations. When taken together with security granted by each SPV over its bank accounts and, potentially, subsidiary/ies, lenders obtain recourse to both any remaining uncalled investor commitments and the net asset value ("**NAV**") of the fund as a whole. The additional security and asset-recourse structure can be simply documented by a new facility request and security documents covering each of the relevant assets. It may, however, be necessary to conduct additional diligence on: (i) the constitutional documents of the fund and the SPV; and (ii) any facilities that have been made available to an SPV (or its subsidiaries).

For example, a key question for funds looking to enter into umbrella facilities (and for lenders looking to provide umbrella facilities) will be whether the existing constitutional documents of the fund permit the provision of guarantees and security in support of facilities to be provided to an SPV of the fund as borrower. A fund's constitutional documents will contain restrictions on the term of any of its borrowings (for example, for a maximum period of 12 months). If the fund is only permitted to provide guarantees and security to support borrowings of an SPV for the same term, this would restrict the tenor of a NAV-based SPV facility, making such facilities less attractive from a borrower perspective as they may not align with the life cycle of the fund's investments.

It will also be necessary to confirm that each SPV can cross-guarantee each other in the manner described in the above paragraph, although a detailed consideration of these issues is beyond the scope of this chapter.

Pros and cons

Viewed from a high level, the pros of using umbrella facilities compared to standard fund finance facilities can be best summarised as offering flexibility. This flexibility may encompass: (i) a facility that develops over the life of a fund, starting off as a capital call facility then potentially becoming a partially asset-based facility towards the end of the life of the fund; (ii) multiple borrowers and funds within one facilities agreement structure; and (iii) flexibility of timing – with the majority of terms pre-agreed, a new sub-facility can be put in place in answer to a sudden need for additional funding. Added to that flexibility, they are generally considered less expensive from both a fees and costs perspective, as explained in more detail below.

Again, from a high level, the cons are that umbrella facilities can be unwieldy and more time-consuming to negotiate, and may not suit all conceivable types of potential fund finance transaction. While the parties can make every effort to pre-empt what they consider will be required throughout the term of the agreement, they are unlikely to be able to predict every eventuality. The umbrella facility may therefore need to be amended if the needs or activities of the fund change materially.

We consider the pros and cons in further detail below in light of the two main characteristics of umbrella facilities.

Flexibility and convenience

Compared to a standard fund finance facility, umbrella facilities can be hugely flexible. They can offer the convenience of an uncalled capital commitment together with an underlying assets (or NAV-based) facility within one agreement. They can provide for either single or multiple borrowers as well as different forms of borrower vehicle (e.g. both fund entities as well as corporate vehicles). They can also be adapted over the life of a fund as its needs change, without having to put multiple standalone facility agreements in place or make extensive amendments to existing standard fund finance facilities.

Umbrella facilities can provide borrowers with greater speed of execution than a standalone facility because they do not have to go through an extensive conditions precedent process or enter into a new suite of finance documents every time they require a new facility, as the documents used are effectively streamlined. This is particularly true in relation to new security (although see above in relation to asset-specific security). In particular, under a Model A umbrella facility, borrowers submit a new facility request each time they want to borrow a new facility, which is typically based on a short-form agreed template. For straightforward transactions, the borrower can prepare the new facility request themselves without needing legal input. This enables the borrower to act quickly and efficiently without needing to instruct lawyers and, because the requests are (usually) substantially the same on each occasion, the borrower will become well versed and ever more efficient in preparing the new facility requests over time.

Umbrella facilities also provide funds with the ability to match their funding requirements to a club of lenders who can provide all of the necessary facilities. The facility should have the discretion to allow lenders to be selected according to their ability to provide certain facilities. Where revolving or ancillary facilities are required, lenders with the ability to provide those facilities (and the requisite rating, if required) will participate. Lenders who can only provide term debt can be selected to provide a proportion of the term debt facilities. The latter point also enhances the ability to syndicate these sorts of facilities to alternative lenders, providing greater liquidity for the lenders and, potentially, greater pricing competition for the borrower. Lenders may also benefit from the increased likelihood that the manager will request a further facility to support a fund's strategy in subsequent investment periods. Where a fund structure involves entities in a number of different jurisdictions, there can be tax issues in respect of certain lenders lending into some jurisdictions, so a club of lenders can be organised so that the appropriate lenders lend to certain entities within the structure, to avoid withholding tax issues.

While we have highlighted ways in which an umbrella facility can make life easier for borrowers and lenders alike, trying to create an all-purpose master facilities agreement may not always end up being as convenient as it seems. The parties (and their legal counsel) might spend a significant amount of time at the outset negotiating provisions into the master facilities agreement that do not end up being utilised (for example, the facilities agreement might provide for a letter of credit facility that is then never used). It is also possible that the fund might negotiate the initial facilities agreement with the expectation that it will last for the full life of that fund, but realise over time that market terms have moved on and/or that it does not require a later life/asset-based facility.

Finally, whilst an umbrella facility being uncommitted might be convenient from a costs perspective, as each new facility will require credit approval, this could potentially delay the borrower's plans to draw down on a particular date. As discussed above, a well-developed relationship between borrower and lender can help to avoid this pitfall.

Fees and costs

As mentioned previously, one of the main features that distinguishes an umbrella facility from a standard fund finance facility is that this type of facility is often partially or wholly uncommitted. The resulting absence of a commitment fee can be a significant cost saving for the borrower. The facility structure can therefore remain in place (albeit uncommitted) without unnecessary ongoing costs accruing. This saves the borrower negotiating a new facility agreement at the point in time where it intends to draw down funds (again, subject to the points discussed above about the uncommitted nature of the structure) without paying a commitment fee for a facility that they are not actively or fully using.

From a lender's perspective, umbrella facilities can be operationally easier to administer than multiple standalone facilities. For example, there is a single relationship between the lender and the fund (on a Model A-type umbrella financing) or between the lender and the manager (on a Model B-type umbrella financing), so lenders are able to pass on their cost savings to the borrower by charging lower fees. On the other hand, and in particular in relation to Model A umbrella facilities, if a borrower requires a complex, bespoke financing arrangement, then the lender may charge more for providing a specialist product at the outset.

Another financial advantage of using an umbrella facility is that legal fees will usually be lower overall because the fund is not entering into multiple facility agreements during its life or because a sponsor does not need to negotiate an entirely new facility agreement for each new borrower or SPV. This reduces the time spent on negotiating finance documents, providing conditions precedent and incurring local counsel fees. However, a complex master facilities agreement or common terms agreement will require more extensive upfront discussion and negotiation than for a standard fund finance facility, so the upfront legal fees are likely to end up being higher than for a standard fund finance facility.

Putting an umbrella facility in place should also save the borrower's key personnel time in the long run as the expectation is that it will become an efficient vehicle to be used by the borrower. A significant amount of time will be needed from these key personnel to negotiate the initial umbrella facility. However, once the facility is in place, each new facility request should require much less time from both lawyers and key personnel than a standard fund finance facility. This will therefore allow the borrower's treasury personnel to spend more time on other day-to-day fund activities, as well as reducing legal costs. Where a manager operates multiple different funds, there is potentially even greater cost and time savings where those funds can all benefit from a single umbrella facility (as discussed further below). As mentioned above in respect of fund set-up, the sponsor can co-ordinate the establishment of its funds that are expected to be borrowers with a degree of confidence that they will be subject to a straightforward route to lender approval if they follow an established format, therefore saving time on restructuring to accommodate lender requirements.

Despite the pros listed above, borrowers need to carefully compare the potential costs savings of an umbrella facility against the potential running costs of a standard fund finance facility. Whilst, as highlighted above, one of the most significant savings of an umbrella facility is the absence of commitment fees, if a fund is very active and is likely to draw a large portion of its available facilities, then the actual level of commitment fees paid for a fully committed facility (i.e. a standard fund finance facility) will be low. For this kind of fund, fee savings will be unlikely to be determinative of whether to use a standard fund finance facility or an umbrella facility.

In addition to the above, it is clearly worth testing whether the flexibility provided by an umbrella facility is actually required by a fund. On the basis that a substantial amount of time and cost will be spent in the negotiation of an umbrella facility, care must be taken to ensure that its use will be frequent enough to justify that initial outlay. There is a danger of flexibility being an end in itself rather than the facility having genuine application to the fund's needs. Having said that, many borrowers will only use an umbrella facility for bridging capital calls, and be perfectly happy that that limited purpose is sufficient to justify the upfront costs.

While the complexity (and as a result, flexibility) of an umbrella facility can be seen as a pro for some sponsors, such complexity is also a potential con. Providing sufficient flexibility in the master facilities agreement (especially if it is the first time a borrower and lender are entering into an umbrella facilities agreement together) takes a significant amount of time. The facilities agreement will need to include more options than a standard fund finance facilities agreement and there will therefore be extensive commercial discussions between lenders and borrowers, and the lawyers will have to spend more time on drafting. Furthermore, in light of this additional complexity, a manager might require additional advice from their legal counsel in order to understand the terms of the facilities agreement (and this has time and cost implications).

Who and where?

The diversity of the types of funds that use umbrella facilities reflects the multi-use nature of such facilities.

Even a single fund with a simple structure (i.e. the absence of a multiplicity of feeder vehicles and SPVs) might take advantage of the umbrella facility's flexibility. This flexibility might be required to ensure that it only has to enter into one facilities agreement during its life. As mentioned above, at the beginning of a fund's life, its value for lenders is in the undrawn commitments of its investors, and, as the fund matures, this will increasingly change to the value of the investments it has made or assets it has purchased with those commitments, and a fund's facility may therefore need to change from a pure capital call facility towards an asset-backed facility. Alternatively, a fund may be planning on carrying out bespoke activities that require something more complex than a standard fund finance facility.

A multi-asset, multi-strategy fund manager (i.e. a fund manager that raises multiple pools of capital across more than one sector (e.g. credit and private equity)) is one of the most obvious beneficiaries of the umbrella facility structure. In addition to its flagship commingled funds, the manager might need the facility to be available for single managed accounts ("**SMAs**") and also require flexibility for parallel funds or feeder vehicles to accede to the facilities. An umbrella facility provides this flexibility from day one as, whatever form the relevant vehicle requiring finance takes, the finance documents already include the framework to allow those different types of vehicle into the facility.

However, for some SMAs, a bespoke individual committed facility may be better than an umbrella facility, if the reality is that their investment activity will be limited. A Model B umbrella facility would be best suited to this kind of situation, especially where a manager is looking to keep its commingled investments separate to those of SMAs. As above, however, a manager would need to assess which facility structure is most likely to be used by its managed funds, and whether the flexibility of having all entities in one structure is of genuine benefit.

The jurisdictions in which a fund can be based to take advantage of an umbrella facility are potentially unlimited. We have advised both borrowers and lenders in relation to facilities agreements governed by English law and with borrowers in onshore (for example, the UK or Luxembourg), near-offshore (for example, the Channel Islands) and far-offshore (for example, the Cayman Islands or Mauritius) jurisdictions.

Conclusion and outlook

We have considered what constitutes umbrella facilities and some of the pros and cons of using them, with a look at which types of funds are using these types of facilities, and in what jurisdictions.

A key driver in the continuing popularity of umbrella facilities is the tendency of managers to establish SMAs (due to the amount of cash investors are looking to invest), which, in turn, drives investors to seek bespoke investment strategies. If a manager can add those SMAs into an existing umbrella structure rather than having to go through the process of establishing a new structure (or indeed, put a single fund finance facility in place for each fund), then this is likely to appeal to investors and set the relationship between the manager and the investors off to a good start. Other positives for a manager are that investors will be attracted by the scope for cost saving (this is a direct benefit for investors as well as managers, because the return on their investment will be higher as fewer fees and costs will be deducted when calculating their profit), and managers will save themselves a significant amount of time and energy by not having to manage multiple single facilities.

On balance, it appears there are more pros than cons for certain types of funds looking to enter into umbrella facilities. In particular, the inbuilt flexibility and the lack of commitment fee are largely what makes an umbrella facility attractive to a fund that: (i) requires such flexibility due to the nature of its activities; or (ii) is part of a structure that is more suited to an umbrella rather than a standard fund finance facility. These two key pros are also the main distinctions between an umbrella facility and a standard fund finance facility. The long-lasting nature of an umbrella facility is itself an advantage – a facility intended to cater to the various life stages and specific investment needs of a fund (as a Model A umbrella facility can) or for several different borrowers (as for a Model B umbrella facility) ensures long-term communication between sponsor and lenders, and the accompanying potential for a firm and rewarding relationship for all parties. However, despite the potential advantages of using umbrella facilities, there are plenty of funds looking to borrow for whom a standard fund finance facility can be more attractive because it is less complicated (and therefore quicker to put in place and easier to manage on an ongoing basis) and better suited to their immediate business needs. In particular, we are currently seeing strong borrowers choose to negotiate a precedent fund finance facility with a lender for one SMA and then replicating this facility with the same lender and same legal counsel for its other SMAs – rather than using an umbrella facility. Nevertheless, umbrella facilities continue to remain popular with sponsors across their commingled fund and SMA portfolios.

Richard Fletcher
Tel: +44 20 7849 2244 / Email: richard.fletcher@macfarlanes.com
Richard is a partner in the finance team at Macfarlanes and advises financial institutions and corporates on a range of financing matters, with a particular focus on fund finance, speciality finance and structured finance.

Richard's fund finance experience includes advising on leverage facilities, investor call bridge facilities and equity bridge facilities.

Yagmur Yarar
Tel: +44 20 7849 2000 / Email: yagmur.yarar@macfarlanes.com
Yagmur is a solicitor in the finance team at Macfarlanes, advising borrowers and lenders on a broad range of domestic and cross-border finance transactions, including fund finance, acquisition finance, real estate finance and leveraged finance.

Macfarlanes LLP
20 Cursitor Street, London EC4A 1LT, United Kingdom
Tel: +44 20 7831 9222 / Fax: +44 20 7831 9607 / URL: www.macfarlanes.com

Side letters: Pitfalls and perils for a financing

Thomas Smith, Margaret O'Neill & John W. Rife III
Debevoise & Plimpton LLP

Overview

Subscription-line (or capital call) facilities (referred to in this chapter as "sub-lines") are, generally speaking, loan agreements provided at fund level, with recourse given to the lender over the right to call uncalled capital of investors in the applicable fund (and related rights). The type of fund-level financing products offered by lenders is continually evolving. One constant is the need to ensure that a fund's governing documents do not prohibit or restrict the financing that the fund wishes to raise.

The terms of an investor's investment in a fund are usually governed by three main types of documents. *First*, a limited partnership agreement ("LPA") containing the primary terms applicable to all investors in the fund. *Second*, a subscription document through which an investor subscribes for an interest in the fund, makes certain representations and agrees to adhere to the terms of the LPA. *Third*, each investor may negotiate a side letter (on a bilateral basis) with the fund's general partner ("GP") or manager. A side letter supplements the terms of the LPA applicable to the specific investor (without modifying the application of the LPA to other investors in the fund). The provisions of a side letter may take into account specific regulatory or tax considerations of an investor or supplement the commercial terms applicable to the investor's investment.

It is critical that the terms of the fund documents accommodate any contemplated fund-level financing. For sub-lines, investors constitute the ultimate source of repayment for lenders if the fund defaults such debt. Lenders will therefore diligence the fund documents to check (among other things) restrictions on borrowing and enforceability of investor obligations to the fund. Issues in the fund documents may preclude the uncalled capital commitment of one or more investors counting towards the amount that a fund can borrow under a sub-line (the "borrowing base"). Worse still, restrictions in the fund documents may even preclude a fund from raising finance at all.

This chapter focuses on the final element of the fund documents framework – side letters. Investors increasingly negotiate side letters in connection with their investment in a fund, and the scope of side letter provisions requested by investors is continually developing. As a result, a fund with a large number of investors will almost certainly have a wide array of side letter requirements to navigate. The terms of those side letters may individually, or collectively, affect a sub-line. Consideration of the terms of side letters is critical to sponsors, lenders and their counsel when contemplating fund-level financing.

We consider in this chapter some of the key issues arising in side letters that may impact sub-lines, and suggest practical solutions to specific issues.

Background to side letter considerations

Disclosure

Lenders generally request copies of all side letters so that they can diligence whether the terms of the side letters impact the proposed financing. There are certain (limited) exceptions to this approach.

First, some sponsors are unwilling to provide side letters to a fund's lenders given the sensitive nature of side letter terms and the sponsor's relationship with the fund's investors. In some cases, lenders may be prepared to allow disclosure of side letters to their counsel only, or be comfortable with a summary of the terms of the side letters prepared by borrower counsel. In limited cases, lenders may accept non-disclosure of side letters and instead rely on a repeating representation from the borrower that there are no side letter terms that are materially adverse to the lenders' interests under the finance documents (other than the terms disclosed). The borrower must therefore disclose any such materially adverse terms (but only those terms) to ensure that there is no misrepresentation.

Second, one or more side letters may be subject to investor-specific confidentiality restrictions on disclosure (see below for an analysis of the consequences of such confidentiality restrictions for the financing).

Impact of investor requirements

There is a third perspective to consider in a fund financing in addition to that of lender and borrower – the perspective of investors. Investors' views will impact side letter terms and, consequently, the ability of the fund and lender to put financing in place.

Investor views continue to evolve. The Institutional Limited Partners Association (a trade association for institutional LP fund investors) released guidance in June 2017 ("ILPA Guidelines") recommending (among other things) increased disclosure to investors with respect to the terms and impact of sub-lines. In response to the issuance of the ILPA Guidelines, the Fund Finance Association (a non-profit industry association in the fund finance market) issued its own analysis and recommendations on the ILPA Guidelines in December 2017 ("FFA Analysis"), emphasising that the ILPA Guidelines should encourage and foster greater dialogue and awareness but should not be viewed as "absolute principles". A fulsome discussion of the ILPA Guidelines and FFA Analysis is beyond the scope of this chapter; however, the views of interested parties will continue to shape the scope of side letter provisions requested by investors and their related impact on fund financings.

Focus on side letter provisions

Lenders place great importance on detailed review of the fund organisational documents, including side letters. That due diligence review focuses primarily on the terms that could impact the lender's right to call capital from the fund's investors and enforce its security. Any restrictions on an investor's funding obligations will be a material lender concern.

Timing

The key to ensuring that the terms of side letters do not adversely impact a financing is to keep the sub-line in mind at the time of side letter negotiation. Sub-lines are generally entered into after a fund has had at least one closing (i.e., after the initial subscription for interests by investors). Side letters are therefore not always negotiated at the same time as the sub-line. Best practice is to involve finance counsel from the outset of a fundraising process to ensure that side letter provisions take into account future financing needs and avoid issues down the line.

Limitations on debt incurrence

The fund must be able to incur the debt contemplated by its proposed fund-level financing. This is an LPA (rather than side letter) point, but is sufficiently fundamental to warrant comment! The LPA should expressly permit the incurrence of debt and the giving of any related guarantees and security. The LPA may contain limitations negotiated with investors in respect of the size of the sub-line (for example, up to a percentage of fund size), the purposes for which the sub-line can be used, and the duration for which borrowings may remain outstanding.

Practical considerations

These are key limitations around the use and structuring of the sub-line. With greater investor focus on LPA debt limitations, the scope of permitted debt incurrence is an increasingly important negotiation point.

In that context, the ILPA Guidelines recommended that investors request reasonable thresholds around the use of sub-lines (indicating, as an example, a limit on the size of a sub-line to around 15–25% of uncalled capital). In response, the FFA Analysis stated that a fundamental concern of the FFA was that a "one size fits all" approach to debt incurrence is not appropriate. Funds do not all have the same structure, investment focus or commercial strategy. For example, funds that may need to complete multiple deals in quick succession should ensure flexibility to draw sufficient amounts under the sub-line. Inclusion of a cap on debt incurrence that is too low could impair the fund's ability to complete one or more investments in the desired timeframe, potentially placing it at a competitive disadvantage.

This developing dialogue with investors emphasises the need to consider financing from the outset of the fund's life. This will avoid inadvertently restricting the viability of a sub-line.

Prohibition of direct obligations to lenders

The sub-line security package typically consists of security over the right to call capital of investors and security over bank accounts into which capital calls are paid. Capital call security allows a lender, on acceleration of the sub-line, to step into the GP or manager's shoes and issue drawdown notices to investors (and often have the right to issue drawdown notices either in the name of the GP or manager or in the lender's own name). Any side letter provisions stating that an investor has direct obligations only to fund parties, or otherwise expressly excluding any direct obligations to a lender, could (but do not necessarily) undermine the lender's ability to enforce its security.

Practical considerations

The drafting of the specific side letter provision matters hugely. The devil is in the detail. There are also supplemental regulatory matters to consider (see below).

First, the GP or manager can assign to a lender as part of the capital call security only those rights given to the GP or manager under the fund documents. The capital call security will not otherwise generally purport to give the lender direct rights against the investors. Some investors are concerned about grants to a third party of broad rights generally against the investor (rather than specific assignment of capital call rights). If this is the investor concern, the side letter restriction should be worded to make clear that it does not prohibit the lender from calling capital on enforcement, while accommodating the investor's broader concern.

Second, as a regulatory matter, in certain jurisdictions, capital commitments (either of all investors or only of certain investors that are subject to specific regulatory requirements) may only be paid into bank accounts of the fund. If so, the side letter restriction should be worded to accommodate both investor concerns and regulatory requirements, while still allowing the lender to call capital (albeit into a bank account of the fund).

Administrative requirements of investors

As an administrative matter, certain investors may request that the fund agree to a formal drawdown process. Investors are normally only concerned with practicalities. For example, investors may ask the fund to use headed notepaper for drawdown notices or provide a certified list of authorised signatories. On their face, these requirements seem unobjectionable. However, although unintended, such procedural mechanics may prevent a lender from calling capital on acceleration of a sub-line.

Practical considerations

If the fund addresses the issue during side letter negotiation, the investor may be prepared to adjust the procedural requirements in the side letter to expressly contemplate capital calls by the lender.

Alternatively, it may be possible to structure a solution in the finance documents. For example, the fund could provide the lender with undated drawdown notices (on headed notepaper, if necessary) signed by the relevant fund party and addressed to the investor for the lender to use on enforcement. The fund could also provide a specimen signature list to the investor, which includes an employee of the lender as an authorised signatory of the manager or GP.

Sponsor co-operation with lenders

Some investors may request that, where the GP or manager has assigned its right to call capital to a lender and that lender has enforced such security by issuing drawdown notices to investors, the GP or manager must provide written confirmation to the investors that those drawdown notices have been validly issued in accordance with the fund documents.

Practical considerations

This type of side letter provision presents a clear issue to lenders: in an enforcement scenario, the lender cannot rely on GP or manager co-operation. It is therefore important to ensure that failure by the GP or manager to provide such confirmation does not preclude the investor from its obligation to fund in response to drawdown notices issued by the lender.

Excuse rights

Many investors, for internal policy reasons, negotiate the right to be excused from specific categories of investments. For example, investors may wish to be excluded from participating in investments in alcohol, firearms and tobacco, or in geographies or industries to which the investor is politically or commercially sensitive. The investor has no contractual obligation to honour a drawdown notice with respect to any investment (or, typically, to repay sub-line debt that was used to make such investment) for which it has an excuse right.

Practical considerations

Excuse rights are relatively common. For many investors, such rights are a core requirement without which the investor will not obtain internal approval to invest. Generally, these rights are not negotiated away but are instead accommodated within the financing structure.

How would excuse rights be accommodated in a sub-line? Lenders generally require that excused investors do not count as part of the fund's borrowing base. The fund should ensure that the lender only excludes the investor from the borrowing base in respect of the portion of that investor's remaining capital commitments attributable to the excused investment, and only for the period for which the borrowing for that investment is outstanding.

Some lenders, particularly in the European and Asian fund finance markets, may also ask that an event of default is triggered if the amount of excused capital contributions at any one time, in aggregate, exceeds a cap (e.g., 15% or 20% of uncalled capital). The fund may wish to negotiate this. Excuse rights, by their nature, are investor-specific and do not indicate an issue with creditworthiness of investors generally, or their appetite to fund capital calls. The fund may therefore view an event of default as too onerous a consequence.

Confidentiality restrictions

Lenders need certain basic information on each investor before they are able to undertake credit analysis on that investor. Certain types of investors (often sovereign wealth funds) insist on provisions that prohibit disclosure of such information, even to lenders. Side letter restrictions that prevent the disclosure of such information are likely to lead to a lender excluding the investor from the borrowing base. For example, if the name and/or contact details of the investor cannot be provided, the lender will not be able to enforce its security against that investor.

Confidentiality provisions also raise additional concerns for lenders that may not be fully addressed by exclusion of the confidential investor from the borrowing base. Fund documents typically require capital calls to be made from all investors, which the lender would be unable to do if the identity of one or more investors is unknown. In addition, lenders are required to carry out certain "know your customer" checks, which can be an issue for lenders if confidential investors make up a significant portion of the investor base.

Practical considerations

It is worth considering the exact scope of an investor's confidentiality requirements when negotiating side letters. The investor may be willing to accommodate exceptions to a blanket restriction on disclosure. For example, an investor may be comfortable with disclosure of its name and contact details to counterparties to the fund (such as a lender), provided the recipient is bound to keep the information confidential and/or the investor is notified of any such disclosure.

Where disclosure of an investor's name is restricted, the sponsor should ensure that it is permitted to provide redacted copies of such investor's fund documents (for diligence purposes). The investor may be willing to agree to disclosure of the investor's name if there is an event of default under the sub-line to enable the lender to serve a drawdown notice on the investor. Alternatively, the sponsor may agree with the lender to call capital from the investor on an event of default, in light of the inability of the lender to do so.

Refusal to acknowledge third-party notifications

Investors may ask for express confirmation in a side letter that they will not have to sign any documentation in connection with a sub-line. These provisions can be problematic if prospective lenders insist on receiving investor letters, investor legal opinions or other additional documents from one or more investors as a condition to providing a sub-line.

Practical considerations

Funds should build into the LPA provisions that will facilitate the incurrence of sub-lines – for example, a waiver by the investors of any rights of set-off or any defences they may have in relation to their obligation to fund capital calls. The LPA should also incorporate certain basic investor representations, covenants and acknowledgments for the benefit of the lenders. If the LPA terms accommodate these points, lenders generally should not require investors to sign a supplemental investor letter in connection with their provision of a sub-line. One exception to this is in the case of separately managed accounts, where, notwithstanding the LPA terms, lenders are likely to require a supplemental investor letter from the single investor.

However, a risk may remain even if the LPA contains terms that the sponsor considers will satisfy lender expectations. If the side letter is entered into before the fund procures financing, the fund will not know for certain at the point of negotiating side letters whether such a restriction could be an issue. The fund could soften any absolute restriction by instead agreeing to use commercially reasonable efforts to ensure that the investor is not required to sign documents in connection with a sub-line.

Similarly, investors may also resist providing financial information to the fund and any sub-line lender. Lenders and investors often get comfortable with limiting the scope of financial information on an investor to publicly available financial information or, in some cases, only to information that is required by the lender in order to assess the creditworthiness of an investor.

Restrictions on jurisdiction of enforcement

Investors may seek to limit the jurisdictions in which a fund can pursue claims against them. This may be problematic for lenders. Lenders expect flexibility to bring claims in any jurisdiction in the event that they enforce rights to call capital and the investor defaults with respect to payment of such capital.

Practical considerations

Investors that are most sensitive to the jurisdiction of proceedings tend to be sovereign investors, including U.S. state pension plans. Principles of sovereign immunity or statutes applicable to any such investor may prohibit the investor from submitting to the jurisdiction of courts outside of its home jurisdiction. Accordingly, this investor request is usually non-negotiable. The prohibition on bringing a claim against the investor other than in its jurisdiction of organisation limits the enforcement rights of lenders. However, certain lenders may accept the limitations (and nonetheless include the investor in the borrowing base) on the basis of the credit quality of the investor.

Sovereign immunity

Certain entities, including sovereign wealth funds and public pension plans, may benefit from sovereign immunity in relation to contractual claims and/or other lawsuits. Funds may seek a waiver of sovereign immunity by investors. Many sovereign investors will not agree to a waiver and may require a side letter provision that overrides the waiver and reserves such immunity. In some instances, investors will also seek express acknowledgment of the scope of their immunities. This can create an enforcement risk for a lender.

Practical considerations

There is limited scope to negotiate a side letter provision reserving sovereign immunity. It is important to understand the scope of the immunity and whether there are exceptions (such as for commercial contracts) to the immunity that preserve the ability for a claim to be effectively brought against the investor. At a minimum, the side letter of an investor that benefits from sovereign immunity should clarify that the reservation of immunity does not limit the investor's obligations to the fund (including making capital contributions when called). Whether or not a sovereign investor is included in the borrowing base will depend on the specific credit analysis of the lenders to the fund.

Transfers to affiliates

Some investors seek enhanced flexibility in connection with the transfer of their interests to an affiliate and may require that the GP or the manager agrees to consent to any such transfer.

Practical considerations

Lenders will consider whether the affiliate transferee is as creditworthy as the transferor. The affiliate transferee may not be given as favourable treatment by lenders in the borrowing base or may be excluded entirely. Funds can mitigate this risk by limiting the affiliate transfer provision to allow transfers only to affiliates of creditworthiness acceptable to the GP or manager.

Funds may wish to negotiate that, under the sub-line, lenders do not have a consent right to investor transfers, or at least no consent right to transfers to affiliates. Historically, many lenders required a consent right to investor transfers above an agreed threshold, although transfers between affiliates were often carved out from the restriction. The primary rationale for such restriction is that an investor transfer may impact the creditworthiness of the lenders' ultimate source of repayment.

Recently, there has been some movement away from such restrictions as a result of objections by investors. The ILPA Guidelines publicly highlighted to investors that lender consent rights would inhibit investors' ability to transfer. Consequently, sub-line terms on investor transfers are evolving. Increasingly, sub-lines allow investor transfers as long as the transfer does not cause a breach of the borrowing base (with the fund able to control whether a breach occurs, because it can repay debt to ensure compliance with borrowing base requirements).

Overcall provisions and concentration limits

LPAs typically include shortfall funding provisions. In the event that an investor defaults or is excused from an investment, the fund may call the shortfall from the other investors. Typically, only investors that have participated in the funding of an investment benefit from the returns that investment may generate. Investors may seek, either in the LPA or in a side letter, to limit the maximum amount they may be required to fund with respect to any investment in excess of the amount that would have been required had all investors participated in the relevant investment. Such overcall limitations can reduce the likelihood of a lender being fully repaid, as the contractual "overcall" protection against one investor failing to fund is weakened.

Concentration limits, which cap an investor's commitment to the fund at a specified percentage of aggregate commitments, similarly serve to restrict the amount of commitments available to repay indebtedness under a sub-line.

Practical considerations

The interests of the lenders are generally aligned with those of the fund with respect to these provisions, so there are no additional side letter points for a fund to negotiate with the sub-line in mind. Overcall and concentration limits will negatively impact a lender's credit analysis. However, lenders may get comfortable if the limitations are not too far-reaching and there is sufficient headroom above which the borrowing base exceeds the size of the facility.

Pay-to-play provisions (and other withdrawal rights)

As a result of regulations governing corrupt practices involving the use of placement agents, many public pension funds and other governmental investors insist on side letter provisions requiring the fund to represent that it has not used a placement agent, or paid any compensation to such investor's employees or related parties, in obtaining such investor's commitment. The consequences of a breach of such representation may include the unilateral right of such investor to withdraw from the fund.

In addition, LPAs often include limited rights for investors subject to the Employee Retirement Income Security Act of 1974 ("ERISA") to withdraw from the fund if continued participation in the fund will give rise to issues for the fund or the investor under ERISA.

Practical considerations

Pay-to-play provisions are generally required by applicable law, so there is limited room for negotiation. However, the potential withdrawal of an included investor will be a major concern for potential lenders, and funds should take potential lender concerns into account in negotiating the side letter. One potential mitigant is to provide that the withdrawal right, or termination of an obligation to fund capital calls, does not apply to capital calls made in respect of debt incurred prior to such withdrawal or termination.

With respect to withdrawing investors, lenders will exclude such investors from the borrowing base. Lenders may also request that an event of default occurs if the aggregate of withdrawn commitments exceeds a threshold percentage of uncalled capital.

MFN provisions

Most-favoured nation ("MFN") provisions may allow investors to elect the benefit of terms negotiated in side letters with other investors (or, often, only other investors with a capital commitment equal to or less than the capital commitment of the electing investor). Only certain side letter provisions will be "MFN-electable". For example, the benefit of investor-specific requirements (such as sovereign immunity or internal policy requirements) cannot generally be elected by other investors that do not have the same requirements.

Practical considerations

If investors elect to take the benefit of side letter terms of other investors under MFN provisions, the adverse consequences for a lender of side letter terms that are detrimental to a financing structure are potentially multiplied. The issue highlights the importance of ensuring that side letters do not contain terms adverse to a lender, as MFN provisions could exacerbate the consequences. The point remains relevant when negotiating a side letter with an investor that will be excluded from the borrowing base, as provisions in such an investor's side letter may be electable by investors that are included in the borrowing base through operation of the MFN. Funds may seek to mitigate this issue by carving out side letter provisions that could impact a financing from the scope of side letter provisions that are available for election under the MFN.

Conclusion

Sponsors and their counsel must consider financing flexibility when negotiating side letters. Investors often request side letter provisions that could reduce a fund's sub-line borrowing base, limit the scope of a fund's financing flexibility, or entirely prevent a fund from raising fund-level financing.

Looking forward, we expect lenders to continue to focus their diligence on the side letter provisions. Anticipating and dealing with potential problems during the side letter negotiation process is critical to ensure that a fund avoids major problems with the financing down the line. Plan ahead for the pitfalls and perils!

* * *

Acknowledgments

The authors acknowledge with thanks the contributions to this chapter of:

Jonathan Adler

Jonathan Adler is a partner in the Funds and Investment Management Group at Debevoise. His practice focuses on advising sponsors of private investment funds, including buyout, growth capital, energy, infrastructure and credit funds.

Pierre Maugüé

Pierre Maugüé is a partner in Debevoise's London office, and a member of the firm's Finance Group. Pierre focuses on acquisition and leveraged buyout financings, structured financings, and fund financings. He brings a global perspective to his work, having lived and worked in Asia, Europe and the United States.

Ramya Tiller

Ramya Tiller is a partner based in Debevoise's New York office, and a member of the firm's Finance Group. She has experience in a broad range of financing transactions, including complex acquisition and leveraged finance transactions, fund finance transactions and other alternative capital transactions.

Alan Davies

Alan Davies is a partner in Debevoise's London office, and a member of the firm's Finance Group. He focuses on acquisition, asset and structured financings, as well as fund-level financing.

Michael P. McGuigan

Michael P. McGuigan is counsel in Debevoise's New York office, and a member of the firm's Finance Group. He advises clients in a broad range of finance transactions, largely in the private equity and project/infrastructure markets.

Felix Paterson

Felix Paterson is an associate in Debevoise's London office. He is a member of the firm's Finance Group, having qualified with the firm in 2014. Felix regularly works with the firm's private equity clients on a variety of financing needs, including fund-level financings.

Thomas Smith
Tel: +44 20 7786 9174 / Email: tsmith@debevoise.com

Thomas Smith is a partner in the London office of Debevoise & Plimpton. Recommended by *Chambers UK*, *The Legal 500 UK* and *IFLR1000*, he acts for borrowers, sponsors, and lenders on a wide range of financing transactions at all levels of the capital structure from fund level to investment level. In fund finance, Tom works on all types of transactions and has particular recent expertise in the growth of ESG-linked financings and NAV financings (across PE, Credit and secondaries markets).

Mr. Smith was named by *The Drawdown* in its list of the most influential experts in fund finance, stating that "Smith has become a key driver in establishing 'what is the market'".

Margaret O'Neill
Tel: +1 212 909 6475 / Email: mmoneill@debevoise.com

Margaret O'Neill is counsel in the New York office of Debevoise, and a member of the firm's Finance Group. Margaret's practice covers a broad range of secured financing transactions. She regularly represents private equity and other investment fund sponsors in connection with subscription credit facilities, co-investment facilities and other fund or management company financings. She also has extensive experience in leveraged acquisition finance.

John W. Rife III
Tel: +44 20 7786 5530 / Email: jrife@debevoise.com

John Rife is a member of Debevoise's Funds and Investment Management Group in the firm's London office. John works with institutional and independent sponsors of buyout, debt, secondaries, real estate, emerging markets, infrastructure and energy funds, as well as funds of funds, in connection with a broad range of matters. These include fund formation and ongoing operational matters, co-investments, carried interest arrangements and internal reorganisations. In addition, John regularly advises sponsors and investors on secondary transactions, including fund restructurings and other sponsor-led liquidity solutions

Mr. Rife was named to *Legal Week*'s Rising Stars in Private Equity list, which represents the finest private practice lawyers under 40 advising in the UK and Europe. He was also named by *Private Equity International* to its Future 40, a list of private equity professionals set to shape the industry over the next decade.

Debevoise & Plimpton LLP
65 Gresham Street, London EC2V 7NQ, United Kingdom
Tel: +44 20 7786 9000 / URL: www.debevoise.com

Fund finance lending: A practical checklist

James Heinicke, David Nelson & Daniel Richards
Ogier

Introduction

In this chapter, we have tried to set out some of the key issues that a lender and its counsel need to consider when entering into a typical subscription or capital call finance transaction.

We have looked at these issues from the perspective of a lender and as its local fund finance counsel. In other words, we have assumed that the fund has been formed in an international fund domicile, such as the Cayman Islands, Luxembourg, Jersey, Guernsey or the British Virgin Islands, and have set out some of the issues that will be relevant for a lender in order to establish that:

- the fund has the capacity to enter into the transaction and perform its obligations thereunder;
- the fund has performed the steps necessary to enable it to enter into the transaction and to ensure the transaction and the relevant finance documents are binding on it;
- the relevant finance documents are enforceable against the fund as a matter of the laws of the jurisdiction in which the fund is formed;
- the transaction and the fund's obligations under the relevant finance documents will not conflict with the fund's constitutional documents or the law of its jurisdiction of formation; and
- all security granted over the assets of the fund in relation to the transaction is first-ranking and properly perfected.

The issues outlined in this chapter are not intended to be exhaustive. In particular, there will be jurisdictional and deal-specific issues that will need to be considered and dealt with. Nor is this a substitute for legal advice. Lenders and funds would be well advised to seek the advice of their legal counsel at the outset of any transaction to ensure these matters are properly addressed on a deal-by-deal basis.

The fund structure

Framework of the fund and its investment structure

Of course, where the fund (and, if applicable, its general partner) is formed will determine: (i) the legislative framework of the relevant jurisdiction that underpins the fund; and (ii) which local fund finance counsel (if any) will need to be involved in the transaction. This will therefore be an important issue for the lender (or its lead counsel) to establish.

However, prior to undertaking a detailed legal analysis of the fund and its constitutional documents, it is important for the lender to understand the fund framework and the way in which the investors' commitments are to be contributed to the fund. The significance of understanding the fund framework is increasingly important, as fund structures become more complex and bespoke. In particular, in recent years we have witnessed a steady increase in deals where closed-ended funds are structured with investors funding a proportion of their commitment with a debt commitment, which, when called, is evidenced in the form of a note or debt advance. This chapter will focus on investors that have capital commitments, but the nature of investors' commitments (be that capital or debt) would need to be determined at the outset of any deal. The fund framework will likely influence a lender's analysis on the scope of the obligor group and the security required in order to ensure there is no leakage of value out of the lender's collateral. Some relevant considerations will be:

- Does the fund have any feeder fund vehicles that invest into the fund? The value of, and potential recourse to, the ultimate investors' uncalled capital commitments needs to be understood and the lender may wish to consider making any such feeder fund an obligor under the facility, and requesting that the feeder fund grants security over the uncalled capital commitments of the investors in the feeder fund and the right the feeder fund has (or the right the feeder fund's general partner has) to make and enforce capital calls on those investors.
- Does the fund have any parallel funds? Generally, parallel funds invest and divest in the same investments as the main fund, at the same time and on the same terms.
- Does the fund have any alternative investment vehicles (**AIVs**)? It may be advantageous for a fund to establish AIVs to hold certain investments for tax, regulatory or other reasons. In such circumstances, a portion of an investor's capital commitment may be invested in the AIV (thereby reducing the investor's capital commitment in the main fund).
- Does the fund have any co-investment or blocker vehicles?

If the fund has parallel funds, AIVs or co-investment vehicles, the lender may wish to treat them in the same way as suggested for feeder funds above. Alternatively, if no parallel funds, AIVs or co-investment vehicles have yet been established, but if the fund has the right to establish them in the future under the fund's constitutional documents, the lender may wish to include a restriction in the subscription line facility agreement prohibiting their establishment unless: (i) the lender provides prior written consent; and/or (ii) those vehicles become obligors and grant capital call and account security upon their establishment.

These points will also be relevant from a capacity and due authorisation perspective, as any such feeder funds or AIVs that are introduced into the obligor group will need to be diligenced by the lender in the same way as the main fund. Whilst it may therefore be possible that the obligor group extends to other entities in the fund group, for simplicity, we have discussed various points in this chapter by reference to the fund (and, where relevant, its general partner) only, on the assumption that the fund (and, if applicable, its general partner) is the only obligor and security provider.

Legal personality of the fund entity

In addition to the fund structure, it is important for the lender to understand the legal personality of the fund and any other relevant entities in the fund group and, if relevant, any regulatory regime applicable to them. The type of legal personality will determine the relevant steps and processes that the fund will need to complete to ensure that it has the capacity and authority to enter into the transaction. For example, some relevant questions will be:

- Is the fund structured as a limited partnership, a company, a limited liability company or some other legal entity?
- Is the fund subject to a regulatory regime and if so, what implications does this have? For example, in a Cayman Islands context, is the fund a "private fund" under Cayman

Islands' Private Funds Law? If it is, evidence of registration of the fund under the Private Funds Law should be obtained.
- Is the fund structured as a regulated investment vehicle? Depending on the type of investment vehicle, certain regulatory restrictions on fund borrowing, or on the ability of the fund to grant security or guarantees, may apply.
- Does the fund fall within the scope of the EU Alternative Investment Fund Managers Directive? In certain circumstances, Luxembourg collective investment undertakings that do not qualify as UCITS (hereinafter referred to as a **Luxembourg AIF**) must appoint an alternative investment fund manager (**AIFM**), and a Luxembourg AIF's financial instruments are required to be held in custody with a Luxembourg-based depositary. As mentioned below, this can have implications for a subscription facility.
- Has the fund been constituted with the ability to create compartments? One Luxembourg fund option available to managers is to utilise a Reserved Alternative Investment Fund (**RAIF**). One of the additional features available to RAIFs is to create compartments, i.e. statutorily ring-fenced pools of assets and liabilities. The lender will wish to diligence the effect of such compartmentalisation on the fund's capacity and authority to enter into the finance documents and the value of related guarantees and security.
- To put legal personality into context – if, for example, the fund is formed as a Cayman Islands exempted limited partnership or a Luxembourg limited partnership, it must have a general partner (and it may actually have a series of intermediate general partners). It is important to understand which entity is the ultimate general partner. The most frequently encountered fund vehicles, Cayman Islands exempted limited partnerships and Luxembourg special limited partnerships (**SCSp**) do not have separate legal personality – they both enter into documents through their general partner (or, in relation to an SCSp, more rarely through the agency of any manager to which such power has been delegated), which undertakes the conduct of the fund's business and, as a general partner, has unlimited liability such that, in the event that the assets of the fund are insufficient, the general partner is liable for all of the debts and obligations of the fund.

Any delegated authority or investment committee

The type of legal personality of the fund, and the extent of any delegated authorities, will, in its relevant jurisdiction, largely dictate the steps that the fund is required to take to ensure it has capacity to enter into, and has properly approved and authorised its entry into, the transaction. However, the lender will need to be aware of other points that may influence this. Some relevant points include:
- Has the fund established an investment committee that needs to provide consent to the transaction? Some funds establish committees that, in addition to usual board/management approval, are required to approve certain business activities of the fund. Sometimes this may include incurring indebtedness (particularly incurring indebtedness above or outside certain agreed parameters set out in the fund's constitutional documents).
- Is there an investment or portfolio management agreement or investment advisory agreement in place? If there is, has the ability to issue capital calls on behalf of the fund been delegated to the investment manager, the AIFM or the investment advisor? If so, any relevant approvals should be obtained from the investment manager, the AIFM or the investment advisor to ensure the transaction is duly authorised, and consideration may also need to be given as to whether the investment manager, the AIFM or the investment advisor ought to be party to the facility agreement and/or grant security over its right, title and interest to issue capital calls to the fund's investors.

- Since a Luxembourg AIF's financial instruments must be held in custody with a Luxembourg-based depositary, consideration ought to be given as to whether any approval of the depositary is required. The depositary agreement may require that the fund notify or obtain approval from the depositary in order for the fund to enter into the finance documents.

Due diligence

As a general point, a significant part of a lender's due diligence analysis will likely be focused on an assessment of the identity and credit quality of each investor in the fund. This will allow the lender to establish which investors will be included in the borrowing base calculation and then set the borrowing base at the appropriate level.[1]

However, to ensure that the financing and the fund's obligations under the relevant finance documents will not conflict with the law of its jurisdiction of formation or, more pertinently, with the constitutional documents of the fund and (if any) its general partner, a detailed documentation review and analysis should be undertaken. We set out below some of the key documentary due diligence points a lender and its counsel should consider when reviewing a limited partnership agreement, where the fund is a limited partnership (**LPA**), investor subscription documents and related side letters.

Deconstructing the LPA

Some key points a lender should consider in the LPA in order to determine whether the proposed subscription financing transaction does not conflict with (or, indeed, is not prejudiced by) the terms thereof, are:

Is borrowing/indebtedness permitted?

The LPA should specifically permit the fund to incur indebtedness (be that borrowing or guaranteeing obligations of an affiliate, should the financing structure require), and any limitations on the purpose, amount or term of such indebtedness should be noted. The lender will need to be aware of any such limitations when agreeing the parameters of these in the facility agreement.

What are the mechanics for capital call notices?

The provisions setting out how capital can be called (including the notice provisions and time frame for payment by investors) and the purpose for which the general partner is permitted to issue capital call notices to the investors need to be understood: specifically, whether the LPA permits capital call notices to be issued in order to repay principal debt, interest accrued thereon and costs related thereto is a relevant consideration, as is whether the LPA makes it clear how the total amount specified in a capital call notice issued in order to fund the repayment of indebtedness would be allocated among the investors.

Is the fund permitted to grant security over the investors' uncalled capital commitments, the right to make and enforce capital calls and its assets generally?

It should be checked that under the LPA, the fund is permitted to grant security over these assets. If the LPA (or any side letter (see below)) designates any investor as a confidential investor, whose identity cannot be disclosed or in relation to whom capital call rights cannot be assigned, these investors will likely be excluded from the borrowing base.

In certain circumstances, in particular for tax, regulatory or ERISA reasons, a feeder fund may be prohibited from guaranteeing and directly granting security to a lender to support the main fund's obligations under a subscription facility. In such circumstances, a cascading pledge, where the feeder fund grants security over its investors' uncalled capital commitments to the fund borrower, which in turn grants security to the lender over its rights under the security granted to it by the feeder fund (in addition to the fund borrower granting security over its rights to receive and call for the uncalled capital commitments of its investors, including the feeder fund), may have to be considered and pledge agreements drafted accordingly.

The LPA should also be checked to establish whether the LPA permits (or at least does not prohibit and permits by way of the general powers) the limited partners paying capital contributions into a specific bank account over which the lender under the finance documents takes a security interest.

What is the term of the fund?

This should be considered in light of the proposed maturity date of the subscription facility. Given that, under the LPA, the fund will be dissolved at the end of its term, the lender should ensure that the maturity date of their subscription facility falls within the term of the fund.

In what circumstances may the fund be terminated and dissolved prior to the end of the term?

The applicable law of the relevant jurisdiction in which the fund is formed will likely set out how a fund can be terminated and the circumstances that result in such termination. For example, in the context of a Cayman Islands exempted limited partnership, Cayman Islands law states that a fund may be voluntarily wound up at the time or on the occurrence of the events specified in the LPA, or otherwise (unless otherwise specified in the LPA) upon the passing of a resolution by all of the general partners of the fund and not less than two-thirds of its limited partners. Similarly, Luxembourg limited partnerships can be liquidated if so resolved by limited partners representing three-quarters of the partnership's interests, unless otherwise provided in the LPA. The LPA may modify the starting position at law (to the extent permitted in the relevant jurisdiction) and will usually also set out other additional early termination events. The LPA will typically provide a contractual "waterfall" for distribution of the fund's assets upon its liquidation, and it should be established whether non-affiliated creditors of the fund are at the top of this waterfall.

What is the investment/commitment period and in what circumstances may it be suspended or terminated?

The right of the general partner to call capital from investors will likely be restricted upon expiry, suspension or termination of the investment/commitment period. Examples of potential suspension or termination events within an LPA are: expiry of the investment/commitment period; the occurrence of a key person event; upon the affirmative vote of a majority of investors; and removal of the general partner for cause. It should be established whether, notwithstanding such restrictions, capital may still be called from investors after suspension or termination of the investment/commitment period in order to fund repayment of the principal outstanding under the subscription facility and related accrued interest and costs.

Has each investor agreed that it will honour capital calls without deduction, set-off, counterclaim or defence?

A lender will want to ensure that each investor's payment obligations to fund capital calls are not capable of being reduced or extinguished by any claim that the investor has against the fund and/or the general partner. If this is not addressed in the LPA, such waivers could instead be provided in investor consent letters. In respect of funds formed in jurisdictions (such as the Cayman Islands) that require notice of security over capital call rights to be delivered to investors in order to fix the priority of such security, such notice will prevent set-offs arising after the date of service of the notice (although it will not affect any potential set-offs that might have arisen prior to the date of service of the notice). Luxembourg pledge agreements will include an acknowledgment of the lender's reliance on such waivers in the LPA (or other fund documents).

Are there overcall provisions in the LPA for any defaulting investor or excused investor?

These are provisions that mean that if an investor has defaulted or is excused from making a capital contribution to fund certain investments, the fund is permitted to call capital from the non-defaulting/non-excused investors up to the amount of such non-defaulting/non-excused investors' unfunded capital commitments. Often, the overcall obligations of other investors are capped under the LPA. For example, they may be limited to the lesser of the relevant investor's unfunded capital commitments and a certain percentage of its total capital contribution. Any such limitation should be noted. It is usual for any defaulting investors to be excluded from the borrowing base.

The excuse provisions in the LPA should be checked to understand whether the capital commitment of an investor that is excused or opts out from making a capital contribution to fund a certain investment would remain unaffected (and so available) for the purposes of repayment of the principal outstanding under the subscription facility and related accrued interest and costs.

Recallable distributions

It should be ascertained whether, under the LPA, the general partner has the ability to "recall" distributions that have been made to investors and, if it does, what the limitations and terms of the recall are. The relevant considerations for a lender are likely to be: whether these distributed and recallable amounts increase the amount of the unused capital commitment of the relevant investor; and whether these distributed and recallable amounts will be available for recall to allow the fund to repay principal, accrued interest and other costs in respect of the subscription facility (including in circumstances where the investment/commitment period has been suspended or terminated). If such distributed and recallable amounts are not so available, a lender may consider excluding these amounts from the borrowing base.

Transfer provisions – limited partners and general partner

The transfer provisions in the LPA should be reviewed to understand in what circumstances an investor may transfer its interest in the fund, grant security over its interest in the fund or withdraw as a limited partner in the fund and, for example, whether prior consent of the general partner is required. As noted above, the identity of the investors in the fund will be an important consideration for a lender in its credit evaluation and in setting the borrowing base level. Changes to the identity of a limited partner may also have know-your-customer and compliance issues for a lender.

The circumstances in which a general partner may transfer ("transfer" is usually a defined term within an LPA and it is common for this to be widely defined to include, amongst other things, the granting of a security interest over the general partner's interest in the fund) its general partner interest in the fund (and whether this needs a certain percentage of investors to give prior consent) or in which the general partner may be removed or replaced (with or without cause) should also be checked. The identity of the general partner will also likely be important to the lender and any change, unless approved by the lender, is likely to trigger an event of default under the subscription facility.

Where these events will cause the investment/commitment period to be suspended or terminated, as mentioned above, it should be established whether capital calls may still be made to repay principal, accrued interest and costs of the subscription facility during such suspension or after such termination (as the case may be).

Are there any key person events under the LPA?

The LPA may name certain key persons who must dedicate a certain amount of their time to the fund during the investment period and/or term of the fund. If any such specified key persons fail to do so, this may constitute a "key person event" under the LPA. The occurrence of a key person event may cause the investment/commitment period to be suspended or terminated. If this is the case, it should be checked whether capital calls may still be made to repay principal, accrued interest and costs of the subscription line facility during such suspension or after such termination (as the case may be).

No third-party beneficiaries/third-party rights provisions

Any "no third-party beneficiaries" or "third-party rights" clauses ought to be checked to ensure that these provisions are consistent with, and do not purport to restrict, the fund and the general partner from granting security over the capital call rights or the lender's reliance on limited partner waivers of any defence, set-off or counterclaim to capital calls. Under the laws of some international fund jurisdictions (such as the Cayman Islands), it is also possible to confer third-party rights on a person who is not party to a contract in order for that person to enforce contractual rights as if it had been party to the contract, i.e. in these jurisdictions it is possible that an LPA could be drafted in a way that allows a lender to directly enforce LPA capital call rights against investors in the same manner as if the lender had been party to the LPA.

Side letters

The terms of any side letters should be reviewed to confirm the absence of provisions that adversely affect any of the findings arising from the LPA due diligence review or any factors that would otherwise conflict with the obligations of the fund or that could potentially prejudice the rights of the lender under the subscription facility or its related security.

For example, we have seen a number of instances where side letters have expressly prohibited the fund from granting a security interest over a particular investor's uncalled capital commitment.

Some additional points to be considered when reviewing side letters are:

- Note any most-favoured nation (**MFN**) provisions. These provisions give an investor (the "subject investor") the right to select that it will get the benefit of provisions that another investor has the benefit of, and that are on better terms than the terms that would otherwise apply to the subject investor. There are sometimes parameters to the exercise by the subject investor of its MFN right. For example, it may need to exercise its MFN right within a certain time period, or the subject investor's MFN right may require it to accept a group of provisions that another investor has the benefit of relating to a certain issue, and prevent the subject investor from "cherry-picking" only certain of those provisions.
- Note any provisions that modify the transfer provisions contained in the LPA.
- Note any confidentiality/confidential investor provisions.
- Note any sovereign immunity provisions. It is not unusual for institutional investors to be connected to the state (for example, public body pension funds and sovereign

wealth funds may make up part of the investor base in a fund). These entities may have sovereign immunity protection by nature of their connection with the state, under certain jurisdictions. The relevant investor may wish to reserve these sovereign immunity protections in a side letter, in line with its internal investment policy or other considerations. The impact of any sovereign immunity on the requirement for the relevant investor to comply with capital calls should be considered.

Security

Another important element that a lender and its local fund finance counsel need to consider when entering into a fund finance transaction relates to the security package. Generally, subscription facilities are secured against the uncalled capital commitments of the investors in the fund, including: (i) the right to make capital calls on investors in respect of their uncalled capital commitments, together with rights to enforce payments of them; and (ii) the right to receive the proceeds of such capital calls. It will generally also include security over the bank account into which investors are required to deposit their capital contributions. The type of security to be created over the capital commitments will be a factor of the legal regime in the jurisdiction of formation of the fund and the governing law of the relevant security document.

For example, in the case of a Cayman Islands exempted limited partnership, where the security is governed by the laws of the Cayman Islands, the security over the right to make capital calls and the right to receive proceeds of capital contributions will technically be granted by way of an assignment by way of security by the fund (acting through its general partner) of those rights as they arise under the fund's Cayman Islands law-governed LPA and any applicable investor subscription documents. For Luxembourg funds the security package is the same, albeit that its legal characterisation is that of a "pledge" rather than an assignment by way of security.

<u>Prior security and/or existing indebtedness within the fund structure</u>

It will be important for the lender to establish whether there is any existing security over the capital call rights and the capital call account they intend to take security over. Given the size of some fund structures, it is not uncommon for certain assets within the fund structure to be subject to existing security in favour of third parties. Clearly to the extent that there is any existing security, this will need to be considered to determine whether it will prejudice the lender's position. The following ought to be considered:

- Can any security or lien searches be carried out to determine the extent of any existing security? For example, in the Cayman Islands, there is no public registration of security interests (other than in respect of security over certain assets such as real estate, aircraft and ships), but the Register of Mortgages and Charges of the fund's general partner (if the general partner is a Cayman Islands company) should be obtained and inspected to see whether it contains any details of any prior security interests that have been granted by the fund over its assets (although this will not be conclusive evidence of the granting of any security, since the entry in the Register of Mortgages and Charges is an internal register only of the Cayman Islands company and making an entry in it does not affect validity or priority of the security). Similarly, in Luxembourg, except with respect to real estate, there is also no publicly available record of pledges or other security interests granted by a Luxembourg entity.
- To the extent that there is any prior security (over any assets), those security documents ought to be reviewed to determine the scope of the security and any applicable negative

pledges contained within the security documents (and whether those negative pledges just pertain to the assets secured under that security document or to all the assets of the fund).
- To the extent that the fund has borrowed from any of the fund's investors, the fund's obligation to repay any such investor loans ought to be contractually subordinated to the debt owed to the fund finance lender. In addition, if the fund is a Luxembourg AIF, its financial instruments must be held in custody with a Luxembourg-based depositary. A release from the depositary may be required in circumstances where the terms of the depositary agreement provide the depositary with a security interest over the bank account into which investors' capital commitments are deposited.
- If there is any existing financing to an investment manager of the fund, the investment manager may have granted security over its right to receive its management fee. Often, the terms of a subscription facility agreement will seek to subordinate payment of any management fee to the manager following the occurrence of an event of default under the subscription facility. This may be incompatible with any such existing financing to the investment manager.
- Have any investors granted security over their limited partnership interests in the fund? If the fund is formed as a Cayman Islands exempted limited partnership, this ought to be established by reviewing the Register of Security Interests of the fund. If so, the implications of such security would need to be considered. There is no equivalent Register of Security Interests for Luxembourg funds, but the fund would be expected to reference in its internal, limited partner register, any pledge of limited partnership interests that has been notified to it.

Priority/perfection of security

A fund finance lender will want to ensure that if the fund defaults on any of its obligations under the facility agreement or becomes insolvent, the lender's security interests will constitute first-ranking and enforceable security interests over the relevant assets of the fund, such that the lender could enforce its security and apply the enforcement proceeds in satisfaction of the obligations that the fund owes to the lender, in priority to the fund's other creditors.

In order to ensure this, the lender should consider at the outset how its collateral is perfected and how it ensures that its rights to the collateral have priority over third parties. The relevant steps that need to be taken will largely depend upon the jurisdiction of formation of the fund (and its general partner), the location of the collateral, and the nature of the collateral (as mentioned above, for a subscription facility the collateral will usually be security over the uncalled capital commitments of investors and security over the bank account into which the capital commitments are deposited). Some issues the lender should consider are:
- Are any security registrations required in the jurisdiction in which the fund or its general partner are formed or in the jurisdiction that governs the finance documents (either on a public register or on internal registers)?
- If security registrations are needed, when should the registrations be made and are there any time periods within which the registrations need to be made?
- What other perfection or priority steps need to be completed?
- What are the implications and risks to the lender of not making the security registrations and/or taking the other perfection or priority steps?
- How can the lender ensure that its security ranks in priority to other creditors of the fund?
- Does notice of the security over the uncalled capital commitments need to be given to the investors for perfection or priority purposes? If notice does need to be given, consider:
  - What form does the notice need to take?
  - When does the notice need to be given?

- How is notice to be delivered (for example, is there any procedure for delivery that must be followed under the fund's constitutional documents)?
- Are any acknowledgments required from the investors?
- What evidence of delivery of the notices should be obtained from the fund?

Enforcement of security

Another crucial point for fund finance lenders is to know how the security interests over the uncalled capital commitments of investors (and the fund's bank accounts) will be enforced upon the occurrence of an event of default under the facility agreement, and in particular, on the fund's and/or general partner's insolvency. Key points to consider will be:
- Will any power of attorney issued in favour of a lender/security agent to issue capital calls survive the fund's/general partner's insolvency?
- Can the lender/security agent exercise any remedies by stepping into the shoes of the fund/general partner and call capital from all investors?
- Should the capital calls made on enforcement be carried out on a *pro rata* basis, pursuant to the provisions of the fund's constitutional documents and the relevant subscription documents, taking into account any existing investor excuse rights under the LPA?

Document execution

Proper execution of the relevant finance documents is also a key component to ensure that the finance documents are enforceable against the fund and/or its general partner. Generally, the lender's lead counsel will be responsible for ensuring that the finance documents are enforceable as a matter of the laws that govern them (unless, in the case of any security documents, these are governed by the law of the jurisdiction of formation of the fund, in which case the lender's local counsel will undertake this task with respect to those security documents). Local counsel input will be needed to ensure that the finance documents are compatible with the laws of the jurisdiction of formation of the fund. The lender's local counsel will also check that the documents have been executed in accordance with the requirements of the jurisdiction in which the fund is formed, the constitutional documents of the fund and the relevant corporate authorisations. The following ought to be considered:
- Certain jurisdictions may have jurisdiction-specific requirements and formalities for execution. Is there any particular form that the execution blocks need to take? Are there any witnessing and/or notarisation requirements?
- Who is signing on behalf of the fund and/or general partner?
- Have the responsible officers that are signing on behalf of the fund and/or general partner been authorised in corporate authorities of the general partner?
- Have such corporate authorisations been validly passed?
- If the investment manager, the AIFM or the investment advisor is signing on behalf of the fund and/or general partner, is such delegation valid?
- Is any stamp duty or other tax or fee payable under the laws of the jurisdiction in which the fund is formed?

Conclusion

The above outlines some of the structural, legal and practical considerations that lenders and their counsel ought to consider when advising on a subscription facility. As we have mentioned, this is by no means an exhaustive list and there will be many deal-specific issues that arise that will need to be considered on a case-by-case basis. However, the content in this chapter illustrates the myriad of issues that lenders (and their local counsel) need to think about when structuring and documenting a subscription facility in order to ensure that the lender's position is protected.

* * *

Endnote

1. The "borrowing base" broadly caps the amount that may be outstanding under the subscription line facility at any time (together with hedging exposure and non-cash-backed letters of credit) to the lesser of: (a) the available commitments under the facility; and (b) the aggregate of the uncalled capital commitments of each eligible investor as multiplied by a specified advance rate that is attributed to that investor, based on its credit quality. Only "eligible" investors to which the lender attributes a certain credit score will be included in the borrowing base calculations, with other investors in the fund being "excluded" investors, whose capital commitments do not form part of the borrowing base, or only being included (and then at a lower advance rate) if they meet certain additional information and due diligence requirements.

James Heinicke
Tel: +1 345 815 1768 / Email: james.heinicke@ogier.com

James is a partner in Ogier's banking and finance team in the Cayman Islands and is the head of Ogier's Fund Finance Practice.

James has significant experience advising on a wide range of banking, finance and corporate transactions. He regularly advises both lenders and sponsors on all types of fund finance transactions and has extensive experience advising on subscription and capital call financings, fund of fund facilities, NAV and hybrid facilities and GP credit lines.

David Nelson
Tel: +852 3656 6018 / Email: david.nelson@ogier.com

David is a partner in Ogier's banking and finance team in Asia, based in Hong Kong. He has extensive experience advising on the BVI and Cayman Islands law aspects of a broad range of debt financing transactions, including leveraged and acquisition finance, fund finance, margin lending, structured finance, real estate finance, and secured and unsecured general corporate lending.

Prior to commencing his practice as a BVI and Cayman Islands lawyer, David worked for a "magic circle" law firm in Hong Kong. There, he advised on several firsts in the Asia fund finance market, including one of the first umbrella facilities for an Asia-based fund manager and one of the first syndicated capital call facilities in Asia.

Daniel Richards
Tel: +352 2712 2011 / Email: daniel.richards@ogier.com

Daniel is a Luxembourg Advocate, Jersey Advocate and English Solicitor. Daniel co-founded Ogier's Luxembourg office in 2012, leading Ogier's Luxembourg finance and private equity teams, prior to becoming practice partner in 2018–2022. He has extensive experience in all aspects of international investment structuring and related financing in Luxembourg, Jersey and the UK.

Having read law at the University of Cambridge, Daniel qualified as an English Solicitor in 1999, practising at Hogan Lovells' City of London office between 1997–2002.

Since moving to Jersey in 2002 and to Luxembourg in 2012, Daniel has acted for leading banks and non-bank lenders to funds as well as fund managers in relation to the financing, establishment and portfolio investment, by regulated and non-regulated funds, securitisation and portfolio acquisition vehicles across the broad range of alternative asset classes, including private equity, real estate, venture capital, infrastructure, infrastructure finance, credit and special opportunities.

Ogier
89 Nexus Way, Camana Bay, Grand Cayman KY1-9009, Cayman Islands
Tel: +1 345 949 9876 / Fax: +1 345 949 9877 / URL: www.ogier.com

Assessing lender risk in fund finance markets

Robin Smith, Alistair Russell & Holly Brown
Carey Olsen Jersey LLP

Risk analysis in an evolving market

Despite being a relatively long-standing lending product, there have been limited public payment defaults by funds in the fund finance space. Consequently, the market has legitimately considered this to be a safe product for lenders and encouraged more market actors to participate. Whilst the market has weathered, even prospered, in the face of certain challenges (such as the 2008 global financial crisis), there are a new set of challenges ahead. The ongoing impact of COVID and the war in Ukraine have caused aftershocks in the wider macroeconomic environment, and the fund finance market is not immune to these wider macroeconomic changes and the uncertainties they create. With these changes in mind, lenders should remain alert to their possible (and changing) exposure.[1]

In 2022, the market has seen a significant increase in the use of NAV facilities. Market changes have also seen an increase in the use of other alternative lending structures, for example, hybrid facilities. There has also been an increase in the number of GP facilities and loans made to single LP funds.

The market has seen global interest rates rise rapidly throughout 2022 and although this has resulted in widening margins, which is clearly a plus for lenders, the higher cost of borrowing could eventually depress utilisations. In that case, lenders may seek to increase commitment fees to make up for the unused portions and in a market that is likely to have less overall liquidity in the short term, ensuring balance sheets are well used will be important.

Given the overall market turbulence, there is an increased focus on mitigating risk and now is a good time for lenders to conduct their gap analysis and to protect against potential future risks in an evolving market. We examine below some of the key and emerging risks that lenders should be aware of and discuss strategies to manage and mitigate these risks.

Our expertise is in advising lenders in relation to funds established in our key jurisdictions, principally the Cayman Islands, Guernsey and Jersey, although we also see activity in the British Virgin Islands and Bermuda. The market in each of these jurisdictions is broad and we see all types of alternative asset classes. The areas of risk that we focus on below relate to:
- complex fund structures, primarily involving fund partnerships; and
- market risk.

Complex fund structures

Typical structures in our jurisdictions

In Jersey and Guernsey, funds are commonly established as either corporate vehicles/corporate group structures (using companies limited by shares, protected cell companies or incorporated cell companies) or, more frequently, limited partnerships with a corporate general partner, often with an interposed GPLP between corporate general partner and the fund limited partner (referred to as the "private equity model", "layering", or "stacking"). To this basic framework is added any number of entities from a variety of jurisdictions: (i) fund asset-holding structures; (ii) carried interest and fee-sharing structures; (iii) feeder funds; and (iv) co-investment and other managed entity arrangements, each of which may guarantee and cross-collateralise lending.

In the Cayman Islands, the exempted limited partnership is the most common form of entity used to establish closed-ended funds, although funds may also be formed as exempted limited companies or limited liability companies.

In the British Virgin Islands, closed-ended funds are most commonly structured as limited partnerships. Less common, but nevertheless possible, funds may be structured as British Virgin Islands business companies.

Feeder vehicles

Investors, for example, US investors, for ERISA purposes, will often invest in a feeder vehicle, which, in turn, invests in a master fund.

The feeder fund may present a greater degree of risk to a lender, as the lender will be a further step removed from the ultimate investors and source of funds for repayment of borrowings, and will need to rely on a chain of drawdowns (both at the master fund level and subsequently at the feeder fund level) in order for capital commitments to be paid down into the master fund borrower. To mitigate this risk, lenders will typically seek to join the feeder vehicle as a party to the finance documents, and take security over the uncalled commitments in the feeder vehicle in addition to that of the main fund, although this is not always permitted under the constitutional documents.

Where this type of security is not possible, either due to restrictions in the security regimes in certain jurisdictions or, if the constitutional documents of the feeder vehicle contain limitations as to borrowing or guaranteeing, preventing the feeder from providing direct security, then the lender may be able to take cascading security as an alternative. Cascading security is where the feeder vehicle grants security over its uncalled commitments to the main fund and, in turn, the main fund grants security over its rights in the feeder vehicle security agreement to the lender (the terms of which would include an appropriate power of attorney and step-in rights).

Legal perspective

Capacity and authority

Complex cross-jurisdictional fund structures can present a number of capacity issues that need to be fully understood in each jurisdiction. This is most evident where there are layered or stacked general partner or manager arrangements across jurisdictions, and it is crucial that the correct capacities are tracked through the relevant transaction documents. In the fund documents, the power to issue drawdown notices to limited partners is almost invariably vested in the manager or general partner on behalf of the fund vehicle, but it should also be considered whether either entity holds any power or right in its own capacity.

Where the general partner delegates any of its powers relating to the calling of capital or the enforcement of the same to a manager, the security should fully reflect that chain of authority and capture both the rights of the general partner in the partnership agreement and also any such rights delegated to the manager pursuant to any management agreement. Failure to do so may cause step-in rights to be ineffective on enforcement.

Similarly, it is surprising how often we come across bank account mandates that do not align with the structure as initially presented to the lending bank, or that do not reflect the correct chain of authority or rights in respect of the monies in the account. In these instances, either the mandate or security agreement should be amended to ensure that the named account holder is the grantor of the account security, and that both reflect the chain of authority for each of the grantor's capacities.

Cross-jurisdictional funds

Where a combination of jurisdictions are involved in a fund structure, there is an added level of complexity in determining the appropriate governing law for the security package, as the contractual arrangements may well be governed by a mixture of regimes.

We are often asked to advise on the most appropriate governing law for this security, particularly where the finance documents are governed by, for example, English law or New York law, and the general partner or the manager is a Jersey or Cayman Islands entity.

In these circumstances, from a Jersey and Guernsey law perspective, we are likely to advise that specific local law security is taken over contractual arrangements where they are governed by such laws. Usually, such structures also have a general partner or manager in Jersey or Guernsey. An added complexity arises where there is a general partner resident in a different jurisdiction to the governing law of the limited partnership agreement. In such case, generally, we would expect the governing law of the security over the capital call rights to follow the governing law of the limited partnership agreement, but careful analysis is required.

In contrast, in the Cayman Islands, it is not particularly common as a matter of market practice to take Cayman Islands security simply because the fund documents are governed by the law of the Cayman Islands or if the general partner or manager is formed within the jurisdiction.

Similar issues may need to be considered in light of the *situs* of the collateral involved. For example, some security regimes (such as Jersey) provide that security must be taken in the jurisdiction where the asset has its *situs*. Therefore, where a Jersey bank account is to be secured, a Jersey security interest will need to be obtained over that account, irrespective of the existence of any foreign law debenture.

Again, in contrast, the Cayman Islands do not generally have any mandatory provisions of law that would require Cayman Islands security be taken over assets with their *situs* within the jurisdiction, and courts will generally respect and give effect to valid foreign law security. However, it is worth noting that, notwithstanding the governing law of the security taken, there are a number of standard provisions that should invariably be included within Cayman Islands security documents that are helpful to lenders and are, in our experience, usually absent from foreign law security documents. It is also of integral importance to ensure that, no matter what the governing law of the security itself may be, any security taken properly reflects the perfection requirements applicable to the Cayman *situs* property.

Overall, we would also note that there is a relatively clear difference in practice between markets; the US market would tend to use US law security over capital call rights where local law permits, whereas the European market, and in particular in the UK, will largely see taking local law security as the preferred approach even where English law security is considered sufficient under local law. The former US-style approach is not possible in respect of security over Guernsey or Jersey law-governed capital call rights unless the security agreement complies with all local law requirements and the relevant provisions are governed by local law. It is usually much more efficient to start with a local law document.

Contractual matrix

As noted above, a careful review of the full contractual matrix is vital in ascertaining the extent of the parties' capacities, rights and powers. In time-limited situations or repeat transactions, there may be pressure from parties to undertake a limited review of documents in an attempt to shorten the transaction time and lower the legal spend. This is likely to be a false economy, as the review may identify gaps and issues that, left unchecked, could have expensive consequences.

For example, investors will regularly seek to effect changes to the terms of the partnership/constitutive documents to meet their requirements, whether by way of direct amendment to the documents themselves, or by way of side letter. If a complete and timely review is not conducted, relevant contractual provisions may be missed or discovered too late in the process. Indeed, what may seem a minor amendment from the perspective of an investor or a fund (such as restrictions on the power of attorney or additional procedural hurdles for the delivery of drawdown notices) could, for a lender, result in costly consequences; for example, by defeating an integral aspect of the security package or rendering it difficult or impractical to enforce the underlying commitments.

Any introduction of conditionality to an investor's obligation to fund a drawdown may put the ability to draw the capital at risk. If lenders require the full pack of fund documents at an earlier stage, before they are executed, and allow due time for these to be reviewed, this situation can largely be avoided. Further, if engaged early enough during the period when the fund is negotiating its constitutive documents and/or side letters with cornerstone investors, lender counsel can often add value by suggesting minor clarifications and amendments to the drafting, which could avoid the need for future complex drafting in the facility, or worse lending terms for the fund. There has been a notable shift in the market as both borrowers and lenders appreciate the value in this type of due diligence, as well as the potential exposure where it is not undertaken.

Technological assistance

When used in conjunction with a traditional review, technology can be a useful aid to reduce document review times and ensure there are no gaps or new contractual limitations introduced.

As technology develops, contract mapping, legal automation and smart contracts will likely become more widely adopted in legal and banking practice. There are numerous blockchain initiatives in the banking and finance space, which shows that contracting by smart contract is increasingly seen as a credible means of contracting, for example, blockchain solutions for standardised contracts such as ISDA[2] and discussion around the digital future for syndicated loans.[3]

In parallel fund arrangements, there are often either prohibitions or intra-fund limits in the parallel investment agreements or co-investment agreements, making guarantees subject to either a specific limit (being the lower of a percentage of the fund commitment or the aggregate of undrawn commitments) and/or requiring they be given in accordance with the partnership proportion (often linked to the capital commitments in each fund), effectively capping the ability of each parallel fund to guarantee the liabilities of the other. Practically, this means: (i) there will need to be amendments to the standard facility agreement drafting; and (ii) it is hard, or even impossible, for a lender to adequately monitor whether such caps have been breached, particularly as committed levels in parallel funds may shift as a result of defaulting or excused investors or due to secondary movements where the transferee prefers to be an investor in the other parallel fund. Not only does this highlight the importance of robust information covenants within facility agreements and/or third-party security documents, but also the importance of relationships with fund administrators who will be in possession of key information, in the event that step-in rights are exercised following a default.

The biggest leaps in technology for the fund finance market have likely been in the fund administration space. This could assist:
(i) before a facility is put in place, where automation should provide for easier lender due diligence;
(ii) if conditions and data contained in loan agreements are captured and monitored from the moment the facility is in place on an ongoing basis and generating an automatic notification if certain thresholds are reached or in relation to certain breaches, allowing for the constant monitoring of caps and covenants; and
(iii) giving lenders "live" access on a blockchain platform to account information for all accounts (even those not held with them) and if automated payments were set up on certain trigger events (e.g. payments in and out).

Waiver of commitments

Though clearly a notably rare event, and indeed, one that many lenders would perhaps see as a diligence matter, recent cases have demonstrated that it is perhaps worth considering how to prevent or protect against the unilateral waiver or release of investor commitments by a fund, notwithstanding that it may be a breach of the finance documents to do so.

Some jurisdictions have enacted specific statutory provisions to mitigate the risk of waiver in certain circumstances by enabling lenders to enforce the original fund obligations directly against the investors. While in the Cayman Islands this statutory protection has been introduced with respect to limited liability companies, it is not something that applies to exempted companies or exempted limited partnerships, which represent the majority of Cayman Islands funds. Similarly, under Jersey or Guernsey law, in the absence of express statutory provisions regulating lending to fund vehicles, lenders would only have access to more practical solutions (such as notifying the investors about the granting of security to the lenders) and traditional remedies.

Market practice has developed to mitigate such risks through practical means by ensuring that borrowers give their investors notice of the security being granted as well as relevant covenants in the facility agreement, including the usual covenant prohibitions on the general partner as manager from cancelling or waiving investor commitments. Jersey practice remains pragmatic and does not usually require a signed acknowledgment of the notice to be provided by each investor (although this would be preferred), but lenders are advised to request and obtain evidence of notice being given to investors. Notice can be given: (a) in the traditional manner by hard copy; (b) by uploading the notice in investor portals; or (c) by emailing the investor. If notice is given using method (b), we advise lenders to request evidence that each investor has accessed and reviewed the notice if uploaded to an investor portal (wherever possible).

These steps are not required under statute but are practical steps to evidence that actual notice of the security has been given to investors, and may go some way to mitigate certain risks or enforcement.

Remedies: The principal remedy for balance-sheet-solvent structures is to call an event of default, accelerate the debt and enforce the transaction security. However, for insolvent structures or where the default prompts insolvency, the remedies include:
(i) redress under the relevant statutory framework relevant to fraud and solvency generally and, in respect of corporate entities, transactions at an undervalue and fraudulent trading;

(ii) equitable remedies including claims against the management and dishonest assistance;
(iii) tortious remedies including inducing a breach of contract and lawful or unlawful means of conspiracy; and
(iv) customary law remedies in relation to fraud and, particularly, defrauding creditors.

These are explored in greater detail in respect of funds domiciled in the Cayman Islands in the article by Alistair Russell, Richard Munden and Ardil Salem entitled: *"Fund finance and releases of investor commitments: How can lenders protect themselves?"*[4]

In Jersey, the relevant factual matrix will dictate the most appropriate course of action for the lender and clarify why the manager agreed to the waiver in the first place, but the starting point will usually be to consider what consideration (monetary or otherwise) the manager received in return for granting the waiver.

In our view, fund documents should ideally be drafted so as to provide lenders with a direct contractual right against investors preventing such a waiver, or release without lender consent. While this may not be practicable in many cases, efforts to move the market in this direction for certain types of fund would no doubt be welcomed by lenders. Notably, this is a right they are afforded statutorily in certain jurisdictions (for example, in the State of Delaware).

Where such a right is not granted (for instance, because the fund documents have already been executed), we would recommend that lenders ensure that the usual contractual restrictions on the fund's ability to waive or release the commitments are clearly communicated to the investors. This may help a lender seek a variety of remedies in the event of an unauthorised waiver, given that many such remedies will involve demonstrating such level of dishonesty or knowledge on the part of such investors.

There is also an added protection in the form of a statutory clawback in the Limited Partnerships (Jersey) Law 1994, which provides that, for a period of six months from the date of receipt, a limited partner is liable to repay (in whole or part) a payment it received representing a turn of its contribution to the partnership with interest to the extent necessary to discharge a debt or obligation of the limited partnership incurred during the period that the contribution represented an asset of the limited partnership.

A waiver would probably hold if an investor would not reasonably be expected to know that it was given without lender consent or in breach of the fund's obligations and such investor had provided consideration or altered its position in reliance on the waiver. For these reasons, it is worthwhile that a lender seeks to protect its position in this regard.

Market risk

As lawyers, we generally leave technical market analysis to those better qualified; however, in the course of our work, certain trends do become apparent that are of note in the context of risk. We look at four of those trends below, being:
- competition in the market;
- concentration risk;
- liquidity in the market; and
- the impact of environmental, social and governance (ESG) factors on credit risk.

Competition in the market

Recent years have seen an appreciable increase in the number of lenders and borrowers in the fund finance space, a fact echoed by many advisors and market participants.

The fund finance market has benefitted from lower margins, serving to increase further the need to avoid unnecessary structural (or other) concerns, which is no doubt popular with borrowers; margins predicated on lenders rarely or never losing money require deals to be structured accordingly. There has been a shift away from the increased pressure on lenders to accept greater levels of risk (for example, in the form of a more lenient covenant package, including hitherto "unfashionable" classes of investor within the borrowing base, or lending to funds whose managers have a shorter track record) and a move to increased scrutiny on the investor base and fund track records.

The macroeconomic climate has, unsurprisingly, impacted lenders. One notable change, as briefly mentioned below, is as a result of the "stress capital buffer" regime established by the Federal Reserve, which has required certain lenders to reduce their exposure to certain types of subscription-line financing.

Lenders and borrowers alike should remain vigilant in ensuring that they and their counterparties are sufficiently familiar with the product and its pitfalls and are being properly advised.

Concentration risk

Central to any lender's risk-management strategy will be how it approaches concentration risk and, more specifically, its exposure to specific investors, fund managers and fund sectors.

In relation to investors, lenders will often encounter the same entities across multiple funds (in particular, large institutional investors such as pension funds and sovereign wealth funds). Over-exposure to such an investor will increase the risk that its default on its commitments will translate into a lender ultimately being out of pocket.

European Banking Authority Guidelines[5] address, among other things, the aggregation of bank exposures, and in particular, exposures to connected clients.[6] The guidelines aim to help lenders identify all relevant connections among their clients, and specifically, two types of interconnection: (i) control relationships; and (ii) economic dependencies that lead to two or more customers being regarded as a single risk (subject to certain exceptions).

A control relationship is deemed or likely to exist where, for example, an entity appears in the consolidated financial statements of a structure or holds, with respect to another entity, a majority of the voting rights, the right to appoint or remove management, or the right to otherwise exercise a dominant influence.[7]

An economic dependency is deemed to exist where the financial difficulties or failure of an entity would be likely to lead to funding or repayment difficulties for another. For example: (i) where the source of funds to repay the loans of two or more borrowers is the same and there is no independent source of income to service the loans (for example, parallel funds with the same borrowing base); or (ii) where there are common investors or managers that do not meet the criteria of the control test (for example, there are common shareholders but no controlling shareholder, or they are managed on a unified basis).

Notwithstanding the foregoing, in the context of many fund structures, a lender may often be able to demonstrate an exception to the need for aggregation. In particular, this may be the case where the lender can show that:
(i) there is no economic interdependence;[8]
(ii) the entity is bankruptcy remote – this will normally be the case for funds that are limited partnerships, as there should be no commingling of partnership and general partner assets (even where the general partner is general partner of multiple partnerships), as

the general partner will have access to its own assets on a bankruptcy only and not partnership assets (save in relation to partner liabilities owed to the general partner such as for fees); and/or

(iii) there is structural de-linkage of the obligations of an entity from its parent.

Nevertheless, lenders are advised to exercise caution in relying on an exception because, in practice, in the case of affiliated funds or funds under common management, they are more likely to be "connected" and will be affected by the success and reputation of the other funds and their managers, irrespective of ring-fencing of assets.

To that end, it is essential that lenders assess a fund functionary's credentials whether they are managers, sponsors, or administrators. For experienced lenders active in the fund finance market, existing relationships with fund functionaries will enable lenders to have visibility on a given manager's track record and performance. Funds promoted by high-quality and established sponsors with a track record would be expected to be lower risk. However, for more recent entrants to the market, relevant information will be less readily available. It is therefore important for lenders to understand both the expertise and experience of the functionaries' key people in terms of portfolio management, investment criteria, business plan and financial model.

At the investor level, the most active lenders will generally hold significant information in relation to the investors and their participation in calls made by funds with which such lenders have an existing relationship. The more informed the lender when assessing whether to include or exclude an investor from a fund's borrowing base, the more reliable the borrowing base should arguably be. Many institutional investors are themselves subject to various reporting standards, including in relation to the provision of financial and other key investor and stakeholder information. Further, there is a wealth of publicly available information in relation to many pension funds and sovereign wealth funds including their financial accounts, their executive managers, their organisational structure and details as to their investment portfolio. In addition, lenders that act as account bank to fund entities can also leverage their overview of account activity.

There is a range of sophistication in the financial modelling carried out by lenders and the monitoring thereof. Newer entrants to the fund finance sector may not have the same resources available to them, and this can lead to different conclusions being drawn by such lenders in relation to the inclusion of investors in borrowing bases, which can be apparent on syndicated or club transactions.

Conducting a thorough review of all the investor side letters and expanding the covenant package in the facility agreement to include: (i) covenants relating to concentration risk; and/or (ii) concentration limits in the borrowing base provisions relating to the calculation of the borrowing base, will assist the lender in managing concentration exposures.

As above, with the increased use of automation, artificial intelligence and data science in the financial services industry and more widely, lenders are becoming increasingly aware of the value of the data they hold in the course of, and for the purposes of, carrying out their business and understanding the dynamic between behavioural science and risk. By deploying new technology such as blockchain or other distributed ledger technology, innovation, and data analytics, lenders can use the data that they hold to build a clearer picture of market activity and, in turn, to determine and anticipate risks. The most obvious form of technology would be to use artificial intelligence to conduct due diligence on funds, sponsors, and investors and keep up to date with sector trends and risks, valuations of fund assets, portfolio companies and net asset values (NAVs).

A lender's success will be intrinsically linked to its identifying to which parties to extend financing. Lessons can be learnt from the tech giants in modelling and manipulating data to establish trends and map the behaviour of key market players, noting the confines of ensuring that this is done for proper purposes in accordance with the prevailing data protection regimes.

In a syndicated loan context, the more efficiently data is shared among the syndicate, the quicker the syndicate will be able to react to situations such as requests to increase facilities and amend terms. The developments in the syndicated market space, and Loan Market Association (LMA) initiatives to explore technology and automation, should mean that in the future, a common syntax is applied to syndicated lending, and a common standard can be applied that will improve the customer experience.

Liquidity risk

Liquidity is a perennial risk attached to lending and lenders will be familiar with the challenges this presents post-financial crisis, in the wake of the **Basel III Framework** and the introduction of liquidity ratios.

The revised regulatory landscape post-financial crisis required banking institutions to increase their capital and liquidity buffers, to help alleviate certain liquidity pressures and equip lenders to tolerate greater stress in financial markets, including due to the continuing economic fallout of COVID-19 and Brexit.

However, recent equity market volatility, liquidity tightening, widening funding spreads, operational fails, and other challenges have put significant pressure on the financial markets. We are aware that certain bank lenders have taken steps to strengthen their liquidity and reporting capabilities and, in some cases, to monitor them more frequently. There is also the introduction of new capital rules by the Federal Reserve that will force certain US lenders to hold more capital relative to their "risk-weighted assets".[9]

Generally, lenders may take a number of steps to manage exposure, including: (i) stress-testing the loan book; (ii) monitoring for concentrations of investors, functionaries and sectors as outlined above; (iii) considering the profile of investors with higher potential for exposure (including in terms of jurisdiction of domicile, ticket size, track record of making payments following drawdown requests, likelihood of themselves being a levered fund) and other reputational matters, noting that if a borrower is at the later stages of the fund cycle or the fund is fully committed, the lender may be less sensitive to the inclusion of such investors and borrowing base requirements may be relaxed accordingly; and (iv) considering whether there are any mismatches between the level and frequency of fund distributions made to investors and the level and frequency of capital calls made by the fund.

In terms of NAV and hybrid facilities, there is an additional liquidity risk to lenders, where assets provided as collateral for the facilities are overvalued or lose value and become insufficient to meet the borrower's obligations under the facility. Inability of lenders to challenge valuations could also play a role here.

Facility information covenants, requiring borrowers to obtain robust and frequent asset valuations or requiring notification of any significant change in NAV, would assist the lender to monitor downstream valuations, *and* in addition to the typical loan-to-value covenants and other financial covenants within facility documents.

ESG risks

ESG risks have been recognised as credit risks in their own right as early as late 2019 (if not earlier).[10] Most lenders have adopted explicit ESG policies, and an increasing number of institutions have an ESG-dedicated resource in their credit risk teams. Lenders are therefore both increasingly aware of the risks and actively managing these risks as part of their usual assessments of credit risks. This should serve them well when the legal and regulatory framework moves to requiring more rigorous reporting standards in line with various taxonomies and local law requirements. As reporting standards and regulations continue to develop, we are likely to see ESG provisions given more prominence in the substantive fund constitutive documents, rather than left as an optional extra for investors to request in their side letters. As a result, more fund managers and lenders alike will need to ensure that a fund's performance is monitored against the ESG key performance indicators (KPIs).

A backdrop of rising interest rates has seen a more cautious approach from some lenders concerned about regulatory risk, in particular after the US Securities and Exchange Commission fined BNY Mellon's investment adviser division for "greenwashing",[11] and borrowers switching away from ESG-linked loans.[12]

However, in light of the wider social and political climate and in the face of investors pushing for ESG factors to play a greater role in investment decisions, it is difficult to imagine that those factors will not also play a greater role in lending. Further, one perspective is that such requirements, driven by legislation and regulation, will become mandatory for lenders. Of the risks noted above, many of these may be managed and mitigated by real-time access to information (e.g. by way of blockchain or otherwise), as it adds colour to the facts, which are borne out through the financials, and facilitates better-quality decision-making by the lender. In the near future, technology could provide solutions to data management and analysis, making it easier and quicker to access, record and analyse data collated by the lender. In addition, artificial intelligence programmes may be implemented to assist with collating due diligence, monitoring and harnessing publicly available information.

There are steps that lenders can introduce now to maximise the information they receive, such as placing the burden on fund functionaries to store, maintain and share management information, financial information and investor lists on systems that can be readily accessed such as private web portals or a private blockchain, for the lender to freely access. This would increase transparency, as such information could be made available in real time to lenders and assist in easing the burden of monitoring the performance of the loan.

Conclusion

This chapter has shown that, despite having a reputation as a low-risk product, the fund finance sphere is not without risk, but rather is a low-risk product due to the effective management of the risk present. In managing the current and evolving risks, we highlight the importance of engaging lender counsel at an early stage, both to conduct full diligence on the structure and to manage the documentation risk.

As the fund finance market continues to evolve, lenders will need to remain alert to the risks associated with lending in the market, notwithstanding the continued low default rate. In particular, the rapidly evolving macroeconomic picture may require the re-balancing of lending books or new approaches to risk migration.

* * *

Endnotes

1. This is in addition to the complexity and cross-jurisdictional dimensions of many fund structures, the size of the financial transactions and, in some cases, relatively slim margins.

2. ISDA has issued a number of whitepapers and academic papers in relation to the broader legal and regulatory aspects of distributed ledger and smart contracts technology. See: https://www.isda.org/2019/10/16/isda-smart-contracts [accessed on 11 December 2022].
3. Clifford Chance (2021) "The digital future of syndicated loans 2021" https://www.cliffordchance.com/briefings/2021/06/the-digital-future-of-syndicated-loans.html [accessed on 11 December 2022].
4. Russell, A, Munden, R and Salem, A (2018) "Fund finance and releases of investor commitments: How can lenders protect themselves?" [online] available at: https://www.careyolsen.com/briefings/fund-finance-and-releases-investor-commitments-how-can-lenders-protect-themselves [accessed on 11 December 2022].
5. Committee of European Banking Supervisors (CEBS) (2018) "Final Report, Guidelines on institutions' stress testing" CEBS [online] available at: https://eba.europa.eu/documents/10180/2282644/Guidelines+on+institutions+stress+testing+%28EBA-GL-2018-04%29.pdf/2b604bc8-fd08-4b17-ac4a-cdd5e662b802 [accessed on 11 December 2022].
6. As defined in Article 4(39) of Regulation (EU) No 575/2013.
7. Although these criteria are non-exhaustive, and other aspects may be relevant.
8. For completeness, there should also not be a material positive correlation between the credit quality of the parent and subsidiary entities in a control relationship; however, this should not apply to fund structures either.
9. See: https://www.ft.com/content/e594087e-126b-4376-90ad-2a245c8313f3 [accessed on 11 December 2022].
10. See: https://www.spglobal.com/marketintelligence/en/news-insights/blog/esg-investing-is-becoming-critical-for-credit-risk-and-portfolio-management-professionals [accessed on 11 December 2022].
11. See: SEC fines BNY Mellon over ESG in first case of its kind, *Financial Times* (https://www.ft.com) [accessed on 11 December 2022].
12. See: https://www.privatefundscfo.com/lenders-get-cautious-on-esg-linked-lines-but-issuance-remains-resilient [accessed on 11 December 2022].

Robin Smith
Tel: +44 1534 822264 / Email: robin.smith@careyolsen.com

Robin is consistently recognised for his ability to deal with a wide range of international corporate and finance transactions. He has acted on numerous significant portfolio acquisitions and disposals. He often acts for both lenders and borrowers on complex financings, refinancings and restructurings and has significant experience in relation to the financing of investment funds.

Robin advises global banks and large corporates as well as smaller privately held entities. He also has experience advising in relation to the establishment, transfer and redomiciliation of banking business in Jersey.

Robin is ranked as a leading lawyer by *The Legal 500*, *Chambers and Partners* and *IFLR1000* and has been recently described as "the stand-out Jersey banking and finance lawyer". Robin has a particular interest in sustainable finance and recently advised the Government of Jersey on the establishment of the loan guarantee scheme to support local businesses through the coronavirus pandemic.

Alistair Russell
Tel: +1 345 749 2013 / Email: alistair.russell@careyolsen.com

Alistair is a partner in the corporate and finance group of Carey Olsen in the Cayman Islands and advises on all aspects of finance, corporate, investment funds and commercial law.

He has advised clients on a broad range of transactions including financing, private equity, joint ventures, mergers and acquisitions and capital markets, and is described by clients in *IFLR1000* as "the best Cayman lawyer we've ever worked with".

Alistair is rated as a Leading Lawyer – Highly regarded in *IFLR1000*.

Holly Brown
Tel: +44 1534 822231 / Email: holly.brown@careyolsen.com

Holly is a senior associate in Carey Olsen's Jersey corporate team. She assists with a range of corporate, banking and finance matters.

Holly is an advocate of the Royal Court of Jersey. She was educated at King's College London and joined Carey Olsen in 2013.

Carey Olsen Jersey LLP
47 Esplanade, St Helier, Jersey JE1 0BD, Channel Islands
Tel: +44 1534 888900 / Fax: +44 1534 887744 / URL: www.careyolsen.com

Fund finance meets securitisation

Richard Day & Julia Tsybina
Clifford Chance LLP

The substantial and rapid growth of the European fund finance market over recent years has been well documented in the pages of this book and elsewhere. We have seen a diversification of both financing techniques and willing financiers and a consequent proliferation of deals looking not only to undrawn limited partner commitment, but also to manager fee income and dividends from underlying assets together with asset-based deals based on portfolios of secondary or fund of fund managers, as well as co-investment lines, GP-led restructurings, dividend recaps and preferred equity transactions. The world of fund finance today is a vibrant and diverse market. The increasing number of deals being carried out by way of securitisation is one aspect of the ongoing evolution of fund financing techniques. In this chapter, we summarise typical features of a securitisation-based fund financing transaction and outline key points to consider when documenting one.

On 1 January 2019, the EU Securitisation Regulation (the "**Securitisation Regulation**") came into effect and largely replaced prior sectoral legislation and regulation applicable to banks (the Capital Requirements regime), insurers (the Solvency II regime) and fund managers (the Alternative Investment Fund Managers Directive regime). It recast those provisions in a new harmonised securitisation regime applicable to a broad range of institutional investors. From 1 January 2021, the Securitisation Regulation was onshored into the domestic law of the UK with relatively few changes (the "**UK Securitisation Regulation**") as part of the Brexit process. Except where otherwise noted, discussions of the Securitisation Regulation below are also applicable, *mutatis mutandis*, to the UK Securitisation Regulation.

The Securitisation Regulation is therefore still relatively new, and there are aspects of it that are untested and where the requirements have not been fleshed out in detail. It is wide ranging in scope and there is a fair degree of complexity in its terms that the market is required to interpret. There are serious consequences for failure to comply with the Securitisation Regulation for an in-scope entity, so there are pitfalls (including large fines of up to 10% of annual net turnover on a consolidated basis for non-compliance) for the unwary. Prior to the Securitisation Regulation, individual compliance obligations were largely on investors rather than the sell-side entities (originator, sponsors, original lenders and issuers). This meant that treating a transaction as a securitisation for the benefit of an investor did not impose regulatory obligations on sell-side entities. This is no longer the case under the Securitisation Regulation, as determining that a transaction is a securitisation will carry much more onerous obligations imposed directly on the sell side.

In a fund finance context, this means that there is a different community of investor and a different type of expertise required of legal advisors as compared to the more traditional forms of fund finance deals, as it is important both to understand the nature of a fund and also to be familiar with securitisation as a form of structured finance technique, as well as with the regulatory backdrop that underpins it.

Why securitise?

If a securitisation is more specialised and relatively complex, the question arises: why would a fund consider taking this financing route as opposed to the more traditional NAV (net asset value or asset-backed) financing facility? As fund managers seek increased returns and more innovative portfolio management techniques to release value, a securitisation is a useful leveraged financing tool to provide a flexible, long-term liquidity solution at an attractive price utilising a type of securitisation – usually referred to as a private securitisation – that is not as complex as a full-blown public securitisation, which would likely not be available or attractive to funds. For investors, this is giving exposure to a broader spread of asset classes with an attractive risk return profile without the need to set up the origination or servicing infrastructure and a preferential capital regime for certain securitisation positions held by credit institutions and investment firms. Notwithstanding the additional operational and structural complexity that it brings, for the lender, a securitisation structure can be attractive from a commercial perspective as, in some cases, it will lead to a reduction in the amount of regulatory capital that the lender is required to hold in respect of its exposure to the fund. Typically, most funds will be unrated and, accordingly, an exposure to a fund by a lending institution will attract a 100% risk weight. Conversely, if the lending institution is able to treat the loan as an exposure to a senior tranche of securitisation (rather than as an exposure to the fund itself), the risk weight associated with the senior tranche may be significantly lower, normally subject to a floor of 15%. By reducing the amount of capital that the lender is required to hold against the exposure, the lender's cost of providing the funding will be significantly reduced, thereby allowing it to offer more competitive pricing and improve its return on the transaction.

What is a securitisation?

In Europe, the relevant definition of a securitisation (under Article 2(1) of the Securitisation Regulation and Article 2(1) of the UK Securitisation Regulation) is based around tranched credit exposures. It is a transaction or scheme where "the credit risk associated with an exposure or a pool of exposures is tranched, having all of the following characteristics:

(a) payments in the transaction or scheme are dependent upon the performance of the exposure or of the pool of exposures;

(b) the subordination of tranches determines the distribution of losses during the ongoing life of the transaction or scheme; and

(c) the transaction or scheme does not create specialised lending exposures (as defined)".

It should be noted that the definition of a securitisation in the US is different and so, for regulatory purposes, it is key to understand which jurisdiction matters. Depending on the parties involved, there could be multiple jurisdictions that are relevant to any given transaction. This chapter will focus exclusively on the rules that apply to European (including UK) securitisations under the Securitisation Regulation and UK Securitisation Regulation.

The various elements of that technical definition are not necessarily intuitive and so this requires further explanation, as follows:

(i) **A pool of underlying exposures**

The main requirement here is that there is a pool of underlying exposures on which there is credit risk. For these purposes, credit risk means risk of principal losses. So, a pool made up of owned real estate, for example, would not meet this requirement because the risk in that scenario is market risk on the value of the real estate. However, a pool of leases over those same properties or a pool of mortgage loans secured on those properties would meet the requirement because the risk is credit risk on the lessees or borrowers. This means that the underlying assets will usually be financial assets.

(ii) **Tranching**

To meet the regulatory requirements, tranching must be contractual (so structural subordination, subordination in time or subordination arising purely by operation of law, will not suffice), it must be done at the transaction level (not investor level), and it must come from an assumption of risk more junior or senior to another tranche. The consequence of this requirement is that many arrangements that may have the appearance of a securitisation or that would economically produce the effect of tranching are not caught by the regulatory definition. Single tranche securitisations that are common in the US are not securitisations for EU or UK regulatory purposes.

(iii) **Distribution of losses**

It has to be possible for junior tranches to suffer losses whilst senior tranches continue to perform. For this reason, a single asset securitisation will not generally be possible as that single asset either defaults, leading to a default on all tranches of debt, or it does not. Tranching may determine the distribution of losses but it will only do so at a single point of default, not on an ongoing basis. A securitisation will feature tranches of debt where the probabilities of default, and hence the allocation of losses during the life of the deal (and not just the loss on a given default), will be different.

(iv) **The specialised lending exception**

Even where a transaction meets the criteria described above, "specialised lending arrangements" will not count as securitisations for EU or UK regulatory purposes. Specialised lending exposures are, broadly speaking, debt exposures related to a physical asset, typically lending to an entity specifically created to acquire and/or operate that physical asset where the debt is repaid primarily by the income from operating that asset and where the lenders have a substantial degree of control over the asset and the income it generates. Aircraft or project finance, for example, would often meet these criteria.

Who are the parties caught by the Securitisation Regulation?

If a transaction meets the definition of a securitisation, certain parties to that transaction will have obligations under the Securitisation Regulation. Those parties are the originator, sponsor, original lender, issuer and any institutional investors. These terms require more explanation, as set out below:

Originator – someone who was directly or indirectly involved in the original creation of the asset or someone who acquired the asset for its own account and then securitised it. Note, however, that "sole purpose" originators are not allowed to fulfil certain required regulatory responsibilities. See below under the heading "Risk retention".

Sponsor – broadly, an entity that sets up and manages a securitisation but who does not actually securitise its own assets. Historically, an entity has only been capable of being a "sponsor" if it had one of a limited number of EU regulatory permissions. There is a view that third-country (non-EU) sponsors may be permitted under the Securitisation Regulation, which is particularly relevant post-Brexit. Although clarification on this point from the relevant EU authorities has been expected, at the time of writing, it has not yet been provided. The UK Securitisation Regulation is clear on this point that non-UK sponsors are permitted for UK regulatory purposes.

Original lender – defined in a way that is generally agreed to be included in the concept of originator of financial assets.

Issuer – this is the entity that borrows the loan from the investors or issues the securities purchased by the investors. The regulatory term used in the Securitisation Regulation is a "securitisation special purpose entity" or "SSPE".

Institutional investor – the definition includes credit institutions, investment firms (or a "CRR firm" in the UK), UCITS (whether self-directed or UCITS management companies), alternative investment fund managers, insurers, reinsurers and pension funds (institutions for occupational retirement provision in the EU or occupational pension schemes in the UK).

Main regulatory obligations associated with securitisation

Once it has been determined that a transaction meets the definition of a securitisation and it has been determined which parties to the deal have obligations under the regulatory regime, the next question is: what are those obligations? We explain below three of the most important, being risk retention, transparency and due diligence.

Risk retention

One of the key reforms to the regulation of securitisation that was introduced in Europe following the global financial crisis of 2007 was the requirement for an originator, sponsor or original lender of a securitisation to retain a material net economic interest in the transaction – this is known as risk retention. One of the originator (or original lender) or sponsor must retain 5% of risk in the securitisation. As yet, the detailed technical rules contained in regulatory technical standards ("**RTS**") (or binding technical standards in the UK) have yet to be adopted, but the market has sufficient certainty based on the level 1 text, final draft RTS published by the European Banking Authority (which is still persuasive in the UK) and existing market practice that it is possible to structure even relatively complex deals with a reasonable degree of legal certainty. "Sole purpose" originators who exclusively exist to securitise assets are now banned from retaining risk. Since fund structures are often complex (certainly as compared to a typical bank originator of loans), a key part of the legal analysis required is the identification of an eligible risk retainer with sufficient substance. "Substance" in this sense is measured via a combination of asset-related factors and governance factors. Securitised assets should not be chosen because they perform significantly worse than comparable assets retained on the balance sheet of the originator over the life of the transaction.

Transparency

There are detailed disclosure requirements that apply regardless of the regulated status of the originator, sponsor or issuer (although such entities do still have to be in scope in terms of the Securitisation Regulation, which, broadly speaking, means that they will not have direct obligations if they are established outside the EU or the UK, although the diligence obligations may bring them back into scope indirectly if they are selling to EU or UK institutional investors). Detailed disclosure is required in all cases regardless of whether the transaction is a public or private transaction. The audience for this disclosure in private securitisations is investors, competent authorities and, upon request, potential investors. Private transactions do not have a prescribed mechanism for disclosure although national competent authorities may prescribe the method, frequency and content of information to be reported to them, and the Financial Conduct Authority and Prudential Regulation Authority have done so for the UK in a joint direction. In the EU, the European Central Bank adopted a notification guide for EU "significant institutions" that covers this ground as well. The content that must be disclosed is full documentation essential for the understanding of the transaction, including a deal summary where there is no prospectus, loan-level data on a prescribed template, investor reports on a prescribed template and reports of any significant events/material changes (also on a prescribed template but where the deal is public, which is unlikely to apply to a fund finance transaction).

Due diligence

The Securitisation Regulation sets out detailed requirements for due diligence that must be conducted by institutional investors and harmonises the specific items to be diligenced for all categories of institutional investor. Generally, due diligence must be carried out on the underlying assets of the securitisation and the transaction structure surrounding them. Therefore, before holding a securitisation position, institutional investors are required to verify that the originator or original lender has appropriate credit-granting standards and processes to enforce them, risk retention requirements have been fulfilled, and information about the securitisation transaction has been made available as required by the transparency rules in the Securitisation Regulation. Institutional investors are permitted to delegate the obligation to carry out regulatory diligence to a third party, but this delegation is only effective to transfer the regulatory obligation (and sanctions for failure to comply) where that third party is itself an institutional investor and makes investment decisions on behalf of the principal. These broad investor due diligence requirements mean that non-EU securitisations need to comply if they are to be sold into the EU and likewise for the UK.

Common structures for fund financing

Whilst we have seen a number of different structures, the common features we see in fund financings that are to qualify as securitisations may be summarised as follows.

Private deals – these transactions are private securitisations rather than full public securitisations and so are less complex and cheaper to establish. They are usually unrated, although often capable of being rated at some point if required.

Eligibility criteria for assets – the portfolio will generally be required to comply with certain eligibility criteria, concentration limits and diversity tests that have been agreed between the originator and the investor. These criteria generally relate to the types of exposures that may be included, the number of exposures, the jurisdictions of the underlying obligors of the assets within the portfolio, the credit grade of the exposures, the maturity profile of the exposures and the industry to which the underlying obligors belong. This is formulated on a bespoke basis for each transaction depending on the fund and the nature of the assets comprised within the portfolio. Generally, eligibility criteria will only be tested at the outset of the deal rather than on an ongoing basis. It is still possible for the fund to purchase assets that do not meet the eligibility criteria, provided it is funded by way of equity. Whilst some deals will have a static portfolio of exposures that does not change over the life of the transaction other than to reflect repayment of the exposures, many securitisations will permit additions to the portfolio, particularly to replenish the portfolio as original exposures are repaid or otherwise disposed of by the originator. It is a commercial question as to how additions to the portfolio are treated, with some deals only permitting it on the satisfaction of pre-agreed criteria and others where investors have no approval or veto rights.

Borrowing base – this is clearly a key commercial component of the transaction and to settle it requires agreement on the advance rates for the eligible assets, the valuation procedures (including the identity of the valuer), the thresholds at which a mandatory prepayment event is triggered and detail of any cure rights.

Form of debt – we have seen investors fund deals by way of revolving loan facility and deals done by way of variable funding notes issuance. There is often the ability to increase the size of the financing subject to agreed tests, which provides an important element of flexibility for funds. The financing can be repaid and redrawn, providing added flexibility for new acquisitions during the life of the deal subject to pre-agreed criteria.

Tranching – the junior tranche is funded by way of income tracking bonds or loan facility by another entity within the fund structure.

Issuer – in a public securitisation, this would usually be an orphan special purpose vehicle issuer, whereas in a private securitisation for fund finance, it is common for the issuer to be part of the originator's group. We see different types of fund utilising this structure but usually it is a credit fund of some description as the underlying portfolio of exposures to be securitised are financial assets. In a securitisation, there are usually standard "separateness" and "special purpose" representations and undertakings given by the issuer to underpin its special purpose vehicle status so that it is clearly acting on arm's length terms and has undertaken limited activities outside of what is required for the transaction. In a private fund securitisation, these provisions will be necessarily more limited or tailored given the issuer's status as part of the group. The analysis here can become nuanced and the relevant provisions may need to permit certain intra-group arrangements, for example, in relation to cost sharing and intra-group debt (subject to group claims being subordinated), as well as the use of premises and branding.

Originator – in a private securitisation for a fund, it is usually the case that an analysis will need to be conducted involving the fund and the relevant lawyers to determine which entity within the fund structure is the originator and which entity is undertaking the risk retention.

Limited recourse – the investors will be expected to agree that the financing is limited in recourse to the secured portfolio. There will be a strict waterfall of payments setting out all payment flows from the designated account structure set up for interest and principal collections in relation to the portfolio with reserve accounts and operating accounts (and separate regimes that are applicable depending on whether an event of default is continuing). In some deals there will be a cash manager, often a professional entity that is unrelated to the originator. There will also be non-petition provisions where investors agree not to institute or join in insolvency, winding up or similar provisions in relation to the issuer.

Servicer/administrator – to be discussed on each transaction, but it is important to have an entity that is undertaking the regular reporting on the portfolio for the investors, which is an important role underpinning the integrity of the payment waterfall.

Security – security will be taken over the assets in the portfolio and all the bank accounts. As with any financing, it is necessary for investors to do a cost-benefit analysis as to how the security package is structured but, in many deals, there is no local security that is taken in relation to each asset comprised within the portfolio given the time and expense involved in creating it. Therefore, an English law debenture is common. Also, in most cases, there will be no upfront notification of the security given to the underlying borrowers in the portfolio.

Securitisation analysis on a fund finance

It will be clear from the preceding paragraphs in this chapter that because these transactions are creatures of regulation, there is a fair amount of analysis to be undertaken to understand whether the regulatory components of a securitisation are present as defined within the

Securitisation Regulation, which parties in the fund structure are carrying out the roles of the various entities described as falling within the Securitisation Regulation, and whether the various requirements of the Securitisation Regulation in terms of risk retention, transparency and due diligence in particular are met. Private securitisations for funds need to be structured in such a way that the regulatory hurdles are met, but in a way that makes legal and commercial sense given the structure of a fund group and the nature of the portfolio that is to be securitised.

Richard Day
Tel: +44 20 7006 4233 / Email: richard.day@cliffordchance.com
Richard is a Partner in the London office of Clifford Chance. He advises lenders and borrowers across the full spectrum of fund-level finance solutions as well as facilities for general partners. Richard's experience spans capital call (subscription) bridge finance, leveraged NAV facilities and hybrid financing including transactions featuring preference interests, securitisation treatment or other specialist solutions.

Julia Tsybina
Tel: +44 20 7006 4368 / Email: julia.tsybina@cliffordchance.com
Julia is a Partner in the London office of Clifford Chance. She specialises in structured finance and derivatives, including fund finance private securitisations, CLOs, complex structured products and repackagings, representing a wide range of asset managers, originators and investors. She also advises on regulatory matters impacting the securitisation and banking industries, including the EU Securitisation Regulation and UK Securitisation Regulation, as well on ESG matters relating to CLOs and structured products.

Clifford Chance LLP
10 Upper Bank Street, London, E14 5JJ, United Kingdom
Tel: +44 20 7006 1000 / Fax: +44 20 7006 5555 / URL: www.cliffordchance.com

Fund finance in Ireland and Luxembourg: A comparative analysis

Jad Nader, Ogier, Luxembourg
Phil Cody, Arthur Cox LLP, Ireland

Introduction

Ireland and Luxembourg have long been the preferred jurisdictions in which to establish a fund in Europe, and the prevalence of funds established in Ireland and Luxembourg make them important jurisdictions for lenders to understand. The ever-increasing use of Ireland and Luxembourg funds for private equity structures and the long track record in both jurisdictions, combined with the continued impact of Brexit, mean that the importance of Irish and Luxembourg funds is likely to further increase, both for capital call/subscription line facilities and net asset value ("**NAV**")/asset-backed facilities. Each jurisdiction offers managers access to the EU-wide marketing passport for Undertakings for the Collective Investment in Transferable Securities ("**UCITS**") and alternative investment funds ("**AIFs**"). The use of Irish and Luxembourg structures continued unabated throughout the pandemic.

This chapter addresses, on a comparative basis, a number of key legal and practice issues that should be considered when an Irish or Luxembourg fund is a borrower (or other obligor) in a fund finance structure. Although Ireland and Luxembourg have different legal systems (Ireland is common law; Luxembourg is civil law), as each is an EU Member State, they share much in common when it comes to fund finance. Both jurisdictions facilitate credit lines to investment funds in a manner that allows flexibility to borrowers, and certainty and robust security to lenders. In each jurisdiction, the following pieces of EU legislation play an important part in fund finance structures: the Alternative Investment Fund Managers Directive (Directive 2011/61/EU) ("**AIFMD**"); and the EU Directive on financial collateral arrangements (Directive 2002/47/EC) (the "**Collateral Directive**").

Legal entity types and introduction to regulatory framework

<u>Common considerations</u>

Each of Ireland and Luxembourg have a number of different legal entity structures: corporate; partnership; contractual; and, in the case of Ireland, trusts. Umbrella funds with segregated liability between sub-funds/compartments are a feature of each jurisdiction. In each jurisdiction, a sub-fund may, as an economic matter, be analysed as a separate entity.

Both Irish and Luxembourg sub-funds benefit from legislative ring-fencing, and each jurisdiction allows a sub-fund to be wound up and liquidated, leaving the remainder of the umbrella structure intact. However, and importantly, a sub-fund of an Irish/Luxembourg fund does not have separate legal personality. Accordingly, care needs to be taken, in drafting the parties' clauses, granting clauses and execution blocks, that the appropriate legal entity is expressed to be the party (with further care taken where, as is common, an investment manager is entering into the financing as agent of the fund).

Ireland

Irish structures can be broadly divided into regulated and unregulated structures. Regulated structures are regulated by the Central Bank of Ireland ("**CBI**") under the Irish law implementation of the UCITS Directives or, much more commonly for fund finance, AIFMD – as considered in detail further below. The main types of regulated fund structures in Ireland are: (i) variable capital investment companies; (ii) Irish collective asset-management vehicles ("**ICAVs**"); (iii) unit trusts; (iv) common contractual funds ("**CCFs**"); and (v) investment limited partnerships ("**ILPs**"). Each of these entity types (other than ILPs) may be established as AIFs or UCITS. ILPs are AIFs, only. The limited partnership (under the Limited Partnership Act 1907) is the most favoured structure for unregulated investment funds in Ireland.

At present, the ICAV (a corporate entity that can elect to be fiscally transparent for US federal tax purposes) is the most common Irish structure encountered in fund finance. ICAVs may be UCITS or under AIFMD. In fund finance, they will invariably be under AIFMD. Changes to the ILP legislation in the past year have seen ILPs used more frequently and will be so more frequently seen in fund finance in the years ahead. The Irish ILP product now allows for the umbrella structure within the partnership and we have seen this feature used in practice.

Luxembourg

Luxembourg offers a wide range of vehicles that may suit various needs and expectations that fund initiators may have. Luxembourg funds may either be regulated or non-regulated vehicles, with or without a legal and/or tax personality, with the possibility of using an important number of corporate entities, to which a regulatory framework may be added.

There are various structuring options, particularly in an AIFMD context. The fund-specific legislation is rich and mainly composed of the following: the Luxembourg law of 12 July 2013, as amended, on alternative investment fund managers (the "**Luxembourg AIFM Act**"), implementing AIFMD, as well as the law of 15 June 2004, as amended, on risk capital investment companies ("**SICARs**"); the law of 13 February 2007, as amended, on specialised investment funds ("**SIFs**"); the law of 23 July 2016 on reserved alternative investment funds ("**RAIFs**"); and the law of 17 December 2010, as amended, on undertakings for collective investment ("**UCIs**", which are covered by the Luxembourg AIFM Act and UCITS). RAIFs bearing the corporate form of a special limited partnership ("**SCSp**") have recently been extremely successful given the important flexibility that they offer (most aspects may be contractually agreed).

AIFMD and other regulatory considerations

AIFMD

Regulatory considerations deserve close attention as part of the due diligence on a fund finance deal. Non-compliance with the regulatory requirements by a fund adversely impacts the financing transaction. Although Irish and Luxembourg funds may also be UCITS, in fund finance structures, lenders will typically encounter only AIFs, so the AIFMD considerations should be noted in financings involving Irish or Luxembourg funds.

Under AIFMD, the relevant fund (Irish or Luxembourg) will have appointed to it an alternative investment fund manager ("**AIFM**"). The AIFM is responsible for the risk management and portfolio management functions of the fund, and will typically delegate (under an investment management agreement) the portfolio management function to an investment manager (as agent of the AIFM). This chain of delegated authority, and in particular, the terms of the investment management agreement, should be verified as part of the diligence process. AIFMs are typically required to be regulated by their home member regulator (CBI, in the case of Ireland; the *Commission de Surveillance du Secteur Financier* ("**CSSF**"), in the case of Luxembourg).

Another key requirement of, and actor in, the AIFMD structure is the depositary – which must be a separate entity to the AIFM and will have its registered office or a branch in the AIF's home Member State (Ireland or Luxembourg). The depositary is responsible for the safekeeping of the fund's assets. The depositary is also generally liable for the failure of its delegates.

Another key actor is the administrator. The administrator plays an important role in processing subscriptions, and recording and registering subscriptions. In addition, the administrator performs the role of calculating the NAV of the fund and its units/shares.

Other EU regulatory regimes may require close attention when dealing with an Irish or Luxembourg fund. Where derivatives are used at the fund level, the European Market Infrastructure Regulation (Regulation (EU) No 648/2012, known as "**EMIR**") will apply (and, as an EU Regulation, its terms should not vary between Ireland and Luxembourg). EMIR is, insofar as derivatives are concerned, broadly the EU equivalent of the relevant aspects of the Dodd-Frank Act in the US.

Where the transfer to the lenders of personal data relating to natural persons is involved (for example, in the case of a subscription line involving investors who are high-net-worth individuals), the General Data Protection Regulation (Regulation (EU) No 2016/679, known as "**GDPR**") may be relevant. This privacy law is an EU Regulation that should apply equally as between Ireland and Luxembourg.

Ireland

A typical Irish fund structure is set out below in simplified form (Fig. 1) and illustrates the AIFMD architecture. In fund finance, lenders dealing with Irish funds will typically encounter qualifying investor alternative investment funds ("**QIAIFs**"), whose corporate structure will most commonly be an ICAV, but increasingly an ILP. A QIAIF is marketed to professional investors only. It is not subject to any investment or borrowing limit. In Ireland, the AIFM may be an external manager of the AIF or, in the case of an ICAV or investment company, the fund itself.

Luxembourg

The Luxembourg financial supervisory authority, CSSF, has not specifically addressed fund finance activities. Nevertheless, fund finance is considered as being covered by the general regulatory framework applicable to a fund entering into a financing and to its manager, and in particular, the guidelines on portfolio management. A typical Luxembourg fund structure is set out below (Fig. 2). As with Fig. 1 (for Ireland), the AIFMD "actors" are the same – AIFM and depositary.

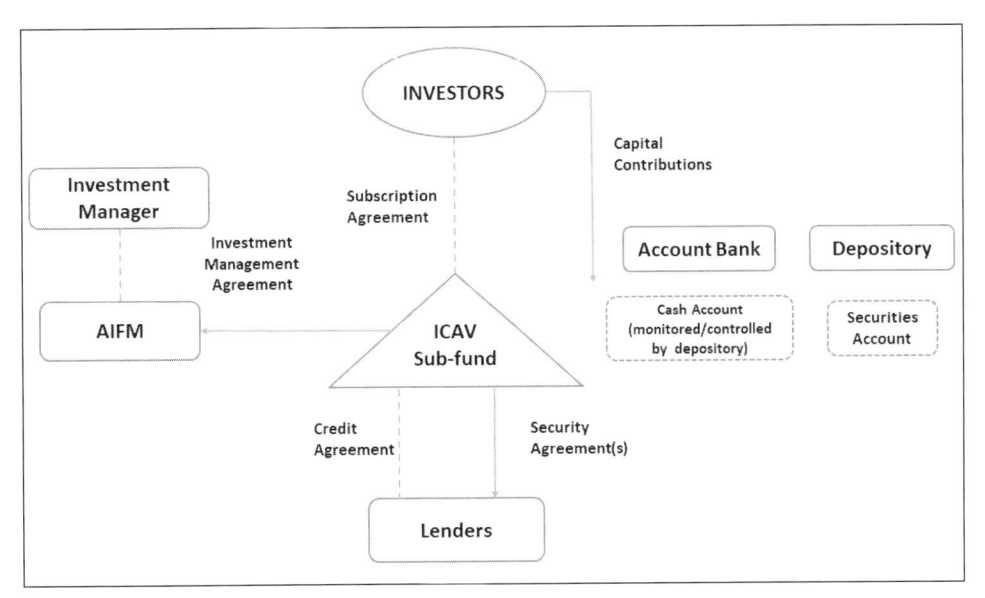

Fig. 1 – Ireland

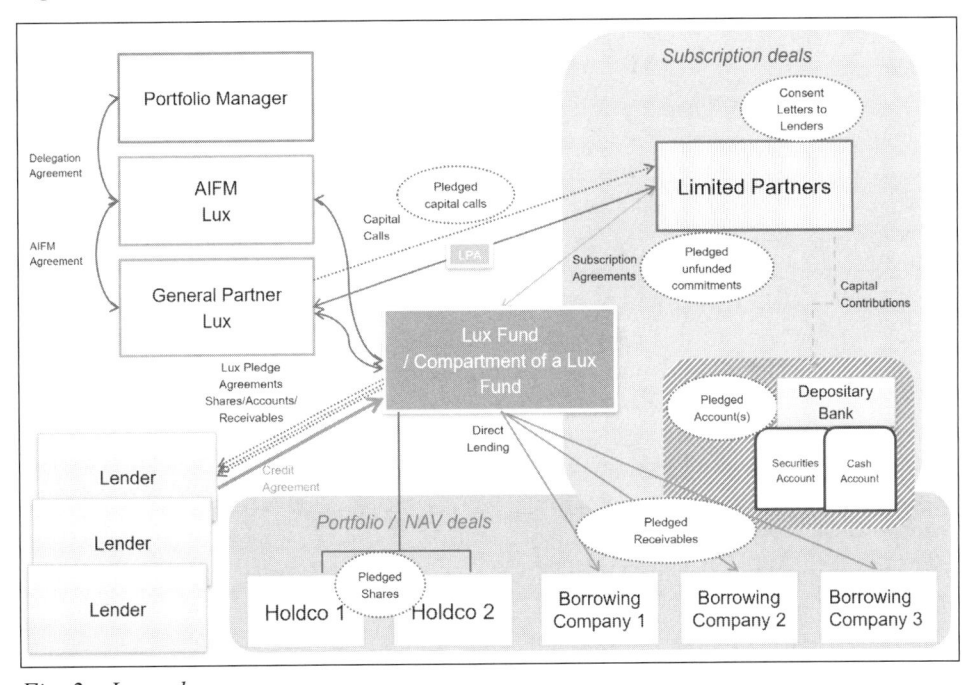

Fig. 2 – Luxembourg

Diligence

Common considerations

In any lending structure, it is essential that appropriate due diligence is undertaken in good time. As in any jurisdiction, the usual issues of capacity and authority need to be examined at an early stage so that any issues may be identified and addressed early in the transaction. The AIFMD aspects introduce additional diligence requirements (for example, on the AIFM (or its delegates) and the regulatory authority of the fund), all of which underline that in the case of Irish or Luxembourg funds, early engagement on diligence is recommended. In the case of both Irish and Luxembourg funds, typically there are no leverage limits imposed, but this needs to be verified by reference to the nature of the fund and any self-imposed leverage restrictions.

In addition, AIFMD, adopted in the wake of the financial crisis and the Madoff scandal, has put increased liability on the depositary, who holds a duty to monitor and reconcile the fund's cash flows and supervise its assets, and a prevention and detection role (the scope of obligations may vary depending on the type of fund used but, in general, the foregoing applies to all funds that are subject to AIFMD).

Any action that might affect the fund's assets requires the approval of the depositary. Hence, a smooth enforcement of the pledge requires that the depositary be informed beforehand of the existence of the pledge and acceptance by the depositary of its terms (it might even be a party to the pledge agreement). Contractual arrangements would normally be included to ensure a periodic valuation of and reporting on the pledged portfolio, with the consent and contribution of the depositary. Moreover, the depositary arrangements commonly provide for a pledge over all or part of the fund's assets in favour of the depositary. Any security to be granted over such assets will need to take into account the existing pledge in favour of the depositary, either by releasing such pledge or by creating a higher-ranking pledge in favour of the lenders.

Ireland

The establishment documents of the fund should be carefully reviewed. Subject to any self-imposed leverage limit (for which the prospectus should be reviewed), the fund can be expected to have broad powers, in its establishment documents, to borrow and create security. It is particularly important, in a subscription line facility, to determine that the power to create security extends to security over the fund's uncalled capital commitments.

In a subscription line facility, plainly the agreement between the fund and investor in relation to the subscription is a key document. Typically, this document is set out in a subscription agreement. It is important to determine in the subscription process: (i) who can make calls on investors; (ii) who determines the price at which units or shares are issued and by what means; (iii) when capital calls can be made on investors; (iv) what an investor can be asked to fund; (v) the implications of an investor not funding a capital call; and (vi) to what account subscription proceeds are paid.

Finally, as the management function of the fund is vested in the AIFM (or an investment manager as its delegate), the correct authorisation of, and approval of the transaction by, the AIFM (or the investment manager) should be appropriately addressed.

Luxembourg

The fund's organisational documents (limited partnership agreement, subscription agreement, articles of association, AIFM and/or portfolio management agreements, depositary agreement, etc.) set the rules governing commitments and any limits on the involvement of each of the fund parties.

It is important to make sure from the outset that there are no contradictions between the facility agreement and the organisational documents. In the context of the Luxembourg AIFM Act, for instance, the AIFM bears the regulatory responsibility as part of its portfolio management responsibilities; consequently, the financing transaction must be approved by the AIFM and, if applicable, the party to which the AIFM has delegated the portfolio management function.

In the last few years, it has become increasingly accepted to have specific provisions on fund financing included in the fund's organisational documents. This is particularly helpful in the context of subscription facilities, for which – as stated earlier – provisions on capital calls, disclosures, escrows, clawbacks and certain waivers are included.

Most Luxembourg AIFs (within the meaning of the Luxembourg AIFM Act) are not subject to statutory limitations on leverage, although there may be some limitations – resulting mainly from the fund's organisational documents. A Luxembourg AIF is required to conduct a self-assessment of its leverage level in order to determine whether or not it must appoint an authorised AIFM. If exceeded as a result of the bank financing, leverage level might trigger statutory obligations to appoint an AIFM and a depositary.

Common features for security interests

Collateral Directive

The Collateral Directive is important in relation to taking and enforcing collateral. It has been implemented into both Irish and Luxembourg domestic law and is an important feature of security arrangements in each jurisdiction.

The Collateral Directive provides to collateral takers, in the case of qualifying collateral arrangements, a number of perfection and enforcement benefits. This includes rights of rehypothecation, substitution of collateral, disapplication of stays, and a right of appropriation on enforcement.

As regards the Collateral Directive and its impact on perfection, first, a preliminary note on what we mean by the term "perfection". When used in some jurisdictions, "perfection" is taken to mean the steps needed to ensure a first-ranking security interest. In each of Ireland and Luxembourg, "perfection" generally refers to the steps that, if not taken, mean that the security is void but which steps, by themselves, will not necessarily render the security interest first-ranking. In this regard, it should be noted that the Collateral Directive disapplies, in respect of any qualifying collateral arrangement, any filing or registration requirements that may otherwise apply under the domestic regime of the applicable EU Member State.

Security agency

Both Irish and Luxembourg law accommodate security being held by one entity for the benefit of many, whether through a security trustee or security agent structure in Ireland, or a security agent structure in Luxembourg.

Security through insolvency

In general terms, security granted by an Irish or Luxembourg fund is effective on and through insolvency and may be enforced without court intervention.

No stamp or transfer taxes

Generally speaking, no stamp, transfer or other similar taxes are typically payable under Irish or Luxembourg law on the creation of security or execution of security documents.

Conflicts-of-law considerations

Due to the multi-jurisdictional nature of finance transactions involving Irish and Luxembourg funds, it is essential to properly address questions of private international law. This is the case for the choice of law and choice of jurisdiction in the finance documentation, but more specifically, as it relates to the recognition of the right *in rem* over the collateral and its enforceability against the pledgor, the investor and any other third party (competing creditors) in a context where all such parties are located in different jurisdictions. Moreover, the impact of an insolvency of the fund or of any other guarantor or security provider should be considered in an international context.

Whereas it is fairly typical for the lending documents to be governed by New York law or another law chosen by the lender, local law considerations come into sharper focus in relation to collateral arrangements. In general terms, similar conflicts-of-law principles arise for consideration in Ireland and Luxembourg. In each case, for the creation, perfection and enforcement of collateral, the law of the location (or deemed location) of the secured asset (the *lex situs*) is very relevant.

Accordingly, whereas there is no concern with the credit agreement or other document regulating borrowing being governed by the law preferred by the lender (typically New York law or English law), in each of Ireland and Luxembourg, there is a preference for security to be taken under the *lex situs*. The *lex situs* will often be Irish law or Luxembourg law (as the case may be). Claims governed by Irish or Luxembourg law or owed to a debtor located in Ireland or Luxembourg, or cash or securities accounts in Ireland or Luxembourg, will generally be regarded as having an Irish or Luxembourg *lex situs*.

Regulation (EC) No 593/2008 is also relevant. Better known as the Rome I Regulation, or simply Rome I, it applies equally in Ireland and Luxembourg and refers to the law chosen by the parties for all contractual aspects. Article 14 of Rome I also addresses the relationship between assignor and assignee under a voluntary assignment of a claim against another person (the debtor). This is relevant to security over capital calls exercisable against investors. Article 14 provides that the relationship between assignor (i.e. the fund) and assignee (i.e. the lender or the security agent) under a voluntary assignment of a claim against the debtor is governed by the law that applies to the contract between the assignor and assignee (i.e. the governing law of the subscription agreement or, as applicable, limited partnership agreement). Article 14 also provides that the law governing the assigned claim shall determine its assignability, and certain effects against the debtor of such claim (investor).

As fund documentation is typically governed by the law of the location of the establishment of the fund (so Ireland or Luxembourg, as the case may be), Irish or Luxembourg law will apply to such matters and such application will, throughout the EU, be supported by Rome I. However, Rome I does not expressly provide for conflicts-of-law rules as regards the enforcement of such security interests against third parties. The impact on third parties is dealt with by national rules, which often designate the law of the location of the relevant investors to govern the effect on third parties. Investors in funds (whether Irish or Luxembourg) are typically located outside the fund jurisdiction (and often outside Europe), so this is something to be taken into account. A draft EU Commission proposal for a regulation on the law applicable to the third-party effects of assignments of claims, published on 12 March 2018, is set to deal with this question. The draft proposal aims to reduce the uncertainty as to the law applicable to perfection requirements and the enforceability of security interests over claims against third parties. The proposal provides that, as a rule, the law of the country where the assignor has its habitual residence will govern the third-party effects of the assignment of claims.

Cascading pledges

Driven by considerations from the US market, the use of cascading structures has become very common in financings involving master-feeder fund structures spanning across the Atlantic. Irish and Luxembourg fund structures with US nexus are no exception to this. The implementation of such security structures has been accepted and built into the local security documentation.

In the case of Irish funds, cascading pledges can also be a useful solution to issues otherwise presented by certain restrictions on third-party credit support.

In the case of Luxembourg funds, cascading pledges can pose some challenges in structuring and drafting the security to dovetail with civil law concepts applicable in Luxembourg. Despite the absence of case law and a number of questions on the efficiency of such security structures in distressed situations, practitioners in Luxembourg have found an agreed position to implement these structures based on the general principle of freedom of contracts and a pragmatic approach.

Typical security package

The security package for a financing of an Irish or Luxembourg fund will, as with any other jurisdiction, depend on the nature of the financing – subscription line or NAV facility (or hybrid). Typically, in each of Ireland and Luxembourg, a combination of at least the following is used: a security interest over unfunded capital commitments, together with security over the bank account into which investors are required to pay subscription/commitment amounts. NAV and other asset-backed facilities will involve collateral over other of the fund's assets and, in particular where this involves securities owned by the fund, the role of the depositary in the security arrangement becomes of central importance.

Typical security package for subscription line deals

In both Ireland and Luxembourg, security interests provided by a fund in respect of capital call rights against an investor are recognised and enforceable against the fund, even if no notice is given to the investor. As regards enforcement against the investor, until the investor is given notice that its rights have been assigned, it may be validly discharged (including by set-off) as against the fund. For this reason, consideration is given to notifying investors of the creation of such security, where practicable. Ideally, such notice is acknowledged by the investor.

Ireland

As with any financing, there is no universal security package. That said, the following are typical features. In a capital call/subscription facility, a typical security package includes security over the fund's rights on capital calls against investors, and security over the relevant bank account into which the subscription monies are to be credited. In addition, a security power of attorney is usually sought from the fund.

As mentioned, the administrator plays a key role in the subscription process. In certain cases, it is appropriate to seek security over the fund's interest in the related administration agreement to provide a lender with "step-in" rights. In other cases, a side letter to the lender is obtained from the administrator in relation to the performance of its duties following enforcement. Control agreements in respect of the subscription proceeds account may be appropriate. The appearance of an Irish fund in a financing will not necessarily be limited to the Irish fund in the role of borrower. The use of Irish funds (particularly ICAVs) in feeder fund structures is common.

One issue that will require careful consideration in this context is the issue of guarantees and other third-party credit support (including joint and several liability). An Irish AIF cannot generally provide "guarantees" (which is generally taken as including third-party credit support more generally) to collateralise the obligations of third parties. The use of "cascading pledges" can be a useful tool in this regard. In the case of security created by an Irish fund, the Collateral Directive, where applicable, displaces any security filing requirements. Nonetheless, it is market practice to consider precautionary security filings (particularly where contractual rights are secured). These are made at the Companies Registration Office or (in the case of ICAVs) CBI. Unless there is a transfer of the security interest to a new lender, these are one-time filings with no renewal requirement (unlike, for example, financing statements in certain jurisdictions). It is permitted under Irish law to take security over future assets.

Luxembourg

The collateral package in Luxembourg subscription deals usually consists of security over: (i) the unfunded commitments by the fund's limited partners to make capital contributions when called by the general partner; and (ii) the account where the contributions are funded. The Luxembourg law of 5 August 2005 on financial collateral arrangements implementing the Collateral Directive, as amended (the "**Luxembourg Financial Collateral Act**"), captures these two types of assets to offer lenders a secure and bankruptcy-remote pledge while allowing the fund, as pledgor, to benefit from a continuing and flexible management of the collateral.

Pledges under the Luxembourg Financial Collateral Act can be granted over virtually all types of securities and claims (the latter include bank accounts and receivables). In addition, they can be granted under private seal and, in principle, are not subject to any filing or publication requirements in Luxembourg.

Contributions in the form of equity, notes or loans can be captured by the Luxembourg Financial Collateral Act, with flexibility as to any contractual arrangements on timing and mechanics. Furthermore, the Luxembourg Financial Collateral Act allows pledges to be granted not only over present assets, but also over future assets. Consequently, counsel in Luxembourg have a large degree of flexibility in structuring the security package for subscription facilities.

In order to be fully effective, a pledge over a claim, including bank accounts, must be notified to and accepted by the debtor of the relevant claim. There are no stringent rules with respect to the form of the notification. Acknowledgment of the notice by the investor may be sought, for evidence purposes only.

More recently, we have seen the use of dual security structures becoming common in US fund finance involving Luxembourg funds. This emerging trend consists of taking two layers of security over capital calls, one under New York law and the other under Luxembourg law. Counsel are more and more comfortable having such "local" Luxembourg security be paired with a New York law security over capital calls, hence allowing for multiple routes of enforcement as available options to the lenders. Generally recommended, a Luxembourg law pledge over capital commitments provides an enhanced protection to the lender in case of enforcement given the important number of connecting factors leading to Luxembourg (governing law of the fund, the limited partnership agreement, the subscription agreements, the depositary agreement, etc.).

Typical security package for NAV deals

Ireland

NAV facilities, involving as they do, security over the fund's securities and other assets within the fund's investment portfolio, invariably involve account security. Control agreements may be an important feature of this. As the depositary is charged with safekeeping of a fund's financial instruments and has an overall supervisory obligation, the role of the depositary in taking and enforcing collateral is important. As with subscription line facilities, the security may benefit from the Collateral Directive even if precautionary security filings may be made. Where security requires enforcement over an Irish-situated account or other asset in the investment portfolio located in Ireland, there is a strong preference, from a lender perspective, to take Irish law security.

Luxembourg

When structuring a NAV facility involving a Luxembourg fund, the Luxembourg counsel to the lenders will always seek to ensure that the security package is structured under Luxembourg law to avoid discrepancies upon enforcement and, in particular under the Luxembourg Financial Collateral Act, to take full advantage of a bankruptcy-remote security package recognised across the EU.

In terms of composition of the security package, in addition or as an alternative to the deposit accounts on which the capital contributions are funded, NAV facilities are mainly granted against the fund's investment portfolio. Depending on the investment policy of the fund, and the way it is structured (whether it is a fund of fund or not, and the way the holding of the underlying assets is structured), the collateral might fall into a different class of assets, and hence be subject to a different form of pledge.

The most common approach in Luxembourg is to have the security package in a NAV facility include a pledge over the portfolio companies (HoldCos), a pledge over receivables (in particular, for credit funds), and a pledge over bank accounts. All such pledges can be governed by the Luxembourg Financial Collateral Act and take advantage of its flexible and efficient regime. With a flexible legal framework, variations are possible around these types of pledges, which can be adjusted to align to the type of transaction and the structure involved. For funds of funds, when the portfolio is composed of hedge funds, certificates are held within a bank account chosen by the lender, who further benefits from a control agreement.

Under Luxembourg law, the terms that are normally used in a control agreement may be incorporated in a pledge over bank account receivables, so that they may take advantage of the robust protections offered by the Luxembourg Financial Collateral Act.

Execution formalities

Both Irish and Luxembourg law facilitate ease of execution by powers of attorney and (as assumed increased importance during the COVID-19 pandemic) electronic signature.

ESG

Environmental, Social and Governance ("**ESG**") factors are assuming increasing importance on both sides of the Atlantic. As members of the EU, both Ireland and Luxembourg are subject to and benefit from the same ESG regime. With the aim of furthering sustainable finance and ESG integration, the EU Commission introduced a package of legislative measures in 2018 that includes three key regulations: the Taxonomy Regulation; the Sustainable Finance Disclosure Regulation; and the Low Carbon and Positive Impacts Benchmarks Regulation. The Sustainable Finance Disclosure Regulation came into effect on 10 March 2021 ("**SFDR Level 1**"), which required all financial market participants ("**FMPs**"), including AIFMs, UCITS management companies and self-managed UCITS, to consider sustainability from a number of perspectives and to: (1) publish information on their websites regarding their policies on the integration of sustainability risks in their investment decision-making process; (2) make pre-contractual disclosures on how they incorporate sustainability risks in their business; and (3) comply with pre-contractual transparency rules on sustainable investments.

The high-level principles-based requirements contained in SFDR Level 1 are supplemented by more detailed Level 2 requirements ("**SFDR RTS**"). SFDR RTS requires FMPs to comply with more detailed pre-contractual disclosures and annual reporting disclosures. FMPs must make these disclosures in the mandatory templates that are set out in the annexes to SFDR RTS for relevant products.

To ensure there is a single rulebook for sustainability disclosures, the European supervisory authorities determined that the additional taxonomy-related requirements should be incorporated into SFDR RTS. These requirements become effective as of 1 January 2023.

Conclusion

The ongoing impact of Brexit has seen asset managers increasingly attracted to Ireland and Luxembourg, resulting in ever-increasing importance of Ireland and Luxembourg in fund finance. The continued importance of Ireland and Luxembourg as fund domicile jurisdictions will ensure that Irish and Luxembourg funds will continue to be prominent in financing structures, whether as borrowers or part of a broader master-feeder structure. The laws of both Ireland and Luxembourg, although different in many respects, allow lenders to obtain a comprehensive security package in relation to an Irish or Luxembourg fund. The importance of fund financing during times of market dislocation (as evidenced by the resilience of fund financing through the early days of the pandemic) will see Ireland and Luxembourg funds be a feature of cross-border financings in all market conditions into the future.

Jad Nader
Tel: +352 2712 2047 / Email: jad.nader@ogier.com
Jad Nader is a partner with Ogier in Luxembourg and a member of the firm's Banking & Finance group. Jad has an important fund finance practice in the US and in Luxembourg. He covers cross-border lending transactions in general and also advises on AIFM licensing requirements and listing regulations. Jad holds a Ph.D. on the taking of collateral over financial assets and has been involved in a number of publications and legal opinion working groups.

Phil Cody
Tel: +353 1 920 1238 / Email: phil.cody@arthurcox.com
Phil Cody is a partner in the Finance group at Arthur Cox LLP. He is based in Dublin, Ireland. Phil advises on a broad range of finance and financial services matters, including fund finance. Phil is a trusted adviser to many of the leading Irish and international financial institutions on Irish law matters and is a go-to Irish counsel for foreign market participants and law firms. In addition, Phil leads the firm's derivatives and trading practice. As the outgoing partner-in-charge of Arthur Cox's New York representative office, Phil has particular experience of US fund financings and strong relationships with US market participants.

Ogier
2–4 rue Eugène Ruppert, PO Box 2078 L-1020
Luxembourg, Grand Duchy of Luxembourg
URL: www.ogier.com

Arthur Cox LLP
Ten Earlsfort Terrace, Dublin 2,
D02 T380, Ireland
URL: www.arthurcox.com

Fund finance facilities: A cradle to grave timeline

Bronwen Jones, Kevin-Paul Deveau & Brendan Gallen
Reed Smith LLP

Introduction

This chapter looks at the different types of fund finance that may be available to funds at the various stages of a fund's life. The following diagram sets out in linear form the typical life cycle of a closed-ended private equity fund, although the diagram would equally apply to closed-ended funds of most asset classes, albeit possibly on a different timeline.

As mentioned, we have picked a private equity fund as the fund on which to base this chapter. The other common asset classes – credit funds, real estate funds, infrastructure funds, secondary funds and funds of funds – are mentioned where relevant.

Start of fund life

The three-month period before first closing of a fund (or typically longer for nascent, early-stage fund managers – or in more challenging economic times) is characterised by management time spent on investor negotiations coupled with the structuring and financing of pipeline transactions expected to complete shortly after closing. The fund will typically have a capital-raise period of 12–18 months following first close, although there is now an increasing number of funds managed by more experienced management teams, which often hold a "one and done" closing. At first close, undrawn commitments will be equal to total commitments. The first drawdown date following first close may depend on whether a transaction needs to be consummated shortly following first close and the extent to which financing is in place to enable speedier execution of that transaction. The fund will also need to pay formation expenses, service provider costs and often the first quarter management fee to the general partner (as the management fee/general partner share is typically payable quarterly in advance) in addition to due diligence costs on pipeline deals.

Subscription line facilities

These fees and costs are funded by drawing investor commitments or by debt, which will most likely be made available by way of a subscription line facility, also often called a capital call facility. This type of facility will be made available to the fund as borrower in an amount calculated – in general terms – by reference to the amount of the undrawn commitments and the creditworthiness of investors. This calculation provides the borrowing base for the fund's debt, and it allows the fund to access debt during its investment phase, before it owns significant assets, by allowing it to use investor commitments as collateral for debt. Whilst the amount of undrawn commitments is a purely empirical and straightforward question, the determination of investor creditworthiness – the other half of the borrowing base calculation – leads to more variation in the subscription line market. Typically, the lender will determine investor creditworthiness on a per-investor basis or by reference to the overall investor base of the fund. In the former case, a discount (called an "advance rate") is applied to each investor's undrawn commitments, and that discount is inverse to that investor's creditworthiness.

Fund and Fund Financing Life Cycle
Typical PE Fund

YEARS	Fund Stage	% UCC	Investments	Financing
-1	First Close Start of Investment Period	100%		
0	Final Close Investment Period	100–90%	None	Sub line
	Investment Period	90–70%		
2.5	Investment Period	80–60%	Some (4–8)	Sub line/hybrid
	Investment Period	50–60%	Probably as many as going to have (e.g. 10–12)	NAV/hybrid
5	End of Investment Period Divestment Phase	20/15%	10–12	NAV
	Divestment Phase	15%	8–10	NAV
7.5	Divestment Phase	15%	6–8	Concentrated NAV
	Divestment Phase	10%	4–6	Concentrated NAV
10	Original Fund Termination Date Divestment Phase	5/10%	2–4	Very Concentrated NAV/Continuation
11	One-Year Extension Divestment Phase	5/10%	2–4	Very Concentrated NAV/Continuation
12	One-Year Extension Divestment Phase	5/10%	2–4	Continuation

Where an investor is not rated, or does not publish financial information that the lender can access and verify, the discount is total (or very high), and the undrawn commitments are zero (or very low) for the borrowing base calculation. This per-investor approach to determining the borrowing base accordingly looks in detail at the creditworthiness of each investor on a reasonably granular basis and can be sensitive to investor-specific events. In the latter case – where the borrowing base is calculated by reference to the overall investor base of the fund – the lender applies a single advance rate against all of the investors, taking into consideration a blended metric of the creditworthiness of investors and the likelihood of investor defaults.

In this way, the investor base is critical at this stage of the fund's life, and the undrawn commitments and the bankability of the investor base will dictate the availability and quantum of finance. Accordingly, the subscription facility market tends not to distinguish significantly between the different types of funds – private equity, private debt, venture capital, etc. – because the facility is granted and sized principally by reference to the investor base. However, certain types of fund, such as earlier stage venture capital funds, may encounter greater difficulties than, for instance, well-established private equity or private debt funds, as they will often have a less sophisticated or institutional investor base. A private equity fund could quite easily have a subscription facility that looks broadly similar to that of a private debt fund. The fund assets do not drive the lending terms for subscription facilities to any significant degree.

The key documentary variations in the subscription facility market are primarily driven by (1) borrowing base methodology and other investor metrics as described above, and (2) variations in fund structures, such as parallel funds and feeder funds (which could result in some degree of documentary complexity to ensure, for example, that the lender has access to the uncalled capital of the actual investors, rather than pass-through vehicles). Other variations emerge where lenders provide debt products that move away from the typical feature of a subscription line described above – i.e. a facility calculated by reference to the undrawn commitments of a diverse (or reasonably diverse) investor base. For example, some lenders are able to make available multi-fund facilities, which aggregate undrawn commitments across funds and provide a framework financing solution to managers, whilst other lenders provide facilities for single-investor funds (also known as separately managed accounts, or "SMAs") that invest alongside a manager's other funds.

Across the subscription facility market, however, facilities are fundamentally calculated by reference to undrawn commitments and investor creditworthiness, and it is this key feature that has contributed to the increasing popularity of subscription facilities amongst lenders in the last decade or so, particularly in the European and (more recently) Asian markets. Lenders take risk not on fund assets, but on a clearly ascertainable and quantifiable amount that investors – often highly rated entities, such as development finance institutions, pension funds and insurance companies – are contractually obliged to make available to the fund and which can be applied to repay the lenders. Lenders typically take a secured position in relation to undrawn commitments in the form of security over the rights to issue drawdown notices to investors and security over the bank account to which commitments are funded by investors. In the event of an enforcement or work-out situation for lenders, which is rare in the subscription line market, the lenders are protected by this secured position against the contractual obligations of investors to fund their uncalled capital, and lenders are further protected in a default scenario by the discount mechanism described above, which should be largely insulated from asset value or market movement fluctuations. In an overall lending market affected by increasing volatility and ever-growing valuations and EBITDA multiples, the subscription line market continues to prove very attractive to lenders.

Midway through the investment period

On final closing, the fund will have a fixed commitment level that will correlate to the size of the deals that the fund may undertake, subject to investment restrictions, whether based on deal size as a proportion of total commitments, geography or asset class. A private equity fund will typically terminate its investment period on the earlier of the five-year anniversary of the final closing date (or the six-year anniversary of the first closing date) or the date on which the fund manager starts to invest in and earn a management fee on a successor fund (within permitted parameters under the fund limited partnership agreement, or "LPA"). One would expect at least 40–50% of commitments to be deployed, committed or allocated for deployment by years three to four. Successor fund formation restrictions are usually relaxed when 70–80% of commitments have been drawn and/or reserved for investment and expenses (or otherwise on termination of the investment period). Consequently, by year four, the key executives of the fund manager may begin thinking about the appropriate time to gear up for the next fundraise within that strategy. The fund manager will also focus on ensuring that commitments are deployed to a sufficient level before the close of the investment period while being mindful of the extent to which follow-on investments may be desirable or required thereafter. The fund manager will be on the lookout for exit opportunities and consider divestment structures for current fund assets.

Hybrid facilities

At this stage, a subscription facility could very well continue to satisfy the fund's need for finance, but as investor capital is deployed, the borrowing base would start to reduce in line with the reduced undrawn commitments, which could have the effect of restricting borrowings. The manager might consider moving to a net asset value ("NAV") facility, which (as described below) would have a borrowing base shaped on the NAV of the fund's assets. Another option could be to obtain a hybrid facility, which combines elements of a subscription facility and a NAV facility, with the borrowing base being calculated by reference to a combination of (1) undrawn investor commitments, and (2) the NAV of the underlying assets acquired by the fund. A hybrid facility (and a NAV facility) typically applies diversity and concentration limits to the asset value element of the borrowing base calculation in order to ensure that debt is not made available by reference to a small number of assets concentrated in a particular region or industry. As a result of this, a hybrid facility frequently starts out with a borrowing base calculated on the basis of undrawn commitments only.

Whilst this combination of borrowing base contributors spanning both uncalled capital and underlying assets would seem a sensible way to increase access to finance, hybrid facilities remain less common – and less popular – than might be expected. This results from a combination of factors. It is difficult for some banks to combine subscription lines and NAV facilities, particularly where those product groups sit in different parts of the bank. More significantly, managers continue to have doubts about the economics of a hybrid facility. Suspicion remains that the margin for a hybrid facility is not a "pure" blend of that for a subscription facility and for a NAV facility, but rather results in the fund paying a margin that is higher than it should be during the initial period where it relies principally on the uncalled commitments of highly rated investors, without sufficient compensation in the form of lower margin for the period when the hybrid facility relies principally on the underlying assets of the fund. Also, for managers who have managed to raise multiple funds, and who have tried and tested subscription facility and NAV facility products agreed with lenders, the prospect of combining those products into a hybrid facility for the prospect of a slight degree of convenience or better pricing has not resulted in a significant move in the market toward hybrid facilities.

That being said, hybrid facilities have become a bigger element of the market for funding private debt funds, which reflects that the life cycle of such funds can be shorter and that the time it takes to deploy investor capital can be much shorter for private debt than private equity. These shorter time horizons make a hybrid facility more attractive. It simplifies the documentary process by only needing to negotiate and agree one facility agreement (and related documents), not two. It can reduce spend on bank fees and legal costs. And it can mitigate financing risk for the fund over its investment life. A manager of a private debt fund is more likely to take the view that a hybrid facility is more attractive than putting in place a subscription facility in the first instance only to find, maybe 12 months later, that the fund needs to move to an asset-backed NAV facility. The window for moving from one to the other could be very limited, and failing to execute a NAV facility in that period could risk either (1) the fund not having access to sufficient bridge facilities to facilitate completions (which can be essential where a private debt fund is buying into private equity-backed acquisition facilities that require "certain funds" on short time schedules), or (2) deploying investor capital too quickly without the ability for strategic short-term investment opportunities and the ability to reinvest capital commitments.

Termination of the investment period

On termination of the investment period, 70–80% of commitments should be drawn down, or allocated to service existing assets and costs. The fund will typically have acquired between 10 and 15 underlying assets, depending on its strategy. Following termination of the investment period, fund LPAs usually only permit drawdowns to complete new investments that were secured (i.e. by way of letter of intent or legally binding undertaking) before termination of the investment period, to make follow-on investments and to satisfy liabilities, including fund financing and guarantees, management fee payments, ongoing partnership expenses, taxes and indemnification expenses. The fund LPA typically enables 15–25% of commitments to be drawn down to make follow-on investments that are intended to preserve or enhance the value of the fund's primary assets.

NAV facilities

NAV facilities are facilities made available to a fund with secured recourse to the portfolio of assets of the fund, and no recourse to the uncalled commitments of the investors of the fund. What that portfolio of assets will be will depend on the strategy of the fund in question. At one end of the asset class scale, a credit fund will have a pool of possibly several hundred loans and bonds. At the other end of the scale, a private equity fund will have a pool of what may be as little as a dozen private equity assets. The original popular asset classes for NAV facilities are credit funds, secondary funds and funds of funds, but NAV facilities in the real estate, infrastructure and private equity asset classes have increased significantly over the last few years as well.

At this point, the different fund structures become important again. In the same way that, for a subscription facility, the fund structure as it relates to investors is important (so bringing in parallel funds, feeder funds, etc.), for a NAV facility, the fund structure as it relates to assets is important. Are the fund assets owed directly by the fund or through a series of holding companies – and if so, do those holding companies hold several assets or only one each? In the case of a private equity fund, the fund will often form chains of three or four (or more) special purpose vehicles ("SPVs"), the "top" SPV being owned by the fund and the "bottom" SPV being the entity that buys the private equity asset. The private equity fund will therefore have a separate chain of SPVs for every asset. In the case of a credit fund, however, the underlying loan assets are very often held by one or a small number of holding companies, each of which holds a pool of loans. Real estate funds, infrastructure funds and secondary funds also all have varying asset structures.

The asset structure determines how the asset security is most efficiently taken. A typical credit fund structure is perhaps the most simple. Assuming the fund has a single holding company that it owns directly, and that holding company owns all the loans, the security package will normally be security from the fund over all the shares in the holding company, and security from the holding company over all its assets, which will include all the loans and all its bank accounts. This gives the lender the ability, on enforcement, either to sell the holding company through a straightforward share sale, taking with it all the underlying loans, or to sell the loans individually or in bundles. Plus, of course, it will have access to the bank accounts of the holding company where proceeds from the underlying loans, whether of principal, interest or fees, are paid in the meantime.

A typical private equity fund is often the most complex in terms of the necessary security structure. Whilst not unheard of, it is not usual for private equity funds to use common holding companies through which they hold their assets, preferring instead a chain of SPVs for each asset with each chain held directly by the fund as described above. This gives rise to two possible security structures. First, the fund can grant share security over each of the "topco" SPVs, giving rise (using our private equity fund example) to a dozen separate share charges. Each share charge needs to be granted under the jurisdiction of the relevant topco SPV, i.e. a Luxembourg share charge for a Luxembourg topco SPV, an English share charge for an English topco SPV and so on. This would allow the lender on enforcement to sell each of the assets separately through individual sales of the topco SPVs, or a bundled together sale of all 12 (or however many) topco SPVs at the same time to the same purchaser.

Alternatively, the fund sometimes carries out a restructuring exercise before the NAV facility is put in place, to insert one, or sometimes two, common holding companies between the fund and each of the topco SPVs. The security package would then be (1) a share pledge over the shares in the new common holding company that now owns all the topco SPVs (the "common asset holding company"), whether that company is a direct subsidiary of the fund or has the second common holding company between it and the fund, (2) bank account security over the accounts of the common asset holding company and/or the bank accounts of the fund (and/or the second common holding company), depending on where distributions from the underlying assets are paid – it is often logistically easier to leave the bank accounts at fund level even though the assets move down to below the common asset holding company, and (3) all asset security from the common asset holding company over the topco SPV in each chain of SPVs. This security structure would allow the lender to sell the shares in the common asset holding company on enforcement, taking with it all the underlying assets, or the direct sale of the individual assets through sales of their respective topco SPVs. Even if security is not taken from the common asset holding company over each topco SPV, as is sometimes the case, a sale of individual assets could be achieved on enforcement by taking control of the common asset holding company (rather than immediately selling it) and through that control selling the assets individually or in bundles. That said, this sort of restructuring to include a common asset holding company at the time of agreeing a NAV facility is not common.

The loan-to-value ("LTV") covenant in NAV facilities is critical to lenders, and the constituent elements are usually heavily negotiated and very specific to the asset class concerned. Eligibility criteria, concentration limits and related "haircuts" are usual. The valuation methodology, frequency of valuations and the ability to challenge and require third-party valuations are also heavily negotiated.

A further feature of some NAV facilities, which is frequently seen for asset classes such as private equity, is a mandatory prepayment sweep of disposal proceeds if assets are sold if the LTV is above a certain level. The sweep may not be 100% of net proceeds, or may be at a lower percentage at a lower LTV and rise to 100% if a higher LTV arises.

The lenders in the market who offer NAV facilities to funds overlap significantly with, but are not identical to, the lenders who offer subscription line facilities. And the NAV lenders vary from asset class to asset class, there being, as you would expect, more active lenders in the credit fund NAV facility market than in the private equity fund NAV facility market. Pricing, and LTV levels, are very different across the asset classes too, as, in reality, what was a broad single product at subscription line facility level, agnostic to asset classes, splinters into different NAV facility markets for each asset class. As a result, pricing and LTV comparisons between asset classes are not particularly helpful.

Midway through the liquidation period

The main focus following termination of the investment period, alongside active monitoring of the portfolio and ongoing engagement with investors, is maximising exit opportunities for the underlying assets so that the general partner can generate a positive distribution curve and therefore carried interest. By this time, assuming the current fund has performed well, the fund manager will likely have formed and may well have started to already invest a successor fund. The fund may make follow-on investments during this phase to protect or enhance the value of the underlying assets, subject to the typical limitations noted above. One would expect 80–90% of commitments to be drawn down as the fund life nears its close.

Concentrated NAV facilities

Continuing the theme of our private equity fund, as it moves through its divestment phase and successfully sells assets, it will reduce from having a pool of perhaps a dozen assets to a smaller pool of perhaps five or six assets. At this point, the original NAV lenders may wish to be repaid because the concentration risk with only five or six assets is too high for them, and new NAV lenders who are more comfortable with increased concentration risk will step in to provide a concentrated NAV facility. The small number of assets, which will continue to reduce as divestment continues, becomes a strong focus for the lender.

Valuations become more critical, and the lender will usually have stronger rights to challenge and require third-party valuations, at the cost of the fund. A cash sweep for asset distribution proceeds is more likely to be required, and more likely to be 100% or 75% of net proceeds rather than the lower percentages found for earlier fund life NAV facilities. The lender will have a more granular view of each of the assets, and may require full repayment upon a sale of the most valuable one or two assets. The lender will probably also require more asset-level reporting, and more frequent face-to-face meetings with the private equity executives in order to better understand and remain close to the asset disposal plans, process and progress.

End of fund life

Nearing termination of the fund's fixed term, typically 10 years following first closing, albeit fund terms are gradually becoming longer and contain multiple extension rights, the general partner in most cases will be unable to draw down commitments from investors to fund further follow-on investments and can probably draw those uncalled commitments solely to meet expenses and liabilities relating to the fund and its assets. Leading up to expiry of the fund term, the general partner will be considering whether to extend the life of the fund to maximise its ability to source exit opportunities and create value.

Very concentrated NAV facilities

At this point, the number of remaining assets is very low. NAV facilities at this time are much less available in the market, or at least not at a price and LTV attractive to the fund. The facilities at this point broadly fall into two categories. It may be that all that is needed is a small working capital line to continue to fund the ongoing costs and expenses until the assets are sold. There will usually, at this end point in a fund's life, still be a small amount of uncalled capital that can, as indicated above, be called for these costs and expenses. Security over these uncalled commitments, when teamed with security over the underlying assets, can be sufficient for a facility with a very low LTV to be implemented.

The other type of facility at this point is where some limited partners do not want the assets to be disposed of just because the fund life happens to be ending, whilst other limited partners do want such a disposal. If a NAV lender can be found willing to provide a facility, this can be used to fund the final return of capital to the "want to leave" investors whilst the "want to stay" investors can remain. There are lenders that will provide these facilities, but they are typically relationship-driven lenders who will be very focused on the remaining assets. They will require considerable asset diligence, assuming they are not already familiar with the remaining assets, more akin in some respects to the diligence exercise required by a leveraged finance lender. They will want to understand in detail the rights of any remaining asset-level (acquisition finance) lenders, and the rights of any joint venture partners or minority equity holders.

Leveraged preferred equity facilities

It is at this point, when concentrated NAV facilities become more difficult to implement, that another product seen in the market may make an appearance – a leveraged preferred equity facility. A preferred equity provider will provide an additional limited partnership interest to a fund in return for a preferred limited partner position, ahead of the "ordinary" limited partners, as and when further distributions from the remaining assets are received. The position is akin to the position of a preferred shareholder in a company. It is possible for that preferred equity position itself to be leveraged, with security over that preferred equity position granted by the preferred equity provider to its lender. Whilst sometimes seen implemented at other stages of the life of a fund, leveraged preferred equity facilities can also make an appearance in place of the second form of concentrated NAV facility referred to above – i.e. when you have "want to leave" and "want to stay" investors.

Fund extensions

Most fund LPAs empower the general partner to extend the life of the fund by 12-month increments. While the subject of investor negotiation, it is common for the first 12-month extension period to be solely at the general partner's discretion, with further 12-month extensions available after that, typically with the consent of the Limited Partner Advisory Committee for the next extension, followed by some form of investor consent thereafter, e.g. a majority or super majority of investors. The decision whether to opt for the first extension will have been made before expiry of the term so, during the first year, the general partner will be monitoring divestment opportunities and the activities of the portfolio companies to assess whether a further extension may be required. If the general partner is of the view that opportunities cannot be maximised during the extension period, then it may seek to run a general partner-led secondary process. This can take the form of: (a) a tender offer of limited partner interests or of one or more of the fund's portfolio companies; or (b) a more complex secondary transaction, such as a stapled secondary transaction where investors in the fund are given the option to cash out their interests in the existing fund or elect to have their in-kind interests in the fund transferred to a new continuation fund, which may also be coupled with a refinancing and new capital being injected into the continuation vehicle, and the admission of new investors who are particularly interested in the one or two portfolio assets.

Continuation facilities

Facilities that are available at this late stage of a fund's life are very bespoke and provided by only a few lenders who, for relationship reasons, are comfortable with these facilities. In respect of the second option mentioned above, a stapled secondary transaction, a facility could be provided to the continuation fund, which could be a hybrid facility if the continuing investors and any new investors have provided additional uncalled commitments or a simple NAV facility based purely on the asset value of the assets transferred to the continuation fund. The proceeds of this type of facility are used to repay those original investors who do not wish to participate in the continuation fund. The terms of this kind of facility are essentially the same as any very concentrated NAV facility: much asset diligence or pre-existing familiarity for the lender; details of the proposed exit plans for the assets; mandatory prepayment on disposals; and low LTV.

* * *

Acknowledgment

The authors would like to thank Shervin Shameli for his contribution to this chapter. Shervin has particular experience advising fund managers on all aspects of the establishment, structuring and operation of a wide range of private investment funds, including in the private equity, private credit, infrastructure, growth capital and venture capital asset classes. In addition, Shervin advises fund managers on their internal matters, including management vehicle set-up and structuring and carried interest arrangements, as well as their co-investment activities.

Shervin has particular experience advising fund managers on all aspects of the establishment, structuring and operation of a wide range of private investment funds, including in the private equity, private credit, infrastructure, growth capital and venture capital asset classes. In addition, Shervin advises fund managers on their internal matters, including management vehicle set-up and structuring and carried interest arrangements, as well as their co-investment activities.

Tel: +44 20 3116 3087 / Email: sshameli@reedsmith.com

Bronwen Jones
Tel: +44 20 3116 3052 / Email: bjones@reedsmith.com

Bronwen acts for banks and other financial institutions, sponsors, general partners and fund managers on the whole range of fund finance matters including capital call (subscription line) facilities, NAV facilities, hybrid facilities and general partner and co-investment facilities. She also has experience of asset finance, project finance, acquisition finance, intercreditor issues, work-outs and restructurings, and investment grade and corporate facilities, and is co-head of the Funds Finance practice at Reed Smith.

Kevin-Paul Deveau
Tel: +44 20 3116 2874 / Email: kdeveau@reedsmith.com

Kevin-Paul is a banking and finance partner with Reed Smith in London. He advises clients on a broad range of domestic and cross-border debt finance transactions, including fund finance, acquisition finance, real estate finance, project finance, general corporate lending, and restructuring. Kevin-Paul specialises in fund finance, and he regularly advises funds on financing matters, including bridge and gearing facilities, intra-fund finance and structuring issues, and finance considerations related to fund formation. He also regularly provides finance advice to private equity clients. Kevin-Paul also has extensive experience in emerging markets, including advising on market-leading transactions in Central and Eastern Europe, Turkey, the Middle East, Africa, and Asia.

Brendan Gallen
Tel: +44 20 3116 3487 / Email: bgallen@reedsmith.com

Brendan is a fund formation partner in Reed Smith's London office. Brendan's practice focuses on advising clients on the structuring, establishment and operation of (and investment into) alternative investment funds across all major asset classes including credit, private equity, infrastructure and real estate. He also advises in relation to spin-outs, secondary transactions, GP-led restructurings, managed accounts, carried interest and other co-investment schemes.

Reed Smith LLP

Broadgate Tower, 20 Primrose Street, London EC2A 2RS, United Kingdom
Tel: +44 20 3116 3594 / Fax: +44 20 3116 3999 / URL: www.reedsmith.com

Newer liquidity solutions for alternative asset fund managers – increasingly core

Jamie Parish, Danny Peel & Katie McMenamin
Travers Smith LLP

In previous iterations of this chapter, the original of which was written in late 2020, we concluded that the combined impact of COVID-19 and other developments in the market was that the concept behind some of the more innovative liquidity solutions adopted by alternative asset managers during the COVID-19 pandemic had been proven. The economic headwinds currently facing global financial markets will add further drivers for the increased use of these liquidity products. We now assess again the current fund finance market and liquidity solutions available to alternative asset fund managers – from traditional subscription facilities through to net asset value (NAV)/hybrid facilities and preferred equity products, as well as broader general partner (GP)-led fund restructurings – each in light of the impact of current economic pressures and prevailing market trends. We also now explore in more detail some of the considerations that liquidity providers may have when looking to enforce security over a fund's NAV.

Introduction

It became clear almost immediately that the impact of the COVID-19 pandemic in 2020 would be severe and long-lasting. Many asset managers, nervous about the potential of their (fundamentally healthy) investments to weather the storm, were forced to seek ways to ensure they had the ability to shore up the balance sheets of their portfolio companies if this was required.

In the short term, that meant finding liquidity. Some managers found themselves considering funding sources that had previously been talked about, but not seriously explored, which were suddenly seen as genuine and potentially the only options for providing that much-needed liquidity to support portfolios. That, in turn, had a longer-term impact, to which the prevalence of these solutions (long after the initial liquidity concerns caused by the pandemic abated and indeed the pandemic more generally ceased to be such a significant driver of behaviour) attests. These sources of liquidity, having been given the chance to prove concept and to demonstrate that they are both structurally feasible to execute and sufficiently flexible to suit a broad range of liquidity requirements, have increasingly cemented themselves in the asset manager's toolkit of core financing options throughout the traditional fund life-cycle. COVID-19 had a permanent impact on how some asset managers structure their funds and finance their investment activity and, with recessions looming across the globe, these types of financing solutions will only becoming increasingly prevalent.

A changed market

The fund finance market has undergone significant expansion in recent years. NAV facilities in particular, traditionally the preserve of secondaries fund managers looking for leverage to finance their portfolio acquisitions of limited partner (LP) interests, have increasingly become standard fare across other asset classes. More recently, preferred equity structures have been used by fund managers willing to embrace more structured solutions. COVID-19 not only accelerated the uptake of these types of products for fund managers that had already started using them, but also meant that others began viewing them as viable options.

The subscription finance arena remains a huge and thriving market that is utilised by the overwhelming majority of fund managers. Subscription facilities constitute a cheap, flexible and now (broadly) investor-accepted route to putting debt in place at the fund level. However, subscription facilities are predicated on a fund having enough uncalled capital to borrow against to enable it to obtain a facility at the quantum required. When COVID-19 hit, funds of a certain vintage that were fully (or mostly) invested had little or no remaining uncalled capital. For these funds, a purely subscription facility-based solution was off the table.

In a volatile economic environment, cash is paramount. As COVID-19 spread rapidly across the globe, fund managers undertook an urgent review of their investment portfolios in order to ascertain (i) which of their portfolio companies were likely to need additional funding as a result of their business being hit by the pandemic, and (ii) whether their funds had sufficient firepower to meet those requirements. The conclusion, in the case of some older vintage funds in particular (and especially those with retail and/or leisure-heavy portfolios), was that the worst-case scenario could see the short-term funding quantum required far exceeding the financing currently available (whether from existing cash resources at portfolio company level, headroom on asset-level facilities, additional leverage at the asset level, or investor capital (especially if this had largely been deployed already)). Fund managers feared the value they had created during years of sourcing, investing in and developing businesses would be destroyed overnight – not due to investment decisions they had made, but due to the immense strain arising from an almost entirely unforeseeable global pandemic that threatened the financial health of even the best businesses.

The liquidity solutions that gained the most traction in the market were NAV or hybrid facilities and preferred equity solutions. These products look to tap liquidity from assets other than investor commitments, principally the fund's equity in existing investments within its portfolio, as a means to generate immediately available cash. These tools have gained increasing popularity in recent years due to the greater flexibility they afford asset managers in maximising returns from their investments. For example, a fund later in its life (and therefore with limited investor capital available to call upon) may not have funding available for follow-on investment but may hold assets that would benefit from bolt-ons or additional capex. Rather than the arbitrary timing of the stage of the fund's life-cycle meaning these assets are left underfunded, NAV facilities and preferred equity products can be used to release capital for this purpose. COVID-19 meant that, for different reasons, readily available cash was a premium asset, and so unlocking value from the equity in the portfolio via a NAV facility or a preferred equity product became a necessary option to explore for a broader range of funds. A similar fact pattern is likely to arise again as global markets navigate increasingly uncertain economic conditions, challenged by rocketing inflation, rampant interest rates, supply chain issues and the war in Ukraine.

NAV facilities *versus* preferred equity – the details

In simple terms, the distinction between these products is that NAV facilities comprise fund- (or fund holdco-) level debt secured against the value of the assets in the investment portfolio (paired with, in the case of a hybrid facility, uncalled investor commitments), whereas preferred equity products comprise prior ranking third-party equity invested in the fund in return for priority claims over future distributions. Managers using these products for the first time might choose to run dual tracks until relatively late in the process (to ensure they have a full understanding of the pros and cons of each) before settling on the most appropriate solution for their specific needs.

NAV facilities, being a debt product, are typically cheaper. However, the lender will usually take at least some security (direct or indirect) over the assets and will require a reasonably wide-ranging suite of covenants that partially restrict the fund's ongoing activities. In addition, the facility will have a fixed tenor (which may be difficult to refinance at expiry if exit horizons are not clear) and there are likely to be ongoing finance costs such as servicing cash-pay interest payment obligations (which may be challenging for a non-cash generative portfolio).

In contrast, a preferred equity provider will not require security or typically as much by way of behavioural controls. Equally, it is unlikely to require payments of principal or cash-pay interest on set dates (although, where the cost of capital becomes increasingly punitive as time passes, funds may be so heavily incentivised to realise value and return capital to the provider that these effectively are time-limited products). Instead, the provider will receive a specified percentage of future distributions from investments until it has received a pre-agreed return on the capital provided, typically set at an internal rate of return (IRR) hurdle with a minimum multiple on invested capital requirement. Preferred equity products are by their nature very flexible and will often be bespoke, with providers marketing themselves as having the creativity to tailor solutions to suit the specific requirements of individual funds.

The principal trade-off between these two products is cost of capital (which can be a challenge for preferred equity providers to justify) *versus* loss of control over the portfolio (which is a preferred equity provider's sell to managers when compared with a debt product). However, there are a number of other detailed considerations for fund managers when putting in place these types of products, including:

- <u>Investor relations considerations</u>: Even if investor consent is not required (or the transaction can be structured such that consent is not required), keeping investors fully appraised of the rationale for (and impact on investor returns and risk profile of) putting a product of this nature in place is of paramount importance. In particular, managers should have regard to (i) investors' concerns around assets within the fund being cross-collateralised, which runs contrary to the general expectation of a series of silo'd investments, and (ii) the fact that the different products can have different impacts on individual investors – for example, some investors' cost of capital will increase if a fund in which it has invested becomes "leveraged" for the purposes of the Alternative Investment Fund Managers Directive (AIFMD) (and it should be noted that AIFMD II will bring further regulatory considerations on this front). From a commercial perspective, key messages a manager needs to be able to give to investors are that (i) the manager will retain control of the assets, even following a loan-to-value (LTV) breach, such that it can avoid a fire sale, and (ii) the nature of their investment in the fund as part of a non-leveraged, long-term investment strategy remains.

- <u>Fund documentation considerations</u>: It may be the case that the fund documentation does not specifically envisage this type of product and so LP/Limited Partner Advisory Committee (LPAC) consent is required (which, depending on the consent threshold required, will impact on timing). For newer funds, a NAV facility will often not require investor consent, but leverage limitations in the fund documentation will invariably apply to a NAV facility and so managers must ensure these will be respected. Preferred equity products typically require an amendment to the waterfall set out in the fund's limited partnership agreement (LPA), which would always require investor consent, but it may nonetheless be possible to execute such a transaction without requiring investor consent – particularly where undertaken at a holdco/aggregator level (see below).

- Structuring considerations: Both NAV facilities and preferred equity deals are simplest to structure where there is an aggregator vehicle in place between the fund partnership and the underlying portfolio assets. The existence of such a vehicle enables a single clean security interest to be granted over the equity in that vehicle (in the case of a NAV facility) or that vehicle to issue the preferred equity instrument (in the case of a preferred equity transaction) without the direct involvement of the fund. If there is no such existing aggregator, then ideally one would be introduced into the structure. This requires an analysis of any transfer or change of control provisions in the underlying equity or debt arrangements relating to each portfolio asset. It also requires consideration of any tax implications of doing so to ensure that dry tax charges are not inadvertently triggered. Ultimately, if it is not practicable to put this structure in place, it may still be feasible to execute a NAV facility where the investment agreements in relation to the various investment holdcos do not prohibit the grant of security over the shares in that investment holdco, but the cost of this may be significant – especially if the holdcos are incorporated across multiple different jurisdictions.
- Regulatory considerations: It may be that putting a product of this nature in place impacts the regulatory status of the fund – for example, causing a previously non-leveraged fund for AIFMD (and upcoming AIFMD II) purposes to be "leveraged" for the purposes thereof (which may also impact the manager itself if it was previously a manager only of non-leveraged funds). If Financial Conduct Authority (FCA) (or its equivalent in other jurisdictions) approvals are required, this will of course impact on timing, but in addition it may affect the compliance requirements applicable to the manager, reporting requirements (to regulators and investors) and (as alluded to above) the capital treatment of investors' own interests in the relevant fund.
- Valuation considerations: Agreeing which assets will be (and will remain) "eligible" for inclusion in the LTV covenant, and the basis on which those assets will be valued, is fundamentally important to the viability of the transaction. A manager will push for its own internal valuations to be used for all purposes, but a liquidity provider is likely to require a third-party valuer's input either at the outset or (at the very least) if there is subsequently a dispute over valuation or a default. These valuations will be used to size the funding that will be made available originally and to set the financial covenants and/or drawdown conditions going forward – with the value of an asset in default or forecasting a covenant breach under its asset-level debt often excluded from these calculations. In addition, certain assets (such as credit assets, which are more liquid) are much easier to value than others (such as buyout assets), with more liquid assets having obvious appeal to financiers. Providers of these products need to understand both fund structures and the underlying asset class in order to price the risk correctly. It is for this reason that such providers often combine internal expertise from their fund finance and asset-level debt teams when negotiating the commercial terms of these facilities.
- Enforcement considerations: If security is granted (directly or indirectly) over a fund's underlying portfolio assets as collateral for a NAV facility, the debt provider will have enforcement options and priority of repayment *versus* other creditors of the fund (though typically not asset-level debt providers) in a distressed scenario. The position is different for holders of a preferred equity product, who typically do not have direct enforcement options and would be subordinated to other agreed creditors of the fund. Managers

must be acutely aware of the rights of NAV facility lenders before entering into these arrangements, especially given the investor relations considerations referred to above. As noted above, lenders under a NAV facility may request security over the equity in the aggregator vehicle, which itself ultimately holds the equity in the underlying assets and security over the bank accounts of that aggregator vehicle, into which any distributions and other proceeds from the fund's investments will be contractually required to be paid. NAV lenders may or may not also require direct share security over each individual portfolio asset holding company stack. Depending on the jurisdiction(s) involved, the nature of the equity holding in each relevant portfolio asset (for example, majority *versus* minority) and the direct or indirect nature of the agreed security package, this may mean that the lenders have powers in an enforcement scenario to sell the shares over which they have security and/or exercise the powers of shareholders, which can include the ability to replace board members and therefore take control of underlying investments. Lenders may also be able to appropriate the value of any funds standing to the credit of the secured bank accounts at aggregator vehicle level to the extent that distribution proceeds are received from the underlying portfolio assets.

Whilst some clearing banks were prepared to consider providing products of this nature during the pandemic, it was only for their most valued and long-standing customers (and only on a NAV facility basis). For the most part, managers had to look to institutions that, for some time, had been specifically focusing on NAV facilities and preferred equity products – including funds dedicated to these strategies, traditional secondary players and investment banks. These institutions were in many cases far better placed to design and provide the bespoke solutions individual funds needed. Many of these entities have been extremely successful at grasping the opportunity to demonstrate their structuring capabilities and knowledge of the underlying portfolio asset classes – such that they are now very much part of the mainstream fund finance universe.

As an aside, it is interesting to note that – although some clearing banks have selectively widened their offering (including making available products that they would not previously have had the risk appetite to provide, to both existing and to new customers) in order to compete with the newer liquidity providers – there remains a relative paucity of providers of NAV facilities, particularly in the mid-market. Subscription finance remains the primary offering of the clearing banks. Investment banks may require a minimum ticket size that is well beyond the liquidity a fund requires and is willing to pay for. Sector focus may limit what other banks are able to provide. All of which means that the field remains open for specialist providers to continue to embed themselves in the market. However, it also means that there is an opportunity for lenders who, through different parts of the same institution, understand (and likely frequently leverage) a fund's underlying assets, and have (or are building) expertise in the subscription finance market, to develop an attractive and lucrative line of business through internal collaboration.

All of this means that managers have become increasingly familiar with products of this nature and are more actively seeking them out. Whilst remaining some way off the subscription facility as the staple debt facility for a fund, these products are becoming increasingly mainstream. Far from being a source of liquidity available as a last resort, these products are now being seen by managers as an option to be used in the ordinary course.

In addition, more sophisticated LPs have recognised the benefits of using products of this nature to leverage their portfolios of LP interests, not least to help them better manage the capital call profiles of the funds in which they have invested and to navigate recent intense liquidity squeezes. A NAV facility to an LP secured by its investment portfolio is fundamentally similar to a NAV facility to a secondaries fund. This area of the market is ripe for further expansion, with those institutions that have, for some time, underwritten facilities to secondaries funds well placed to take advantage of current liquidity demands amongst the wider institutional investor universe.

A shout-out to GP-led restructurings

Those funds employing the most sophisticated financing structures have, for some time, been using NAV facilities and preferred equity products not just to protect value, but more proactively to create, release and extend value. For example, by generating cash for distributions to investors earlier in the fund's life-cycle than would otherwise be available because exits from investments are not envisaged in the imminent future – which can be used to enhance IRRs or release capital to investors at an opportune moment when fundraising for a successor fund. In these respects, these types of products are a legitimate alternative to secondaries transactions, which are used to generate liquidity for investors as well as (potentially) the funds themselves.

Trading in LP interests on the secondaries market has become a mainstream method for new entrants on the investor side to gain exposure to alternative assets without having blind pool investment risk, as well as for investors with large portfolios of LP interests to manage their cashflows and asset allocations by realising value in advance of receiving distributions. The emergence of GP-led fund restructurings, whereby a continuation vehicle is managed by the same GP and funded by new investors and/or investors in the existing fund that choose to roll their position into the new vehicle, is testament again to the increasing proactivity that managers are showing in finding different liquidity solutions, both for themselves and their investors. These are involved and complex transactions, requiring delicate structuring (for example, to ensure any rollover structured as tax-free genuinely does avoid any tax obligations being crystallised – noting that the position may be different for individual investors – and to ensure that the assets are transferred to the new vehicle at the correct value).

GP-led restructurings have the significant benefit of allowing managers to offer their investors a liquidity option (but not a requirement) – roll into the new structure, thereby maintaining their exposure to the portfolio, or realise value and cash-out now. In that respect, they differ from NAV facilities and preferred equity products in that they can give rise to different outcomes for the existing investor base. They also enable fund managers to hold on to assets for longer where they see additional value-creation opportunities, rather than being forced to exit because the closed-ended fund is reaching the end of its defined life-cycle.

Another key difference is in relation to valuations. Secondaries transactions necessarily must land on a fixed value for the NAV of the portfolio, with the purchase price typically being a set discount to that NAV. These transactions therefore require greater conflict management, with increasingly sophisticated investors expecting robust, market-tested pricing and typically fairness opinions to ensure they are not being prejudiced – whether they are an existing investor exercising the option to take liquidity out, an existing investor rolling into the new structure, or a cornerstone secondary investor providing liquidity to capitalise the continuation vehicle.

In our view, the trend towards increasing volumes of secondaries transactions (with GP-led solutions forming an ever-larger part of that) will continue. Investors will continue to look to more actively manage their investment portfolios, and the denominator effect is felt from proportionate allocations to alternative assets increasing as public markets continue to fall. In complete contrast, and to demonstrate the complexity of what underpins market participants' engagement with these types of products, where a NAV facility or preferred equity product is being put in place, some investors are actively seeking to participate as providers of these – thereby further blurring the boundaries between investors, traditional lenders and providers of capital throughout the fund structure.

Conclusion

These products are now firmly in the consciousness of managers that had not previously considered using them and are now, beyond doubt, here to stay. Fund managers across asset classes have, for some time, sought an array of funding solutions provided on a fund-wide basis that are more flexible than the traditional pairing of a subscription facility at fund level (used to bridge capital calls) and asset-level debt packages (put in place for each investment individually). As fund managers navigate the increasingly uncertain economic outlook, these funding solutions will become an increasingly important and core part of their toolkit.

The market is also reacting to the increasing prevalence of whole portfolio financing structures, including the use of technology from the securitisation markets. At a purely documentation level, LPAs are increasingly providing for much greater clarity and flexibility in what liquidity solutions the fund may put in place. At the other end of the spectrum, there are questions as to whether funds using these types of structures as a matter of course (with leverage throughout the capital structure of the fund rather than just at asset level) have a different risk profile from that traditionally associated with "unlevered" funds.

Expect these products to become ever more commonplace and, given the range of institutions that provide them and their innovative approaches in doing so, to continue developing to adapt to fund managers' increasingly sophisticated requirements.

* * *

Acknowledgments

This chapter was authored by Jamie Parish, Charles Bischoff, Danny Peel, Katie McMenamin and Kirsty Emery.

Jamie Parish
Tel: +44 20 7295 3464 / Email: jamie.parish@traverssmith.com
Jamie Parish is a partner in the Finance Group at Travers Smith specialising in fund finance and real estate finance. He advises some of the most active participants in the fund finance space on the full spectrum of products, in particular investor call bridge/subscription facilities, NAV and hybrid facilities, GP support/co-invest facilities, and equity commitment-backed facilities to funds, GPs, managers and investors across a range of asset classes. Jamie's clients include numerous private equity real estate funds that, in addition to advising on fund finance products, he advises on all aspects of real estate debt financing, at all levels of the capital structure. He previously completed a secondment at the Royal Bank of Scotland in the Financial Institutions Group.

Danny Peel
Tel: +44 20 7295 3441 / Email: danny.peel@traverssmith.com
Danny Peel is a partner and Head of the Finance Group at Travers Smith where he also co-heads the Fund Finance team alongside Charles Bischoff. Danny specialises in fund finance and has a long-established lender-side practice where he regularly advises many of the most active lenders in the market on subscription, co-invest, NAV and hybrid facilities for private equity, private equity real estate, infrastructure and private credit funds. He also has a burgeoning borrower-side practice. Danny also specialises in real estate finance, advising lenders, sponsors and borrowers on investment and development facilities across the full range of asset classes.

Katie McMenamin
Tel: +44 20 7295 3350 / Email: katie.mcmenamin@traverssmith.com
Katie McMenamin is a partner in the Finance Group at Travers Smith specialising in fund finance, leverage finance and general corporate lending. She regularly advises some of the most active fund finance providers and borrowers on some of the most highly structured and complex facilities across the spectrum of fund finance products available in the market, from subscription facilities to GP-led secondary transactions, preferred equity investments and NAV-based debt financings. Katie is a key member of the firm's cross-practice team supporting asset management clients and she was featured as a 'Private Equity Rising Star' by *Legal Week* in 2020.

Travers Smith LLP
10 Snow Hill, London EC1A 2AL, United Kingdom
Tel: +44 20 7295 3000 / URL: www.traverssmith.com

The rise of ESG and green fund finance

Briony Holcombe, Robert Andrews & Lorraine Johnston
Ashurst LLP

Introduction

There is an ever-increasing focus on how financial instruments and every participant in financial markets from banks to fund managers to investors can positively impact climate change.

With this ever-increasing focus on the correlation between finance and climate change as well as other changes considered beneficial to society as a whole, green and environmental, social or governance ("**ESG**") or sustainability-linked lending ("**SLL**") in the fund finance market has become a core part of many fund finance facilities. ESG and SLL provisions are now incorporated in several large, high-profile multi-bank facilities and are starting to be seen in smaller and bilateral facilities too, across a wide range of asset classes. This general market movement towards cleaner and greener investing through either a use of proceeds-based approach or an overall ESG metrics approach has limited partners ("**LPs**") increasingly interested in ESG factors. For funds and fund managers, this has resulted in an increasing inclusion of ESG provisions/obligations in side letters entered into with LPs. With more rigorous ESG obligations entering into force, particularly as a result of key ESG regulatory developments, this is evolving to become a core element of limited partnership agreements. While we saw a slight pause in some markets with regard to the growth of SLL and ESG financing due to the impacts of macroeconomic events, we expect that ESG will remain at the forefront of LPs', and therefore fund managers', minds.

Along with mounting public pressure to evidence ESG credentials, one of the key aspects driving this change is new regulation that has been introduced in Europe and shortly the UK and which sets ambitious objectives in reorienting capital towards more sustainable investments. The regulatory drivers will have a significant impact on funds and fund managers, how ESG factors and risks are incorporated into investment decisions and financing arrangements. As the pressure for funds to focus and report on ESG metrics increases, the question for funds will no doubt arise as to how this may flow through into their financing documentation.

Likewise, lenders are increasingly keen to be at the forefront of driving green and ESG change through financing products, and increasing the amount of lending linked to green objectives (also known as use of proceeds lending) or ESG objectives (also known as SLL) is becoming a board-level imperative for financial institutions as market participants realise that financial stability is intrinsically tied to sustainability and ESG risks. For a lender thinking about its own ESG strategy, there is awareness that funds with sustainability on their agenda are arguably those that are more likely to be better prepared for future risks and opportunities and, therefore, perhaps, a better credit risk. This, however, has to be tempered against an increased focus on claims of greenwashing and an overstatement of a firm's product or service's sustainability profile. Lenders are also becoming more sophisticated in mitigating the risks of greenwashing and also in their role as Sustainability Coordinators (a role where one of the lead banks has a separate role in agreeing ESG terms that work for all parties).

A quick overview

By now we are no doubt all very familiar with both use of proceeds and ESG financing, but by way of a quick overview:

Green or use of proceeds financing

While much of the focus on ESG lending in the fund finance market focuses on "ESG" lending, we should not discount green lending as also having a role to play in the fund finance market. Green loans are loans made for a specific green purpose that do not necessarily have pricing mechanics attached to them but rather a specific (usually green) commitment to making investments that meet this green purpose.

While being lent for a specific purpose has the potential to make them less flexible than their sister, the ESG loan, this does not prevent their use in the impact or green fund space – where the loans can be utilised to invest in "green" investments that meet the criteria set out in the loan agreement. For example, funds with a particular green or sustainable strategy (e.g. investment in renewable energy) may be well suited to a green loan. Similarly, 2021 saw the introduction of the Social Loan Principles by the Loan Market Association ("**LMA**"), which, like a green loan, are extended on the basis of a particular "purpose". While we have not yet seen these arising in the fund finance market, recent world events are likely to see this product come into our market in the coming years.

ESG financing

ESG SLL is the provision of (usually) a revolving credit facility that includes certain ESG-related key performance indicators ("**KPIs**"), achievement of which links to a pricing toggle. In a nutshell, ESG or SLL is like any other loan to a fund, except with an additional layer of reporting (whether by a third-party verifier, auditor or the fund itself) on specific ESG/sustainability KPIs developed in respect of that fund or its investments. This expands the universe of borrowers and industries that can access the sustainable finance market by enabling funds that do not have an eligible project to still incorporate ESG considerations into their financing.

To date, much of the green or ESG financing we have seen in the fund finance space has been linked to an ESG financing as it provides funds and fund managers with the ability to retain a revolving credit facility at the fund level similar to that which they may have otherwise had in place, and rewards or (sometimes) penalises them for general ESG performance across the board or specific KPIs (rather than linking it to a specific investment/limiting the fund to making specific approved investments).

As ESG finance becomes increasingly popular, we have no doubt that market norms will emerge (particularly with the introduction of the LMA SLL provisions that are currently being developed) but, at this stage, no substantive market norms as regards documentation and practices have been established. Key characteristics of an ESG or SLL financing are:

Margin adjustment

A margin discount goes hand in hand with ESG or sustainability-linked finance (unlike green loans/finance, which does not necessarily offer a pricing adjustment) but consideration will need to be given as to what the appropriate level is to which this discount should be applied.

Generally, the market appears to have started from a position where a simple discount is applied when the relevant fund hits the requisite KPI and the discount is then disapplied when the relevant KPI is not met. However, as the market becomes more sophisticated, the spread for the margin incentive linked to KPIs becomes wider. In particular, an upwards and downwards margin ratchet linked to KPIs is now trending in certain markets, and we have already seen it appear in a number of ESG financings in the fund finance market. This means that if the KPI is met, then there is a downwards movement and if the KPI is not met, then the margin goes up.

Thought should also be given to what the fund will be encouraged to do (if anything) with any discount achieved. We have increasingly seen examples in some markets of borrowers agreeing to donate any discounts achieved to environmental charities or to demonstrate that such savings are applied to ESG purposes, and we expect this to also become a feature of fund finance ESG or sustainability-linked financings. Although, donations can present KYC and reputational challenges for lenders. A more recent development has been the discussion of whether penalties or benefits from SLL or ESG financing should be used to buy voluntary carbon credits to offset emissions. This of course negates the ability of the fund/borrower using any discount to drive further efficiencies within their own organisations and for this reason is being approached with caution by most lenders. There is also the argument that voluntary carbon credits encourage offsetting, which many sustainability advocates are actively trying to discourage as it is not seen as driving actual change in behaviours.

Key performance indicators

KPIs are at the heart of an ESG financing and the KPIs for each financing in the fund finance market will be unique and accordingly will need to be discussed and considered in context. In the fund finance space, the underlying investment strategy of the fund and what it would like to change within its business will also be an important factor in this discussion. While discussions regarding ESG finance often focus on the environmental gains to be made, consideration should also be given to the social and governance aspects – are there, for example, gender, diversity or governance improvements that could also be measured?

Similarly, while there is a tendency to focus on KPIs at the investment level, consideration should also be given as to whether fund-level KPIs may be appropriate (i.e. governance or social) or potentially even higher up the structure?

Regardless of what they relate to, we expect the KPIs to take into account considerations such as:

- **The term of the loan** – the longer the term of the loan, the more consideration should be given to the suitability of the KPIs towards the end of the loan. Should the KPIs be incremental, increasing year on year? Or is a mechanism required to revisit the KPIs periodically to reassess their suitability?
- **Number and nature of KPIs** – where there are numerous or complex KPIs, thought should be given to whether these are likely to be better monitored by third parties with appropriate knowledge of the complexities of said KPIs. Consideration should also be given to the administrative burden (for both the borrower and lender) resulting from including numerous KPIs and whether quality should be preferred over quantity.
- **What is being measured** – is it just the investment portfolio that should be tracked against KPIs? Or are there other fund-level metrics that should be considered whether ESG-related (e.g. a recycling target, reduction in energy use, moving away from single-use plastics or diversity KPIs)?

- **How should it be measured** – should there be a weighting given to the ESG score of the fund depending on the percentage of investment of the fund in a company against the fund's total portfolio? Should consideration also be given as to the timing of when the investment is made when calculating the relevant ESG score?
- **What are the consequences of non-compliance with that KPI** – while the obvious answer here is some upwards adjustment to the margin, query whether that should be the only consequence. Should some KPIs be hurdles/ones that have to be achieved before any other discount flowing from KPI achievement can be unlocked? Could KPIs be included that are not linked to margin adjustments but rather aimed at reputational motivation? This will likely require public disclosure of the relevant KPIs but, to the extent that funds are simultaneously making public commitments to ESG goals, funds are being increasingly held to account by stakeholders.

The unique challenge of setting KPIs for the fund finance market

One of the unique challenges the fund finance market faces with ESG financing is how we set appropriate, challenging KPIs for those financings put in place early in the life of a fund when few or potentially no investments have been made. While previous fund performance on similar ESG metrics may help to inform this process, thought should be given to whether there is a requirement for an ability to review KPIs on a regular basis (e.g. every 12 months to consider whether they remain appropriate and sufficiently challenging). Other ways in which to approach this may include an ability for either the borrower or finance parties to bring the parties to the table to discuss certain KPIs should they feel they are no longer appropriate (with a right to disapply a KPI if agreement cannot be reached on any necessary amendments).

Will there be regulatory drivers for KPIs going forward?

There are already a number of existing international standards and guidelines that fund managers may voluntarily disclose against with respect to ESG factors. Most recently, the EU – followed by the UK – has sought to codify these reporting obligations and harmonise what can and cannot be deemed "sustainable".

EU position

The new EU regulation that seeks to achieve this is the **EU Taxonomy Regulation**, which creates a framework for what can and cannot be considered an environmentally sustainable financial product. The regulation introduces an EU-wide classification system (or taxonomy) of environmentally sustainable activities, which aims to provide more clarity for investors concerning financial products that purport to invest in sustainable activities or to promote environmental objectives. The EU Taxonomy Regulation sets out the criteria for determining whether an economic activity constitutes an environmentally sustainable activity that includes the requirement that the activity does "no significant harm". This is intended to facilitate (or reduce the burden of) investors' own due diligence with regard to a product's environmental sustainability and eliminate the practice of greenwashing (where financial products are inaccurately marketed as "green" or "sustainable"). The EU Taxonomy Regulation goes hand in hand with the EU's proposal for a Corporate Sustainability Due Diligence Directive as well as the Corporate Sustainability Reporting Directive, both of which aim to increase production of ESG data by in-scope corporate entities and reduce the burden for investors of ESG due diligence.

The second piece of the jigsaw puzzle is the **EU Disclosure Regulation**, which seeks to harmonise existing provisions on sustainability-related disclosures by imposing requirements on so-called financial market participants (e.g. EU AIFMs and EU UCITS management companies (or non-EU AIFMs marketing funds into the EU) and EU investment firms or EU credit institutions carrying out portfolio management) in relation to financial products.

The EU Disclosure Regulation requires certain information to be made available either at entity level or at product level, irrespective of whether sustainability risks are integrated into financial market participants' investment decision-making processes. Further measures seek to increase transparency as regards financial products that target sustainable investments, including reduction in carbon emissions.

The final key regulatory development is the **Low Carbon Benchmark Regulation**. The Low Carbon Benchmark Regulation creates disclosure requirements on benchmark administrators as to ESG considerations for various different benchmarks. It also creates two new categories of benchmarks – the Paris-aligned benchmark and the climate transition benchmark – which will help fund managers measure performance against the Paris Agreement climate targets, if that is the objective of the fund.

UK position

The UK has lagged behind the EU in terms of the introduction of sustainability-related disclosures, mandating Task Force on Climate-Related Financial Disclosures ("**TCFD**") reports for the largest UK asset managers.

More recently, it has been announced that the UK will, like the EU, introduce its own UK Taxonomy by the end of 2023 as well as Sustainability Disclosure Requirements ("**SDRs**"), which will create an integrated framework for "decision-useful disclosures on sustainability". The SDRs will apply to asset managers and asset owners.

The UK's approach to SDRs is in contrast to the EU Disclosure Regulation. Despite the name on the tin, the UK SDRs are a labelling regime with three categories of labels available:

(a) sustainable focus – products that invest predominantly in assets that can be deemed to be sustainable;
(b) sustainable improvers – products that aim to improve the sustainability of the portfolio over time; and
(c) sustainable impact – products that seek to achieve impact through the provision of finance, typically to underserved markets.

To meet any of these classifications, a product will need to meet:

(d) five overarching principles, referred to as general criteria, which will cover: sustainability objective; investment policy and strategy; KPIs; resources and governance; and/or investor stewardship;
(e) a number of key cross-cutting considerations; and
(f) certain key category-specific requirements.

Compared to the EU regime, the UK SDRs will provide a sustainability framework that in-scope asset managers and owners will need to embed within their processes for all aspects of the investment lifecycle. The UK will also implement its own taxonomy that will be largely based on the EU Taxonomy, although the underlying eligible economic activities may differ to take into account the distinction in the UK economy and industry focus. The UK Taxonomy classifications will in time flow through into the disclosures to be made under the UK SDRs.

Taken together, these EU and UK regulations are likely to shift behaviour in the fund market and in the fund finance market. With more focus on fund managers' own ESG approach, there is a likely impact on the fund finance market with respect to the characteristics set out above. KPIs and reporting in particular are likely to be highly impacted with the data flow requirements that fund managers will be subject to as a result of the EU Disclosure Regulation and UK SDRs once these are in force.

Sustainability performance targets

Once you have set your KPIs, one of the unique challenges of the post-COVID world is how to set sustainability performance targets ("**SPTs**"). With few exceptions, carbon emissions, travel, use of plastics, waste, etc. across all industries were significantly reduced due to arrangements put in place to deal with COVID, and with few expecting to return to pre-COVID levels, how do you set SPTs? Are 2019 numbers the best to use? The LMA Sustainability Linked Loan Principles recommend three years of historic data to measure track record. Allowing for the interference of COVID, that three years of data is starting to look a bit out of date. Similarly, most industries are looking at returning to a "new normal" but what that looks like, and how much travel, emissions, etc. that will involve, remains unclear.

We have seen increasing use of side letters or "ESG Ready" facilities as a workaround to this problem, where facilities are put in place with the mechanics for an SLL or ESG financing but the KPIs and SPTs that will apply are agreed at a future date in a side letter. Sometimes, these are utilised to work around tight timing requirements for getting facilities in place. This approach, while giving more time (although query how long/whether it solves our out-of-date data issue), also brings with it its own challenges – in particular, reputational issues. For example, do we need to introduce publicity restrictions to ensure that one party does not unilaterally publicise the facility as being an SLL or ESG facility before that side letter is agreed? If we introduce such a restriction, should breach of it lead to an event of default? As alluded to above, SLL/ESG mechanics have traditionally remained outside the event of default regime but, without bringing this into the event of default regime, what teeth will such a restriction have?

Reporting obligations

There will also be a discussion to be had as to the reporting obligations of the fund and whether reports produced internally by the fund, and which are provided to investors, will be sufficient for the finance parties, and whether there should be an audit of internal ESG reporting or whether a third party should be engaged to provide an ESG report. Ultimately, there are a number of factors that will feed into this discussion, including:

- **Existing practices of the fund** – does the fund have a track record of disclosing ESG information to investors? Is the information disclosed sufficiently detailed to provide the requisite comfort to the lenders and measurement of the proposed KPIs?
- **Underlying investments** – depending on the fund, it may be that there are already reports being obtained from third-party providers; in which case, can these reports be made available to the lenders? Do these existing reports cover all the KPIs in sufficient detail?
- **Cost-benefit analysis** – if third-party reports are to be obtained, are the costs associated with obtaining such reports reasonable in the context of the transactions, or, more importantly, will the cost of procuring such a report exceed any gain in margin reduction? This will be a particular focus for the fund finance market where, unlike a corporate group, reporting might need to be carried out on an investment-by-investment basis. Particularly for funds with a large number of investments, this may put the possibility of third-party reporting out of reach.
- **Timing of reports** – at present, reporting obligations are usually on a semi-annual or annual basis. There may be consideration of increasing the frequency, but this will have a corresponding effect on cost as identified above.
- **KPIs** – what is being measured and can that information reliably be reported on by a third party?

Thought should also be given to whether the failure to provide an ESG report should trigger an event of default. Many will argue that the failure to provide a report should trigger an event of default in the same way a failure to comply with any other reporting obligation would under the facility. Alternatively, there is an argument to be made that failure to provide a report should have no more severe a consequence than delivering a report that shows a failure to meet the relevant KPIs (i.e. a margin premium/removal of discount applied).

What do we see for green and ESG/SLL fund financings in the next 12 months?

It would be remiss of us to write this chapter and not consider some of the challenges we see coming for ESG/SLL fund financings in the next 12 months. In our view, the likely headwinds will be:

- **Greenwashing**: greenwashing is, broadly speaking, providing inaccurate or misleading information about the environmental impact of a product or service. In the fund financing space, it is most likely to be of concern if the KPIs and SPTs that are set for an SLL financing are not sufficiently robust or challenging, or for a green financing if the green project or asset is not sufficiently green.

  There is renewed focus from regulators on greenwashing, which brings with it regulation risk but also the risk of reputational damage or greenwashing litigation for fund managers and lenders alike.

  For fund managers and lenders, the focus on greenwashing risks in the next 12 months will mean a renewed focus on:
  - **KPIs/SPTs**: have they been adequately diligenced? Are they sufficiently challenging or do they simply require the fund to do what they were already doing? Are the KPIs encouraging the right behaviours? Are they consistent with those of peers in the market? If not, why not?
  - **ESG/green information**: linked again to the point above, is the data used to set KPIs/SPTs sufficiently robust? Has it been adequately tested?
  - **Refinancing risk**: as the lifecycle of green and SLL financings rolls around to refinancings, fund managers and lenders will need to be careful to ensure that refinancings do not run into greenwashing territory. For example, if a green loan for a particular asset is being refinanced, is the asset still sufficiently green by the market standards at the time of the refinance? If the original green loan has been paid down, is the "green" portion of the new loan of a reduced value to reflect that reduced value (i.e. not just lending against the full asset value as this may not meet the green purpose requirements)?
- **Macroeconomic influences**: the macroeconomic headwinds in recent months are likely to continue in some form in the next 12 months and we can foresee a situation in which green or SLL financings take a backseat to more pressing considerations for fund managers. Hopefully this is not the case – sustainability is a long-term project and important to keep on everyone's agenda, even when times are tough.
- **Capital treatment**: providing beneficial capital treatment for lenders in relation to green or SLL financings has long been a topic of discussion, the argument being that if the underlying fund/business is more sustainable, the likely better the credit risk. On this point, we do not think regulators are likely to move any time soon (and certainly not in the next 12 months) but it is nonetheless a worthy consideration as there is little doubt that beneficial capital treatment would encourage more green or SLL financings and hopefully have the flow-on effect of ensuring that funds and their investments are greener and more sustainable. Certainly a space to watch.

- **ESG litigation**: as ESG disputes and litigation become more prevalent, will we see this impact the fund finance market? At this stage, we think this is unlikely to have a direct impact but there is no doubt that this may play into the KPI/SPT setting and focus the minds of fund managers and lenders, particularly in relation to greenwashing concerns.

While we expect continued focus on the social and governance elements of ESG as well as green loans and continued interest in this product in the longer term, it remains to be seen whether the headwinds of the next 12 months will impact appetite for these products in the short term.

Further Ashurst ESG-related articles/publications can be found at https://www.ashurst.com/en/news-and-insights/hubs/sustainability/.

Briony Holcombe
Tel: +44 20 7859 1067 / Email: briony.holcombe@ashurst.com
Briony Holcombe is a senior associate in Ashurst's Global Loans practice in London. Briony advises global financial institutions and funds on fund financing transactions including subscription/capital call facilities, umbrella facilities, hybrid, NAV, co-investment, GP and asset-backed facilities in both the domestic and international arena. Briony has particular experience acting on fund financing financial institutions as well as a wide variety of private equity funds, real estate funds and direct lending funds. Briony was named as a Next Generation Partner in *The Legal 500* rankings (2022) with the Ashurst team ranked in Tier 1 in Fund Finance.

Robert Andrews
Tel: +44 20 7859 1091 / Email: robert.andrews@ashurst.com
Robert Andrews is a partner in Ashurst's Global Loans practice in London. He specialises in advising financial institutions and funds on subscription/fund finance, including capital call facilities, NAV facilities, facilities for SMAs and hybrid financings as well as GP Co-Invest facilities. Robert was named as a Leading Individual in *The Legal 500* Fund Finance rankings (2022) with the Ashurst team ranked in Tier 1 in Fund Finance.

Lorraine Johnston
Tel: +44 20 7859 2579 / Email: lorraine.johnston@ashurst.com
Lorraine Johnston is a partner in Ashurst's Global Finance Regulatory practice. Lorraine works with institutions across the financial sector, including banks, asset managers, brokers and others, specialising in a broad range of conduct and technical matters. Lorraine has a particular focus on the governance of large financial services firms, including Senior Managers & Certification Regime rules. She led the widest review to date of the impact of SMCR within banks on behalf of UK Finance, the leading bank industry body, leading to the publication of *SMCR: Evolution and Reform*.

Lorraine is leading Ashurst's practice on Environmental, Social and Governance regulation in Europe and the UK.

Ashurst LLP

London Fruit & Wool Exchange, 1 Duval Square, London E1 6PW, United Kingdom
Tel: +44 20 7638 1111 / URL: www.ashurst.com

Robust liquidity solutions for complex Cayman Islands fund structures

Agnes Molnar, Richard Mansi & Catharina von Finckenhagen
Travers Thorp Alberga

Background

Merely saying that private equity deal value set a new record in 2021 hardly does the industry justice. Investment activity surpassed the trillion-dollar mark. In total, 24,520 deals were closed with an aggregate value worth USD1.04 trillion,[1] nearly double the amount from the year before. North America led the surge with USD537 billion in deals transacted and on its own matched the global total of a year ago. Buyout funds raised USD387 billion in 2021, their second-best year ever. Technology funds and those that invest in tech-enabled sectors like fintech or health tech have become by far the dominant theme in the buyout world. Growth, venture, and infrastructure all grew faster relative to their five-year averages, and buyout's share of the total has flattened at around 30% over the past several years. The appetite for diversification has led investors to pump capital into areas they never would have considered in the past. New funds have sprung up to serve them, and older ones – particularly the large, diversified buyout funds – have pivoted accordingly. Growth investing has rapidly emerged as one of the most dynamic segments of the private equity industry, and growth and late-stage venture capital assets under management (AUM) have grown at around twice the pace of buyout AUM over the past decade.[2]

Private credit, as the second-largest alternative asset class after private equity, has performed strongly mainly as it offers benefits for investors looking for strong growth opportunities at a time of constrained mainstream lending. For those investors who were exploring private credit in 2022, inflation seems to be less of a concern as they see private credit as a safer bet in volatile/inflationary times. Other reasons for private credit allocations included low fixed income yields, unfulfilled target allocations and exciting new opportunities around distressed assets. Distressed assets and direct lending are currently the most sought-after private credit strategies, making up 60% of AUM in the asset class.[3] According to the Alternative Credit Council (ACC), the estimated AUM of private credit is at USD805 billion,[4] out of which direct lending's AUM of USD452 billion is now double that of the second-largest private credit strategy, distressed debt's AUM at USD277 billion. ESG is also of growing importance for both investors and fund managers, and some of the largest private credit funds have launched record-breaking funds with ESG considerations.

The fund finance market remained buoyant in 2022 as more sponsors turn to fund-level financing solutions. Recent trends behind more sophisticated products such as NAV facilities, preferred equity and hybrid facilities have accelerated and boosted the array of flexible financing solutions for funds. Although pricing has widened modestly in the capital call financing market,[5] we still see increasing demand for the product and new funds are now formed to have a subscription facility in place at first closing.

Continuing its multi-decade dominance, the Cayman Islands remains the leading offshore jurisdiction for the establishment of private equity funds, private credit funds and hedge funds and stands at the centre of these capital flows and sophisticated legal structures. As of 30 September 2022, the number of closed-ended funds registered with the Cayman Islands Monetary Authority (CIMA) as private funds under the Private Funds Act was 15,662,[6] with a further 8,780[7] open-ended investment funds and 3,233[8] master funds regulated by CIMA. Based on CIMA figures, we estimate that the total US dollar value of Cayman Islands regulated open- and closed-ended funds stands at USD7.5 trillion. CIMA has no statutory authority to restrict a fund's investment strategy and Cayman Islands funds are thus employed by sponsors to pursue the full range of alternative strategies, including private equity, private debt, hedge, venture capital, infrastructure and real estate as well as traditional long-only investing. Main fund vehicles aside, Cayman Islands structures are also used for managed accounts, incentive compensation vehicles and co-investment structures as well as holding vehicles and blocker entities.

In this chapter, we examine some of the typical Cayman Islands fund structures throughout their life cycle and their liquidity options. Ensuring that the fund and its parallel, feeder, master, blocker, portfolio entities and related vehicles (the Multi-Fund) have sufficient liquidity is an important factor in the success of the fund. Leverage, if structured and priced correctly, can enhance a fund's returns significantly by reducing the cost of capital while offering attractive income returns to lenders. During the investment period, borrowings can smooth out cash flow issues and flatten the J-curve. Leverage can recapitalise fund assets and provide returns to investors without needing to exit underlying positions. We therefore look at some of the possible funding structures for complex Cayman Islands fund structures to obtain secured or unsecured debt financing throughout their full term. It is clearly important for lenders to understand such structures, their operation and cash flows in order to protect their positions; for instance, in terms of ensuring that guarantees and/or security arrangements are implemented at the correct level and cannot be avoided. Prior to fund formation and as part of structuring, sponsors must anticipate with their fund finance and fund formation counsel the liquidity and structural requirements of the entire fund structure during its life cycle.

Common Cayman Islands structures

When establishing a fund with investors from multiple jurisdictions who are subject to different local tax and regulatory regimes, a multi-tiered 'master-feeder' structure is often used. In this structure, one or more Cayman Islands or onshore feeder funds (complying in each case with the local offering and tax requirements of the specific jurisdiction) raise investor funds and 'feed' the combined proceeds into a single Cayman Islands master fund in or through which underlying assets are held. For example, US taxable investors will often invest in a Cayman Islands master fund through a US-based feeder fund, while non-US investors and certain non-taxable US investors typically invest in the Cayman Islands master fund through a Cayman Islands feeder partnership fund or 'blocker' corporate entity in order to address their tax and regulatory requirements. Each feeder issues shares or interests to its investors in return for capital commitments from those investors, which the feeders onward invest in subscribing for interests in the Cayman Islands master fund. In turn, the Cayman Islands master fund uses those investment proceeds to acquire underlying investments, directly or through subsidiaries. Multi-Fund structures can also, and very often, employ parallel fund arrangements, which invest and divest in the same investments on a side-by-side basis without the use of a master fund. Alternative investment vehicles (AIVs) are often used for tax or regulatory reasons to hold a particular investment, and investors might be required to make their capital contributions directly to the AIV (hence reducing their capital commitment to the main fund).

Depending on the investment strategy of the fund or the various tax, regulatory or legal considerations of its investors (e.g. ESG or *Sharia* compliance), the fund might consider, for example, co-borrowing with and/or guaranteeing and/or securing the borrowings or other indebtedness of its related entities in the Multi-Fund structure. The constitutional documents of the fund and the related group entities should be drafted in a manner that enables the desired funding and security structure to be implemented. Finance lawyers understanding the legal issues of complex fund structures must review the draft constitutional documents to ensure that the liquidity requirements of the fund and its related entities can be achieved under the organisational documents, and that any appropriate entities are duly registered under the Private Funds Act.[9]

In many respects, the needs of the fund, its investors, sponsors and lenders are highly aligned; for example, ensuring that the available capital is precisely defined in a robust manner in both the fund and finance documents. Lenders must understand how available capital may be impacted by, for example, such vital provisions as the equalisation upon subsequent investor closings or the capital recall arrangements to meet the expense or indemnity liabilities of the fund (or indeed the clawback on the general partner's carried interest or on distributions to limited partners). In single fund transactions, these require close attention, and matters become all the more acute in a complex fund structure spanning many parallel, feeder and blocker entities. Any weakness in these arrangements may constitute the basis of the defence of an investor who is subject to a capital call from an insolvent fund or its receiver.

Capital call funding of Cayman Islands fund structures

There are various ways to 'insert' debt into a master-feeder structure, ranging from the fairly straightforward to more complex, albeit increasingly common, methods. Given the pre-eminence of Cayman Islands fund vehicles, it is unsurprising that they are at the forefront of innovative and intricate financing structures. We select some interesting practical considerations below.

<u>Cascading *vs* guaranteed structures</u>

In master-feeder structures, in order to gain recourse against the capital commitments of the ultimate investors, subscription credit lenders may request guarantees or cascading security from feeder funds. As a feeder fund invests all of its investors' investment proceeds into the master fund (or a lower fund-related entity) and does not hold assets directly, it should seek to avoid securing or guaranteeing the borrowings of the master fund (e.g. through the 'covenant to pay') in excess of its capital on grounds of commercial benefit and insolvency risk. Even in situations where a guarantor feeder fund limits its guarantee, it should give consideration to a potential double exposure, on the one hand under its guarantee to the lender and on the other hand under its capital commitment to the master fund. Any subrogation arising upon paying the debt of the master fund gives little comfort as it is invariably subordinated to the debt owed by the master fund to the lender and will be deferred until all liabilities are cleared.

<u>Hybrid capital commitments</u>

For tax structuring reasons, investors and intermediate entities often make use of hybrid capital commitments to the fund in the form of equity and debt obligations. These structures are often flexible as to whether capital is called as debt or equity in order to mitigate taxes on a particular investment based on evolving tax policy. From a sponsor's perspective and in anticipation of the needs of future lenders, the right to cause the debt financing to be advanced will require careful drafting to ensure it is assignable by way of security and cannot be avoided in an insolvency situation. Moreover, the debt advanced by investors or intermediate entities will need to be thoughtfully subordinated from the outset to contemplate the requirements of an external lender financing the fund.

Intermediate blockers

It is common for fund structures to be layered, with blocker or other intermediate entities between fund vehicles, through which subscription funds flow to reach the ultimate master fund (in a master-feeder structure) or portfolio investment (in a parallel structure). In the case of a Cayman Islands company, the right to call capital vests in the company itself, and where the company is a typical exempted company limited by shares (rather like a US C Corp), the directors have the power and authority to make calls for uncalled capital and to receive into the company capital contributions from shareholders in accordance with their subscription agreements. The Companies Act of the Cayman Islands allows flexibility in the structuring and as such, partly paid shares (whereby the investor only pays part of the subscription price upon its subscription and the unpaid part remains outstanding as a capital commitment of the investor) and shares issued in tranches (whereby the issued shares are fully paid upon issuance but the company may issue further shares up to the amount of the investor capital commitment) may both be used in Cayman Islands fund structures. Sponsors and lenders need to appreciate the features and indeed characteristics of each, as the two approaches may provide different consequences in terms of the lawfulness of release of capital commitments, the ability to increase the commitment on shares (perhaps upon subsequent closing equalisation or recallable distributions), the validity and consequences of forfeiture upon a breach, the flexibility that can be afforded for custodian or other pass-through investors, and the risks of any defect or delay in share issuance. The share structuring of a blocker or similar entity may also need close consideration in order to reflect the flows of capital to and from, and any associated commitment, excuse, exclude or default adjustment between, the feeder entities to the blocker. Where tax analysis allows, we anticipate an increase in the use of the 'limited liability company' (LLC) form, which follows the Delaware model and envisages the LLC issuing members' interests of variable commitment amounts similar to a flexible partnership format.

Pass-through investors – custodians and feeder structures

It is well recognised by sponsors and lenders that custodians acting on behalf of investors have a cautious approach to commitment-based structures, and typically, custodians will ensure that the underlying investor substantially collateralises the custodian in respect of the initial commitment to the fund. Difficulties may arise towards the end of the life of a fund where there have been distributions that may be recalled by the fund for indemnification matters. At the point of initial fund structuring, from a sponsor perspective, it may be advisable to include a mechanism that permits the custodian to substitute its underlying investor in a manner that still gives sufficient comfort to a lender. This should neutralise the risk position substantially for custodians and reduce their concerns as investor.

In a related vein, it is common for master funds to limit their recourse against a feeder fund upon a subscription default by the feeder fund, so that the default only applies to the portion derived from a default of an investor in the feeder fund. This is commercially common and well recognised. From a structuring perspective, sponsors must ensure that the default management arrangements are sufficiently robust and be certain that the rights of the lender are not hollowed out, though equally not at the risk of reintroducing contagion within the feeder fund impacting all feeder fund investors upon the default of one of their number. Particular consideration should be given to feeder-on-feeder structures.

LP Givebacks *vs* Recallable Capital

Almost all long-form partnership agreements (and the ILPA Model Limited Partnership Agreements) include a 'return of distributions' provision whereby limited partners are required to contribute capital to the partnership to cover obligations of the partnership out of distributions previously made by the partnership (LP Giveback). The LP Givebacks are heavily negotiated between sponsors and seed investors and usually limited by cut-off times and/or percentage amounts of distributions or commitments. The general partner of the partnership may only exercise its right to 'claw back' distributions from the limited partners under the LP Giveback where the partnership agreement explicitly authorises the general partner to do so. Naturally, the general partner may only operate the LP Giveback provisions where the uncalled capital commitments of the limited partners are exhausted. The obligation of the limited partners to inject capital to fund liabilities of the fund (including indebtedness) as an LP Giveback would not increase (nor, if paid, discharge) their uncalled capital commitments.

We must distinguish LP Givebacks from recallable commitments. 'Recallable commitments' usually means the unused capital contributions of the limited partners returned to them by the general partner and the recycled distributions of the partnership, which are liquidity proceeds of realised investments distributed to the limited partners with a provision that they could be recalled later (Recallable Capital). Recallable Capital, once it is returned to the limited partners, is added back to the limited partners' uncalled capital commitments, thus increasing the uncalled capital commitments of the limited partners.

Under capital call financing, a security interest is created over the general partner's right to call uncalled capital commitments from the limited partners of the partnership. Most security assignment agreements fail to create security over the general partner's right to demand capital from the limited partners beyond the uncalled capital commitments. As uncalled capital commitments decline during the life of the financing, lenders may wish to consider requesting that the general partner grant a security interest over its right to demand funds from the limited partners under LP Givebacks. The fact that LP Givebacks are not part of the borrowing base of the facility should not necessarily mean that the LP Givebacks are excluded from the collateral package. Lenders would of course prefer to be overcollateralised.

Islamic fund financing

Islamic finance is a type of financing activity that must comply with *Sharia* (Islamic Law). The main difference between conventional finance and Islamic finance is that some of the practices and principles that are used in conventional finance are strictly prohibited under *Sharia* laws. In addition to the well-known prohibitions such as interest payment and speculation, Islamic finance is based on two other crucial principles. One is the requirement to have material finality of the transaction so each transaction is related to a real underlying economic transaction. The second principle is profit and loss sharing pursuant to which the parties entering into the contracts must share the profits and the risks associated with the transaction.

In large, Multi-Fund structures, it is not uncommon to create one or more investment vehicles dedicated for *Sharia*-compliant investors. Those investment vehicles cannot participate in conventional fund financing transactions, and we have seen an increase in *Sharia*-compliant *Murabaha* fund financing facilities.

Murabaha is a financing transaction based on purchase and sale, whereby the 'lender' purchases an underlying asset (usually commodities) from a broker and sells it to the 'borrower' with a set markup either in the form of a lump sum or percentage. Such purchase and sale comprises several inter-linked transactions. First, the 'lender' entity purchases commodities from a broker with immediate payment and delivery of the commodities. The 'lender' then on-sells the commodities to the 'borrower' under the *Murabaha* agreement with a markup on the deferred sale price basis. The 'borrower' further on-sells the commodities via the 'lender' (acting as agent) to a second broker. At this point of time, the 'lender' will receive the proceeds from the sale of the commodities and pay that to the 'borrower' as part of the financing. On maturity, the 'borrower' repays the deferred purchase price to the 'lender' together with the markup.

Such *Murabaha* financing could then be secured by the uncalled capital commitments of the limited partners of the borrower partnership or other assets of the borrower, similar to conventional fund finance facilities.

NAV-oriented funding of Cayman Islands fund structures

NAV-oriented borrowing looks to the NAV of the fund's portfolio of investments in determining borrowing ability, and lenders are sought to underwrite the assets of the fund or to lend against the future cash flows of the portfolio of investments. In implementing the financing, it is crucial that NAV-oriented borrowing and related fund-level leverage are not prohibited in the constitutional documents of the fund. These types of asset-backed fund finance facilities are often sought by funds to finance the acquisition of investments or to inject recapitalisation funding to release distributable proceeds for investors. Funds may also require liquidity at the portfolio company level for bolt-on or opportunistic investments. We have witnessed a recent shift away from single-asset lending (i.e. leveraged loans and real estate financing) towards portfolio-based financing where leveraged, real estate and project financing transactions are structured as lending against a diversified portfolio of assets. Such structures may provide enhanced flexibility to funds, as they may be able to invest and divest assets without needing to obtain lenders' consent or to amend security documentation, while still affording lenders an acceptable level of diversified security.

We examine below some important legal aspects of certain funding products and how the strategy of a fund will influence its financing structure.

Private equity funds – share security

As private equity funds typically hold investments through holding companies, the ability to grant security over the equity interests of the fund in companies is fundamentally important in a NAV-oriented funding structure. Lenders must review the constitutional documents of the company to ensure that granting and enforcing security is fully effective. Detailed due diligence should reveal whether the shares are subject to restrictions such as consents, rights of first refusal or first offer, tag-along or drag-along rights. Difficulties may also arise if third-party leverage is in place at the asset level. Asset-level lenders are structurally senior to any fund-level lenders, and their facility agreements typically prohibit a change of control at the asset company level. Fund lenders enforcing their security over the shares of the asset company would trigger a change of control and, due to the structural subordination, the fund-level lender's recovery will be net of, and subsequent in priority and timing of payment to, the liabilities owed to the asset-level lender. If the asset company is incorporated in the Cayman Islands, lenders should require its constitutional documents to be amended to restrict the transfer of the secured shares, to eliminate the discretion of the directors to refuse to register a transfer of the secured shares upon enforcement of the security, and to disapply the company's lien in respect of secured shares. The loan and security documentation should also prohibit the company whose shares are secured from amending its constitutional documents without the consent of the lender.

Private equity funds – LP Interest Security

When the investments of a private equity fund are held through exempted limited partnerships (Asset Holding Partnership), lenders usually request the fund borrower to grant a security interest over its partnership interest in the Asset Holding Partnership (LP Interest Security) to secure its NAV-oriented borrowing. Lenders must review the partnership agreement of the Asset Holding Partnership to ensure that the requirements of granting and enforcing such LP Interest Security are followed. As both the creation of any security interest over the partnership interest and the enforcement of the LP Interest Security typically constitute a 'transfer' under the limited partnership agreement of an exempted limited partnership formed in the Cayman Islands, the consent of the general partner will be required.

In a Multi-Fund structure, the consent of the general partner can easily be obtained prior to granting such LP Interest Security. Enforcement, however, could be trickier, as a lender (or its transferee) will become a limited partner of the Asset Holding Partnership and acquire all of the rights and assume all of the obligations of the fund borrower attached to the acquired partnership interest. Lenders must consider the liabilities that may arise under the partnership agreement of the Asset Holding Partnership as LP Givebacks, clawback and other indemnity obligations or uncalled capital contributions might make the LP Interest Security less desirable. Respectively, the general partner of the Asset Holding Partnership will be concerned as to the credit rating of the lender or its transferee.

In addition, the loan and security documentation should prohibit the amendments to the partnership agreement of the Asset Holding Partnership without the consent of the lender.

Secondary funds

Due to the typical requirement that the consent of the general partner must be obtained prior to granting and/or enforcing security over a limited partner's interest in a Cayman Islands exempted limited partnership, secondary funds have moved away from providing direct security over limited partnership interests[10] when structuring their acquisitions of large portfolios of such secondary limited partnership interests. One structural solution involves employing a Cayman Islands special purpose vehicle (SPV) to purchase the interests. The fund and/or the SPV could borrow funds to finance the acquisition. No direct security over the limited partnership interest would be granted and instead, the distribution proceeds generated from holding those interests will be secured in favour of the lender (enhanced by regular cash sweeps, if applicable), and security over the shares of the SPV will also be granted so the lender could 'step in' to the structure upon enforcement and look to sell the underlying portfolio as a whole. In addition, the SPV might be 'orphanised' by appointing an independent board, perhaps with its voting management shares held under an independent purpose trust, to give additional protection to the lender.

Another alternative is to establish a custody arrangement whereby the investments of the fund are transferred to and held by a custodian under suitable control arrangements. Distribution proceeds arising from those underlying investments (which may be swept on a periodic basis in order to service the financing) will also be held by the custodian. The fund might create security over its rights arising under the custody agreement in respect of the custodian assets in favour of the lender, which would be able, for example, to direct the custodian to dispose of the investments in an enforcement scenario. Similarly, trust arrangements may also be used.

Financing future income streams

We have observed an increase in the use of GP-support and management fee facilities where lenders advance funds to the sponsor against management fees or the profit share of the general partner of the fund. Those income streams are generated under the partnership agreement or the management agreement of the fund. Lenders' due diligence must examine how those fees are calculated and reveal whether sponsors are able to reduce or delay the payment of management fees/profit shares, for example, due to poor portfolio performance or tax planning. In addition, the lender should consider including a prohibition on the ability of the sponsor to waive, reduce, or defer the payment of management fees. It is important to note that fund-level lenders may also subordinate the payment of management fees in the facility agreements of the fund, which may have the effect of reducing or prohibiting the payment of management fees. In addition, fees may be subject to deductions in respect of service fees paid to the manager by the portfolio companies.

In co-invest facilities, lenders provide leverage based on the borrower's return on the fund. In co-invest facilities (similar to financing a secondary partnership interest), a lender ultimately lends against the co-investor's portion of the underlying investments. To enhance the lender's position, the co-investor borrower will be prohibited from disposing of its investment in the fund and moreover, distributions from the underlying investments might be used to fully or partly repay the borrowings. As the lender will not have any recourse to the underlying investments (and only to the cash flow arising from the investments), it may require a personal guarantee from the co-investor to overcome the limited recourse restriction.

Preferred equity

Portfolio finance (capital advanced based on the value of a fund's portfolio) has grown rapidly in the years since the global financial crisis and as the onset of the pandemic has dramatically increased funds' demand for liquidity, traditional secured financing has been boosted by preferred equity financing. These facilities have been deployed by general partners to fund follow-on, opportunistic or bolt-on investments, or as a cash advance of future cash flows (e.g. accelerating distributions to satisfy investor liquidity demands). Preferred equity solutions offer the funds liquidity by unlocking the equity value of the portfolio so the fund will be able to grow the value of the portfolio and benefit from future upside without the need to sell the assets. It provides capital to a private equity fund via issuance of equity capital. Preferred equity can be used for the same purposes as asset-based facilities but, as it has no debt-like covenants or restrictions, it provides a valuable tool for funds when valuations are volatile. Preferred equity solutions have no maturity and typically offer higher advance rates against the underlying investments than traditional asset-based lending. Preferred equity providers usually obtain a priority right to receive distributions up to a multiple of the price of the preferred equity whilst the benefits of upside performance remain with the existing investors. Funds or portfolio companies that cannot borrow due to regulatory, tax, accounting or legal reasons (or are already highly levered at fund level) should consider preferred equity financing because the preferred equity, if properly structured, should not appear on their balance sheet as a liability. Although preferred equity provides economic exposure to a portfolio of investments, that exposure is provided through securities issued by a single fund. Due diligence of the constitutional documents of the fund and the underlying portfolio companies and their cash flows are crucial for a successful financing.

Crypto funds

The digital asset market size is projected to grow from USD4.2 trillion in 2022 to 8.0 trillion by 2027[11] (including pure cryptocurrencies such as Bitcoin or Litecoin, platform coins such as Ethereum, and stablecoins). The digital asset market extends beyond the assets themselves and includes other market participants such as online exchanges, payment processors and mining companies.

The Cayman Islands, being a leading global financial centre and having a reputation as one of the world's most innovative business-friendly jurisdictions in which to operate, became an obvious choice for many of those wishing to establish fintech structures. We have seen the growth of Cayman Islands crypto funds (investment funds established with the purpose of investing in various cryptoassets), exchanges and decentralised trading platforms. The Virtual Asset (Service Providers) Act (2022 Revision) (VASP) regulates businesses providing services related to digital assets and cryptocurrencies in the Cayman Islands. A virtual asset service provider is an entity that is incorporated or registered in the Cayman Islands and provides a virtual asset service as a business or in the course of business. Although the VASP regime is beyond the scope of this chapter, it is clear that blockchain technology and cryptoassets are impacting how people invest, borrow and save. For example, major crypto exchanges or decentralised credit platforms allow users to earn 'interest' on balances of certain cryptoassets and clients may borrow with cryptoassets as security to back their loans.

In terms of investment strategies of crypto funds, growth strategies are focusing on long-term investments, investing either directly in certain digital assets or in entities developing goods or services to the fintech industry. Other strategies include hedge fund strategies such as long/short funds, which often use derivatives and seek to capitalise on the price volatility across various exchanges. In addition, fund managers have been experimenting in revenue-generation strategies and adopting credit fund-type strategies. In terms of financing crypto funds, the method will depend on the investment strategy and the underlying investments of the fund. Given that cryptoassets do not typically amount to a recognisable chose in action, financing direct investments in digital assets entails derivatives and synthetic structures utilising title transfer quasi-security arrangements (or other control strategies) over the underlying cryptoassets/security tokens. Investments in underlying fintech entities can be financed by any traditional fund finance products. Crypto credit funds will have flexible funding options as detailed below.

Private credit funds – part of two worlds

Private credit funds, as both borrowers and lenders, merit particular mention, not least as the private debt market (which includes distressed debt and venture capital) has experienced impressive and sustained growth over the last several years, increasing from USD42.4 billion in AUM in 2000 to USD776.9 billion in 2018. Experts say that the AUM of private credit currently stands at USD1.187 trillion.[12] Private credit funds as lenders are extremely active in financing private equity funds and portfolio companies and providing credit for their acquisition, real estate, infrastructure and development activities. A large portion of private credit funds are now offering ESG-focused private credit products incorporating ESG-linked financial incentives in their loans.[13] Private credit funds have demonstrated their ability to provide bespoke expertise and flexible capital and are able to finance beyond the traditional means of bank lending. According to one survey, over half of the funds now use private credit as the preferred choice over traditional bank financing in their buyouts as private credit lenders are typically able to customise borrowing terms to a far higher degree, which can result in an extra level of leverage and tailored borrowing covenants for funds.[14] Flexibility is crucial for fund borrowers especially at times of uncertainty. As the landscape is shifting towards flexible financing solutions, we expect that private credit fund lenders will continue to grow their market share in the fund finance market.

For private credit funds as borrowers, clearly the earlier points apply as they do to any private fund when anticipating future financing requirements. As the underlying loan portfolios are income-generating assets, private credit funds typically have flexible funding options. They can borrow against the cash flow of the portfolio of loans on a secured or unsecured basis. They can securitise the portfolio or use other synthetic structures (for example, using credit default swaps or risk participations) to transfer some of the risks of holding the loan positions. Private credit funds can even raise collateralised loan obligation financing over larger portfolios by issuing sophisticated risk and return-based tranches of securities. Generally speaking, the private credit fund, as a loan originator, has the opportunity to structure their portfolio of loans to be suitable for a wide range of financing, refinancing and realisation transactions. Where the loan portfolio cannot be so easily assigned or secured, then the Cayman Islands SPV, custodian or trust-based structures come to the fore and can be deployed to house the loan portfolio in anticipation of future needs.

Outlook and conclusion

While the outlook remains strong in 2023, several important factors will weigh on investors' and managers' minds as they think about doing deals. The macroeconomic environment, market volatility and heightened regulatory oversight present challenges for the industry. Increased inflation and Russia's invasion of Ukraine have dialled up global disruption, causing geopolitical and economic uncertainties around supply chains, energy prices, and other economic factors, as well as untold human suffering. The question of outflows of capital from China remains another known unknown.

Inflation, tightening Central Bank monetary policies, the appreciation of the US dollar and rising commodity, oil and food prices are contributing to currency depreciation in emerging markets. Private equity managers will continue to prepare their portfolios for difficult market conditions. For a continued bear market, private equity managers are pumping up the liquidity.[15] Uncertainty around the sustainability of the current growth rate is likely to persist, and inflation and tax rises will remain a major concern. For the financing market, the combination of lower asset prices and increased financing costs may increase competition in fundraising, and we expect the increasing use of bespoke structures that are tailored to sponsors' needs. Collateralised fund obligation structures aggregating multiple funds assets, rated note structures or an increasing use of continuation funds are all part of those bespoke solutions. We expect the further growth of secondaries markets using deferred consideration, flexible debt financing and cross-fund equity financing as useful tools. Private equity and venture capital investments in Central and Eastern Europe are ready to ride the rising tide of growth as private credit managers expect growth to take place across emerging markets.[16]

With the continuous rise of preferred equity and hybrid facilities, the fund finance market is poised for more growth with the increase of alternative credit providers and we expect that sponsors will be turning to fund-level credit to fill liquidity needs both as a defensive measure and for opportunistic investments.[17] Flexibility will remain paramount when those private equity sponsors are looking for robust liquidity solutions for their complex and bespoke fund structures.

We have no doubt that the growth of the private equity and private credit markets will continue with considerable pace and with that, we anticipate increasingly complex fund structures paired with flexible liquidity solutions. We also anticipate that these increasing complexities will solidify the position of the Cayman Islands as an offshore jurisdiction for investment funds due to its sophisticated legal and regulatory framework, and we expect that some of the robust liquidity solutions will become core financing options throughout the life cycle of investment funds.

* * *

Endnotes

1. S&P Global Market Intelligence 2022.
2. Global Private Equity Report 2022 – Bain & Company.
3. Prequin Global Private Debt Report 2022.
4. Alternative Credit Council and AIMA, Financing the Economy 2022 – published on 23 November 2022.
5. Debevoise & Plimpton – 2022 Private Equity Mid-Year Review and Outlook.
6. 'Number of Private Funds' Q3 2022 published by CIMA.
7. 'Number of Mutual Funds' Q3 2022 published by CIMA.
8. 'Number of Mutual Funds-Master' Q3 2022 published by CIMA.
9. From 7 August 2020, Cayman Islands closed-ended funds that fall under the Private Funds Act (2021 Revision) must register with CIMA before they can accept capital from investors.
10. If, however, security is granted over a partnership interest in a Cayman Islands exempted limited partnership, the general partner is required under the Exempted Limited Partnership Act (2021 Revision) to note the security interests in respect of which it has received valid notice in the register of security interests of the partnership.
11. MarketsandMarkets.
12. Private Credit Association, https://privatecreditassociatioin.com.
13. Global Private Equity Report 2022 – Bain & Company.
14. Global Private Equity Outlook 2022 – Dechert LLP and Mergermarket, published on 9 November 2021.
15. Institutional Investors: Private Equity's Outlook Is Mixed as They Prepare for Headwinds, published on 14 October 2022.
16. Private Equity and Venture Capital in Central and Eastern Europe – Bain & Company.
17. Debevoise & Plimpton – 2022 Private Equity Mid-Year Review and Outlook.

Agnes Molnar
Tel: +1 345 623 2376 / Email: amolnar@traversthorpalberga.com

Dr. Agnes Molnar, formerly a member of the banking and fund finance team of a leading international law firm, is a finance and funds partner and a member of the Fund Finance Team and the Investment Funds Team. Agnes is a recognised expert across a broad range of fund finance products including subscription financing, asset-backed financing (NAV facilities), hybrid, preferred equity, GP-support and co-invest facilities. Agnes also advises on investment schemes and financing real estate, distressed assets and acquisition of loan portfolios. Triple qualified with a Doctorate in Law (*Dr. iur.*), Agnes is admitted to practise in Hungary, England and Wales and the Cayman Islands. Agnes was recommended by *Chambers Global* (2016) as a leading lawyer in banking & finance and recognised by *The Legal 500* (2019) as a next generation lawyer for emerging markets and as a rising star for fund finance and non-performing loans.

Richard Mansi
Tel: +1 345 949 0699 / Email: rmansi@traversthorpalberga.com

Richard Mansi is a leading corporate, funds and banking expert with over 20 years of experience who heads up the Investment Funds Team. He advises on the launch of particularly complex private equity and hedge funds, on their fund-linked financing and derivatives businesses, and represents leading funds, lenders, managers, derivative parties, distributors, investors and service providers on the full range of fund activity and wind down. Richard, formerly of Linklaters, ran Maples and Calder's funds and fund-linked products practice in London before becoming a director in Deutsche Bank's fund-linked financing and derivatives front office structuring team and thereafter a managing director at RBS/ABN leading a similar structuring team. He holds an M.A. in Mathematics from the University of Oxford.

Catharina von Finckenhagen
Tel: +1 345 949 0699 / Email: cvf@traversthorpalberga.com

Catharina von Finckenhagen is a banking and finance partner in the Fund Finance Team having previously worked at Norton Rose Fulbright LLP in London, Hong Kong and Bahrain as a corporate finance, banking and investment funds lawyer and thereafter with an offshore firm in Singapore. Catharina is the only dual qualified Cayman Islands attorney and Luxembourg *avocate* specialised in fund finance, and advises major US and foreign banks and other financial institutions on structuring subscription credit facilities, hybrid facilities and other secured and unsecured lending arrangements, management fee lines, GP lines, co-invest loans and complex syndicated and bilateral credit facilities for funds. Catharina is recommended by *Chambers Global* (2022) and by *The Legal 500* (2022) as a leading banking and finance lawyer, is recognised by *IFLR1000* as a rising star and won the Fund Finance Association rising star award in 2020. Catharina is admitted as a lawyer in England and Wales, the Cayman Islands, Luxembourg and Ireland.

Travers Thorp Alberga

Harbour Place, 2nd Floor, 103 South Church Street, P.O. Box 472, George Town,
Grand Cayman KY1-1106, Cayman Islands
Tel: +1 345 623 2376 / URL: www.traversthorpalberga.com

More than a decade of global fund finance transactions

Michael Mbayi
Pinsent Masons Luxembourg

Introduction

The purpose of this chapter is to examine how global fund finance practices have evolved for more than a decade. Luxembourg is a unique jurisdiction from which to observe the evolution of fund finance globally, as it is a domicile of choice for private equity funds and there are often Luxembourg aspects in global fund finance transactions.

This chapter will examine how practices have evolved in the Grand Duchy of Luxembourg, the United States, England and Wales, France, and will also briefly consider the Asian market.

From subscription credit facilities to NAV, hybrid and other types of facilities

The typical fund finance transaction a decade ago was carried out via a subscription facility agreement. In this type of transaction, a loan facility is granted at fund level based on the creditworthiness of the investors. Hence, the credit underwriting is against the investors and security interest is taken over both the undrawn commitments of the investors and the bank account of the fund where such commitments are to be paid. The purpose is that in the event of default, the lenders may "step into the shoes" of the general partner or the manager of the fund and claim to the investors direct payment of their undrawn commitments.

Over the course of the last decade, other types of transactions have emerged, such as net asset value (NAV) credit facilities and hybrid credit facilities. The difference between subscription credit facilities and NAV credit facilities is that the credit underwriting exercise is performed against the assets of the fund rather than against the investors. Such facilities are also known as being "asset-based". Security is taken over the shares of the portfolio companies and/or on the accounts where the proceeds deriving from the investments are to be received. Hybrid credit facilities combine aspects of both subscription credit facilities and NAV credit facilities.

More recently, we have also seen the emergence of fund finance solutions designed to provide liquidity options to general partners and fund managers; namely, general partner credit facilities and management fee facilities. The most common global set-up for a private equity fund is a partnership with a general partner and limited partners. However, the general partner may choose or may be required, depending on the relevant jurisdiction and the regulatory requirements, to delegate the management to a fund manager (such as an alternative investment fund manager). As such, there are fund finance solutions tailored by lenders in favour of the general partner. Here, the general partner will grant a pledge over the management fees to be received by it (if any), the distributions to be received from the fund, and over the bank accounts where the proceeds related to such distributions will be paid.

Similarly, there are fund finance solutions that exist for fund managers, which are secured by a pledge granted over the management fees to be received from the fund and over the relevant accounts where such fees are to be paid. Finally, we have seen increased interest in bespoke transactions as preferred equity solutions.

From investor letter transactions to non-investor letter transactions

A decade ago, a fund finance transaction would not close if satisfactory investor letters were not provided for the investors to be included in the borrowing base. In a typical subscription credit facility transaction, collateral is granted over the undrawn commitments of the investors. As a consequence, in the event of default, the lenders may claim direct payments from the investors. That being said, the investors may have legal grounds to refuse payment, such as a right of set-off or counterclaim. Since the credit of the investors is the core element of this type of transaction and the loan is granted on the assumption that the investors will pay in the event of a default of the fund under the facility agreement, it is of paramount importance to ensure that there is no legal gap. To close the gap, the lenders seek to receive letters from the investors waiving any right of defence, set-off, counterclaim and other similar rights in respect of the payment of their commitments to the lenders. However, with the progressive increase of lenders and competition in the market, and the progressive recalibration of bargaining power between lenders and borrowers, it has become increasingly difficult for lenders to obtain investor letters. Consequently, solutions needed to be found in order to provide a similar level of comfort to lenders, and the necessary waivers started to be included directly in the fund documents, for the benefit of the lenders, in order to achieve such a purpose. This is based on different legal grounds depending on the law of domicile of the relevant fund. As to funds domiciled in Luxembourg, the technical legal grounds to achieve this were found in the toolkit provided by the Luxembourg Civil Code and the Luxembourg law of 5 August 2005 on financial collateral arrangements (the Luxembourg Financial Collateral Law). The Luxembourg Civil Code provides for the mechanism of third-party stipulation (*stipulation pour autrui*), whereby a party to an agreement may agree with its counterparty to grant rights in favour of a third party. In the context of a fund finance transaction, the investor will agree with the fund to grant rights to the lender. With the third-party stipulation mechanism, the fund and the relevant investor may agree to confer certain rights to the lenders, such as an undertaking from the investor to pay to the account determined by the lender pursuant to a drawdown notice sent by the lender in the event of default. Such mechanism needs to be captured in a contractual document, which, in the context of a fund finance transaction, would be the limited partnership agreement and/or the subscription agreements. On the basis of article 2 (5) of the Luxembourg Financial Collateral Law, the investor may waive any defence, right of set-off, counterclaim or any other similar type of right *vis-à-vis* the lender. Such waiver needs to be documented in a document signed by the investor, which may be the limited partnership agreement and/or a subscription agreement. Hence, in a transaction with a Luxembourg fund, in order to ensure that there is a similar level of comfort for the lenders than in a transaction with investor letters, both mechanisms should be appropriately captured in the fund documents.

Investor letters should not be confused with notices of security interest. Notices of security interest generally have two main functions. The first function is a legal technical function, where a notice of the collateral over the undrawn commitment is necessary for the perfection of the security, in light of the law governing such a security. The second function is a more commercial or informative function, where notice is not necessarily legally required but is requested by the lender to ensure that the investors are aware that the relevant security agreement is in place. Concerning Luxembourg more specifically, the Luxembourg Financial Collateral Law provides that the perfection (*dépossession*) of security occurs by the mere conclusion of the pledge over claims, which is the form of pledge commonly used to have a security interest over the undrawn commitments of the investors. Although, the debtor may be validly discharged if he pays his creditor as long as he is not aware of the pledge. Fund finance transactions are generally cross-border and involve investors outside Luxembourg, so conflict of law rules must also be considered to determine the perfection requirements for the enforceability of the Luxembourg pledge *vis-à-vis* third parties. In this respect, Regulation (EC) 593/2008 of the European Parliament and of the Council of 17 June 2008 on the law applicable to contractual obligations (Rome I) is silent concerning the law applicable to determine the enforceability of a pledge over claim *vis-à-vis* third parties. Therefore, we need to look into specific Luxembourg conflict of law rules. In this respect, there is both a traditional view and a modern view. Under the traditional view, the perfection formalities applicable in the domicile of the debtors (i.e. the investors) are considered. In application of the modern view, perfection formalities of the law governing the relevant claim (i.e. Luxembourg law, in the context of investors' commitments governed by Luxembourg law) are considered. Therefore, these points need to be discussed between counsels, and the Luxembourg security needs to be appropriately structured in order to grant sufficient comfort to the lenders in this respect. Hopefully, such questions will soon be settled by the European Union as part of the Capital Markets Union initiative, which aims to set conflict of law rules applicable to the third-party effects of assignments of claims. The applicable law on the basis of the envisaged rule would be Luxembourg law.

Evolution of the security over undrawn commitments

In a subscription facility transaction, in terms of collateral over the undrawn commitments of the investors, the objective has not evolved as such. The idea is to have the possibility for a lender to step into the shoes of the general partner or the manager of the fund in the event of default and to claim direct payment to the investors. However, in some jurisdictions, the technical means of achieving this have evolved. To achieve this objective in Luxembourg, at the start of the last decade, there was generally a transfer of property for collateral purpose of the undrawn commitments from the fund to the lenders. However, the market has evolved to a pledge over claims whereby the undrawn commitments of the investors are pledged. The Luxembourg Financial Collateral Law provides that a pledge over claims encompasses the exercise of the rights attached to the pledged claims (*droits liés à la créance gagée*), hence, in respect to undrawn commitments, the right to claim payment of the same (i.e. the capital call right). Originally, for this type of transaction in England and Wales, a power of attorney by way of security was granted, so that in the event of default, the lender would have the possibility to exercise such power of attorney and send drawdown notices to the investors. Such a set-up evolved to an assignment of rights of the general partner and the manager of the fund under the limited partnership agreement to the lenders. In the United States, the approach has been consistent over the last decade: the state involved is generally Delaware; and a UCC-1 financing statement is filed against the fund and the general partner in order to have the possibility to call capital and enforce such right in the event of default. In France, to achieve the envisaged objective, the mechanism used is a stipulation for a third party. We see here the difference with Luxembourg where a pledge, which is a security interest as such, is used. Such difference is explained namely because, in France, the types of funds generally involved in fund finance transactions are not subject to bankruptcy; therefore, a third-party stipulation is sufficient. Conversely, in Luxembourg, the funds may be subject to bankruptcy proceedings, but Luxembourg financial collateral arrangements are bankruptcy-remote and remain enforceable even when bankruptcy proceedings occur. We see here two different ways in two different jurisdictions to reach the same objective.

Cross-border and domestic Luxembourg market

At the beginning of the last decade, the clear tendency was for foreign law-governed subscription credit facility agreements (generally New York law or the law of England and Wales), as the main actors granting facilities to Luxembourg funds were established in the United States or the United Kingdom. More recently, we have seen more local lenders and a tendency to have Luxembourg law credit facility agreements when local lenders are involved. That being said, in most fund finance transactions for Luxembourg funds, the facility agreements tend to be governed by New York law or the law of England and Wales.

Legal opinions

The position regarding responsibilities in relation to the issue of legal opinions has been quite consistent. In Europe, there is generally a split of opinion: the fund's counsel provides the capacity opinion, while the lender's counsel provides the validity and enforceability opinion. Conversely, in the United States, it is generally the fund's counsel that provides the full set of opinions. It should also be noted that, in practice, different lenders may have different requirements in terms of the content of opinion and so requesting the relevant lender's opinion checklist at the outset of the transaction is advised.

ESG fund finance, the last child

We have recently observed an increased demand for fund finance solutions with Environmental, Social and Governance (ESG) features. First, a clarification of terminology is necessary. There are typically two main types of loan involved in this field: green loans; and ESG-linked loans. A green loan is a loan granted whose proceeds are used exclusively for green or environmental purposes. Conversely, for an ESG-linked loan, there is no limitation on the use of the proceeds, but the focus is on key performance indicators (KPIs) to be met in order to obtain a decrease of the pricing. Green loans are more suitable for impact funds while ESG-linked loans are more suited to private equity funds.

In this context, we have recently seen the emergence of ESG-linked subscription facility agreements. The mechanic and the security package are mainly the same as for a standard subscription facility agreement, but a margin ratchet mechanism is embedded in the documents so that there is a reduction of pricing where the agreed KPIs are met. One important step for ESG-linked subscription facility transactions is the prior due diligence, where the lender tries to understand the ESG policy of the relevant fund and agrees with it on the KPIs. The idea is generally to build on the existing policy, the existing standard adopted by the relevant funds, and the existing frequency of reporting. Examples of KPIs seen include gender diversity in management, certain carbon emission targets, and specific governance requirements. In order to avoid "greenwashing", it is of paramount importance to have measurable KPIs, and another core aspect in this respect is monitoring. Monitoring may be done externally, by a rating agency, for instance, or internally by the relevant lender where it has the qualified personnel in this respect. In terms of volume of this type of fund finance transaction, Europe is leading the way. It should also be noted that fund finance lawyers advising on this type of transaction in the European Union need to master the increasing EU regulation around sustainability; for instance, Regulation (EU) 2019/2088 of the European Parliament and of the Council of 27 November 2019 on sustainability-related disclosures in the financial services sector (the Disclosure Regulation) and Regulation (EU) 2020/852 of the European Parliament and of the Council of 18 June 2020 on the establishment of a framework to facilitate sustainable investment (the EU Taxonomy). The EU Taxonomy may be seen as a framework, a classification, or a dictionary setting out what is sustainable or not, so that there is a common understanding on the subject. The EU Taxonomy will be completed by delegated acts from the European Commission setting up relevant technical screening criteria.

Fund finance in Asia

Fund finance has become a very active market in Asia in approximately the last seven years. Generally, the set-up of a fund finance transaction in Asia is somewhat similar to some fund finance transactions seen in the United States: there is typically a Cayman fund and a credit facility agreement governed by New York law, with a similar security interest to that in a standard US fund finance transaction. The difference is simply that the investors are located in Asia. That being said, while the Cayman Islands remains the domicile most commonly seen in Asian fund finance transactions, there is an emergence of Singapore and Hong Kong funds. In Hong Kong, the Limited Partnership Fund Ordinance (Cap. 637) entered into force on 31 August 2020 and introduced a new limited partnership fund regime to enable private funds to be registered in the form of limited partnerships in Hong Kong. The idea is to foster the development of private equity funds in the special administrative region. From a Luxembourg perspective, there have been more and more fund finance transactions involving Asia. Luxembourg remains the domicile of choice for European investors. In such context, where European and Asian investors invest in the same pool of assets, European investors would invest through a Luxembourg fund while Asian investors would invest through a fund most commonly used in Asia. In such a configuration, Luxembourg legal requirements are implied in Asian fund finance transactions.

New entrants

During the last few years, we have seen many new entrants in the market. From the lending side, this concerns not only credit institutions but also alternative lenders that raise funds specifically to enter into the fund finance market.

We will continue to see new entrants in the market since there is still significant space for growth. In this respect, many strategies are available. In this competitive environment, new lenders will need to find their own niche within fund finance, specialising in light of the type of product, the profile of the sponsor, the size of the fund, the geography, or the asset class, while the vast majority of lenders currently acting in the subscription finance space are generally asset-class agnostic.

With the increased complexity of the transactions, we have also seen debt advisors entering into the market to assist fund managers to determine and tailor, with the assistance of specialised lawyers, the appropriate fund finance solution.

Fund finance 3.0

We often say that we are currently in the fund finance 2.0 era, and we believe that this sophistication will continue as the industry enters into a fund finance 3.0 era.

We expect to see an increasing number of fund finance solutions for securitisation vehicles, taking into account that, in this respect, the lawyer involved would have to be able to navigate a sea of EU regulations combined with local law requirements. We will also see more and more fund finance solutions provided in the form of bonds or other forms commonly seen in the capital market space.

Furthermore, we expect to see continuing advancement of the industry globally, with significant development in Africa and South America, while North America, Europe and the APAC region will continue to grow and perform.

Resilience of the fund finance market

One of the key features of the fund finance market has been its resilience over time. Indeed, during the last major crises, such as the global finance crisis and the COVID-19 pandemic, the fund finance market remained resilient, and activity continued to develop considerably. This is because fund finance technology is an essential tool for fund managers, even in a crisis period. Indeed, as explained in this chapter, there are a wide variety of fund finance products, and there is always a product tailored to provide an optimal solution.

Conclusion

Global fund finance is constantly evolving and is an industry where innovation is always present. The fund finance market will certainly continue to evolve and grow in the coming years in view of the number of outstanding and innovative experts in this industry.

Michael Mbayi
Tel: +352 40 49 60 245 / Email: michael.mbayi@pinsentmasons.com
Michael Mbayi is a Legal Director at Pinsent Masons Luxembourg, in the Finance & Projects, Banking & Restructuring group. He leads the fund finance practice of the firm in Luxembourg and was awarded in 2021 by the Fund Finance Association for his contribution to the industry. Michael has also been included in the list of the Most Influential Fund Finance Experts of 2022 established by The Drawdown. He has an in-depth knowledge of the fund finance market and long-standing experience in fund finance. Michael advises financial institutions as lenders and investment funds as borrowers in a wide range of transactions including subscription facilities, hybrid/NAV facilities, and other bespoke fund finance solutions. He is the host of the Fund Finance Series, an industry-driven webinar where he regularly meets with global experts for in-depth discussions and analysis. He is also the host of Fund Finance Expert Talks, where he has extensive one-to-one discussions with industry experts. Michael is the author of various fund finance publications and has been quoted by *The Legal 500 EMEA 2022* as "*very knowledgeable on fund finance matters*", "*responsive*" and "*particularly active on behalf of a lender focused client base*".

Pinsent Masons Luxembourg

69, Boulevard de la Pétrusse, L-2320 Luxembourg
Tel: +352 40 49 60 1 / URL: www.pinsentmasons.com

NAVs meet margin loans: The rise in single asset financings

Sherri Snelson & Juliesa Edwards
White & Case LLP

The markets for financial products made available to private equity, venture capital and other investment funds ("Funds") and the ultra-wealthy are ever-evolving.

Margin lending has a well-established presence in the financial markets, long pre-dating fund finance and, for that matter, Funds as we know them. Traditional margin loans rely on daily mark-to-market pricing and margin call mechanics to ensure that the agreed loan-to-value ratio ("LTV ratio") is maintained. Whether the underlying collateral is a single publicly traded security or a portfolio of securities, the mechanics are the same. The reliance on a publicly reported market price, however, renders margin loans *per se* ill-suited when the asset to be financed is equity in a privately held company.

Chapters in previous editions of this book, including our own,[1] have chronicled the rise of the net asset value ("NAV") lending market in the Funds space. By enabling financial sponsors to leverage their aggregate net equity across a portfolio of assets, NAVs provide an additional source of liquidity for sponsors seeking funding for additional and follow-on investments or to return capital to investors. An important source of comfort for NAV lenders, however, is the ability to rely on collateral support from a diverse portfolio of assets.

So, what do you do when the leverage needed is for a highly concentrated portfolio or even a single privately held asset? A bit of match-making.

In recent years, we have seen rising interest in what you might call "private margin loans" to provide financing to company founders and other high-net-worth individuals ("HNWI") collateralised by their shares in the still-privately-held companies they founded. In the Funds realm, similar loans are being used to provide "back levering" for individual portfolio investments. In both scenarios, a bespoke combination of NAV and margin lending techniques tailored to the underlying asset provide the valuation and margin maintenance mechanics and other lender protections necessary to make these loans feasible.

In this chapter, we will outline the key features of NAV facilities and traditional margin loans as well as the limitations of each type of facility when applied in the context of a single privately held asset. We will then explore the myriad of ways these features are being mixed and matched to facilitate financings for single privately held assets.

NAV facilities – background

Enterprising Funds have many options to source quick liquid capital. Funds are consistently taking advantage of third-party financing opportunities from lenders to assist with the running of the Fund or improve returns to investors. These financings are often secured. The traditional form of such financing is a revolving subscription line facility, which "looks up" toward the investors and helps bridge the gap between the Fund's need for capital to make an investment and the investors' ability to provide the capital in a timely fashion. A lender's collateral for a revolving subscription credit facility is each investor's promise to provide capital to the Fund when called upon to do so by its general partner or manager (such promise, the investor's "capital commitment"). The lender(s) will provide a revolving commitment, which may be borrowed from time to time up to the borrowing base amount. Such borrowing base amount will be a percentage of the uncalled capital commitments of certain eligible creditworthy investors. Due to how this borrowing base amount is calculated, the subscription line financing option is not ideal for all Funds. In particular, when a Fund has matured beyond its investment period and has utilised all or substantially all of its capital commitments to make investments, the subscription line financing option is no longer available. At this stage in its life, the Fund may consider entering into a facility where the borrowing base amount is based on the NAV of the portfolio investments rather than its uncalled capital commitments.

NAV facilities – structure

NAV facilities "look down" toward the portfolio investments for collateral, security and borrowing base purposes. In a NAV facility, one or more banks, financial institutions, or other lenders will provide a term or revolving loan secured, directly or indirectly, by the underlying portfolio investments of the Fund and related cash flows. The borrower under these facilities may be the Fund itself (including any parallel vehicles) or a subsidiary of the Fund (referred to as an "aggregator") established to hold the Fund's interest in its underlying investments. In some cases (often where private equity assets are involved), the borrower may be an "orphan" special purpose vehicle ("SPV") that holds a preferred equity interest in an aggregator vehicle. Importantly, the NAV facility should be structured to ensure that any cash proceeds from portfolio investments are routed to the NAV borrower for deposit to a pledged account subject to the control of the lender(s) pending application of any amounts necessary to prepay the NAV facility so as to maintain the requisite LTV ratio. Absent a default, upon satisfaction of those prepayment (or "cash sweep") requirements, any remaining proceeds are permitted to be distributed to the Fund and its investors.

NAV facilities – features

NAV facilities can be distinguished by (1) the nature of their collateral, (2) how the borrowing base is determined, and (3) prepayment and cash retention triggers. We will review each of these features below.

Collateral

The collateral for a NAV facility will typically consist of (i) the proceeds of any portfolio investments, and (ii) equity interests in the borrower and any entity or other investments owned directly by the borrower. In some cases, the assets being pledged may be the portfolio investments themselves, but more often, those portfolio investments are held via a series of intervening holding companies. In the typical NAV structure, the only equity pledged is the equity of the borrower itself and the borrower's interest in the top-tier investment holding companies. Where the borrower is an aggregator, the obligations may also be guaranteed by the Fund parent. For purposes of this chapter, it is sufficient to focus on the fact that lenders "look down" to the assets held indirectly by the Fund for their collateral protection rather than "looking up" to the investor capital commitments.

Borrowing base

The borrowing base for a NAV facility is typically determined by looking at the LTV ratio – that is, the ratio of the outstanding loans provided (before and after giving effect to the proposed use of each borrowing) to the net fair market value of the included portfolio assets (as valued by the sponsor in accordance with its usual valuation policy – see more on this below).

In calculating the numerator of the LTV ratio, lenders often incorporate concentration and diversity requirements for the underlying assets. For example, a lender might require a certain number of assets be held within the portfolio at any given time and/or include concentration limits to govern how much of each type of asset may be "included" for purposes of the LTV ratio calculation. Not all assets are created equal for lenders evaluating the riskiness of their loans and the appropriateness of the LTV calculation and maximum permitted LTV ratio, and the "haircuts" derived by application of the diversity and concentration limits reflect this.

Cash monitoring and retention

The LTV ratio regulates how much credit may be extended under the facility at a given time. In that respect, a NAV might look similar at first to an ordinary asset-based loan ("ABL") or subscription credit facility. However, when one looks to what happens when the requisite LTV ratio is exceeded (i.e. a "borrowing base deficiency" in ABL parlance), a NAV facility behaves much differently. In an ABL or subscription facility context, a borrowing base deficiency triggers an immediate obligation to prepay the loan to the extent necessary to bring the borrowing base back into compliance. Those prepayments are funded either from other cash resources of the borrower (in the case of an ABL) or from capital calls issued to investors (in the case of a subscription facility). One of the key features of a NAV facility, however, is that it relies on the (often illiquid) investments of the Fund for collateral support, and the remaining uncalled capital available to fund prepayments of the NAV facility may well be insufficient to cover a borrowing base deficiency. The borrower thus has no guaranteed ready access to cash with which to fund a prepayment. In light of this, a borrowing base deficiency – or LTV breach – does not trigger an immediate obligation to prepay the NAV facility. Instead, a cash sweep event goes into effect such that, as and when cash proceeds are received from portfolio assets, 100% of those proceeds will be swept to prepay the loan until the required LTV ratio is reached, after which the sweep percentage returns to its normal level. Unlike the ABL or subscription facility contexts, there is no stated deadline by which those proceeds must be received and/or such prepayments completed.

To ensure that this cash sweep mechanism is complied with, the NAV facility documents will require that all cash proceeds received by the borrower from its interest in the portfolio investments are deposited into a pledged account that is subject to the control of the NAV lender. These proceeds must be used first to satisfy any outstanding cash sweep obligations. Subject to certain exceptions,[2] proceeds may only be withdrawn from the secured account and used for other purposes of the Fund (including distributions to investors) once all cash sweep obligations have been satisfied and provided that no default or event of default is otherwise ongoing.

NAV facilities – valuation of assets and lender dispute rights

One of the trickiest parts of a NAV facility – and the technology of the NAV most relevant for this chapter – is answering the question of how to value the assets when there is no publicly available reference price.

The process for valuation of portfolio assets is fairly straightforward, but frequency, intra-period adjustments and lender dispute rights can be highly negotiated. Typically, the NAV of the portfolio is determined by the sponsor on its usual schedule and in accordance with its usual methodology for reporting to its investors. For private equity Funds, this most often means that the value of the portfolio investments is marked quarterly in accordance with the Fund's stated valuation policy. For Funds holding debt positions or a range of debt and equity investments, some of which may be traded in a liquid secondary market, monthly or even more frequent marking and reporting may be required.

Whether the portfolio values are determined quarterly or more frequently, there is an inherent lag between the as-of date of the valuation and the time it is reported to the NAV lender. For quarterly valuations, for example, the value will be determined as of the last day of the fiscal quarter but not reported to the lender until 45 to 60 days thereafter. Year-end valuations have an even greater lag, with 90 to 120-day reporting periods.

To be comfortable lending based on LTV ratios that are subject to the sponsor's discretion and which, in a rapidly changing market climate, may materially overstate current market value of the asset at the time of reporting, lenders generally require that dispute rights be included in the NAV facility documentation. These provisions provide the lender with the right to substitute its own opinion of the value of relevant assets or, if the borrower objects to the substitute value, to obtain two to three firm market bids and/or an independent third-party valuation. If the third-party bids or valuation result(s) in a value that is a specified percentage (often 5 to 10%) lower than that reported by the sponsor, the third-party bids/valuation will control. Until the third-party bids or valuation are obtained or the valuation dispute is otherwise resolved, additional borrowings and distributions to investors will generally be permitted only to the extent they would be allowed using the lender's proposed valuations. Cash sweep requirements that would be triggered by the lender's proposed valuations may be deferred pending resolution of the dispute.

Margin loans – background

As alluded to earlier in this chapter, single asset or "private margin loan" facilities also make use of familiar concepts from traditional margin loans.

Margin loans were originally conceived in the second half of the 19th century to provide capital to finance the buildout of railroads and other infrastructure projects across the United States. Investors combined their own available cash with borrowings from banks or brokers to plow ever-greater investments into railroads and other publicly traded companies using the purchased securities as collateral. Purchasing shares in this manner has become known as "buying on margin".

Margin loans – structure

Like NAVs, margin loans "look down" toward the pledged company stock for collateral and borrowing base purposes. In a margin loan facility, one or more lenders provide(s) the borrower with a term or revolving loan that is secured by publicly traded equity securities. The collateral may be securities of a single company or a portfolio of multiple companies. Like the NAV facility, a margin loan facility will be structured to trap proceeds from the underlying collateral to fund any required prepayments before such proceeds may be withdrawn by the borrower and used for other purposes.

Margin loans – features

As with NAV facilities, we will review the following margin loan facilities features: (1) collateral; (2) the borrowing base; and (3) prepayment and cash retention triggers. In addition, we have included a brief note about U.S. securities regulations. While not directly applicable to NAV facilities or margin loans over privately held shares, this regulatory background is important to understand when structuring private margin loans over shares in companies that may become publicly traded during the life of the facility or which are being taken private as a result of the relevant transaction.

Collateral

The collateral for a margin loan will consist of (i) shares in one or more publicly traded companies, (ii) the pledged securities account subject to lender control to which such shares are credited, and (iii) any proceeds of those shares. The shares will be required to be held in a pledged securities account maintained with a third-party custodian and subject to an account control agreement in favour of the lender. Absent a default or event of default under the margin loan, the borrower will typically be permitted to issue buy and sell orders with respect to securities in the account, but any withdrawals from the account will be subject to the conditions specified in the margin loan agreement and will require the instructions of the lender.

Borrowing base

As with NAV facilities, the borrowing base for a margin loan is determined by looking at the ratio of the outstanding loans to the value of the collateral on deposit in the custody account. However, unlike for NAV facilities, the publicly traded nature of the collateral permits daily recalculation of the LTV ratio based on observed market prices without a reporting delay. For facilities supported by multiple underlying securities, concentration limits and diversity criteria will apply to ensure that the collateral value supporting the loan is not overly reliant on a particular position, country, industry, etc. In addition, the facility may feature limits on the exchanges on which underlying collateral may be traded and their currencies, and may feature an outright prohibition on credit for securities in certain industries (such as weapons manufacturing).

Cash monitoring and retention

Margin calls

If the value of the collateral supporting a margin loan declines such that the LTV ratio exceeds a specified "margin call LTV", a margin call will occur. This means that the lender will require the borrower to deposit additional collateral into the custody account in order to bring the LTV ratio back down to the maintenance level. The additional collateral may consist of additional shares in companies already included within the portfolio, cash and/or, where the borrower is controlled by a Fund, a standby letter of credit or an equity commitment letter from the Fund. If the borrower does not respond to the margin call by submitting additional collateral or calling capital by the stated deadline, an event of default will occur and the lender may call the loan immediately due and payable and foreclose on the collateral.

Mandatory prepayments/issuer events

In addition to margin calls, certain events may result in mandatory prepayments of the entire margin loan. These events typically include a change of control of the borrower and so-called "issuer events" with respect to the issuer(s) of securities included in the collateral. Issuer events may include: (i) the market reference price for the assets falling below a minimum required reference price at the close of business on any trading day; (ii) the issuer's announcement that its shares will no longer be listed for trading on the relevant exchange; (iii) a suspension of trading of issuer's shares in the market for two/three or more consecutive trading days; (iv) the announcement or occurrence of a tender offer, exchange offer or takeover of the issuer wherein any person acquires more than a specified percentage of the outstanding shares; (v) the issuer's shares are nationalised or otherwise required to be transferred to a government agency; and (vi) the average daily trading volume of the listed shares is less than a minimum volume required by the margin loan agreement. In addition, other events affecting the collateral shares, such as share splits, reclassifications of shares, share dividends, share repurchases by the issuer, mergers and other transactions that could have a dilutive or concentrative effect on the value of the collateral shares may result in a "facility adjustment event" giving the lender the right to readjust the LTV thresholds, concentration and diversity criteria and other metrics in the loan so as to counter the effect of the facility adjustment event and ensure the loan continues to reflect the original commercial arrangement. If the lender concludes that no adjustment of the facility is possible that would maintain the commercial intent, then an issuer event will be deemed to have occurred and the facility will be required to be repaid.

Regulation

One of the key differences between traditional margin loans, on the one hand, and NAV facilities and private margin loans, on the other, are the U.S. government regulations that apply to margin loans. As noted above, margin loans became popular in the late 1800s, driving not only the intended increase in investment into infrastructure but also rapid rises in the stock markets. As with any asset bubble, so long as money kept flowing into the system and prices kept rising, everyone was happy. Until they were not. Margin lending regulations were virtually non-existent at the time, and many people, from Wall Street financiers to the local newspaper boy, were caught up in the mania. As prices began to decline in 1929, borrowers were forced to sell increasing amounts of shares to fund margin calls, which only drove prices lower and fuelled the contagion. Successive waves of margin calls and panic selling in late October 1929 resulted in what is still the worst percentage decline in the U.S. stock market, wiping out fortunes, bankrupting banks and companies across the country and giving way to the Great Depression.

Having seen the effects of over-reliance on margin lending, the U.S. Congress included restrictions on margin lending by brokers and other lenders in the Securities Exchange Act of 1934 ("Exchange Act") in the hopes of preventing similar financial devastation in the future. Those statutory enactments authorised the Board of Governors of the Federal Reserve System ("Federal Reserve") to adopt regulations to establish margin requirements and to prevent the excessive use of credit for the purchasing or carrying of or trading in securities. The Federal Reserve then adopted Regulation T (governing securities credit by brokers), followed soon thereafter by Regulations U (governing margin lending by banks) and G (governing margin lending by lenders other than banks or brokers). The Federal Reserve harmonised Regulations U and G over the ensuing decades and in 1997, merged former Regulation G into Regulation U, with the latter regulation now governing margin lending by all lenders in the United States other than brokers. Additionally, in 1970, Congress amended the Exchange Act to restrict U.S. persons or foreign persons controlled by or acting on behalf of or in conjunction with U.S. persons from obtaining margin credit from a lender outside the United States to purchase or carry securities of U.S. issuers where the credit does not conform to the requirements of the margin regulations. That statutory provision has been implemented by the Federal Reserve in Regulation X.

Broadly speaking, for loans by bank or non-bank lenders other than brokers that are secured, directly or indirectly, by "margin stock" and which are borrowed for the purpose of purchasing or carrying margin stock, Regulation U caps the LTV ratio at 50% of the current market value of any margin stock collateral, with most other types of collateral having "good faith" loan value. "Margin stock" is generally any equity security that is traded on certain exchanges in the United States, including exchange-listed American depositary receipts ("ADRs") of foreign issuers.

The Federal Reserve generally views loans to investment funds differently from loans to industrial or commercial companies for purposes of Regulation U, with a loan to such a fund being presumed to be indirectly secured by the securities in the fund's portfolio even in the absence of any indirect security-type arrangements (such as a negative pledge) in the credit agreement. As a result, unless not more than 25% of the value of the Fund's assets consist of margin stock, a loan by a bank or non-bank lender to such a fund would generally be presumed to be indirectly secured by margin stock.

The margin regulations are highly complex and an exploration of the details is beyond the scope of this chapter, but it is important to be aware that these regulations exist to ensure that NAVs and private margin loans do not fall foul of them if there is a potential for the underlying collateral to include or become margin stock.

Margin loans – valuation of assets

Valuation of assets for a margin loan is relatively straightforward due to the availability of mark-to-market reference prices. Margin loans will have a "calculation agent" responsible for the daily determination of asset values and LTV ratios. Unlike the NAV facilities, here, the secured parties (and specifically the calculation agent) are responsible for determining LTV ratio levels in the first instance.

Application to single privately held assets

Neither NAV facilities nor a traditional margin loan approach work well by themselves when the underlying asset to be financed is equity in a single privately held company.

In the case of NAV facilities, the lenders lose the benefit of spreading risk across a diverse portfolio of assets. Moreover, without the ability to rely on cash flows resulting from transactions involving different portfolio companies at different times, the cash sweep mechanisms of a NAV facility are ineffective in keeping the LTV in line if values decline. Instead, there would be an undesirable all-or-nothing aspect to the loan, with the entire loan coming due if the default LTV is triggered. The discretionary element of sponsor-driven valuations and the lag in reporting discussed above add to the heightened risk of concentrated NAVs and single asset financings.

In a similar vein, traditional margin loan mechanics that rely on daily marking to market based on public reference asset prices cannot function where the underlying asset is privately held.

The answer: Private margin loans/back-levering facilities

Over the course of the pandemic, we have seen a marked rise in concentrated NAVs and single-asset back-leveraging transactions. These have come about for a variety of reasons, including providing protective liquidity for portfolio companies to weather market uncertainty, financing opportunistic add-ons and returning capital to investors while extending holdings periods for portfolio companies to await better market conditions for exits. Prior to the more recent freeze in the syndicated loan market, we also saw sponsors using back-leveraging transactions as an additional layer of financing for acquisitions, providing the "equity" for their portfolio acquisitions at a lower cost of capital *vis-à-vis* capital calls from their investors.

Outside the Fund world, we have also seen these facilities being used by family offices who may hold only a limited number of investments and by HNWIs, typically company founders. In the latter case, the borrowings enable the founders to monetise a portion of their shareholdings to provide capital for other start-ups or simply to de-risk their personal financial position via diversification into other investments.

To overcome the weaknesses of both NAV facilities and traditional margin loans discussed above, concentrated NAV and single asset facilities typically mix and match concepts from both domains to tailor a solution that works for the asset in question.

Single asset financings – valuation

There is a spectrum of mark-to-market and valuation techniques that may be employed depending on the underlying asset.

On one end of the spectrum are companies that, although privately held, have public-traded bonds or other liquid debt instruments for which there is an available market quote. In those cases, more traditional margin lending mark-to-market and margining techniques may be employed, either using the debt trading price as a proxy for the underlying equity value or tying margin requirements directly to the trading price of the debt. There is an important catch, however, that must be addressed. If the reference asset is a debt instrument rather than the common equity, that instrument can disappear by refinancing or repayment or its validity as a proxy for the equity value may be compromised by amendments that affect the trading price (e.g. juicy increases in interest or fees or addition of collateral) or by the issuance of more junior tranches of debt. In these transactions, much time is often spent negotiating the scope of facility adjustment events and replacement reference asset provisions to protect lenders in the event of post-closing amendments to the original reference asset or other changes to the issuer's capital structure that could artificially inflate the LTV ratio being relied on by the lender.

On the other end of the spectrum are companies that rely on quarterly sponsor valuation in the same manner as typical NAVs. For these transactions, more fulsome dispute rights, margin loan-style margin call mechanics and Fund recourse are often key to offsetting the increased risks of inferior access to regular third-party market price quotes.

In the middle lie a variety of alternative valuation methods that may be applicable. Non-sponsor-owned companies, especially tech companies, for example, may require quarterly independent valuations ("409A valuations") for tax reasons in connection with their issues of stock options to employees. Lenders may also require independent valuations, at least annually if not quarterly, to obtain a disinterested opinion as to the equity value. In any case, incorporating dispute rights into the documentation, to enable the lender to seek its own independent valuation if it believes the value being reported by the borrower is overly optimistic, provides important comfort to lenders to address the risks of uncertainty and reporting delays inherent with private assets.

Single asset financing – margin calls and recourse

Single asset financings most often employ margin call mechanisms from traditional margin lending rather than relying on the cash sweep mechanics more often seen in NAV facilities. As there is no diversification of risk and cash flow generation across a range of assets, the lender has an immediate right to be repaid as needed to maintain the requisite LTV ratio. As with traditional margin loans, acceptable additional collateral may include cash, cash equivalents, letters of credit or equity commitment letters (in sponsor-driven transactions) or additional shares in the underlying issuer (in non-sponsor-driven deals where less than 100% of shares owned by the Fund or HNWI are subject to the financing).

For a variety of reasons, these financings may be put in place at a level beneath the main Fund vehicles or, outside a Fund context, at an SPV wholly owned by the HNWI or other party seeking the financing. They may or may not be recourse to the Fund or HNWI. If the financing is full recourse to the Fund or HNWI via a guaranty or Fund equity commitment letter, margin calls resulting from a decline in value will trigger a payment obligation under those credit support documents. If recourse is limited to the SPV borrower and the posted collateral for the loan, the Fund or HNWI has a decision to make. To prevent a default, it can inject further assets into the SPV or provide credit support of its own in satisfaction of the margin call. Given that LTV advance rates for these transactions are typically well south of 50%, the normal expectation is that the economically rational response for any Fund or HNWI with the wherewithal to do so is to provide the additional collateral to protect its equity in the underlying asset. If it opts not to do so, an event of default will result, and the lender will be entitled to foreclose on and sell the collateral, resulting in the Fund's or HNWI's loss of control of the asset.

Single asset financing – ensuring the ability to enforce

In a traditional margin loan, the collateral is publicly traded securities, so enforcement is straightforward – the lender simply sells the shares into the market on the exchange on which it is listed, subject to potentially applicable securities law limitations. If the size of the position in relation to the average trading volume is such that an immediate sale may negatively affect the market price or may prove difficult to execute, the lender may opt for smaller transactions over an extended period of time or execute a block sale to maximise foreclosure proceeds, but generally speaking it will have an unfettered right to dispose of the collateral in any commercially reasonable manner, subject to potentially applicable securities law limitations.

Where the underlying asset is a privately held security, by contrast, the lender needs to be mindful that practical and/or contractual limitations may impact its ability to quickly convert the collateral to cash.

As with any NAV loan over private equity interests, a foreclosure by a lender may trigger change of control provisions in underlying opco debt agreements and/or regulatory consent requirements that would be less likely triggered in the sale of the shares of a public company. Given that, here, we are dealing with a single or possibly handful of assets, however, negotiating those consents or otherwise addressing those issues is less daunting than it would be for a large portfolio of assets. Consequently, rather than put in place more complex structures designed to create a liquid collateral instrument (for example, a pref LP interest), which can be sold without triggering a change of control of the issuer, the lender may opt to accept the pledge of the issuer shares and take the risk of obtaining consents at the time of foreclosure or may structure the transaction with recourse to the Fund to create other, hopefully easier, avenues for collection if things do not go to plan.

In many cases, especially outside the Fund sponsor context, the limitations on enforcement will arise not from change of control issues but from transfer restrictions in the charter documents and shareholders' agreements governing the issuer's shares. Whether the financing is for a company founder or to back-lever a Fund's share of a consortium investment, transfer of the issuer's shares is likely to be subject to restrictions, including rights of first refusal, pre-emptive rights, tag-alongs and drag-alongs and even outright prohibitions on transfer without consent of the issuer board or specified groups of shareholders. In these instances, the lender will want to ensure before making the loan that it has all consents necessary to permit a foreclosure transfer free of these burdensome limitations. As a condition to making the loan, the lender will customarily require that it receive a consent signed by the issuer, as well as consents from any required shareholders, to waive transfer restrictions that would otherwise apply to a foreclosure sale. These can be highly negotiated, as the issuer and shareholders will often preclude a sale to a competitor of the issuer or others. In addition, the issuer will want to ensure that any transfer by the lender does not jeopardise the tax or regulatory status of the issuer or risk resulting in a public offering of its shares. These are fair concerns, and must be balanced carefully against the lender's desire for a quick and easy recovery.

Conclusion

In summary, the ability of the financial markets to create new product lines and find ways to solve liquidity needs is limited only by the imaginations of market participants. Over and over again, we have seen the market pull tools from a variety of toolboxes and use them to solve new problems or respond to changing market conditions. This is illustrated well by the combination of NAV and traditional margin lending techniques to extend the concepts to cover single or highly concentrated interests in privately held shares. As market participants, both on the lender and borrower side, become more familiar with these products and more comfortable with how they operate, we have no doubt that the market for these financings will continue to expand.

* * *

Endnotes

1. See "NAVigating the collateral waters: You have a boat but will it float?", *GLI – Fund Finance 2022*, Sixth Edition.
2. Such exceptions often include (i) funding investments that the Fund had contractually committed to make prior to the cash sweep going into effect, and (ii) funding certain operating expenses of the Fund, which may include (often subject to a cap) management fees payable to the Fund sponsor.

Sherri Snelson
Tel: +1 212 819 8430 / Email: sherri.snelson@whitecase.com
Sherri Snelson is a partner in White & Case's Debt Finance practice and is based in New York. She has extensive experience acting as lead counsel for lenders, private equity funds and their portfolio companies in connection with leveraged finance and fund/portfolio finance transactions across numerous jurisdictions and industries. In particular, Sherri has over 20 years of experience structuring and negotiating subscription finance and various NAV and asset-based fund finance solutions in the US, Europe and Asia. She received her J.D. with high honours from the University of North Carolina, an M.B.A. from New York University, and a B.A. *magna cum laude* from Wake Forest University, and is dual-qualified in New York and England and Wales.

Juliesa Edwards
Tel: +1 713 496 6137 / Email: juliesa.edwards@whitecase.com
Juliesa Edwards is an associate in White & Case's Americas Debt Finance practice in the firm's Houston office. Her experience includes the representation of private equity funds, financial institutions and commercial borrowers in financial transactions of all types, including fund finance transactions, acquisition financings, syndicated financings, reserve-based financings, reorganisations, workouts and debt restructurings. Juliesa graduated *cum laude* with a Bachelor of Science Management in Legal Studies in Business and in Management from Tulane University before graduating from Vanderbilt University Law School.

White & Case LLP
1221 Avenue of the Americas, New York, New York 10020-1095, USA
Tel: +1 212 819 8200 / URL: www.whitecase.com

Regime change but business as usual – updates to sanctions and restructuring regimes in the Cayman Islands

Alexandra Woodcock & Danielle Roman
Mourant

Introduction[1]

The Cayman Islands is one of the largest offshore fund jurisdictions globally, with over 15,600 closed-ended private equity funds and 13,000 open-ended funds[2] registered with the Cayman Islands Monetary Authority (**CIMA**) at last count. For that reason, most fund finance lawyers practising in onshore jurisdictions will be accustomed to seeing Cayman Islands borrowers, guarantors, feeders and other relevant credit parties in their transaction structures.

The Cayman Islands has recently experienced some important legal updates that, while not specific to fund finance law and practice, are nonetheless relevant in that context. These developments include an unprecedented number of new designations under the Cayman Islands sanctions regime following the Russian invasion of Ukraine in February 2022. A new restructuring regime has also been introduced to provide the Cayman Islands with a modern, accessible and flexible restructuring process while also demonstrating the jurisdiction's commitment to adapting its laws to meet the ongoing needs of the global economy. Finally, two recent Cayman Islands cases regarding the proper procedure for winding up exempted limited partnerships (**ELPs**) have led to some judicial debate as to whether such a winding-up action can be brought against an ELP itself (as opposed to its general partner). In this chapter, we take the opportunity to comment on these recent developments in a fund finance context.

Sanctions regimes

The financial sanctions in force in the Cayman Islands are in essence those implemented by the United Kingdom (**UK**), reflecting sanctions adopted by the UK in response to resolutions of the United Nations (**UN**) Security Council and domestic UK sanctions regimes. Those sanctions regimes are extended to the Cayman Islands (and other British Overseas Territories) pursuant to UK Overseas Territories Orders in Council, though the Cayman Islands may also impose domestic sanctions. All legal and natural persons located or operating within the Cayman Islands are subject to the sanctions regimes regardless of where their activities are conducted.

The key sources of sanctions to be considered in the Cayman Islands are as follows:
- Overseas Territories Orders in Council extending UK sanctions to the Cayman Islands with certain amendments;
- the Consolidated List of Financial Sanctions Targets published by the UK's Office of Financial Sanctions Implementation (**OFSI**), a division of His Majesty's Treasury, which provides a list of individuals and entities designated as being subject to UK financial sanctions;

- any 'list of designated persons' (meaning sanctioned persons) that may be published by the Governor of the Cayman Islands; and
- in certain circumstances, the UK Sanctions List published by the UK Foreign, Commonwealth & Development Office, which contains all individuals, entities and ships designated under the UK's Sanctions and Anti-Money Laundering Act 2018.

Additional sanctions regimes such as those of the European Union (**EU**) and the United States (**US**) are not in force in the Cayman Islands as a matter of law; however, they may still be applicable in practice. Many Cayman Islands funds, specifically those with jurisdictional overlap between various regimes, may choose to monitor and comply with non-UK/Cayman Islands sanctions, particularly the US regime administered by the Office of Foreign Assets Control. Situations where there is jurisdictional overlap between various sanctions regimes can be difficult to navigate, especially in areas where the Cayman Islands/UK regime differs from the EU/US sanctions regimes.

Aggregation

Aggregation is one of the areas that differs between the Cayman Islands/UK and EU/US sanctions regimes. Aggregation refers to an instance where a fund has more than one sanctioned investor/limited partner, neither of whom individually 'own or control' the fund for the purposes of the relevant legislation.[3] In situations where aggregation is possible, the Cayman Islands follows the UK position; that is, when making the assessment on ownership and control, the OFSI would not automatically aggregate sanctioned persons' holdings unless there is evidence of a joint arrangement between those parties or one party controls the rights of another, or evidence that a sanctioned person controls the fund for the purposes of the relevant sanctions legislation.[4] This approach is markedly different than that under the EU and US sanctions regimes, which would both aggregate the ownership interests of multiple sanctioned investors in a fund to determine whether the applicable ownership threshold is satisfied.

Sanctioning process

The Cayman Islands anti-money laundering, counter-financing of terrorism and counter-proliferation financing regimes require that applicable sanctions lists (as set out above) must be checked frequently to identify whether a fund maintains any accounts or holds any funds or economic resources for designated persons or entities, whether directly or indirectly. This raises the question of the frequency of which these screenings are required. This type of screening should be conducted on an ongoing basis since ownership and control may change over time. Ultimately, however, frequency is a risk-based decision and what is appropriate for one financial service provider, such as a bank, may not be appropriate for another, such as an open-ended fund. In practice, the screening of sanctions lists is often conducted on a daily basis via third-party service providers. Notably, the fund is responsible for looking through to the ultimate beneficial owners of their direct clients or investors. Where a sanctions hit occurs, the fund is required to do the following:

- immediately freeze any accounts, funds or economic resources (which are defined broadly) that are owned or controlled (directly or indirectly) by designated persons or entities;
- cease dealing (also defined broadly) with the funds or assets, or from making those funds or assets available (directly or indirectly) to, or for the benefit of, the designated person or entities, unless an appropriate licence is held;

- report any findings to the Cayman Islands Financial Reporting Authority (**FRA**) as soon as practicable by completing and submitting a compliance reporting form in the prescribed form; and
- consider whether a suspicious activity report (**SAR**) also needs to be made to the FRA.

What is an asset freeze?

An asset freeze in the context of a fund with a sanctioned or designated investor usually means that the fund may not process any redemptions, withdrawals or transfers of, or make any distributions in respect of, the frozen interest; nor may the fund accept any additional subscriptions from or make capital calls on the relevant investor. Additionally, the fund must not otherwise alter, move or allow the designated person(s) to access or receive the benefit of the investment. The current industry recommendation is to ensure that there is a clear process in place for dealing with freezing funds or ceasing transactions or the provision of other financial services. Firms are not legally required to inform clients who are targets that their accounts have been frozen but there should be appropriate systems in place to report or provide other necessary information to the FRA. The impact on day-to-day activities is expected to be minimal where a designated person holds a minority interest in a fund.

Penalties and exemptions to sanctions

Breaches of financial sanctions are considered serious criminal offences and, under the Overseas Territories Orders in Council, generally carry a maximum of seven years' imprisonment on conviction on indictment and/or a fine. Persons may apply for licences that allow certain activities or transactions to take place that would otherwise be prohibited by the Cayman Islands sanctions regime. Licences may only be issued where one of the grounds, or 'derogations', provided by the applicable sanctions legislation has been met. In addition, the Governor of the Cayman Islands must either obtain the consent of, or consult with, the UK Secretary of State prior to issuing any licence.

On 4 October 2022, the Governor of the Cayman Islands issued a general licence (**General Licence**) in relation to the Cayman Islands/UK sanctions regimes. The General Licence took effect immediately and will expire on 4 April 2023. The General Licence was issued under Regulation 64 of the UK's Russia (Sanctions) (EU Exit) Regulations 2019, as extended to the Cayman Islands, with modifications, by the Russia (Sanctions) (Overseas Territories) Order 2020 (**Modified Regulations**). In accordance with the General Licence, a 'Relevant Investment Fund'[5] (or the fund manager on its behalf) may redeem, withdraw or otherwise deal with an investment interest of a non-designated person and make payments for basic needs, routine holdings and maintenance and legal fees from frozen accounts. The General Licence only permits redemptions of non-designated investors, subject to the fund's constitution and terms, and does not allow for redemption of any position owned or controlled, directly or indirectly, by a designated person.

Under the General Licence, the permissible payments are 'basic needs' payments (including professional service provider fees, corporate and regulatory fees, director fees and audit and accounting fees), payment of reasonable legal fees and payment of reasonable fees or service charges arising from the holding and maintenance of frozen funds or assets.

The General Licence provides that service providers will not breach the Modified Regulations by receiving fees permitted under the General Licence in exchange for providing the relevant services to the Relevant Investment Fund. Service providers located outside the Cayman Islands will, however, need to ensure compliance with the sanctions legislation applicable to them.

Where the General Licence is relied upon, the following notification requirements apply:
- the Governor's Office must be notified by email as soon as practicable the first time the General Licence is relied upon;
- subsequently, monthly reporting must be provided to the Governor's Office on 16th of each month setting out the use of the General Licence in the previous month; and
- if the Relevant Investment Fund is regulated, CIMA must be provided with notice of use of the General Licence within three business days.

Impact of sanctions on the fund finance industry

Most credit agreements include express representations and restrictive covenants, which require the borrower to actively monitor for sanctions risk at the investor level where the possibility arises of controlling persons, individual officers or employees becoming sanctioned. The term 'sanctions' is typically broadly defined in credit agreements to include all economic or financial sanctions imposed, administered or enforced by any governmental authority with jurisdiction over the borrower or its affiliates. However, the exact wording of any sanctions provision must be considered on a case-by-case basis.

In scenarios where an investor in the fund is sanctioned, the borrower will need to take active steps to ensure it remains compliant with these contractual provisions. In particular, a sanctions covenant will usually strictly prohibit any proceeds of a sanctioned transaction being used to repay advances under the facility and will prohibit any proceeds of the facility being made available, directly or indirectly, to any sanctioned person. Nonetheless, both the lender(s) and borrower(s) need to remain aware that under a typical credit agreement, an investor (including those holding a minority interest) becoming sanctioned is likely to, at the very least, result in that investor being excluded from the borrowing base. This may in turn trigger a prepayment requirement if the borrowing base is exceeded.

General Licence

The initial hope for the recently issued General Licence was that it would allow funds to redeem out the problem/sanctioned investor, without making any payment of redemption or withdrawal proceeds to the designated person, allowing the fund to continue to operate as usual with the non-sanctioned investors. However, the General Licence, in practice, will not accommodate this approach since the definition of Relevant Investment Fund does not apply to funds with minority sanctioned investors. Even if the definition of Relevant Investment Fund included funds with minority sanctioned investors, the permissions in the General Licence would not necessarily be helpful to most funds since it only provides for the redemption/withdrawal of non-sanctioned investors. Notably, practitioners should be mindful that the General Licence does not override the contractual position of a fund's constitutional documents in relation to any actions required to withdraw/redeem an investor. Currently, it is unknown whether any further general licences will be issued and, if so, whether they would provide the operators and managers of funds with frozen investors a way forward to improve the position of the funds and remediate any technical breaches of credit facility terms.

The previous restructuring regime

The Cayman Islands as a jurisdiction is no stranger to complex corporate restructurings. In recent years, the Cayman Islands courts have been involved in multiple high-value corporate restructurings of global businesses.[6] However, unlike the bespoke UK administration or US Chapter 11 restructuring regimes, the Cayman Islands has, up until now, facilitated restructuring using the process of provisional liquidation.

Provisional liquidation was not ideal for the purposes of restructuring for a number of reasons. In order to apply for the appointment of a provisional liquidator, first a petition to wind up the company had to be presented to the court. The presentation of a winding-up petition was perceived quite negatively for obvious reasons and, therefore, had limited use as a restructuring process. Further, the presentation of a petition did not commence insolvency proceedings for the purposes of foreign recognition and did not give rise to any moratorium on claims being brought against the company. These only occurred when the court made the order appointing the provisional liquidator. This resulted in timing issues around foreign recognition of the restructuring proceedings and left a potential opening for third parties seeking to frustrate the proceedings.

A further challenge during the old regime, which was brought to light by the case of *China Shanshui Cement Group Ltd*,[7] was that a company's directors could not present a winding-up petition without either shareholder sanction or an express provision in the articles of association of the company authorising the directors to do so on behalf of the company.

The new restructuring regime

The Cayman Islands Companies (Amendment) Act 2021 came into force on 31 August 2022, addressing many of the issues with the old restructuring regime and, in particular, the use of provisional liquidation as the sole tool for corporate restructuring where an automatic stay on creditor claims was necessary to implement the restructuring successfully. Notably, the new regime is also expressed to apply to Cayman Islands ELPs, although exactly how ELPs will be treated will be subject to further consideration.

The new restructuring regime will facilitate the efficient restructuring of companies by:
- retaining the flexibility of the existing regime, specifically the courts' ability to adopt powers of the restructuring officer in particular circumstances;
- improving accessibility to the restructuring regime, particularly dispensing with the need to present a winding-up petition to commence a court-supervised restructuring;
- providing additional debtor protection to facilitate restructuring beyond the existing regime, such as by imposing an automatic stay, with extraterritorial effect, upon presenting a restructuring petition; and
- preserving and enshrining in statute important creditors' rights, specifically the right to receive notice of any application in the ordinary course.

In terms of procedural steps, the new regime allows for the following:
- the presentation of a petition to the court for the appointment of a restructuring officer on the grounds that the company is or is likely to become unable to pay its debts and intends to present a compromise or arrangement to its creditors. A restructuring officer is required to be a qualified insolvency practitioner in the Cayman Islands, but the court may appoint a foreign practitioner to act together with the Cayman Islands insolvency practitioner. Notably, any time after the appointment of a restructuring officer, the company, the restructuring officer, any creditor or any contributory may apply to the court for the variation or discharge of the order appointing the restructuring officer;
- a petition for the appointment of a restructuring officer can be presented by the directors of a company without a resolution of its member or express power in its articles of association; and
- an automatic global moratorium on the filing of a petition for the appointment of a restructuring officer. Notably, this prohibition has extraterritorial reach and expressly applies to proceedings brought against a company in a foreign jurisdiction.

It is not proposed there be any substantive changes to the manner in which a restructuring may be implemented under Cayman Islands law. For instance, the regime continues to allow for a restructuring to be achieved by use of a scheme of arrangement if the unanimous consent of all parties cannot be reached. The new restructuring regime provides the Cayman Islands with a modern and flexible restructuring process, which should enable the Cayman Islands to continue to facilitate high-value, complex corporate restructurings.

Impact of the new restructuring regime on the fund finance industry

There are many aspects of the new restructuring regime that benefit both secured and unsecured creditors of a Cayman Islands debtor, including:
- creditors are not bound by the restructuring moratorium. This means that creditors with security over the assets of a Cayman Islands debtor may continue to take steps to enforce their security, provided those steps do not necessitate commencing any legal proceedings against that debtor;
- the regime sets out advertising requirements that will ensure that the application petitioning for the appointment of a restructuring officer is brought to the attention of all relevant shareholders whether within or outside the jurisdiction. However, these requirements may be varied with leave of the Cayman Islands court;
- creditors have standing to participate and make their views known in the court proceedings in various ways, such as:
  - applying for the restructuring moratorium to be lifted;
  - seeking leave to bring a winding-up petition against the Cayman Islands debtor;
  - making an application to set aside the appointment of restructuring officers or to have their powers varied; and
  - nominating alternative restructuring officers to those proposed by the Cayman Islands debtor during the hearing of its application before the court; and
- in a scenario where the Cayman Islands debtor seeks to undergo restructuring through a scheme of arrangement, those creditors caught by the scheme will additionally have the option to vote in favour or against the proposed restructuring.

Ultimately, the enforcement of the new regime and automatic global moratorium does not alter the current Cayman Islands law position as regards secured creditors. The automatic stay does not extend to enforcement of security, and a secured creditor may enforce security in accordance with its terms without reference to the restructuring officer or obtaining the consent of the Cayman Islands courts.

Generally, it is not expected that the new restructuring regime will result in any necessary drafting changes to credit agreements. The typical definition of 'Debtor Relief Laws' (or any analogous definition) in most modern credit agreements will usually be drafted broadly to cover any other liquidation, conservatorship, bankruptcy, insolvency, fraudulent conveyance, reorganisation/restructuring, or similar laws affecting the rights or remedies of creditors. Again, however, Cayman Islands counsel will review the wording on a case-by-case basis.

Overall, the new regime is a welcome development in the Cayman Islands market, in that it provides a restructuring procedure more aligned to administration in the UK or Chapter 11 in the US.

Proper procedure for a creditor to commence winding up a Cayman Islands ELP (two perspectives)

There are two key recent cases in relation to determining the proper procedure for a creditor to commence winding-up proceedings against a debtor that is a Cayman Islands ELP. The first of these cases presented to the Cayman Islands court was *In the matter of Padma Fund L.P.* (**Padma**),[8] and the most recent case is *In the matter of Formation Group (Cayman) Fund I, L.P.* (**Formation**).[9] Prior to these cases, the generally assumed position in the Cayman Islands was that a creditor could commence winding-up proceedings against the ELP itself.

Padma

In *Padma*, certain creditors presented a petition to the Cayman Islands court seeking the winding up of Padma Fund L.P. (**Partnership**) on the basis that the Partnership was unable to pay its debts and should therefore be wound up. The court held that a creditor's winding-up petition could only be presented against the general partner of an ELP and not against the ELP itself. The bases of the court's decision were as follows: (i) the general partner is responsible for the debts of the ELP; and (ii) section 33(1) of the Exempted Limited Partnership Act (as amended) (**ELP Act**) absolutely prohibits proceedings being issued against the ELP itself.[10]

Formation

In *Formation*, an application to strike out a limited partner's petition to wind up an ELP was made on the basis that, following *Padma*, such proceedings had not been instituted against such ELP's general partner. In this instance, the court held, contrary to the decision in *Padma*, that the ELP Act under section 36(3) does allow a winding-up petition to be brought against an ELP.[11]

Conflicting decisions

The conflicting decisions of *Padma* and *Formation* from the Cayman Islands courts has resulted in uncertainty in the current state of the law in relation to the proper procedure for a creditor to wind up a Cayman ELP. A difficulty that arises from the courts' approach in *Padma* is that section 35 of the Partnership Act (as amended) only provides partners with the right to apply to dissolve a partnership and does not confer this right on creditors, which means that a creditor (such as a bank) could not apply to dissolve a debtor being an ELP. Although the judgment in *Formation* appears to disagree with this, it is important to note that: (i) this case involved a winding-up petition brought by a limited partner (therefore, strictly speaking, *Padma* is still the authority on the appropriate route for a creditor petition); and (ii) the views expressed by the court in *Formation* as to whether legal proceedings may be commenced against an ELP were expressed in *obiter* and, therefore, are not legally binding.

There is obvious uncertainty in this area of the law that will need to be clarified either by way of amendments to the ELP Act and Partnership Act or by a judgment from the Cayman Islands Court of Appeal. In the meantime, the safest course of action for a creditor is to seek to enforce their debt against the general partner instead of attempting to present a winding-up petition against the ELP.

Impact of *Padma* and *Formation* on fund financing

It is important to note that, even based on the court's view in *Padma*, the position is a purely procedural matter in that it does not prevent a creditor from getting an order for the winding up of an ELP, but simply requires a creditor to bring the proceedings against the general partner.

Subsequent to the initial decision in the *Padma* case, it has become common to update the drafting in certain credit agreement forms, which include limited recourse/non-petition language relating to the general partner of an ELP fund borrower or guarantor. The drafting updates will typically add a carve-out to clarify that proceedings can still be brought against the general partner in relation to a winding up of the ELP borrower or guarantor. Of course, any required carve-out will be specific to the drafting of the provision in question.

Additionally, given the variety of different fund borrowing structures, it is worth noting that:
(i) generally, a creditor would have jurisdiction in the Cayman Islands courts to commence winding-up proceedings against a foreign general partner (for example, a Delaware general partner) that is the sole general partner of a debtor that is an ELP; and
(ii) in the case of an ELP with more than one general partner, it is the natural reading of the ELP Act and consistent with the general law relating to partnerships that all general partners would be jointly and severally liable for the debts and obligations of the ELP. As such, a creditor would be able to commence proceedings against one or more of the general partners in relation to a debtor that is an ELP. Notably, where there are multiple general partners, only one general partner is required to be: (a) a Cayman Islands person or entity; or (b) registered as a foreign entity in the Cayman Islands. In such a situation, we would advise commencing proceedings against a general partner that is either a Cayman Islands person or entity or is registered as a foreign entity in the Cayman Islands.

The apparent judicial debate over the proper procedure for a creditor to wind up a Cayman ELP will need to be considered by an appellate-level court or clarified by amendment to the relevant legislation to provide welcomed certainty on the topic. In the meantime, using the drafting approach to the recourse provisions (as outlined above) appears to be an adept solution that has proven uncontroversial in the Cayman Islands market.

Conclusion

Although there have been some significant legal developments in the Cayman Islands in the last year, the overall effect of these changes to the fund finance industry has been minimal and have not led to any fundamental changes in approach among Cayman Islands fund finance attorneys. Ultimately, the recent updates in the Cayman Islands legal sphere continue to allow the Cayman Islands to be a modern, flexible and co-operative jurisdiction capable of performing high-value and complex fund financing transactions.

* * *

Endnotes

1. The content of this chapter relates to developments up to 31 October 2022.
2. As at 30 September 2022.
3. Under the Russia (Sanctions) (EU Exit) Regulations 2019 (as amended), an entity is 'owned or controlled, directly or indirectly' by another person if:
   (a) the person holds (directly or indirectly) more than 50% of the shares or voting rights in an entity;
   (b) the person has the right (directly or indirectly) to appoint or remove a majority of the board of directors of the entity; or
   (c) it is reasonable to expect that the person would (if they chose to) be able, in significant respects, by whatever means and whether directly or indirectly, to achieve the result that the affairs of the entity are conducted in accordance with their wishes.
4. Paragraph 4.1.4, OFSI General Guidance – UK Financial Sanctions.
5. Under the General Licence, a **Relevant Investment Fund** means an investment fund whose assets are frozen under and pursuant to the Modified Regulations due to its assets being 50% or more owned or controlled by a designated person.
6. These include the cases of *Ocean Rig UDW, Inc*, *LDK Solar Co Ltd*, *Suntech Power Holdings Co Ltd*, *Arcapita Investment Holdings Limited*, *ATU Cayman Holdco Limited* and *Tailored Brands Worldwide Purchasing Co*.

7. 2015 (2) CILR 255.
8. Unreported, 8 October 2021.
9. Unreported, 21 April 2022.
10. The Exempted Limited Partnership Act, section 33(1) provides that:

    'Subject to subsection (3), legal proceedings by or against an exempted limited partnership may be instituted by or against any one or more of the general partners only, and a limited partner shall not be a party to or named in the proceedings.'

11. Under the Exempted Partnership Act, section 36(3) provides that:

    'Except to the extent that the provisions are not consistent with this Act, and in the event of any inconsistencies, this Act shall prevail, and subject to any express provisions of this Act to the contrary, the provisions of Part V of the Companies Act (as amended) and the Companies Winding Up Rules 2018 shall apply to the winding up of an exempted limited partnership and for this purpose … (g) on the application by a partner, creditor or liquidator, the court may make orders and give directions for the winding up and dissolution of an exempted limited partnership as may be just and equitable. (13) Following the commencement of the winding up of an exempted limited partnership its affairs shall be wound up by the general partner or other person appointed pursuant to the partnership agreement unless the court otherwise orders on the application of any partner, creditor or liquidator of the exempted limited partnership pursuant to subsection (3)(g).'

* * *

Acknowledgments

With special thanks to Gabrielle Myers, Sara Galletly, Andrew B Grant, Finn Howie and Marianne Wilson for their contributions to this chapter.

Alexandra Woodcock
Tel: +1 345 814 9183 / Email: alexandra.woodcock@mourant.com

Alexandra is a Partner in the firm's Cayman Islands Corporate and Finance practice and specialises in banking and finance work.

Alexandra frequently advises many of the world's leading finance institutions and private fund sponsors on the structuring and execution of finance transactions and restructurings involving secured lending to Cayman Islands companies, partnerships and unit trusts (including hedge funds and private equity funds). She has extensive experience in fund finance matters and has worked on some of the largest and most high-profile cross-border consensual restructurings.

Before joining Mourant, Alexandra was a Partner at another offshore law firm in the Cayman Islands for 12 years, and prior to moving offshore she worked at a US law firm in London.

Danielle Roman
Tel: +852 3995 5705 / Email: danielle.roman@mourant.com

Danielle is a Partner at Mourant Ozannes (Hong Kong) LLP and the Local Practice Leader of the firm's Banking and Finance team, having practised in Asia for over 15 years. She advises on a broad spectrum of cross-border transactions, including asset finance (in particular aviation and shipping), fund financing, acquisition and leveraged finance, debt restructurings and general corporate lending.

In fund financing, Danielle regularly represents private and commercial banks on subscription credit facilities, hybrids, NAVs and GP/Management facilities. She is on the global board of the Fund Finance Association, and is also a board member of Women in Fund Finance.

Prior to joining Mourant in 2012, Danielle worked at Clifford Chance in Hong Kong and Dentons in London.

Mourant

PO Box 1348, 94 Solaris Avenue, Camana Bay, Grand Cayman, KY1-1108, Cayman Islands
Tel: +1 345 949 4123 / URL: www.mourant.com

VC *vs* PE: Comparing the venture capital and private equity fund financing markets

Cindy Lovering & Corinne Musa
Cooley LLP

Overview

Market trends in the fund finance space have been well documented over the years. Following the collapse of Dubai-based Abraaj in 2019 and the JES Global Capital fraud in 2021, lenders have bolstered their diligence and compliance processes to ensure that their collateral in the historically safe subscription facility product – the rights to capital contributions from investors – is well vetted and secure. More recently, (i) pricing for capital call facilities has trended up in line with interest rate hikes by the Federal Reserve, (ii) banks are re-evaluating their portfolios in response to market conditions, internal depository requirements and regulatory mandates, (iii) new lenders continue to enter the market, (iv) alternative lenders are edging into the market as well, particularly looking for the higher returns associated with asset-backed leverage, including net asset value ("NAV") facilities backed by a fund's underlying investments, and (v) demand for debt facilities from general partners ("GPs") and their principals, to fund GP commitments or for personal capital, continues to be on the rise. As trends in the fund financing market continue to evolve, it is also important to consider key differences in how private equity funds and venture capital funds use the variety of available financing products. This chapter explores some of those differences and analyzes the benefits and challenges from both the fund and lender perspectives.

Fund-level financings

At the fund level, capital call facilities or subscription credit facilities are a standard product used by both private equity and venture capital funds primarily as a bridge loan to receipt of capital contributions. There is a huge competitive advantage for a fund in having a capital call facility, because it can boost its internal rate of return by borrowing and investing prior to an investor having to part with any cash or make its investment. The benefits for a private equity fund can be significant, given that there is sometimes no requirement to repay borrowings within a specified time frame in the underlying fund documentation, or any such requirement can be fairly lengthy (usually, up to 12 months, since that time frame helps mitigate risks of generating unrelated business income tax for certain tax-exempt investors). This allows the private equity fund to generate returns for an extended period of time before an investor pays a dime of its investment. Venture capital funds, however, frequently rely on an exemption to the U.S. Investment Advisers Act of 1940 (the "Advisers Act"), which significantly limits this benefit. The Advisers Act, which requires investment advisers to register with the Securities and Exchange Commission, provides for exemptions, including a venture capital exemption. The analysis of the venture capital exemption can be complex, but one prong of the analysis requires that a venture capital fund does not borrow or incur leverage in excess of 15% of the fund's aggregate capital commitments and any such borrowing is for a "non-renewable term of no longer than 120 calendar days." Thus, some of the instinctive benefits frequently touted as relevant metrics for funds using subscription facilities are less relevant for venture capital funds, and may not be a significant part of the value proposition for the fund in using a subscription facility. That being said, subscription facilities remain attractive to venture capital funds for other reasons, such as the administrative convenience of making multiple investments and paying expenses without troubling investors with multiple capital calls.

Relatedly, a useful feature of most fund-level credit facilities is the ability of the fund to add holding company or portfolio company entities as borrowers on the facility, backed by a secured guarantee from the fund. This feature usually labels the holding company or portfolio company borrower as a "qualified borrower," which is generally subject to limited covenants given that the lender's source of repayment is the underlying commitments from the fund investors and not the assets of the qualified borrower itself (although the scope of covenants/representations applicable to qualified borrowers is often a point of negotiation between the lender and fund). While the qualified borrower feature has gained substantial traction in the private equity market, where funds frequently add holding companies or operating companies that have had difficulty getting third-party financing on attractive terms, the feature is rarely used in the venture capital market. Venture capital funds usually only take minority positions (i.e., less than 50% ownership) in emerging companies, and qualified borrowers are often required to be wholly owned subsidiaries of the applicable fund for the lender to provide financing to the entity on the subscription facility. For this reason, the trend of adding qualified borrowers on capital call credit facilities appears to be limited to private equity financings.

Another development in subscription facilities is that lenders are more frequently requesting investor letters for anchor investors (usually, investors with capital commitments in the 25–35% range). Investor letters add another layer of comfort for lenders with respect to their ability to obtain capital contributions from investors upon a forced capital call. Such investor letter requirements seem to affect both private equity and venture capital funds in a similar vein. Whether investor letters become a sticking point in negotiations depends primarily on the investor make-up and/or any underlying concerns with the partnership agreement/side letters not sufficiently protecting the lender's interests. Either type of fund may have a narrowly concentrated investor base where the request for an investor letter may come into play. However, funds should equip their partnership agreements with (arguably) standardized lender protections (e.g., express authority of the fund to enter into subscription facilities and the GP's right to pledge capital commitments and the right to call capital, waiver of investor defenses, lender exclusion from the no-third-party beneficiary clause, etc.) to best position themselves in a negotiation to limit or waive investor letters. Funds may also benefit from having their draft partnership agreement borrowing language reviewed by potential lenders prior to execution to help streamline the financing process, and limit, to the extent possible, the likelihood of requiring separate investor letters.

GP-level financings

An investment fund's GP may need to access liquidity for purposes of supporting its own commitment to the related fund. These facilities often take the form of a term loan credit facility amortizing over time, to align with the fund's investment period. A GP facility will almost always also involve a pledge of collateral from the GP, which can range from an "all assets" pledge to the economic (not management) rights in the related fund. Creative approaches to financing the GP position for large sponsors can involve notes offering and securitization structures. Large private equity sponsors often have easier access to these types of structures, and GP financing generally, because of their established track records and deep relationships with lenders. Venture capital firms, in contrast, may be looking to fund individual founder positions, and therefore generally confront more challenges in finding lenders that are comfortable with the GP collateral and/or are willing to accommodate a structure that does not fit easily into their credit underwriting regime. Despite some reluctance, however, lenders to venture capital funds may accommodate GP financings despite credit concerns in order to strengthen ties with established clients or as an investment in new client relationships. Thus, in the venture capital space, a GP-level financing may bear similarities to an LP-level financing (discussed further below). GP financings can raise a number of key issues relating to the collateral, including that a pledge of collateral needs to be narrow so as not to conflict with any pledge by the GP to a subscription line lender, and the scope of collateral *vis-à-vis* the GP's interest in a particular fund needs to account for any conflicts in those fund-level limited partnership agreements. Both GPs and lenders should take heed of such collateral issues and address them in the loan documentation early on to obviate unintended consequences and costs down the line. Another common feature of GP-level financings is financial covenants, either loan-to-value or liquidity requirements. Similar to limited partner ("LP") financings, GP financings can sometimes require firm guarantees from the fund's management company, and/or personal guarantees from individual members of the GP. Whether these features are included in GP financings in a private equity or venture capital context can depend on the overall strength of the firm and practical considerations in terms of near-term future facilities with the particular proposed lender.

Management line of credit

Management companies can also play an important role in a fund's overall financing structure, and lenders frequently provide liquidity options to assist management companies, primarily for working capital to help a management company manage payments for expenses between the receipt of management fees from the funds. Occasionally, management company lines are also used to warehouse investments prior to an anticipated fundraise, but in the ordinary course, these facilities are meant to assist a firm with "keeping the lights on" in between fee payments. Strong sponsor borrowers often have management facilities that are unsecured, with just financial covenants relating to assets under management or the amount of expected management fees received. For newer or less established fund managers (and generally, in the current economic environment), these management facilities will be secured by all assets of the management company, including the rights to management fees and any related bank accounts. Diligence for management company facilities requires review of any management company agreements, investment advisory agreements and the partnership agreements of the relevant funds to ensure that a pledge of the rights thereunder is permitted, and to determine potential offsets that may reduce anticipated management fees.[1] Complications may arise if the management company and GP are the same entity, which occurs more frequently in the Asia market. In this circumstance, an all-asset lien over the management company/GP would conflict with subscription facilities under which the manger/GP has pledged its right to call capital from fund investors. Differences in the use of management company facilities in the venture capital and private equity space are minimal, as the primary driver of terms is ultimately the size of the sponsor (venture capital or private equity), whether it has an established track record and how comfortable the lender is with the relevant fee streams. The less comfortable a lender is, the more likely it will be to look for additional credit support, including by way of guarantees from the founders of the particular firm at issue.

LP financings

In both private equity and venture capital funds, the LPs in the fund frequently seek various forms of third-party financing to help the LPs of the fund or GP to fund their capital commitments. The most typical form of these is usually a partner loan program, where the fund manager will arrange for a loan program for certain affiliated LPs with a bank lender. The bank offers loans directly to the LPs, and the management firm assists by providing regular information to the bank, and, occasionally guaranteeing the individual partner borrowings (allowing the partners to secure advantageous pricing with minimal ongoing obligations). The collateral for an individual borrower's loan is usually its individual LP interest in the particular fund, which the fund acknowledges as part of the loan documentation and initial set-up. The individual borrower's loan may also be secured solely by the management fees of the management company in the case of partner programs that are linked to a management company facility. A potential drawback to this type of facility when utilized by partners of the GP, however, is the possible tax ramifications. A partner's capital interest in the GP that is funded with the proceeds of a loan made or guaranteed, directly or indirectly, by the underlying partnership, a partner or any related person may be treated as carried interest, and would therefore be ineligible for the capital interest exception set forth in Section 1061 of the Internal Revenue Code. This means that any allocation to a partner that is attributable to a contribution funded by such loan would be subject to the longer, three-year holding period applicable to carried interest rather than the one-year holding period that would apply if the allocation were subject to the 1061 exception and treated as capital interest. Care should be taken to ensure that the financing of a partner's capital commitment to the GP is structured in a manner that considers any negative tax consequences that may result if the facility is made or guaranteed by a fund-related party (e.g., in some cases, if the partner of the GP is "personally liable" for the loan, these adverse rules may not apply). While these programs are popular, they can be burdensome on a new manager, and if they are not otherwise available, LPs will occasionally enter into bespoke negotiations with a private bank to fund their positions. These loans can be used either for general liquidity (in an attempt to monetize their otherwise illiquid fund interests) or to allow for funding of capital commitments. LP financings of this type often involve negotiations between the LP and the fund or GP itself, in order to address any transfer restrictions set forth in the related fund limited partnership agreement. Because the collateral for these financings is by its nature illiquid, advance rates against the LP interest collateral can be quite low and lenders may require additional financial covenants and minimum cash liquidity amounts for their borrowers.

There are other debt financing options available to LPs based on their fund positions. LPs sometimes obtain loans from the applicable GP or management company for the related fund. These can be easier to obtain since the affiliated entity is familiar with the collateral (i.e., the LP's interest in the fund) and has a deep understanding of the valuation of the interest. That said, in the venture capital space in particular, there are frequently limitations in the fund documents about loans among affiliated parties where conflicts of interest or other disclosure issues may be in play. Some of these restrictions may pertain in the private equity market as well, and it is important to check the underlying fund documents and to consider any tax implications from any related party loans when pursuing these transactions.

Another financing option for LPs that seems to be gaining more traction lately with third-party financiers is restructuring an LP investment to allow a preferred equity provider to provide liquidity to the LP. The preferred equity would then receive distributions from the fund until a negotiated hurdle rate is achieved. This arrangement provides some of the benefits of both debt and equity treatment.

LP borrowers in both the venture capital and private equity spaces continue to look into creative ways to monetize the value of their portfolios by relying on banks and non-bank lenders to provide liquidity solutions. In doing so, fund LPs are acting similarly to the investment funds themselves, looking to lever their portfolio company assets in pursuing a NAV or other asset-based facility.

Understanding the different objectives, limitations and credit underwriting considerations of private equity and venture capital funds and appreciating perspectives on both sides of the negotiating table will help counsel negotiate meaningful terms that are relevant for their clients, and thought should be given to these considerations at every level of the fund structure.

* * *

Endnote

1. Notably, notwithstanding any anti-assignment provisions in the applicable management agreement, terms that restrict assignment of payment obligations (i.e., management fees) are unenforceable under Section 9-406 of the Uniform Commercial Code.

* * *

Acknowledgment

The authors would like to thank Jamee Lewis for her valuable contribution to this chapter.

Cindy Lovering
Tel: +1 858 550 6186 / Email: clovering@cooley.com
Cindy Lovering represents lenders in fund finance transactions, including syndicated and bilateral subscription credit facilities, hybrid and NAV credit facilities and management company credit facilities. She also advises lenders and companies on venture capital and middle-market financing transactions in the technology and life sciences industries.

Corinne Musa
Tel: +1 212 479 6369 / Email: cmusa@cooley.com
Corinne Musa focuses her practice on the representation of borrowers and alternative lenders in fund financing transactions, particularly subscription credit facilities, NAV and hybrid credit facilities, and management fee and GP lines of credit. She has been lead counsel on many of the largest and most complex credit arrangements to funds affiliated with pre-eminent fund sponsors, and has experience with ESG subscription credit facilities. Corinne is also an active participant in her community and has a vibrant *pro bono* practice.

Cooley LLP

3175 Hanover St, Palo Alto, CA 94304, USA
Tel: +1 650 843 5000 / URL: www.cooley.com

Subscription facilities: Key considerations for borrowers – a global experience

Jean-Louis Frognet, Caroline M. Lee & Eng-Lye Ong
Dechert LLP

Introduction

As the number of new entrants to the fund finance market both on the fund and lender side has swelled, we have also experienced an increasing demand for subscription facilities and other related fund finance products from fund sponsor clients throughout the U.S., Europe and Asia. Fund sponsors who did not previously use subscription facilities have begun utilising them for their new funds and those that have used a subscription facility before have returned to the market.

This chapter outlines some of the legal and practical aspects that fund sponsors and their counsel should consider when structuring, documenting and/or maintaining a subscription facility, with a particular focus on the issues relating to fund documentation and collateral. This is not an exhaustive list of the issues that are pertinent to sub line borrowers but rather a roadmap or even a conversation starter for a fund sponsor in any jurisdiction interested in exploring using a subscription facility as a financing option.

Fund documentation

A subscription facility generally takes the form of a revolving credit facility secured by the contractually committed but unfunded capital commitments of the investors in a fund. The size of the facility is determined by reference to the borrowing base, which is calculated (in the case of some sub line lenders) on the basis of the unfunded capital commitments of so-called "included investors" that meet certain credit criteria or (in the case of other sub line lenders) on a global view of the investors and their capital commitments. Given that such unfunded capital commitments are rights of a fund arising from its fund documentation and the sub line lenders' collateral and source of funds for repayment are closely tied to such unfunded capital commitments and related assets as provided therein, having "bankable" fund documentation with top-of-the-market financing provisions is the crucial first step towards a successful subscription financing.

The term "fund documentation" generally refers to the following documents in the collective: (i) the fund's limited partnership agreement (the "***LPA***"), which sets forth the relationships governing the fund, the general partner of the fund and the investors;[1] (ii) the subscription agreements, which are entered into by each investor in the fund and the general partner of the fund, whereby such investor subscribes to the fund as an investor; and (iii) any applicable side letters, which are agreements between an investor and the fund that, among other things, can alter the terms in the LPA or subscription agreements to address any tax, regulatory or legal requirements, investment policy considerations, immunities and/or other issues that are specific to such investor.[2] The fund documentation is the backbone of any subscription financing as it will set the bounds of what is permissible under a subscription facility.

Considerations

If a fund sponsor has decided to explore a subscription facility as one of its financing options, first and foremost, the fund sponsor should engage a finance counsel (if and to the extent possible, during the drafting stage of the LPA and related fund documents) to ensure that the fund documentation has robust language to address the potential sub line lenders' underwriting needs.

While the question of what makes an LPA "bankable" would inevitably involve an extensive discussion of legal and business considerations, it is probably fair to say that, at a minimum, sub line lenders and their counsel generally expect a "bankable" LPA to: (i) expressly permit the fund and/or its general partner to borrow (and if multiple vehicles are parties to, or are expected to be joined as parties to, a subscription facility, to borrow, guarantee and/or incur other credit support obligations on a joint, several, joint and several and cross-collateralised basis); (ii) expressly permit the fund and/or its general partner to call capital from the investors in the fund to service any debt incurred by the fund; (iii) expressly permit the fund and its general partner to pledge their respective collateral (*see* the "*Collateral*" section below); (iv) include the investors' acknowledgment, whereby each investor in the fund expressly confirms its obligation to fund capital contributions without any counterclaim, defence and offset; and (v) designate the sub line lenders as third-party beneficiaries of the financing provisions of the LPA.

Further refinements would be necessary if the fund sponsor is aiming for a subscription facility with optimal flexibility. For example, if the fund sponsor wants to keep a subscription facility and/or the ability to draw from a subscription facility for a longer period, the LPA should expressly permit the fund and/or its general partner to call capital to repay debt even after the investment period is suspended or terminated. If the fund sponsor does not want to be subject to any cap or restriction on the use of proceeds under a subscription facility due to any concentration and overcall limits in the LPA,[3] it should consider adding a 5–10% cushion to the investor-by-investor concentration limit so that limit is always higher than the fund-level concentration limit and thereby overcall protection is preserved.

Fund sponsors should also be mindful that older LPAs tend to be silent on, or expressly limit, certain "bankable" financing provisions. As such, if a new LPA is being drafted based on an older model, even if the investor base is exactly the same and the same sub line lenders are involved or expected, finance counsel should be engaged to review the LPA and bring its terms up to the most current "bankable" standard. For example, the older LPAs often lack a built-in investor acknowledgment, whereby each investor confirms its funding obligations without any setoff, counterclaim or defence (including bankruptcy), because such investor acknowledgment used to be included in separate investor consent letters that were routinely requested by the sub line lenders and delivered by the investors as part of standard subscription financing process in the past. Now that the LPAs (or subscription agreements) typically include such investor acknowledgment and investor consent letters are no longer delivered to the sub line lenders except in certain limited circumstances (*see* the "*Investor consent in the fund-of-one context*" section below), if a fund sponsor follows an older model LPA without consideration of its "bankable" credentials for cost, investor relations and/or other reasons and the subscription agreements also fail to include such investor acknowledgment, the fund sponsor could run the risk of drafting an LPA that would not be sufficiently "bankable" for a subscription facility, which will likely trigger a request for an investor consent letter (to address any perceived gaps in the LPA), increased pricing and/or tighter covenants.

Robust side letter provisions will help the fund mitigate the risk of the applicable investors being excluded from the borrowing base and achieve sufficient borrowing capacity under a subscription facility. As such, promptly upon receipt of any side letter request from an investor, fund sponsors, with the assistance of their finance counsel, should ask for buffers to mitigate any potential adverse effects of any relevant side letter provisions. If an investor requests a side letter provision entitling such investor to withdraw from the fund and/or cease making capital contributions upon the occurrence of certain events that may cause issues from a reputational perspective (e.g., pay-to-play) or breach of specific provisions in the organisational documents or the internal policy of such investor (e.g., excuse from participating in investments in gambling or tobacco businesses), the fund sponsor should ask that such right be conditioned upon the payment of debt incurred prior to such event. If a governmental investor requests that its sovereign immunity be expressly reserved in a side letter, the fund sponsor should propose that such investor acknowledge and agree that its funding obligations under the LPA and subscription agreement constitute a private commercial action. If an investor requests a side letter provision exempting such investor from a requirement to deliver financial or other information and/or documents, the fund sponsor should offer to limit the scope of such deliverables to publicly available information and/or those required by the sub line lenders in order to assess the creditworthiness of such investor. If an investor requests that its identity be kept confidential, the fund sponsor should ask that there be an exception for disclosure, on a confidential basis, of such information to the sub line lenders. Borrower counsel should also make sure to ring fence any limitations imposed by any side letter so that such limitation does not spread to other investors in the fund via a "most favoured nation" election.

Delivery of the fully executed and enforceable fund documentation is the first step of any subscription financing process. Fund sponsors should be mindful that all fund documentation (as well as information and documentation related to the underlying investors)[4] should be ready to be shared with the potential sub line lenders upon execution of a non-disclosure agreement and at the commencement of the term sheet and indicative borrowing base solicitation process. Accordingly, fund sponsors should consider running an inventory of, and reviewing, all fund documentation to make sure that all such documents are properly dated and fully executed with all the investor questionnaires and signature blocks correctly filled out. Such preparation will significantly reduce the number of follow-up lender requests and the need to go back to the investors to get the documents re-executed during the diligence period. To the extent any confidentiality restrictions are contained in any subscription agreement or side letter, the fund sponsor should allow itself sufficient lead time to obtain such confidential investor's waiver or consent prior to sharing their information and documents with the potential sub line lender.

Lastly, fund sponsors and their counsel should remember that given the importance of the fund documentation, the sub line lenders will often require prior notice of any proposed amendment to the LPA, subscription agreement and/or side letter and that the administrative agent or the sole lender, as applicable (not the fund sponsor or its counsel), will have the right to determine the materiality of such proposed amendment. In the case of a syndicated deal, if the administrative agent determines that such proposed amendment is a material amendment that would impact the collateral and/or the sub line lenders' related rights, the required lenders' consent will be required. Given that the lender approval process could take more than two weeks from the date the administrative agent or the sole lender, as applicable, receives a notice of such proposed amendment from the fund or its general partner and failure to so notify and/or obtain the necessary lender approval is an event of default under a subscription facility, the fund sponsor should always be mindful that any request or need for an amendment or modification to any fund documentation (regardless of how immaterial it may be) is a material issue to the sub line lenders and should set up a system of notifying such lenders at the earliest opportunity to ensure timely execution of such amendment without breaching any covenants under the subscription facility.

Investor consent in the fund-of-one context

With a growing number of funds utilising fund-of-one structures, we have seen an uptick in the number of fund-of-one facilities in recent years.

In the case of a subscription facility for funds-of-one or separately managed accounts for a single investor, due to the increased concentration risk and lack of overcall protection, most sub line lenders will require an investor consent letter, which will, among other things, establish direct privity of contract between such investor and the sub line lenders and address any pertinent issues (e.g., sovereign immunity as a defence to funding obligations).[5]

Considerations

If a fund sponsor is interested in exploring a subscription facility for a fund-of-one or a separately managed account, the fund sponsor should start socialising with the investor the need for such subscription financing and potential requirement to deliver an investor consent letter early in the financing process (or if possible, during the fund formation process) as the investor's willingness to provide such a consent letter and cooperate with the sub line lenders' credit diligence and reporting obligations under the subscription facility will be vital to the success of the fund-of-one subscription facility.

Fund sponsors should be mindful that investors often resist the sub line lenders' request for an investor consent letter. From an investor's perspective, not only is it an additional, if not unnecessary, contract to be entered into in favour of the fund's third-party lender, but also the notion of expressly and contractually waiving any counterclaim, offset or defence it may have with respect to its funding obligations certainly does not make it an attractive one. Further, the execution and delivery of an investor consent letter is often subject to a lengthy administrative review, approval and/or execution process, particularly with governmental investors that are investing in a fund-of-one structure. Putting the need for such investor consent letter on the investor's radar early in the financing process will give the investor sufficient time to understand the reason for such letter and therefore increase the likelihood of the investor's cooperation.

In terms of the actual documentation required, it may be appropriate for the fund sponsors and their counsel to review and reach an agreed form of the investor consent letter with the sub line lenders and their counsel first, and thereafter send the mutually agreed form to the investor for review. Such initial review process provides the fund sponsor and its counsel an opportunity to: (i) make sure that the obligations of the investor set out in the investor consent letter are not more onerous than those under the LPA, such investor's subscription agreement and any side letter; and (ii) present a form of investor consent letter with the standard representations, warranties and covenants that are absolute must-haves for the sub line lender's underwriting needs and that are consistent with the market standard, which will help the investor's review and often result in an easier sign-off.

Collateral

Scope

A subscription facility generally takes the form of a senior revolving credit facility secured by: (i) the unfunded capital commitments of the investors; (ii) the right to call capital from the investors and receive capital contributions; (iii) the deposit or securities accounts into which the capital contributions are deposited or credited (each, a "*collateral account*"); and (iv) the right to enforce the investors' funding obligations and other enforcement rights under the LPA.

Considerations

Given the limited nature of the sub line collateral, it is vital that there is a clear business understanding of the scope of the agreed-upon collateral and an accurate reflection thereof in the finance documents. Borrower counsel should carefully review the granting provision of the applicable security documents and ensure that the collateral description does not go beyond what is typically required in a subscription facility unless otherwise agreed as a business matter. For example, sub line lenders or their counsel may inadvertently request for expanded collateral that includes investment assets and/or equity interests in a subsidiary holding investment assets in addition to the capital call-related assets. Although such expanded collateral may be appropriate in a hybrid facility with a hybrid capital call-portfolio investment borrowing base, which is often utilised early in the life of the fund until the fund acquires a sufficient amount of assets and becomes ready for a more permanent "asset-based lending" facility backed by such investment assets, it should not be included in a pure subscription facility where the borrowing base is determined by the uncalled capital commitments of the eligible investors only.

Setting the correct parameters around the collateral is an important point to remember as lien restrictions in subscription facilities often take the form of a negative pledge on the collateral. Any inadvertent over-pledge may create a problem if the fund plans to do an asset-based facility supported by its investment assets while the subscription facility remains in place.

Collateral accounts

Because all investors' capital contributions to the fund must be deposited or credited to one or more collateral accounts, the collateral accounts are a material part of any sub line collateral package. All collateral accounts must be pledged, directly or indirectly, to the sub line lenders at the initial closing (and at each joinder or accession of the related vehicles to the extent applicable) of any subscription facility. Each collateral account must be set up in the name of the fund and each other vehicle (other than any pass-through blockers) where capital contributions are or will be received. If such account is located in the U.S. and is not held with the administrative agent or with the sole lender, as applicable, an account control agreement over such collateral account will need to be put in place at the initial closing (or, if applicable, at such joinder or accession closing) to provide a perfected security interest to the sub line lenders. For accounts located in other jurisdictions, such as England and Wales and Hong Kong, it is sufficient that notice of the security interest be given to the account bank. In certain jurisdictions, such as Luxembourg, the account bank may be required to acknowledge the granting of the pledge and waive pre-existing rights it may have on the collateral account to ensure the sub line lender has a first ranking security interest.

Considerations

As soon as a fund sponsor has made a decision to enter into a subscription facility and identified the sub line lender(s) and the fund's related vehicles to be joined to the subscription facility as co-borrowers and/or pledgors, the fund sponsor should start the process of opening the collateral accounts at an eligible financial institution. It is important that the opening process is started early as the depositary bank or the securities intermediary, as applicable, will need sufficient lead time to conduct their "know your customer" diligence on each of the applicable entities and, depending on the number of such entities and/or location of such accounts, a longer lead time and additional steps and documentation (e.g., a foreign-law security agreement) might be required to open and pledge a collateral account.

A fund sponsor should also ensure that each applicable borrower and/or pledgor (i.e., main fund, parallel funds, alternative investment vehicles ("*AIVs*") and/or feeder funds) is the actual named account holder of the related collateral account. If any such collateral account is held in the name of the investment manager, the related master fund or any other entity for the benefit of the applicable borrower and/or pledgor, it is likely that a new account will need to be opened in the name of the correct entity. Any lack of clear ownership with respect to any collateral account could alert the sub line lenders and trigger additional lender requests, including, but not limited to, the opening of a new account, all of which could potentially delay the facility closing.[6]

Furthermore, extra time should be allocated if the transaction requires an account control agreement as it is a tri-partite agreement among the account holder, the administrative agent or sole lender (as applicable), as secured party, and the depositary bank or securities intermediary, which will typically be based on the depositary bank or securities intermediary's standard form but will often take time to negotiate.[7]

Lastly, the fund sponsors should remember that only the capital contributions received from the direct and indirect investors should be deposited or credited to the collateral accounts as the facility documents will not permit the borrowers and/or pledgors to commingle the capital contributions in such collateral accounts with other funds of such borrowers and/or pledgors. To avoid any inadvertent commingling of funds, fund sponsors should consider setting up the accounts designated for capital calls only and direct the investors to fund capital contributions to only such designated account(s) from the outset (or, by no later than when a subscription facility is put in place). It is also worth noting that in the unlikely event that an event of default or a cash control event, as applicable, occurs, such segregation will ensure that the borrowers and/or pledgors are only blocked from accessing the funds in their collateral accounts and that all other funds that are not part of the subscription facility collateral package remain accessible to the borrowers and/or pledgors.

Capital calls

Any actual or perceived delegation of the fund and/or its general partner's right to call capital to a party that is not an obligor under a subscription facility may be deemed potential collateral leakage by the sub line lenders.

Considerations

It is imperative that the fund and/or its general partner retain the right to call capital from the investors of the fund at all times during which the facility is in place. Ideally, neither any fund documentation nor investment management agreement should delegate the fund and/or its general partner's right to call capital to the investment manager, as in such a case, the sub line lenders may ask the investment manager to be a party to the subscription facility and to grant a security over its right to issue capital calls to the investors. While an investment manager typically signs the subscription facility with respect to the subordination covenant, whereby such investment manager acknowledges and agrees to subordinate its claims against the fund and its affiliates to the obligations owed to the sub line lenders under a subscription facility, any further exposure to the subscription facility and restrictions therein should be avoided. Similarly, if and to the extent a fund and/or its general partner has retained a third-party service provider to handle its capital calls, it should make it very clear, both in writing as well as in practice, that the authority to call capital remains with the fund and/or its general partner and that such provider is acting at the direction of the general partner. Otherwise, the sub line lenders may ask the third-party service provider to become a party to a subscription facility and to grant a lien on its right to call capital, and it is unlikely that any third-party servicer provider would agree to do so.

Investor notices

In certain jurisdictions, in light of the law governing security with respect to the unfunded capital commitments of the investor of a fund (which is generally the law of the jurisdiction where such fund is formed and/or registered as that will be the governing law of the fund documentation), such fund and/or its general partner must notify the investors that their unfunded capital commitments have been pledged or assigned to the sub line lenders as collateral as such notice is required for the perfection of the security with respect to the unfunded capital commitments of the investors. The Cayman Islands, England and Wales and Hong Kong are examples of the jurisdictions requiring an investor notice to be delivered to perfect the security. An acknowledgment of the notice from the relevant investor is not strictly necessary for perfection of the security, although it is desirable as evidence that the notice has been given. Security agreements in such jurisdictions will typically include an obligation on the fund and the general partner to use "reasonable endeavours" to obtain acknowledgments from the investors. In Luxembourg, a pledge over unfunded capital commitments is perfected by the mere conclusion of the pledge agreement between the fund and the sub line lender or the security agent. However, given that investors may validly discharge their obligation in the hands of the fund as long as they are not aware of the conclusion of the pledge, the pledge agreement usually includes an obligation to notify them of the granting of the pledge.[8] It is generally not required to obtain acknowledgments from the investors.

Considerations

Method of delivery of the investor notices often becomes a point of negotiation as this is closely related to the collateral as well as the day-to-day administration of the fund. A fund sponsor, particularly if such fund is an open-ended fund, should find the appropriate timing and method of delivery that can be easily complied with during the life of the subscription facility.

Subject to the terms of the LPA notice provisions and applicable law, investor notices are commonly delivered in one or more of the following ways: (i) by hard copy; (ii) by uploading the notices on investor portals; and/or (iii) by emailing directly to the investors. If the investor notices are delivered via investor portal, lenders and their counsel may require that the fund and/or its general partner provide evidence that each investor in the fund has actually opened such investor notice. If and to the extent any such investor notice has not been accessed by the designated time, the sub line lenders and/or their counsel may require that additional actions be taken (i.e., sending follow-up emails with a copy of the investor notice attached, obtaining receipt confirmation from the investors and submitting such confirmation to the sub line lenders and their counsel as evidence of delivery), which can be onerous and administratively burdensome from a fund's perspective especially if it is an open-ended fund where such delivery must be repeated every time new investors are admitted to the fund. To ensure that the fund is in compliance with such notice covenant, the fund sponsor should consider establishing and maintaining a system (e.g., an investor portal) where such information can be easily and timely delivered and reaching an agreement with the lenders as to the most commercially sensible timing and delivery method that is not administratively burdensome but still effectively achieves a first priority security interest.

Dual security structures

As the private funds market has matured and fund structures have become increasingly more complicated, many subscription facilities now include one or more borrowers and/or pledgors organised in multiple jurisdictions pledging their respective collateral to the sub line lenders.

In certain jurisdictions (e.g., England and Wales, Ireland, Luxembourg, etc.), the law of the location of the pledgor's assets (the *situs*) will dictate how security is taken over such asset. It is important that the specific assets or rights that are the subject of the security in question are carefully considered. For example, for an LPA and subscription agreements governed by the laws of Luxembourg, the unfunded capital commitments and other LPA-derived capital call right security will be taken under the laws of Luxembourg as the investors' funding obligations derive from Luxembourg-law governed documents. This will be the case even though the subscription facility will be governed by New York or English law.

Considerations

In the case of a U.S. subscription facility, if it is agreed that the collateral includes foreign assets, then if and to the extent the sub line lenders feel strongly that an additional set of security documents is necessary to preserve its enforcement rights in such foreign jurisdiction, a second set of security documents under such foreign law are prepared. For example, in U.S. subscription facilities involving Luxembourg parallel funds, usually two sets of security are granted with respect to such Luxembourg parallel funds – one under New York law and the other under Luxembourg law. When dealing with such dual security structures, the fund sponsors and their counsel should make sure that the business terms do not differ under both security structures. Borrower counsel should closely coordinate with its local counsel and carefully cross-check the scope of the collateral, representations, covenants and events of default under both security documents.[9]

Conclusion

Despite the current economic situation, we are optimistic that the subscription facility will remain resilient as it has done so in numerous past downturns and will continue to be an attractive source of financing for many fund sponsors.

As discussed above, the best sub line financing terms are the final product of the robust bankable fund documentation as well as early and continuing cooperation among fund sponsors, sub line lenders, investors and their respective counsel. This is because the subscription facility terms will always be limited to the bounds of the fund documentation, and the more robust financing provisions are in the fund documentation, the less restrictions and limitations to which the fund will be subject under a subscription facility.

Given the importance of fund documentation and cooperation among the finance parties and investors, it is recommended that the fund sponsor engage finance counsel early in the financing process (and to the extent possible, during the fund formation process) and have them steer the way to avoid unnecessary pitfalls and maximise the chances of obtaining and successfully maintaining a subscription facility.

Endnotes

1. Certain types of funds in certain jurisdictions are established as corporate entities and not as partnerships, are governed by articles of incorporation or similar organisational documents and not by LPAs, and are managed by a board of directors or similar governing body and not by a general partner.
2. Certain types of funds in certain jurisdictions (e.g., Luxembourg and other European countries) are also required to issue a prospectus or an offering document, which will also need to be considered in the context of a subscription facility.
3. LPAs may include overcall provisions, which allow the fund to overcall capital from its non-defaulting or non-excused investors to make up for any shortfalls created by the defaulting or excused investors' failure to fund the initial capital call. Investors often put a cap on the maximum amount they may be required to fund with respect to any investment in excess of the amount that would have been required had all investors participated in the relevant investment funded.
4. In the case of deals involving a European fund, additional documents such as an offering memorandum, depositary agreement and alternative investment fund manager agreement will need to be delivered to the sub line lenders for diligence.
5. An investor consent letter may also be used in other contexts to address any actual or perceived deficiencies or gaps in the fund documentation.
6. A master account structure is an exception, whereby the master fund (i.e., main fund or parallel fund) opens an account in the name of the master fund and agrees to act as agent for each of the appointing entities (e.g., AIVs) and agrees to grant a lien in favour of the sub line lenders on the amounts in the account that are held for any such entity.
7. Similarly, most account banks in Luxembourg have their standard forms of notices and reaching out in advance to the relevant account bank to ensure its most up-to-date forms are used in the legal documentation will definitely facilitate and speed up the negotiation and the establishment of the collateral account pledge.
8. In Luxembourg, some take the view that, based on the conflict of law rules, non-Luxembourg investors in a Luxembourg fund must be notified according to notification rules applicable in their local jurisdiction, which could end up being an onerous and administratively burdensome process for fund sponsors.
9. In contrast, in our experience lenders to Cayman Islands funds do not require a separate set of security documents governed by Cayman Islands law as the Cayman Islands courts generally respect and give effect to valid foreign law security.

* * *

Acknowledgments

The authors wish to thank Jay Alicandri, a partner and co-head of global finance practice at Dechert LLP, Karen Stretch, a partner in the Financial Services and Investment Management Group at Dechert LLP, and Nathalie Sadler, a partner in the Financial Services and Investment Management Group at Dechert LLP, for their assistance in the preparation of this chapter.

Jean-Louis Frognet
Tel: +352 45 62 62 29 / Email: jean-louis.frognet@dechert.com
Jean-Louis Frognet is a partner in Dechert's financial services practice group, based in Luxembourg. Mr. Frognet has extensive experience advising asset managers, financial institutions and other clients on a wide range of financing transactions for regulated and non-regulated entities on the borrower or on the lender side, including fund financing transactions (such as subscription facilities, hybrid facilities and NAV facilities), acquisition finance and real estate finance. Mr. Frognet's practice also includes advice on securitisation and other structured finance transactions as well as public offerings and listing of bonds and shares (including of investments funds) on the Luxembourg Stock Exchange.

Caroline M. Lee
Tel: +1 212 649 8797 / Email: caroline.m.lee@dechert.com
Caroline M. Lee is a counsel in Dechert's global finance practice, with extensive experience in complicated financings designed to provide fund-level leverage to facilitate and support investment activities. Ms. Lee regularly advises various financial sponsors, asset managers, business development companies and other financial institutions on a wide variety of fund financing transactions, including: subscription (capital call) facilities secured by uncalled capital commitments and related rights, with borrowing base capacity for the fund, as well as its parallel funds, alternative investment vehicles and portfolio companies; unsecured demand lines with an uncalled capital coverage requirement; hybrid facilities; NAV facilities; asset-based revolvers and Loan-to-SPV financings; margin loans; fund guarantees of portfolio-level investments; management lines provided to investment advisors for working capital purposes; and employee co-investment credit facilities secured by their fund interests.

Eng-Lye Ong
Tel: +65 6730 6968 / Email: eng-lye.ong@dechert.com
Eng-Lye Ong is a partner in Dechert's global finance practice, based in Singapore. Mr. Ong has extensive experience advising private equity sponsors, corporate borrowers and financial institutions on a broad range of complex financing transactions in the U.S., European and Asian markets. His practice focuses on advising private equity sponsors on their financing needs across the capital structure, including at the fund, acquisition and portfolio company levels. Mr. Ong's fund financing experience includes subscription line facilities, NAV facilities and GP/management lines.

Dechert LLP

Three Bryant Park, 1095 Avenue of the Americas, New York, NY 10036-6797, USA
Tel: +1 212 698 3500 / URL: www.dechert.com

Innovative rated note structures spur insurance investments in private equity

Pierre Maugüé, Ramya Tiller & Christine Gilleland
Debevoise & Plimpton LLP

As insurance companies look for opportunities to invest in a diversified portfolio of funds, and funds look for ways to access additional capital, there is increasing demand for innovative rated note structures. Such investments are typically structured in one of two ways: (i) through a rated note feeder fund for investment in a single fund; or (ii) through a special purpose vehicle structure for investment in a portfolio of funds, creating a fund of funds structure. For investment in a single fund, the master fund typically creates a feeder fund that issues rated debt and equity through which the insurance company can participate as a debt-only investor or as a debt and equity investor, depending on the structure of the deal. For investment in a portfolio of funds, the special purpose vehicle is typically structured to include one or several tranches of rated debt supported by limited partnership (LP) interests in the underlying funds that comprise the investment portfolio and a tranche of equity commitments (structured as straight equity or subordinated notes), which, as the first-loss tranche, is important for the ratings analysis. The past year has seen an increase in the use of such note structures, and we expect their popularity to continue even if market conditions tighten so long as the insurance regulators do not change the investment classification of the notes issued by, or the loans incurred by, these structures.

This chapter reviews how these investments are typically structured, some important parameters that need to be determined in their structuring, the current regulatory environment, and recent trends.

Key characteristics

- *Basic Single Fund Structure*: Structured notes obligations invested in a single master fund usually take the form of a feeder fund that issues one or more tranches of debt and equity. Typically, the investor purchases debt and equity, with the substantially larger commitment taking the form of debt (for example, 80% debt and 20% equity). This structure relies on the ability to map steady cash flows from the master fund for the ratings analysis and we therefore usually see this structure used to invest in debt funds. If the sponsor needs the ability to adapt terms for the rated debt that would not be available in a feeder fund structure, the sponsor may choose to create a parallel fund structure instead, although such a structure may add complexity.
- *Basic Fund of Funds Structure*: Structured notes obligations invested in a portfolio of funds generally involve two entities: an issuer, which is a special purpose vehicle that issues debt and equity; and an asset holdco, which is a special purpose vehicle that is a direct subsidiary of the issuer and is the entity that holds the investment portfolio. The issuer then pledges its ownership interest in the asset holdco for the benefit of the noteholders. Some transactions do not use a separate asset holdco, in which case the issuer directly pledges the underlying portfolio of fund interests.

- *Debt-like Characteristics*: Insurance companies rely on the debt characterisation of the structured notes obligations for more attractive risk-based capital (RBC) treatment, which, for U.S. insurance companies, depends on whether the investment is categorised as a bond under statutory accounting and RBC rules that benefit from more attractive RBC charges compared to equity investments. To support the accounting and RBC analysis, the return on the debt is generally structured as regular interest payments and repayment of principal, subject to a priority of payments waterfall. The equity in the issuer gets the benefit of the upside once the scheduled debt payments have been made pursuant to the priority of payments.
- *Priority of Payments Waterfall*: Structured notes issued in these structures typically have long maturity (for example, 10–15 years), although the notes are generally expected to be repaid much faster. Because of this, a structured notes obligation that relies on market performance and is supported by alternative investments that are inherently illiquid assets requires some protection from economic downturns. Common terms used to provide that protection include:
  - Payment of interest is generally required only to the extent that cash is available; otherwise, the interest is deferred until cash is next available in the priority of payments.
  - The amortisation schedule is usually a target amortisation schedule that requires amortisation payments only to the extent that cash is available in the priority of payments (with cumulative catch-up payments in subsequent periods). The amortisation schedule is often supplemented by a cash sweep if certain loan-to-value tests are not satisfied.
  - Full repayment of the debt can be targeted within a relatively short period of time (e.g., four to five years) based on modelled cash flows, but final legal maturity will often be set at 10–15 years to provide flexibility, in particular in case of an economic downturn.
  - Distributions are made to equity only once interest and target amortisation have been paid in accordance with the target schedule. Distributions to equity are also generally subject to *pro forma* satisfaction of a loan-to-value ratio and, sometimes, a liquidity ratio.
- *Funding Capital Calls*: There are certain structural holes that the investors need to be prepared to either address in the documentation or, more commonly, accept as deal risk:
  - The debt and equity committed to the issuer is generally (but not always) equal to the LP commitments made to the underlying funds. If the underlying funds can call capital to pay fees and expenses in addition to the LP capital commitment, in the absence of adequate reserve or sufficient distributions to supplement existing reserves, there is a possibility that there will not be sufficient cash available to fund a capital call to pay fees or expenses.
  - Many funds permit recycling of commitments. However, if the issuer has received a cash distribution from the underlying funds, and that cash is run through the waterfall, it is no longer available for recycling. While it is not uncommon to allow distributions to equity to be recalled, the cash may have been paid to the rated notes under the waterfall and it would be unusual to allow payments to rated notes to be recycled. The portfolio needs to provide sufficient cash into the structure to be able to cover these additional calls on capital.

  In these cases, the issuer would become a defaulting limited partner if the investment portfolio does not generate sufficient cash to service these capital calls, thereby impairing the debtholders' collateral. It is therefore important to control when and how much cash leaves the structure.

- *Investment Grade Rating*: Insurance companies rely on the investment grade or quasi-investment grade rating of the debt for their RBC analysis. For U.S. insurance companies, favourable RBC asset charges are assigned based on the investment's National Association of Insurance Commissioners (NAIC) designation, which is typically determined based on the credit ratings assigned to the investment by nationally recognised statistical rating organisations. If the debt is downgraded to the extent that the rated notes are funded on a delayed draw basis, the debtholders might request an Event of Default or a draw stop on unfunded commitments until the investment grade rating is restored.

Critical single fund structuring parameters

When structuring these rated note feeder fund investments, issuers must determine certain key parameters. We list four of them here, and discuss each in turn:
- whether the structure will be through a feeder fund or a parallel fund;
- whether the holder of the debt and equity commitments will be the same;
- whether the master fund will seek to pursue a subscription line facility; and
- what type of fund would support a rated note feeder.

<u>Feeder fund or parallel fund</u>

Sponsors typically choose to structure a rated note through a feeder fund to accommodate insurance companies interested in participating in a fund. Creating a feeder fund allows the sponsor to simplify the overall fund structure and keep the terms of the debt investment structure the same as the equity investment structure but for the specific debt characteristics required to make the rated notes debt. The feeder fund structure, however, does not allow the sponsor to make adjustments to the investment structure that may be necessary to achieve or maintain a particular rating or to address particular insurance company issues. To the extent that the feeder fund structure does not allow enough flexibility to make the necessary adjustments (for example, the fund is levered, which impacts the rating), the sponsor could create a standalone parallel fund. While this may add complexity to creation and maintenance for the sponsor, a parallel fund structure allows the sponsor to more closely manage the parallel fund to maintain the necessary rating and to adjust the terms as may be required by the insurance company.

<u>Debt, equity or both</u>

Typically, a rated note feeder fund is structured so that the issuer issues debt and equity interests to each investor. Subject to the ratings constraints, the interests are heavily weighted towards debt commitments in recognition of the insurance companies' preference for debt investments. When the holders of the debt and equity investment own a vertical slice of the structure, it streamlines documentation and assures that the insurance companies' investment more closely aligns with the pure equity investors. For example, the equity component allows for recycling and clawbacks. However, certain insurance companies are subject to specific internal policies, or regulatory requirements, that make any equity investment a significantly more cumbersome undertaking. For example, Korean insurance companies face a lengthy regulatory approval process for any equity investment. In such cases, the sponsor is sometimes required to structure the rated note feeder fund as a strictly debt investment for the insurance company investors. A significant complication this presents is trying to replicate equity concepts, such as recycling and clawbacks, in a purely debt structure. Another concern a sponsor may have is that if the issuer files for bankruptcy, the debt commitments are no longer enforceable against the investor, whereas equity investors would still have to fund a capital call. To address this concern, the sponsor may structure the debt commitment as convertible to an equity commitment upon bankruptcy of the issuer.

Subscription line facilities

If a master fund intends to utilise a subscription line facility, early discussions should be had with the subscription line lenders regarding treatment of the rated note feeder fund in their borrowing base calculations. Subscription line lenders are often concerned about the quality of a debt commitment as collateral because, as noted above, in the event that the issuer enters bankruptcy, creditors are not required to fund their debt commitments. This is as opposed to the equity holders, who are required to fund capital calls even in the event that the issuer enters bankruptcy. Sponsors have tried to address this concern in various ways, including by (i) creating a mechanic that converts the debt commitments into equity commitments in the event of bankruptcy, (ii) creating the commitments as debt/equity commitments from day one pursuant to which the debt/equity commitments are shared and the issuer can choose whether to draw on the commitments as debt or as equity, or (iii) creating the feeder fund as a bankruptcy remote vehicle to dramatically decrease the likelihood that the feeder fund will enter bankruptcy. None of these methods have been truly tested in the courts, so it is unclear which method is most effective to address the subscription lenders' concern.

Ratings and cash flows

Another consideration for a sponsor is what type of fund could support a rated note feeder suitable for insurance companies to invest in. In order to achieve the necessary rating, the issuer will need to show the ratings agency sufficient regular cash flow to support the issued debt. If the investment is in a single private equity fund, there is no pool of cash flows to rely upon, as many private equity funds do not expect distributions until five to seven years after inception. Such delayed cash flows will likely not be acceptable to a ratings agency and could result in an investment's classification as equity resulting in less favourable RBC charges under the insurance company's accounting and RBC analysis. We therefore typically see rated note feeder funds invested in debt funds, as debt investments typically produce cash flows immediately and those cash flows are regular and predictable.

Critical fund of funds structuring parameters

When structuring these fund of funds investments, issuers must determine certain key parameters. We list three of them here, and discuss each in turn:
- whether the investment portfolio will be set as of the closing date;
- whether the commitments to the issuer will be funded in full on the closing date; and
- whether the issuer will be consolidated with its parent's balance sheet and whether that parent has other obligations that subject the parent and its subsidiaries to covenants with which the structured notes obligations might conflict.

Setting the investment portfolio

The issuer needs to determine whether the asset holdco will have set the investment portfolio as of the closing date, or whether the asset holdco will build or adjust the portfolio after the closing date based on agreed investment guidelines. If the investment portfolio may change after the closing date, it is important to ensure that the investment portfolio will be sufficiently diversified to support an appropriate rating. In addition, the issuer needs to be prohibited from committing more than the aggregate principal amount of debt and equity that has been committed to the issuer. Alternatively, noteholders will have to be comfortable that expected distributions on the underlying funds will be sufficient to fund capital calls for which no matching source of funding is identified at closing.

Funded or unfunded commitments

Another important parameter is whether the debt and equity commitments will be fully drawn on the closing date, or whether there will be a delayed drawing schedule. Having some or all of the commitments unfunded as of the closing date presents additional considerations. There needs to be a comfort level regarding the credit worthiness of the relevant debtholders and equity holders. Protections may be necessary to ensure that the issuer receives the full draw amount needed, including defaulting noteholder or equity investor provisions and a requirement that the relevant debtholder or equity investor be an entity with an acceptable rating or benefit from parent support from a rated entity, or post a letter of credit from an acceptable letter of credit issuer to support its unfunded commitment. Finally, investors investing on a delayed draw basis may require drawing conditions, such as a ratings downgrade or a loan-to-value breach, in the event that the condition of the structured notes obligation has changed since the closing date. However, the matter of drawing conditions should be approached cautiously, as a draw stop may cause the issuer to become a defaulting limited partner with respect to some or all of the underling funds, thereby exacerbating the problem.

Balance sheet considerations

While the issuer of a structured notes obligation is a special purpose vehicle, the equity in the issuer may be owned by a company that itself has debt obligations. If the issuer ends up being a subsidiary of an equity investor, the covenants in the parent's debt agreements may extend to the parent's subsidiaries and must be considered to ensure that the debt issuance by the issuer does not conflict with those covenants. In addition, the parent should consider whether it will be required to consolidate the notes issued by the issuer as debt on its balance sheet.

Liquidity facility

Many fund of funds structured note structures include liquidity support, in the form of a revolving facility provided by a third-party lender, that can be used to bridge a funding shortfall. These liquidity facilities are generally available to fund fees and expenses, interest on the debt tranches and, usually, capital calls from the underlying funds. While these liquidity facilities are rarely used, including a liquidity facility in the structure provides stability to the structured notes obligation by supporting the ratings analysis and reducing the possibility that the structure will fail.

Regulatory treatment

For U.S. insurance companies, the transaction structure for structured notes obligations is typically designed to achieve favourable RBC treatment of the notes' debt investments, which will be determined based on whether the investment is classified as a "bond" under statutory accounting rules. The NAIC, the standard-setting and regulatory support organisation created and governed by state insurance regulators, has for a number of years been exploring changes to statutory accounting principles and securities valuation office (SVO) procedures that could affect the reporting and capital treatment of structured notes obligations rated note feeder vehicles and similar structures.

Currently, the NAIC is working on significant revisions to Statement of Statutory Accounting Principles (SSAP) No. 23R and No. 43R to implement a principles-based bond definition to determine whether an investment should be considered and reported as a bond on Schedule D-1 (Long-Term Bonds) of an insurance company's statutory financial statements. The proposed statutory accounting rules define a bond as "any security representing a creditor relationship, whereby there is a fixed schedule for one or more future payments, and which qualifies as either an issuer credit obligation or an asset backed security". Structured notes obligations fall under the asset-backed security classification. In order to receive bond treatment, the notes' debt obligations will generally need to have pre-determined principal and interest payments with contractual payments that do not vary based on the appreciation or depreciation of underlying collateral value or other variables and reflect underlying assets (e.g., the LP interests of debt funds) that generate a "meaningful" level of cash flows to service the debt obligations. In addition, the insurance company holder of the notes' debt obligations must be in a different economic position than if the holder owned the underlying fund investments directly. The NAIC's principles-based bond proposal also contemplates a rebuttable presumption that debt investments collateralised by equity interests would not qualify as bonds because they would not reflect a creditor relationship in substance. Notwithstanding this rebuttable presumption, it is possible for such a debt investment to represent a creditor relationship if the characteristics of the underlying equity interests are expected to produce predictable cash flows and the underlying equity risks have been sufficiently redistributed through the capital structure of the fund issuer.

The NAIC continues to consider comments from industry participants and the proposed revisions are not yet final. Currently, the proposed principles-based bond definition and the revisions to the statutory accounting principles relating to structured notes are expected to be finalised by May 2023 with a January 1, 2024 effective date.

Although the proposed changes to the statutory accounting rules and treatment of structured notes are not yet final and may impact the RBC treatment of these investments, we generally see the insurance company debtholders assume the risk of a change in law or of the structured notes obligation not achieving the desired capital or reporting treatment.

Tax considerations

The principal tax considerations of a rated note structure for a single fund or portfolio of funds are largely the same. The tax structure of these vehicles depends on a number of factors, including whether they are being marketed to U.S. or non-U.S. insurance company investors and the nature of the underlying investment strategy. For U.S. insurance company investors, the issuers are typically structured as partnerships for U.S. federal income tax purposes to avoid entity-level tax leakage. For non-U.S. insurance company investors, issuers may be structured as either a partnership or non-U.S. corporation for U.S. federal income tax purposes depending on whether the underlying fund or funds are expected to generate (or have options to block at the fund level) U.S. tax filing and payment obligations. If structured as a partnership, transfer restrictions may apply to both the debt and equity interests in the fund in order to mitigate the risk that the fund will instead be treated as a corporation for U.S. federal income tax purposes under the "publicly traded partnership" rules (the "taxable mortgage pool" rules should also be considered if the underlying portfolio includes real estate-secured debt). In addition, equity and potentially debt tranches may be restricted such that they can only be owned by U.S. holders, to avoid the risk of subjecting the structure to U.S. withholding tax. If structured as a non-U.S. corporation (and a concern for non-U.S. investors more generally), the issuer may need to "block" income effectively connected with a U.S. trade or business via a subsidiary entity and may incur U.S. withholding tax. In each case, the associated leakage will reduce returns to investors and should be taken into account in modelling. If it is important that a tranche of debt be respected as indebtedness (rather than treated as equity) for U.S. tax purposes (e.g., because the debt is not subject to transfer restrictions and the issuer is a passthrough entity), then the terms of the debt, expected ratings and repayment expectations will need to be scrutinised to ensure that they support such treatment – with investment grade ratings often used as the proxy for whether there is doubt as to the right characterisation.

Recent trends

- *Decoupling of Debt and Equity Commitments in Fund of Funds Structures*: While investors in some structured notes obligations are purchasing a vertical slice of the structure that includes both debt and equity, we are increasingly seeing structures that decouple the two. This strategy works well for insurance companies that wish to invest in rated debt instruments but not the equity. The equity is then purchased by investors such as a balance sheet fund of the firm forming the structured notes obligation, family offices and other third-party investors attracted to the combination of levered exposure to multiple funds and the potential for high returns. While equity holders may be required to make an initial funding, sometimes no further funding is required (subject to certain downside events such as a loss of rating for a period of time) until the debt has been funded in full. If the portfolio produces sufficient cash flows to service future capital calls, it is possible that the equity is never drawn again but still gets the benefit of excess cash distributions out of the system. Equity funded on a delayed draw basis may be an attractive investment for insurance companies to the extent that the unfunded commitment does not attract a capital charge.
- *Equity Credit Support*: In the fund of funds structure, to the extent that equity commitments are not funded in full on the closing date, equity holders may be required to have an eligible rating or provide adequate credit support from a person with an eligible rating. This credit support frequently takes the form of a parent guaranty, a letter of credit or cash collateralisation, in each case for the full amount of the equity commitment. This credit support not only supports the ratings analysis, but also provides comfort to the debtholders that the equity holders will fund when required to do so under the terms of the transaction documents.

Conclusion

In the current market environment, we expect to see more private equity firms and insurance companies develop and invest in these structures to maximise their access to liquidity and as a new investment opportunity. We also expect further innovations as market participants react to regulatory and other developments.

* * *

Acknowledgments

The authors acknowledge with thanks the contributions to this chapter of Alexander Cochran (partner), Daniel Priest (partner), Matthew Parelman (counsel), Christopher Rosekrans (counsel), and David Rock (associate).

Pierre Maugüé
Tel: +44 20 7786 9190 / Email: pmaugue@debevoise.com

Pierre Maugüé is a partner in the London office of Debevoise & Plimpton LLP. His practice focuses on acquisition and leveraged buyout financings and structured financings.

Mr. Maugüé is recommended by *The Legal 500*, which has described him as "exceptional", "responsive, commercial and creative", "technically very strong" and a trusted adviser who helps clients achieve goals in the most efficient manner. Mr. Maugüé is also recommended as a leading lawyer by *IFLR1000*.

Mr. Maugüé brings a global perspective to his work, having lived and worked in Asia, Europe and the United States.

Mr. Maugüé writes frequently on legal matters related to finance topics and is also a regular contributor to the Debevoise & Plimpton Private Equity Report.

Ramya Tiller
Tel: +1 212 909 6204 / Email: rstiller@debevoise.com

Ramya S. Tiller is a partner in the New York office of Debevoise & Plimpton LLP. She has experience in a broad range of financing transactions, including complex acquisition and leveraged finance transactions, fund finance transactions and other alternative capital transactions.

Ms. Tiller is ranked as a Next Generation Partner by *The Legal 500 US*, where she has been described as an "ultimate professional", and "highly rated". She is also recognised as a Notable Practitioner by *IFLR1000*.

Prior to joining the firm, Ms. Tiller worked for a leading Indian law firm in Mumbai, India. Between 2010 and 2012, she served as a member of the Finance group at an international law firm in Munich, Germany.

Ms. Tiller is a frequent speaker on finance-related topics for the Practising Law Institute.

Christine Gilleland
Tel: +44 20 7786 5520 / Email: csgilleland@debevoise.com

Christine Shu Gilleland is an associate in the London office of Debevoise & Plimpton LLP.

A member of the firm's Finance group, Ms. Gilleland has experience in a range of financing transactions, including major capital markets financings, leveraged financings, and structured and fund financings.

Debevoise & Plimpton LLP

919 Third Avenue, New York, NY 10022, USA
Tel: +1 212 909 6000 / URL: www.debevoise.com

Financing secondary fund acquisitions

Ron D. Franklin, Jinyoung Joo & Allison F. Saltstein
Proskauer

Introduction

The private equity secondary market had a strong year in 2021 and, while 2022 did not see quite as much activity overall, an uptick in demand from investors looking to sell their investments in private equity funds in the secondary market seems likely in 2023.[1] To access this ever-growing market and sell their investments, investors are increasingly looking to experienced secondaries buyers who manage fund vehicles that specialise in purchasing these interests (these buyers referred to herein as secondary funds). To fund the acquisition of these private equity fund interests, secondary funds are increasingly using leverage in the form of debt financing.

A secondary fund invests in other private investment funds that have largely completed their investment periods, with portfolio investments that are often already generating cash flow. In a secondaries transaction, a secondary fund acquires the existing seller's commitments to a private equity fund (referred to herein as the underlying fund), replaces the seller as a new limited partner in the underlying fund and assumes all of the seller's rights and obligations under the underlying fund's partnership agreement. A purchase agreement is signed between the secondary fund, as buyer, and the outgoing limited partner, as seller. As the underlying funds are structured so that the general partner's consent is required for the actual transfer of the existing investor's interest, a transfer agreement among the secondary fund, the seller and the general partner of the underlying fund is then negotiated and signed at the closing of the transfer. The transfer agreement is the means by which the secondary fund becomes a limited partner in the underlying fund and a party to the underlying fund's partnership agreement. The closings of the transfers themselves usually occur at fiscal quarter-end because general partners of the underlying funds typically only allow transfers of limited partnership interests to occur at that time. Secondary funds use debt to acquire existing limited partnership interests in order to decrease the amount of equity the secondary fund needs to use for both the purchase of the existing investor interests and to meet capital call obligations over the remaining life of the underlying fund.

This chapter examines the typical structure of debt facilities for secondary funds (secondaries facilities), outlines market financing terms and covers specific concepts and issues that often arise during negotiations.

Basic structure

Unlike capital call facilities, which look up to the uncalled capital commitments of the limited partners in the relevant fund as the borrowing base, and thus a source of repayment, secondaries facilities, like other net asset value (NAV) facilities, look down the structure to the underlying assets of the secondary fund. In a typical secondaries facility, the secondary fund establishes a special purpose vehicle for the purpose of obtaining the financing and holding the portfolio investments included in the borrowing base. The vehicle's permitted activities are often limited in scope to ensure that it is free from any potential competing creditors. This is the entity that serves as the borrower and, in most cases, takes the form of a limited partnership.

Obligations under a secondaries facility are secured by a pledge of 100% of the limited partnership interests in the borrower and either a pledge by the borrower's general partner of its general partner interest therein or a pledge by the parent entity of the borrower's general partner of its equity interests in the borrower's general partner. Additionally, the borrower will pledge its deposit and securities accounts into which distributions and proceeds of the portfolio investments are paid. The lender will perfect its security interest in the collateral by filing Uniform Commercial Code (UCC) financing statements against the applicable pledgors and will enter into control agreements with the deposit banks or securities intermediaries of the respective deposit and securities accounts. In the event that the pledged equity interests constitute "securities" under Article 8 of the applicable UCC, the lender will also perfect its security interest by taking control of the securities under one of the available perfection methods under the UCC. Ultimately, there are two main objectives in structuring the collateral package for a secondaries facility. The first is to put the lender in the position of a senior secured creditor to its obligors to enable the lender to monetise the value of the portfolio investments following an acceleration of the loan and an exercise of remedies, and the second is to ensure that cash proceeds from the portfolio investments are paid to the borrower so that any required repayments of the loan are made before any distributions are paid to the secondary fund.

A simplified diagram of this structure is set forth below.

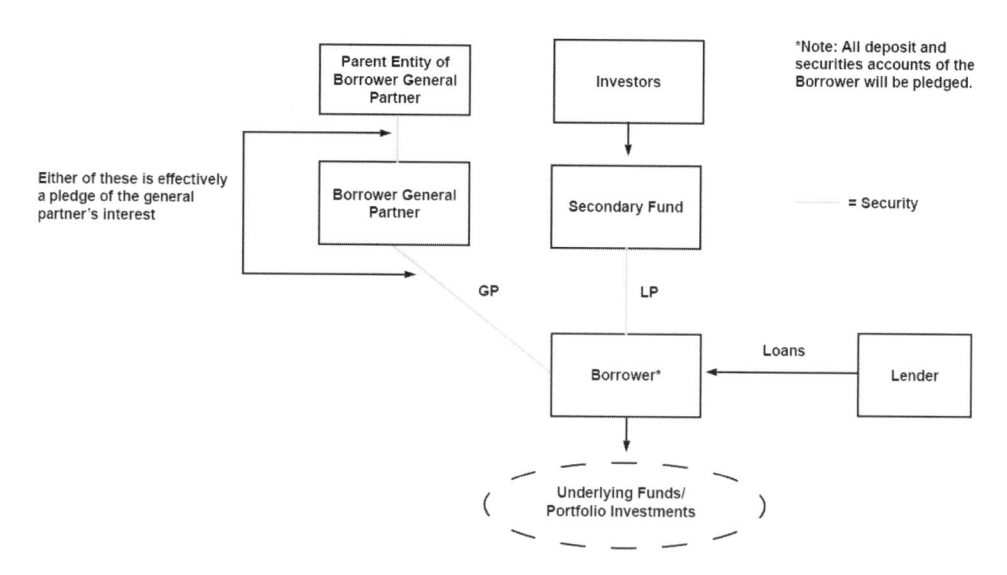

Although the underlying assets of the borrower serve indirectly as the primary credit support, lenders may request additional forms of credit support. This additional credit support can take the form of a guaranty, where the secondary fund guarantees the obligations of the borrower and agrees to call capital from its investors to satisfy the guaranteed obligations. Additional credit support can also be achieved indirectly by the borrower pledging the unfunded capital commitments of the secondary fund to the borrower. This is often paired with a restriction on over-commitment, where the borrower agrees to maintain unfunded capital commitments from the secondary fund in an amount equal to or greater than the amount of the borrower's unfunded capital commitments to the portfolio investments. Depending on the structure, this covenant may also include liquidity requirements for entities further up in the structure.

Typical financing terms

Secondaries facilities are usually term loan facilities (either a single borrowing at closing or delayed draw availability) with a term of three to five years. The amount available to be drawn by the borrower is limited by the value of the borrowing base. Secondaries facilities can include some form of mandatory amortisation, expressed either as maximum outstanding principal amount or maximum loan-to-value (LTV) ratios on certain dates. They also often include a partial sweep of distributions from the underlying portfolio investments on a quarterly basis as mandatory prepayments. Each of these concepts is discussed below.

Borrowing base

The borrowing base is calculated by reference to the NAV of the portfolio investments plus, to the extent negotiated, cash and/or securities in the borrower's accounts. For a portfolio investment to be an "eligible" portfolio investment included in the borrowing base, the investment must satisfy specific negotiated investment criteria. These criteria typically include the absence of certain adverse investment events in respect of an underlying fund, such as bankruptcy events, insolvency events, existence of unpermitted liens and material breaches of the underlying fund documents. Because one of the attractive features of secondaries facilities for lenders is the diversity of the pool of portfolio investments held by the borrower, the borrowing base is often subject to concentration limits to ensure that the portfolio remains sufficiently diverse. Concentration limits may constrain (i) the percentage of total NAV attributable to a single fund, or fund sponsor, or to a single portfolio company or the largest few portfolio companies, (ii) particular investment strategies, and/or (iii) the geographic locations of sponsors outside the United States and Europe. Concentration limits are included to allow for some degree of investment management flexibility by the borrower while also maintaining the overall diversification of the portfolio investments that support the credit.

LTV financial covenants and related events of default

The LTV ratio is a key component of a secondaries facility, which assesses the risk to the lender by comparing the outstanding principal amount of the debt drawn under the facility to the aggregate borrowing base valuation. Similar to a leverage ratio covenant based on cash flow, the higher the LTV ratio, the riskier the loan. Breach of the maximum LTV ratio covenant acts as a trigger for various lender protections, including mandatory prepayment events, cash sweeps, and events of default.

The LTV ratio covenant generally requires that the amount of debt outstanding under the facility does not exceed a given percentage of the aggregate NAV of the portfolio investments owned by the borrower at any given time. It is a dynamic metric that fluctuates over time as portfolio investments are acquired, gain or lose value, and are ultimately sold. The LTV ratio covenant is tested periodically and is also tested intra-period on an incurrence basis as a *pro forma* compliance condition to certain actions (e.g., additional borrowing, distributions to the secondary fund, disposal of a portfolio asset, or withdrawal of cash from the borrower's account). The borrower is required to provide relevant calculations and compliance certificates to the lender when the covenant is tested. The maximum permitted

LTV ratio may step down over time during the term of the secondaries facility to force a paydown of the loan if the portfolio investments are not appreciating in value (alternatively, the loan documents may simply require certain scheduled prepayments of the loan).

The LTV ratio also interacts with another common provision in secondaries facilities, which is the mandatory prepayment cash sweep. The goal of the mandatory cash sweep is to reduce the outstanding balance of the loans and consequently the lender's exposure to the borrower by periodically sweeping the cash in the borrower's account and applying it to repay the debt. In a secondaries facility, the mandatory cash sweep provision may also require that a higher percentage of distributions from the portfolio investments be used to prepay the loans depending on the LTV ratio at the time.

While a breach of the LTV ratio covenant is usually not an immediate event of default, it will trigger a mandatory prepayment event. If the borrower does not pay down the loan in an amount sufficient to reduce the LTV ratio below the maximum permitted LTV ratio within the prescribed period of time, a payment default would be triggered.

Specific issues relevant to secondaries facilities

This section focuses on some of the common issues that arise when negotiating secondaries facilities: the importance of diligencing transfer and pledge restrictions in the underlying fund documents and the impact of that diligence on the structure of the security package; negotiations around confidentiality restrictions in the underlying fund documents that might limit the borrower's ability to fulfil its reporting obligations; and the parties' diverging incentives concerning valuation of the portfolio investments, together with contractual provisions that attempt to bridge that gap.

Transfer and pledge restrictions

A common structuring issue for secondaries facilities involves the restriction on transfers and pledges in the underlying fund documents (i.e., the limited partnership agreements). The value of the borrower's portfolio investments supports its loan obligations. However, the lender typically will not have a direct security interest in the portfolio investments but instead will have an indirect pledge. The terms of the underlying fund documents governing each of the portfolio investments almost always provide that granting a direct security interest in the portfolio investment, as well as any future transfer of the portfolio investment (e.g., in connection with a foreclosure by the lender), requires the consent of the underlying fund's general partner. In most cases, obtaining such consents would be impractical given that general partners are almost universally wary of admitting a lender (or its transferee) as a limited partner in their funds upon a foreclosure, thus preventing the borrower from directly pledging its limited partnership interests in the underlying funds as collateral. As a result, as discussed above, secondaries facilities are typically structured so that the borrower directly holds the portfolio investments and the secondary fund pledges the equity interests in the borrower to the lender.

The pledge of the equity interests in the borrower is an indirect pledge of the portfolio investments and raises a few different potential issues. In addition to requiring general partner consent to granting a direct security interest in the portfolio investments, in some cases the terms of the underlying fund documents may also prevent a limited partner from granting the indirect pledge that arises from the pledge of the equity interests in the borrower and/or the indirect transfer of the portfolio investments via a foreclosure sale of the equity interests in the borrower by the lender. In this scenario, the lenders cannot rely on the Article 9 override on transfer restrictions found in the Delaware UCC (often the governing law of the relevant underlying fund documents) because the override is statutorily inapplicable to pledges of limited partnership interests. Accordingly, careful diligence of the underlying fund documents is necessary. Lenders, borrowers and their respective counsel must review the underlying fund documents for any such prohibitions on indirect pledges and transfers, and the consequences of a breach of these provisions, in order to determine whether consent from the underlying fund's general partner would be required in connection with the pledge of the equity interests in the borrower. In this regard, the interests of both the borrower and the lenders are aligned in that neither wants the borrower to be in breach; the borrower, as a limited partner in the underlying fund, because it does not want to be subject to a contractual claim for a breach of the limited partnership agreement and the lenders because such breach could ultimately impair the value of the underlying funds.

Any necessary consent would normally be included in either the relevant transfer agreement between the seller, the borrower and the general partner of the portfolio investment, or in a separate side letter between the relevant general partner and the borrower, as the incoming limited partner. In order to avoid breaching the underlying fund documentation in the event that the borrower is unable to obtain the necessary consent in respect of any portfolio investment, a separate holding vehicle may be set up to hold the relevant portfolio investment, and the equity interests in that holding vehicle would not be pledged as collateral. Distributions from the portfolio investments that are not subject to a pledge can still be swept to prepay the loans, but the pledged holding vehicle (the entity whose equity interests are pledged) only holds the assets for which indirect consents could be obtained or were not required based on the underlying fund documentation. A simplified diagram of this structure is set forth below.

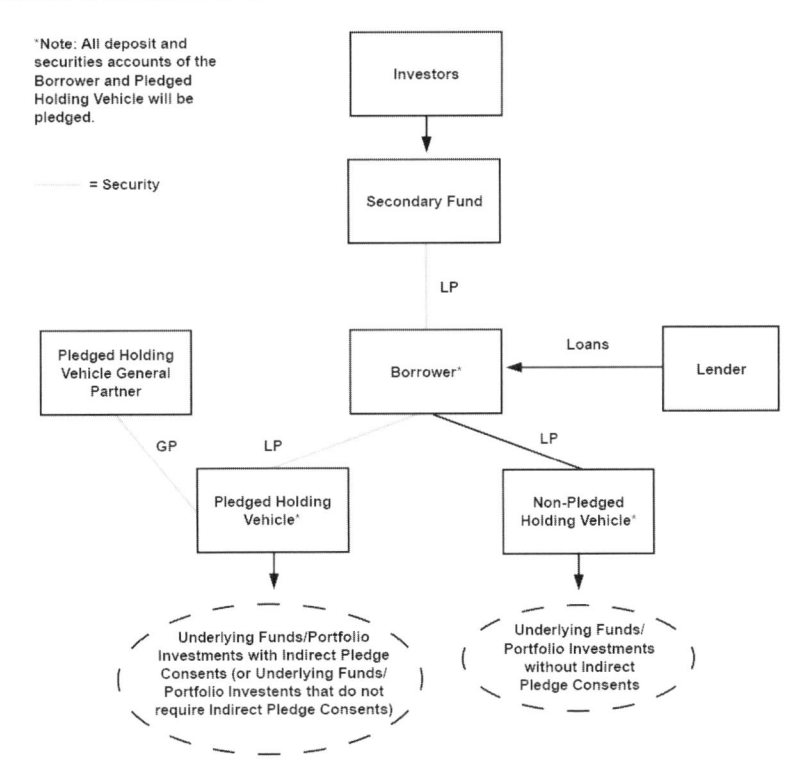

The consequence of these indirect pledge structures is that upon an event of default under a secondaries facility, while the lender could take control of the borrower, it would not be able to quickly liquidate the portfolio investments. Rather, the lender would be limited to foreclosing on the assets that actually constitute the collateral (i.e., the equity interests in the borrower or pledged holding vehicle), which is itself an indirect foreclosure on the portfolio investments. Practically speaking, this means that in an enforcement scenario, the lender would need to sell the entirety of the portfolio investments together via a sale of the equity interests in the borrower (or the pledged holding vehicle) since this type of sale would not constitute a change of the record owner of the portfolio investments. Any direct sale of a portfolio investment would still require the consent of the general partner of the portfolio investment. To address this lack of flexibility, parties often negotiate a contractual obligation in the relevant pledge agreement where the borrower agrees to follow the lender's instructions following an event of default with respect to the disposition of individual portfolio investments.

Confidentiality

In addition to transfer and pledge restrictions, confidentiality provisions in the underlying fund documents for each portfolio investment do not typically allow their limited partners to share information about the underlying fund and its underlying assets with third parties, including the lenders to such limited partners. This of course presents a disclosure problem in secondaries facilities, since the lenders are lending against the value of the portfolio investments and expect to receive appropriate reporting from the borrower. Accordingly, the borrower will often need to negotiate an exception to the confidentiality restriction with the underlying fund's general partner to allow the borrower to share relevant information with its lenders and comply with the reporting obligations under the secondaries facility. Any confidentiality carveout should be sufficiently broad to comply with the reporting requirements to the lenders, which may include (i) the portfolio investment documents (the partnership agreement, the transfer agreement or capital account statement and/or any side letter) that evidence the borrower's ownership of the portfolio investment, (ii) quarterly NAV statements, (iii) the amounts of capital contributions and distributions for any relevant period, and (iv) underlying portfolio company information, with appropriate redactions as may be necessary. The carveout is normally included in either the relevant transfer agreement or a side letter between the borrower and the relevant general partner, along with any necessary pledge consents discussed above.

In practice, it is important for borrowers, lenders and their respective counsel to secure the confidentiality carveout and any general partner consents to disclosure upfront to avoid any mismatch between what is required to be delivered under the secondaries facility and what is permitted to be disclosed under the underlying fund documentation. Both the disclosure consents and the pledge consents discussed earlier often must be negotiated with a large number of sponsors in a very short amount of time; therefore, experienced fund finance counsel for both the borrower and the lender is essential.

Valuations

As there is no public market price for the private portfolio investments included in the borrowing base or the LTV ratio calculation (with the value instead being reported by the general partner of each portfolio investment), there may be divergent interests between the lender and the general partner of the underlying fund, with the lender tending to value the portfolio investments more conservatively than the general partner. This is particularly the case during periods of extreme market volatility, when there can be a greater range of scenarios for defensible valuations. Additionally, due to the nature of private equity funds, the borrower as a limited partner must wait to receive the NAV statement from the underlying fund's general partner, which is typically only prepared by the general partner as of the end of each fiscal quarter and often not provided to the borrower until 60 to 90 days after the quarter-end. Given this time delay, by the time the LTV ratio calculation is updated, it is possible that market conditions may have changed since the record date of the NAV statement. Lenders raise the issue of delayed reporting particularly when there are public securities in the underlying portfolio. While, in theory, valuation information about any public assets that are included in the overall NAV can be updated in real time, doing so from the borrower's perspective is administratively burdensome and impractical.

Generally, for purposes of determining the LTV ratio, the NAV of a portfolio is calculated as the lesser of (i) the value of the portfolio investment provided to the borrower from the general partner of the portfolio investment as of each quarter-end record date, and (ii) the value that the borrower has assigned to the portfolio investment on its own books and records. The value is then adjusted when reported to the lender to account for any capital contributions of the borrower to the portfolio investment and/or distributions from the portfolio investment to the borrower made after the most recent record date. In order to address the fact that there is no public market price for private assets as well as the lag in reporting, secondaries facilities may include a write-down mechanism or provide for third-party valuations, as described below.

- *Write-Down for Stale Portfolio Investment Valuations.* To the extent an updated quarterly NAV statement for a portfolio investment is not provided by its general partner within the prescribed amount of time after a quarter-end, the lender may view the last reported valuation as stale and may seek to write down the NAV of the portfolio investment for purposes of the borrowing base calculation.
- *Third-Party Valuations.* Occasionally, lenders in secondaries facilities ask to include a third-party valuation concept, where the parties agree to a list of acceptable valuation agents that either provide valuations in connection with a periodic review of the portfolio investments or, more commonly, to settle a dispute raised by the lender, that in its reasonable belief, there has been a material deterioration of the value of a portfolio investment as reported by the borrower. However, from the perspective of the borrower, because the assets are private investments and illiquid, the portfolio investment's general partner is likely best positioned to value the assets, and the borrower would want to avoid the expense of engaging a third-party valuation agent and potentially having to reconcile two different values being assigned to a portfolio investment. Even in situations where the lender is able to negotiate for the right to challenge the reported valuation, there is usually a threshold mechanism used to determine whether the new value from the valuation agent will be adopted. For example, if the borrower's value is $300 and the lender obtains a third-party valuation appraisal at $298, there would be no change because the $2 difference is not material. The point of the threshold is therefore to align the parties' incentives and put reasonable limits on third-party valuation changes.

Conclusion

As the private equity secondary market has grown, so too has the emergence of secondary funds that specialise in purchasing the interests of investors in private equity funds. For these investors, secondary funds expand the market of potential buyers, enhancing investors' opportunities for dynamic portfolio management. By using financing to fund the purchase of these investments, secondary funds are able to remain competitive on pricing and also enhance their returns by reducing the amount of equity required to be contributed at the time of the purchase. It is therefore no surprise that sophisticated market participants are finding secondaries facilities to be an increasingly valuable tool in their investment toolkit.

* * *

Endnote

1. See Lazard, Sponsor-Led Secondary Market Report H1'22, August 2022.

* * *

Acknowledgment

The authors would like to thank their colleague, Carolyn Killea, for her valuable contribution to this chapter.

Ron D. Franklin
Tel: +1 212 969 3195 / Email: rfranklin@proskauer.com
Ron D. Franklin is co-head of Proskauer's Finance Group and leads the Firm's Fund Finance practice. He advises clients across a broad spectrum of finance issues, including secured and unsecured lending transactions, domestic and cross-border acquisition financings, all types of fund financings, project financings, workouts, restructurings and general banking concerns. He also counsels corporate clients regarding stock and asset acquisitions, contract negotiations, and general corporate matters.

Jinyoung Joo
Tel: +1 212 969 3334 / Email: jjoo@proskauer.com
Jinyoung (Jin) Joo is a partner in Proskauer's Corporate Department and a member of the Finance Group. He represents borrowers, lenders and private investment funds on a wide range of financing transactions, including acquisition financings, fund finance transactions, restructurings and other secured and unsecured lending transactions. As a U.S. Air Force veteran, Jin also devotes a significant amount of time providing *pro bono* legal services to disabled veterans.

Allison F. Saltstein
Tel: +1 212 969 3734 / Email: asaltstein@proskauer.com
Allison F. Saltstein is an associate in Proskauer's Corporate Department and a member of the Finance Group. Allie represents both borrowers and lenders in a variety of complex financing transactions, including fund financings, acquisition financings and other secured and unsecured lending transactions. Prior to joining Proskauer, Allie was an associate in the financial services group at a Wall Street law firm, where she represented banks and other financial institutions in bilateral and syndicated transactions, with a particular emphasis on NAV-based and secondary portfolio acquisition facilities. Allie also serves as co-chair of Proskauer's LGBTQ+ Affinity Group.

Proskauer
Eleven Times Square, New York, NY 10036, USA
Tel: +1 212 969 3000 / URL: www.proskauer.com

Australia

Tom Highnam, Rita Pang & Jialu Xu
Allens

Overview

The Australian private capital and fund finance markets maintained strong levels of activity in 2021 and 2022, continuing the momentum in recent years spurred on by the near-zero interest rate environment and government stimulus packages as the world began to emerge from the pandemic. However, as 2022 draws to a close, global economic trends, such as rising inflation, higher interest rates and the risk of recession, are starting to impact on deal appetite and fundraising activity. Geopolitical turmoil (including the war in Ukraine) has also contributed to uncertainty and exacerbated global economic headwinds. Deal activity towards the end of 2022 has been motivated by borrowers attempting to lock in pricing and ensure certainty of funding for future acquisitions. The outlook for 2023 remains uncertain.

As in previous years, Australian domestic banks, offshore commercial banks and investment banks have remained active in providing liquidity in the Australian fund financing market with new entrants of credit funds also expanding into this space. Capital call (or subscription finance) facilities remain the dominant type of facilities used in Australia, albeit with a noticeable growth in sponsor appetite for, and lender offerings of, net asset value-based (*NAV*) facilities. Diversification of the market continues with the use of subscription finance technology for debt investors (rather than equity investors) and some superannuation funds and other significant investors taking advantage of single investor/separately managed account (*SMA*) facilities.

Sovereign wealth funds and superannuation funds remain key investors in Australian funds and with it brings the associated considerations and complications in deal structuring. Green and sustainable financing has become increasingly prevalent in the Australian debt market. In line with this trend, sustainability-linked loans are continuing to emerge in the fund financing market. As the traditional domestic and offshore banks continue to be subject to stringent regulatory conditions, this has propelled the growth of direct lending activities of credit funds and superannuation funds, as well as further developing fund financing opportunities in the Asia-Pacific region.

The funds landscape in Australia

During 2021 and early 2022, private capital assets under management continued to increase in Australia. Dry powder was slightly down throughout 2021, suggesting commitments have been utilised in investment opportunities that have been identified by fund managers. There was a marginal reduction in fundraising in 2021 compared to 2020; however, there was a marked reduction in the number of funds closed in 2020 and 2021, when compared with pre-pandemic levels.[1] This suggests a flight to quality from fund investors.

Australia-focused private capital assets under management, 2020–2021

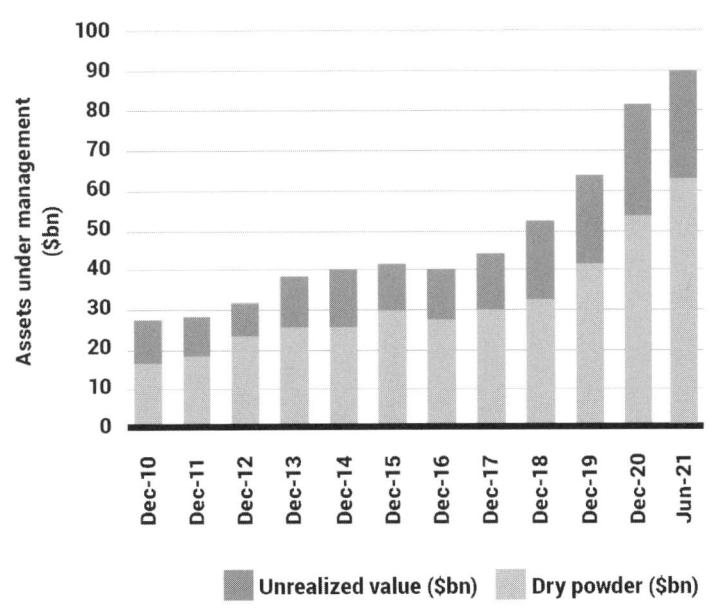

[Bar chart showing assets under management ($bn) from Dec-10 to Jun-21, with Unrealized value ($bn) and Dry powder ($bn) components. Values rise from approximately 27 in Dec-10 to approximately 90 in Jun-21.]

Australia-focused private capital fundraising, 2010–2022 YTD (data as of February 2022)

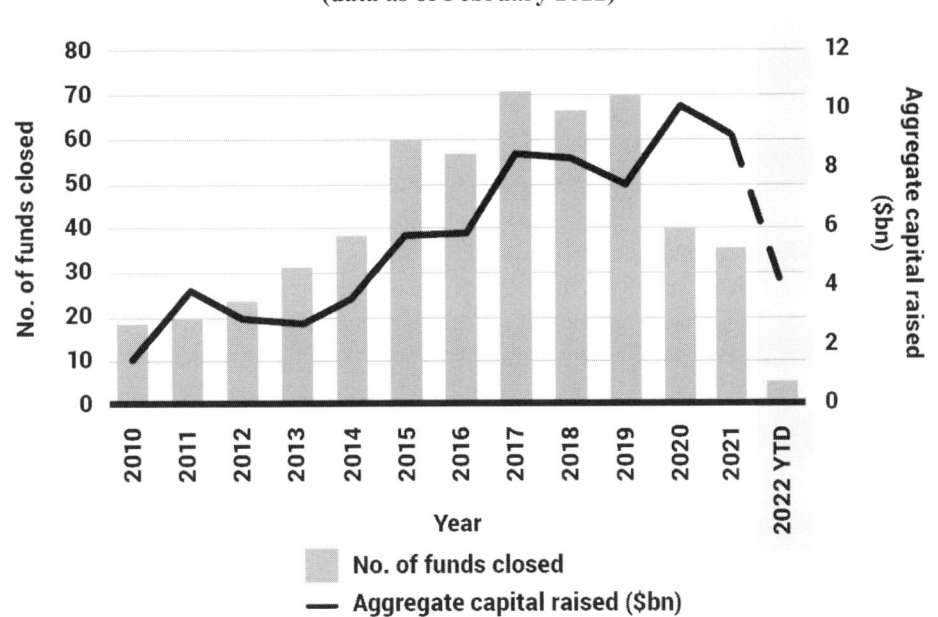

[Bar and line chart showing No. of funds closed (bars) and Aggregate capital raised ($bn) (line) from 2010 to 2022 YTD. Number of funds closed peaks around 70 in 2017 and 2019; aggregate capital raised peaks around 10 in 2020.]

Source: Preqin and Australian Investment Council, 'Australian Private Capital Market Overview: A Preqin and Australian Investment Council Yearbook 2022', pages 14 and 15.

Private equity and venture capital remain the dominant class for alternative assets in Australia. Aggregate private equity deal value reached a record A$20.1bn in 2021, a 30% increase year on year, while aggregate venture capital deal value also doubled year on year with A$7.9bn invested (although venture capital fundraising slowed in 2021).[2] Investment in real estate also continues to grow, with A$35.2bn assets under investment, which represents 39% of all assets under investment in Australia.[3] As in other areas, recent years have seen an increase in fundraising volume in real estate funds, although the number of fund closes has decreased.

Australia-focused closed-end private real estate fundraising, 2010–2022 YTD

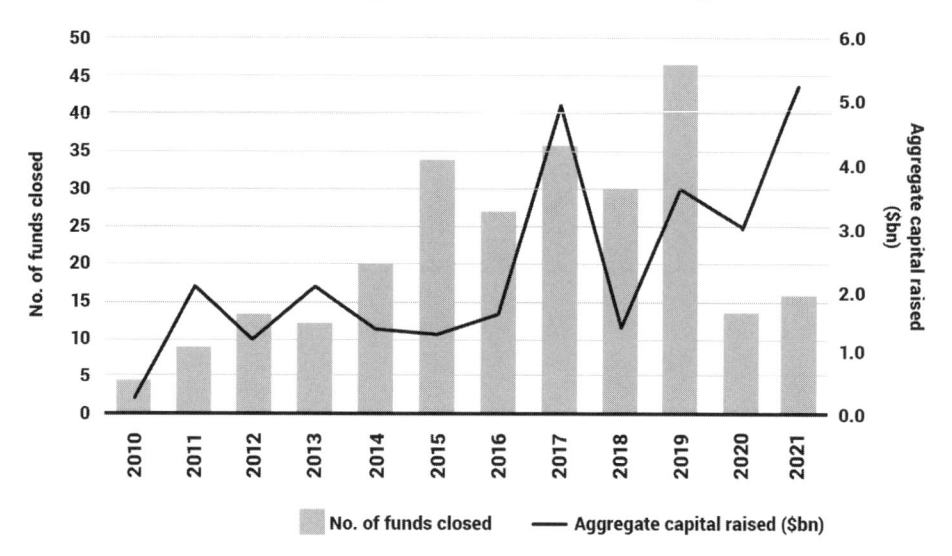

Source: *Preqin and Australian Investment Council, 'Australian Private Capital Market Overview: A Preqin and Australian Investment Council Yearbook 2022', page 24.*

Investment in infrastructure continues to be a key aspect of fund investment in Australia, with public and private sector superannuation funds and sovereign wealth funds demonstrating greater appetite for infrastructure over the past year, both by way of equity and private debt investments.

Australia's private debt market has also continued to mature and grow during recent years, with a marked increase in the number of debt funds entering the market – both local and global players – whose sole mandate is to invest in debt assets and find higher yields. The Australian private debt market currently represents 2% of the private capital market in Australia, with a growth of 144% in assets under management from December 2020 to June 2021. Indeed, six of the top 10 Asia-Pacific-based private debt investors by allocation are based in Australia.[4]

Fund formation and finance

Fund formation and other developments

In regard to fund structure, Australian funds are predominantly set up as a unit trust or a series of stapled unit trusts. Typical limited partnership structures do not offer the same beneficial tax treatment afforded to a trust and are therefore a less popular funding structure in Australia. While common in Australia, a unit trust is not considered a standard investment vehicle in many other jurisdictions.

Australian funds may also be set up as venture capital limited partnerships (***VCLPs***) under the *Venture Capital Act 2002* (Cth) to take advantage of certain tax benefits, especially for foreign investors. However, VCLPs can only invest in Australian businesses with total assets of not more than A$250m by acquiring shares, options or units.[5] It is not uncommon for Australian mid-market private equity funds to be structured with a VCLP stapled with one or more trusts in order to provide greater flexibility for investment, with eligible investments held through the VCLP and all other investments held through the parallel trust(s).

On 1 July 2022, a new corporate collective investment vehicle (*CCIV*) commenced in Australia. As mentioned in our previous chapters, this was introduced as a tax-effective alternative to current Australian pooled investment trusts, the aim of which is to grow Australia's share of the global mobile capital. The CCIV is a company limited by shares that has sub-funds that do not have separate legal personality. Each sub-fund's assets and liabilities are segregated from those of other sub-funds of the same CCIV. The CCIV is subject to regulatory requirements that reflect a mixture of those applying to companies and those applying to registered (retail) managed investment schemes, and taxation treatment of each sub-fund is (in broad terms) assessed as if each sub-fund were a separate unit trust.[6] However, in the new Albanese Labor Government's first federal budget handed down in October 2022, plans by the previous government for a limited partnership collective investment vehicle (*LP CIV*) separate to the CCIV were scrapped.[7] It remains to be seen the extent to which the CCIV will be taken up by Australian fund managers in the coming years. Although a lighter touch regulatory approach has been adopted for wholesale CCIVs as compared to retail CCIVs, wholesale CCIVs are more heavily regulated than unregistered (wholesale) managed investment schemes (including those structured as unit trusts), which may mean that the CCIV may be less attractive to wholesale fund managers and their investors.

Fund documentation

Unlike many offshore funds, it is less common for Australian fund documentation to include provisions that expressly contemplate fund financing facilities, including the grant of the required specific security over capital commitments, the ability to make capital calls by the fund to repay debt during and after the investment period, or mechanics to facilitate investors consenting to security being given by the fund. Typically, the fund documentation does contain a general permission for the fund to borrow, give guarantees and the ability to grant security. As the market is maturing, we have seen Australian fund documentation develop – albeit the process remains gradual – to import the technology utilised in offshore fund documents to cater specifically for capital call financing, particularly for new vintage funds raised by managers that have utilised these fund financing facilities in the past.

Fund document terms vary depending on the asset classes and investment strategy of the particular fund. Accordingly, it is essential to ensure that the credit and security terms are consistent with the fund document terms, and that the lender is able to properly enforce its securities. While investor side letters are a common feature, financing provisions are seldom integrated in those documents. Where there is a stapled fund structure, one focus for lenders is whether the trust deed or partnership agreement allows for cross-collateralisation of investor commitments in the stapled funds.

Another key consideration when drafting the fund's governing documents is to ensure that investors explicitly allow the fund to pledge all capital commitments. There should also be express wording included whereby each investor acknowledges its obligation to make the capital contributions without any right of set-off, counterclaim or waiver. If this authorisation is not included in the partnership agreement/trust deed, lenders will generally require that investors deliver consent letters in connection with a fund financing.

Governing documents of Australian fund entities typically also contain consent rights for the fund or other limitations as to transferability of fund interests and potentially the giving of security or guarantees by the fund. Depending on the proposed security structure, any restrictions on the powers of the fund entities to provide security and give guarantees should be checked. If security is taken as part of an asset-level facility over a borrower fund's interests in other downstream funds, there should also be a review of the underlying funds' governing documents and any applicable unitholder agreements to ensure that any transfer restrictions on the borrower fund's interests in those downstream funds are accounted for.

Types of financings

In the Australian market, fund financing facilities are more commonly provided on a bilateral or club basis rather than syndicated. In terms of product diversification, capital call facilities are the predominant product types used in Australia, with pockets of activity in relation to NAV facilities, hybrid facilities, umbrella facilities and unsecured facilities. There has been marked growth in the use of facilities by 'Funds of One' and SMAs, and interest in general partner facilities remains strong.

Australian fund financing facilities are typically traditional capital call facilities, generally structured as senior-secured, revolving-loan facilities. While documentation may limit the use of borrowings to relatively short-term borrowings (90 to 364 days), in our experience this has become less common. Terms of facilities are generally structured in alignment with a fund's investment period, and are usually for less than three or four years. While term and revolving loans are the norm, lenders are also open to providing letters of credit and bank guarantee facilities to meet the financing and investment needs of the fund.

Lenders have also provided NAV-based financing to funds, which are secured against the underlying cash flow and distributions that flow up from the underlying portfolio investments or the debt or equity interests of holding companies through which the fund may hold such investments. These types of facilities are attractive to funds, particularly private equity or special situations funds, where there is an urgent requirement for liquidity at the fund level, but no distributions from the portfolio imminent. They require the lender to 'look down' for recourse against the underlying investments, rather than 'looking up' to the investor commitments. The creditworthiness of the investors of the fund is less important than the value of the underlying assets. The returns for lenders are generally higher than the returns for traditional capital call facilities or asset-backed facilities. However, lenders providing these facilities may be structurally subordinated to other lenders that have provided finance that is secured directly against the underlying portfolio companies. We have seen these facilities increase in popularity as the 'dry powder' of private equity and venture capital funds in Australia decreases, and as funds approach the end of their investment periods.

Hybrid facilities, where the facility is secured by both the uncalled capital commitments of the fund as well as the underlying portfolio assets of that fund, may be used by funds that have started to mature in terms of their investment lifecycle.

Facilities provided to a 'Fund of One' are provided on the back of the credit of the uncalled capital commitment of that investor in the fund through which it holds a portfolio of assets. Given the dependence on the single investor commitment, among other things, a clean due diligence of that investor and its unconditional commitment is often mandated by lenders. In the case of a general partner facility, the facility is used to finance the general partner's commitment, as well as associated working capital expenses, into the fund.

Hybrid, general partner and 'Fund of One' facilities, while less prevalent, are growing in popularity in Australia. These facilities are bespoke in structure and, in the case of hybrid facilities and general partner facilities, are often provided by incumbent financiers that have previously provided the capital call facilities to those funds.

Security arrangements

Capital call facilities

The defining characteristic of the capital call facility is the security package, which comprises the fund granting security over:
- the rights to call the unfunded capital commitments of the fund's investors and to enforce the associated rights under the fund documents to call capital; and
- the deposit account into which the investors deposit their capital call proceeds.

Security is not typically taken over the underlying assets of the fund. The specific security is usually supported with an express power of attorney granted by the general partner of the fund in favour of the lender. This allows the lender to exercise capital call rights in a default scenario.

Where the fund is Australian or is otherwise subject to the *Corporations Act 2001* (Cth), the specific security may be accompanied by an all-assets security interest that operates as a 'featherweight' security to minimise moratorium risk on an administration of the fund. This all-assets 'featherweight' security only secures a small amount of debt (typically the final A$10,000 owing), and is typically requested because under Australian law, there is a stay on the enforcement of certain rights that one party (**Enforcing Party**) may have against a counterparty under a contract, agreement or arrangement due to specified insolvency events (**Trigger Events**). Rights stayed include acceleration, termination and enforcement of security. Where the stay applies to a right, the Enforcing Party needs permission of the court or the relevant insolvency practitioner to enforce the relevant right. One of the notable exemptions from this stay is where the financier has security over all or substantially all of the assets of the borrower, and a 'featherweight' security will fall within this exemption.

Security is typically granted by the fund and the trustee or general partner (as applicable), as they will hold the deposit account, the rights to call capital and related rights. Where the borrower is a portfolio special purpose vehicle (**SPV**) of the fund, a guarantee from the head fund may also be required. In Australia, it is common for the general partner or trustee to delegate the power to call capital and other functions to a manager. If there is a delegation of the power to call capital to a manager, or a custodian arrangement is put in place, security is usually sought from the manager and custodian, as applicable. Nevertheless, the security structure depends on the nature of the fund and the credit requirements of the respective lender.

The lender will need control over the deposit account to enable it to secure capital call proceeds upon a default. The deposit account may be required to be opened with the lender on day one of the facility, but this is not always mandated. Where the deposit account is held by another Authorised Deposit-taking Institution (**ADI**)[8] who is not the lender, an appropriate account control arrangement between the lender, the ADI and the account holder will be required, such as an account bank deed (although, in recent years, we have started seeing various ADIs becoming less amenable to entering into such account control mechanisms). Where the lender holds a security interest over an account maintained by another ADI, the security interest in that ADI account is perfected by registration of a financing statement on the Personal Property Securities Register (**PPSR**).

However, without an account control arrangement, any security interests that the ADI takes in respect of the account will have priority over the lender's security interest (even if perfected by registration on the PPSR), because the ADI is said to have perfected its interest by control over the account for the purposes of the *Personal Property Securities Act 2009* (Cth). Where the bank accounts are held outside of Australia, it is necessary to seek advice from foreign counsel regarding the fund documentation and security arrangement.

NAV facilities

As with capital call facilities, the security structure seen on NAV facilities depends on the nature of the fund and the credit requirements of the respective lender. Typically, the security package will include an all-assets security from the borrower fund to capture its equity interests in the holding entities of each downstream investment asset of the fund. Guarantees may also be provided by various fund entities to support the security.

As previously mentioned, there should be a diligence process undertaken as to the governing documents of each relevant Obligor to ensure that the proposed security or guarantee can be given. This is particularly the case where there may be any shareholder or unitholder agreements for co-investment vehicles that may mean that additional consents or approvals need to be received. If equity interests in any downstream entities are proposed to be part of the security, review of the constituent documents and shareholder/unitholder agreements relating to those downstream entities should also be undertaken for any transfer restrictions or pre-emptive rights applicable to those interests.

Investor consent

An investor consent letter serves three main purposes:
- The fund gives notice to the investor of the loan facility, the security over the trustee/general partner's rights to make a capital call against that investor and, upon a default, the ability of the lender to make such a call to the exclusion of the trustee/general partner.
- The fund directs the investor to pay any capital calls at the direction of the lender upon a default under the financing.
- The investor acknowledges such arrangements in favour of the lender, giving the lender privity of contract and, accordingly, the ability to have direct recourse to that investor.

The letter can also be the instrument under which the investor waives certain of their set-off rights and immunity rights. In particular, for 'Funds of One' or where there is a small club of investors to the fund, such letter is of importance as it typically operates to restrict the amendment of underlying fund documents. In some situations, funds may be sensitive about approaching investors to obtain such a letter because of the administrative burden. The investors may themselves be reluctant to provide such acknowledgment. In these situations, the lender needs to evaluate the reputation and creditworthiness of the underlying investor to see whether the uncalled capital commitments remain commercially 'bankable' despite the lack of a direct acknowledgment.

More sophisticated funds (particularly those established in the Cayman Islands and British Virgin Islands) have investor acknowledgments built into the fund documents, which avoids the need for separate investor consent letters. Older vintage Australian fund documents generally do not contain such an acknowledgment.

In Australia, investor consent letters are still obtained but have become less common, with a number of fund borrowers having successfully resisted these requirements, particularly where the relevant provisions are included in the fund documentation in a form acceptable to the lenders. That said, investor consent letters (or other forms of direct investor acknowledgment) are more common where there is greater concentration risk on investors. In our experience, for funds where investor consent letters cannot be obtained, notices of the assignment and security interest may be given at the time of the grant of security or by way of notice in the next regular newsletter to the investors. However, the latter approach has become increasingly uncommon as a repercussion of the *Abraaj* case. The form of this notice is agreed in advance with the lenders and the actual issue of such notice is monitored. However, as is always the case, each transaction is determined on its merits, and rarely does one deal replicate the next.

Key developments

Sovereign wealth funds and sovereign immunity

In recent years, sovereign wealth funds have been a dominant investor in funds, both in terms of the number of funds as well as the size of their investments. By the end of 2021, state-owned investors (including sovereign wealth funds and public pension funds) jointly managed US$32tn in assets.[9]

Accordingly, sovereign immunity, which may protect a sovereign wealth fund or other foreign or domestic government body from enforcement action or shield them from liability in its entirety, is a key focus area for lenders. Whether an entity has the benefit of immunity is a matter of the local law where the sovereign wealth fund or government body is established, and a function of the ambit of the local law as to which matters the immunity applies. It is worth noting that commercial transactions of a sovereign entity tend to be an exception to the immunity coverage.

In Australia, the *Foreign States Immunities Act 1985* (Cth) provides that a foreign state is not immune from execution with respect to a commercial transaction.[10] A commercial transaction is a commercial, trading, business, professional, industrial or like transaction into which the foreign state has entered, or a like activity in which the state has engaged. It is a broad concept and includes an agreement for a loan or some other transaction for, or in respect of, the provision of finance and a guarantee or indemnity in respect of a financial obligation. Therefore, entry into a subscription agreement with respect to a fund will be considered a commercial transaction rather than a governmental action, so immunity will not apply.

In our experience, where an investor has the benefit of sovereign immunity, no express waiver of such immunity will be provided. Rather, the investor typically expressly restates such immunity and requires the fund to acknowledge this. Where there is an investor consent letter provided in favour of a lender, a similar acknowledgment of sovereign immunity is usually required in the consent letter, with a further acknowledgment from the investor that, notwithstanding the immunity, the investor's obligations under the fund documents, including to make payment to the fund, apply. Lenders with longstanding relationships with the relevant investors may be willing to allocate borrowing base credit for their commitments based on prior dealings with them, but this is carefully analysed on a case-by-case basis and advance rates are generally discounted.

SPV investor structural issues and confidential investors

Some investors may choose to invest in a fund via an SPV rather than investing directly into that fund. Where an investor implements an SPV structure, one issue that the lenders face is to determine where the ultimate credit of the investor lies.

While lenders can obtain a level of comfort by performing due diligence on the SPV and the financial robustness of that SPV to assess whether that entity is sufficiently capitalised to meet capital calls, lenders will generally look for recourse to the ultimate investor. Under Australian law, in order to get direct recourse to the ultimate investor of that SPV, a contractual nexus between the ultimate investor and the lender will need to be established. In practice, lenders will often receive an acknowledgment from the ultimate investor in favour of the lender with regard to its liability in respect of the obligations of the SPV entity. It is usually a matter of commercial negotiation as to the level of assurance the ultimate investor is required to provide. This ranges from a direct acknowledgment that it guarantees the performance of the SPV's obligations, to letters of comfort from the ultimate investor that the SPV is its subsidiary and that it will use best efforts to ensure that the SPV has sufficient resources to meet its limited partnership agreement of fund document obligations.

Moreover, where confidentiality provisions in investor side letters may restrict a fund from disclosing certain investor details, including the identity of that investor or the ultimate investor, to a lender, we have found that funds are more willing to engage with their investors to obtain the necessary information the lenders require to assess that investor's creditworthiness to facilitate its inclusion in the borrowing base.

Superannuation funds

Superannuation funds remain key candidates for continued development in the Australian fund finance field. At the end of the June 2022 quarter, the assets under management of Australian superannuation funds in aggregate were approximately A$3.30tn, which reflects a 0.5% decrease when compared to June 2021 on account of global interest rates, supply chain issues and the war in Ukraine.[11] The superannuation industry has been undergoing consolidation over recent years and this has only accelerated with the 'Your Future, Your Super' reforms that aim to increase accountability and transparency of superannuation funds and scrutinise underperformance by performance testing superannuation funds.[12] There were 15 mergers of superannuation funds in the 12 months to October 2021.[13] Larger superannuation funds continue to grow in sophistication, evolving from being passive investors by investing through fund managers to becoming actively involved in direct investment in assets via co-investment structures or in their own capacity. In addition, like the pressures of other private capital funds, the pursuit of positive returns by superannuation fund managers has also seen superannuation funds becoming increasingly active in direct lending more generally, and not just in areas where it is necessary to 'plug the gap' in industries where typical lenders are pulling back.

It is important to note that there is a prohibition in the *Superannuation Industry (Supervision) Act 1993* (Cth) that restricts the scope of the types of borrowings a superannuation fund may undertake and the granting of security over the fund's assets. Subject to certain exceptions, a trustee of a regulated superannuation fund must not borrow money, or maintain an existing borrowing of money.[14] One innovative funding structure to account for these requirements is the 'equity level gearing' structure, under which the superannuation fund subscribes into an SPV entity which then incurs the debt. Lenders then have recourse against the superannuation fund itself using the usual capital call security mechanics.

Superannuation funds are also subject to regulatory and prudential review as to performance. Under the relevant legislation, the Australian Prudential Regulation Authority (***APRA***) has a directions power that allows it to take civil action against trustees and their directors to address underperformance/breaches of obligations by superannuation trustees.

Separately managed accounts

There has been a noticeable increase in interest to use SMAs as a way of investing, with this trend expected to continue. SMAs are a managed investment product held by an investor and overseen by an investment manager. The demand for SMAs is driven by the need of investors for investment solutions that are more tailored than those available via a sponsor's main commingled fund. In line with the proliferation of SMA activity is the potential for a new market for financing opportunities for such investors. However, with the single investor concentration risk, the credit underwrite for such financings is bespoke, and very much dependent on the identity of the relevant investor.

Green shoots for ESG

In recent years, there have been significant developments in the Australian debt market in the uptake of green and sustainable finance products. In the fund finance space, we are seeing increasing interest from both funds and lenders alike in implementing ESG or, more specifically, sustainability-linked loans. Such loans are provided on the basis that the fund is incentivised to meet pre-agreed sustainability-related performance targets through a pricing toggle based on its compliance. This is monitored by specific and regular reporting on the ESG/sustainability performance targets in relation to the fund or its investments. While it is still early days, with the increasing focus on ESG issues globally, we expect that such products will only become more pervasive.

The year ahead

In our view, it is likely that the global economic uncertainties as to interest rates and inflation, recession risk, as well as ongoing geopolitical tensions and the war in Ukraine may have an impact on fund financing in the near to medium term. However, deal activity continues to be high at the moment as borrowers attempt to lock in pricing and secure borrowing for uncertain times to come. Regardless, we anticipate that there will continue to be long-term growth in the Australian fund finance market from the new offshore lenders and credit funds that are looking to expand their portfolios in fund financing in Australia. Lending to private equity, venture capital and infrastructure funds will remain dominant in the Australian fund financing market; however, real estate funds, debt funds and superannuation funds will remain the key potential growth areas.

We expect that there will be greater take-up of ESG and sustainability-linked loans in the market. Utilisation of NAV, hybrid, general partner and 'Fund of One' facilities will continue to grow. Australia is still considered an attractive investment destination with its favourable political and economic stability in comparison to other jurisdictions. To that end, we are optimistic that the strong demand for fund financing capabilities to support the ongoing investment mandate of funds in the region will remain robust.

* * *

Endnotes

1. Preqin and Australian Investment Council, '*Australian Private Capital Market Overview: A Preqin and Australian Investment Council Yearbook 2022*', page 14.
2. Preqin and Australian Investment Council, '*Australian Private Capital Market Overview: A Preqin and Australian Investment Council Yearbook 2022*', page 8.
3. Preqin and Australian Investment Council, '*Australian Private Capital Market Overview: A Preqin and Australian Investment Council Yearbook 2022*', page 24.
4. Preqin, '*Preqin Territory Guide – Private Debt in APAC: Japan, South Korea & Australia*', page 11.
5. Section 118-425 *Income Tax Assessment Act 1997* (Cth).
6. For further details on the CCIV, see the Insight article published by Allens, '*Five years on: the new CCIV regime is here*', 16 February 2022, available at: https://www.allens.com.au/insights-news/insights/2022/02/Five-years-on-cciv-is-here.

7. Commonwealth of Australia, Budget October 2022–2023, Budget Measures – Budget Paper No. 2, page 19.
8. Authorised Deposit-taking Institutions are corporations that are authorised under the *Banking Act 1959* (Cth).
9. Global SWF, 2022 Annual Report, available at: https://globalswf.com/reports/2022 annual.
10. Section 11 *Foreign States Immunities Act 1985* (Cth).
11. APRA Statistics – Quarterly Superannuation Performance, June 2022 (issued 23 August 2022).
12. See *Treasury Laws Amendment (Your Future, Your Super) Bill 2021* (Cth), *Treasury Laws Amendment (Your Future, Your Super – Addressing Underperformance in Superannuation) Regulations 2021* (Cth) and *Treasury Laws Amendment (Your Future, Your Super – Single Default Account) Regulations 2021* (Cth).
13. Preqin and Australian Investment Council, '*Australian Private Capital Market Overview: A Preqin and Australian Investment Council Yearbook 2022*', page 15.
14. Section 67 *Superannuation Industry (Supervision) Act 1993* (Cth).

Tom Highnam
Tel: +61 2 9230 4009 / Email: tom.highnam@allens.com.au

Tom Highnam is a Partner in the Banking and Finance department at Allens. He is recognised as having a leading position in the Australian subscription finance market. He acts for all of the leading banks operating in the market including NAB, CBA, ANZ, Westpac, Macquarie Bank, MUFG, SMBC, UOB, and Standard Chartered Bank. He also acts for key sponsors in the Australian market, including IFM, ESR, Aware Super, and PEP. He is active across the spectrum of funds in the Australian market, being private equity funds, infrastructure funds and offshore funds accessing Australian capital.

He graduated from the University of Cambridge in 1996. He is recognised in *Chambers Asia-Pacific* 2015–2022 as a notable practitioner in corporate finance and acquisition finance, and by *Best Lawyers* 2022 in Banking and Finance Law and Derivatives.

Rita Pang
Tel: +61 2 9230 5836 / Email: rita.pang@allens.com.au

Rita Pang is a Partner in the Banking and Finance department at Allens. She is recognised as a fund financing specialist in the Australian market. Rita has extensive experience representing funds as well as domestic and offshore lenders active in the Australian subscription finance market in connection with domestic and offshore private equity, private debt, venture capital and infrastructure fund financings. Rita has experience in the development of hybrid, NAV and separately managed account facilities for funds investing in the Australian market. In 2022, she acted on fund finance transactions having an aggregate value in excess of A$12bn.

Recognised as a Next Generation Partner in *The Legal 500* in Banking and Finance, she has broad experience acting for lenders, borrowers and sponsors in relation to various types of financing, including leveraged acquisition financing, corporate finance, asset and structured finance, property financing and restructuring.

Jialu Xu
Tel: +61 2 9230 4198 / Email: jialu.xu@allens.com.au

Jialu Xu is an Associate in the Banking and Finance department at Allens. He advises both borrowers and lenders on a range of financing transactions, with a particular focus on fund financing transactions for both Australian and international funds in the private equity, infrastructure, and venture capital spaces. He also has experience acting in a range of leveraged finance, corporate finance, and property finance transactions.

Jialu holds a Bachelor of Arts and Bachelor of Laws from the University of Sydney, at which he has also taught as a casual academic.

Allens

Deutsche Bank Place, Level 28, 126 Phillip St, Sydney NSW 2000, Australia
Tel: +61 2 9230 4000 / URL: www.allens.com.au

Bermuda

Matthew Ebbs-Brewer & Arielle DeSilva
Appleby

Bermuda is a major centre in the international offshore investment fund industry, with an estimated over USD225bn of fund assets domiciled in the jurisdiction with *c.*800 investment funds authorised or registered in Bermuda under the Investment Funds Act 2006, as amended (**IFA**).

The Bermuda fund industry sees investment predominantly from North America and Europe, and therefore trends in the Bermuda fund finance market track the major onshore markets. Although there is no overall data reporting service for the local fund finance market, anecdotal reports from many of the major facility lenders, as well as Appleby practitioners, anticipate that there will continue to be a high demand for capital call or subscription line facilities. That is not to say, of course, that other structures such as NAV facilities will not be utilised.

Bermuda as a jurisdiction is highly responsive to evolving market demands and benefits from years of experience providing services to a number of high-profile asset management companies, cementing Bermuda's position as one of the premier offshore jurisdictions for private equity funds in addition to those investing in insurance-linked securities.

Fund formation and finance

Investment funds – overview

The IFA governs the registration and authorisation of investment funds and contains certain requirements for the formation of investment funds, their operation, and the offering of shares or interests of investment funds, the key point being that investment funds are prohibited from operating in or from Bermuda unless they are authorised or registered under the IFA.

An "investment fund" is broadly defined under the IFA and means any arrangement with respect to property of any description, including money, the purpose or effect of which is to enable persons taking part in the arrangements to participate in or receive profits or income arising from the acquisition, holding, management or disposal of the property or sums paid out of such profits and income.

In addition, investors must not have day-to-day control over the management of the fund's property, whether or not they have the right to be consulted or to give direction. There also needs to be a pooling of investor contributions together with the profits or income out of which payments are to be made to them and/or the property is managed as a whole by or on behalf of the operator of the fund.

Whilst this may appear to be a relatively broad definition at first, there is a supplemental piece of secondary legislation that narrows down the scope to exclude those arrangements, such as joint ventures, that may not truly be considered funds.

Regulatory approval and requirements

The formation of companies, partnerships and limited liability companies (**LLCs**) is subject to the approval of the Registrar of Companies (**Registrar**) and the Bermuda Monetary Authority (**BMA**) (the Registrar and BMA being the principal regulatory bodies). The BMA is the principal body responsible for the regulation of investment funds, including those listed on the Bermuda Stock Exchange (**BSX**). The Registrar is responsible for the registration of companies, partnerships and LLCs and has powers pursuant to, *inter alia*, the Companies Act 1981 (**Companies Act**), the Partnership Act 1902, the Limited Partnership Act 1883, the Exempted Partnerships Act 1992, the Segregated Accounts Companies Act 2000, the Limited Liability Company Act 2016 and the Incorporated Segregated Accounts Companies Act 2019 (**ISACA**). While the Registrar and BMA do not regulate the formation of unit trust funds, a unit trust fund is required to apply to the BMA for authorisation or exemption under the IFA, and must also seek the permission of the BMA under the exchange control regulations (**Exchange Regulations**) to issue units.

<u>Anti-money laundering and anti-terrorist financing and economic substance</u>

The Bermuda government and BMA are committed to ensuring that Bermuda's anti-money laundering and anti-terrorist financing (**AML/ATF**) requirements are aligned with the highest international standards.

The Bermuda AML/ATF framework requires that certain persons, including AML/ATF regulated financial institutions such as investment funds, establish policies and procedures to forestall and prevent money laundering and terrorist financing. Such policies and procedures must cover:
(a) customer due diligence measures and ongoing monitoring;
(b) reporting;
(c) record keeping;
(d) internal control;
(e) risk assessment and management; and
(f) the monitoring and management of compliance with and the internal communication of such policies and procedures in order to prevent activities related to money laundering and terrorist financing.

The policies and procedures should be developed using a risk-based approach. The nature and extent of such policies and procedures will depend on a variety of factors, including: the nature, scale and complexity of the business; the diversity of its operations, including geographical diversity; and its customer, product and activity profile.

In keeping with other onshore and offshore jurisdictions, economic substance requirements were introduced in Bermuda. Assuming that an investment fund does not conduct any activity that would be a relevant activity (operating an investment fund is not such an activity), economic substance requirements should not apply to the fund itself. If the fund has a Bermuda investment manager, then that vehicle would most likely be in scope and specific advice should be sought to ensure that manager complies with the applicable requirements.

<u>Beneficial ownership regime</u>

Bermuda has also adopted legislation to implement international standards in order to enhance transparency while combatting money laundering and terrorist financing. The standards that the legislation implements were initially adopted by the Financial Action Task Force (**FATF**), with the Organisation for Economic Co-operation and Development incorporating key FATF requirements into their proposals. The Bermuda beneficial ownership regime has certain exemptions where considered appropriate, including with respect to investment funds.

Private equity funds

Closed-ended private equity funds are typically formed as limited partnerships or companies incorporated with liability limited by shares; although, in our experience, the former is the more popular.

Following the developments discussed further below, whilst such funds were historically often outside the scope of the IFA, we would now typically expect such funds to be registered as professional closed-ended funds.

Investment funds

Historically, investment funds have typically been formed as mutual fund companies or limited partnerships, the optimal structure depending on a number of factors, including where and to whom the investment opportunity is to be marketed, the nature of the investor base, and the identified portfolio of investment assets.

Mutual fund companies

A mutual fund company is a company incorporated with limited liability that is incorporated for the purpose of investing the monies of its members for their mutual benefit, having the power to redeem or purchase for cancellation its shares without reducing its authorised share capital, and stating in its memorandum of association that it is a mutual fund. In the case of a mutual fund company, the shares of which are to be sold in overseas markets, an exempted company is the appropriate vehicle. However, shares of a Bermuda mutual fund company, which is an exempted company, may also be offered inside Bermuda to both local and international investors.

Typically, a mutual fund company is incorporated with two share classes: ordinary voting shares (non-participating) held by the investment manager; and non-voting, participating, redeemable shares held by the investors.

The timeline for incorporation of a mutual fund company, after submission of the application to the BMA, is usually three to five business days. A mutual fund company may only commence business and issue shares after it has been organised and the consents under Bermuda's Exchange Regulations, the IFA (if required) and the AML/ATF framework (if required) have been obtained.

Following certain amendments to the legislative framework, it is no longer a requirement that a Bermuda company meet the definition of a "mutual fund company" in order be considered an investment fund. However, given that certain provisions of the Companies Act do not apply, or apply in an amended form that is conducive to the operation of a fund, it would be unusual to proceed with a company structure without it being a mutual fund company.

Limited partnerships

Investment funds may also be formed as exempted limited partnerships. A limited partnership consists of one or more general partners (which may be bodies corporate, or general or limited partnerships, formed under the laws of Bermuda or another jurisdiction) and one or more limited partners (namely investors) whose relationship is governed by a partnership agreement.

In Bermuda, partnerships (both general and limited partnerships) are not legal entities separate from their partners unless a specific election has been made by the partnership to have separate legal personality.

Nevertheless, a partnership may in any event function as an "entity", and may sue and be sued and carry on business in its own name. In the event that a partnership does not elect to have separate legal personality, any actions brought against the partnership shall be, in the first instance, brought against the general partner of said partnership. If an election is made by the partnership to have separate legal personality, such election is irrevocable and the partnership will continue regardless of whether all the partners die or are declared bankrupt or if there is a change in its constitution.

General partners are fully liable for partnership debts and obligations. In the case of limited partnerships, the general partners will have such general liability to third parties, while, generally speaking, the liability of the limited partners is limited to the value of the money and any property that they contribute (or agree to contribute) to the limited partnership. It should be noted that the limited partners may forfeit their limited liability status in certain circumstances if they participate in the management of the partnership.

Limited liability companies

LLCs were introduced to the Bermuda regulatory landscape in 2016 as a result of the Limited Liability Company Act 2016, as amended (**LLC Act**). An LLC is a hybrid legal structure allowing the contractual and operational flexibility of a partnership to be housed within a corporate entity.

Like a Bermuda exempted company, an LLC has separate legal personality and the liability of its members is limited. Whilst members of a Bermuda company receive shares, members of a Bermuda LLC will each have an interest in a capital account in a similar way to partners in a partnership. Under the LLC Act, parties can create bespoke vehicles, having the contractual freedom to set out in the LLC agreement the terms of operation and management of the LLC as well as expressly agreeing the allocation of profits and timing of distributions amongst its members. A Bermuda LLC may be managed by one or more members (a **managing member**), or a manager may be appointed who may or may not be entitled to share in the profits of the LLC.

Whilst the LLC vehicle may be utilised by clients in a broad range of sectors, the Bermuda LLC is an attractive structuring option for operators of investment funds and, in particular, closed-ended private equity funds, as the flexible corporate governance structure allows "managing members" to manage the fund (in a similar way to a general partner) but without unlimited liability for such members in respect of the fund's losses. At the moment, it is not yet clear what the lender collateral package will look like in respect of LLC funds, although arguably the use of LLCs, as opposed to partnerships, may serve to simplify the security package, as security would only have to be granted by the LLC itself and not its manager.

Security package in fund financings

A key consideration in any fund financing transaction (whether it be a capital call facility, subscription facility or equity bridge facility) is the collateral package that the lender can secure. Typically, security will be granted over the rights to call for contributions from investors, with the security interest in uncalled capital commitments perfected by the delivery of a notice of the assignment of such capital commitments to the investors, where the document granting the security is governed by Bermuda law. Where the security document is not governed by Bermuda law, local counsel should be engaged to determine any perfection requirements. Additionally, the lender will want security over the account into which investors' capital contributions are funded.

There is no Bermuda law requirement that the collateral account be a local one (although, of course, the local banks are very familiar with such requirements, should it be preferable to secure a local account). Bermuda law does not stipulate that the security package must be governed by Bermuda law, and most often we see the security agreements mirroring the governing law of the applicable credit facility. Bermuda as a jurisdiction is very familiar with New York law as the preferred governing law for US facilities, and English law for European facilities. Of primary concern, therefore, from an offshore perspective, is to review the validity and priority of the offshore-based security.

Bermuda recognises the concept of a security agent and there are no restrictions under Bermuda law on the enforcement of rights or security interests solely because those rights or security interests are held by an agent. An agent is treated in the same way as any other secured party and is subject to any applicable Bermuda law. It should also be noted that there are no Bermuda law restrictions on granting security to foreign lenders and that it is not necessary under Bermuda law for a security agent to be registered, licensed or otherwise qualified in Bermuda in order to enforce any of its rights.

There are no restrictions under Bermuda law on a company or partnership making payments to a foreign lender under a security document, guarantee or loan agreement, and exempted companies and partnerships are designated by the BMA as "non-resident" for exchange control purposes, which means that they are free to deal in any currency of their choosing, other than "resident" Bermuda dollars.

The Stamp Duties (International Businesses Relief) Act 1990 abolished stamp duty on most documents executed by exempted undertakings (including exempted companies and partnerships, and this also applies to LLCs).

Following execution of the security document, lenders will want to ensure that their security package is appropriately registered. Charges over the assets of Bermuda companies in Bermuda (except charges over real property in Bermuda or ships or aircraft registered in Bermuda), which are granted by or to companies incorporated outside of Bermuda, are capable of being registered in Bermuda in the office of the Registrar, pursuant to the provisions of Part V of the Companies Act. Registration under the Companies Act is not compulsory and does not affect the validity or enforceability of a charge, and there is no time limit within which registration of a charge must be effected. However, in the event that questions of priority fall to be determined by reference to Bermuda law, any charge registered pursuant to the Companies Act will take priority over any other charge that is registered subsequently in regard to the same assets, and over all other charges created over such assets after 1 July 1983 and which are not registered. The provisions of Part V of the Companies Act are also extended by section 61 of the Act to charges on property in Bermuda that are created, and to charges on property in Bermuda that are acquired, by a company incorporated outside Bermuda.

Partnerships that have elected to have separate legal personality can also register with the Registrar and thereby ensure priority in a similar way to the regime for companies. In the event that a Bermuda partnership has not elected to have separate legal personality but has a Bermuda company as its general partner, the charge can be registered against the general partner acting in its capacity as general partner of the partnership. Additionally, in instances where the partnership has not elected to have separate legal personality, charges are capable of being registered in Bermuda against the partnership, in the office of the Registrar General pursuant to the provisions of the Mortgage Registration Act 1786 and Regulations enacted pursuant thereto.

Key developments

Professional closed-ended funds

There has been an increased focus within the jurisdiction over the last three years to comply with the heightened global standards being set in relation to the regulation of licensed and registered entities, including investment funds vehicles. With this we have seen key stakeholders, including the Bermuda government, the BMA as the financial services regulator and investment industry professionals, collaborating to make necessary legislative changes to facilitate this.

A key change to the investment funds landscape in Bermuda was seen in January 2020 when professional closed-ended funds were brought within the scope of the IFA. Closed-ended funds were previously outside the scope of the IFA as the IFA only applied to certain arrangements that entitled participants to have their units redeemed in accordance with the fund's constitution and offering document at a price determined in accordance with the constitution and offering document (open-ended investment fund).

The definition of "investment fund" has been amended to include both open- and closed-ended investment funds. A closed-ended investment fund means an arrangement in which the participants are not, at their election, entitled to have their units redeemed.

With this change in definition, the legislation also introduced a new class of fund for closed-ended investment funds, namely the professional closed fund.

A fund may register as a professional closed fund if it satisfies the following requirements:
(a) it is a closed-ended investment fund;
(b) it is open only to qualified participants;
(c) the qualified participants are provided with an investment warning prior to the time of the purchase of units;
(d) its operator has appointed a licensed local service provider or an officer, trustee or representative resident to Bermuda who has access to its books and records; and
(e) its operator has appointed an auditor, and its financial statements are prepared in accordance with recognised standards (i.e. IFRS or GAAP).

Market trends

We have seen a number of market trends in the fund finance sector globally, making their way into transactions involving Bermuda domiciled investment vehicles.

Where market practice changes onshore or in other international financial centres, lenders involved are now seeking to apply the same approach to transactions involving Bermuda.

A key component of operating offshore is being able to quickly identify these trends and adapt our services and advice, to provide the necessary agility required. The flexibility of our legislative regime lends itself well to being able to facilitate these changes in the market, and deliver on lender requests.

The year ahead

We are seeing an increase in the number of tailored investment structures and single investor vehicles being utilised in Bermuda. These "fund of one" structures are often popular with institutional investors, whereby they are the sole investor in a specific vehicle or fund. These structures allow the institutional investor to create a bespoke investment rather than investing in a target fund as an ordinary limited partner. As "fund of one" structures continue to grow in popularity, we anticipate that the subscription credit and NAV facility markets will continue to expand their offering to facilitate lending to these types of structures.

Another innovative legal structure that Bermuda offers, and where there is increasing interest, is the segregated accounts company. Under the provisions of the Segregated Accounts Companies Act 2000, a mutual fund company may be registered as a segregated accounts company, enabling it to create different share classes, each representing a segregated portfolio of assets. Accordingly, where a multi-class structure is desired with a separation of liability between classes, it is not necessary to incorporate multiple companies in an umbrella form. Instead, a single segregated accounts company may be incorporated, with segregated accounts representing each share class. Such accounts enjoy a statutory division of liability, effectively ring-fencing each segregated account from the general liabilities of the company, and from other segregated accounts. Bermuda segregated accounts can invest in other segregated accounts in the same company, creating a master/feeder structure, making it possible to invest and redeem without the capital leaving the company and creating a capital transfer.

Whilst Bermuda has offered the use of segregated accounts in this way for quite some time, such segregation does not create separate bodies corporate. The ISACA has now introduced the incorporated segregated accounts company (**ISAC**) to provide another option whereby segregation is provided within a structure that does create a new body corporate. It will be interesting to see whether this structure sees increasing utilisation going forward as parties evaluate how it may compliment or provide an alternative to existing structures.

Bermuda will continue its commitment to developing new and innovative products, and we will continue to see a "collaborative effort" by regulators, government and industry professionals to ensure that Bermuda continues to provide innovative fund products and maintains its position as a leader in the offshore funds world.

Matthew Ebbs-Brewer
Tel: +1 441 298 3226 / Email: mebrewer@applebyglobal.com

Matthew Ebbs-Brewer is a partner in the Corporate department of Appleby's Bermuda office and leads the funds and investment services team in Bermuda. He is also a member of Appleby's global Technology & Innovation group, providing comprehensive advice in connection with all aspects of digital asset issuances and the carrying on of digital asset business. Matthew has advised corporations, funds and high-net-worth individuals on a range of both contentious and non-contentious matters with notable experience in cross-border mergers and acquisitions, as well as the establishment and development of multinational group structures, joint ventures and both standalone and master/feeder fund structures (including those investing in insurance-linked securities).

Arielle DeSilva
Tel: +1 441 295 2244 / Email: adesilva@applebyglobal.com

Arielle DeSilva is an associate in the Corporate department of Appleby's Bermuda office.

Arielle has acted in connection with the establishment and development of multiple fund structures, including both standalone and master/feeder fund structures, with a particular emphasis on those investing in insurance-linked securities.

Arielle regularly assists on multijurisdictional fund finance transactions, including advising on related matters of company law, partnership law and the grant and appropriate registration of security. Additionally, Arielle has gained regulatory experience, with a focus on the areas of anti-money laundering and anti-terrorist financing.

Appleby

Canon's Court, 22 Victoria Street, PO Box HM 1179, Hamilton, Bermuda
Tel: +1 441 295 2244 / URL: www.applebyglobal.com

British Virgin Islands

Andrew Jowett & Johanna Murphy
Appleby

Overview

The British Virgin Islands (**BVI**) fund finance market has seen continued growth during 2022, with increasing numbers of fund formations and general transactional activity. With a sophisticated commercial court for fast-track dispute resolution, international recognition as a well-regulated jurisdiction, a tax-neutral environment and competitive fees for incorporating, launching and maintaining investment funds, the BVI is one of the most popular offshore jurisdictions for fund formation.

The growth in the BVI fund finance market over the past few years has been driven in part by: expansion into a broader range of fund types; increasing take-up by fund sponsors who had not traditionally used the product in their fund families; record levels of fundraising; and an increasing number of bespoke transaction structures, including net asset value (**NAV**) and hybrid facilities, as well as equity commitment deals. It is apparent that as the demands and needs of sponsors and funds have diversified, lenders have become more innovative and specialised in their approach. While certain banks have continued to build their book of business, new alternative lenders have also emerged on the scene. The BVI has also seen steady increases in funds focused on climate tech, as environmental, social and governance (**ESG**) factors become an increasing priority for investors, as well as significant numbers of blockchain and cryptocurrency funds.

Types of investment funds

Investment funds can be structured as a BVI business company, segregated portfolio company (**SPC**), limited partnership (**Partnership**) or unit trust. The most popular vehicle for BVI funds has historically been companies, which is largely attributed to the modern and flexible framework provided by the BVI Business Companies Act 2004, as amended (**BCA**). However, Partnerships are becoming increasingly popular for joint venture funds since amendments were made to the Limited Partnership Act 2017, pursuant to the Limited Partnership (Amendment) Act 2019 (together, the **LP Act**).

The vast majority of BVI private equity funds are private investment or closed-ended funds, which are defined as companies, Partnerships, unit trusts or any other BVI entities that:
a) collect and pool investor funds for the purpose of collective investment and diversification of portfolio risk; and
b) issue fund interests, which entitle the holder to receive an amount computed by reference to the value of a proportionate interest in the whole or in part of the assets of the entity.

An open-ended fund is defined as a company, Partnership or unit trust that collects and pools investor funds for the purpose of collective investment and issues fund interests that entitle the holder to receive on demand, or within a specified period after demand, an amount computed by reference to the value of a proportionate interest in the whole or in part of the net assets of the company or other body, Partnership or unit trust, as the case may be. The categories of open-ended funds are:
a) professional fund (open to professional investors only, with a minimum investment of US$100,000);
b) private fund (not more than 50 investors and promoted on the basis of private offers only);
c) public fund (carrying a higher level of regulatory oversight);
d) recognised foreign fund (foreign funds authorised to be marketed in the BVI);
e) incubator fund (for start-ups); and
f) approved fund (for family offices).

Companies

A BVI company is incorporated under the BCA with separate legal personality. A BVI company for use as a private equity fund will typically have a range of share classes, allowing for the shares held by the manager (or its affiliates) to have different rights from those of investors. Shares can be issued with or without a par value. As shareholders in a BVI company, liability will be limited to: (i) the amount, if any, unpaid on the shares it holds; (ii) any liability expressly set out in the articles of the company; and (iii) any liability to repay a distribution.

Segregated portfolio companies

Previously limited to certain regulated entities and open-ended funds, the Segregated Portfolio Companies (BVI Business Company) Regulations 2018 allow a private investment fund and other BVI entities to be structured as an SPC. An SPC is a single company whose assets and liabilities can be allocated and ring-fenced between separate sub-funds or segregated portfolios, similar to the concept of "protected cell" or "segregated account" companies in other jurisdictions. Shares may be issued in respect of a certain portfolio, and investors will be entitled to receive distributions from that portfolio alone. Similarly, creditors may contract with a particular portfolio, and only have recourse to assets from that portfolio. This development allows private equity funds to house multiple funds within one centralised body, providing cost and administration savings.

Limited partnerships

While a common structure for funds in other jurisdictions, Partnerships have traditionally been underused in the BVI, partly as a result of outdated and imprecise legislation. The LP Act sought to address this by introducing commercial and flexible provisions, aimed at both private equity and open-ended mutual funds. For example, it is now possible for a Partnership to choose to have legal personality and register security interests.

Under the LP Act, a Partnership can be established either with or without separate legal personality, making them suitable for both funds and carried interest distribution vehicles. For Partnerships established after the LP Act, the choice of whether or not the Partnership has legal personality is irrevocable. All Partnerships in existence prior to the new LP Act coming into force may be re-registered with or without legal personality, at the election of the general partners.

Investors join as limited partners. Subject to the fund's limited partnership agreement (**LPA**), a limited partner may, but is not required to, make a contribution to the Partnership. Save in circumstances where limited liability is lost (for example, by holding an office (including a directorship) or acting as a consultant, contractor or agent of the general partner), a limited partner's liability for the debts and liabilities of the Partnership will be limited to the amount of the limited partner's contribution or unpaid commitment to the Partnership, if any.

A Partnership must also have at least one general partner, often controlled by the fund manager, who will be responsible for managing the Partnership. Provided the LPA does not provide otherwise, the general partner is liable for the unpaid debts and liabilities of the Partnership incurred while they are a general partner. Where there are multiple general partners, each general partner is jointly and severally liable. There is no requirement for the general partner to be established within the BVI.

In most cases, the general partner will be a company with limited liability, acting as a "liability blocker" to prevent liability from flowing higher up the chain of ownership.

Unit trusts

Unit trusts are recognised under BVI trust law. Unit trusts are not separate legal entities and are established by way of a deed of trust. The principal benefit of offshore unit trusts for private equity vehicles (being that units could be redeemed without issuing new shares) has been reduced with the ability of companies to issue shares with no par value and, accordingly, this vehicle is not commonly used.

Fund formation

Once the constitutional documents (being memorandum and articles for a company and a written LPA for a Partnership) and any other commercial matters are agreed between any interested parties, a company or a Partnership can be established relatively quickly (normally within one to two working days). The incorporation of a company will require the filing of the following with the BVI Registrar of Corporate Affairs (**Registrar**):

a) memorandum and articles; and

b) a document from the proposed registered agent, consenting to their appointment.

If the company is to be incorporated as an SPC, prior approval from the BVI Financial Services Commission (**FSC**) must be obtained. We would expect this to take one to two weeks.

The formation of a Partnership will require the filing of the following with the Registrar:

a) a statement confirming the Partnership's name, address, registered agent, name and address of each general partner and a confirmation of whether the Partnership has an unlimited duration or a fixed term;

b) if desired, an election by the general partners for the Partnership to be formed without legal personality (the default position being a Partnership with legal personality); and

c) a document from the proposed registered agent, consenting to their appointment.

The LPA is not filed and is not otherwise made public.

A registered agent, within the BVI, will need to be engaged in order to establish either a company or Partnership. Only a registered agent is permitted to file registration documents with the BVI Registry of Corporate Affairs (**BVI Registry**). Provided the Registrar is satisfied that the registration requirements for the company or Partnership (as applicable) have been complied with, it shall issue a certificate of registration, being conclusive evidence that the requirements have been met and that the company or Partnership (as applicable) has been established.

Private investment funds (whether companies or Partnerships) do not have any minimum capital requirements.

Regulation, licensing and registration

The Securities and Investment Business Act 2010 (**SIBA**) is the primary legislation regulating funds in the BVI and is monitored by the FSC. SIBA is supplemented by various regulations, including the Private Investment Funds Regulations (**PIF Regulations**) and the Financial Services Commission (Securities and Investment Business Fees) Regulations 2010 (as amended). Further regulations apply to open-ended funds. As the vast majority of private equity funds are closed-ended, this chapter focuses primarily on closed-ended structures.

Prior to 2020, private investment funds (or closed-ended funds) were not regulated in the BVI. On 31 December 2019, the BVI amended SIBA to bring "private investment funds" into the scope of the regulatory regime.

As a BVI entity, a fund (whether open- or closed-ended), if structured as a company, will be registered with the BVI Registry and its corporate affairs will be governed by the BCA. BVI entities structured as a Partnership will be registered with the BVI Registrar of Limited Partnerships and its corporate affairs will be governed by the LP Act.

In order to obtain recognition, the fund is required to submit to the FSC an application in the approved form, accompanied by copies of:
a) the fund's constitutional documents, register of directors (where applicable) and certificate of incorporation;
b) formation or registration;
c) the fund's valuation policy;
d) the fund's offering document or term sheet, where the fund intends to issue such document; and
e) CVs or biographies of each director, general partner or trustee, or the underlying individuals where such entities are corporate entities.

Where the fund does not intend to issue an offering document or term sheet, the fund must provide its reasoning for doing so and explain how investors will receive pertinent information concerning the fund. Any offering document or term sheet must include information prescribed by the PIF Regulations (including a disclaimer, the investment objectives and details of any fees).

Once an entity is incorporated, it can operate as a private investment fund for a period of 14 days before submitting the application to the FSC for recognition. In order to be recognised by the FSC, BVI private investment funds must either:
a) be authorised to have no more than 50 investors;
b) invite investors to subscribe for, or purchase, fund interests on a private basis only; or
c) only issue fund interests to professional investors, each with a minimum initial investment of US$100,000 (or the equivalent in any other currency and subject to certain exemptions to be outlined by the FSC).

The fund's constitutional documents must specify which of these restrictions apply to the fund.

Registration of investment advisers and fund managers

Where fund managers, advisers, administrators or appointed persons are established outside the BVI, they (and their directors and officers) will not normally need to be registered or licensed in the BVI, provided that they have no physical presence in the BVI, and the fund has no presence in the BVI save for its registered office and agent.

Where a manager, adviser, administrator or appointed person is either BVI-incorporated or physically operates within the BVI, such persons will normally be required to obtain an investment business licence under SIBA. Licensees under SIBA are subject to requirements to, among other things, file audited financial statements and seek approval from the FSC for any change in its directors, officers or significant interest holders, for any business carried on outside the BVI and any establishment of a subsidiary.

For BVI-incorporated investment managers or advisers, an alternative option to SIBA licensing is to register as an approved manager under the BVI Investment Business (Approved Managers) Regulations, which impose lighter requirements (including no requirement to appoint an auditor). The approved manager regime is available for BVI-incorporated investment managers or advisers to closed-ended funds whose aggregate assets under management do not exceed US$1 billion (or its equivalent in another currency).

Registration under either SIBA or the approved manager regime will require payment of an initial application fee and recurring annual fee.

BVI security package

The BVI is an attractive jurisdiction for financing structures with lender-friendly insolvency laws (modelled on the English legal system) and a simple, yet robust, regime for secured financing transactions.

Under the BCA, and subject to the constitutional documents of a BVI company or Partnership, the BVI entity may, by an instrument in writing, create a mortgage, charge or other encumbrance over any of its assets situated in any part of the world in accordance with the law of relevant jurisdiction, and the mortgage, charge or other encumbrance will be binding on the BVI entity to the extent, and in accordance with the requirements, of the chosen law. Assuming that the execution and delivery of a foreign law security document (**Foreign Security Document**) creates a valid charge under the chosen foreign law, then such security interest will be recognised in the BVI. Upon registration of the Foreign Security Document with the Registrar, all registrations, filings and other actions necessary or desirable to protect priority of the Foreign Security Document in the BVI will have been taken, subject to any priority afforded to pre-existing registered charges.

With the majority of BVI investment funds being structed as companies, a BVI security package will typically include an equitable mortgage or charge over shares in the BVI company. Under BVI law, there are no steps required to "perfect" a security interest; however, in order to protect a security interest granted by a chargor over shares that it holds in a BVI company, the chargor should deliver to the secured party a signed but undated share transfer form and signed directors' resolutions authorising the registered agent of the company to register the name of the secured party in the company's share register. The BVI company's register of members is *prima facie* evidence of title, so it is important to ensure that steps are taken to include the entry of the secured party's name in the BVI company's register of members. If the shares are over 100% of the BVI company, or a significant enough percentage to allow the shareholder to control the board of directors, it is prudent to also request signed but undated letters of resignation from the current directors (should the secured party wish to change the board upon enforcement of the charge).

A BVI chargor will typically also grant security over:
a) bank accounts into which any distributions are placed from the underlying investments;
b) contract rights under any custodian agreement (including security over the relevant custodian accounts); and
c) any other asset security.

We would not normally expect the relevant security instruments for the above assets to be governed by BVI law because these assets are generally not located in the BVI.

Where a BVI investment fund or obligor grants security over any of its assets, to establish the priority of a security interest created by that BVI company, the secured party should request that particulars of the security interest are publicly registered with the Registrar, in accordance with the BCA. Under BVI law, public registration of security is not necessary to perfect the security interest; however, where there are two security interests that relate to the same collateral, the timing of the public registration of the security interest will, in the majority of cases, determine priority. Public registration in the register of registered charges also provides constructive notice to third parties.

As previously noted, a Partnership may be constituted with or without legal personality. Where a Partnership does not have legal personality, the Partnership merely reflects a contractual agreement between the partners, where the general partner is vested with certain duties and powers with respect to the Partnership's business and assets. Conversely, a Partnership that is registered with legal personality, which is the default position unless the general partners elect not to have legal personality on registration, will be able to grant security over its assets. The legal treatment of a Partnership and the corresponding role of the general partner will therefore have a number of implications for lenders offering subscription credit facilities to BVI vehicles when structuring the related security package. Subject to the LPA, a Partnership with legal personality may, by an instrument in writing, create a charge over the assets of the Partnership, including uncalled capital commitments (**Uncalled Capital**). The contractual obligation of a limited partner to make capital contributions, to the extent that they have not already been called, and the corresponding right of the general partner on behalf of the Partnership to call for any Uncalled Capital (**Capital Call Rights**), are at the core of the typical subscription credit facility security package. Security over the Uncalled Capital and/or Capital Call Rights would be granted in respect of a BVI obligor's contractual obligations/rights under the subscription agreement (rather than the memorandum and articles of association or LPA). We note that security over contractual rights is granted only by way of an equitable assignment because it is not possible to grant a legal assignment of contractual rights under BVI law.

Key developments

Access to information

Since December 2019, the FSC has maintained a register of recognised funds, which identifies each fund's service and business addresses (within and outside the BVI), authorised representative, date and status of recognition, whether the fund is up to date with its FSC fees and such other information the FSC considers appropriate. Such information will be available for public inspection, for which the FSC may charge a fee.

Other than as set out above, limited information is available publicly about entities established in the BVI and, where information is available publicly, such documents are generally only accessible through the FSC's online database, which requires registration with the FSC to access and the payment of fees. Such available information includes registered office and agent details, name and registered number and any publicly registered charges over its assets. For companies, the memorandum and articles (and any resolutions amending these) will also be available. For Partnerships, the identity of general partners will be available (but not the LPA). Entities are required to keep filed information up to date and any failure to do so may result in a fine.

A BVI company is also required to file a copy of its register of directors (and any changes thereto within 30 days) with the Registrar. The register of directors has not previously been publicly available, except on an order of the court, on a written request by a competent authority (for tax compliance or other law enforcement purposes) or at the election of the company. However, with effect from 1 January 2023, certain authorised users of the BVI Registry's system (generally, only BVI service providers) will be able to search for the names of the current directors of a BVI company. We note that the search results are limited in scope to include the name of the current directors; accordingly, it will not be possible to obtain the date of birth, nationality, address and other personal information of a director or the names of former directors.

Although this remains to be determined, we expect that there will be some form of fee to access the names of directors (as with all company searches in the BVI).

The identities of shareholders in a company and limited partners in a Partnership, and the amounts of their capital commitments, are not publicly available. However, both a limited partner and a member of a company is entitled to inspect, on giving written notice, the records, the register of limited partners (in the case of a Partnership and subject to the LPA) and the registers of members and directors (in the case of a company). For a Partnership, the LPA may restrict these inspection rights. For a company, subject to its memorandum and articles, a director may refuse an inspection request if they are satisfied that it is contrary to the company's interests. The articles of a company, or the LPA for a Partnership, may allow for further inspection or information rights for investors.

In 2017, the BVI introduced a centralised system for recording the beneficial owners of BVI entities (being persons who ultimately own or control more than 25% of an entity). While open-ended mutual funds and any licensed BVI entities are exempt from this regime, closed-ended funds are not. The system is not available to the public and can only be accessed following a formal request from the BVI Financial Investigation Agency, the FSC, the BVI International Tax Authority or the Attorney General's Chambers, who will in turn be bound by strict confidentiality rules. Non-compliance can result in a fine, imprisonment or both.

Economic substance regime

The BVI introduced the Economic Substance (Companies and Limited Partnerships) Act 2018, as amended, and the Economic Substance (Companies and Limited Partnerships) (Amendment) Act 2001 (together, the **ES Act**), which applies to all companies and Partnerships incorporated or registered in the BVI (these are referred to as "relevant entities"). All relevant entities that are classified as "resident" in the BVI and as carrying on a "relevant activity" will need to demonstrate that they have "adequate substance" in the BVI or they will be subject to administrative penalties and, ultimately, strike-off for failure to comply.

The ES Act lists nine "**relevant activities**", the most relevant of which for the purposes of this chapter being "holding company business" and "fund management business"; however, "investment fund business" is excluded from this list.

A corporate entity that carries on "**holding company business**" is defined as a "pure equity holding business" (meaning a BVI entity that only holds equity participations in other entities and only earns dividends and capital gains) and is in scope of the ES Act, but is subject to a reduced economic substance test. In practice, this should be met by its ongoing compliance with existing statutory obligations.

"**Fund management business**" includes taking decisions on the holding and selling of investments, calculating risk and reserves, taking decisions on currency or interest fluctuations and hedging positions and preparing regulatory and other reports for government authorities and investors. This means that it is likely that an investment manager would be classified as carrying on fund management business and will fall in scope of the ES Act.

The exemption for legal entities that carry on "**investment fund business**" means that: (i) most BVI entities in a fund structure will not be classified as carrying on a relevant activity under the ES Act; and (ii) equity funds, which would otherwise have been considered a pure equity holding business, are also out of scope.

For completeness, the activities of an approved manager would need to be reviewed on a case-by-case basis to determine whether it will fall within the definition of fund management business and, therefore, whether there is an obligation for the approved manager to have substance in the BVI (other than to have a registered office and authorised representative).

Compliance should, nevertheless, be initially assessed by lenders' counsel and all corporate vehicles should be monitored on an ongoing basis to ensure compliance with the ES Act.

The year ahead

The forecast for private equity fundraising over the next few years remains optimistic and, given the ability of top US-based sponsors to raise money from institutional investors based in the US, we anticipate that the North American market will continue to dominate. The BVI will remain relevant for North American and Asia-focused funds in particular, while continuing to be a popular jurisdiction for UK managers establishing offshore funds with a transatlantic nexus. As the industry matures further, the demand for fund finance solutions throughout the lifespan of the fund will likely increase, as will the need for its underlying portfolio companies to be supported. We anticipate that the types of fund-level financing and the purposes for which such financing is used will continue to diversify in 2023 and we expect an increase in not only subscription facilities, but the more bespoke NAV facilities, management fee facilities and hybrid facilities. Continued focus on ESG will inevitably lead to an increasing number of funds and lenders incorporating ESG into their strategies.

Given that strong credit performance remains the norm in this market, the relatively low-risk profile of the product will continue to make it attractive for lenders. The strength of the fund finance market is bolstered by strong collaborative relationships between lenders and fund sponsors alike. Continual development and innovation will likely remain a feature of the industry, with the BVI market ever willing to evolve and adapt to meet the requirements and expectations of our onshore counterparts.

We anticipate that the BVI will maintain its position as one of the most popular offshore fund jurisdictions, for reasons including the range of vehicles that can be utilised to meet a fund's structuring requirements, investor familiarity with the jurisdiction and a proportionate and adaptive regulatory framework. Due to the popularity of the BVI as a fund jurisdiction, coupled with the growth of the finance market generally, we expect 2023 to be another extremely busy year in the BVI fund finance market.

Andrew Jowett
Tel: +1 284 393 5316 / Email: ajowett@applebyglobal.com
Andrew Jowett is a Group Partner in the Corporate and Regulatory BVI practice groups and of the Jersey office at Appleby. Andrew has extensive experience in corporate, banking and finance, and capital markets transactions. Andrew's corporate practice involves advising a range of clients from large blue chip listed companies to small private companies on multi-jurisdictional mergers and acquisitions, public takeovers, IPOs, private placements, corporate reorganisations, joint venture arrangements, continuations, voluntary liquidations, shareholder rights, corporate governance, and directors' duties. Andrew's banking and finance practice involves advising both large financial institutions and corporate borrower groups in relation to fund finance, acquisition finance, asset finance, debt restructuring, security enforcement, insolvency, real estate finance, and project finance.

Andrew has been consistently recognised across international legal rankings, most recently praised for his "commercial savvy, leadership and responsiveness" (*Chambers Global* 2021).

Johanna Murphy
Tel: +44 7829 931 811 / Email: jmurphy@applebyglobal.com
Johanna Murphy is a Senior Associate within the firm's Corporate departments in both Jersey and the BVI. She advises clients on a broad range of corporate finance and general corporate matters, regularly providing corporate finance, real estate finance, fund finance, debt restructuring and regulatory advice to leading financial institutions and corporate borrowers. She also has significant experience in corporate transactions, including advising on multi-jurisdictional mergers and acquisitions, corporate restructurings, shareholder rights, voluntary liquidations and migrations, in relation to transactions that involve Jersey and BVI structures.

Appleby

Jayla Place, Wickham's Cay I, PO Box 3190, Road Town, Tortola, VG1110, British Virgin Islands
Tel: +1 284 393 4742 / URL: www.applebyglobal.com

Canada

Michael Henriques, Alexandra North & Kenneth D. Kraft
Dentons Canada LLP

General industry overview

Though not as large as the corresponding markets in the United States and the UK, the market for the subscription credit facility (commonly referred to in Canada as a "**capital call financing**") and other fund finance products continues to evolve. Generally speaking, the market continues to see an uptick in terms of lenders (both Canadian and foreign banks) and borrowers (particularly with respect to venture capital and real estate funds), and the product continues to evolve to meet an increasing number of requirements, complexities and/or demands in the Canadian market. For the funds that seek out financings of this nature, capital call facilities have proven to be an efficient tool to provide for, among other things, a more predictable capital call schedule, payment of normal-course operating expenses, more flexible timing of fund investments, long-term leverage not previously available at the fund level, smoother capital call processes, cross-leverage between funds, and enhanced internal rates of return. In short, the market in Canada has continued to thrive.

Subscription financing in Canada

Acquisition finance transactions aside, capital call financings continue to be the most common form of credit made available to private equity funds, and are on the rise for venture capital funds and real estate funds, in Canada. In their purest form, capital call financings are not secured by the general assets of the fund (or those of its operating or project-level subsidiaries) but rather, as the name suggests, by the unfunded capital commitments of the investors in the fund. As is the case in other markets (where capital call financings are more common due to the depth and breadth of the private equity markets), lenders on these capital call financings generally focus on, and follow a comprehensive due diligence regimen in order to confirm, the underlying credit strength of the investors and their legal obligation to fund capital commitments pursuant to the applicable fund documents.

Like other jurisdictions, the core collateral package on a typical capital call financing in Canada includes: (i) a pledge of the unfunded capital commitments of the investors in the fund; (ii) an assignment of the fund's right to make a call on such capital commitments and the right to enforce payment of the capital commitments once called (including a covenant to ensure all payments are made into certain bank accounts); and (iii) a pledge of such bank accounts into which the capital commitment proceeds are to be deposited. Unlike certain other jurisdictions, however, and notwithstanding that the market in Canada has evolved significantly, certain differences in approach still exist from lender to lender and by fund type (private equity *vs* venture capital) with respect to certain of the remaining characteristics of the structure.

What makes Canada different?

In Canada, it is not uncommon (particularly for mid-market or small funds) for lenders to provide capital call financing facilities based on varying security packages, varying covenant packages and varying reliance on capital call diligence. Though we are cautious not to generalise (we acknowledge that a number of factors contribute to the structure and security package on any financing), we believe this reflects, at least partially, the fact that a certain segment of the capital call financing market in Canada is still heavily relationship-based, particularly in the burgeoning venture capital fund space. We have set out below some of the key differences or attributes of a capital call financing in Canada.

Account control agreements – Unlike the United States, the common law jurisdictions in Canada do not require an account control agreement (or any other form of control) to perfect a security interest over bank accounts. Perfection of a security interest over a bank account happens by way of registration pursuant to the applicable provincial *Personal Property Security Act*. Furthermore, most structures in Canada include deposit accounts with the applicable lender or agent. Consequently, on a purely domestic transaction (Canadian lender(s) and a Canadian borrower with bank accounts in Canada only), lenders do not generally require account control agreements. Account control agreements can provide other benefits and foreign lenders (accustomed to taking them in their home jurisdiction) often require them, but many of those benefits can be addressed in the other loan documents.

Limited partner acknowledgments – The requirement for limited partner acknowledgments varies greatly from transaction to transaction in Canada, based in large part on the quality of the applicable fund documents. We still see transaction structures with: (i) no such requirement; (ii) limited requirements where only certain investors are required to provide acknowledgments; (iii) a requirement for every investor to provide an acknowledgment of a limited nature; and (iv) a requirement for every investor to provide a comprehensive acknowledgment. We continue to see a fifth requirement on certain deals that notice of the capital call facility and the security relating thereto be provided to each limited partner notwithstanding that such notice is not otherwise required by the applicable limited partnership agreement or for perfection of security. It is important to note that certain large institutional investors have a significant influence on the fund documents and that limitations may be imposed on the managers to prevent them from approaching investors for acknowledgments (and certain diligence materials like financial statements) in connection with third-party financings. This can lead to significant issues where the fund documents do not otherwise contain capital call-friendly provisions regarding, among other things, authorisation to enter into such facilities, setoff, waiver of certain defences, investor reporting and the assignment of the capital call commitments.

Included and excluded investors – A limited number of capital call financings in Canada do not contain "included investor" and "excluded investor" concepts. Instead, the borrowing base will include all investors, and do so on an equal basis. Given the typical reliance on the strength of the investor capital call commitments, it might seem particularly strange to treat all investors equally, but this particular approach is generally paired with other attributes (a lower margin rate, small deal size, 90- to 120-day demand-bridge loan, a general security agreement ("GSA"), etc.) that mitigate overall risk. The more common approach in Canada aligns with what you might expect to see in other jurisdictions: a strong focus on the investors of the fund, including detailed investor eligibility criteria in the credit facility; and a list of ongoing exclusion events that operate to remove an investor from the borrowing base during the life of the facility. Certain credit facilities in Canada also include multiple margining rates.

Diligence – As can be expected in a jurisdiction where a meaningful portion of the capital call financings are relationship-based, we still see a broad range of approaches to diligence in Canada. Our general advice on any capital call financing is to follow a comprehensive and regimented review of the fund documents, including, among other things, the offering materials, limited partnership agreements, subscription agreements and side letters. Some lenders obtain comfort based on a limited review of certain key issues: authorisation regarding borrowing and assignment of the capital call commitments; limited partner acknowledgments; investment periods; defaulting investors provisions; capital call periods; and use of capital calls to repay loans. Other lenders take a more comprehensive approach and request the same of their counsel.

To be clear, there is nothing particularly special about the structure of a Canadian capital call financing (*versus* a capital call financing in the United States or the UK, for example) that allows for or encourages a more limited approach to diligence. Furthermore, given the make-up of the fund market in Canada (like many jurisdictions, it includes a broad range of funds in terms of size, fund formation experience and capital call financing experience), a comprehensive and regimented approach is warranted in almost all cases – even where cost sensitivities, relationship, timing, additional general security or other factors might suggest otherwise.

Notwithstanding that many funds in Canada are extremely sophisticated and are both proactive (in their fund formation documentation) and protective (with respect to what they accept in subscription agreements and side letters), we still experience situations where the diligence leads to: (i) amendments to the fund formation documents; and/or (ii) a request for acknowledgments from fund investors where acknowledgments were not originally contemplated. This is never the intended purpose of the diligence process, and we are very mindful of the investor/fund relationship, but we raise these examples to highlight the importance of the diligence process on these transactions.

General security agreements – The GSA operates to grant a security interest in all of the personal property of a fund. In certain limited circumstances, lenders in Canada still require a GSA in connection with a capital call financing (we note these are used less frequently every year). This, of course, reflects a divergence from the premise that the lender is focused solely on the investors and the legal obligation of such investors to provide capital contributions once called upon, pursuant to the fund documents. For some funds (particularly those accustomed to capital call financing structures in the United States), this is of material concern. In certain instances, after accounting for the fund's future acquisition financings with third-party lenders, the overall benefit of the GSA is limited and can result in the need for future intercreditor agreements and/or waiver letters with such third-party lenders. Furthermore, certain of the risks addressed by the GSA can be addressed in the credit agreement and the other loan documents through the use of more stringent operating and reporting-related covenants. After taking into account where the general global market has been heading for a number of years, we expect GSAs to be used less frequently in connection with capital call financings in Canada.

Mature market structures – Though the market in Canada continues to evolve, we acknowledge that Canada still trails more established markets such as the United States and the UK. As previously mentioned, the depth and breadth of the fund markets in those jurisdictions are far greater than Canada's. Consequently, the capital call finance markets in those jurisdictions have evolved at a quicker pace. That said, and notwithstanding that single borrower, demand-bridge loan structures are still prevalent in Canada, lenders have also become comfortable with more sophisticated fund structures involving committed facilities, single investor funds, umbrella facilities, multiple funds (feeders, alternative investment vehicles, parallel funds, etc.), a more singular focus on the investors and the capital call rights in the fund documents and, in limited circumstances, cascading security and/or mixed asset/hybrid borrowing bases. Most importantly, though, structures that involve leverage for the managers and the principals/employees are also becoming more common.

Multiple fund structures – Certain multiple fund structures have become more common in Canada. Most lenders are now comfortable lending into funds with borrowing bases that involve multiple levels of funds (including, for example, feeder funds in the Cayman Islands for international investors) on closing, and/or allow for multiple levels of funds to be used going forward. The key to these arrangements is a strong understanding of the fund documents in connection with, among other things: the mechanics of how each fund operates on its own and with the other funds in the structure; what each fund can or cannot be jointly liable to pay; the comfort of lenders with the manager and general partners; and how the capital call rights may be impacted by the use of additional funds.

Cascading security – Cascading security packages are a viable option in Canada and have been implemented by certain lenders (for example, where certain feeder funds cannot be directly liable to the lender for tax or other reasons). As described in greater detail in other chapters of this book, this structure relies on multiple levels of pledges and security to ultimately put the lender in a position similar to the position it would have otherwise been in, had each of the funds guaranteed and provided security packages directly to the lender. As is the case in other jurisdictions, lenders in Canada generally try to avoid cascading security packages and prefer to rely on direct guarantee and assignment structures.

Hybrid borrowing bases – Again, these are not as common in Canada as they might be in more mature capital call finance markets. These facilities combine standard capital call borrowing bases (based on investor capital commitments) with asset-based borrowing bases for other asset classes (for example, real estate assets held in the fund's subsidiaries) under one credit agreement. These structures generally involve coordination among multiple groups within a particular lender organisation and we have seen fairly limited use and/ or consideration of hybrid borrowing bases in the Canadian market. That said, where the desire for such a structure exists, there are no issues (from a purely legal perspective) to structuring these facilities in a manner that properly protects the lender's interests.

Enforcement

Typical steps to enforcement in a subscription credit facility – Though there may be slight variations in enforcement depending on whether the lender has obtained a GSA, proceedings will be identical so far as the capital call enforcement is concerned. Therefore, in this section, our intention is to focus on that latter aspect of enforcement.

(a) Notice

Enforcement in Canada will generally require the lender to give the debtor notice of the default under the loan agreement and a reasonable amount of time to cure the default, before any enforcement action can be taken. This notice period is usually 10 days although, in some cases, the courts have extended the length of time for which notice is required. In cases of urgency (e.g. fraud), an application to the court can be made to waive or abridge the 10-day period. Once this default notice period expires, the lender would then be in a position to enforce its security interest. Where the lender has the typical capital call security package, the lender would not have to send notice to all creditors of the fund, only the investors.

(b) Enforcement

Where the lender has the typical capital call security package, enforcement will involve taking possession of the fund's deposit account(s), and advising the fund and its investors that the lender is enforcing its security interest and exercising its capital call rights pursuant to the pledge (and any power of attorney granted thereunder) of the investors' unfunded capital commitments. The notice to investors would direct them to deposit their unfunded capital contributions into the debtor's deposit account, of which the lender would have taken possession.

Ability to appoint a receiver – Where appropriate, a lender in Canada may choose to apply to a court to appoint a receiver for the purpose of enforcing the lender's security interest in the specific collateral. This results in additional professional costs but provides court protection for the lender's enforcement. It may also ensure that the investors in the fund are obliged to comply with any capital call requirements that the court-appointed officer may assert pursuant to the fund formation documents. This may be beneficial where limited partner acknowledgments have not been obtained, or the fund formation documents do not make it expressly clear that the capital call rights can be assigned as part of any permitted financing. In such a scenario, the receiver would be exercising the rights of the fund to call on the capital commitments of the investors.

Insolvency – The foregoing analysis is not impacted should the fund become subject to insolvency proceedings, either voluntarily or involuntarily. The rights and remedies available to the lender in any type of insolvency proceeding are not altered regardless of the type of security package.

Insolvency proceedings in Canada can be either voluntary or involuntary. If the fund owes CA$5 million or more, then the fund can initiate proceedings for protection under the *Companies' Creditors Arrangement Act*, R.S.C. 1985, c. C-36 ("CCAA"), or it can opt to reorganise under the *Bankruptcy and Insolvency Act*, R.S.C. 1985, c. B-3 ("BIA"). The BIA has no minimum debt requirement. The commencement of proceedings results in an initial 30-day stay of enforcement proceedings against both secured and unsecured creditors under the BIA or 10 days under the CCAA. After the initial stay period lapses, there is no limit on how long the court can authorise further CCAA extensions, while BIA stays can only be extended in 45-day increments to a maximum of six months (from the initial filing date). A stay of proceedings could prevent exercise of the assignment rights, and the lender may have to apply to the court to seek permission to enforce. It is uncertain how a court in Canada would address the competing interests. There is one notable BIA exception: if the lender has delivered a notice of intention to enforce its security more than 10 days before the BIA proceeding commenced, then the stay will not apply to that lender under that statute (but would still apply under the CCAA).

The future of capital call financing in Canada

The Canadian market with respect to capital call financings continues to evolve in all respects, including ancillary or complimentary fund finance offerings that are now available here. New lenders and new funds continue to enter the market in Canada. A number of those new participants are foreign-based and enter the Canadian market with experience in, or as part of a cross-border structure originating from, the United States or the UK. Ultimately, the bifurcation still exists between the purer capital call financings provided by certain Canadian and international lenders to the larger or more experienced funds at one end of the spectrum, and the more traditional, smaller, relationship-based demand-bridge facilities being provided at the other end of the spectrum.

In the face of global uncertainty, we continue to witness positive momentum and an increasing awareness of the potential of the fund finance market. Almost all lenders have dedicated fund finance teams that review, promote, sell, lead or participate in capital call financings (and related fund finance products) within the Canadian market. Furthermore, the size and number of venture capital funds continue to increase, thereby creating further demand for this product – and that, in our view, generally bodes well for the market here in Canada.

* * *

Note

At this time, we do not have access to year-end industry statistics.

Michael Henriques
Tel: +1 416 361 2355 / Email: michael.henriques@dentons.com

Michael Henriques is a partner in Dentons' Banking and Finance group in Toronto. He represents both domestic and international financial institutions and borrowers, with a greater focus on lender-side work. His practice covers all areas of financial services with a particular focus on sponsor/fund finance transactions (including capital call, NAV, manager/employee programme and acquisition financings). His practice also involves negotiation of complex intercreditor or sharing arrangements on hybrid facilities and split collateral structures. First recognised in 2018, Michael has been commended for his extensive knowledge and experience in a variety of respected publications, including:

- *The Legal 500 Canada*: Banking & Finance.
- *Chambers Canada*: Ranked as a Leading Lawyer in Banking & Finance 2023 edition.
- *Best Lawyers in Canada*: Banking and Finance Law; Asset-Based Lending Practice.
- *Canadian Legal Lexpert Directory* – Repeatedly Recommended: Banking and Financial Institutions.
- *IFLR1000*: The Guide to the World's Leading Financial Law Firms – Leading Lawyers: Banking and Finance.

Alexandra North
Tel: +1 416 863 4412 / Email: alexandra.north@dentons.com

Alex North is a partner in Dentons' Banking and Finance group in Toronto. With more than 13 years' experience, Alex represents domestic and international financial institutions and borrowers, with an emphasis on lender-side work. Her practice encompasses all areas of financial services, including real estate, cross-border, cashflow, construction, syndicated, condo and sponsor/fund financings (including subscription and acquisition facilities). She regularly acts as Canadian counsel on complex cross-border fund financing transactions. Alex has been recognised by the *Canadian Legal Lexpert Directory* – Repeatedly Recommended: Banking and Financial Institutions since 2020 and by *Best Lawyers* – Banking and Finance Law since 2022.

Kenneth D. Kraft
Tel: +1 416 863 4374 / Email: kenneth.kraft@dentons.com

Ken Kraft is a partner in Dentons' Banking and Finance group and leads Dentons' Toronto insolvency team. He focuses his practice on insolvency and finance, both secured and unsecured. Acting for lenders as well as borrowers, his expertise encompasses receiverships, informal work-outs and all manner of restructurings under the Companies' Creditors Arrangement Act and the Bankruptcy and Insolvency Act. He is recommended as a leading insolvency practitioner for Canada in the *Restructuring and Insolvency Handbook* of the *Global Counsel Handbook* series and has been listed as a leading lawyer in restructuring and insolvency in editions of *Chambers Global (Canada)*, *Best Lawyers in Canada*, the *Canadian Legal Lexpert Directory* and *The Legal 500 Canada* since 2010.

Dentons Canada LLP
77 King Street West, Suite 400, Toronto, Ontario M5K 0A1, Canada
Tel: +1 416 863 4511 / Fax: +1 416 863 4592 / URL: www.dentons.com

Cayman Islands

Simon Raftopoulos & Georgina Pullinger
Appleby

Overview

The year to date could perhaps be described as a bit of a rollercoaster for the finance markets, with a record-breaking start that then veered into significant macroeconomic and geopolitical headwinds as the year progressed. Despite the recent economic uncertainty, however, the global fund finance market has generally remained extremely active and has had another successful year so far, with the Cayman Islands fund finance market reflecting that trend.

Cayman has seen significant private equity activity throughout 2022, with large numbers of fund formations and general transactional activity, although, unsurprisingly, not at the same record-breaking numbers of 2021. New fund finance facilities involving Cayman vehicles continued to increase throughout the first half of 2022 and although this slowed coming out of the end of Q3, it has still been a generally impressive year for the Cayman fund finance market, which has also been bolstered by ongoing amendments and joinders.

From a Cayman perspective, we have seen that growth in the fund finance market over the past few years was driven in part by the continued expansion of the product into a broader range of fund types, increasing take-up by fund sponsors who had not traditionally used the product in their fund families and also increasing numbers of net asset value (**NAV**), hybrid, general partner (**GP**) and separately managed account (**SMA**) facilities. It is apparent that as the demands and needs of sponsors and funds have diversified, lenders have become more innovative and specialised in their approach. While some established banks are coming up against capital and balance sheet constraints, we are seeing an increase in the role of the mid-cap lenders, while non-bank lenders, including insurance companies and private credit funds, have also increased their presence in the market, helping to meet the ongoing mismatch between supply and demand for capital this year.

The Cayman Islands continues to be a pre-eminent offshore jurisdiction for the establishment of private equity funds, having previously been named "Best Private Equity Fund Domicile" by industry publication *Private Equity Wire*. The exempted limited partnership (**ELP**) continues to be the private equity fund vehicle of choice. According to figures published by the Cayman Islands Registry of Exempted Limited Partnerships, 2021 saw 5,778 new ELPs registered in the Cayman Islands, bringing the total number of active ELPs as at the end of 2021 to 34,343, which is a 10% increase on 2020. As at the end of Q3 2022, a total of 15,662 private funds were registered with the Cayman Islands Monetary Authority (**CIMA**) under the Private Funds Act (please refer below to "Ongoing considerations and key developments – The Cayman Islands Private Funds Act" for further details).

No doubt buoyed by the familiarity of US counsel and fund managers with Delaware limited liability companies (**LLCs**), the use of the Cayman LLC as a business vehicle has generally been on the rise since its introduction in July 2016. According to figures published by the Cayman Islands Companies Registry, there are around 4,400 active LLCs registered to date in the Cayman Islands. The success of the Cayman LLC can, at least in part, be attributed to the decision by legislators, in collaboration with the private sector, to introduce a vehicle that is similar to the Delaware LLC. Familiarity with this type of vehicle facilitates usage and offers the benefit of operational consistencies across the onshore and offshore segments of fund structures. Cayman LLCs are most commonly used as joint venture vehicles, carried interest vehicles, downstream blockers, and investment management vehicles. We are also aware that a handful of Cayman LLCs have been used as investor-facing fund vehicles, including by Asia-based fund managers.

Successful public and private sector consultation and collaboration are but two of the factors contributing to Cayman's market-leading position in this space. Others include: (i) investors' and fund sponsors' historical familiarity with the jurisdiction; (ii) the increasing convergence of hedge fund and private equity sectors, as more fund managers offer and operate both products from the same platform; and (iii) Cayman law's English common law roots, supplemented, as necessary, by local legislation, which ensures that Cayman Islands funds are recognised as internationally accepted vehicles.

Fund formation and finance

Lending to Cayman Islands funds

Cayman Islands private equity funds have historically been registered as ELPs under the Exempted Limited Partnership Act, as amended (**ELP Act**), particularly for the North American and European markets. The appeal of this type of entity is often the ability to provide operational consistencies as between the offshore fund vehicles and their equivalent onshore counterparts (often, Delaware or Luxembourg limited partnerships). The Cayman LLC, registered under the Limited Liability Companies Act, as amended (**LLC Act**), is a hybrid form of business vehicle, merging certain characteristics of a Cayman Islands exempted company and an ELP. The LLC has been an appealing alternative for general partner, upper tier, manager and co-investment vehicles. Cayman Islands exempted companies are also occasionally used as investment vehicles, although, given their corporate structure, they are more commonly used as general partner, manager, blocker or holding vehicles.

Though registered pursuant to the ELP Act, an ELP is not a separate legal entity. Rather, an ELP reflects a contractual agreement between the partners, where the general partner is vested with certain duties and powers with respect to the ELP's business and assets. Any rights and obligations of the general partner and the limited partners are therefore contractual in nature and will be governed by the provisions of the limited partnership agreement (**LPA**) and any subscription agreements (and/or side letters). The ELP's rights and property of every description, including all choses in action and any right to make capital calls and to receive the proceeds thereof, are held by the general partner in trust as an asset of the ELP. A Cayman LLC, on the other hand, is a body corporate with separate legal personality and limited liability. It can therefore hold such property and assets and incur obligations and liabilities in its own name.

The legal treatment of an ELP and the corresponding role of the general partner have a number of implications for lenders offering subscription credit facilities (**Subscription Facilities**) to Cayman Islands vehicles when structuring the related security package.

Limited partners of an ELP will usually commit in the LPA and/or subscription agreement to fund investments or to repay fund expenses when called upon to do so by the general partner from time to time. This contractual obligation of a limited partner to fund capital, to the extent that it has not already been called (**Uncalled Capital**), and the corresponding rights of the ELP to call for Uncalled Capital (**Capital Call Rights**), are the backbone of Subscription Facilities. Given that these rights, or choses in action, are contractual in nature, the appropriate form of Cayman law security over such rights is an assignment by way of security. As discussed above, legal title to such assets ultimately vests in the general partner of the ELP and, being contractual in nature, such rights are exercisable by the general partner for the benefit of the ELP. Consequently, the proper parties to any grant of security in a Subscription Facility are the general partner as well as the ELP (acting through the general partner), as the beneficial owner of such assets.

Where the obligor in a Subscription Facility is a Cayman LLC, however, legal title to Uncalled Capital and to Capital Call Rights should vest in the Cayman LLC itself, with the manager (or managing member, if applicable) having such power and authority as set out in the LLC Agreement to make calls for Uncalled Capital and to receive capital contributions from the members in accordance with the terms of their subscription agreements. The LLC Act allows considerable flexibility in the structuring, governance and administration of the Cayman LLC, as it defers in many instances to the LLC Agreement. Members of a Cayman LLC will therefore have relative freedom to introduce features typically associated with ELPs such as capital accounts, capital commitments and capital calls, provided that the provisions of the LLC Agreement do not contravene the LLC Act or any other laws of the Cayman Islands. Each member of the Cayman LLC will also typically enter into a subscription agreement, setting out the terms on which it agrees to be a member, and to fund its capital commitment to the Cayman LLC.

In all instances, the optimal security package would incorporate (i) an express irrevocable power of attorney in favour of the lender to exercise effectively the general partner's or the Cayman LLC's Capital Call Rights following the occurrence of an event of default, and (ii) the grant of a security interest over a designated bank account under the control of the lender.

Although the security over Capital Call Rights can be granted under a Cayman law document, the governing law of the security will generally depend on the market practice of the jurisdiction of the main transaction documents; for example, in facilities governed by English law, it is customary to enter into a separate Cayman law security agreement creating security over such collateral, whereas it is unusual to take additional Cayman law security in the US fund finance market, where facilities generally rely on security governed by the relevant US law. Assuming that the grant of security is permitted under the Cayman law-governed LPA or the LLC Agreement (as applicable), Cayman courts would recognise the grant of security even if such security were granted under a foreign law-governed security agreement. In such a situation, the lender will need to ensure that the local law opinion covers not only the assignability of the Capital Call Rights, as a matter of Cayman law, but also the recognition of the security assignment, the choice of foreign law to govern the same, and the steps taken to establish priority as a matter of Cayman law.

The terms of the LPA or the LLC Agreement (as applicable) play an integral role in the structuring of the Subscription Facility collateral package and must be reviewed in detail in order to ensure that a number of key elements are present, including but not limited to: (i) the ability of the ELP or the Cayman LLC to incur indebtedness and enter into the transaction; (ii) the ability to grant security over (x) the Uncalled Capital, (y) the Capital Call Rights, and

(z) the related contributions; (iii) the ability to apply the capital contributions towards the secured obligations; (iv) the ability to call on non-defaulting investors to make up a shortfall in the event that an investor defaults on a capital call; and (v) acknowledgment by the limited partners of the ELP or the members of the Cayman LLC that such security assignment is permitted and confirmation of their obligation to fund their capital commitments without set-off, counterclaim or defence.

Perfection of security

As a general rule, no perfection steps are required in the Cayman Islands, except with respect to land located in the Cayman Islands, vessels flagged in the Cayman Islands, Cayman Islands-registered aircraft and interests of limited partners in an ELP or members of an LLC in the LLC. There is also no general register of security interests in the Cayman Islands accessible to the public.

Perfection (by which we mean, in this instance, that security interests over the encumbered property will be enforceable as against third parties claiming to have a security interest in the same property) and priority over the Capital Call Rights are achieved through the delivery of written notice of the grant of security (**Notice**) to the ELP's limited partners or the members of the Cayman LLC. Where a security interest is granted over Capital Call Rights set forth in a Cayman law-governed LPA or LLC Agreement, priority of the security interest as against any competing security interest will be determined in accordance with Cayman Islands law. As a matter of Cayman Islands law, where successive assignments of a chose in action are concerned, priority as between creditors is determined based on the English court decision in *Dearle v Hall* (1828) 3 Russ 1, according to the order in which written Notice is given to a third-party obligor (i.e. the limited partners of an ELP or the members of a Cayman LLC). Priority is not established in accordance with the time of creation of the relevant security interests. Delay in the delivery of the Notice will therefore expose the lender to the risk that the Cayman LLC, or a general partner on behalf of the ELP, may (quite unintentionally) subsequently grant a competing security interest or an absolute assignment over Capital Call Rights to another secured party; if Notice of the second security interest is given to the investors ahead of Notice of the first security interest, the subsequent secured party will rank for repayment ahead of the first secured party.

Investors in Cayman Islands funds are increasingly aware of Subscription Facilities, with sponsors and lenders alike agreeing that investors should expect transparency insofar as the use of subscription lines by fund managers is concerned. Familiarity with the product means that there is now far less resistance from funds to giving Notice to investors. In addition, a general "tightening up" by lenders of certain aspects of their facilities has led to less flexibility around timing for delivery of Notices, which are typically circulated to the investors either immediately upon execution of the security documents, in order to ensure that priority is achieved at closing of the Subscription Facility, or within three to five business days of closing, depending on the commercial agreement between the parties.

Given the importance of actual delivery of the Notice to investors, evidence of the Notice having been received also assumes some importance. With advances in the technology of delivery of Notices and reports to investors, such as posting to secure web portals and other similar platforms, the discussion of the appropriate evidence of delivery of such Notices becomes crucial. If the applicable LPA or LLC Agreement specifically contemplates how Notices are actually delivered to investors, then this may prove helpful to the discussion. Where LPAs or LLC Agreements include provisions that specify the circumstances in which Notices delivered in accordance with their terms are "deemed" to have been received by the investors, a lender might take some comfort in proof of delivery of the Notices in accordance with the provisions of such LPA or LLC Agreement, rather than proof of receipt by way of a signed acknowledgment by the investors. In all cases, the recommendation would be that the general partner of the ELP, or an authorised person on behalf of the Cayman LLC, sign and deliver the Notices to the investors in accordance with the provisions of the LPA or the LLC Agreement governing service of Notices on the investors, with a copy delivered to the lender.

Apart from establishing priority, delivery of a Notice to investors of an assignment of Capital Call Rights has certain other distinct advantages. Firstly, service of the Notice prevents investors from obtaining good discharge for their obligations to fund their Uncalled Capital in any manner other than as specifically indicated in the Notice. Once Notice has been delivered to each investor, indicating that investors are to make all payments with respect to Uncalled Capital into a designated lender-controlled account, the investors will not be in a position to discharge their obligations to make such payments in any other manner.

Service of the Notice also prevents set-offs from arising after the date of service of such Notice. This rationale is based on the common law principle that set-off works between the same parties in the same right. If there is Notice to one party of the assignment of a right to a third party (i.e. a lender), set-off will no longer operate in the same manner. The service of Notice on investors does not, however, have the same effect with respect to claims that might have arisen prior to the date of service of the Notice. Most LPAs, LLC Agreements and/or the accompanying subscription documents will now incorporate express waivers on the part of investors confirming that they will not rely on any right of set-off in order to reduce their obligations to fund their Uncalled Capital when called by a lender to repay a Subscription Facility. Usefully, these contractual waivers survive the insolvency of the ELP or the LLC, as the case may be, as the insolvency provisions of the Cayman Islands Companies Act (which apply to ELPs by virtue of section 36 of the ELP Act and to Cayman LLCs by virtue of section 36 of the LLC Act) expressly provide that the collection in and application of property on the insolvency of a company (or partnership, as the case may be) is without prejudice to and after taking into account, and giving effect to, any contractual rights of set-off or netting of claims between the entity and any persons, and subject to any agreement between the entity and any persons to waive or limit the same. As a final point, the Notice also serves as an important informational tool insofar as investors are concerned. Once an investor has taken delivery of the Notice, it becomes more difficult for that investor to challenge the enforceability of a capital call (made in a facility default scenario) based on a lack of knowledge or awareness of the existence of the Subscription Facility.

Although there is no public registry relating to the grant of capital call security in Cayman, the Companies Act requires exempted companies and Cayman LLCs to enter particulars of all security created over their assets (wherever located) in a register of mortgages and charges (**ROMC**) maintained at their registered office. Importantly, the statute does not aim to impose perfection requirements and failure to enter such particulars will not invalidate the security; however, exempted companies and Cayman LLCs are expected to comply with the requirement, and failure to do so will expose such companies to a statutory penalty.

While there is no corresponding requirement for an ELP to maintain an ROMC with respect to security over its assets, where the general partner of an ELP is a Cayman Islands exempted company or a Cayman LLC, then (i) the general partner is required to update its ROMC with details of security granted in its own right, and (ii) it is advisable for the general partner to update its ROMC with details of the security granted on behalf of the Cayman ELP. In practice, this puts any person inspecting the ROMC on notice as to the existence of the security.

Ongoing considerations and key developments

The Cayman Islands Private Funds Act

The Private Funds Act, as amended (**PF Act**), came into force on 7 February 2020 and created an entirely new regulatory regime for private investment funds. Although investors and lenders alike are fairly familiar with the PF Act by now, given its significance, it is worth revisiting the applicable requirements and impact on a Subscription Facility. As an indication of the significant reach of the PF Act on the Cayman private equity market, 15,662 private funds were registered with CIMA as at the end of Q3 2022.

The PF Act applies to any "private fund" carrying on business in or from the Cayman Islands other than a mutual fund or an EU-connected fund regulated under the Mutual Funds Act. The PF Act defines a "private fund" as a company, unit trust or partnership that offers or issues or has issued investment interests, the purpose or effect of which is the pooling of investor funds with the aim of enabling investors to receive profits or gains from such entity's acquisition, holding, management or disposal of investments, where:

1. the holders of investment interests do not have day-to-day control over the acquisition, holding, management or disposal of the investments; and
2. the investments are managed as a whole, by or on behalf of the operator of the private fund, directly or indirectly,

but a "private fund" does not include:

1. a person licensed under the Banks and Trust Companies Act (2021 Revision) or the Insurance Act 2010 (which can be searched on the CIMA online database at https://www.cima.ky/search-entities);
2. a person registered under the Building Societies Act (2020 Revision) or the Friendly Societies Act (1998 Revision); or
3. any non-fund arrangements.

Single investor funds are out of scope and are therefore not required to register. Non-fund arrangements such as joint ventures, pension funds, holding vehicles and securitisation special purpose vehicles are expressly excluded from the ambit of the regime. Following certain legislative updates, Cayman Islands alternative investment vehicles may be relieved from the burden of certain provisions associated with registration as a private fund.

All private funds must apply to be registered with CIMA within 21 days after accepting capital commitments from investors. Failure to register within such time exposes the fund to an administrative penalty. Significantly for Subscription Facilities, an in-scope fund must be registered by CIMA before it accepts capital contributions for investments, which is obviously of primary importance for the security package of a Subscription Facility. The PF Act facility language has, for the most part, settled down and market positions in relation to conditions precedent, covenants and events of default have emerged.

An issue that is still arising now is one of timing, in the situation where a Cayman fund is not PF Act-registered with CIMA by the time the sponsor wishes it to join a facility. This has led, in some instances, to closings being delayed until the applicable private fund is registered or, more frequently, the exclusion of such fund from the initial closing or borrowing base, to be subsequently added once CIMA registration has occurred; however, given that CIMA continues to process PF Act registrations efficiently and that its website is regularly updated to demonstrate evidence of registration (although there have still been some delays with receiving the PF Act certificates of registration), we are not seeing many significant transaction delays resulting from delayed PF Act registration.

Economic substance regime

The Cayman Islands introduced the International Tax Co-Operation (Economic Substance) Act, as revised (**ES Act**) in January 2019. The ES Act requires certain "relevant entities" incorporated or registered in the Cayman Islands, and carrying on any "relevant activity", to demonstrate that they have "adequate substance" in the Cayman Islands. Such entities will be subject to administrative penalties and, ultimately, strike-off for failure to comply.

At the time that the economic substance regime was initially implemented, "relevant entities" were: (i) Cayman companies (including exempted companies and LLCs); (ii) limited liability partnerships; and (iii) non-Cayman companies that are registered in Cayman (which would include a foreign company that acts as a general partner of an ELP), but *exclude* (x) investment funds, and (y) entities that are tax-resident outside of the Cayman Islands. As a result of the International Tax Co-Operation (Economic Substance) (Amendment of Schedule) Regulations 2021, which came into force on 21 June 2021, the category of relevant entities was expanded to include, *inter alia*, limited partnerships and foreign limited partnerships registered in the Cayman Islands. While all "relevant entities" are required to declare their ES Act status in their annual filing, only those entities that are carrying on "relevant activities" are required to comply with economic substance requirements.

The ES Act lists nine "relevant activities", the most relevant for these purposes being "holding company business" and "fund management business".

Cayman corporate blocker entities or corporate vehicles that are not classified as investment funds and not otherwise tax-resident outside of the Cayman Islands will be subject to the ES Act. A corporate vehicle carrying on "holding company business", which is defined as "pure equity holding business" – i.e. only holding equity participations in other entities and only earning dividends and capital gains – is in scope, but is subject to a reduced economic substance test. In practice, this should be met by its ongoing compliance with existing statutory obligations. Compliance by other relevant entities should, however, be initially assessed by lenders' counsel, and all corporate vehicles should be monitored on an ongoing basis to ensure continued compliance with the ES Act.

A foreign corporate or foreign limited partnership general partner registered in the Cayman Islands would be considered a "relevant entity", but would not likely be carrying out a "relevant activity" such as "fund management business" (except in unusual situations). As such, while it would need to declare its status in its annual filing, it would not otherwise be subject to any economic substance requirements.

Beneficial ownership registration regime

Cayman companies and Cayman LLCs are required to maintain registers of beneficial ownership at their registered offices, pursuant to legislation that came into force on 1 July 2017 (as amended, **Beneficial Ownership Regime**). As a result, barring any applicable exemptions, in-scope companies must take "reasonable steps" to identify individuals qualifying as "beneficial owners" or corporate vehicles qualifying as "relevant legal entities". Beneficial owners are those individuals who hold: (i) directly or indirectly, 25% or more of the shares, Cayman LLC interests or voting rights in the company; or (ii) the right to appoint or remove a majority of the board of directors or managers of the company. If no individual meets these conditions, the Beneficial Ownership Regime looks to those persons who directly or indirectly exercise significant influence or control over the company through direct or indirect ownership or interests. Generally, "relevant legal entities" are intermediate holding companies registered in the Cayman Islands through which beneficial owners hold their registrable interests. Subsequent amendments to the Beneficial Ownership

Regime added certain exemptions that broadly seek to exempt entities already subject to a certain level of regulatory oversight (e.g. certain regulated or licensed entities) and any company that claims such an exemption must provide its corporate services provider with written confirmation of the exemption relied on.

The potential significance of the Beneficial Ownership Regime for lenders in a financing transaction lies in the possible consequences to a "registrable person" in the case of its non-compliance with a request for beneficial ownership information. If an in-scope company fails to maintain the register or keep it up to date, its corporate services provider is required to issue to the company a notice requiring compliance. If the information requested is not received within one month of receipt of the notice, the corporate services provider must issue to the registrable person whose particulars are missing a "restrictions notice" in respect of the relevant interest held by that person. Subject to that person's right to apply to court to object to any restrictions imposed, until the restrictions notice is withdrawn by the corporate services provider or ceased by court order, any transfer or agreement to transfer the interest is void, no rights are exercisable in respect of the interest and, except in liquidation, no payment may be made in respect of the interest.

Given that: (i) the Beneficial Ownership Regime currently applies only to Cayman companies, LLCs and limited liability partnerships (and not to ELPs) and only where an exemption is not applicable; (ii) regulated investment funds and funds (including private equity funds) having a manager or administrator who is regulated in Cayman or in an equivalent legislation jurisdiction (i.e. designated as having measures for combatting money laundering and the financing of terrorism that are equivalent to those of the Cayman Islands) remain outside the scope of the Beneficial Ownership Regime; and (iii) a restrictions notice may not be served in respect of an interest that is subject to the security interest of an arm's length security holder, the enforceability of an unaffiliated lender's security package in a Subscription Facility should remain relatively unaffected by the Beneficial Ownership Regime. Lenders should, however, be aware of any possible consequences that may be applicable to in-scope companies in the context of the wider fund structure (e.g. an in-scope downstream entity), particularly given the more diversified security packages that we are currently seeing.

The Beneficial Ownership Regime reflects the Cayman Islands' commitment to help combat tax evasion, terrorist financing, money laundering and other serious and organised crimes, by providing greater transparency on beneficial owners.

The year ahead

The forecast for the fund finance market over the coming year remains cautiously optimistic, and, given the ability of top US-based sponsors to raise money from institutional investors based in the US, we anticipate that the North American market will continue to dominate. Cayman will remain relevant for North American and Asia-focused funds, in particular, while continuing to be a popular jurisdiction for UK managers establishing offshore funds with a transatlantic nexus.

We anticipate that the types of financing and the purposes for which financing is used will continue to diversify in 2023 and we expect that lenders and sponsors alike will continue to increase their focus on more bespoke fund finance solutions, including NAV, hybrid and management fee facilities. The historically strong credit performance and relatively low-risk profile of the subscription product will continue to make it attractive for lenders, although we note that being "selective" seems to be the current theme in a capital-constrained environment, which may, in turn, impact pricing, availability and facility sizes (leading to further opportunity for non-bank lenders). ESG will remain a focus for investors, sponsors and lenders alike, and we are interested to see the new approaches that will come out of the increase in ESG-focused facilities.

The fund finance market will continue to be bolstered by strong collaborative relationships between lenders and fund sponsors, and the Cayman market will continue its track record of being ever willing to evolve and adapt to meet the requirements and expectations of our onshore counterparts.

We expect Cayman to maintain its position as the principal offshore fund jurisdiction, for reasons including the range of vehicles that can be utilised to meet a fund's structuring requirements, investor familiarity with the jurisdiction and a proportionate and adaptive regulatory framework. There are certainly many unknowns and potential headwinds going into the next year; however, given the popularity of Cayman as a fund jurisdiction, as well as the ever-increasing size and innovative capabilities of the industry, we remain cautiously optimistic that 2023 will be another busy year in the Cayman fund finance market.

Simon Raftopoulos
Tel: +1 345 814 2748 / Email: sraftopoulos@applebyglobal.com

Simon Raftopoulos is the Local Corporate Practice Group Head in the Cayman Islands and a member of the Corporate Finance and Private Equity teams.

He represents clients in a wide variety of corporate finance transactions, including private equity and fund finance, joint ventures, mergers, acquisitions, leveraged buyouts, initial and secondary public offerings and private placements of equity and debt securities. Simon also represents clients on large private equity transactions and his team has a deep PE formation and transactional presence in Cayman.

Simon is currently recognised by *Who's Who Legal* 2022 as one of the world's leading banking and M&A lawyers and is named in the *Asia Business Law Journal*'s A-List of top 50 offshore lawyers. Since 2012, he has consistently been ranked and is highly regarded globally across many leading legal directories. *Chambers Global* reported that clients laud him for his skills and describe him as "…extremely supportive, responsive and always provides sound guidance on all manner of things" as well as being "…practical and creative".

Georgina Pullinger
Tel: +1 345 814 2089 / Email: gpullinger@applebyglobal.com

Georgina Pullinger is a Partner within the Corporate Practice Group, who specialises in banking and finance and general corporate matters. She has extensive experience in all aspects of finance transactions, with a particular focus on fund finance and corporate finance, and represents leading financial institutions and private equity funds on lending transactions, deal structures and on all types of secured transactions. Georgina also advises on a wide range of general corporate and commercial matters.

Georgina is currently ranked by *The Legal 500* as a "Next Generation Partner – Banking, Finance & Capital Markets" for 2023 and previously ranked as a "Rising Star" (2020, 2021 and 2022).

Appleby
71 Fort Street, George Town, Grand Cayman KY1-1104, Cayman Islands
Tel: +1 345 949 4900 / URL: www.applebyglobal.com

England & Wales

Sam Hutchinson & Nathan Parker
Cadwalader, Wickersham & Taft LLP

Summary

What makes a fund finance transaction "English"?

There are a number of features of a fund finance transaction that can give it a significant nexus to England & Wales, including:
- the facility agreement being governed by English law;
- a lender or the arranger being incorporated in, operating from, or leading the transaction from England & Wales;
- the fund manager or fund vehicle being formed, incorporated in or operating from England & Wales (usually as an English limited partnership);
- one or more investors being domiciled in England & Wales; or
- particularly in the case of net asset value (NAV)-based facilities, the assets being located in England & Wales.

In practice, it is the first two of these factors that most clearly define a fund finance transaction as "English", and it is the market of transactions with those two features that this chapter is chiefly focused on. However, these transactions are rarely domestic in nature. The location of the fund manager and investors varies significantly from transaction to transaction, and the fund vehicles used in these transactions are often domiciled in other jurisdictions, as explained in more detail below. Fund financiers operating from other jurisdictions (such as continental Europe and Asia) also use English law to govern some of their facilities, and so commentary below on English contractual matters is also potentially relevant to fund finance transactions that are not, in other respects, strictly "English".

When and why did the English fund finance market develop?

Outside North America, England & Wales is the most mature fund finance market, having its genesis in the early 2000s. The main drivers for its initial development were:
- a growing need and desire for fund-level liquidity from (principally) private equity managers; and
- the close relationship between the small group of financial institutions that first began to provide these types of products and the end-user private equity managers (sometimes in an investor capacity), giving them access to fund-level information essential for the assessment of the credit quality of the collateral underpinning the financing.

While many very large transactions were being carried out at this time (generally bilaterally), the size of the market was comparatively small as a result of:
- a limited number of financial institutions offering this type of product and offering it as a relationship-enhancing product in conjunction with more traditional credit lines, such as portfolio company leverage; and

- a limited number of fund managers being considered an appropriate user of this type of financing – typically top-quartile European and global private markets managers with high-quality, diversified investor bases and underlying assets, and proven track records.

How has the English fund finance market faired in 2022?

In previous editions, this chapter considered the impact of the pandemic and its related supply chain issues on the fund finance market in Europe, and we discussed how favourably the markets had responded, showing a resilience and sophistication that allowed sponsors to tap into the liquidity they needed at that time. 2022 has seen that resilience continue in the face of energy, war and inflation crises. During 2022, we have continued to advise on a multitude of subscription, umbrella, hybrid, general partner (GP), co-invest, back-levered, NAV and preferred equity financings, allowing us to observe and participate in the "bedding-in" of the more sophisticated market that developed during 2020–2021. We have been involved in some of the largest subscription facilities to come to the market and some of the most structured and complex NAV and preferred equity-based financings.

The main drivers of growth in the fund finance market in England have traditionally been:
- an increasing number of financial institutions, insurance companies and asset managers with capital to deploy looking to these products to deliver attractive risk-adjusted returns and, in the case of financial institutions, to facilitate a wider and deeper relationship with private markets fund managers;
- the attractiveness of the "low default" record of these transactions;
- as the products have become better understood and more widely used and recognised, a greater willingness and appetite to make these products available to managers across all asset classes, sizes and jurisdictions across Europe (including Germany, Spain and Italy) where English law generally remains the governing law of the financing;
- an increase in the prevalence of different types of fund finance products as alluded to above, including an increase in the number of GP/exec. financings, umbrella and co-invest facilities and separately managed account (SMA) financings and the continued development of preferred equity and NAV financings; and
- the desire of fund managers to use fund finance products to facilitate the use of their dry powder capital as efficiently as possible, with an intelligent use of fund finance facilities providing a competitive edge.

Looking at these drivers, it becomes clear why the fund finance market has again out-performed itself in 2022. Some key observations regarding the development of the market over 2022 are as follows:
- **Market players**. The interest of non-bank lenders in fund finance products has continued to grow during 2022 and in many respects is one of its most defining features. Preferred equity financings in Europe are now (and have been since the first few months of the year) regularly funded by syndicates composed entirely of non-bank lenders, and with the increase in syndication for these products we have seen lenders focus in on their voting rights and minority protections with increased scrutiny.

  Another significant development is the interest being shown by LP investors in participating in the preferred equity/NAV part of the fund's capital structure – are these the new co-invest opportunities perhaps? The inviting coupon coupled with the fact that the investor is already well versed in the underlying assets provides a compelling proposition. This can cause some tension with the "unaffiliated" lenders in the syndicate (due to a perceived conflict position for the LP investor as lender), which again gives rise to intercreditor and voting considerations that are not the usual staple of fund finance.

- **Developments in subscription facilities**. After the reversal of any pandemic-related upward swing in pricing during 2021, as 2022 draws to a close we are again seeing pricing beginning to increase as a result of global uncertainties and liquidity constraints. It will be interesting to see what 2023 will hold in terms of pricing.
- **ESG**. The ESG market now seems to have reached a level of understanding with respect to ESG metrics and mechanics and 2022 has continued to see ESG feature in a large number of deals, with certain banks stepping forward into a role of ESG Co-ordinator or ESG Agent, to represent the lenders in negotiations to agree suitable key performance indicators and reporting given the underlying business. We expect to see ESG receiving increased focus from lenders, funds and investors during 2023.
- **Developments in NAV and pref. products**. 2022 brought with it new and interesting preferred equity structures that top-tier European private equity sponsors employed to leverage their portfolios. These financings are highly structured and heavily negotiated by the participants. Will 2023 see these structures employed by mid-market funds as well? Time will tell, but we expect to see increased interest in these products from both the non-bank lenders providing the credit and the funds keen to lock in liquidity ahead of possibly turbulent times.
- **GP and co-invest financings**. GP financing activity remained at more normal levels this year, but there is clearly an increased demand for these products that non-banks are beginning to fill. Interestingly, this year the largest GP financing we closed was originated and underwritten solely by a non-bank. The trend toward platform-wide (multi-vintage) financings unsurprisingly continued and, given market conditions, we expect to see activity increase next year.
- **Single account financings**. We reported over the last few editions of an increase in the number of single account financings from the levels of previous years and this continued, perhaps to a slightly lesser extent, in 2022. Given the increased prevalence of these deals over recent years, as managers have looked to meet the needs of investors that want to deploy their investment through a segregated account, and as lenders have become increasingly comfortable with the concentration issues that arise on these deals, this increase in deal numbers may well have occurred anyway. But, at a time when fundraising faces potential challenges due to global financial pressures, SMAs continue to provide a useful solution both for managers keen to maintain and grow fee revenue, and for investors looking to deploy capital with managers that may be delayed in their usual fundraising programmes. The trend toward "near-SMA" deals that we saw in 2020/2021 (i.e., deals with two or three investors, not strictly a single-asset deal but having a sufficient lack of investor diversity for similar principles to apply) continued in 2022, with many of these deals involving continuation vehicles or vehicles to bring increased liquidity into structures involving mature funds in the later stages of their investment and divestment cycle. We have continued to see an increased focus on not just investor letters (creating a direct relationship between the lender and the investor), but on lenders tracking through the investor holding company structure and requiring this comfort to come from the money vehicle behind the investor (where the investor on record is a special purpose vehicle).

Subscription finance structures

In the past, subscription credit facilities advanced against diversified limited partner pools have been the most prevalent product in the English fund finance market. The product has developed over time to become far more sophisticated, both because of the natural development and deepening of the market and because managers are increasingly looking to their subscription credit line to do more and more things. Gone are the days when there was a straightforward revolving credit line; subscription facilities now allow for letters of credit, bilateral ancillary facilities, swing-lines, portfolio-level borrowings, separate feeder and parallel-level borrowings, secured hedging and umbrella arrangements for commonly managed funds – to name just a few of the features that managers now expect to see. As subscription facilities retain such a prominent position in the market, it is worth looking at some of the key areas of development:

- **Secured or unsecured**. Prior to the global financial crisis, many subscription line facilities in the English market were provided on an unsecured, uncommitted basis with a security power of attorney often being the only piece of (quasi-) security taken by the lenders. The rationale for this was:
  - the market at this point comprised only very high-quality, experienced private markets managers with whom lenders had close institutional relationships;
  - importantly, the terms of the facilities precluded any other indebtedness within any fund vehicle sitting between the lender and the lender's ultimate source of repayment, i.e., the contractually committed and uncalled capital of the investors and very often, the underlying assets of the fund as well;
  - these facilities were niche bespoke products at that time and, whilst the fund documentation expressly contemplated the fund having the power to borrow, the security package that is now widely accepted as a staple part of these transactions was often not expressly contemplated;
  - these transactions were accompanied by a legal opinion from the fund's counsel confirming that the lender's claims under the finance documents ranked ahead of the claims of the investors (being the only other potential "creditors" of the fund); and
  - utilisation of these facilities was largely short term, so the periods during which lenders were on risk was generally less than one year.

  As the market has grown and developed, with the funds using fund finance products no longer having these relationships or features, so the emphasis on security has become greater, such that we now rarely see unsecured lines.

  We have also seen an acceptance by sponsors (and a raised awareness of lenders as to the importance) of properly perfecting security prior to the first utilisation of the facility. Investor notices are now rarely provided any length of time after closing, but we now generally expect to see that evidence of delivery of investor notices is required if not on the closing date then as a condition to the initial drawdown. We have also seen a trend toward the more formal agreements with English account banks that we were previously more accustomed to seeing where the account bank was in a continental jurisdiction such as Luxembourg or in the US (where there would be a deposit account control agreement).

- **Committed *versus* uncommitted**. Historically, many subscription line facilities were structured on an uncommitted basis, enabling lenders to benefit from favourable regulatory capital treatment under UK regulation. Private markets managers using these facilities had done so on a regular basis for many years and took comfort from their experience with the lenders providing uncommitted facilities over this time that they would not be withdrawn without serious cause. The size of these facilities ran into the hundreds of millions, if not billions, and the savings made by private markets managers on commitment fees were considerable, particularly given that, historically, these facilities tended not to be heavily drawn. We still see a number of uncommitted transactions (or transactions with an uncommitted element) in the English market, but as the market has opened up to new entrants, some managers have become less confident with uncommitted lines and many banks now do not have the ability to provide such lines. However, we are seeing an increasing use of uncommitted facilities to facilitate non-bank money into the subscription facility market, e.g., insurance companies.

- **Side letters.** As a result of fund finance facilities becoming better understood and more widely used across the private markets, the use of debt by fund managers has become a focal point for investors when negotiating the limited partnership agreement and side letters and we are seeing side letter arrangements become more bespoke and detailed (and longer), including with respect to provisions that relate to, restrict and otherwise impact on a manager's use of subscription lines. We are increasingly seeing restrictions around who can serve drawdown notices on investors and restrictions on the amount that can be called from investors by lenders providing subscription lines, including some provisions that may seem innocuous but that may have a material impact on a lender's recovery. There is also an increasing trend to include requirements for the delivery of information to investors together with a capital call notice, which raises practical questions as to how a lender will be able to obtain and deliver such information in an enforcement scenario. Another aspect of side letters that we have seen gain increased prominence in 2022 are restrictions on overcall for defaulting investors with respect management fees, which can have implications for the financing where the purpose provisions allow the facility to be used to finance management fee amounts.

Fund domicile in English law fund financings

Guernsey, Jersey, Ireland and Luxembourg continue to be the most popular when it comes to fund domiciliation in English law fund financings, and based on our 2022 dealbook, Luxembourg continues to be the most prevalent of those four.

Comparatively few English fund finance transactions involve English-domiciled funds. This is at least in part because, until relatively recently (2017), the law governing English limited partnerships was antiquated, with the key statutes, the English Limited Partnership Act 1907 and the Partnership Act 1890, having changed little since they were originally introduced.

The introduction of English "private fund limited partnerships" in 2017, in respect of which some of the traditional rules, restrictions and administrative burdens that previously applied to all English limited partnerships and their limited partners no longer applied, does not appear to have resulted in any material increase in the number of funds choosing to domicile in England & Wales, perhaps because English limited partnerships still do not provide all of the advantages of limited partnerships in some other jurisdictions.

With the use of Luxembourg, Ireland and the Channel Island jurisdictions, we have seen an increasing number of different types of vehicles being used as fundraising vehicles – particularly corporate structures – which can present challenges in terms of putting a subscription or hybrid line in place. The challenges depend on the structure, jurisdiction and terms of the fund documents, but include addressing and providing the lender with control over any additional steps that need to be taken in order to complete the call-down process on investors.

Looking back and looking forward

At the time of writing this chapter, we look back at a year that thankfully saw the impact of the pandemic lessen but a year that also brought with it war, inflation, rising interest rates and economic and social pressures from energy and petrol price increases.

We also look back, as this is a fund finance publication, on yet another remarkable year for the fund finance market in Europe. The growth of the market in size over 2020/2021 is now matched by a sophisticated and diverse product base. In this context, we stand at the end of 2022 with a fund finance market that covers a panoply of financing tools, and with lender participants more diverse than ever before and willing to engage with sponsors on developing the financing options to allow the private capital markets to continue to grow and sustain in what are potentially the choppy seas of 2023.

Sam Hutchinson
Tel: +44 20 7170 8700 / Email: samantha.hutchinson@cwt.com
Sam Hutchinson advises both financial institutions and private markets managers on the full range of fund finance products across all asset classes. Sam has advised on some of the largest subscription and leverage deals in the market, including a $2 billion secondary financing for a leading European secondary manager, a $1.5 billion hybrid umbrella facility and a €5 billion subscription line to a leading global primary fund. In the past 12 months, she has advised on more than 50 new fund financings exceeding £15 billion in value.

Sam has been advising financial institutions and private markets managers for over 15 years, and her practice covers the full range of fund lending products, including subscription lines, primary and secondary leverage and liquidity lines, GP and executive financings and co-invest facilities delivered via a number of different structures including framework and umbrella facilities. She is recognised as a preeminent banking lawyer by *Chambers UK*, *The Legal 500 UK* and *IFLR1000*. *The Lawyer* featured Sam in its 2020 "Hot 100" list, which highlights the UK's "most daring, innovative and creative lawyers".

Nathan Parker
Tel: +44 20 7170 8700 / Email: nathan.parker@cwt.com
Nathan Parker is a partner in the Finance Group in Cadwalader's London office. He has worked in the City for over a decade advising on a wide range of financing transactions. Nathan's practice focuses on acting for financial institutions and private markets managers across a full range of fund finance products, including subscription facilities, NAV and hybrid products and GP and co-invest facilities. His background and understanding of the market is extensive, having previously advised exclusively on financings outside of fund finance for private sponsors in their leveraged buyout and high-yield offerings, as well as direct lenders in the special situations space.

Prior to joining Cadwalader, Nathan worked in the acquisition finance and fund finance practices in Debevoise & Plimpton's London office.

Nathan is admitted to practise in England and Wales.

Cadwalader, Wickersham & Taft LLP
100 Bishopsgate, London EC2N 4AG, United Kingdom
Tel: +44 20 7170 8700 / URL: www.cadwalader.com

France

Philippe Max & Meryll Aloro
Dentons Europe, AARPI

Overview[1]

2021 was a record-breaking year both in terms of fundraising, with €24.5bn raised by French private equity players, members of France Invest (the French private equity and venture capital association), up 33% from 2020 and up 17% from the previous record of 2019, and on the investment front with €27.1bn deployed, up 53% from 2020 and up 41% from the pre-COVID era of 2019.[2]

Activity of French private equity players in the first half of 2022 was in line with the levels observed in 2021. French private equity raised €16bn in H1 2022 (+€6bn *vs* H1 2021) from a wide range of subscribers: insurers accounted for 20% of inflows (+124% *vs* H1 2021); pension funds for 16% (+152% *vs* H1 2021); funds of funds for 15% (-11% *vs* H1 2021); and individuals and family offices for 12% (+14% *vs* H1 2021). This performance was boosted by fundraisings of more than €1bn, which represented 41% of the total fundraisings for the first semester of 2022.[3]

The growth in the size and number of funds has led to a mechanical increase in demand for equity bridge facilities. With demand for subscription lines at around 20–30% of capital raised, the fund finance industry in France has experienced exponential growth in the last few years. While equity bridge financings have been readily available on the market since the early 2000s in the United States and the United Kingdom, French funds for professional investors only started using bridge loans in 2015. With the rising demand for financing, the French market has seen new foreign banks entering into the market in the last few years and an increase in club deals in order to meet the large amounts of debts required. Non-bank lenders are still rare on the French market due to, among other things, the French banking monopoly rules, which prohibit institutions other than licensed credit institutions or licensed financing companies from carrying out credit operations in France on a customary basis.

Net asset value ("**NAV**") facilities and general partner ("**GP**") financings are still in their early stages in France, with a shortage of liquidity in this market and only a few established providers on the French market.

French funds overview

A French alternative investment fund reserved for professional investors ("**Professional Fund**") is usually structured as a:
- *Fonds Professionnel de Capital Investissement* ("**FPCI**"), which can be established as a mutual fund or as an investment company with variable capital; or
- *Fonds Professionnel Spécialisé* ("**FPS**"), which can be established as a mutual fund (*Fonds d'Investissement Professionnel Spécialisé*, "**FIPS**"), as an investment company

with variable capital (*Société d'Investissement Professionnelle Spécialisée*, "**SICAV**") or as a *société en commandite simple* (*Société de Libre Partenariat*, "**SLP**") comparable to the English limited partnership or the Luxembourg *société en commandite spéciale* ("**SCSp**").

A mutual fund does not have legal personality, whereas an investment company or SLP does.

Professional Funds are subject to the provisions of the Alternative Investment Fund Managers Directive 2011/61/EU ("**AIFMD**") as implemented in France and related EU Delegated Regulations. Professional Funds are not subject to approval by the French Regulator ("**AMF**") but shall only be declared to the AMF at the latest within the month following their constitution. The legal documentation of such Professional Funds ("**By-Laws**") can be drafted in French or in any other commonly used language in the financial sector (usually English).

Changes in French law

Article R. 214-206 of the French Monetary and Financial Code has been amended further by Decree n°2019-1172 of 14 November 2019 to increase the borrowing limit of the FPCI from 10% to 30% of its assets, which has an impact on the former practice where, before such Decree, borrowings were made at the level of a special purpose vehicle set up by the FPCI, with the FPCI granting to the lenders a guarantee (*cautionnement*) of the obligations of such special purpose vehicle. The establishment of a special purpose vehicle should, therefore, in most cases, no longer be necessary since most of the funds borrow under an equity bridge financing less than 30% of their assets and consequently, an FPCI will be able to borrow directly without the need to set up a special purpose vehicle, provided that the financing is put in place after the first investment(s) of the FPCI and the FPCI has enough assets to comply with the above threshold at that time.

Structuring of the financing

In France, an equity bridge facility will usually be structured via a committed term facility (which can be "replenished" upon repayment of each loan), but the facility also often includes an uncommitted line, such uncommitted line reducing the costs of the facility for the lenders in terms of regulatory capital and for the fund in terms of commitment fees, but leaving the commercial risk for the fund if a lender refuses to commit. During the subscription period of the fund, the uncommitted line enables the fund, through an increase mechanism, to increase the maximum facility amount each time a substantive closing of investors is achieved, subject to the lenders' consent. In order to avoid the management company being considered to be using leverage for the purposes of Commission Delegated Regulation n°231/2013 of 19 December 2012, "supplementing Directive 2011/61/EU of the European Parliament and of the Council with regard to exemptions, general operating conditions, depositaries, leverage, transparency and supervision", loans should be temporary in nature and should relate to and be fully covered by capital commitments from investors, while revolving credit facilities should not be considered temporary in nature.[4] It is usually considered in France that loans with a maximum duration of 364 days should be considered temporary, provided that they relate to, and are fully covered by, capital commitments from investors. Depending upon the activity of the fund, the facility can be utilised only by way of loans or by way of loans and letters of credit.

Finally, depending upon the size of the facility, such facility is either syndicated or bilateral.

French law security package

Usually, the lenders under the facility agreement will benefit from: (i) a pledge over the bank account of the fund into which the investors pay their capital calls (and possibly, over certain other bank accounts of the fund); (ii) a pledge over certain bank accounts of the special purpose vehicle (if any); and (iii) the right to draw down investors' undrawn commitments if (a) there is a payment default or an acceleration, and (b) the management company has not sent drawdown notices to such investors or the management company has sent drawdown notices to such investors but such investors have failed to pay the amounts due and payable under the facility agreement.

Certain transactions are also secured by way of a pledge over the undrawn commitments of the investors. However, under most transactions, the lenders have relied on a third-party drawdown right granted by the investors in the By-Laws of the fund, called *stipulation pour autrui* or, to a lesser extent, on a power of attorney granted by the management company in order to call the investors, both the power of attorney and the *stipulation pour autrui* being exercisable upon the occurrence of the two enforcement events listed in the above paragraph.

Under French law, a power of attorney can always be revoked by the donor, even if stated to be irrevocable, subject to damages being due by the donor to the beneficiary of the power of attorney.

A *stipulation pour autrui*, as used in France in equity bridge financings, is an undertaking made by the investors (at the request of the fund), directly in the By-Laws of the fund, pursuant to which each investor agrees to pay, at the request of the lenders, its undrawn commitments into the collection account of the fund, opened usually with its French depositary, up to the amount owed by each investor to the fund pursuant to its subscription agreement. Under a typical equity bridge financing, such collection account is pledged to the benefit of the lenders. Since, as at the fund's creation, the lenders' identity is usually still unknown, such *stipulation pour autrui* cannot refer to the names of such lenders. However, the lenders can rely on the terms of the *stipulation pour autrui* notwithstanding the fact that their names are not specifically indicated in the By-Laws of the fund, since such *stipulation pour autrui* is a third-party right that may benefit any future lenders. As soon as the *stipulation pour autrui* has been accepted by the lenders, it cannot be revoked by the fund. Such acceptance is typically made by way of a simple one-page letter executed by the lenders on the facility agreement signing date.

A *stipulation pour autrui* is not a security *in rem* as such and does not grant any preference right to the lender, which means that if another creditor of the fund wants to seize the undrawn commitments of the investors or if the fund has granted a pledge over such undrawn commitments (even if this would be done in breach of the negative pledge provisions of the facility agreement or in breach of the limits to indebtedness inserted in such facility agreement), such seizure would prevail at the time it is carried out and the pledge would prevail at the time it is notified to the investors or enforced. Lenders on the French market have obtained comfort from the absence of a pledge due to (i) the specific nature of the funds, dedicated to investments, which means that, in principle, a fund should not have other financial indebtedness and, therefore, should not have other competing debt creditors with respect to such indebtedness, (ii) the negative pledge clause inserted in the facility agreement, and (iii) the fact that the By-Laws of the funds usually provide that the investors' commitments shall be paid on the collection account of the fund opened with its depositary (which would, in practice, render such pledge less attractive for the pledgee). From what we have seen, lenders have also taken a view on the quality of the investors and the potential side business that could be generated as a result of entering into an equity bridge financing with such fund. A lender may avoid this risk by taking security *in rem* in respect of the undrawn commitments of the investors. However, as noted, as a matter of French market practice, if lenders benefit from such a *stipulation pour autrui*, we have not seen pledges being granted to such lenders over the undrawn commitments of the investors, although we are seeing certain lenders considering such possibility.

A pledge of receivables can be enforced by notification to the investors, asking them to pay the pledgee. A pledge can also be enforced by contractual attribution of the claim that has been pledged, without the need to go to court. Such pledge could, in theory, also be enforced by way of judicial attribution but, due to the existence of the two above enforcement methods, such judicial method, in practice, is never used. There are no judicial expenses related to an enforcement by way of notification or contractual attribution. Depending upon the law applicable to the By-Laws and the location of the investors, formalities may be required in order for the pledge to be enforceable, as detailed, among other things, in Regulation (EC) n°593/2008 of the European Parliament and of the Council of 17 June 2008 on the law applicable to contractual obligations (Rome I) and in French case law.

French insolvency issues

Neither an FPCI, an FIPS nor an SLP can be subject to insolvency, to the extent the FPCI or FIPS is established as a mutual fund. For such FPCI and FIPS, this is due to the fact that they do not have legal personality, since they are co-ownerships of assets. For an SLP, the French Monetary and Financial Code has specifically provided that the French insolvency proceedings regime does not apply to SLPs.[5] Since the French insolvency proceedings regime does not apply to such funds, the enforcement regime of the abovementioned security interests is not affected by the French rules applicable to insolvency proceedings (Book VI of the French Commercial Code) and enforcement is very much based on the principle of "first come, first served".

However, under Article 1343-5 of the French Civil Code, a borrower may ask a judge for a grace period, which the judge may or may not grant, of a maximum period of two years. The criteria according to which a borrower can apply for a grace period will be decided on a case-by-case basis by the judge. Article 1343-5 of the French Civil Code is very general, and the judge will mainly decide on the basis of the situation of the borrower and the needs of the lender. The judge can decide that the rescheduled amount owed by the borrower will bear interest. The judge can also provide that such grace period will be subject to the accomplishment by the borrower of certain acts that may facilitate or secure the payment of the debt. Article 1343-5 of the French Civil Code cannot be excluded from the scope of the security or disapplied since it is a mandatory provision of French law. In practice, however, we are not aware of any instances of a judge having granted such grace period in a fund finance context.

Contrary to an FPCI or an FIPS, to the extent that such FPCI or FIPS is established as a mutual fund, or an SLP, the management company of a French fund can be subject to insolvency proceedings. Although insolvency of the management company would have an impact on the power of attorney referred to above, the insolvency of the management company would not have an impact on a *stipulation pour autrui*.

Key developments

Equity bridge financings have traditionally been viewed as presenting a low risk for lenders. The only significant default that has been largely publicised is that of Dubai-based Abraaj Group. To a lesser extent, the press also reported, in March 2021, the alleged fraud by JES Global Capital GP III under a subscription line facility.

Abraaj's default was caused by the manager's deceit towards investors, the misuse of funds and the release of the investors while it acquired a business with a subscription line from a French bank just prior to its default.[6] Although this is a very rare and unusual situation, lenders who operate in the fund finance sphere in France have sought to strengthen their contractual positions following this default, in particular, by requesting early disclosure to the investors of the existence of the facility, of the drawdown right and of the security interests securing such facility.

French law does not require notices to be sent to the investors in order (i) to perfect the *stipulation pour autrui*, or (ii) for the *stipulation pour autrui* to be invoked against the investors. It is now standard for lenders to request a notification of all existing investors upon the closing of the facility (or the first drawing under the facility) and of all new investors after the closing date (at the latest on the date on which each new investor becomes an investor in the fund), thus avoiding leaving a three-month window (corresponding to the time period between quarterly reports) during which the investors could be released from their commitment (even if this would be done in breach of the various undertakings and covenants of the facility agreement) without being aware of the equity bridge financing.

In particular, the knowledge by the investors of the equity bridge financing, the drawdown right and the security interests makes it possible to:

- ensure that the investors will cooperate in case of enforcement and will respond to the drawdown notices received from the lenders or their agent, without being able to argue that they were not aware of the existence of the financing (although such argument should, in practice, not be accepted by a French court); and
- in the event of a release by the fund of its investors (as in the case of Abraaj) and, therefore, in the situation where the undrawn commitment of the investors would be reduced to zero, establish that the investors allegedly knew about the fraud and to have the release declared unenforceable (*inopposable*) vis-à-vis the lenders via an "*action paulienne*".[7]

It is worth noting that the guidelines on equity bridge facilities published by the Institutional Limited Partners Association ("**ILPA**"),[8] which have been widely discussed (including in previous editions of this publication and by the Fund Finance Association),[9] include extensive recommendations covering disclosure and encourage greater transparency from management companies.

The year ahead

Due to inflation, supply chain issues and wider macroeconomic uncertainty, it seems that a wait-and-see attitude and caution may be the key themes in the French private equity market for the second semester of 2022 and probably for the beginning of 2023. The subscription finance market will largely be dictated by the fundraising markets. Anything that lengthens fundraising cycles or reduces fund sizes may impact demand for equity bridge financings.

In light of the inflationary pressures and conflict in Ukraine impacting equity markets and valuations, we expect the demand for NAV facilities to increase; however, given that this market is not mature in France and in view of the current economic climate, lenders will likely be more conservative when it comes to NAV lines.

Endnotes

1. We state the law as of 31 October 2022.
2. These data are based on a report entitled "*Activité du non-côté français: capital investissement et infrastructure*" from France Invest and Grant Thornton, which can be accessed at https://www.franceinvest.eu.
3. These data are based on a report entitled "*Activité des acteurs français du capital-investissement S1 2022*" from France Invest and Grant Thornton, which can be accessed at https://www.franceinvest.eu.
4. Whereas (14) of Delegated Regulation of Commission Delegated Regulation n°231/2013 of 19 December 2012 supplements Directive 2011/61/EU of the European Parliament and of the Council.
5. Article L. 214-162-1.I. of the French Monetary and Financial Code.
6. "What have cheap bank loans done to private equity funds?" by Florin Vasvari, which can be accessed at https://www.london.edu/lbsr/what-have-cheap-bank-loans-done-to-private-equity-funds.
7. Article 1341-2 of the French Civil Code provides that "a creditor may, also, in its own name, attack the acts made by its debtor in fraud of its rights to have them declared unenforceable (*inopposable*) against it, on the condition that, in the case of an act for consideration (*acte à titre onéreux*), it establishes that the third contracting party knew about the fraud".
8. "Subscription Lines of Credit and Alignment of Interests – Considerations and Best Practices for Limited and General Partners" published by the ILPA in June 2017, which can be accessed at https://ilpa.org/wp-content/uploads/2017/06/ILPA-Subscription-Lines-of-Credit-and-Alignment-of-Interests-June-2017.pdf.
9. Fund Finance Association Analysis on ILPA Guidelines, which can be accessed at https://www.fundfinanceassociation.com/wp-content/uploads/2018/12/FFA-Analysis-on-ILPA-Guidelines.pdf.

Philippe Max
Tel: +33 1 42 68 44 78 / Email: philippe.max@dentons.com
Philippe Max is a finance partner in Dentons' Paris office. He works on domestic and international banking and finance transactions. He is specialised in structured finance, cross-border finance and acquisition finance, with a strong focus on fund financing facilities (acting for both borrowers and lenders).

Meryll Aloro
Tel: +33 1 42 68 44 82 / Email: meryll.aloro@dentons.com
Meryll Aloro is an associate in Dentons' Paris office. She concentrates on banking and finance law and works on domestic and international banking and finance transactions, with a particular focus on funds financing.

Dentons Europe, AARPI

5 boulevard Malesherbes, 75017 Paris, France
Tel: +33 1 42 68 48 00 / URL: www.dentons.com

Guernsey

Jeremy Berchem
Appleby

Overview

Guernsey is a leading funds domicile with a proven track record of more than 50 years as an international financial centre, and as such, is recognised by fund sponsors and promoters as a leading centre for the formation, administration and cross-border distribution of investment business such as private equity, alternative investments, property funds, hedge funds and funds of hedge funds. As at the end of June 2022, there were over 1,400 funds and sub-funds administered in Guernsey, with the overall value of institutional and retail funds under management and administration in Guernsey standing at £302.8 billion. Over the past year, total net asset values have increased by £30.2 billion (11.1%).

There are a range of factors contributing to Guernsey's leading position in this space, including: (i) over 800 years of independent self-governance as a Crown Dependency of the United Kingdom; (ii) an AA-/A-1+ credit rating from S&P Global Ratings, representing Guernsey's very strong capacity to meet its financial commitments; (iii) historical familiarity with the jurisdiction by investors and fund sponsors; and (iv) the increasing dominance of the private equity sector in the funds market.

In addition, Guernsey law, which is derived from a combination of English common law, Norman customary law and local legislation, ensures that Guernsey funds are recognised as internationally accepted and well-recognised vehicles for all kinds of fund-related activity.

Collaboration between the Guernsey government and the private sector also ensures that Guernsey laws keep pace with market evolution and demand. New products are being introduced to the market regularly to keep Guernsey at the forefront of the international funds market; previous products include private investment funds (**PIFs**) and the Alternative Investment Fund Managers Directive (**AIFMD**) marketing passport-ready, manager-led products (**MLPs**) – including the Guernsey limited liability company, which is expected to be open to the market in the upcoming year.

The Guernsey Green Fund regime was established in 2021 to provide a transparent product that contributes to agreed objectives of mitigating environmental damage and climate change. More than £4.9 billion has been channelled into green investments through the Guernsey Green Fund regime. In September 2022, the criteria in the regime was expanded to include the EU Taxonomy for Sustainable Activities' technical screening criteria for activities contributing to climate change mitigation and adaption.

Building on the success of the Guernsey Green Fund regime, Guernsey launched the Natural Capital Fund regime in 2022. This regime creates a regulatory designation for funds to help channel investment into biodiversity and natural capital products that make a positive contribution and/or significantly reduce harm to the natural world.

The growth in this area shows a strong correlation with the fund finance space, where Appleby's Guernsey office continues to see steady growth year on year in the subscription credit facility market. Indeed, Appleby's Guernsey office continues to be a market leader in this area, representing the majority of the largest global banks on a variety of different financing structures.

An increase in fund size across the globe has meant higher commitments being expected of general partners, and this in turn has given rise to market demand for general partner support facilities over and above the standard subscription lines. These facilities tend to bring with them more bespoke security packages, tailored depending on the make-up of each individual general partner and the fund it manages.

Fund formation and finance

Lending to Guernsey funds

Guernsey private equity funds have typically been registered as limited partnerships (**LPs**) under the Limited Partnerships (Guernsey) Law, 1995, as amended (the **LP Law**). Though registered pursuant to the LP Law, an LP is not generally a separate legal entity (although it can elect to have separate legal personality from its partners at the time of registration).

An LP reflects a formal legal arrangement between one or more general partners of the LP and one or more limited partners of the LP. A general partner of a Guernsey LP is liable for all of the debts and obligations of an LP and is vested with certain duties and powers with respect to the business of the LP. On the other hand, limited partners contribute or agree to contribute specific sums to the capital of the LP only, and have no liability for any of the debts or liabilities of the LP beyond this amount so long as they refrain from taking part in its management.

Any rights and obligations of the general partner and the limited partners are governed by the LP agreement and any subscription agreements or side letters entered into by the limited partners, and are therefore contractual in nature. The LP's rights and property of every description, including any right to make capital calls and to receive the proceeds thereof, are held by the general partner in trust as an asset of the LP (and this remains the case even if an LP elects to have separate legal personality).

The typical security package

This contractual arrangement and ownership structure largely dictates the structure of the security package available to lenders offering subscription credit and general partner support facilities to Guernsey vehicles. As previously mentioned, limited partners of an LP will usually commit in the partnership agreement and/or subscription agreement to fund investments or to repay fund expenses when called upon to do so by the general partner from time to time. It is this contractual obligation of a limited partner to make these capital contributions, to the extent that they have not already been called (**Uncalled Capital**), and the corresponding right of the general partner on behalf of an LP to call for Uncalled Capital (**Capital Call Rights**), which is at the core of the typical subscription credit facility security package. Given that these rights are contractual in nature and will be governed by the laws of Guernsey, the appropriate form of security over such rights is an assignment of title in the form of a security interest agreement in accordance with section 1(6) of the Security Interests (Guernsey) Law, 1993, as amended (the **Security Law**).

As legal title to the assets of the LP ultimately vests in the general partner, the Capital Call Rights are exercisable by the general partner for the benefit of the LP. As such, the proper parties to any grant of security over the LP's assets (and in particular, the Capital Call

Rights) must be the general partner as well as the LP (acting through the general partner). The security package must be in strict compliance with the requirements of the Security Law and, ideally, should incorporate an express irrevocable power of attorney in favour of the secured party, entitling the secured party to exercise the general partner's Capital Call Rights following the occurrence of an event of default.

It should not be assumed that the assignment of Capital Call Rights is necessarily permitted under the LP agreement governing the LP (although it is common enough that the requisite changes to an agreement to permit such security are fairly uncontroversial). The terms of the LP agreement can have a fundamental effect on the structuring of the collateral package and must be reviewed in detail in order to ensure a number of key elements, including but not limited to:
- the ability of the LP to incur indebtedness and enter into the transaction;
- that security may be granted over (a) the Uncalled Capital, (b) the right to make and enforce capital calls, (c) the related contributions, and (d) the general partner's share; and
- that Uncalled Capital may be applied (when called) towards the secured obligations.

In general partner support facilities, security is also taken under this section of the Security Law, with the collateral consisting of less well-known receivables than Uncalled Capital, such as general partner investor distributions.

Service of notice in respect of security over Capital Call Rights

In order to be effective and comply with the Security Law, any security over a contractual right must satisfy the following two limbs (the **Two Limbs**): firstly, the secured party must have title to the collateral assigned to it under a security interest agreement; and secondly, express notice in writing of that assignment must be served on the person from whom the assignor would have been able to claim the collateral (for example, in the case of Capital Call Rights, the limited partners).

On this basis, the serving of notice under the Security Law is a matter not just of the perfection of the security; the service of notice is crucial to the creation of the security interest, and without it, no security interest exists. Attention must therefore be given to the sometimes tricky issue of the service of notice on limited partners who may otherwise be unaware of the financing arrangements proposed for the LP in which they invest; funds are often reluctant to serve notice promptly following the signing of the security interest agreement, and it can be important to educate lenders and fund managers as to the implications of not doing so.

Where a security interest is granted over Guernsey Capital Call Rights, priority of the security interest over any competing security interest will therefore be determined in accordance with Guernsey law and, given that a valid security interest is only created once both of the Two Limbs have been satisfied, priority may not be established in accordance with the time of execution of the relevant security interest agreements. A delay in the delivery of the notice will therefore open up the secured party to the possibility that a general partner, on behalf of the Guernsey LP, may (quite unintentionally) grant a competing security interest or an absolute assignment over Capital Call Rights to a subsequent assignee. If both security interest agreements have been executed, provided that notice of the second assignment is provided to the limited partners ahead of notice of the first assignment, the second assignee will rank for repayment ahead of the first assignee.

Limited partners are increasingly aware of subscription facilities, and familiarity with the product means that there is now, generally, less resistance by Guernsey LPs to giving notice to limited partners. This has led to notices typically being circulated to the limited partners immediately upon execution of the security documents in order to ensure that security is created and priority is achieved at closing of the subscription credit facility.

Given the importance of actual delivery of the notice to the limited partners, evidence of the notice having been received also assumes some importance. In general, where the limited partners are not part of the same borrower group, it is unlikely that any form of acknowledgment of the notice will be received. It is increasingly common for Guernsey LP agreements to build in provisions that specify the circumstances in which notices delivered in accordance with their terms are "deemed" to have been received by the limited partners. Where an LP agreement contains such provisions, lenders can take some comfort in proof of delivery of any notice in accordance with the provisions of that agreement (rather than proof of receipt by way of a signed acknowledgment by the limited partners, which is the ideal). On the other hand, due to recent judicial cases, there has been a particular focus on limited partners receiving actual notice of the security being granted. That being so, we would typically require the general partner or manager (as the case may be) to give back-to-back notice to the limited partners, and confirm that it has done so.

In all cases, the recommendation would be that the general partner sign and deliver the notice to the limited partners in accordance with the provisions of the LP agreement governing service of notices on the limited partners, with a copy delivered to the secured party. Where no such provisions are included regarding the service of notice and deemed delivery, it is important to obtain proof of delivery to limited partners (such as receipt of copies of courier delivery slips).

We have also seen an increasing prevalence of limited partners, within the terms of the LP agreement, appointing an agent specifically to receive notice of this nature on their behalf (and indeed, sometimes, to also acknowledge receipt of the notice on their behalf). Wording of this nature should be examined with caution to ensure compliance with the requirements of the Security Law. Increasingly, local market practice is to have the agent sign an acknowledgment to the notice of assignment, containing a specific confirmation that they (the agent) will send the notice on to the limited partners in satisfaction of the requirements of the Security Law (although, see below under "Key developments").

In addition to facilitating the creation of a security interest, delivery of a notice to a Guernsey LP's limited partners of an assignment of Capital Call Rights has other distinct advantages. Two of the more important advantages of delivery of the notice include preventing: (i) the limited partners from obtaining good discharge for their obligations to fund their Uncalled Capital in any manner other than as specifically indicated in the notice; and (ii) set-off arising after the date of service of such notice (on the basis of the common law principle that set-off works between the same parties in the same right).

Other elements of a typical security package

The typical security package will also include the grant of a security interest over a designated bank account under the control of the lenders into which any capital call proceeds must be paid. Although the security interest agreement over Capital Call Rights in a Guernsey LP must be granted under a Guernsey law security interest agreement that complies with the requirements of the Security Law, security over such designated bank accounts should usually be governed by the law of the jurisdiction in which the account itself is situated.

Whilst Guernsey is a popular choice for the accounts of both Guernsey and non-Guernsey private equity funds due to the well-established and regulated status of the jurisdiction, it is equally common for such accounts to be sited in the United Kingdom or United States and, in such instances, it would be usual for such security to be granted under a New York or English law-governed security agreement. If the account is Guernsey situate, security should be taken in compliance with the requirements of the Security Law and take the form of a security interest agreement. Assuming that the secured party is not also the account bank, then notice is once again a key factor, and time should be factored in to deal with the requirements of individual account banks who maintain the accounts that are the subject of the security.

Less typical security elements

Other, less typical security packages may include security directly from the limited partners over their interests in the LPs themselves, and, particularly in relation to hybrid facilities and funds nearing the end of their life cycle, security is often taken over underlying assets of the fund, as this is where the fund's value lies. In Guernsey, these might include shares in Guernsey-registered subsidiary companies, units in Guernsey unit trusts, and/or contract rights arising under Guernsey law contracts. In respect of these asset types, security is taken by way of a Guernsey law security interest agreement, and the formalities to finalise the creation of the security are as follows:

- Shares – notice of the assignment is given to the company whose shares are secured, possession is taken of the share certificates (together with blank stock transfer forms), and the register of members is annotated to reflect the security interest.
- Units – notice of the assignment is given to the trustee of the unit trust whose units are secured, possession is taken of the unit certificates (together with blank unit transfer forms), and the register of unit holders is annotated to reflect the security interest.
- Contract rights (including rights to management or general partner fees) – notice of the assignment is given to the contract counterparty and acknowledgment obtained.

Registration requirements

With the exception of land located in the Bailiwick of Guernsey, vessels flagged in Guernsey and Guernsey-registered aircraft, there are no registration steps required in Guernsey and there is no general register of security interests in Guernsey accessible to the public. There is similarly no statutory requirement that a Guernsey entity keeps a private register of security interests.

Other products

The protection afforded to investors in funds proposed by AIFMD has been at the forefront of the minds of the entire Guernsey funds industry and has seen increased emphasis on the substance of both funds and fund managers, in particular.

Guernsey has worked hard to ensure that from the outset, its regulatory infrastructure is suitable to enable the distribution of Guernsey-domiciled funds to both EU and non-EU countries. In July 2016, the European Securities and Markets Authority announced its recommendation that Guernsey be included in the first round for the granting of a third-country passport for the purposes of AIFMD. Guernsey is still one of only five non-EU jurisdictions to be given such an assessment, and the recommendation (subject to relevant approvals at an EU level) will enhance Guernsey's position as a gateway to the European funds market.

Guernsey publicly stated its intent to participate in the OECD's Base Erosion and Profit Shifting (**BEPS**) Project as an Associate in March 2016 and remains committed to the collective aim to reach a globally fair and modern international tax system. Accordingly, it has signed a Multilateral Agreement to exchange tax information. The Multilateral Competent Authority Agreement provides for automatic exchange of information in accordance with country-by-country reporting by large, multinational enterprises. BEPS refers to tax planning strategies that exploit gaps and mismatches in tax rules to artificially shift profits to low- or no-tax jurisdictions where there is little economic activity, resulting in little or no overall corporate tax being paid.

Manager-led products

In May 2016, the Guernsey Financial Services Commission (the **GFSC**) launched the MLP. The MLP is aimed at alternative investment fund managers (**AIFMs**) seeking to market into one or more EU Member States under national private placement regimes.

Under the MLP regime, all regulatory standards are borne by the AIFM and, by virtue of the AIFM's sponsorship, no alternative investment fund or underlying licensee will have rules imposed on it. The MLP regime avoids duplicating regulatory requirements over several entities. Further, derogation requests acceptable to the host country will be considered by the GFSC. The GFSC will be able to register a fund and license an underlying licensee within 24 hours of notification.

The regime is intended to be used by AIFMs seeking to market an AIF into an EU Member State under its national private placement regime. In addition, it is anticipated that the MLP regime will assist Guernsey AIFMs in utilising the EU AIFMD third-country passport (once available) in order to market in the EU. For that reason, the MLP regime anticipates that the AIFM will opt into the Guernsey AIFMD Rules – which replicate the rules of the EU AIFMD.

Until the EU AIFMD third-country passport has been extended to Guernsey, it is unlikely that a Guernsey AIFM would wish voluntarily to submit to the additional regulatory burden of Guernsey's AIFMD Rules. For that reason, the GFSC has indicated that significant derogations from the MLP regime requirements may be available.

The GFSC intends to extend Guernsey's suite of MLPs to include a similar offering for marketing outside the EU.

Private investment fund

In November 2016, the GFSC introduced a PIF regime that provides fund managers with greater flexibility and simplicity. The PIF, which was developed in response to market demand by the GFSC in consultation with the island's funds industry, recognises that certain investment funds are characterised by a relationship between management and investors that is closer than that of a typical agent. The PIF dispenses with the formal requirement for information particulars, such as a prospectus, in recognition of that relationship, significantly reducing the cost and processing time of launching of a fund.

The PIF, which can be either closed- or open-ended, should contain no more than 50 legal or natural persons holding an economic interest in the fund. A key strength of the product is that, where an appropriate agent is acting for a wider group of stakeholders, such as a discretionary investment manager or a trustee or manager of an occupational pension scheme, that agent may be considered as one investor. While there is a limit imposed on the number of investors in the PIF, no attempt has been made to limit the number of investors to whom the PIF might be marketed – a feature not available under comparable regimes.

The PIF is predicated on a close relationship between investors and the licensed manager, who will be responsible for providing warranties on the ability of the investors to assume loss. Under the new rules, both the PIF and its manager benefit from an application process that can be completed in one business day. The two processes may be completed in tandem by the GFSC, ensuring a short regulatory timescale.

Key developments

As a result of certain judicial cases in the last year, we have seen a tightening of legal structures, with increased scrutiny of the way in which security in fund finance transactions is created, or perfected, in foreign jurisdictions.

From a Guernsey perspective, as noted above, service of a notice of assignment under the Security Law is fundamental to the creation of a Guernsey security interest, and so due service on the counterparty must occur contemporaneously with completion occurring.

Where we have seen key developments in the market is in lenders' internal policy requirements for the service of such notices of assignment. The internal policies often contain little to no room for flexibility in the mode of service, regardless of the terms of the partnership agreement, so as to minimise the risk of a counterparty challenging the security on the grounds of non-receipt.

Such a clear movement in internal thinking has given rise to multiple market discussions around the mode of service of notices to bigger funds with larger pools of limited partners, discussions that will no doubt continue to develop over the coming year.

The year ahead

While we expect a busy year ahead, we anticipate that growth will be tempered from the dizzying heights recently experienced. Competition between lenders in this space will still be strong, especially as we see new entrants looking to capitalise on the well-performing fund finance market.

Accordingly, the Guernsey market continues to see sophisticated lenders providing increasingly complex and tailored solutions to the funds market, with loans being made to the full cast of players in the funds market including funds, secondary funds (against their LP interests, to finance the acquisition of LP positions and release capital to investors), limited partners and general partners (to help finance general partner and fund commitments). More products to funds to assist with end-of-life options are expected as funds seek to maintain options and flexibility with their investments. We are increasingly seeing "series funds", which may previously have flirted with other jurisdictions, returning to Guernsey's shores, which will bolster activity.

Jeremy Berchem
Tel: +44 1481 755 601 / Email: jberchem@applebyglobal.com

Jeremy Berchem is the managing group partner of Appleby (Guernsey) LLP. He has a well-established fund finance practice, acting for major financial institutions in a wide variety of corporate finance transactions. Jeremy is a market-leading finance lawyer and is highly regarded and rated globally across the leading legal directories. *Chambers UK* 2022 recognises Jeremy as a notable practitioner, and he was named as highly regarded in the 2021 edition of *IFLR1000*. He is described as an "expert in the niche area of fund finance, commercial, responsive, solution focused", and "our first port of call when it comes to fund financing advice in Guernsey offering fantastic partner led advice". Jeremy was named as a "Leading Individual" in *The Legal 500 UK* 2022. Jeremy is praised for having a "wealth of experience and knowledge in the sector. He is well known to clients and counterparties alike and is very good to work with".

Appleby

Hirzel Court, Hirzel Street, St Peter Port, GY1 3BN, Guernsey
Tel: +44 1481 755 600 / URL: www.applebyglobal.com

Hong Kong

James Ford, Patrick Wong & Charlotte Robins
Allen & Overy

Overview

An overview of the Hong Kong fund landscape

Against the backdrop of uncertainties generated by the ongoing challenges of managing COVID-19 and an increasingly complex global market environment, the Hong Kong Government and various regulatory authorities continue to take steps to further develop Hong Kong as a preferred jurisdiction for fund domiciliation and strengthen its position as an international funds hub.

Public funds and open-ended fund companies (**OFCs**) are regulated in Hong Kong by the Securities and Futures Commission (the **SFC**). As at 31 December 2021, there were 865 Hong Kong-domiciled SFC-authorised funds (a year-on-year increase of 7%) with a net asset value (**NAV**) of HK$1,497 billion (US$192 billion), representing a year-on-year increase in NAV of 5%.[1] 2021 was a particularly busy year for registrations of OFCs, with an increase in the number of registered OFCs to 48 with 95 sub-funds, including 21 exchange-traded funds (a year-on-year increase of 500%), with a market capitalisation of HK$16.7 billion (US$2 billion).[2] This increase in registrations was helped by the availability of a grant scheme introduced by the SFC in May 2021, which subsidises eligible investment managers who have successfully incorporated an OFC or re-domiciled a non-Hong Kong fund corporation in Hong Kong as an OFC.

The SFC has also continued to expand the mutual recognition of funds scheme, which allows for securities of public funds domiciled in Hong Kong to be offered directly to investors in recognised markets (and *vice versa*). As of the time of writing, mutual recognition arrangements exist with the People's Republic of China (the **PRC**, which, for the purposes of this chapter, excludes Hong Kong, Macao and Taiwan), Australia, France, Luxembourg, Malaysia, the Netherlands, Switzerland, Taiwan, the United Kingdom and, most recently, Thailand.[3] It is expected that this list will grow as the SFC continues to hold discussions around similar arrangements with other jurisdictions.

In connection with the development of the Greater Bay Area (which consists of Hong Kong, Macao and nine other cities in Guangdong, Mainland China), Hong Kong has also been taking steps to promote the growth of the wealth management industry. In September 2021, the SFC and various regulators in Mainland China and Macao launched the Cross-boundary Wealth Management Connect Scheme in the Guangdong-Hong Kong-Macao Greater Bay Area (**Cross-boundary WMC**), which focuses on the flow of supervisory information, investor protection and co-operation on enforcement, signifying Hong Kong's ongoing engagement and collaboration with Mainland China in this area. Under the Cross-boundary WMC, eligible Mainland, Hong Kong and Macao residents in the Greater Bay Area can invest in wealth management products distributed by banks in each other's market through a closed-loop funds flow channel established between their respective banking systems. This provides a higher degree of flexibility to individual retail investors, who are able to open and operate cross-boundary investment accounts directly in order to choose their preferred products.[4]

While there are roughly 359 fund managers based in Hong Kong,[5] the majority of private funds are historically domiciled overseas due to preferable tax arrangements and lack of legal support for complex private fund structures in Hong Kong. However, Hong Kong has made great strides recently to bolster its position as a leading jurisdiction for fund domicile. On 31 August 2020, the Limited Partnership Fund Ordinance (Cap. 637) (the **LPFO**) came into force, establishing a new limited partnership fund (**LPF**) regime enabling private funds to be registered in the modernised form of limited partnerships in Hong Kong. As of October 2022, around 550 LPFs had been registered (a year-on-year increase of 51%), and it is expected that this will continue to increase rapidly.[6] Market participants have been taking advantage of amendments made to the Inland Revenue Ordinance (the **IRO**) in 2019 establishing a unified fund exemption regime, allowing all privately offered onshore and offshore funds operating in Hong Kong, regardless of their structure, their size or the purpose they serve, to enjoy profits tax exemption for their transactions in specified assets (including in investments in both overseas and local private companies) subject to meeting certain conditions. On 7 May 2021 (but with retrospective effect from 1 April 2020), the Inland Revenue (Amendment) (Tax Concessions for Carried Interest) Ordinance (the **Tax Concession Amendments**) was enacted to give profits tax and salaries tax concessions in relation to eligible carried interest received by qualified investment managers for certified investment funds. Further, passage of the Securities and Futures (Amendment) Bill 2021 and the Limited Partnership Fund and Business Registration Legislation (Amendment) Bill 2021 (the **Re-domiciliation Bills**), which each came into effect on 1 November 2021,[7] created a statutory re-domiciliation mechanism for foreign funds to re-domicile in Hong Kong as OFCs or LPFs.

As fund finance activity is very much concentrated in the private funds domain, the remainder of this chapter will focus more on the private funds market in Hong Kong.

Recent trends in the Hong Kong and PRC private equity funds market

Fund managers and fundraising: The PRC continues to produce the largest number of private equity and venture capital investors in the region. However, as demonstrated in the following table, which shows a breakdown of the numbers between Mainland China, Hong Kong and Taiwan as of October 2022, given its size relative to Mainland China, Hong Kong has performed impressively – having 8.4% of the number of fund managers compared to that of China, and having raised 12.5% in terms of fund value compared to that of China, over the last 10-year period.[8]

Region	No. of Active Members	Total Funds Raised in the Past 10 Years (US$bn)
China	4,287	1,280
Hong Kong	359	160
Taiwan	81	4

Source: *Preqin Pro (data as of 6 October 2022).*

In terms of year-on-year numbers, capital raised in Mainland China and Hong Kong increased sharply by 28% and 35% (respectively) in 2021 as the region started to recover from COVID-19 restrictions. In the year to date, the amount of capital raised has fallen drastically in Mainland China but continued to rise, albeit markedly more slowly, in Hong

Kong (down 86% and up 7.6%, respectively). This pattern of volatility can be seen across the Asia-Pacific region, with Australia showing a decrease year-on-year in 2021 (down 29%) but a strong recovery in 2022 (up 74%) while India increased 31% year-on-year in 2021 but has fallen 6% in 2022 so far. It is worth noting that Taiwan did exceptionally well in 2021 with a year-on-year increase of over 3,500% and only a 16% reduction to date in 2022.[9]

Aggregate capital raised by fund manager location, 2012–2022

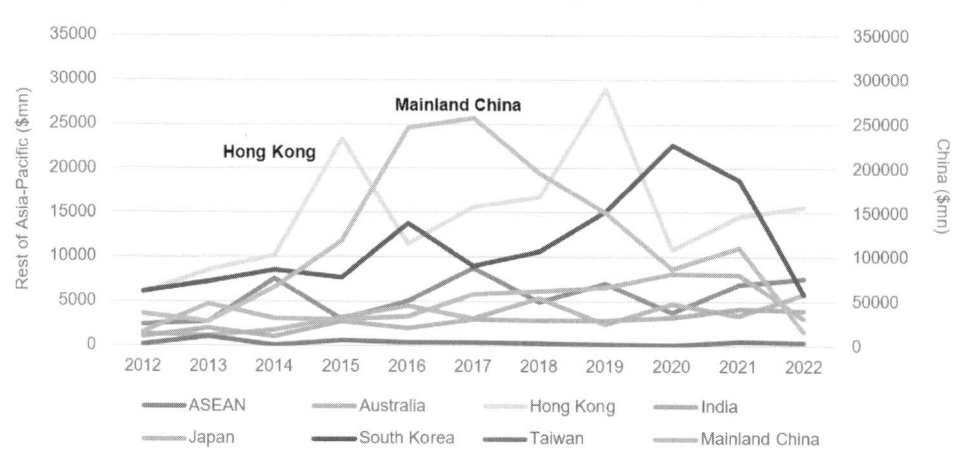

Note: China is plotted on a secondary axis as its numbers are on an order of magnitude far higher than the rest of Asia-Pacific.

As was witnessed in the last couple of years, it has appeared that the larger and more established fund players were able to raise capital and close their funds more expeditiously than the start-ups, as they have strong track records and limited partner relationships. With fundraising ongoing and the ability to deploy that capital continuing to be hampered (see further below), Asian-based fund managers were holding a record US$654 billion of dry powder at the end of 2021, considerably higher than the figure of US$477 billion in 2020.[10]

Dry powder grew to US$654 billion in 2021, setting another record

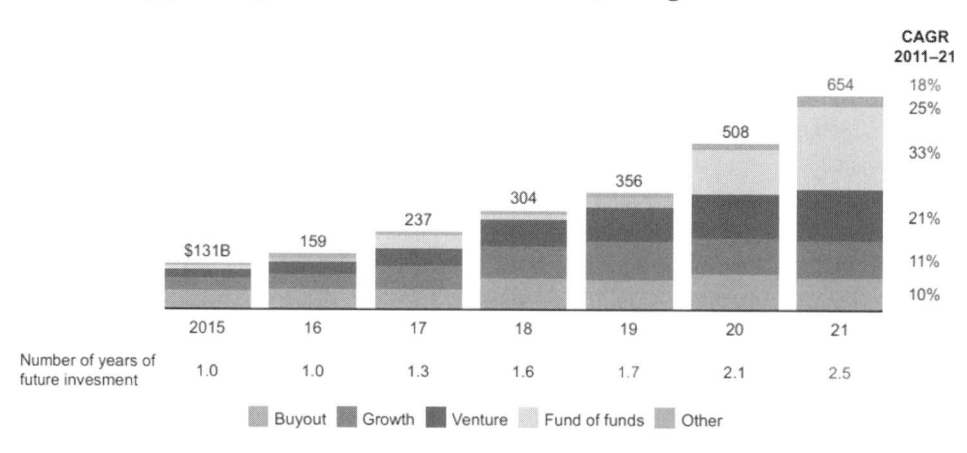

Note: Growth for 2017–20 partly reflects greater coverage from the data supplier in China; "other" includes distressed and mezzanine funds, and excludes real estate and infrastructure funds; number of years of future investment based on estimated growth of the private equity market (factoring debt). Source: Preqin.

Private equity buyouts and exits: According to industry analysis, exit value more than doubled in Asia-Pacific in 2021, which was a 54% increase over the previous five-year average (representing approximately US$172 billion in deal value).[11] A record 61 buyouts were completed in Greater China in 2021, which is 46% higher than the previous year,[12] with one of the top 20 global private equity buyouts being of Chinese portfolio 51job, Inc. for US$5,700 million.[13]

While initial public offerings (**IPOs**) are the most popular form of exit in the Asia-Pacific region (accounting for 47% of the exit market),[14] there has also been an increase in trade sales (where a company is sold to another business typically operating in the same industry or sector, with an independent intermediary acting on behalf of the sellers) and secondary exits through fund restructuring (where an asset or portfolio of assets is sold from an existing vehicle to another (usually newly formed) vehicle under the same management). Some of the largest venture capital IPOs globally were Chinese portfolios, including Beijing Kuaishou Technology Co. Ltd. and Didi Chuxing (with exit values of US$5,418 million and US$4,435 million, respectively).[15] Trade sales included the sale of Hong Kong-based Apex Logistics International to Kuehne + Nagel, a Swiss logistics provider.[16]

Exit activity declined significantly in the second half of 2021, when more stringent rules were set by the Securities and Exchange Commission (**SEC**) under the Holding Foreign Companies Accountable Act, requiring foreign, United States-listed companies' auditors to comply with certain requests for information or risk being delisted.[17] This has made United States listings a much less attractive exit option.

Sectors: Technology and the Internet made up nearly half of the deal values across Asia-Pacific in 2021, being the largest sectors for the 10th year running.[18]

Technology and advanced manufacturing produced more than 60% of deal value in 2021

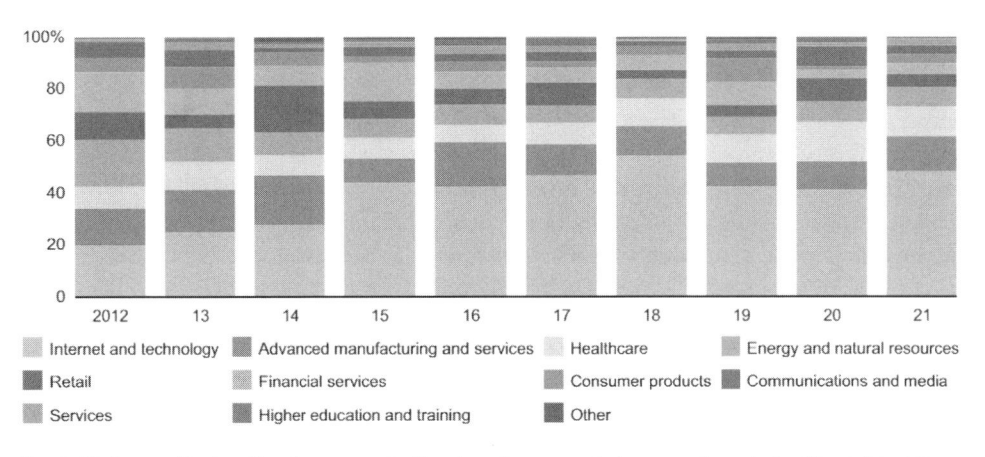

Note 1: The bars on this chart (from bottom to top) reflect the various sectors in the same order as the key (from left to right, top to bottom).

Note 2: "Other" includes deals tagged private equity, and no industry; data excludes real estate and infrastructure; industry sectors with a share under 5% are not labelled. Source: AVCJ.

ESG: In the last decade or more, the focus on environmental, social and corporate governance (**ESG**) has become a requirement of public shareholders and private investors alike, with governments and businesses across the Asia-Pacific region focusing on ESG as a top priority. The way in which ESG metrics and associated incentives are being calculated and assessed is ever evolving, providing interested parties the opportunity to be flexible and inventive. Measures of impact across a diverse range of sustainability metrics are increasingly becoming relevant in fund financing transactions. A notable example is the up to US$3.2 billion sustainability-linked credit facility obtained by Hong Kong-based Baring Private Equity Asia in October 2021. A recent survey has highlighted an intention of 57% of general partners in the region to significantly increase ESG efforts in the next three to five years, which is a marked increase as compared to surveys in prior years (41% in 2020 and 30% in 2019).[19]

Factors affecting the market

As the world started to acclimatise to new ways of working and COVID-19 vaccination programmes were rolled out in the first half of 2021, new investment highs were recorded across the region. However, fundraising did slow significantly in Greater China in the second half of the year as a result of China's slowing economic growth and tightening political tensions with the United States, both in respect of the Russia-Ukraine war and the tightening of regulatory oversight in the United States' markets of foreign companies, which add to the ongoing souring of relations between the United States and China.

In July 2021, China's Ministry of Education issued new rules banning private tutoring firms within Mainland China and required all private education firms offering tuition of core subjects to be registered as "not-for-profit" organisations. The extent of the ban was an unexpectedly strict game-changer, after private equity firms had channelled huge sums of capital into the education sector. Although some clarity on the new regime was announced in early September 2021, it remains to be seen how investors will recover from such announcement.

The Qualified Domestic Institutional Investor (**QDII**) regime allows qualified domestic financial institutions to invest in securities and bonds in offshore capital markets. In 2015, the QDII regime was unofficially suspended – reportedly, amongst other reasons, to reduce capital outflow. The relevant PRC regulator revived the regime in April 2018 and, since then, the total QDII quota has increased to US$159.7 billion (as of October 2022).

Generally, given the limited channels through which onshore capital can be repatriated outside the PRC, it is not surprising to see a lot of private funds based in Asia (including those managed in Hong Kong) having an investor base that is dominated by offshore investors. Despite regulatory relaxations in recent years in the PRC, there are still limited opportunities for onshore investors to commit onshore capital directly to offshore private funds.

Fund formation and finance

What is a "Hong Kong" fund and what is "Hong Kong" fund financing?

Until the LPFO was introduced, a reference made to a "Hong Kong" fund would typically be a reference to foreign funds administered out of Hong Kong or managed by a fund manager based in Hong Kong. Similarly, we would classify a fund financing as a "Hong Kong" financing if it is provided by a lender operating in Hong Kong and/or if the fund obtaining the financing is administered or managed out of Hong Kong. In practice, the reality is that Hong Kong fund financing typically involves various parties across a number of jurisdictions (especially as we see more financing provided on a club rather than on a bilateral basis). With the introduction of the LPFO, we would also classify an LPF as a "Hong Kong" fund and fund financing provided to an LPF a "Hong Kong" fund financing.

Fund formation in Hong Kong

Cayman Islands Exempted Limited Partnership: Currently, the vast majority of private investment funds in the Asia-Pacific region are set up as Cayman Islands Exempted Limited Partnerships (the **Cayman ELP**). The Cayman ELP structure provides great flexibility to investors and fund managers looking to organise and structure their investment vehicle. Specifically, a Cayman ELP is governed by its partnership agreement, and is free from the many legal constraints that otherwise exist in companies. For example, a Cayman ELP can distribute capital to its partners without being subject to capital maintenance rules for companies. Further, because Cayman ELPs do not have a separate legal personality, they are considered tax-neutral and treated as a "flow-through" entity. This means that the partners will only be taxed based on their income distributed by the fund and there will be no taxation at the fund level. As a result, the Cayman ELP structure has long been one of the most commonly used structures for private funds for Hong Kong fund managers. However, the International Tax Co-operation (Economic Substance) Law (2021 Revision) (the **Economic Substance Law**) enacted in the Cayman Islands brought about significant changes for fund managers. As a member of the Organisation for Economic Co-operation and Development (**OECD**) Inclusive Framework on Base Erosion and Profit Shifting, the Economic Substance Law was enacted as part of the OECD's efforts in tackling tax avoidance and money laundering by imposing substantive requirements for applicable entities carrying out investment management business in the Cayman Islands, including, without limitation, incurring an adequate amount of expenditure, having sufficient management presence and having an adequate number of employees. As a result, because of increased operational costs arising from the Economic Substance Law, we have seen a trend of onshoring efforts by fund managers, and Hong Kong is expected to benefit greatly from this trend as a result of its recent legal developments.

Hong Kong limited partnership fund: The development of the Hong Kong private funds industry had long been impeded by the outdated Limited Partnership Ordinance (Cap. 37), and Hong Kong was rarely the choice of domiciliation for private funds despite its thriving private equity market. Hong Kong's introduction of the LPF regime in 2020 was a much-needed and accommodating development for the private funds industry. The LPF structure shares many of the characteristics and aforementioned benefits of the Cayman ELP structure. Under the LPFO, a fund can be registered as an LPF if it is constituted by a limited partnership agreement between a general partner and limited partner(s). The general partner of an LPF will have unlimited liability for all the debts and obligations of the LPF, and the limited partner(s) will not be liable for such debts and obligations beyond their agreed contribution (unless the relevant limited partner has taken part in the management of the fund). The general partner will be required to appoint an investment manager to carry out the day-to-day investment management functions. Other features of LPFs include flexibility in relation to capital contribution, distribution of profits, contractual flexibility and a straightforward and cost-efficient dissolution mechanism. These features make the LPFO comparable to the limited partnership regimes in other popular fund domicile jurisdictions. As noted above, as of October 2022, around 550 LPFs had been registered in Hong Kong, demonstrating enthusiastic adoption of the structure from the outset.

Tax concession for carried interest: Further to the LPFO, the introduction of the Tax Concession Amendments was also a major milestone for the private funds industry. A carried interest is a fund manager's share of profits generated by an investment fund. Along with management fees, carried interest is the largest source of a fund manager's income and is naturally one of their biggest concerns when deciding their funds' domicile. The Tax Concession

Amendments provide unprecedented certainties in the taxation of carried interest in terms of its competitive rate and clear classification. Currently, under the IRO, carried interest received by investment managers derived from the provision of investment management services is considered chargeable income for either profits tax or salaries tax. Under the Tax Concession Amendments, eligible carried interest received by eligible recipients arising from qualifying transactions through qualified funds would be charged at a 0% profits tax rate. Alongside the unified fund exemption regime, funds domiciled in Hong Kong will now benefit from tax exemption at the fund level as well as the fund manager level.

Re-domiciliation of foreign funds: While the LPFO and Tax Concession Amendments greatly increased Hong Kong's competitiveness as a fund domicile, the majority of existing private funds managed by Hong Kong fund managers are currently still largely operating in offshore jurisdictions. The Re-domiciliation Bills, which came into operation on 1 November 2021, aim to further enhance Hong Kong's position as a preferred funds domicile and provide a formal statutory re-domiciliation mechanism for existing non-Hong Kong investment funds. The amended ordinances provide mechanisms for the re-domiciliation of non-Hong Kong funds into Hong Kong via registration as OFCs and LPFs and provide certainty of operation and continuity upon registering in Hong Kong. This process will not discontinue the foreign fund's existence nor affect the existing contractual relationships and rights of its partners. Further, this allows Hong Kong fund managers and investors to operate within a single jurisdiction, thereby providing a unified and consistent regulatory and legal framework for different stakeholders, minimising costs and outsourcing needs.

Open-ended fund companies: The introduction of the OFC structure in 2018 has also increased Hong Kong's competitiveness with other sophisticated investor markets such as the United Kingdom (whose equivalent structure is known as the "open-ended investment company"). The OFC structure allows funds to take on a limited liability corporate structure, with the flexibility to vary their share capital to meet shareholder subscription and redemption requests. Sub-funds allowing for segregated liability within an overall umbrella OFC may also be established. OFCs have requirements such as: (i) mandatory delegation of investment management functions to an investment manager in Hong Kong; (ii) mandatory entrustment of scheme property to an eligible custodian; and (iii) disclosure requirements. OFCs can either be set up as public or private vehicles. Public OFCs are authorised and regulated in accordance with the existing authorisation regime for SFC-authorised funds, whilst private OFCs are not. Further, in September 2020, the SFC revised the *Code on Open-Ended Fund Companies* to, amongst other things, expand the investment scope for private OFCs and the entities eligible to act as private OFC custodians.

Investment managers: Any entity that holds responsibility for managing investments in Hong Kong must hold a Type 9 (asset management) licence with the SFC, regardless of whether the fund itself is incorporated onshore or offshore (as a unit trust, OFC or LPF). Type 9 intermediaries are required to comply with the Fund Manager Code of Conduct, which sets out organisation, conduct and disclosure requirements in connection with managing collective investment schemes. In August 2021, the SFC issued the *Consultation Conclusions on the Management and Disclosure of Climate-related Risks by Fund Managers*, confirming that it would amend the Fund Manager Code of Conduct to require fund managers to take climate-related risks into consideration in their investment and risk management processes. The introduced requirements cover governance, investment management, risk management and disclosure obligations. Depending on the activities and size of the fund manager, baseline or enhanced requirements will be applicable (with a corresponding transition period). It is worth noting that, in instances where the main commercial substance of a fund is located in another jurisdiction, the investment manager would most likely be domiciled in that jurisdiction and subject to any local regulatory requirements. In order to manage the Hong Kong aspects of that fund, the investment manager would then appoint a sub-advisor or sub-manager in Hong Kong. Such sub-advisor or sub-manager would be subject to the same licensing requirements as described above, and would manage the local aspects of the fund only.

Hong Kong fund financing

Capital call (subscription) financing: Subscription line financing has become significantly more common in the Hong Kong market in recent years, with established funds continuing to put in place larger and more sophisticated fund financing facilities for their ever-growing number of successive funds and co-investment funds, largely unhampered by COVID-19. As in other markets, traditionally, subscription line facilities are used as a bridging loan facility to allow investment managers to close deals in a tighter timeframe than would be possible by calling capital from investors (as amounts can often be drawn down under a subscription line facility within a matter of days, while notice periods for calling capital from investors can (as a matter of practice) extend into a number of weeks). Due to the previously low interest rate environment, funds were using subscription line facilities more frequently and more extensively for longer-term borrowings than the original bridging financing they were intended for. However, with the recent hikes in interest rates, fund managers and lenders will become increasingly cautious in assessing how subscription line facilities are to be used going forwards. In recent years, as well as becoming larger (as noted below) and individual borrowings being permitted to have longer tenors, subscription line facilities have become more flexible for borrowers with a combination of one or more of committed and uncommitted tranches sitting together under a single facility, conversion mechanics (which allow the borrower to elect to convert the uncommitted tranche into a committed tranche when required) and multi-currency and ancillary facilities being common features. As noted above, we have also seen Asia take the lead on ESG-linked subscription line facilities, which afford those funds with a clear ESG strategy the ability to reduce margin on their borrowings, subject to certain targets linked to sustainability principles being met. The Baring Private Equity Asia sustainability-linked subscription line credit facility is one of the first and largest to be launched in Asia by a private equity firm.[20]

In Hong Kong, as is the case in the United States, Europe and Australia, security under a subscription line facility is twofold: firstly, an assignment of the fund's and the general partner's right to make capital calls on the limited partners' unfunded capital commitments; and secondly, a fixed charge over the collection account into which the proceeds of such capital calls are paid. The assignment is typically governed by English or Hong Kong law (as the governing law of the facility agreement) and the security interest can be a legal or equitable assignment. However, market practice in Hong Kong is to give notice of the assignment to the limited partners (and, although not a legal perfection requirement, use reasonable endeavours to obtain an acknowledgment) in order to perfect the legal assignment (and, in this respect, the law in Hong Kong relating to charges and assignments follows the same principles as English law).

As suggested above, the market indicates that there may be an increased number of larger-sized funds in the Asia-Pacific region and, since the market for subscription facilities generally tracks that of fundraising of the larger-sized private funds, the prevalence of large, multi-bank subscription line facilities is likely to continue to increase in the next few years, particularly if the PRC relaxes its restrictions on outbound investment over time.

While international banks (many with a strong track record in fund financing in the United States, Europe and Australia) still dominate the mid- and large cap fund finance market in Hong Kong, regional banks based in Hong Kong and other parts of Asia are also starting to become increasingly involved in subscription line financings. Given their extensive network in the region, these domestic champions are well placed to assess the credit of funds with a large regional investor base. They also have a robust appetite for country-specific risk.

Umbrella financing: Many funds choose to set up as an umbrella fund: a single legal entity with a number of separate sub-funds that each operate as an individual fund. For investors, this provides the benefit of economies of scale and, for the investment manager, it is more efficient, as the same terms and conditions tend to apply to each of the sub-funds and to the umbrella fund, reducing administrative time and costs. A subscription facility may be provided either to the umbrella fund or to any one or more of the sub-funds against the usual security package. Umbrella financings are becoming increasingly common in the Hong Kong market, as a number of Asia-domiciled funds are choosing to establish themselves using this structure.

General partner financing: We continue to see general partner financings, with a number of new lenders in the market offering variations on this product as a differentiator in order to secure a right to participate in the underlying subscription line facility. Under a general partner financing, financing is provided to the general partner of a fund in order to finance its working capital needs and, sometimes, its capital contributions into the underlying fund. Under these facilities, security is taken by way of an assignment of all or some of the general partner's partnership interests in the fund (including, for example, its right to receive management fees, performance fees, carried interest and any other related income) in addition to a fixed charge over the relevant collection accounts. This structure is the same in Hong Kong as it is in the United States, Europe and Australia, where these types of financings are much more common in the respective markets.

Alternative models: As the Hong Kong market becomes increasingly sophisticated, both lenders and borrowers are beginning to ask more questions of alternative financing structures that may be more suited to their requirements. Mature funds, which have already called all or a significant portion of their investors' capital commitments, funds that do not permit traditional subscription financing or single investment, and sub-funds looking to obtain financing without recourse to the master fund (amongst others), may, for example, benefit from a NAV-based financing. Instead of being backed by the uncalled capital commitments of the fund's investors, NAV facilities are backed by the underlying cashflow and distributions that flow up from the fund's underlying investments via security interests over the portfolio assets.

As parties search for other available liquidity outside the more traditional financing products, NAV financings are expected to become much more prevalent as a product in Hong Kong.

Another alternative option is the hybrid facility, which offers maximum flexibility to both lenders and borrower funds. These are particularly useful for funds, as they provide financing with a long maturity, utilising a traditional subscription financing structure in the early stages and switching to a NAV-based structure later in the life of the fund, after a certain proportion of commitments has been drawn from investors. This affords lenders recourse to both the undrawn commitments of the fund and the fund's underlying assets, while borrowers are presented with a more flexible solution that may suit their investment needs over time.

In general, there is continuing appetite for managers in the Greater China region to explore either the NAV or hybrid structures; however, most credit providers in the market are still finding it challenging to offer bespoke financing solutions to meet such demand, mainly due to the difficulties in assessing these structures from a credit perspective. The more traditional fund finance products such as subscription line facilities and the general partner/limited partner financings continue to constitute a large majority of the fund financings seen in the market over the past year.

Key developments

Other key developments

ILPA guidance: As mentioned above, a subscription line facility allows a fund to delay calling capital. In addition to being used as a tool to manage the timing of capital calls, it can also be used to boost a fund's internal rate of return by shortening the time that investors' capital is deployed during the fund's investment cycle, which, it is argued, can be used to artificially inflate performance. While many investors do favour subscription line facilities due to the decreased number of capital calls, others are more hesitant because of the additional expenses and this perceived ability to manipulate the internal rate of return. This led the Institutional Limited Partners Association (**ILPA**), following consultations with various interested parties, to issue best practice recommendations in respect of subscription line facilities in June 2017, which were supplemented in June 2020. Generally, these recommendations focus on increased transparency and disclosure to investors.

In the Asia-Pacific region in particular, where investors may be less sophisticated and familiar with the financing product, the market view is that this guidance may lead to increased discussions and interest from investors, helping the investors to better understand subscription line facilities, and in turn perhaps enabling them to better utilise the product. Over time, it is becoming more prevalent to see new funds being established with limited partnership agreements that are more favourable to creditors and expressly contemplate subscription line facilities and related security interests, cross-collateralisation between funds and alternative investment vehicles, and more flexible financing terms including longer-dated facilities. We have also seen an increase in fund financings (both on a bilateral and syndicated basis) being documented on a fully or partially uncommitted basis as lenders compete to offer ever more cost-efficient financing solutions to their fund clients.

Regulatory environment in the PRC: Since the summer of 2016, the Asset Management Association of China (**AMAC**) has opened up the private funds market to foreign asset managers. As at December 2021, there were 57 private Sino-foreign joint-venture (**JV**) or wholly foreign-owned securities investment fund management companies with licences granted by AMAC, including Fidelity International and UBS Asset Management. Such a licence enables them to market funds to qualified domestic companies and high-net-worth individuals in the PRC. The opening of the public fund management sector to foreign investors has also made landmark progress. The first wholly foreign-owned public fund manager BlackRock has received a licence from the China Securities Regulatory Commission (the **CSRC**) and commenced its operation, while Fidelity has received the CSRC's approval for its establishment and is in the process of preparing to commence operation. It is expected that a few other reputable players will also enter the market in the coming years. Another noticeable type of platform is the bank wealth management JV, which allows foreign asset managers to set up majority foreign-owned JVs with Chinese banks and offer both public and private bank asset management products in the Chinese domestic market. Several reputable foreign asset managers have formed JVs and have been exploring entering into the Chinese asset management market under this structure. Such JVs include Amundi BOC Wealth Management, BlackRock CCB Wealth Management, Bank of Communications Schroder Fund Management and Goldman Sachs ICBC Wealth Management.

The year ahead

Looking forward

In the past few years, the Hong Kong Government has pushed forward many much-needed measures and reforms to strengthen Hong Kong's position as a leading international fund centre, and we continue to see encouraging signs in the form of expanding mutual recognition of funds, the introduction of the OFC and the LPF regime, the establishment of the unified fund exemption regime, the Tax Concession Amendments and the operations of the Re-domiciliation Bills for re-domiciliation of non-Hong Kong funds to Hong Kong. With a large number of global asset managers already having significant presence in Hong Kong, this jurisdiction will no doubt continue to be a key player in the private funds market in Asia.

As lenders, funds and investors in Hong Kong develop a more mature understanding and appreciation of the funds market and attempt to transfer more sophisticated products and tailor-made solutions from the United States and Europe (such as NAV and hybrid financings), we have no doubt that Hong Kong and Greater China will see an intriguing evolution in the years ahead.

* * *

Endnotes

1. Asset and Wealth Management Activities Survey 2021 (Securities and Futures Commission July 2022).
2. Asset and Wealth Management Activities Survey 2021 (Securities and Futures Commission July 2022).
3. Website of the Hong Kong Securities and Futures Commission: https://www.sfc.hk/en/Regulatory-functions/Products/List-of-publicly-offered-investment-products/Mutual-recognition-of-funds-arrangements.
4. Website of the Hong Kong Monetary Authority: https://www.hkma.gov.hk/eng/key-functions/international-financial-centre/wealth-management-connect.
5. Data provided by Preqin.
6. Based on a search of ICRIS, Cyber Search Centre of the Hong Kong Companies Registry website, as of 10 October 2022.
7. See https://www.elegislation.gov.hk/hk/2021/33!en and https://www.elegislation.gov.hk/hk/2021/34!en, respectively.
8. Data provided directly by Preqin.
9. Data provided directly by Preqin.
10. Asia-Pacific Private Equity Report 2022, Bain & Company.
11. Asia-Pacific Private Equity Report 2022, Bain & Company.
12. Preqin Territory Guide: Greater China 2022, Preqin.
13. 2022 Preqin Global Private Equity Report. Private Equity: Year in Review, Cameron Joyce & Grant Murgatroyd.
14. Asia-Pacific Private Equity Report 2021, Bain & Company.
15. 2022 Preqin Global Venture Capital Report, Preqin.

16. Preqin Territory Guide: Greater China 2022, Preqin.
17. Preqin Territory Guide: Greater China 2022, Preqin.
18. Asia-Pacific Private Equity Report 2022, Bain & Company.
19. Asia-Pacific Private Equity Report 2022, Bain & Company.
20. Website of Baring Private Equity Asia: https://www.bpeasia.com/bpea-establishes-asias-first-sustainability-linked-credit-facility-at-us3-2-billion.

* * *

Acknowledgment

The authors would like to thank Ernest Yim, a lawyer in Allen & Overy's Asia-Pacific Funds & Asset Management group based in Hong Kong, for his important contribution to this chapter. Ernest advises clients on fundraisings, establishment of and participation in private equity investment funds, and secondary transactions.

James Ford
Tel: +852 2974 7085 / Email: james.ford@allenovery.com
James is a partner in Allen & Overy's Asia-Pacific Funds & Asset Management group. His practice focuses on clients active in private equity and other alternative assets, where he has a broad range of experience covering traditional fundraisings, secondary transactions, mergers and acquisitions, strategic investments and capital markets transactions. He regularly guides clients in structuring funds and transactions to address a wide range of regulatory, tax and transactional issues. James is recognised as a leading lawyer by the industry's most prestigious legal publications, including *Chambers Asia-Pacific*, *Chambers Global*, *The Legal 500*, and *IFLR1000*.

Patrick Wong
Tel: +852 2974 7260 / Email: patrick.wong@allenovery.com
Patrick is a partner based in Allen & Overy's Hong Kong office. He has experience in a wide range of banking and finance transactions, including fund financings, bilateral and syndicated corporate lending, acquisition financings, equity margin financings, pre-IPO investments and other event-driven financings. Patrick regularly represents banks and non-bank financial institutions in structured cross-border financings in the Asia-Pacific region with a particular focus in Mainland China and Hong Kong.

Charlotte Robins
Tel: +852 2974 6986 / Email: charlotte.robins@allenovery.com
Charlotte is a partner based in Allen & Overy's Hong Kong office. She acts for a wide range of national and international financial institutions including investment and private banks, asset and wealth managers (including hedge fund and private equity managers and advisors) and insurance companies. Her practice includes advising on setting up regulated businesses in Hong Kong, ongoing compliance with regulatory laws, codes and guidelines, and the impact of regulatory change. Some selected areas of expertise include licensing, product offering, regional and global cross-border issues, regulatory corporate governance, ESG, anti-money laundering and data privacy. She has been actively involved in responding to regulatory consultations, recent examples including: client suitability requirements; manager-in-charge regimes; amendments to the SFC Fund Manager Code of Conduct and the Hong Kong Monetary Authority's regulation; and supervision of Trust Business.

Allen & Overy

9th Floor, Three Exchange Square, Central, Hong Kong
Tel: +852 2974 7000 / URL: www.allenovery.com

Ireland

Kevin Lynch, Ian Dillon & Ben Rayner
Arthur Cox LLP

Overview of the Irish funds industry

Overview of the Irish regulated funds market

Ireland is regarded as a key strategic location by the world's investment funds industry. Investment funds established in Ireland are sold in 90 countries across Europe, the Americas, Asia, Africa and the Middle East. Over 1,000 fund promoters have funds domiciled and/or serviced from Ireland.

As of July 2022, there were 8,497 Irish-domiciled funds (including sub-funds) with net assets of almost €4 trillion. While the majority of these fund assets are held in Undertakings for Collective Investment in Transferable Securities ("**UCITS**"), Irish-domiciled alternative investment funds ("**AIFs**") had in excess of €890 billion in net assets as of July 2022. Ireland is also the largest hedge fund administration centre in the world.

Given the scale of the funds industry in Ireland and the global reach of its distribution network, it is not surprising that the vast majority of the investment in these regulated investment funds comes from non-Irish, predominantly institutional, investors.

Regulatory framework

The Central Bank of Ireland (the "**Central Bank**") is responsible for the authorisation and supervision of regulated financial service providers in Ireland, including regulated investment funds and investment managers. The powers delegated to the Central Bank are set out in the laws and regulations applicable to the relevant financial services sector. In addition, the Central Bank issues guidance in relation to various aspects of the authorisation and ongoing requirements applicable to financial service providers and investment fund products in Ireland.

Common fund structures

Ireland as a domicile provides a variety of potential fund structures, which can be broadly categorised as regulated by the Central Bank or unregulated.

Regulated structures

There are five main types of regulated fund structure in Ireland (as described below): (i) variable capital investment companies ("**Investment Companies**"); (ii) Irish collective asset-management vehicles ("**ICAVs**"); (iii) Unit Trusts; (iv) common contractual funds ("**CCFs**"); and (v) investment limited partnerships ("**ILPs**"). Investment Companies, ICAVs, Unit Trusts and CCFs may be established as UCITS pursuant to the European Communities (Undertakings for Collective Investment in Transferable Securities) Regulations 2011 (as amended) or as AIFs pursuant to the EU (Alternative Investment Fund Managers) Regulations 2013 (as amended) (the "**AIFMD Regulations**"). An AIF may also be established as a regulated ILP. The Irish legislation governing ILPs was overhauled by the enactment of the Investment Limited Partnerships (Amendment) Act 2020 (the "**ILP 2020 Act**") in late December 2020. The ILP 2020 Act modernised the law governing ILPs in Ireland. As well as modernising the ILP in line with other types of Irish investment fund structures, the amendments to the existing legislation brought the ILP in line with comparable partnership structures in other leading jurisdictions by incorporating "best in class" features for this type of vehicle.

These structures may be organised in the form of umbrella schemes with segregated liability between compartments ("**sub-funds**").

Investment Companies

An Investment Company is established as a public limited company under the Irish Companies Act 2014. They have a separate legal identity and there is no recourse to the shareholders. There is a requirement to spread risk if the fund is established as an Investment Company. It is typically the board of directors of the Investment Company that will approve any decision to borrow, grant security or enter into derivatives, although it will be important in each case to review the Investment Company's constitutional documents, including its memorandum and articles of association, prospectus and/or supplement thereto, and any management agreements to determine who has the authority to execute the necessary agreements.

ICAVs

The ICAV is an Irish corporate investment fund that was introduced to meet the needs of the global funds industry, pursuant to the Irish Collective Asset-management Vehicles Act 2015 (the "**ICAV Act**"). The ICAV is now the most commonly used structure for newly established funds in Ireland. The ICAV is a bespoke corporate structure that is specifically designed to give more administrative flexibility than an Investment Company. For example, the ICAV may:
- amend its constitutional documents without shareholder approval in respect of changes that do not prejudice the interest of shareholders and do not come within certain categories of changes specified by the Central Bank;
- where established as an umbrella fund, prepare separate financial statements for each sub-fund;
- issue debenture stock, bonds and any other securities; and
- allow directors to dispense with the holding of an AGM by giving written notice to all shareholders.

In addition and unlike Investment Companies, the ICAV may also be eligible to elect to be treated as a transparent entity for US federal income tax purposes.

UCITS and AIFs established in Ireland as Investment Companies may convert into an ICAV subject to compliance with the conversion process specified by the Central Bank. Importantly, this conversion process does not affect the legal existence of the fund or any pre-conversion rights or obligations. The ICAV Act also contains a mechanism for existing corporate collective investment schemes established in jurisdictions such as the Cayman Islands, the British Virgin Islands, Bermuda, Jersey, Guernsey and the Isle of Man, to migrate or redomicile to Ireland as an ICAV by operation of law. As the ICAV is a separate legal entity, the analysis in relation to who has authority to contract, e.g. borrow, grant security or enter into derivatives, for an ICAV is the same as for an Investment Company.

Unit Trusts

Unlike an Investment Company or an ICAV, a Unit Trust is not a separate legal entity but rather a contractual fund structure constituted by a Trust Deed between a Trustee and a management company. In a Unit Trust, the Trustee or its appointed nominee acts as legal owner of the fund's assets. As the Unit Trust does not have a separate legal personality, it cannot contract for itself. Managerial authority is exercised by the directors of the management company, which, in the context of an AIF, may also perform the role of alternative investment fund manager ("**AIFM**"). While, in many cases, it is the directors of the management company who execute contracts, the Trust Deed and other relevant documents such as the management agreement should be carefully reviewed to confirm who has signing authority. For example, if assets are registered in the name of the Trustee, the Trustee would need to execute any security agreements required to grant security over the assets of the Unit Trust and, in some Unit Trusts, the Trust Deed may, for example, require joint execution by the Trustee and the management company.

CCFs

A CCF, similar to a Unit Trust and ILP, does not have a separate legal existence. It is a contractual arrangement established under a deed of constitution, giving investors the rights of co-owners of the assets of the CCF. As co-owners, each investor in a CCF is deemed to hold an undivided co-ownership interest in the assets of the CCF as a tenant in common with other investors. The CCF was developed initially to facilitate the pooling of pension fund assets efficiently from a tax perspective and may be treated as transparent for tax purposes, which is a key distinguishing feature from other types of Irish fund structures.

ILPs

An ILP is a partnership between one or more general partners ("**GPs**") and one or more limited partners ("**LPs**") and is constituted by a partnership agreement. As with a Unit Trust, an ILP does not have an independent legal existence. It has one or more LPs (which are similar to shareholders in an Investment Company or ICAV, or a unitholder in a Unit Trust) and a GP who can enter into contracts on behalf of the ILP, which would include any loan agreement or security document. The ILP 2020 Act introduced a number of changes to the ILP structure intended to make the ILP more broadly appealing to promoters of venture capital and private equity funds in particular. The changes included provision for: (i) the establishment of umbrella ILPs; (ii) the broadening of "safe harbour" provisions allowing LPs to take certain actions without being deemed to be taking part in the management of the ILP; (iii) the amendment of the limited partnership agreement ("**LPA**") by majority (rather than by all general and limited partners); and (iv) the streamlining of the process for the contribution and withdrawal of capital.

Unregulated structures

Limited partnerships

The limited partnership established pursuant to the Limited Partnership Act 1907 is the favoured structure for unregulated investment funds in Ireland.

A limited partnership is a partnership between one or more GPs and one or more LPs, and is constituted by a partnership agreement. To have the benefit of limited liability, the LPs are not permitted to engage in the management of the business of the partnership, or to contractually bind the partnership – these functions are carried out by the GP.

There is a general limit of 20 partners in a limited partnership, although this limit can be raised to 50 where the limited partnership is formed "for the purpose of, and whose main business consists of, the provision of investment and loan finance and ancillary facilities and services to persons engaged in industrial or commercial activities". The analysis in relation to who has authority to contract, e.g. borrow, grant security or enter into derivatives for an unregulated limited partnership, is similar to that for an ILP.

Section 110 companies

Section 110 is a reference to section 110 of the Taxes Consolidation Act 1997 (as amended), which provides for a specific tax regime for certain qualifying companies. They are most commonly incorporated as Irish designated activity companies (or "**DACs**") and are used in structured finance deals, but we also see them being used as vehicles for loan book transactions and being dropped under regulated fund structures as an investment vehicle. To qualify for the beneficial tax treatment, certain conditions must be satisfied. Where a section 110 company is borrowing under a financing transaction, it is common to include certain representations and covenants in a loan agreement to give a lender comfort that the relevant conditions are being satisfied. The section 110 is often, but not always, established as a "bankruptcy-remote" vehicle, and a common ask from section 110 borrowers is that recourse to the borrower is limited to the secured assets and that a "non-petition" clause is included. From a borrower perspective, this should be raised at term sheet stage to avoid the need for a further credit approval on this point. Developments in response to the interest limitation rules under the EU Anti-Tax Avoidance Directive may result in the restructuring of certain stand-alone section 110 structures in favour of a structure that utilises a regulated fund vehicle as part of the overall structure, and this may have implications for existing deals where security or other elements must be re-papered.

Regulation of Irish funds

Broadly speaking, regulated investment funds in Ireland can be established as either UCITS or AIFs.

UCITS

UCITS were first introduced in 1985 in the EU with the introduction of the UCITS Directive. Although UCITS are a regulated retail investment product, subject to various liquidity constraints, investment restrictions (both in terms of permitted investments and required diversification), borrowing and leverage limits, they are predominantly held by institutional investors and are firmly established as a global investment fund product (being widely distributed both inside and outside of the EU). Irish UCITS may avail of the UCITS passport regime, which allows for UCITS to be marketed publicly across the EU subject to limited registration requirements.

AIFs

AIFs are defined under the Alternative Investment Fund Managers Directive ("**AIFMD**") as "any collective investment undertaking [...] which raises capital from a number of investors, with a view to investing it in accordance with a defined investment policy for the benefit of those investors", and that does not require an authorisation under the UCITS Directive. Therefore, all non-UCITS funds may be considered AIFs. Irish AIFs are established pursuant to the AIFMD Regulations, which implement AIFMD in Ireland. AIFMD regulates both EU AIFMs that manage AIFs in the EU, and non-EU AIFMs that manage or market AIFs in the EU. The main types of AIFs in Ireland are Qualifying Investor Alternative Investment Funds ("**QIAIFs**") and Retail Investor Alternative Investment Funds ("**RIAIFs**").

QIAIFs can be marketed to professional investors and there is a minimum subscription requirement of €100,000 (which may be disapplied in respect of certain categories of investor). They can avail of the right to market across the EU using the AIFMD passport. A QIAIF can be managed by an EU or non-EU AIFM and can also be internally managed (see below). A QIAIF is not subject to any investment or borrowing limit, but it is obliged to spread risk if established as an Investment Company.

The RIAIF replaced the previous retail non-UCITS regime and has no minimum subscription requirement, but there is a restriction on it borrowing more than 25% of its net assets. As the RIAIF is a retail fund, it cannot use the AIFMD passport that is available to QIAIFs marketing to professional investors. Unlike a QIAIF, RIAIFs cannot be managed by a non-EU AIFM. AIFs are required to appoint an AIFM, which can be either an external Manager of the AIF or, where the legal form of the AIF permits, such as in the case of an Investment Company or ICAV, and the AIF chooses not to appoint an external AIFM, the AIF itself.

Real Estate Investment Trusts ("**REITs**")

REITs were first introduced in Ireland in 2013 under the Irish Finance Act with the purpose of attracting capital and thereby improving the stability of the Irish property market. Irish REITs are established as companies under the Companies Act 2014 and can gain classification as a REIT when notice is given to Irish Revenue and applicable conditions are met. While REITs are not collective investment undertakings as such, the Central Bank has indicated that REITs are *prima facie* AIFs for the purpose of AIFMD (requiring the appointment of an AIFM) unless the REIT can demonstrate otherwise. Furthermore, the Central Bank has indicated that REITs structured as unauthorised AIFs must comply with the Central Bank AIF Rulebook provisions for retail AIFs.

Regulatory and market update

Developments in relation to sustainable finance

With the aim of furthering sustainable finance and ESG integration, the European Commission (the "**Commission**") introduced a package of legislative measures in 2018 that includes three key regulations: the Taxonomy Regulation; the Disclosures Regulation; and the Low Carbon and Positive Impacts Benchmarks Regulation. The Disclosures Regulation came into effect on 10 March 2021 ("**SFDR Level 1**"), which required all financial market participants ("**FMPs**"), including AIFMs, UCITS management companies and self-managed UCITS, to consider sustainability from a number of perspectives and to: (1) publish information on their websites regarding their policies on the integration of sustainability risks in their investment decision-making process; (2) make pre-contractual disclosures on how they incorporate sustainability risks in their business; and (3) comply with pre-contractual transparency rules on sustainable investments.

The high-level principles-based requirements contained in SFDR Level 1 are supplemented by more detailed Level 2 requirements ("**SFDR RTS**"). SFDR RTS requires FMPs to comply with more detailed pre-contractual disclosures and annual reporting disclosures. FMPs must make these disclosures in the mandatory templates that are set out in the annexes to SFDR RTS for relevant products. In addition, certain Taxonomy Regulation-related disclosures will apply to those products/funds that are categorised as "Article 8" or "Article 9" under the Disclosures Regulation. This subset of Article 8 and Article 9 funds will be subject to additional disclosure requirements regarding the alignment of their investments with the Taxonomy Regulation. Further, the Taxonomy Regulation requires that so-called "Article 6" funds include a negative statement in their offering documents and annual reports that underlying investments do not take into account the EU criteria for environmentally sustainable economic activities.

To ensure there is a single rulebook for sustainability disclosures, the European Supervisory Authorities determined that the additional taxonomy-related requirements should be incorporated into SFDR RTS. These requirements become effective as of 1 January 2023.

Central Bank consultation in relation to macroprudential measures for the property fund sector

As noted above, Irish AIF structures are not typically subject to borrowing limits. However, in November 2021, the Central Bank published Consultation Paper 145 ("**CP145**"), consulting, *inter alia*, on the possible introduction of limits on the permitted level of leverage in an Irish fund investing in Irish property. Detailed submissions on the consultation paper have been received from many interested parties. The final position has now emerged and a 60% leverage limit has been set, which will include lending from the Sponsor into a property fund by way of "quasi-equity". Certain transitional or grandfathering arrangements will apply to existing structures, lessening the need for restructuring existing debt arrangements.

Fund financing and security

Overview

Lending to Irish funds is typically structured as either a bilateral or syndicated facility, or a note issuance agreement whereby the issuer (the fund) issues a note in favour of the note holder. Lending by AIFs is restricted, although (as discussed above) it is possible to establish an AIF that is focused on loan origination, including investing in loans. While the majority of deals we see are capital call/subscription line deals, in the last number of years, we are seeing more net asset value ("**NAV**"), hybrid, umbrella and preferred equity transactions. Irish fund structures, particularly Investment Companies, ICAVs and ILPs, are also commonly used as property investment vehicles.

The lenders and governing law

At present, the majority of deals in the Irish market are being financed by international financial institutions, although one of the Irish "pillar" banks is in this market. Reflecting the international nature of the financiers, the relevant loan agreements for such transactions are commonly governed by the laws of New York or England & Wales, although there is no legal reason why they could not be governed by Irish law. The terms of the loan agreement will very much depend on the type of facility being advanced.

While many lenders in Irish fund financings hold a bank licence or have "passport" rights to lend into Ireland, it should be assessed on a case-by-case basis whether a bank licence or passporting rights are required on a particular transaction, particularly where the relevant lender(s) do not have either a banking licence or passporting rights and the transaction involves "banking business" as a matter of Irish law. Lenders should also assess with local counsel whether they need to register summary details of the loan with the Irish Central Credit Register maintained by the Central Bank.

Security package

A key consideration in every fund financing is the security package. This will vary depending on the type of financing involved. For example, on many financings, the security package will consist of a fixed charge over the fund's rights, title and interest in and to the securities and/or cash account recorded in the books and records of the Depositary (or Trustee, in the case of a Unit Trust; as such, any references hereafter to a Depositary should be read to include Trustee in the context of a Unit Trust) and an assignment of the fund's rights in the Depositary Agreement (or Trust Deed, in the case of a Unit Trust or deed of constitution in the case of a CCF). Such a security package is also commonly coupled with a control agreement, which will give the lender or its security agent control over relevant rights or assets either on a "day-one" or more commonly on a "springing lien" basis, which gives control to the security agent upon the occurrence of a future enforcement event.

A properly drafted and structured Irish law security document should also be able to obtain the benefits of being considered a "financial collateral arrangement" pursuant to the European Communities (Financial Collateral Arrangements) Regulations 2010 (as amended) in respect of a securities account. For cash accounts, relevant bank mandates should be reviewed and, where necessary, amended to be consistent with the terms of the control agreement. It is very important in this context to also verify where the account is located, whose name the account is opened in and who has signing rights on the account. The International Bank Account Number ("**IBAN**") for the account is an important piece of information to obtain in order to determine the *lex situs* of a cash account and, therefore, the appropriate governing law for the account security. In many cases, the account holder may be a Depositary or sub-custodian, and the cash account for an Irish fund may not be located in Ireland, particularly where cash is held by a sub-custodian. In this context, and to satisfy the Depositary's obligations to maintain control over the assets, consideration should be given as to whether the Depositary also needs to be party to the control arrangements. Any party with signing rights should also be a party to the control arrangements. Equally, in structures where the connection with Ireland is only that the Depositary is Irish-incorporated, it is not uncommon that one or more cash accounts may also be held by sub-custodians outside Ireland. In our experience, lenders will frequently weigh the cost of taking security in potentially multiple jurisdictions against the benefit of obtaining such security. One important consideration we have seen recently is that while, in Ireland (which has a common law system), we recognise the concept of legal and beneficial ownership of assets, this may not necessarily be the case in other jurisdictions, particularly jurisdictions that have a civil law system. By way of example, if a cash account is held in a custodian's name in Luxembourg (rather than being held in the name of the relevant fund, and including situations where the custodian holds the account on behalf of the fund), from a Luxembourg law perspective, any purported security granted by the fund under Irish law in respect of its beneficial interest in the cash account will not be enforceable under Luxembourg law, and consideration should therefore be given as to whether such security should be taken under Luxembourg law from the account holder, i.e. the custodian. As with any financing, there is no "one size fits all". In this regard, the typical security package for a capital call/subscription facility is quite different, commonly consisting of security over the right to call on investors for further contributions and security over the account into which such subscription monies are lodged, coupled with a robust power of attorney either prepared on a stand-alone basis or forming part of the relevant security document.

The fund's constitutional documents, prospectus, as well as the administrative services agreement, other fund service provider appointment documents and the Subscription Agreement, need to be carefully reviewed to verify who has the right to make the subscription call. For example, in the context of a corporate fund such as an Investment Company or ICAV, most commonly it is the directors of the fund that make the call, but sometimes the constitutional documents also give the Manager (where the corporate fund is externally managed) the power to make the call. It is not uncommon that subscriptions into an Irish entity, particularly in structured finance transactions, may consist of a subscription for shares but also a subscription for profit-participating notes, which are, in essence, a form of debt instrument. The issues that must be checked for/addressed will be similar in many respects to those for a Subscription Agreement for shares.

The Administrator also plays an important role in processing subscriptions and recording and registering them. Depending on the extent of the role performed by the Administrator, consideration could be given to taking specific security over the rights of the fund in and to the administrative services agreement, which would afford the lender "step-in" rights *vis-à-vis* the Administrator in any further enforcement. However, in practice we do not see this, and more usually a side letter addressed to the lender/agent is obtained from the Administrator in relation to the performance of their duties under the administrative services agreement; such side letters would typically, amongst other things, give the lender (or its security agent) a right to issue instructions to the Administrator following an Event of Default. Depending on the extent of the role of other fund service providers, further side letters may be required.

Over the last number of years, we have also seen a steady growth in financings involving Feeder Fund structures. From an Irish law regulatory perspective, this can require careful structuring of the security package. One of the issues that requires consideration in this regard is that an Irish regulated fund cannot give "guarantees" to support the obligations of a third party (which may include another sub-fund within the same umbrella fund structure).

Unfortunately, the term "guarantees" is not defined, and it would be prudent to take it that this term also captures "security" to support the obligations of a third party. In Feeder Fund structures where, for example, the Main Fund is the borrower and the Feeder Fund is an Irish fund that is expected to guarantee the obligations of the Main Fund, the rule against giving third-party guarantees is very relevant and the structure and security package will need to be carefully considered and tailored to ensure that this rule is not infringed.

The use of "cascading pledges" can also, depending on the structure, be a useful tool in the security package. It is also possible to apply for an exemption from the Central Bank but, even if given, this takes time to obtain. Other structuring solutions do exist, and we would always recommend local advice be sought at term sheet stage so the solutions can be "baked" into the deal. Guarantees by an Irish regulated fund of the obligations of a 100%-owned subsidiary are not captured by the prohibition.

Governing law of security package

Irish law does not strictly require that the security package be governed by Irish law. We commonly see transactions where security is taken under the laws governing the relevant financing agreement, e.g. New York or England & Wales law. However, where the relevant secured assets are in Ireland, e.g. the securities or cash account or, for a subscription call deal, the governing law of the Subscription Agreement is Irish law, we would always also take Irish law-governed security. Typically, any control agreement would be governed by the laws of the country where the account is located; however, if this is not the case, local law guidance (and preferably a legal opinion) should be obtained to ensure that the use of a different governing law will be enforceable in the relevant jurisdiction.

Security agent

As a common law jurisdiction, there is no issue as a matter of Irish law with security being granted in favour of a security agent or security trustee and, subject to the bank licensing considerations referred to previously, it is not necessary under Irish law for the security agent to be licensed in Ireland to enforce its rights. A point to note in relation to the enforcement of Irish security is that on enforcement, it is typically a receiver appointed by the lender/security agent who will be appointed over the secured assets, and realise the same on behalf of the secured parties. One advantage of this, from a lender/security agent perspective, is that the Irish security document will contractually provide that the receiver is the agent of the borrower rather than the lender/security agent, thereby insulating the lender/security agent from potential claims arising from the actions of the receiver as part of any enforcement.

Consents and stamp duty

No Irish governmental consent or stamp duty is generally required/payable in connection with the execution of security in fund financing. However, where a security assignment is being taken over the funds' rights in and to the Depositary Agreement, the Depositary Agreement should be carefully reviewed to check that the prior consent of the Depositary and/or the Central Bank is not required. In cases where the assignment is taken by way of security rather than being a true assignment, the consent of the Central Bank will not be required, as it permits funds granting such security in connection with its borrowings, and for receivers appointed by the lenders enforcing such security.

Security over the appointment documents of other fund service providers is not common, but should be assessed on a case-by-case basis, depending on the extent of the relevant role of such fund service providers in relation to the secured assets.

Security filings

Once security has been created, lenders will need to ensure that the security, if created by an Irish entity or an entity required to be registered in Ireland as a branch, whether governed by Irish law or otherwise, is registered against the correct entity in the appropriate Irish registry. For example, (1) security created by an Investment Company will be registered on the file of the Investment Company in the Irish Companies Registration Office (the "**CRO**"), and (2) security created by a Trustee or its nominee as part of a Unit Trust structure will be registered on the file of the Trustee/its nominee in the CRO.

Importantly, as ICAVs are established under the ICAV Act rather than the Companies Act, registrations for ICAVs are made on the file of the ICAV with the Central Bank rather than the CRO. Particulars of all such security in the form prescribed by the CRO (Form C1) or the Central Bank (Form CH1) must be filed within 21 days of the date of creation of the security, and in the absence of such, filing is void against a liquidator and any creditor.

Property fund financing

Irish funds are also popular vehicles for investment in Irish real estate by both Irish and non-Irish investors. In our experience, ICAVs, since their introduction in 2015, have been the most popular platforms used by investors, but some investors have also used Unit Trusts due to their familiarity with same in their home jurisdictions. While many investors establish their own fund platforms, it is also possible to establish a sub-fund as part of an existing platform set up by a service provider, a so-called "rent a fund". This can save on the establishment cost. In some deals, ILPs are also set up under the relevant Investment Company or ICAV sub-fund, for finance structuring reasons.

The loan agreement in financings for such funds is typically based on the Loan Market Association ("**LMA**") Real Estate Finance form of loan agreement. This is commonly governed by Irish law but, if necessary, could equally be governed by the laws of England (adapted as required). There are a number of key modifications that need to be made to the LMA form, in particular to reflect the role and importance of the relevant service providers in such structures, such as the management company, AIFM and the Depositary, the applicable Events of Default, regulatory compliance matters, the change-of-control provisions and the security package.

The security package will always consist of security over the relevant property and related assets and in many, but not all, cases, security over the shares/units in the fund/sub-fund. Where the fund/sub-fund has invested in real estate through an ILP, security can also be taken over the sub-fund's interest in the ILP, and security is also taken over the shares held by the shareholder of the GP of the ILP. This is important as, in an ILP, it is the GP who contracts for the ILP and, on an enforcement, having security over those shares means that the lender can exercise control over the GP and its contracting powers.

As with all fund financing structures, it is crucial at an early stage of any property fund financing deal to ascertain who has title to the assets and who has contracting power. An additional point to note in this regard is that the Depositary of the fund investing in real estate is obliged to maintain "control" over the property and related assets, such as rental income. Previously, this was interpreted by Depositaries to mean that title to the property had to be registered in their name.

However, this potentially exposes the Depositary, as registered owner of the property, to claims, for example, in relation to environmental liability, but also to being named in court proceedings if, for example, there is a rent dispute. The practice that has emerged in this regard is that either the Depositary has title registered in the name of a nominee company it establishes or, more commonly, title is registered in the name of the fund, and the Depositary registers a caution on the relevant property title that restricts future disposals, including on any enforcement.

It is crucial in this context to obtain a control letter/deed of control from the relevant Depositary to regulate the rights and duties of the Depositary on any future enforcement by the lenders but also, for example, to regulate how the Depositary operates the fund's bank accounts to ensure compliance with the account control and waterfall provisions of the facility agreement. Commonly, the rent account in such transactions is opened in the name of the Depositary, and it is Depositary signatories who are named on the bank mandate. Certain Depositaries also interpret their duty of "control" to extend to limited partnership assets where the relevant Irish regulated fund controls the GP and is the sole LP.

Hotel financing can also be accommodated through a fund structure. Particular issues can arise in relation to this type of structure, where a separate operating company/property company ("**OpCo/PropCo**") structure is used, and advice should be sought at an early stage to optimise the structure and ensure that financing can be put in place.

Due diligence

Before deciding on the final lending and security structure, it is of critical importance that the requisite due diligence is undertaken. A good deal of management time, both on the lender and borrower side, can be saved by clearly setting out the proposed structure, the proposed security structure, including what will be required from all stakeholders, including investors, and what amendments will be required to constitutional documents.

Identifying and seeking to address issues in relation to any of the above in the course of the transaction will lead to additional costs, tension and potentially, in the worst cases, the deal not completing. In this update, we focus on some issues that lenders should bear in mind when undertaking their due diligence for subscription facilities.

<u>Power and authority to borrow and give security</u>

Subject to any self-imposed leverage limits, as mentioned below, most AIFs will have broad powers, in their constitutional documents, to borrow and create security. For a subscription call facility, it is preferable that the constitutional documents, when describing the assets over which security can be taken, explicitly refer, for example, to "unfunded capital commitments". But even where they do not, the lender should be satisfied that the constitutional documents refer to the fund's ability to create security over all of its "assets", as the unfunded capital commitments will constitute an asset of the fund.

Borrowing and leverage limits

As referenced above, there are a variety of available fund structures in Ireland, ranging on the regulated side from Investment Companies, ICAVs, Unit Trusts, ILPs and CCFs, to limited partnerships and section 110 vehicles on the unregulated side. The constitutional documents of each type of fund, while bearing similarities to each other in terms of regulatory content, can be quite different structurally and will always need to be carefully reviewed to establish who has the authority to borrow and provide security on behalf of the fund. Such authority should reflect the legal structure of the fund and should be set out in the relevant constitutional document. Typically, the following parties will have authority to borrow and provide security on behalf of a fund:

- **Investment Company**: The directors of the Investment Company.
- **Section 110**: The directors of the section 110 company.
- **ICAV**: The directors of the ICAV.
- **Unit Trust**: The Manager commonly has the power to borrow, and frequently also has the power to create security, although this varies and sometimes requires execution by the Trustee.
- **CCFs**: As per Unit Trust, above.
- **ILPs and limited partnerships**: The GP.

Regulated Irish funds may be established as umbrella funds with one or more sub-funds and segregated liability between sub-funds. Importantly, sub-funds do not have a separate legal personality, so the finance documents are typically entered into by: the corporate entity itself, in the case of a corporate fund such as an Investment Fund and ICAV; the Manager, in the case of Unit Trusts and CCFs; and the GP, in the case of a limited partnership.

In each case, the relevant entity is acting for and on behalf of the relevant sub-fund, and this should be reflected in the finance documents. Segregation of liability means that the assets of one sub-fund cannot be used to satisfy another sub-fund's liabilities. This is achieved by statute in the case of Investment Companies and ICAVs, and by contract in the case of Unit Trusts, CCFs and limited partnerships.

While statute implies the concept of segregated liability between sub-funds in an umbrella in every contract entered into by Investment Companies, ICAVs and ILPs, it is customary practice to include segregated liability language in any finance document to which the Irish fund is a party, irrespective of the legal form of the fund. Segregated liability is not important for unregulated fund structures, i.e. limited partnerships and section 110 companies, but as previously mentioned the concepts of limited recourse and non-petition will be key concerns for section 110 companies.

The constitutional documents – due diligence

Irish funds may be open-ended, open-ended with limited liquidity, or closed-ended. In the context of a capital call facility (in the case of closed-ended funds or limited liquidity funds with a capital commitment structure), it is crucial to understand: (i) the subscription process, including who can make calls on investors; (ii) who determines the price at which units or shares are issued and by what means; (iii) when capital calls can be made on investors; (iv) what an investor can be asked to fund; (v) the implications of an investor not funding a capital call; and (vi) what account subscription proceeds are paid to.

The subscription process, who can make calls?

The agreement between the fund and the investor in relation to subscriptions is typically enshrined in a Subscription Agreement. This tends to be a relatively short document, but must be read in conjunction with the constitutional documents and the fund service provider documents. Most commonly it is the fund, through its directors, GP or Manager (as applicable), who will be authorised to make the calls on investors, although this is sometimes a role that is delegated by the directors, GP or Manager (as applicable) to either the Investment Manager or the Administrator. For entities such as a Unit Trust or a CCF, which are constituted by deed between the Manager and the Trustee/Depositary, it is usually the Manager who is authorised to make calls.

How and who determines the price at which units or shares are issued?

For Irish regulated funds, it is not just the fund itself acting through its directors, GP or Manager (as applicable) that has a role. Other service providers, such as the Administrator of the fund, also play a crucial role. The Administrator in an Irish regulated fund assumes, for example, the role of calculating the NAV of the fund and its units/shares. This calculation is crucial in determining the number of units/shares that will be issued to the investor in return for their subscription/capital call proceeds.

Once the proceeds are received, the Administrator will then issue all of the relevant shares/units to each relevant investor. In Irish regulated funds, the constitutional documents commonly provide that physical unit/share certificates are not issued but rather the unitholder/shareholder register is evidence of ownership. Due to the important role played by the Administrator, it is common that an Administrator side/control letter is obtained as part of the security package.

When can calls be made on investors?

Calls are typically made on a Dealing Day, which will be a defined term in the constitutional documents. It is important to check that this definition accommodates calls being made by the lender, if they need to, on a future enforcement. The definition of Investment Period is also relevant in this regard. Many constitutional documents only permit calls to be made during the Investment Period, subject to limited exceptions; for example, where the call is made to satisfy sums due for an acquisition that has contracted but did not complete prior to the expiry of the Investment Period.

As noted above, one of the key first steps in making a call is for the Administrator to determine the NAV and how many units/shares will be issued. The constitutional documents must be carefully reviewed to determine what events are specified, the occurrence of which gives the directors the right to suspend calculation of the NAV. The concept of suspension is an important safeguard for the fund to deal with; for example, *force majeure* market events that prevent the fund from valuing a substantial portion of the assets of the fund, or generally where it is deemed in the best interests of the investors in the fund.

However, in practice, while the NAV is suspended, calls may not be able to be made. This risk can be mitigated by having all shares potentially issuable to an investor being issued on a partly paid basis on day one, but the ability to use this mechanism needs to be assessed on a case-by-case basis. A suspension of the NAV where enforcement is necessary is not ideal! A carefully drafted investor consent letter, or drafting included in the Subscription Agreement, in which the investors expressly agree to fund a capital call during a suspension of the NAV, can give lenders additional comfort on this issue.

What can an investor be asked to fund?

As you would expect, investor calls are primarily made to fund the acquisition of investments. Preferably, the constitutional documents should also explicitly permit calls to be made to repay sums due to the lenders. Importantly, most Irish funds will operate on the basis that *pro rata* calls are made on investors. This may not be explicit in the constitutional documents, and sometimes may be reflected in an investor side letter.

What are the implications of an investor not funding a subscription call?

The constitutional documents and/or the Subscription Agreement will usually provide for a period of time in which the investor must remit the call proceeds. If they are not received in that period, the documents will commonly provide that the fund may then issue a default notice and, if the default is not remedied within any applicable remedy period, the fund will have the right to charge default interest and ultimately to realise the defaulting investor's shares/units to meet the call. From a lender perspective, the constitutional documents need to be checked to determine whether they contain "overcall" provisions. Such provisions permit the fund to call on the other investors to fund another investor's defaulted call, subject of course to the investors' maximum commitment not being exceeded.

As noted above, this needs to be carefully considered in the context of any potential conflict with any "*pro rata*" call provisions in the constitutional documents, any side letter, or the commercial practice of the particular fund. The constitutional documents should also be checked to determine whether the investor has any right of set-off, defences, counterclaim, etc., in respect of unpaid calls against amounts that may be owed by the fund to the investor. If possible, it should be made explicitly clear that the investor must fund even if the fund is insolvent, and that they will meet calls by the lender upon enforcement. If a borrower is asked to give an undertaking to a lender in the finance documents that all sums due to an investor are subordinated to sums due to the lender, the borrower should check that its fund documents and contractual arrangements with its investors are consistent with this. If such subordination provisions are not included, an amendment may be required to the constitutional documents or the fund may need to obtain a side letter from the investors. We also see appropriate wording being built into notices of creation of security and the investor agreeing to the wording by signing an acknowledgment of the notice.

What account are subscription proceeds paid to?

A key part of the security package for a capital call facility is security over the Subscription Proceeds Account. There can be some variation between funds as regards how and in whose name their bank accounts are established. For example, it may be in the fund's name, which is the most straightforward position from a lender's perspective, but may also be in the AIFM's or the Depositary's name. The bank account mandates should also be checked to see who has signing rights, and it should be checked with the Administrator/Depositary whether the proceeds move through any other accounts *en route* to the Subscription Proceeds Account and whether there are any automatic sweep mechanics on the account. Appropriate control arrangements should also be considered, to include the above-referenced service providers, where necessary.

The Subscription Agreement, investor side letters and notice of security

As mentioned above, the typical Subscription Agreement is quite short but is nevertheless a crucial document. As part of the security package, security is taken over the fund's rights therein by way of security assignment. The Subscription Agreement and any side letters need to be checked to ensure there are no prohibitions or restrictions on such assignment. For subscriptions into a section 110 company, investors commonly invest by subscribing for profit-participating notes rather than by subscription for shares, but a security assignment can still be taken over the section 110's rights therein.

Upon execution of the security, an equitable assignment is created as a matter of Irish law. From a priority perspective, however, it is better to convert this to a legal assignment. There can be some reluctance on the part of the fund to have notices of assignments sent to investors and relevant acknowledgments obtained, particularly where there is a large number of investors. In this regard, some lenders will agree that notices are not served until a future Event of Default. One possible compromise between these two positions is that the relevant notice of creation of security is communicated in the next investor communication. Most commonly, we see notices served on investors at closing of the facility.

Securitisation Regulations

The European Securitisation Regulations (2017/2402) came into force in Ireland on 1 January 2019. If a section 110 company is in the deal structure, it is important that an analysis is carried out at the beginning of the deal as regards whether the financing could be considered to be a securitisation and if the Regulations are applicable. An important part of the analysis in relation to applicability of the Regulations will be determining whether the lender is relying, partly relying, or not relying on the underlying cash flows or assets of the section 110 company. The analysis may therefore reach different conclusions for subscription line facilities, NAV, other asset-based facilities or hybrid facilities.

The year ahead

The Irish financial services sector has continued to provide market-leading solutions for its international client base, which is reflected in significant increases in total assets in the Irish funds sector as well as the continued increase in the number of asset managers establishing management companies in Ireland.

Irish Funds, the industry body for the Irish funds sector, forecasts the level of international assets in Irish-domiciled funds to top €5 trillion by 2025, with the number of people directly employed in the industry, across asset management, Depositaries, Administrators, professional advisers, transfer agents, and other specialist firms, set to increase by 25% to over 20,000 in the same period.

Ireland is an open and international economy. In the fund finance space, lenders are currently dominated by the major players from the US and UK and continental Europe. Bank of Ireland has developed a visible and growing market presence over the last number of years and it is to be hoped that it will be joined by other domestic banks and direct lenders in the near future. The cautious optimism that predominates amongst our clients seems to be echoed on an international level; for example, in Cadwalader's recent lender survey with some well-placed words of caution, as expressed in Jeff Johnson's excellent article "A discussion on Bank Regulatory Capital and other Factors Impacting the Fund Finance Market".

We are excited for what 2023 will bring and look forward to working on innovative and market-leading transactions with you.

Kevin Lynch
Tel: +353 1 920 1199 / Email: kevin.lynch@arthurcox.com
Kevin Lynch is the Head of the Arthur Cox Banking & Finance Group. Kevin has extensive experience in banking and finance transactions with an emphasis on domestic and cross-border finance transactions and financial services. Kevin acts for a wide range of financial institutions, funds (both Irish and non-Irish domiciled), corporates and corporate service providers (including AIFMs and Depositaries), advising on funds lending transactions including subscription call, hybrid and NAV facilities. Kevin's practice also includes asset/property finance, acquisition finance and structured finance.

Ian Dillon
Tel: +353 1 920 1788 / Email: ian.dillon@arthurcox.com
Ian Dillon is a Partner in the firm's Asset Management and Investment Funds Group with experience in all aspects of Irish fund law and regulation. Ian's particular focus is on alternative investments including all aspects of AIFMD as well as real estate, hedge, private equity, credit, infrastructure and liquid fund formation. Ian has extensive experience advising both borrower- and lender-side clients on the regulatory and practical aspects of fund financing transactions in Ireland. Ian has worked in the investment funds industry in Ireland and internationally and both in practice and in-house roles for over 20 years and is the current Chair of the Irish Funds AIF Regulatory Working Group.

Ben Rayner
Tel: +353 1 920 2332 / Email: ben.rayner@arthurcox.com
Ben Rayner is a Senior Associate in the Arthur Cox Banking & Finance Group. He has extensive experience advising on domestic and cross-border finance transactions in Ireland and whilst working at international law firms in London, and acts for a range of financial institutions and funds on subscription, NAV and hybrid facilities. Ben's practice also includes advising on acquisition and leveraged financings. He has spent time on secondments to the legal teams of an alternative asset manager in Dublin and the London office of a leading investment bank.

Arthur Cox LLP
Ten Earlsfort Terrace, Dublin 2, Ireland
Tel: +353 1 920 1000 / URL: www.arthurcox.com

Italy

Alessandro Fosco Fagotto, Edoardo Galeotti & Valerio Lemma
Dentons Europe Studio Legale Tributario

Overview[1]

According to the annual market overview published by the Italian Private Equity and Venture Capital Association ("**AIFI**"), 2021 was a year that saw significant transactions, also in terms of size of target companies, in relation to which very positive returns were achieved.

This is confirmed by an analysis of the figures. Indeed, it should be noted that the "Cash In" (EUR 1,701 million compared to EUR 5,274 million in 2020) and "Cash Out" (EUR 684 million in 2021 compared to EUR 1,625 million in 2019) amounts recorded in 2021 were lower than in previous years, although these were unique years that are incomparable with others because of some extraordinary "mega deals" with high returns.

More generally, in 2021, 654 transactions were recorded in the Italian private equity and venture capital market, distributed among 488 companies, for a countervalue of EUR 14,599 million. Compared to 2020 (with EUR 6,597 million invested in 471 deals), the figure shows a 121.3% increase in the amount invested, whilst the number of investments grew by 38.8%. With respect to the main types of transaction that were carried out, early-stage investments (371) were clearly dominant, followed by buy-out (159) and add-on (60) transactions.

In terms of amount, infrastructure became the market segment where most of the resources were spent (EUR 7,671 million), with an increase of 480% compared to the previous year (EUR 1,322 million), followed by buy-outs (EUR 5,386 million) and early-stage investments (EUR 587 million).

With reference to the categories of players involved, international operators absorbed 76% of the market in terms of amount invested (EUR 11.138 million), while domestic operators invested an overall amount equal to EUR 3.561 million (24% of the market). In this regard, it should be noted that international operators without an office in Italy invested EUR 5.661 million in the country distributed over 75 deals. On the other hand, domestic operators carried out most of the investments (489, equal to 74.2% of the market).

With respect to the value of transactions, the average amount was equal to EUR 22.5 million, up on the previous year, when it stood at EUR 14 million. More specifically, taking into account the amount invested in each transaction, in 2021, eight deals were present with an equity value between EUR 150 million and EUR 300 million (*i.e.* large deals) and eight deals with an equity value of more than EUR 300 million (*i.e.* mega deals). Overall, large and mega deals attracted resources for EUR 9,821 million, equal to 67% of the total amount invested in 2021. In the previous year, large and mega deals attracted EUR 3,463 million, equal to 53% of the total amount. Deals with an equity value of less than EUR 150 million (*i.e.* small and medium deals) equalled EUR 4,878 million, an increase compared to 2020 (EUR 3,134 million).

In line with the data recorded in the previous year, the geographical distribution of investments shows that 95% of investments carried out in 2020 related to companies located in Italy, corresponding to 98% of the amount invested in such year. If we consider only the activity carried out in Italy, 69% of transactions involved companies located in the north of the country (60% in 2019), followed by the southern region and islands with 9% (23% in 2019), while the central region was stable at 22% (17% in 2019). In terms of amount, the north attracted 79% of the total resources invested in Italy (74% in 2019), followed by the central region with 15% (21% in 2019), while the share of resources allocated to southern Italy stood at 6% (5% in 2019). As per tradition, at regional level, Lombardy confirmed its supremacy, where 40% of the total number of operations completed in 2021 were carried out there, followed by Lazio (13%) and Veneto (8%). In terms of amount, Lombardy took first place, with 60% of the total resources invested, followed by Lazio (11%) and Piemonte (8%).

With respect to the sectoral distribution of investments, in 2021, the ICT sector (communications, computers and electronics) represented the main investment target in terms of number of operations, with a share of 28%, followed by the industrial goods and services sector, with a weight of 14%, and the medical sector (11%). In terms of amount, most of the resources invested during the year went to the ICT sector (51% of the total), followed by industrial goods and services (12%) and environment and energy (14%). The number of transactions carried out in 2020 in favour of companies defined as "high-tech" stood at 185 (181 in 2019), a market impact of 28%. Taking a closer look, the sub-sectors in which the highest number of operations is highlighted are ICT, medical and insurance and financial services, which, in terms of number, accounted for 64% of investments in high-tech companies carried out during 2021. It is significant to point out that 77% of high-tech transactions detected involved start-up companies.

With regard to distribution of the number of investments by size of target companies, the 2021 data show a concentration of operations from small to medium-sized companies (86% of the total number, 90% in 2020), characterised by a number of employees below 250. These companies attracted resources for a total amount of EUR 6,253 million (43% of the total, 42% in 2020), while the rest of the market, with a weight of 14% in terms of number of investments, absorbed 57% of total resources (EUR 8,446 million). The distribution of investments by turnover also shows how small and medium-sized companies (with a turnover of less than EUR 50 million), also for 2021, represented the main target towards which private equity and venture capital investments were directed in Italy, with a share of 79% of the total number of transactions.

In relation to the figures related to disinvestments, during 2021, the relevant amount calculated at the acquisition cost of equity investments reached EUR 2,702 million, showing an increase of 69% compared to the EUR 1,594 million recorded in the previous year. By number, 104 divestments were recorded, an increase compared to the 81 transactions recorded in 2020. Sale to an industrial operator (trade sale) was the preferred channel of divestment (EUR 871 million accounting for 32%) followed by sale to another private equity operator (EUR 814 accounting for 32%). Furthermore, in terms of numbers, the most common type of exit strategy still remained the trade sale (36 exits, equal to 35% of the total), followed by sale to another private equity operator (30% of the total). With specific reference to the type of investor, domestic operators were the most active in terms of the number of divestments (62%), while in terms of amount divested, international operators prevailed (66%). Lastly, if the number of divestments is cross-referenced with the type of original investment, it emerges that the largest number of divestments was attributable to buy-outs (46%), followed by expansions (27%) and replacement (12%).

When looking at the analysis of resources collected by funds, in 2021, the total resources collected by domestic operators were equal to EUR 5,725 million, which shows an increase of 119% when compared to EUR 2,612 million in 2020. In that respect, it shall be noted that 44 operators carried out fundraising activities in 2021, compared to 27 in 2020.

Capital raised in the Italian and international financial markets by independent operators amounted to EUR 5,359 million, up 159% compared to the previous year (EUR 2,072 million). More specifically, with reference to the geographical origin of these amounts, it should be noted that 89% (EUR 3,237 million) were domestic, while the foreign component accounted for 11% (EUR 408 million). In this regard, pension/social security funds were the primary source of capital (26%), followed by institutional funds of funds (15%), insurance companies (14%) and banks (14%).

Finally, in terms of distribution of independent funding by type of target investment, it is expected that most of the capital flowing into the market will be used for buy-outs (54%). This will be followed by investments in infrastructure (25%) and the early-stage sector (15%).

Fund formation and finance

The Italian regulatory field

The transition to a low-carbon, more sustainable, resource-efficient and circular economy in line with the Sustainable Development Goals is key to ensuring the long-term competitiveness of the asset management industry and has been the ground for the drafting of Commission Delegated Regulation (EU) no. 2021/1255 of 21 April 2021 amending Delegated Regulation (EU) no. 231/2013 as regards the sustainability risks and sustainability factors to be taken into account by Alternative Investment Fund Managers ("**AIFMs**"). National competent authorities ("**NCAs**") and AIFMs should be given sufficient time to adapt to the new requirements contained in this Regulation. Its application was therefore deferred to 1 August 2022.

It is also worth noting that Italian regulators have considered the need for aligning Bank of Italy regulations in line with the European Securities and Markets Authority ("**ESMA**") guidelines on performance fees of UCITS and certain types of alternative investment fund ("**AIF**") (ESMA34-39-992) of 5 November 2020. In a nutshell, given this need, the update has driven a simplification and adaptation to market developments.

It is also worth recalling that the European Commission's "*Report assessing the application and the scope of Directive 2011/61/EU on alternative investment fund managers*" (published on 10 June 2020) has provided input for reviewing the national implementation of Directive 2011/61/EU ("**AIFMD**"), considering also the COVID-19-related stresses and emergency temporary regulation. According to the conclusions of the abovementioned report, the Italian harmonised regime delivers a more coordinated supervisory framework based on a set of standards, promoting high-level investor protection and facilitating greater integration of the EU AIF market.

It is a common opinion that improved regulation on both fund formation and fund financing is needed. In this respect, the expected EU review of AIFMD would be an opportunity for envisaging a supervisory convergence in the area of investment management with respect to delegation and substance requirements, in order to reduce the possibility of unfair competition (considering seconded staff, regulatory arbitrages, etc.). This refers also to the possibility of identifying a set of collective portfolio management functions to be regulated in a way that admits the engagement of platforms and white-label service providers to innovate the business of collective portfolio management (considering specific requirements to ensure the reliability of fintech services).

The experience of COVID-19 highlighted the need for additional liquidity management tools, whose regulation should be consistent throughout all EU jurisdictions, as well as the need for aligning investment policy to unexpected temporary market shocks. In this respect, a review of AIFMD is desirable, which would also include availability of a set of these tools, as well as the possibility to regulate the way in which NCAs use their powers to suspend redemptions in situations where there are cross-border financial stability implications.

Besides the above, it is worth considering that the transposition of AIFMD has already changed the Italian regulatory framework on collective portfolio management, which provides a well-tested system for regulating both management companies' organisation and funds' investment activities. In particular, this is the result of integration between clear legislative requirements and the wide freedom of self-regulation (in the drafting of funds' rules or by-laws).

By way of background, collective portfolio management is ruled by the Italian consolidated law on finance (Legislative Decree no. 58 of 24 February 1998) ("**Decree 58/98**"), by a specific Ministerial Decree (no. 30 of 5 March 2015), by the Bank of Italy Regulation on collective portfolio management of 19 January 2015, and by the Bank of Italy Regulation on the corporate governance of management companies of 5 December 2019.

Within the above regulatory framework, the life and operations of each fund are governed by the "funds rules" (*Regolamento del fondo*), set by the asset management company authorised by the supervising authority (except for the fund reserved to professional investors) and accepted by the participants (*i.e.* the investors who have subscribed to the units of the relevant fund).

With specific regard to the formation of Italian funds, the abovementioned regulations leave to the management company a wide range of possibilities in choosing the contents of the fund's rules (in accordance with the provision of article 37 of Decree 58/98). In other words, the management company can set up the investment policy of the fund with a high level of discretion, as the final step of a self-regulation process that governs the fund's formation (prior to the actual provision of collective portfolio management).

Therefore, supervision of management companies, the reserved nature of the activity, and self-regulation are the pillars of the current Italian legislative framework. In particular, the recent amendments to Decree 58/98 have confirmed the basic principles pursuant to which collective portfolio management is reserved to management companies (articles 32 *quater* and 33), and that the obligations assumed on behalf of the fund are satisfied only with the fund's assets (article 37). Moreover, the Bank of Italy can provide specific limits to the leverage of AIFs, in order to ensure the stability and integrity of the financial market (article 6 of Decree 58/98). In addition, Italian regulation has been amended to comply with the provisions of Directive (EU) no. 2019/1160 and Regulation (EU) no. 2019/1156 facilitating cross-border distribution of collective investment undertakings. It concerns new rules about pre-marketing in order to improve information for the market.

With regard to fund financing requirements, it is worth mentioning the requirement for asset managers to set forth in the fund's rules the maximum level of leverage used in the management of the fund, and the way to reach such leverage. In this context, the leverage of real estate AIFs must be below two (even if real estate AIFs that are not listed may borrow money – within the limit of 10% of the net asset value ("**NAV**") – for early reimbursements in case of issue of new units), while the leverage of AIFs investing in credits must be lower than the limit of 30% of their NAV. Other closed-end funds must contain their leverage within 10%.

In 2021, the Bank of Italy issued a second update containing amendments to the regulations on collective asset management, and this update: (i) clarified the possibility of deferred and gradual payment of subscription fees; (ii) extended the possibility to suspend, in exceptional market circumstances, the right of redemption of investors in open Italian UCITS; (iii) eliminated the obligation for management companies of non-reserved closed-end AIFs to purchase on their own account a share of at least 2% of the initial total net value of the AIF; (iv) eliminated the limit of concentration towards the same counterparty for investments in credits in reserved closed-end AIFs; and (v) implemented ESMA guidelines regarding liquidity stress tests, introducing obligations for managers and custodians.

We should also consider that the Italian regulatory framework regulates the establishment of companies with fixed or variable equity, namely SICAFs and SICAVs. In terms of regulatory contents, they are defined as open- or closed-ended undertakings incorporated as joint-stock companies, with variable or fixed equity, and with the exclusive purpose of collective investment in the assets raised by the offering of their own shares (article 1, lett. i e i-*bis* of Decree 58/98). The funding of this kind of company relies on common rules for commercial companies and those relating to collective portfolio management.

Following the latest updates of Italian regulations, the formation of AIFs investing in credits offers a wide range of opportunities in using such vehicle in operations aimed at increasing the performance of the debtor or the value of the assets underlying the relevant guarantees. It is worth recalling that Law Decree no. 18 of 14 February 2016 has provided specific provisions for supporting lending to Italian firms, confirmed by its conversion into Law no. 49 of 8 April 2016. In this respect, EU AIFs aimed at investing into credits of Italian borrowers (other than consumers) must obtain the relevant authorisation in their home country (and adopt a scheme analogous to the one provided for Italian funds, including – among others – the rules on leverage). In such a case, the asset manager of these EU AIFs shall notify to the Bank of Italy the intention to invest in Italy (and shall join the Italian Central Credit Register).

In this respect, this kind of AIF is suitable for supporting non-bank financial intermediation, as they are under public supervision, but out of the scope of capital adequacy requirements. Hence, direct-lending AIFs are in a position to issue the credits and hold or distribute them, depending on the actual set-up of the relevant investment policy. In this scenario, AIF managers may also manage funds aimed at the warehousing of those credits, or their resale on the wholesale market. The last development in this context is the management of funds investing in direct lending to other funds. Such investment policy would create a new market whereby investors could rely on activities aimed at investing in the debt (and not in the equity) of other funds.

From this perspective, UCITS and AIFs shall be considered the products of the asset manager, as in the cases of the European Long-Term Investment Fund ("**ELTIF**") (introduced by EU Regulation no. 760 of 2015), the European Venture Capital Fund ("**EuVECA**") (in relation to a qualifying venture capital fund in the European Union, under EU Regulation no. 345 of 2013), and the European Social Entrepreneurship Funds Regulation ("**EuSEF**") (on European social entrepreneurship funds, under EU Regulation no. 346 of 2013). The relevant regulations of ELTIF, EuVECA and EuSEF are uniform and directly applicable to Member States, so that asset managers are already able to set up such kind of funds, in order to market and manage them across Europe.

In this context, the transposition of Directive 2014/65/EU ("**MiFID II**") has strengthened the transparency of such products in order to allow for safer marketing. However, this Directive did not extend its provision to funds or their management companies, but limits the duty of cooperation between authorities to the supervision of the latter (articles 11 and 68). Therefore, there is still an open question regarding the regulatory path to satisfy the collective need for the portfolio management industry to be competitively set up, in the light of the new standards required for complying with MiFID II.

Financing and collateral structure

The common financing structure for fund financing in Italy reflects the structure applied in other regions, where fund financing was introduced a long time ago. Usually, it is built up as a committed revolving credit facility, and provides for an availability period that starts upon the first closing of the fund. The reimbursement usually does not exceed 12–18 months, which is set out as a target. According to the preference of Italian banks, the relevant facility agreements are frequently governed by Italian law.

The typical security package structure provides for: (i) a pledge over the claims (undrawn commitments) (sometimes substituted by a deed of assignment by way of security) of the fund *vis-à-vis* its investors to make future contributions of previously subscribed capital to the investment vehicle (the "**Pledge over the Claims**"); and/or (ii) a pledge over the credit rights arising from the bank account where the capital contributions of the investment vehicle's equity investors must be made (the "**Pledge over Bank Account**").

In addition to the above and in order to strengthen the lender's security package, banks usually ask (and obtain) from the fund an irrevocable power of attorney (which could also be notarised in order to strengthen its power) that allows them to directly exercise their rights to call for the undrawn commitments. Such power of attorney shall only be exercisable by the pledgee in case of an acceleration event, and to the extent the acceleration event has not been remedied or waived in accordance with the finance documentation.

According to general principles under Italian law, and in line with the majority of academics and Italian Supreme Court case law on this matter, it must be noted that any power of attorney may be revoked by the relevant principal, despite being expressed to be irrevocable. To mitigate such issue, the power of attorney is frequently incorporated in a specific contractual mandate, given also in the interest of the mandator under article 1723, paragraph two of the Italian Civil Code (applicable to all contractual mandates), which sets out that the contractual mandate is not extinguishable by revocation by the principal, unless: (i) it is otherwise agreed between the parties; or (ii) there is a specific hypothesis for just cause (*giusta causa*, *i.e.* as a result of: (i) a breach of contractual undertakings; or (ii) non-compliance with the duties of loyalty, diligence or correctness inherent in the fiduciary nature of the contractual relationship) for such revocation.

It is still a controversial matter whether article 1723, paragraph two of the Italian Civil Code is applicable not only to the contractual mandate but also to a power of attorney linked to this contract: while a minority of academics and a recent Italian Supreme Court case law denied such conclusion, an overwhelming majority of academics, supported also by a dated orientation of the Italian Supreme Court, assert that such paragraph is applicable also to the power of attorney.

Under Italian law, several requirements must be executed in order to perfect the above-mentioned pledges.

With regard to the Pledge over the Claims, according to article 2800 of the Italian Civil Code, the pledge over receivables must be granted by a written deed bearing a certain date at law (*data certa*) and may be enforceable with priority against third parties only when, alternatively: (i) a notice of the pledge has been given to the debtor by a court bailiff or by means of another document bearing a certain date at law; or (ii) the debtor has accepted the pledge by means of a document bearing a certain date at law. The same requirements must be fulfilled in order to perfect the deed of assignment by way of security of the undrawn commitments.

In relation to both such securities, the execution of the relevant deed allows the pledge to be perfected – or the assignment by way of security, as the case may be – between the relevant parties. The notice to the debtor, or instead, its acceptance, is required in order to ensure that the relevant security can be considered opposable towards the debtor in respect of undrawn commitments as well as any third party (including any bankruptcy procedure).

In this regard, for investors located in the European Union, pursuant to article 14.2 of Regulation (EC) no. 593/2008 of the European Parliament and of the Council of 17 June 2008 on the law applicable to contractual obligations (so-called "Rome I"), the formalities for the Pledge over the Claims (or the assignment by way of security), to be invoked against the debtors, are governed by the law governing the document under which the credits that are pledged (*i.e.* the fund documents) were born. Despite the universal nature of such regulation, for investors located outside of the European Union, the formalities to be carried out in order for the Pledge over the Claims (or the assignment by way of security) to be invoked against the debtors and third parties may vary depending upon the law and case law (*jurisprudence*) of the country of residence of said investors.

With regard to the Pledge over Bank Account, according to article 3 of Legislative Decree no. 170 of 21 May 2004, implementing Directive 2002/47/EC on financial collateral arrangements, as subsequently amended and supplemented ("**Decree 170**"), such pledge is perfected, valid and opposable towards the debtors of the undrawn commitments and third parties once the Pledge over Bank Account is signed by the fund and the pledgee. Should the relevant bank account be opened with a bank other than the lenders or the security agent (the "**Depositary Bank**"), according to Italian law it is mandatory that the Depositary Bank also accedes to such pledge agreement in order to make it impossible for the pledgor to dispose of the amounts credited without the consent of the lenders.

While the Pledge over the Claims (or the deed of assignment by way of security) allows lenders to be the beneficiaries of payments of any claims *vis-à-vis* the investors, upon the occurrence of an event of default, Decree 170 allows the lenders to perfect several enforcement methods in order to realise the Pledge over Bank Account and, in particular, lenders shall be entitled, beyond any in-court procedure, to the direct appropriation of any amount credited on the pledged bank account for an amount equal to the outstanding sums due to the lenders at the time of the enforcement.

Taking into consideration that fund financing is spreading in Italy but is still not a common practice, and that Italian funds are still not completely familiar in respect of such transactions, during the structuring of the financing, particular attention should be paid to the partnership agreement of the fund, to confirm that it provides for the same provisions as one would expect to see in limited partnership agreements in jurisdictions more familiar with fund financing (*i.e.* provisions that clearly confirm that the fund can enter into a facilities agreement, as well as provisions that allow the relevant lender to submit, on behalf of the manager of the fund, a drawdown notice to the investors of the fund).

In addition to the above, in the Italian fund financing market, it is not customary to have detailed due diligence in respect of the fund's investors, and funds are not comfortable giving evidence of side letters. In this respect, Italian lenders are frequently asked to rely on specific representation that no side letters exist, which could affect the reimbursement of the financing or the enforcement of the relevant securities.

The year ahead[2]

Italy's economy exceeded pre-COVID-19 levels in the second quarter of 2022. The reopening of the economy, after lifting all pandemic-related restrictions, and policy measures to mitigate the impact of high energy prices on firms and households, contributed to strengthened output growth.

These factors also had an impact on the private equity market. The first half of the year has shown significant growth in the amount invested by private equity on the market (EUR 10.863 million with an increase of 139% compared to the first semester of 2021), whilst the number of investments grew by 34%. Infrastructure has been the market segment where most of the resources were spent (two of the eight mega deals completed during this period are in infrastructure). On the other hand, during the same period, there has been a collapse of expansion operations aimed at developing companies, and there have been a few turnaround deals supporting companies under financial distress. Moreover, the actions taken by the Government have boosted the venture capital sector.

In the third quarter of 2022, the global economy – and Italy's economy, too – slowed down considerably due to exceptionally high inflation, worsening financial conditions, the uncertainty linked to the conflict in Ukraine, weak economic activity in China and, although less than at the beginning of the year, supply chain difficulties. The price of natural gas in Europe reached new heights in August 2022 and decreased after storage targets were met; futures contracts indicate that the prices will remain very high throughout the next year, partly due to the risks weighing on energy supply security. Instead, oil prices dropped due to the widespread deterioration in the economic situation. The latest forecasts of international institutions do expect a slowing down of global growth during the next year, with a high risk that it could turn to a wider decrease.

With regard to Italy's economic situation, the negative impact of high energy prices and inflation rate, which is expected to climb up to 8.7% at the end of this year, are causing a general contraction of the Italian economy. The figures show that a tangible recovery is not expected before the second half of 2023.

Considering the above, the expected public actions to tackle inflation and the implementation of the National Recovery and Resilience Plan are set to play a key part in overcoming the envisaged period of contraction of Italy's economy.

With regard to the Italian private equity market forecast, the onset of new risks – inflation, rising interest rates, geopolitical turmoil – contributed to a surge in volatility and slowdown in private equity deals in the third quarter of 2022. However, the strong resilience showed by the Italian private equity sector during the COVID-19 pandemic, and the data on this market related to the first half of 2022 and the Government measures aimed to stimulate growth and investments, lead us to believe that, despite the uncertainties, the equity bridge financing market will continue to play a leading role in 2022.

Even though the Italian fund finance market is dominated by Italian banks, the past year has shown how it continues to evolve rapidly towards more complex capital call financing structures that are similar to those prevalent in other comparable European markets. This should also increase the potential participants in these transactions, including foreign-based lenders.

Endnotes

1. Source: https://www.aifi.it.
2. Source: European Commission (https://ec.europa.eu/info/business-economy-euro/economic-performance-and-forecasts/economic-performance-country/italy/economic-forecast-italy_en) and Bank of Italy bulletin.

* * *

Acknowledgment

The authors acknowledge with thanks the contribution to this chapter by Alessandro Engst, a partner in the Banking & Finance practice and the head of the Financial Services area.

Tel: +39 06 8091 2000 / Email: alessandro.engst@dentons.com

Alessandro Fosco Fagotto
Tel: +39 02 7262 6800 / Email: fosco.fagotto@dentons.com
Fosco is a partner in the firm's Milan office and the head of Europe Banking & Finance. He gained great experience in advising lenders (his clients are almost all of the most representative Italian banks, and international banks providing financial support in Italy), financial sponsors (private equity and private debt funds), investors, other financial institutions and borrowers, in connection with a very broad range of financing transactions, including acquisition and leveraged finance, structured finance, real estate finance, general corporate lending and refinancing, with great experience in fund financing facilities. He is broadly acknowledged as one of the leading finance lawyers in Italy for his strong presence, over the last 15 years, in the Italian debt market.

Edoardo Galeotti
Tel: +39 02 7262 6800 / Email: edoardo.galeotti@dentons.com
Edoardo is managing counsel in the firm's Milan office and a member of the global Banking & Finance practice. He advises clients such as leading domestic and international banks, financial institutions, private equity funds, private debt funds and corporations (also listed) in matters relating to, mainly: acquisition and leveraged finance; corporate and syndicated lending; and real estate finance. He focuses, in particular, on complex domestic and cross-border leverage buy-out transactions involving banks and financial institutions, with great experience in fund financing facilities.

Valerio Lemma
Tel: +39 06 8091 2000 / Email: valerio.lemma@dentons.com
Valerio is counsel in the Banking & Finance practice. He focuses on asset management, banking, financial and insurance regulation. Valerio has extensive experience in structuring and implementing investment funds (including credit and real estate funds) and regularly advises financial institutions and other regulated entities with respect to a broad range of regulatory matters and dealings with regulators. Valerio is Full Professor of Economics Law at Università degli Studi G. Marconi. He is the author of several monographs and publications in scientific journals and coordinates the second-level Master's degree in "Regulation of financial markets" at Luiss Guido Carli University. Valerio is a member of the ESMA Post Trading Standing Committee (PTSC) Consultative Working Group (CWG).

Dentons Europe Studio Legale Tributario

Piazza degli Affari, 1, 20123 Milan / Via XX Settembre, 5, 00187 Rome, Italy
Tel: +39 02 7262 6884 / +39 06 8091 2000 / URL: www.dentons.com

Jersey

James Gaudin, Paul Worsnop & Daniel Healy
Appleby (Jersey) LLP

Overview

As an international financial centre (**IFC**) of choice for global investments primarily into the UK and Europe, Jersey is currently home to regulated funds with aggregate net assets under management of approximately £458 billion (June 2022).

The continued rise in assets under management reflects Jersey's increasing popularity as a funds jurisdiction and, in particular, as a home for funds investing in alternative asset classes, including hedge, real estate and private equity funds, which make up approximately 89% of funds business in Jersey. In addition, the lightly regulated Jersey Private Fund introduced in 2017 also continues to increase in popularity, with just over 550 launched to date with an increase of 22% over the last 12 months.

Further, significant funds continue to be raised from a wide range of EU countries, with Jersey seeing an annual increase in Jersey fund managers marketing into Europe with more than 200 Jersey-registered alternative managers marketing 374 funds – a 47% increase over the last five years (December 2021).

There are many reasons for the continuing confidence in Jersey as an IFC. With an increasing global need to demonstrate local economic substance, Jersey, with its 13,000-strong financial sector workforce and well-developed local infrastructure, has the edge over competitor jurisdictions who cannot comply with global substance requirements as readily as Jersey.

Unsurprisingly, there has been a corresponding increase in the demand of the size, complexity and frequency of fund finance transactions in Jersey despite the impact of the current economic outlook and the COVID-19 pandemic.

Fund formation

As a leading financial centre, the fund and financial services regimes are well established and there have been no substantial changes that impact on fund formation, lending or security in recent years. The most commonly used fund structures in Jersey follow well-established patterns and remain as companies, limited partnerships or unit trusts.

From September 2022, the Jersey limited liability company (**LLC**) vehicle has been able to be incorporated. The Jersey LLC is expected to prove popular with US investors and managers and build on the strong transatlantic ties Jersey already enjoys. The Jersey LLC has been designed to be as attractive as possible and will be very familiar to those who already use Delaware or Cayman LLCs in their structures, allowing great flexibility while still protecting Jersey's reputation as a leading, regulatory-compliant finance centre. Series LLCs are still to be introduced at a later date.

Jersey has also introduced well-received updates to the Limited Partnerships (Jersey) Law 1994. These amendments are to improve its flexibility and clarity and to reflect modern improvements made to equivalent laws in competitor jurisdictions by providing further protections/rights for limited partners and third parties.

Security and collateral

Security is taken under and governed by the Security Interests (Jersey) Law 2012 (the **2012 Law**). In force since January 2014, the 2012 Law is a stable and well-trodden security regime specifically designed for the needs of financial services. Perfection requirements for a Jersey law-governed security depend on the collateral, and range from possession of the certificates representing certificated investment securities, control of deposit or portfolio accounts by way of notices and acknowledgments with the relevant account bank or custodian, to registration on the public Security Interests Register (the **SIR**), which will perfect security over any collateral and is the most common, and highly recommended, means of perfection.

A registration fee of currently £150 is payable for each security document registered on the SIR. No other stamp duties, taxes or registration fees are due in Jersey for the taking and registration of security.

In a fund finance context, lenders commonly take as transaction security:

Collateral	Market practice comment	Usual perfection method(*)
Call rights	These rights will usually be under the relevant fund documents (e.g. partnership agreement, subscription agreement, articles of association or LLC agreement). Investors are usually notified of the security interest and may be asked to sign an acknowledgment of the notice. The notice and acknowledgment provide an "estoppel" argument, but neither is required to perfect the security interest.	SIR registration
Bank accounts	Notice is served on, and an acknowledgment obtained from, the account bank. In this context, a "bank account" could be a deposit account or a portfolio/securities account. Bank account security, combined with call rights security, is still the most common security package sought.	Control over bank account via notices and acknowledgments and/or SIR registration
Contract rights regarding a custodian agreement	Notice is served on the custodian and an acknowledgment obtained. This is generally combined with a security over any relevant portfolio/securities account – but not often seen in a fund finance context.	SIR registration
Contract rights regarding management or GP fees	Notice is served on the relevant contractual counterparty and an acknowledgment obtained.	SIR registration
Shares, partnership interests, units or LLC interests	Notices and acknowledgments are generally obtained but not required for perfection. Share or unit certificates and blank transfer instruments are delivered at completion.	Possession of share or unit certificates (for certificated securities) and SIR registration

In general, there is no legal or regulatory impediment to lending to funds in Jersey. The fund manager and directors/controllers of the fund can agree limits and restrictions in the constitutional documents of the fund and the investment manager agreement, if they so choose. In particular, the ability of the fund manager to borrow additional sums or grant security over the fund's assets is an important commercial point to consider.

There are no regulatory restrictions on borrowing for Very Private Funds, funds under the Private Placement Funds Regime, Unregulated Funds or Jersey Private Funds.

For slightly more regulated Expert Funds, Listed Funds and Eligible Investor Funds, no legal restrictions are set in stone but the Jersey Financial Services Commission (the **JFSC**) reserves the right to additional scrutiny if the fund is permitted to borrow money in excess of 200% of its net asset value (**NAV**).

For open-ended certified collective investment funds offered to the general public, which are more heavily regulated, the JFSC provides guidance on borrowing restrictions of the following fund type:

Guidance on borrowing restrictions	
Fund type	Limits on borrowing
General Securities Fund	Not more than 25% of the fund's total net asset value.
Fund of Funds	May borrow up to 10% of its total net asset value, but only on a temporary basis for the purpose of meeting redemption requests or defraying operating expenses.
Feeder Fund	May borrow up to 10% of its total net asset value, but only on a temporary basis for the purpose of meeting redemption requests or defraying operating expenses.
Money Market Fund	May borrow up to 10% of its total net asset value, but only on a temporary basis for the purpose of meeting redemption requests or defraying operating expenses.
Warrant Fund	May borrow up to 10% of its total net asset value, but only on a temporary basis for the purpose of meeting redemption requests or defraying operating expenses.
Real Property Fund	May borrow for the purpose of purchasing real property and for short-term purposes like defraying expenses or to facilitate redemption. The maximum aggregate amount that may be borrowed is 35% of the total net asset value. Borrowing for the purpose of purchasing real property must not exceed 50% of the purchase price of the real property. For real property funds with a net asset value of less than £5 million, and especially during the early life of the fund, some relaxation of the above limits may be granted by the JFSC.
Futures and Options Fund	Must be discussed with the JFSC.
Guaranteed Fund	Must be discussed with the JFSC.
Leveraged Fund	Must be discussed with the JFSC.

Economic substance

The economic substance regime is now well established in Jersey and the comparative ease of demonstrating substance has led to an influx of activity.

The economic substance regime applies to limited partnerships as well as companies and LLCs. Collective investment vehicles (but not their subsidiaries) remain outside the scope of the economic substance regime, save in the case of self-managed funds who are subject to the regime in respect of their fund management activities only.

Green and environmental, social and governance

Environmental, social and governance (**ESG**) issues have moved firmly into the mainstream across the globe, and Jersey has taken proactive steps to acknowledge the importance placed on ESG by investors and managers alike. The JFSC has published disclosure requirements applicable to Jersey Funds who reference sustainable investments in their offering materials with the intention of combatting the risk of greenwashing.

When a fund is marketed on the basis of investing in a sustainable investment as part of its investment objectives, it must disclose all material information in relation to the sustainable investment, which may help simplify matters when setting key performance indicators for sustainability-linked lending.

The year ahead: A glimpse into the future of Jersey Funds for 2022/23

We expect the Jersey fund finance market to continue on its current trajectory. A pipeline of new facilities of all kinds is expected in the jurisdiction, but we continue to anticipate that NAV, hybrid and concentrated NAV facilities will remain a popular alternative for private equity sponsors looking to increase leverage. In addition, we expect to continue to see an uptick in GP liquidity solutions as fund managers consider how to best deal with end-of-life options for funds and their investments. We anticipate that funds will look to hold certain investments for longer to see through the expected economic recession. The practical impact of the pandemic, and particularly the time taken to process new deals, seems to have abated, with the deal timelines generally back to pre-pandemic levels.

James Gaudin
Tel: +44 1534 818 337 / Email: jgaudin@applebyglobal.com

James Gaudin is the Office Managing Partner in Jersey and a Partner within Appleby's Corporate department. He specialises in all areas of offshore corporate, finance and restructuring work within Appleby's strong equity and capital markets practice.

James provides legal advice to a number of high-profile clients in relation to real estate and fund finance and has also advised on some of the largest corporate restructurings to have occurred in the Jersey market. James advises banks and other global financial institutions in relation to the Jersey elements of complex cross-border insolvencies and enforcements.

James became a Partner at Appleby in 2011. Prior to joining Appleby in August 2010, he spent six years in the capital markets and structured finance team at a Jersey-based offshore firm, before joining another major offshore firm where he was a Group Partner and Head of Corporate in Jersey. Before returning to Jersey, James worked with Hemmington Scott in London for four years, latterly as Head of Treasury and Banking. James qualified as a barrister in 1996 and has been a Jersey advocate since 2005. He has not always been a lawyer and spent years as a broker and investment banker with Hemmington Scott, Deutsche Bank and ABN AMRO.

Paul Worsnop
Tel: +44 1534 818 225 / Email: pworsnop@applebyglobal.com

Paul Worsnop is a Senior Associate in the Corporate department in Jersey and works closely with James Gaudin, servicing both fund managers and lenders in connection with high-value, secured and unsecured, capital call, NAV and GP support facilities. Paul joined Appleby in June 2016 from a leading international law firm and has an active practice in fund finance, structuring and establishment.

Daniel Healy
Tel: +44 1534 818 010 / Email: dhealy@applebyglobal.com

Daniel Healy is a Senior Associate in the Corporate department in Jersey. Daniel advises lenders and financial institutions across the full fund finance spectrum of subscription facilities, NAV, hybrid and GP liquidity solutions. Daniel was named as a "Key Lawyer" in *The Legal 500 UK* 2022 and is praised as being "responsive, proactive and can [be] relied upon to get the deal done".

Appleby (Jersey) LLP

13–14 Esplanade, St Helier, JE1 1BD, Jersey
Tel: +44 1534 888 777 / URL: www.applebyglobal.com

Luxembourg

Vassiliyan Zanev, Marc Meyers & Maude Royer
Loyens & Loeff Luxembourg SARL

Overview

Luxembourg continues to strengthen its ranking as the world's second-largest fund domicile after the United States: the assets under management (**AuM**) of Luxembourg-domiciled funds stand at around €5 trillion as at September 2022.[1] Luxembourg remains a major centre for traditional Luxembourg-domiciled undertakings for collective investment in transferable securities (**UCITS**) funds, but also for alternative investment funds (**AIFs**), including private equity, real estate, infrastructure and debt. The overhaul of the limited partnership regime in 2013 followed by the successful introduction of the reserved alternative investment fund (**RAIF**) in 2016 reinforced Luxembourg's position as a jurisdiction of first choice for fund managers.

Concurrently with the surge in the AIF market, Luxembourg has seen a significant development in fund finance activity, supported by the possibility of implementing efficient security packages in the context of credit facilities for funds. Recent years have been particularly active as regards fund finance transactions in Luxembourg, with positive growth, strong credit performance and an absence of credit defaults. While capital call credit facilities, also called subscription line facilities, are still used and continue their steady growth, permanent leverage facilities and net asset value (**NAV**) facilities are now frequently used in order to increase investment capacity, optimise performance and provide additional liquidity solutions for the funds.

Fund formation and finance

Legal overview – fund formation

When selecting Luxembourg as their hub for setting up their investment fund, initiators generally opt for either a non-regulated ordinary commercial company (**SOPARFI**) or one of the following (regulated and non-regulated) fund regimes:

- an investment company in risk capital (**SICAR**), based on the Law of 15 June 2004, as amended, on the risk capital investment company (**SICAR Law**) (the SICAR is a vehicle specifically dedicated to private equity and venture capital investments, whether diversified or not);
- a specialised investment fund (**SIF**), based on the Law of 13 February 2007, as amended, on specialised investment funds (**SIF Law**);
- an RAIF, based on the Law of 23 July 2016, as amended, on reserved alternative investment funds (**RAIF Law**); or
- an undertaking for collective investment (**UCI**), based on Part II of the Law of 17 December 2010, as amended, on undertakings for collective investment (**Part II UCI**) –

given the declining popularity of Part II UCIs with fund initiators (in light of the flexibility of the other available AIF regimes), this chapter will not cover any particular aspects related to funds formed as Part II UCIs.

On the basis of Directive 2011/61/EU of the European Parliament and of the Council of 8 June 2011 on alternative investment fund managers (**AIFMD**), implemented in Luxembourg by the Law of 12 July 2013 on alternative investment fund managers (**AIFM Law**), whose impact on financing transactions taking place within the framework of investment funds will be discussed below, an AIF is defined as a collective investment undertaking, or the compartments of which: (i) that raise(s) capital from a number of investors; (ii) with a view to investing such capital in accordance with a defined investment policy for the benefit of those investors; and (iii) which is not covered by Directive 2009/65/EC on UCITS.

While the RAIF must qualify as an AIF within the meaning of the AIFM Law (and must accordingly appoint an authorised alternative investment fund manager (**AIFM**) as well as a depositary), exemptions under the AIFM Law may apply to the SICAR and the SIF (which are only required to appoint an AIFM if they qualify as an AIF).

It is important to note that any unregulated SOPARFI will be considered an AIF if it fulfils all of the above criteria, thereby triggering the application of the AIFM Law, including the obligation to appoint an AIFM and a depository in respect of the assets held by the SOPARFI (except if such SOPARFI is managed by an Exempted AIFM (as defined below)). This is even more relevant as Luxembourg has taken advantage of the AIFM Law to modernise the existing Luxembourg corporate and limited partnership forms and introduce a new special limited partnership without separate legal personality, thereby setting the stage for the use of Luxembourg unregulated limited partnerships as fund vehicles.

Insofar as the AIFM Law applies, an AIFM may freely market the AIFs it manages to professional investors (within the meaning of Directive 2004/39/EC, as amended (**MiFID**)) in the EU.

Leverage under the AIFMD and the AIFM Law

While non-regulated SOPARFIs, SICARs, SIFs and RAIFs are not subject to any legally imposed limits with regard to leverage, insofar as those vehicles qualify as AIFs and are considered leveraged, the AIFM Law may, nevertheless, need to be taken into consideration.

Meaning of leverage

The AIFM Law defines leverage as any method by which the AIFM increases the exposure of an AIF it manages, whether through borrowing of cash or securities, leverage embedded in derivative positions, or by any other means.

The AIFMD gives the European Commission the power to adopt delegated acts to specify the methods of leverage as defined in the AIFMD, including any financial and/or legal structures involving third parties controlled by the relevant AIF when those structures are specifically set up to, directly or indirectly, create leverage at the level of the AIF. It is important to note, in particular for private equity and venture capital funds, that leverage existing at the level of a portfolio company is not intended to be included when referring to those financial or legal structures.[2] The European Securities and Markets Authority (**ESMA**) considers, however, that debt raised by a financial structure held by an AIF that is a private equity fund as referred to in recital 78 of the AIFMD in order to finance the acquisition of assets shall be included in the calculation of the exposure where: (1) those structures are specifically set up to directly or indirectly increase the exposure at the level of the AIF; and (2) the AIF controls such a structure. If these two conditions are fulfilled, the debt raised by the financial structure is to be included in the calculation of the exposure of the AIF. If an AIF does not have to bear losses beyond its investment in a financial structure that is used to acquire non-listed companies or issuers, the financial structure should not be considered as having been set up to directly or indirectly increase the exposure at the level of the AIF.[3]

The European Commission has also used its powers under the AIFMD to clarify that borrowing arrangements entered into by an AIF are excluded from the leverage calculations if they are: (i) temporary in nature; and (ii) fully covered by capital commitments by investors (i.e. a contractual commitment by an investor to provide the AIF with an agreed amount of investment on demand by the AIFM).[4] The Level 2 Regulations give details of the method to be used by AIFMs to calculate leverage in respect of the AIFs they manage.

Impact of leverage under the AIFMD and the AIFM Law

Any leverage at the AIF level may affect whether or not the AIF must appoint an authorised AIFM and a depositary.[5] Under the AIFM Law, any vehicle qualifying as an AIF must appoint an AIFM, although a lighter regime applies to AIFMs managing: (i) AIFs whose total AuM, including any assets acquired through use of leverage, do not exceed a threshold of €100 million; or (ii) AIFs whose total AuM do not exceed a threshold of €500 million and which are unleveraged and have no redemption rights exercisable during the five years following the date of the initial investment in each AIF (each a *de minimis* exemption).

AIFMs qualifying for a *de minimis* exemption (**Exempted AIFMs**) must nonetheless register with the relevant supervisory authority of their home Member State (**Regulator**). When registering, Exempted AIFMs must identify the AIFs they manage and provide the Regulator with information on their investment strategies. Once registered, Exempted AIFMs must regularly (at least annually) provide the Regulator with information on the main instruments in which they are trading, the principal exposures and the most important concentrations of the AIFs they manage, in order to enable the Regulator to monitor systemic risks effectively. If Exempted AIFMs cease to qualify for the *de minimis* exemption, they must notify the Regulator accordingly and apply for a full authorisation.

The AIFM Law also requires AIFMs to set a maximum level of leverage that they may employ on behalf of each AIF they manage, as well as the extent of the right to reuse collateral, or guarantees that could be granted under the leverage arrangement.

For each AIF they manage that is not an unleveraged closed-ended AIF, AIFMs must employ an appropriate liquidity management system and adopt procedures that enable them to monitor the AIF's liquidity risk, and ensure that the liquidity profile of the investments of the AIF complies with its underlying obligations. They must regularly conduct stress tests, under normal and exceptional liquidity conditions, which enable them to assess the AIF's liquidity risk, and monitor that risk accordingly. On 29 September 2020, the Luxembourg supervisory authority for the financial sector (*Commission de Surveillance du Secteur Financier*, **CSSF**) issued a new circular regarding the ESMA guidelines on liquidity stress testing in relation to UCITS and AIFs, which entered into force on 30 September 2020 (**ESMA Guidelines**). With this circular, the CSSF confirms that, as the national competent authority, it applies the ESMA Guidelines and has integrated them into its administrative and regulatory approach. The ESMA Guidelines set out the items to be covered in a liquidity stress testing policy and recommendations on the frequency of the stress tests (quarterly, unless a higher or lower frequency is justified by the characteristics of the fund, and at least annually).

The AIFM concerned must provide investors with disclosures in respect of the AIF in which they intend to invest, including, but not limited to: a description of the circumstances in which the AIF may use leverage; the types and sources of leverage permitted and the associated risks; any restrictions on the use of leverage and any collateral and asset reuse arrangements; and the maximum level of leverage that the AIFM is entitled to employ on behalf of the AIF. In addition, AIFMs managing EU AIFs employing leverage, or marketing AIFs employing leverage in the EU, must disclose, on a regular basis for each such AIF: (i) any changes to the maximum level of leverage that the AIFM may employ on behalf of the AIF, plus any right to the reuse of collateral or any guarantee granted under the leveraging arrangement; and (ii) the maximum level of leverage that the AIFM is entitled to employ on behalf of that AIF.

In addition to the disclosures to be made, AIFMs must also provide the Regulator with information in respect of the AIFs they manage. In this context, AIFs employing leverage on a substantial basis must make available information on: the overall level of leverage employed by each AIF they manage; the breakdown between leverage arising from borrowing of cash or securities and leverage embedded in financial derivatives; and the extent to which the AIFs' assets have been reused under leveraging arrangements. This information includes the identity of the five largest sources of borrowed cash or securities for each of the AIFs managed by the AIFM, and the amounts of leverage received from each of those sources for each AIF. For non-EU AIFMs, the reporting obligations referred to in this paragraph are limited to EU AIFs that they manage and non-EU AIFs that they market in the EU.

Structuring the security package

Capital call credit facilities are typically secured by the available commitments of the funds' investors. These facilities are subject to a borrowing base determined by the value of the pledged/assigned investors' commitments satisfying certain eligibility criteria. Investors' commitments relating to Luxembourg funds may be structured in different ways and may take the form of equity capital commitments (i.e. to make equity contributions to the fund) and/or debt capital commitments (i.e. to provide debt financing to, or to subscribe for, debt instruments issued by the fund).

The security package typically comprises: (i) a pledge by the fund of the rights in and to the available capital commitments of the investors and the claims against the investors in relation to those commitments; and (ii) a pledge over the bank account into which investors are required to pay their contributions. The fund's underlying investments are not usually part of the security package for capital call credit facilities.

Luxembourg law typically governs the security interests granted by the borrowing fund over the rights in and to the investors' available capital commitments, and any claims against the investors in relation to such commitments. The relevant security interest is in the form of a financial collateral arrangement governed by the Law of 5 August 2005 on financial collateral arrangements, as amended (**Collateral Law**). According to the Collateral Law, security interests over claims against the investors may be created by way of a pledge or an assignment for security purposes. Pledges are the most common security interests over investors' commitments in relation to Luxembourg funds. The pledge/assignment agreement must be evidenced in writing, and the relevant security interest agreement must be executed by the fund (as pledgor or assignor), the fund's general partner and the security taker. It may be signed by way of electronic signature, subject to certain conditions. If the AIFM is empowered to make capital calls and/or enter into borrowing and security interest arrangements on behalf of the fund, it must be added as party to the security interest agreement.

According to Luxembourg conflict-of-law rules, the courts in Luxembourg will generally apply the *lex loci rei sitae* or *lex situs* (the law of the place where the asset subject to the security interest is situated) in the case of creation, perfection and enforcement of security interest over the asset. Thus, Luxembourg law will apply in relation to the creation, perfection and enforcement of security interests over assets that are located or deemed to be located in Luxembourg or governed by Luxembourg law. Claims (*créances*) governed by Luxembourg law or owed by a debtor located in Luxembourg, or accounts opened with banks located in Luxembourg, will be considered located in Luxembourg and thus falling within the scope of the Collateral Law. In addition, the provisions of Regulation (EU) 2015/848 of the European Parliament and of the Council of 20 May 2015 on insolvency proceedings (recast), as amended, must be considered. According to that regulation, claims against a third party (other than claims in relation to cash held in bank accounts) will be considered situated in the EU Member State within the territory of which the third party required to meet the claims (i.e. the debtor) has its centre of main interests.

Concerning claims against investors that are subject to security interests, certain conflict-of-law rules must be taken into consideration when structuring the security package. According to article 14 of Regulation (EC) 593/2008 of the European Parliament and of the Council of 17 June 2008 on the law applicable to contractual obligations (**Rome I Regulation**): (i) the relationship between the security provider and the security taker is governed by the law applicable to the contract between the security provider and the security taker under the Rome I Regulation; and (ii) the law governing the pledged/assigned claim will determine its assignability, the relationship between the security taker and the debtor, the conditions under which the pledge or assignment may be invoked against the debtor, and whether the debtor's obligations have been discharged. Because the fund documentation and subscription agreements are typically governed by Luxembourg law, that law will apply to such matters. Since the Rome I Regulation does not provide explicitly for any conflict-of-law rules concerning the enforceability of and possibility to invoke a pledge/assignment over claims against third parties, some Luxembourg legal practitioners consider that a pledge over, or assignment of, claims would become invocable *vis-à-vis* third parties other than the debtor if the legal formalities applicable in the debtor's jurisdiction are duly complied with.

Given that investors in Luxembourg funds are generally located in different jurisdictions outside Luxembourg, the lenders and the security takers will need to take the above considerations into account when structuring the security package.

On 12 March 2018, the European Commission published a proposal for a regulation on the law applicable to the third-party effects of assignments of claims (**EU Commission Proposal**). This proposal will have an impact on the current conflict-of-law rules and will reduce the uncertainties that surround the enforceability of security interests over claims against debtors (including investors) located in different jurisdictions. The new rules clarify which law applies to the third-party effects of assignments of claims in cross-border transactions. The EU Commission Proposal defines the term "assignment" as "a voluntary transfer of a right to claim a debt against a debtor". The term includes outright transfers of claims, pledges, transfers by way of security or other security rights over claims. As a general rule, the law that governs the third-party effects of assignments of claims is the law of the country where the assignor has its habitual residence. If adopted, the new regulation will provide increased certainty with respect to the perfection and enforceability of security interests over claims against investors (located inside or outside of the EU) in relation to their commitments, and it will significantly reduce the discussions around the applicable creation, perfection and enforceability formalities.

The Collateral Law allows a security interest to be created over present and future claims, provided that they are identified or identifiable at the time of entry into the security interest agreement. It is common practice for the security provider to provide the security taker periodically with an updated list of the investors' commitments.

Under Luxembourg law, pledges/assignments for security purposes that are not notified to or accepted by the investors are fully recognised and enforceable. However, the debtor of a pledged/assigned claim may be validly discharged from its obligation *vis-à-vis* the security provider if it had no knowledge of the pledge/assignment in favour of the security taker. It is therefore usual for lenders to require security interests granted by the fund to be notified to and accepted by the investors, in order to ensure that the investors act in accordance with the security taker's instructions and pay the available commitments to the pledged accounts if the security interest is enforced. Another reason for notifying the investors of the creation of the security interest over their commitments is to ensure that the investors will not be able to invoke their good faith if they act in a way that adversely affects the rights of the security taker (for instance, if the investors accept a release of their commitments, which are subject to a pledge). Additional remedies, such as "*action paulienne*", may be available to the security taker in case of detrimental acts of the fund and the investors acting in bad faith in relation to the pledged commitments.

Notices may be served to the investors by different means (registered letters, emails, electronic communications, etc.). Alternatively, notices may be included in the financial reports (distributed to the investors) or published on an investor portal.

It is usually required by the lenders that the investors waive any defences, right of retention or set-off and counterclaim the investors may have with regard to the pledged/assigned claims and any transferability restrictions that may be applicable. According to the Collateral Law: (i) a debtor of a claim provided as financial collateral may waive its rights of set-off in writing or a legally equivalent manner, as well as any other exceptions *vis-à-vis* the creditor of the claim provided as collateral and *vis-à-vis* persons to whom the creditor assigned or pledged such claim as collateral; and (ii) the waiver is valid between the parties and enforceable against third parties. A proper waiver will give comfort to the lenders that the investors will pay their capital commitments upon the enforcement of the security interest without challenging their obligations.

Given the above, and to pre-empt any difficulties with the investors, it becomes usual to include "bankable" financing provisions in advance in the fund documentation (notably the partnership agreements and/or the subscription arrangements), such as: investors' acceptance of the possibility for the fund and its general partner to borrow and pledge the available capital commitments; the security taker's right to initiate and enforce capital calls; waivers of set-off and defences to funding; provisions allowing the security taker to give instructions to the investors upon the occurrence of an event of default; and subordination of the investors' claims, etc. Particular attention should be paid to the "no third-party right" provisions in limited partnership agreements. Lenders and security takers should be expressly mentioned as third-party beneficiaries in order to avoid any interpretation issue as to whether they may benefit from the waivers of the investors' defences and set-off rights, and other "bankable" financing provisions included in the fund documentation. In addition, if the investors' capital commitments are structured as obligation to subscribe for units or shares, a specific undertaking of the investors to fund their commitments, notwithstanding the impossibility of the fund to issue such units or shares (notably in case of bankruptcy), should also be included in the fund documentation. Such undertaking is also important in case of suspension of the NAV calculation of the fund, which may result in a suspension of the issuance of units or shares in certain cases.

Concerning the right of the fund to make capital calls and enforce the obligations of the investors to contribute capital, it should be considered that such right is an ancillary right to the pledged/assigned claim (*droit lié à la créance gagée/transférée*) and, as a result, the security taker may be entitled to exercise that right in accordance with the provisions of the security interest agreement. This view is supported by the Collateral Law, which provides that the pledge/assignment of a claim implies the right for the security taker to exercise the rights of the security provider linked to the pledged/assigned claim. Without prejudice to and independently of the above, Luxembourg security interest agreements provide for a power of attorney granted by the security provider and its general partner in favour of the security taker to make the capital calls, send funding notices and require the investors to make payments into the pledged accounts, it being understood that this power of attorney may be subject to certain limitations arising under Luxembourg law.

The Collateral Law allows the enforcement of a security interest over claims upon the occurrence of any trigger event contractually agreed between the parties (including in the absence of payment default) without prior notice (*mise en demeure*). Until the adoption of the Law of 20 July 2022, the Collateral Law was silent on how to handle, in practice, the application of the enforcement proceeds in the absence of a payment default and acceleration of the secured debt. The Collateral Law, as amended by the Law of 20 July 2022, now expressly allows the security taker to apply the enforcement proceeds against the secured obligations, even when the latter are not yet due and payable at the time of enforcement (unless agreed otherwise). Subject to the terms of the fund documents and certain Luxembourg regulatory requirements, in respect of pledges, the security taker (as pledgee) may, *inter alia*: (i) serve a funding notice on the investors, requesting payment into the pledged accounts; (ii) request direct payment from the investors; (iii) appropriate the pledged claims (at a value determined using the valuation method agreed upon by the parties); (iv) sell the pledged claims by way of a private sale (at arm's length conditions) or a public sale; or (v) request a court to attribute the pledged claims. Concerning assignments for security purposes, in the event of the security provider's failure to perform the relevant financial obligations, the security taker (as assignee) is discharged from its obligations to retransfer the assigned claims up to the amount of the secured obligations.

The security interest over bank accounts (held in Luxembourg) into which investors are required to fund their contributions may be created by way of a pledge in accordance with the Collateral Law. The pledge agreement must be evidenced in writing and perfected in accordance with Luxembourg law. It may be signed by way of electronic signature subject to certain conditions. In practice, as a result of their general terms and conditions, Luxembourg account banks have a first-ranking pledge over such accounts. Provided the terms and conditions do not prohibit pledges, the pledge will become valid and enforceable against the account bank and third parties once the existence of the pledge has been notified to and accepted by that bank.

Luxembourg funds may also use NAV or asset-backed financing arrangements, which have become increasingly popular since 2020. These borrowing arrangements are facilities made available to a fund (or a special purpose vehicle (**SPV**) held directly by the fund) with recourse to the portfolio of assets of the fund. The borrowing base is calculated on the NAV of the assets of the fund (being the primary source of repayment). Lenders will analyse the underlying investments as well as cashflows and other distributions that the fund will receive from those investments. Depending on the investment strategy and the structure of the fund, the security package may be composed of pledges over loans, claims and/or bank accounts into which investments proceeds are to be paid with the aim to allow the lender to control the distributions paid on the underlying assets. Sometimes, the security package may also include a pledge over equity interests issued by any entity holding (directly or indirectly) the underlying investments (to the extent that the constitutional documents of, as well as any shareholders' arrangements governing, such holding entity do not restrict the possibility to pledge its equity interests). These financing arrangements constitute leverage and shall be included in the leverage calculation of the borrowing funds. To the extent that the loan is made available to an SPV of the fund, the lenders will require that the fund guarantees the borrowing obligations of the SPV borrower and/or provide credit support in another form.

Hybrid products mixing capital call financing and NAV financing features may also be used by Luxembourg funds.

Involvement of AIFMs in fund finance transactions

The AIFM being entrusted with the portfolio management and risk management of the AIF, it is important to consider on a case-by-case basis whether the AIFM needs to be involved in relation to subscription line financing arrangements. The review of the AIFM documentation is part of the due diligence made by subscription line lenders to understand whether and how the AIFM should be involved in the financing. Different situations may arise. The general partner of the fund may have delegated to the AIFM the power to issue drawdown notices to the investors and/or the power to enter into financing arrangements on behalf of the fund. In other cases, the fund documents may provide that the AIFM has to consent to the fund's financing arrangements and/or the security interests over the fund's assets.

In relation to NAV and leverage financings, obtaining the AIFM's consent must be considered, given that the entry into such financings may interact with the portfolio management and risk management duties of the AIFM, and such arrangements shall be taken into consideration by the AIFM for leverage calculation and disclosure purposes.

Depending on the powers of the AIFM, the provisions of the fund documents and the type of financing, lenders may require that the AIFM becomes a party to the finance documents or issue a letter confirming its consent or non-objection. Delegation by the AIFM to portfolio or investment managers must also be taken into consideration.

It is also common for Luxembourg funds to be directly or indirectly involved in the financing of their portfolio entities, by issuing guarantees, letters of comfort or equity commitment letters. It must be assessed whether the consent of the AIFM is required, given that such arrangements may be part of the investment strategy and portfolio management of the fund in certain situations. In addition, guarantees, equity commitment letters or similar instruments issued by the fund may constitute leverage at the level of the fund in certain cases. Therefore, the AIFM may need to take the relevant arrangements into consideration for leverage calculation and disclosure purposes.

Involvement of depositaries in fund finance transactions

Authorised AIFMs must appoint a depositary in Luxembourg for each AIF they manage. It is also mandatory for RAIFs, SIFs and SICARs to appoint a depositary in Luxembourg. The depositary of a Luxembourg fund is generally in charge of the safekeeping and supervision of the fund's assets and the control over the transactions of the fund (including compliance with investment policies and monitoring of the cashflows). As the ultimate purpose of depositaries is to enhance investors' protection, lenders should ensure that the legal obligation to appoint a depositary is met by the fund. In addition, lenders must verify whether the depositary should be notified of and/or provide its consent in relation to the financing transaction and the related security package. Certain depositary agreements may contain a pledge over the fund's assets in favour of the depositary. In this case, it must be assessed whether such pledge conflicts with the financing arrangements and, if so, requires a specific release of such pledge from the depositary. On the fund side, the best practice is to inform the depositary of any financing arrangements relating to the fund, in order to allow the depositary to properly perform its duties.

GDPR impact on fund finance transactions

Regulation (EU) 2016/679 on the protection of natural persons with regard to the processing of personal data (**GDPR**) regulates how personal data (relating to natural persons) is processed and transferred. In the context of fund finance transactions, a point of attention is how personal information regarding investors and their commitments may be transferred to the lenders in order to determine the borrowing basis and take the security interests over the available capital commitments. As a result, GDPR provisions and consents are included in the fund documentation in order to authorise the fund and its general partner to share such information with the lenders and transfer such information outside of Europe.

EU Securitisation Regulation

Regulation (EU) 2017/2042 of the European Parliament and of the Council of 12 December 2017, laying down a general framework for securitisation and creating a specific framework for simple, transparent and standardised securitisation (**EU Securitisation Regulation**), came into force on 1 January 2019. Certain fund finance transactions (notably leveraged transactions) and borrowing entities may potentially fall within the scope of the EU Securitisation Regulation, which would trigger a broad array of obligations for the borrowing entity, but also for originators, sponsors and certain investors (among others, requirements with regard to risk retention, due diligence, transparency and disclosure, restrictions on sale to retail investors, etc.). In order to determine whether such obligations would be applicable, one must assess whether the transaction meets the definition of "securitisation" as set out in the EU Securitisation Regulation and whether any of the involved entities may be considered a securitisation special purpose entity (**SSPE**) for the purpose of the EU Securitisation Regulation.

Article 2(1) of the EU Securitisation Regulation defines "securitisation" as a transaction or scheme, whereby the **credit risk associated with an exposure or pool of exposures is tranched**, having both of the following characteristics:
- payments in the transaction or scheme are dependent upon the performance of the exposure or pool of exposures; and
- the subordination of tranches determines the distribution of losses during the ongoing life of the transaction or scheme.

It follows from the above definition that a transaction would only fall within the scope of the EU Securitisation Regulation if the securitised credit risk were tranched. The EU Securitisation Regulation defines "tranche" as:
- a contractually established segment of the credit risk associated with an exposure or a pool of exposures;
- where a position in the segment entails a risk of credit loss greater than or less than a position of the same amount in another segment; and
- without taking account of credit protection provided by third parties directly to the holders of positions in the segment or in other segments.

Furthermore, transactions falling within the "specialised lending" exception (as described in article 147(8) of Regulation (EU) 575/2013 of the European Parliament and of the Council of 26 June 2013 on prudential requirements for credit institutions and investment firms) are not subject to the EU Securitisation Regulation, even if the above conditions are satisfied.

In addition, it must be assessed whether any of the involved entities may be considered an SSPE for the purpose of the EU Securitisation Regulation. According to article 2 of the EU Securitisation Regulation, an SSPE is defined as "a corporation, trust or other entity, other than an originator or sponsor, established for the purpose of carrying out one or more securitisations, the activities of which are limited to those appropriate to accomplish that objective, the structure of which is intended to isolate the obligations of the SSPE from those of the originator".

The definition of securitisation under the EU Securitisation Regulation is thus quite large and it is therefore advisable to assess each transaction (notably any transaction involving entities investing in credit assets and receiving financing with different payment priorities and seniorities) and the involved entities on a case-by-case basis to determine whether the above conditions are met.

Outlook

Significant drivers for the success of Luxembourg as a European hub for the structuring of AIFs, in particular over the past few years, have been:
- the success of the modernisation of the Luxembourg partnership regime, which has been able to offer fund initiators accustomed to Anglo-Saxon partnerships a new onshore alternative for fund structuring; and
- the addition of the RAIF to the Luxembourg fund structuring toolbox, replicating, without any regulatory supervision at product level, the flexibility of regulated AIF regimes.

There is no reason to doubt that this trend will continue and sustain a growing demand from fund managers for financing solutions.

* * *

Endnotes

1. As at 30 September 2022.
2. According to recital 78 of the AIFMD.
3. ESMA questions and answers on the application of the AIFMD, ESMA34-32-352.
4. Commission Delegated Regulation (EU) 231/2013 of 19 December 2012 supplementing Directive 2011/61/EU of the European Parliament and of the Council with regard to exemptions, general operating conditions, depositaries, leverage, transparency and supervision (**Level 2 Regulations**).
5. SIFs, SICARs and RAIFs are obliged to appoint depositaries in any event on the basis of the SIF, SICAR and RAIF Laws, respectively.

Vassiliyan Zanev
Tel: +352 466 230 257 / Email: vassiliyan.zanev@loyensloeff.com
Vassiliyan Zanev co-chairs the Investment Management group of Loyens & Loeff and leads the firm's fund finance practice in Luxembourg. He represents a variety of financial institutions, investment funds and corporations across a range of structured finance and lending transactions, with particular emphasis on fund finance, securitisation and real estate finance. Vassiliyan has extensive experience in the financing of Luxembourg alternative or regulated investment fund borrowers (including by way of capital call subscription credit facilities and permanent leverage solutions). Vassiliyan is a member of the EMEA Advisory Council of the Fund Finance Association.

Marc Meyers
Tel: +352 466 230 306 / Email: marc.meyers@loyensloeff.com
Marc Meyers heads the Luxembourg Investment Management team of Loyens & Loeff. Marc specialises in structuring, regulatory and transactional work for Luxembourg alternative investment fund structures, with a particular focus on private equity, property/infrastructure and debt funds. Before joining Loyens & Loeff, he established the Luxembourg legal practice of another Benelux law firm. He worked for several years in the Luxembourg office of a leading international law firm, as well as in the New York and London offices of the US firm Cravath, Swaine & Moore LLP. Marc is an active member of several working groups within the Association of the Luxembourg Fund Industry, as well as the Luxembourg Private Equity and Venture Capital Association. He is a member of the Luxembourg and New York Bars.

Maude Royer
Tel: +352 466 230 276 / Email: maude.royer@loyensloeff.com
Maude Royer is a Senior Associate in the finance practice of the Luxembourg Investment Management team of Loyens & Loeff. Maude acts on a full range of finance transactions, with particular focus on fund finance. She acts at all levels of the fund capital structure, advising investment funds (including real estate, private equity, infrastructure and debt funds, as well as funds of funds), fund managers and financial institutions. Her expertise includes capital call financing, GP financing, NAV financing and other hybrid products, asset-based financing, real estate financing and general corporate financing.

Loyens & Loeff Luxembourg SARL
18–20 rue Edward Steichen, L-2540, Luxembourg
Tel: +352 466 230 / URL: www.loyensloeff.com

Mauritius

Malcolm Moller
Appleby

Overview

As the end of 2022 approaches, this provides an opportunity to reflect on the current state of play in the fund finance market. The fund finance market has demonstrated its resilience in the face of the challenges of COVID-19 as well as the effects of the Russia-Ukraine war and resulting high inflation and depreciation of the rupee, and, to date, has weathered this storm admirably and we continue to be unaware of any significant institutional default within our subscription finance client base. Similar to the market impact of *Abraaj* and the last global financial crisis, there will be a lot of reflection and revisiting of subscription finance structures – but, ultimately, they will prove robust, and there will not be much in the way of fundamental change to how the market operates. That said, there will be further improvements in reporting to investors and transparency of information about borrowing at fund level and security structures.

We anticipate that the types of fund-level financing and the purposes for which financing is used will continue to diversify in 2023. Many Mauritius private equity funds currently use subscription line facilities to bridge capital calls and reduce administration for their limited partners. Going forward, many funds will find it prudent to consider broadening their use of subscription lines for purposes such as foreign exchange (**FX**) hedging, letters of credit, evidencing certain funds for acquisitions, gaining a competitive advantage and realignment of investment strategies.

We also anticipate broader use of hybrid net asset value (**NAV**)/capital call facilities, particularly by credit funds implementing leveraged investment strategies. Private equity M&A activity continued at a robust pace in 2022, although deal volume dropped in 2020 due to the COVID-19 crisis. Even though many of the COVID-19 storm clouds remain, including a likely increase in interest rates, we believe the imperative to deploy fund capital will propel a very active deal market in the coming year. We have also seen that, positively for the sector, and despite some concern in the early days of the pandemic, credit and liquidity for the fund finance market has proven to be robust. The pool of lenders serving the subscription finance market in Mauritius has grown significantly. There has also been a corresponding ability to provide a greater degree of flexibility, with COVID-19 acting as the catalyst for this evolution. Some in the industry have considered exploring alternate fundraising sources; for instance, general partners (**GPs**) are seeking dedicated debt and/or equity results through new platforms, buy out third-party investors, or make an outsized commitment to their next fund. This not only provides for more flexibility, but equally helps broaden the GP's investor base to more aligned investors. Further, many funds have moved to more robust quarterly portfolio valuations in response to limited partners seeking more timely information so they can take the appropriate asset allocation decisions. In addition, the highest inflation in over

40 years, driven by supply chain disruptions, soaring energy prices and tight labour markets, colliding with the prospect of slower growth coupled with the geopolitical instability tied to the war between Russia and Ukraine, have increased market volatility and resulted in investors paying closer attention to FX rates, leading to a significant increase in hedging activity to protector investments and returns.

Mauritius global funds (that is, investment funds and their intermediaries) in Mauritius are regulated by the Financial Services Commission (**Commission**). The Commission has, since 2001, developed a very flexible set of guidelines as well as a consolidated regulatory and supervisory framework for the regulation of such global funds, namely the Securities Act 2005 (**Securities Act**), the Securities (Licensing) Rules 2007, the Securities (Preferential Offer) Rules 2017 (as recently amended by the Securities (Preferential Offer) (Amendment No. 2) Rules 2021, the Financial Services Act 2007 (**FSA 2007**), the Securities (Collective Investment Schemes and Closed-end Funds) Regulations 2008 (**Securities Regulations 2008**), the Financial Services (Peer to Peer Lending) Rules 2020, the Securities (Solicitation) Rules 2020, the Securities (Real Estate Investment Trusts) Rules 2021, and the Securities (Exemption) Rules 2021.

Fund formation and finance

Global funds – overview

The present regulatory framework contemplates two main categories of global funds, namely: an open-ended fund, also known as a collective investment scheme (**CIS**); and a closed-end fund, commonly known as a private equity fund. Global funds can be structured as companies incorporated under the Companies Act 2001 or as limited partnerships (**LPs**), which came into force pursuant to the Limited Partnerships Act 2011 (**Limited Partnerships Act**), or licensed as companies or partnerships holding a Global Business Licence (**GBL**) under the FSA 2007.

Any CIS or closed-end fund (individually a **Scheme** or, collectively, **Schemes**) wishing to be approved, registered with, recognised and/or licensed by the Commission, under the Securities Act, must first apply to the Commission for authorisation as a CIS or closed-end fund in the manner set out in the Securities Regulations 2008, and obtain a GBL under the FSA 2007. Funds usually take the form of companies, LPs, protected cell companies (**PCCs**) or trusts. The typical vehicle used to structure a closed-end fund is a private company limited by shares or an LP, while a CIS is commonly structured as a public or private company, unit trust or PCC.

The Mauritian LP combines features of both a company and a partnership, and acts as another preferred vehicle for foreign investors that may provide flexibility in structuring a CIS. It can have separate legal personality just like a company, while at the same time enabling some partners, known as limited partners, to contribute and participate in the returns of the LP without being engaged in its day-to-day management. The GP is responsible for managing the business and affairs of the LP and is personally liable for the debts of the partnership. The GPs in an LP can elect for the LP to have a legal personality or not. If they elect so at the time of registration, they must file with the registrar of LPs a declaration signed by one or more of the GPs stating that the LP shall have legal personality. The register of LPs and certificate of registration shall state whether the LP has legal personality or not.

The Limited Liability Partnerships Act 2016 (**LLP Act**) was introduced to further equip the economy's financial sector with innovative tools, as well as alternative and attractive vehicles to investors – the Limited Liability Partnership (**LLP**). Similar to the LP, the LLP combines features of both a company (holder of a GBL) and a partnership, where the LLP is incorporated as a body corporate having separate legal personality from its partners, thus providing the flexibility of a partnership. The LLP Act applies to a person (a) offering professional or consultancy services, (b) holding a Global Legal Advisory Services licence, or (c) engaging in other prescribed activities. An LLP has a separate legal personality from its partners. Under an LLP, the partner is accountable and liable to the LLP only to the extent of its contributions (except in the event of insolvency). The LLP is required to have at least two partners and one manager. The relationship between the partners and the LLP is governed under a partnership agreement.

On 1 January 2000, the Protected Cell Companies Act 1999 came into force, which created an incorporation and registration regime whereby a Mauritian company carrying out global business would be able to register as a PCC. A protected cell (known in some jurisdictions as a 'segregated account' or 'segregated portfolio') is an account containing assets and liabilities (known as 'cellular assets') that are legally separated from the assets of the company's ordinary account, called its 'non-cellular assets', and also separate from assets and liabilities allocated to the company's other protected cells (if any).

A trust, established under the Trusts Act 2001, is a legal relationship created by the beneficial owner creating the trust (the settlor) and the persons willing to undertake the office of trustee (the trustees). As part of this relationship, property (the trust fund) is declared held by the trustees for the benefit of certain parties (the beneficiaries) or for certain purposes, creating a binding obligation on the part of the trustees to act in accordance with the terms of the trust. Trusts are normally liable to income tax on its chargeable income. Chargeable income is calculated as the difference between the net income derived by the trust and the aggregate income distributed to the beneficiaries under the terms of the trust.

The regulatory and supervisory framework for global funds is in line with international principles and practices as laid down by the International Organization of Securities Commissions. Intermediaries ensure the proper functioning of investment funds and hence protect the best interests of investors. All global funds are therefore subject to ongoing reporting obligations, as imposed by the Commission under the Securities Act and the FSA 2007. Reporting obligations include submission of Audited Financial Statements and Quarterly Statutory Returns (Interim Financial Statements), in accordance with the FSA 2007. A fund is required to be managed by an investment manager licensed in Mauritius. A foreign regulated investment manager may alternatively be appointed, subject to the prior approval of the Commission.

Fund financing

As the private funds sector grows and matures in Mauritius, financing solutions are increasingly required by funds and fund managers. The need for finance can vary, from equity bridge or capital call facilities used to assist liquidity and speed of execution for private equity funds, to more esoteric products used by hedge funds in addition to their prime brokerage agreements, such as NAV-based margin loans to provide liquidity or leverage, and equity or fund-linked derivative solutions. In fact, we still have not been consulted on a single facility payment event of default in the first half of 2022. Also, as more investors look to limit their investments to a smaller group of preferred sponsors, sponsors are also diversifying their product offerings. We have, for instance, noticed a trend involving a number of sponsors leveraging their existing investor relationships by creating funds focused on sectors in which they have not traditionally participated (i.e., buyout shops creating direct-lending funds).

General security structure for Mauritius transactions

Historically, funds have predominantly been incorporated as corporate structures. Some companies may have more than one class of shares, which denote various fee structures and/or limitations on the types of investments some shareholders can make. There may also exist multiple series within each class of shares. In order to widen its array of financial products, Mauritius introduced its Limited Partnerships Act, adding a new dimension to the international investment community. This investment vehicle enables global funds to be structured as partnerships in Mauritius, reducing the need for complex master-feeder structures and ensuring tax-efficient structures.

Mauritius has become a central hub for foreign direct investment into India and Africa due to its network of double taxation avoidance agreements and investment protection and promotion agreements with various African countries. However, while investors have been able to form global business companies for foreign direct investment, the more rigid structure of companies means they are not always perfectly suited for these investment projects. For example, for funds structured as a Mauritius corporation, a shareholders' agreement governs the relationship with the shareholders rather than a partnership agreement. The obligation of shareholders to pay in capital contributions is contingent upon the issuance of further shares, and a corporation's ability to issue shares is generally not delegable under Mauritius law, thus limiting the ability to make capital calls on investors in an event of default under the fund financing facility.

Security for the fund finance consists of: (a) a security assignment by the fund of the capital commitments, right to make capital calls, right to receive and enforce the foregoing, and the account into which the capital commitments are to be funded; and (b) a charge on the bulk of its other assets including its accounts, investments compensation from various of its assets including bonds, guarantees, negotiable instruments and the like. The security package relating to the capital calls is tailored in order to account for specifics of Mauritius law and the structure of the fund as a corporation (rather than an LP, as most funds in Mauritius are structured as corporations). In particular, various rights in respect of the fund are vested in the board of directors and cannot be easily delegated. Mauritius law requires that shares be issued in exchange for capital calls.

One would expect security to be taken over bank accounts of the fund and assignment of rights to make capital calls, accompanied by a power of attorney in favour of the lender to exercise such rights on behalf of the fund/GP and/or manager (as the case may be) in a typical fund financing security transaction. So, while one would have a pledge over the security provided above, the ability for a lender to make a capital call on its own would be complicated by the foregoing. In a worst-case scenario, the preferred enforcement mechanism would have the lender appoint a receiver (and, if necessary, a liquidator), as each have statutory authority to make capital calls and issue shares in order to satisfy creditors to whom such security is pledged. Indeed, after an event of default, a lender is entitled to appoint a receiver under the Insolvency Act 2009. Security documents, such as fixed and floating charge documents, would need to provide that if a receiver were appointed, it would have full management powers to the exclusion of the board of directors. Under the Insolvency Act 2009, the receiver would have the power to make calls of unfunded capital to the extent such assets are included in the charge granted to a lender and issue shares.

It is also recommended that a liquidator be appointed in order to avoid certain issues relating to the set-off of claims by shareholders against the called capital (described further below). The liquidator would also be permitted to call capital. For example, various contract law defences may be waived in Mauritius by contract in the situation where the fund is not in insolvency (including non-performance by the fund). Generally, such language is sought for three reasons: (a) to waive contract law defences such as lack of consideration, mutual mistake, impracticability, etc.; (b) to prevent LPs from claiming that they may set off amounts owed to them by the fund against what is due to the lender; and (c) claims that an issuance of shares or some other action by the fund is required as a condition for payment of capital contributions.

We recommend that such language be included in this transaction since, in the event of insolvency of the fund, the language may prove helpful and could avoid other defences raised by shareholders that their commitment to contribute capital is a 'financial accommodation' or otherwise avoidable under insolvency laws. Such ability to waive in advance the right to raise the defence above and other defences by contract could be inserted in the contract (presumably by amendment to the shareholders' agreement or by an investor letter); however, general waivers are not effective, so specific waivers would be required as to each of the possible defences.

Moreover, such contractual waivers would not be effective in a number of circumstances, including rights to set-off pursuant to the Insolvency Act 2009. By statute, under the Insolvency Act 2009, while a receiver is in place, principles of contractual, legal and equitable set-off apply that would permit set-off by shareholders, and such set-off is available to the extent that claims have been incurred prior to the commencement of the liquidation (subject to other limitations). To avoid such risk, we normally recommend the initiation of winding-up by a lender by appointment of a liquidator, as such appointment would crystallise the liability of shareholders as a statutory liability that cannot be set off against amounts owing to the shareholder.

Key developments

Some of the salient amendments made to the present regulatory framework are as follows.

<u>Amendments to the Companies Act 2001</u>

The timeframes under the COVID-19 provisions have been repealed and amended as follows:
- The frequency of the annual meeting of shareholders shall be:
  - not more than once annually;
  - not later than six months after the balance sheet date of the company or such other period as the Registrar of Companies (**ROC**) may determine; and
  - not later than 15 months after the previous annual meeting.
- The disapplication of the duty of directors during insolvency of a company in times that have been decreed by the Government of Mauritius as the COVID-19 period has been removed and the duties are now restored, unless as may be otherwise prescribed.
- Where a company has an obligation to prepare and file financial statements, it shall prepare the financial statements within six months or as may be prescribed by the ROC after the balance sheet and file them with the ROC within 28 days or such other period as the ROC may determine from signing the financial statements.

<u>Amendments to the Securities Act – obligation for auditors to be approved by the Commission</u>

Only audit firms approved by the Commission are authorised to audit the financial statements of a CIS manager or CIS. The Commission must be satisfied that that an audit firm has adequate experience, expertise and resources to audit such financial statements.

Amendments to the Banking Act

Digital currency

The Bank of Mauritius (**BOM**) is entitled to issue rules to provide for the framework under which digital currency will be issued by the BOM and may be held or used by the public. The BOM may, for the purposes of issuing digital currency, open accounts for and accept deposits from such persons as it may determine.

Establishment of a Central KYC System and Central Accounts Registry

The BOM is authorised to establish (i) a Central KYC System for facilitating the electronic verification of the identity of customers, validation and extraction of KYC records of customers by KYC institutions, and collecting KYC records submitted to KYC institutions by their customers, and (ii) a Central Accounts Registry for collecting information on accounts maintained by customers, other than the balance and amount held in these accounts (**Registry**).

The BOM is empowered to require any KYC institution (including financial institutions licensed by the Commission) to furnish to the Registry, on such terms and conditions as it may determine, such information as it may require for the purpose of maintaining the Registry.

The year ahead

As 2022 is coming to a close, we believe that real-time uncertainty about current economic conditions and policy actions will likely keep market volatility high, and investors will remain focused on whether central banks can tame inflation without triggering a global recession. The fund finance market was extremely resilient during and following the global financial crisis (outperforming many other forms of finance) and has benefitted from strong growth since; thus, we remain cautiously optimistic for a robust fund finance market in 2023 – and we further expect the number of facilities consummated to continue to grow at a solid clip as fundraising improves and the product further penetrates the private equity market, and a greater number of existing facilities get refinanced. Our Mauritius Fund Finance Team has worked with the vast majority of market participants over the last 18 months, and while the present uncertainty about current economic conditions and policy actions will likely keep market volatility high, and investors will remain focused on whether central banks can tame inflation without triggering a global recession, we nevertheless remain cautiously optimistic for a robust fund finance market in 2023.

Malcolm Moller
Tel: +230 203 4301 / Email: mmoller@applebyglobal.com

Malcolm Moller, Group Managing Partner – Mauritius, Seychelles and Shanghai, is a member of both the Insurance and Structured Finance Teams of Appleby. He specialises in advising financial institutions on financial regulation, regulatory capital issues, financial institution M&A, and insurance-related transactions. Malcolm advises on private equity funds, hedge funds, derivatives transactions and securities offerings, as well as a range of corporate and corporate finance transactions. Malcolm has extensive experience representing corporations, financial institutions and other principals. His experience spans public and private M&A, subscription credit facilities, restructuring, bankruptcy, capital markets, fund formation and winding up, and a variety of strategic and advisory corporate assignments. As a regular contributor to Mauritius-related articles, Malcolm's writings have been featured in numerous publications, including *The Lawyer*, *The American Lawyer*, *International Investment* and the *Investor Services Journal*.

Appleby

7th Floor, Happy World House, 37 Sir William Newton Street, Port Louis, Mauritius
Tel: +230 203 4300 / URL: www.applebyglobal.com

Netherlands

Gianluca Kreuze, Michaël Maters & Ruben den Hollander
Loyens & Loeff N.V.

Overview

The Netherlands is widely recognised as a leading international financial centre and has a mature investment funds industry with an attractive investment environment due to, amongst others, flexible corporate legislation, various tax structuring options, and an extensive network of bilateral investment treaties and tax treaties.

In terms of both fundraising and invested capital, 2021 and 2022 were successful years for market participants in the Netherlands. The most recent research conducted by the *Nederlandse Vereniging van Participatiemaatschappijen* (the Dutch Association of Private Equity Firms)[1] shows that in 2021 alone, Dutch private equity firms raised around €6.3 billion in new funds, of which approximately €1.6 billion was raised by Dutch venture capitalists. In 2021, 206 Dutch private equity and venture capital firms managed approximately €37.9 billion (committed capital) in 466 funds, and over €8.1 billion was invested by national and international private equity and venture capital firms in Dutch companies.

We have seen a continued and significant increase in the number of fundraisings, investor appetite and fund financings in the Netherlands. The markets for fundraising, fund finance and private equity investments have proven to be resilient (for example, during the COVID-19 pandemic), although it is yet to be seen what impact geopolitical, macroeconomic and interest rate developments will have.

The evolving fund finance market has proven to be of interest to both Dutch and foreign lenders over the past couple of years, and market participants are more actively exploring other (more structural) fund finance solutions on top of the traditional capital call facilities.

Consequently, we are looking forward to an exciting 2023, which will potentially provide for a great investment environment for fund managers and fund finance lenders.

In view of the aforementioned relevance of the Dutch fund formation and fund finance market, this chapter seeks to provide further background on the following relevant aspects: (a) fund formation and the most commonly used Dutch fund vehicles; (b) regulation of fundraising and fund managers; (c) fund finance in the Netherlands; (d) structuring the security package; and (e) the year ahead.

Fund formation and the most commonly used Dutch fund vehicles

A Dutch alternative investment fund (an **AIF**)[2] may be structured in various ways, both as corporate and contractual entities. Corporate entities have legal personality (*rechtspersoonlijkheid*), enabling them to hold legal title to assets, and are governed by mandatory corporate law, whereas contractual entities lack such legal personality and are unable to hold legal title, but enjoy the benefit of more contractual freedom. The most frequently used corporate investment vehicles are the private limited liability company (*besloten vennootschap met beperkte aansprakelijkheid*) and the cooperative with excluded liability (*coöperatie met uitgesloten aansprakelijkheid*). Contractual investment vehicles are most commonly established in the form of a limited partnership (*commanditaire vennootschap*) or a mutual fund (*fonds voor gemene rekening*).[3] The ultimate selection strongly depends on the outcome of relevant tax and legal structuring analyses.

Regardless of whether a contractual or legal entity is selected, an AIF established in the Netherlands should take into account that the European Alternative Investment Fund Managers Directive 2011/61/EU (the **AIFMD**) is applicable and has been implemented into the Dutch Act on Financial Supervision (*Wet op het financieel toezicht*, or the **AFS**). Consequently, the AIFMD and all rules and regulations promulgated thereunder (including Delegated Regulation (EU) 231/2013, the **Delegated Regulation**) must be complied with in the Netherlands by any alternative investment fund manager (an **AIFM**), unless an AIFM can benefit from exemptions (such as, *inter alia*, AIFMs managing AIFs below the Threshold (as defined below)).

In the event that a Dutch licensed AIFM establishes an AIF as a contractual investment vehicle (lacking legal personality), it is – in principle – required under the AFS to also establish a single-purpose corporate entity to hold the assets of one or more of such AIFs set up by the licensed AIFM.

Regulation of fundraising and fund managers

The management or marketing of AIFs in the Netherlands by 'large' AIFMs triggers the obligation to obtain a licence in the Netherlands, subject to certain exemptions and grandfathering rules. AIFMs are considered 'large' if they, directly or indirectly, manage portfolios of AIFs whose assets under management amount to €500 million or more, or – when open-ended or leveraged – €100 million or more (together, the **Threshold**). An AIFM is deemed to manage an AIF in the Netherlands if such AIFM is established in the Netherlands, or if the AIF managed by it is established in the Netherlands.

Dutch AIFMs that fall below the Threshold may manage and market their AIFs without an AIFMD licence in the Netherlands, provided that:

a) the AIF's units or shares are exclusively offered to professional investors within the meaning of the AFS (*e.g.* banks, insurers, pension funds, brokers, AIFMs, AIFs, or qualifying large corporates); or
b) the AIF's units or shares are offered to fewer than 150 persons, or have a nominal value of, or are offered for a consideration payable per investor of, at least €100,000, provided that a banner or selling legend as to the AIFM's unregulated status (in a predefined size and layout) is printed on the AIF's offering documents; and
c) in each case, the relevant AIFM is registered with the Dutch competent authority, the AIFM. The aim of said registration is (amongst others) to ensure that the AIFM can assess whether or not the sub-Threshold regime is legitimately relied upon, and to effectively monitor any build-up of systemic risks. Such Dutch AIFMs are required to disclose to the Dutch Central Bank (*De Nederlandsche Bank*), amongst others, information on the main instruments in which the AIFs are trading, the principal exposures, and the most important concentration of the AIFs managed.

Dutch AIFMs that do not require a licence for managing and marketing their AIFs in the Netherlands may voluntarily apply for such licence, provided such AIFM complies with all applicable AIFMD requirements (as implemented into Dutch law). Not many Dutch AIFMs have chosen to apply for an AIFMD licence voluntarily.

Additionally, considering that AIFs making private equity investments are not excluded from the scope of the venture capital regulation (Regulation 345/2013/EC, or **EuVECA**), EU-based managers of (EU) AIFs that comply with the conditions of EuVECA may benefit from an EU marketing passport as introduced therein. Such passport allows for the marketing of units or shares to potential investors investing at least €100,000 or to investors that are treated as professional clients (within the meaning of Directive 2014/65/EU), in each case provided that they have confirmed their awareness of the risks associated with their investment. Potential investors that do not otherwise qualify as professional investors may opt to be treated as such. Both licensed AIFMs and sub-Threshold AIFMs can benefit from EuVECA: enabling licensed AIFMs to use the EuVECA marketing passport to also market interests to investors that commit to invest at least €100,000 (and not only to professional investors as allowed under Article 32 of the AIFMD). We see that an increasing number of (sub-Threshold) Dutch AIFMs obtain EuVECA labels to benefit from the marketing passport (providing market access in a transparent manner).

Finally, in 2021, two new sets of European laws entered into force that affect how AIFMs can market their AIFs to investors. The first being Regulation (EU) 2019/2088 on sustainability-related disclosures in the financial services sector (the **SFDR**) aimed at prohibiting AIFMs from 'greenwashing' their product through subjecting them to comprehensive disclosure requirements. Both licensed and sub-Threshold AIFMs are required to satisfy the disclosure requirements prescribed by the SFDR. The character of the disclosures that an AIFM is required to make in respect of an AIF depends on how such AIF is categorised (*i.e.* as an AIF promoting environmental or social characteristics, an AIF having a sustainable objective or an AIF that does none of the foregoing). The second being a new set of rules on the cross-border marketing of AIFs, Cross-Border Distribution Directive (EU) 2019/1160 and Cross-Border Distribution Regulation (EU) 2019/1156 (together, the **Cross Border Distribution Rules**). On the basis of the Cross Border Distribution Rules, licensed AIFMs and AIFMs managing EuVECA-labelled AIFs can now benefit, for instance, from an EU harmonised pre-marketing regime, additional rules for marketing to retail investors, transparency on cross-border supervision costs, and the de-notification process of AIFs marketed under the passport. Under the framework of the Cross Border Distribution Rules, the rules applicable to marketing communications issued by AIFMs in respect of their AIFs are also replaced by new, more comprehensive rules that are supplemented by the European Securities and Markets Authority's Guidelines on marketing communications. Since February 2022, qualifying AIFMs' marketing communications must comply with these new requirements.

Fund finance in the Netherlands

With increasing availability of capital for investments and demands for high returns by investors, the need for financing solutions by Dutch AIFMs and AIFs is expected to continue its upturn. Depending on the type of AIF, the need for financing can vary, but is typically limited to (i) the more traditional capital call facilities, and (ii) credit facilities to provide leverage or liquidity for the AIF (often based on the net asset value (**NAV**) of investments).

There is limited data publicly available on the use of the various types of fund financing in the Netherlands, which makes it difficult to assess the size of the Dutch fund finance market. In our experience, traditional secured capital call facilities continue to be the main type of financing selected by AIFMs. It has become customary to explicitly refer in the relevant fund documentation to the possibility to take out this type of financing and the creation of security by the AIF on its assets (including receivables that investors owe to the fund).

The purpose and use of traditional capital call financings are expected to further expand. In addition to bridging capital calls, those financing arrangements are also being used to 'bridge' the third-party financing to be arranged for at the level of the portfolio company (*i.e.* at bidco level) and thus speed up acquisition processes. Recently, there has also been an increasing interest in the ability to obtain NAV or hybrid facilities at fund level, but given that this is a recent development in the Dutch market, the ability to incur (structural) leverage at the level of the fund is not always catered for in fund documents.

An important consequence of incurring such leverage at the level of a Dutch AIF is that, depending on the details of the financing, the relevant AIFM managing such AIF may be required to obtain an AIFMD licence in the Netherlands, as further discussed below.

Whether or not an AIF incurs leverage may affect the relevant AIFM's regulatory status (*i.e.* it may lead to a lower Threshold being applied for purposes of determining whether an AIFMD licence is required in the Netherlands). Additionally, if AIFs deploy leverage, the AIFMD (and rules and regulations promulgated thereunder) imposes additional obligations on an AIFM managing such AIF. Consequently, incurring leverage may affect an AIFM.

The term 'leverage' is defined by the AIFMD as any method by which an AIFM increases the exposure of an AIF it manages, whether through borrowing of cash or securities, or leverage embedded in derivative positions, or by any other means.

While determining whether an AIF deploys leverage within the meaning of the AIFMD and when calculating exposure, the Delegated Regulation dictates that AIFs should 'look through' corporate structures. Therefore, exposure that is included in any financial and/or legal structures involving third parties controlled by the relevant AIF, where those structures are specifically set up to increase, directly or indirectly, the exposure at the level of the AIF, should be included in the calculation. However, for AIFs whose core investment policy is to acquire control of non-listed companies or issuers, AIFMs should not include in the calculation any leverage that exists at the level of those non-listed companies and issuers, provided that the relevant AIF does not have to bear potential losses beyond its capital share in the respective company or issuer.

On the other hand, borrowing arrangements entered into by the AIF are excluded under any of the abovementioned methods if these are:
a) temporary in nature; and
b) fully covered by 'capital commitments' from investors (*i.e.* the contractual commitment of an investor to provide the AIF with an agreed amount of investment on demand by the AIFM).

Even though the Delegated Regulation considers in its recitals that revolving credit facilities (**RCFs**) should *not* be considered as being temporary in nature, it is the prevailing view that capital call facilities (by way of an RCF or otherwise) can be structured as being temporary in nature if certain requirements otherwise applicable to non-RCFs are similarly complied with. In order to structure these facilities as temporary in nature, certain features can be implemented, such as: (i) a mandatory clean down to occur once every 12 months (followed by a period during which the facility is not used); and/or (ii) an obligation to repay each loan, with the proceeds of capital contributions, within 12 months of drawing such loan.

Structuring these capital call facilities as temporary in nature typically fits their purpose, as these facilities are typically utilised to bridge the liquidity gap at the level of the AIF to be funded ultimately out of the proceeds of capital contributions. Such a time gap between inflowing money from investors and outflowing money for investments can be caused by: (a) the period, often 10 business days, it takes before capital drawn by the AIFM is actually contributed to the AIF; (b) the desire of the AIFM to bundle capital calls (so not to burden the investors with drawdowns of smaller amounts); (c) a defaulting investor not contributing; and (d) the AIFM delaying certain capital calls, as this may boost the internal rate of return for investments in and by the AIF.

Structuring the security package

Credit facilities to be granted to AIFs can be secured in a variety of ways. For example, security may be granted over the assets in which an AIF would (indirectly) invest, which is usually the case for NAV facilities. Typically, capital call credit facilities granted to AIFs are secured by a right of pledge over (i) the bank account (which is considered a receivable on the account bank under Dutch law) on which capital contributions are made by the AIF's investors, and (ii) all receivables or contractual obligations that the investors owe to the AIF, such as the right to make drawdowns from the capital commitments.

Bank accounts

Dutch funds are usually set up with one single Dutch bank account per fund entity. With respect to creating a right of pledge over Dutch bank accounts, the applicable general terms and conditions are of relevance. The general terms and conditions used by most Dutch account banks create a first-ranking right of pledge over such bank account for the benefit of the account bank, and state that the bank account cannot be (further) pledged. Consequently, the cooperation of such account bank is required to create a (first-ranking) right of pledge over a Dutch bank account. It is becoming increasingly difficult to convince Dutch account banks to cooperate and consent to the creation of a right of pledge over bank accounts for the benefit of third-party lenders.

Investor receivables

Pursuant to Dutch law, security over receivables can be established by way of a disclosed right of pledge, or by way of an undisclosed right of pledge. A disclosed right of pledge is created by way of a security agreement (or notarial deed) and notification of the right of pledge to the relevant debtors of the receivables that are being pledged. An undisclosed right of pledge is created either by way of a notarial deed or by way of a security agreement that is registered with the Dutch tax authorities for date-stamping purposes. A disclosed right of pledge can be created over present and future receivables, whilst an undisclosed right of pledge can only be created over present receivables and future receivables arising from legal relationships existing at the time of creation of such undisclosed right of pledge. Therefore, for an undisclosed right of pledge, it is common practice to periodically file supplemental security agreements with the Dutch tax authorities to also secure present and future receivables resulting from legal relationships that have been entered into after the date of the initial security agreement (or notarial deed).

With respect to creating a disclosed or undisclosed right of pledge over receivables of the AIF on its investors, choosing one form of pledge over the other depends, to some extent, on whether it is commercially desirable to disclose the right of pledge to the relevant investors, and whether an undisclosed right of pledge is acceptable to the beneficiary of the right of pledge. With pledge notices customary to be sent to investors in key jurisdictions such as Luxembourg, the United Kingdom and the United States, it has become common over the last few years to notify investors of a right of pledge over the investor receivables in the Netherlands as well. Dutch law allows for sufficient flexibility as to the form of such notification to be made; consequently, such notification can be made by uploading the notice to the AIF's investor portal or referencing the right of pledge in any investor reporting document, making the process of serving notice a fairly effortless procedure. Therefore, in the majority of transactions, there will be a disclosed right of pledge over investor receivables notifying the investors not by separate pledge notice, but via the investor portal of periodic investor reports.

The qualification of the receivable owed by the investor to the AIF as either an existing but conditional claim or a provisory future claim is important for determining whether the receivable can be made subject to a bankruptcy proof right of pledge. If the claim is considered a future claim, any right of pledge that is created in advance will only take effect if such claim comes into existence prior to the pledgor being bankrupt; any claim that comes into existence after bankruptcy will fall within the bankruptcy estate of the pledgor.

In Dutch literature and case law, the prevailing view is that the receivable owed by the investor to the AIF qualifies as a future receivable arising from an existing legal relationship, which receivable comes into existence once the AIFM sends the relevant capital call notice to the relevant investor and therefore can also be made subject to an undisclosed right of pledge as of the date of the capital call notice (without periodical supplemental security being required, unless the investor base changes as that will be considered a new legal relationship between the fund and the new investor – in case of a disclosed right of pledge, a change to the investor base will typically require notification to be served on the new investor). However, if the AIFM sends the capital call notice after the pledgor's (the AIF's) bankruptcy, then the receivable comes into existence after such pledgor's bankruptcy and therefore forms part of the pledgor's bankruptcy estate unencumbered by any right of pledge. It is, however, the prevailing view in Dutch legal literature that the parties may agree on the qualification of a receivable – as such, fund documentation will typically contain a clause that explicitly states that any receivable owed by the investor to the AIF is considered an existing but conditional claim, conditional upon the capital call being made. A right of pledge created over an existing but conditional receivable is also valid if the condition (the capital call) is met after the pledgor's bankruptcy.

However, there is limited case law confirming that such a provision would work to avoid any of the aforementioned issues. There is also some debate in literature on whether a pledgee may issue capital call notices solely based on its right of pledge. To mitigate those risks, the pledgee may request to be granted a direct, independent right to issue capital call notices in default situations. Often, a direct agreement to be entered into between the pledgee and the investors is not (commercially) feasible. Nowadays, we do see that fund documentation caters for the possibility for the pledgee (as an independent right) to make capital calls by submitting capital call notices (to avoid the need to arrange this at a later stage via direct agreements). Alternatively, the AIFM may grant a power of attorney to the pledgee to issue, in certain default situations, a capital call notice in the AIFM's name to the investors (again, this right is often acknowledged in the fund documentation). However, as a power of attorney is terminated, by operation of law, in the event of bankruptcy of the entity that has granted the power of attorney, the latter option is less favourable to the pledgee.

Another element to take into consideration when structuring the security over the AIF's assets is that receivables and contractual rights may, through a clause in (the general conditions to) the contract from which such receivables or contractual rights arise, be made non-assignable/transferable or 'non-pledgeable'. Depending on the wording of the relevant provision of the contract, such non-assignability clause could have an effect *in rem*, in which case creating a right of pledge over such receivable or right will simply not be possible. The fund documentation should be carefully checked on this.

The year ahead

As emphasised, 2021 and 2022 have been interesting and important years for Dutch fund formation and fund finance markets. With current national and international political developments confirming and strengthening the Netherlands' position as a mature and well-equipped jurisdiction for funds and investments, we expect that 2023 will be another important year for the Dutch private equity and venture capital markets. With the Dutch fund finance markets maturing, we expect to see an increase in the diversity and volume of the fund finance products offered in the Netherlands; for example, by an increase in the number of hybrid facilities, general partner solutions and co-investment facilities offered. We are seeing an increasing number of fund managers exploring NAV facilities as well and expect that trend to continue in 2023. We are also seeing an increasing number of non-Dutch lenders showing interest in the Dutch market. In view of, amongst other things, the evolving legislation in this respect (such as the SFDR), a key development will likely be the integration of ESG factors in fund facilities, whereby measurable ESG performance indicators can directly impact the applicable interest margin.

* * *

Endnotes

1. An interactive graphic providing an overview of the NVP's findings can be found on its website: https://nvp.nl/feiten-cijfers/marktcijfers (this reference is accurate on the date of this publication).
2. We note that this chapter does not focus on collective investment undertakings that require a licence pursuant to Article 5 of Directive 2009/65/EC (UCITS).
3. It is noted that the Dutch partnership law is currently under review and that a second preliminary draft bill at civil service level (*Tweede Ambtelijk voorontwerp Wet modernisering personenvennootschappen*) was presented on 10 October 2022. If this second preliminary draft bill is implemented in its current form, Dutch (limited) partnerships will be granted legal personality. Having legal personality may affect the treatment of Dutch (limited) partnerships, *inter alia*, from a regulatory perspective (as, for example, a separate entity holding legal title to the assets of an AIF may no longer be necessary).

* * *

Acknowledgment

The authors acknowledge with thanks the contribution to this chapter by Vilmar Feenstra, a partner in the Investment Management practice group.

Gianluca Kreuze
Tel: +31 20 578 55 12 / Email: Gianluca.Kreuze@loyensloeff.com

Gianluca Kreuze, attorney at law, is a partner of the Finance practice group and co-head of the Private Equity team. Gianluca advises lenders, borrowers and "originators" with structuring and documenting finance transactions. Gianluca is specialised in domestic and international private equity matters and his particular expertise concentrates on debt finance transactions with an emphasis on acquisition finance and follow-on recapitalisations and other corporate finance transaction. Gianluca formerly worked at the Loyens & Loeff office in London, where he mainly dealt with structured finance transactions.

Michaël Maters
Tel: +31 20 578 58 64 / Email: Michael.Maters@loyensloeff.com

Michaël Maters, attorney at law, is a senior associate of the Investment Management practice group and member of the Private Equity team. Michaël focuses on investment management, Dutch partnerships, corporate fund structures and AIFMD-related matters, specialising, in particular, in the civil, corporate and regulatory aspects of (international) fund formation. He acts both on behalf of managers in the formation of their alternative investment funds as well as on behalf of (institutional) investors, assisting them with their investments in such alternative investment funds. Additionally, Michaël also publishes on the various civil, corporate and regulatory aspects of fund formation (such as asset segregation and management participation structures). Michaël was seconded to the Loyens & Loeff office in Zürich in 2017.

Ruben den Hollander
Tel: +31 6 10 90 14 82 / Email: Ruben.den.Hollander@loyensloeff.com

Ruben den Hollander, attorney at law, is an associate of the Finance practice group and member of the Private Equity team. Ruben specialises in secured lending, advising both financial institutions and private investors on structuring and documentation. He focuses on leveraged finance and fund finance.

Ruben worked in the firm's Investment Management practice group in 2016 and 2017 where he assisted managers with the formation of their funds and institutional investors in respect of their investments in funds. Ruben worked in the firm's New York office from 2020 to 2021 and was seconded to Mayer Brown (Banking & Finance) in New York in 2020.

Loyens & Loeff N.V.

Parnassusweg 300, 1081 LC Amsterdam, Netherlands
Tel: +31 20 578 57 85 / URL: www.loyensloeff.com

Norway

Snorre Nordmo, Ole Andenæs & Karoline Angell
Wikborg Rein Advokatfirma AS

Overview

Overview of the Norwegian market

Although the Norwegian asset management market is small in a global context, it has shown solid growth over recent years. Established players observe rapid growth in assets under management, and there is a steady increase in the establishment of new asset managers, funds, and service providers. Even during the market turmoil at the beginning of the pandemic, the net inflow in Norwegian funds grew rapidly.[1] The amount invested by Norwegian alternative investment fund ("**AIF**") managers by the end of 2021 was record high with a total of NOK 403 billion – an increase of more than 35 per cent from the year before.[2] Furthermore, 2021 saw record investment levels. Norwegian companies received investments of NOK 66.8 billion from Norwegian and foreign private equity funds, beating the record of NOK 36.8 billion in 2019. The majority of the capital (NOK 60 billion) was invested by foreign fund managers, showing that foreign fund managers find Norwegian companies attractive.[3] Never before has the proportion of Norwegian private retail investors saving in funds been higher than in 2021, and as much as 46 per cent of the population now has money invested in equity funds, according to a new survey conducted on behalf of the Norwegian Fund and Asset Management Association.[4] However, this trend and the financial market in general have faced certain challenges in the latter half of 2022 with higher market volatility and geopolitical issues, and net inflow in the capital market seems to have abated somewhat.[5]

The increased number of asset managers and assets under management in Norwegian funds is driven by many features. In broader terms, we think that the continuing growth of wealth is one of the main factors. We also think that the political stability, financial predictability and general economic growth in the region has made Norway an attractive harbour for making investments.

The two main categories of funds in Norway are Undertakings for Collective Investment in Transferable Securities ("**UCITS**") and AIFs. As of today, there are 58 full-scope authorised managers of AIFs in Norway, and 194 registered ("sub-threshold") AIF managers. There are 30 managers of securities funds (consisting of managers of UCITS and national funds, as further described below).

Further, there is a growing number of family offices in Norway. A family office can only manage a family's own assets, a so-called "pre-existing group", and therefore cannot be considered to constitute an AIF, as further outlined in the European Securities and Markets Authority's ("**ESMA**") guidelines on Key Concepts of AIFMD (ESMA/2013/611).

Another trend is the continuing growth in establishment of Norwegian fund structures, in contrast to establishing funds in offshore jurisdictions. At the same time, it is still common for Norwegian fund managers to establish fund structures in jurisdictions such as Delaware, Guernsey, Ireland, Jersey, Luxembourg, etc.

The continuing growth in the Norwegian asset management market, both in terms of capital under management and the number of Norwegian funds and managers being established, has resulted in a subsequent growth of service providers (e.g., administrators, depositary services, fund compliance and risk management services, research firms, etc.).

Regulatory framework

The Norwegian regulatory framework is, to a large extent, based on EU legislation.

Norway is not a member of the EU; however, it is part of the European Economic Area (the "**EEA**"), which is established and regulated through the EEA Agreement. EU legislation does not automatically transform to Norwegian law, but such legislation is incorporated into the EEA Agreement and subsequently incorporated into Norwegian law by the Norwegian parliament (the lawmaker in Norway).

Norway is obligated under the EEA Agreement to implement most of the financial legislation from the EU. However, due to the rapid change and growth in EU financial legislation, there is more or less a constant backlog in the Norwegian implementation.

Directive 2009/65/EC relating to undertakings for collective investment in transferable securities (the "**UCITS Directive**") and Directive 2011/61/EU on alternative investment fund managers ("**AIFMD**") are implemented in Norway through the Securities Funds Act (the "**SFA**") and the Alternative Investment Fund Managers Act (the "**AIFM Act**"), respectively. Although both directives seek harmonisation to a large extent, the flexibility for national specific regulation and gold plating has been used to some extent.

The Norwegian Financial Supervisory Authority (the "**FSAN**") is responsible for supervision of the regulated actors in Norway.

Fund formation and finance

Types of funds

Broadly speaking, the various fund structures in Norway may be divided into two main groups, i.e., regulated and unregulated fund structures. UCITS funds are naturally regulated, while unregulated fund structures are currently dominating the Norwegian AIF market.

Unregulated fund types

Prior to the implementation of AIFMD in Norway in 2014, the AIF market (non-UCITS) was more or less unregulated. Since the implementation of AIFMD, AIF managers are now regulated; however, AIFs themselves may be unregulated.

The definition of an AIF in Norway corresponds with that of AIFMD: "*[A] collective investment undertaking which is not an UCITS, and which raises capital from a number of investors with a view to investing the capital in accordance with a defined investment strategy for the benefit of the investors.*" In this context, the ESMA guidelines on Key Concepts of AIFMD and the FSAN's circular no 9/2019 provide further guidance on the interpretation of the definition. Companies falling within the scope of the holding company exclusion will not be considered AIFs. The Norwegian definition of a holding company corresponds with AIFMD Article 4 no 1 (o).

Under the AIFM Act, there are no limitations on the legal form of an AIF, and an AIF can be organised as a private limited liability company, public limited liability company, limited partnership, etc.

Regulated fund types

There are, in total, six regulated fund types in Norway, those being UCITS, national funds, special funds (which are also national funds), EuVECA, EuSEF and ELTIF (where the latter is still not implemented in Norway).

The **UCITS** rules correspond to a large extent with the UCITS Directive. UCITS may be marketed to both professional and non-professional investors.

As an alternative to UCITS, **national funds** are a separate class of securities funds (also being an AIF), which deviate from the main rules that apply to UCITS funds, primarily related to investment restrictions and diversification rules. When approved by the FSAN, national funds may be marketed to both professional and non-professional investors.

Special funds (also being AIFs), a subcategory of national funds, are securities funds that, compared to UCITS and regular national funds, have greater flexibility in terms of investment strategy, investment techniques and redemption requirements. A specific authorisation regime applies for marketing to non-professional investors.

After the implementation of AIFMD in Norway, national funds (including special funds) are not as common as unregulated AIF structures, mainly due to the lack of flexibility on investment strategy and redemptions compared to unregulated AIFs.

Regulation (EU) 345/2013 on European venture capital funds (the "**EuVECA Regulation**") and Regulation (EU) 346/2013 (as amended) on European social entrepreneurship funds (the "**EuSEF Regulation**") have been implemented in Norway, and entered into force in August 2021. Regulation (EU) 2015/760 on European long-term investment funds (the "**ELTIF Regulation**") is yet to be implemented, but is expected to enter into force sometime in 2023.[6]

Specifically on finance funds/credit funds

While other EU/EEA countries have various forms of specialised credit funds (and mezzanine funds), credit funds are not defined in Norway and lending activities are strictly regulated, as described in further detail below.

Fund finance

Financing activities in Norway

Lending and other forms of financing by extension of credit (including leasing and furnishing of guarantees, and the intermediation and facilitation of such activities) are defined as "financing activities" under the Norwegian Financial Institutions Act of 2015 (the "**FIA**"), *cf.* FIA section 2-1 (2).

Carrying out "financing activities" is subject to licensing requirements under the FIA, and can only be carried out by institutions duly licensed in Norway or EEA-based credit or financial institutions that have the benefit of EEA "passporting rights", unless an exemption applies.

As a starting point, the definition of financing activities includes both granting credit in the primary market (originating) and purchase of loans in the secondary market. The purchase and collection of overdue claims is regulated by the Norwegian Debt Collection Act of 1988.

Investments in bonds (whether on the primary or secondary market) are generally held not to constitute financing activities. In addition, activities such as operational leasing (in contrast to financial leasing) or investing through structured equity do not constitute financing activities under the FIA.

It should also be noted that financing activities are only licensable if the activities take place "in Norway". This qualification is also the basis for the Reverse Solicitation Exemption, as further described below.

In addition, there are certain general exemptions to what constitutes a financing activity. For funds, the main exemptions are (i) the access to grant loans in accordance with EuVECA (and ELTIF and AIFMD II, when implemented in Norway), (ii) to conduct financing activities on an isolated or one-off basis, (iii) to conduct financing activities to companies within the same group, and (iv) reverse solicitation.

Please see above for more information on EuVECA and ELTIF.

FIA section 2-1 (3) provides several exemptions from the licensing requirements, where one of the most relevant for funds is to conduct financing activities on an isolated or one-off basis and to conduct financing activities to companies within the same group.

FIA section 2-1 (3) letter f) is an exemption for financing activities that are only granted on an isolated or one-off basis. The scope of exemption is generally interpreted as very limited and must be assessed on a case-by-case basis, where relevant considerations are the size and the number of loans, the frequency of lending and the duration of the lender's financing activities.

Previously, it was long-standing market practice for the exemption to be used by various types of special purpose vehicles when financing major projects, for example, in shipping and infrastructure. Subsequent practice from the regulator and relevant authorities indicates that the exemption is not available for such special purpose vehicles, when the main purpose of the special purpose vehicle is to provide loans/financing, even when it is only a single loan. As a consequence, the exception may only apply for entities where loans are granted in isolated instances alongside other activities (and the other activity does not constitute financing activity, neither in nor outside Norway).

FIA section 2-1 (3) letter c) includes a general exemption for providing credit to, or granting guarantee for, own employees or legal entities within the same group of legal entities as the credit or guarantee provider. This exemption is, for example, commonly used for private equity funds (or underlying companies in the fund structure) to grant loans to their portfolio companies (provided that the relevant fund has controlling influence over the portfolio company).

The general perception is that there is a limited exception for foreign lenders to carry out financing activities on a so-called "reverse solicitation basis" in Norway (for foreign funds), often referred to as the "first approach exemption" (the "**Reverse Solicitation Exemption**"). The Reverse Solicitation Exemption is not a defined concept under Norwegian law (i.e., there are no statutory rules on reverse solicitation under Norwegian law), but it is based on an interpretation of what constitutes "financing activities" in Norway under the FIA. A concrete assessment has to be conducted in each case to determine whether the Reverse Solicitation Exemption may apply.

Security

Generally speaking, it should be noted that in Norway, security may only be taken in the manner and to the extent explicitly permitted by Norwegian law (which is referred to below as "statutory authority"). Any security held that is subject to Norwegian law and that lacks statutory authority will be invalid.

The statutory authority to take security is scattered in various laws in Norway, although a majority of such authorities, and the main principles for taking security in Norway, are included in the Norwegian Mortgage and Pledges Act of 1980.

Key developments and the year ahead

As mentioned above, we have seen great growth and development in the Norwegian fund market, and it is expected that the current trends will continue to evolve in the long term.

During the year ahead, it is expected that the ELTIF Regulation will enter into force in Norway. Further, we expect the following EU legislation to be implemented in Norway during or after 2022.

Securitisation in Norwegian law

The current rules under the FIA do not include specific rules on securitisation. As a consequence, the licensing requirements for financing activities apply for securitisation special purpose entities that acquire underlying financial assets in a traditional securitisation transaction.

However, amendments to the FIA implementing the EU Securitisation Regulation (Regulation (EU) 2017/2402), which consequently make it possible to conduct securitisation transactions in Norway, was passed on 23 April 2021. The amendments have not yet entered into force as the EU Securitisation Regulation is not yet incorporated into the EEA Agreement, and the timing for incorporation into such Agreement is currently unknown.[7]

The amended rules will apply to securitisation as defined in Article 2 (1) of the EU Securitisation Regulation, which captures both traditional and synthetic (on-balance sheet) securitisations. The amended rules will create new and better opportunities for funds and investors who seek to obtain exposure to the Norwegian financing market.

SFDR in Norwegian law

The Sustainable Finance Disclosure Regulation (Regulation (EU) 2019/2088 (the "**SFDR**")) imposes mandatory environmental, social and governance ("**ESG**") disclosure obligations for asset managers, including a requirement to provide prescript and standardised disclosures on how ESG factors are integrated, both at an entity and a product level. The SFDR framework also requires asset managers to classify their fund product and sets forth three categories: (i) the Article 6 category (a "normal fund"/"grey fund"); (ii) the Article 8 category (a "light green fund"); and (iii) the Article 9 category (a "dark green fund").

In December 2021, the new Norwegian Act on Sustainable Finance was passed, which includes the implementation of two important pillars in the EU's work on sustainable finance, the taxonomy regulation and the SFDR. The Act on Sustainable Finance has not yet entered into force, and enforcement has been delayed to sometime in 2023.[8]

The new SFDR and taxonomy regulation impose various disclosure and reporting obligations. We have experienced that fund managers managing Norwegian AIFs have started to prepare for the new legislation prior to implementation in Norway, as the funds are often also marketed in other EU states where the SFDR is already in place. In general, we have seen a great focus on ESG-driven investments and the implementation of sustainability risk factors in investment strategies in the Norwegian market, in addition to establishment of reporting routines and preparation of ESG policies.

Cross-Border Distribution of Funds Directive

The Cross-Border Distribution of Funds Directive 2019/1160 was implemented by amendments to the AIFM Act and the UCITS Act on 22 June 2022. Accordingly, once the implementing law comes into effect (which is expected to take place sometime in Q4 2022 or early 2023), the harmonised rules for marketing funds from other EEA states and possibility for EU/EEA AIFMs to undertake pre-marketing will apply in Norway. The amended AIFM Act does not allow for non-EEA managers and funds to conduct pre-marketing in Norway.

Other

Prospectus Regulation

Regulation (EU) 2017/1129 on prospectus requirements was implemented in Norway in 2019, by way of reference in the Securities Trading Act. Prospectus requirements are applicable for investments in funds unless any of the relevant exceptions apply: (i) an offer of securities is addressed to fewer than 150 natural or legal persons (as defined in the Prospectus Regulation); or (ii) an offer of securities whose denomination per unit amounts to at least EUR 100,000. For UCITS and national funds, there exist separate prospectus requirements as set out in the SFA.

* * *

Endnotes

1. Norges Bank, *Norway's financial system: An overview 2021* (available at: https://www.norges-bank.no/contentassets/97a4fd6249bb48c0a80cfef7ff64ddb1/nfs_norways-financial-system-2021.pdf?v=09/01/2021102524&ft=.pdf).
2. The Financial Supervisory Authority of Norway, *Report on alternative investment funds 2021* (available in Norwegian at: https://www.finanstilsynet.no/publikasjoner-og-analyser/rapport-om-alternative-investeringsfond).
3. Norwegian Venture Capital & Private Equity Association (NVCA), *Private Equity Funds in Norway: Activity report 2021* (available at: https://www.nvca.no/wp-content/uploads/2022/04/Private-Equity-Funds-in-Norway-2021-revidert.pdf).
4. Norwegian Fund and Asset Management Association, *The fund survey 2021* (available in Norwegian at: https://vff.no/storage/Dokumenter/2021/Fondsunders%C3%B8kelsen-2021-hoved.pdf).
5. The Financial Supervisory Authority of Norway, *Performance report: Investments Firms and Fund Managers H1 2022* (available in Norwegian at: https://www.finanstilsynet.no/contentassets/e3e990e7ea6d4b27b7d5bad3f30581fc/resultatrapport-for-verdipapirforetak-forste-halvar-2022.pdf).
6. The Norwegian Government, *EEA note on ELTIF* (available in Norwegian at: https://www.regjeringen.no/no/sub/eos-notatbasen/notatene/2013/okt/eltif/id2434707).
7. EFTA, *Legal status: Securitisation Regulation* (available at: https://www.efta.int/eea-lex/32017R2402).
8. The Norwegian Government, *News: The Act on Sustainable Finance will enter into force in 2023* (available in Norwegian at: https://www.regjeringen.no/no/aktuelt/lov-om-barekraftig-finans-vil-tre-i-kraft-i-2023/id2940988).

* * *

Acknowledgments

The authors would like to thank Karoline Ulleland Hoel and Stina Tveiten for their valuable contribution to this chapter. They both work at Wikborg Rein's Oslo office and are part of the firm's Asset Management and Financial Regulatory practices.

Snorre Nordmo
Tel: +47 22 82 76 09 / Email: sno@wr.no

Snorre Nordmo is a Partner at Wikborg Rein's Oslo office and head of the firm's Asset Management practice.

Snorre is specialised in asset management and financial regulatory matters and has broad experience within the industry from both a service provider and client perspective. He advises both regulated and unregulated asset managers, including investment firms, alternative investment managers (within private equity, hedge funds, real estate, private debt, infrastructure, etc.), securities fund managers, investment banks and financial institutions, pension funds, insurance companies, family offices, consultants, advisers and service providers within the asset management industry. Snorre has previously worked as General Counsel at Sector Asset Management (the largest hedge fund manager in Norway) and as an Attorney at Norges Bank Investment Management (NBIM, the manager of the Norwegian sovereign wealth fund).

Ole Andenæs
Tel: +47 22 82 76 61 / Email: oea@wr.no

Ole Andenæs is a Partner at Wikborg Rein's Oslo office and heads the firm's Financial Regulations practice.

Andenæs previously worked as Head of Legal in investment bank Carnegie AS, and he has in-depth and practical knowledge about the regulatory framework surrounding investment firms, asset managers, investor behaviour and adjacent regulations. Prior to this, Andenæs worked as a Senior Lawyer at the law firm Thommessen, where he mainly worked with financial regulations, advising a wide range of regulated entities, as well as company law and disputes within these areas. He is also a specialist in company law, and is the co-author of *"Aksjeselskaper og allmennaksjeselskaper"* (3rd edition 2016) (*"Public and Private Limited Company Law"*).

Karoline Angell
Tel: +47 22 82 75 10 / Email: ang@wr.no

Karoline Angell is an Associate at Wikborg Rein's Oslo office and is part of the firm's Asset Management and Financial Regulations practices. Karoline works primarily with financial regulatory issues and securities law. This includes advising Norwegian and foreign regulated entities on matters related to licensing, operation and organisation of activities in line with applicable laws and regulations.

Wikborg Rein Advokatfirma AS

Dronning Mauds gate 11, PO Box 1513 Vika, NO-0117 Oslo, Norway
Tel: +47 22 82 75 00 / URL: www.wr.no

Singapore

Jean Woo, Danny Tan & Cara Stevens
Ashurst LLP

Fundraising activity in Southeast Asia – 2022[1]

Looking back

2022 has not been the best of years for fundraising, and activity has slowed down dramatically. As of September 2022, only one Southeast Asia-focused private equity fund had achieved closing. This was Mitsubishi-backed, ASEAN-focused AIGF Advisors, which announced the final close of its second fund at US$126 million in August. This is in stark contrast to the record year in 2021 in which seven funds achieved nearly US$3 billion in fresh capital. At the time of writing and considering the current pace towards year end, 2022 is likely to go down as the weakest of the past five years.

Reasons for slowdown

Southeast Asia has not been immune to the macro-economic and geopolitical turbulence. The strong economic rebound early in 2022 for most countries is losing momentum. Russia's invasion of Ukraine and China's strict zero-COVID policy and related lockdowns together with the deepening turmoil in its real estate sector have dampened deal-making sentiments in this region.

Looking ahead – 2023

Fortunately, the outlook for 2023 looks more promising based on interim closings data published by DealStreetAsia, and the following six Southeast Asia-focused funds achieved interim close to raise US$1.47 billion: Hildrics Asia Growth Fund I; Fullerton Thai PE; Growtheum Capital Partners Fund I; Tropical Asia Forest Fund 2; ASEAN Frontier Markets Fund; and Creador V.

More broadly, Southeast Asia remains one of the brighter spots and is expected to enjoy a strong recovery. IMF expects Vietnam to benefit most from disruption of global supply chains with an expected 7% growth. The Philippines is also expected to see a 6.5% expansion, while growth in Indonesia and Malaysia will top 5%.[2]

Is Southeast Asia attracting more liquidity?

It appears so. Despite the marked slowdown in fundraising activity, the rate of investments in the digitalisation and technology sector in Southeast Asia has grown. The number of venture investments rose by 4.3% to 862 and the aggregate deal value grew by 158% to over US$21 billion in 2021.

According to the World Economic Forum, during the COVID-19 pandemic, over 60 million people in ASEAN became online consumers. The pandemic has pushed a vast number of people to embrace technology as a means of mitigating COVID-related challenges, particularly lockdowns.

Now, two-thirds of Asia's population are mobile users and many predict that there is still room for expansion, with the fastest growing regions being Indonesia and the Philippines.

Despite worldwide and regional slowdown, Southeast Asia still continues to be one of the top investment destinations. In particular, there are news reports of continued flow of liquidity from Greater China to Southeast Asia. Perhaps reflective of this, the SuperReturn Asia conference held in Singapore in September 2022 created a buzz when it saw a record 1,500 delegates, including 500 limited partners, attending in person.

In the same month, digital financial services group Fazz raised US$100 million and Indonesia's Xendit, which bills itself as Southeast Asia's alternative to payments processing platform Stripe, announced fundraising of US$300 million in May 2022.

According to Preqin's forecast,[3] venture capital in the Asia-Pacific (APAC) region will still be the strongest asset class where the Compound Annual Growth Rate (CAGR) for 2021–2027 (forecast) is expected to be 16.04%, followed by infrastructure at 12.51%, private equity at 11.59%, natural resources at 11.15%, private debt at 9.14% and real estate at 9.12%.

Denominator effect in public market affecting private market

Preqin highlighted that, following a strong sell-off in public markets, some allocators are grappling with a phenomenon known as the "denominator effect": some investors have found that the sharp fall in public markets since the beginning of 2022 has led to an over-investment in illiquid assets such as, for example, real estate and infrastructure.

Private Equity International reported[4] in November 2022 that private equity's stellar performance in 2021 and resilience relative to the public markets in 2022 has left some investors overallocated to the asset class. This denominator effect has prompted some to reduce their ticket sizes or commit to fewer vehicles, affecting fundraising in the private markets.

The article cited that Apollo Global Management will keep its latest flagship fund open well into 2023 as potential investors grapple with the allocation constraints described above.

In Singapore, the outlook for the SPAC market is reflective of the sentiments towards the public market between 2021 and 2022.

The Business Times wrote an article on 5 June 2022 titled "SPACs were all the rage. Now, not so much". The listing of SPACs led Singapore's IPO market to its busiest half year in five years in the first half of 2021. SPACs are special purpose acquisition companies; more specifically, shell entities that sell shares to the public and use those funds to buy an operating business. Investors get their money back if the SPAC has not found a business to buy within a two-year window.

The global SPAC boom is now cooling, having been fuelled by long periods of low interest rates that pushed investors to riskier corners for higher return. Most venture capitalists regarded SPACs as a quicker way to take technology startups public.

Unfortunately, with the rapidly rising interest rate environment, investors have more frequently invoked their contractual right to redeem their shares in a SPAC. However, experts feel that it may be too early to tell whether Singapore SPACs will lose steam, as three of Singapore's SPACs are backed by experienced and reputable sponsors in the mergers and acquisitions space and have ample time to look for targets.[5]

Conclusion

In view of the above, it is not surprising to learn that, according to the Preqin Insights survey, private equity investors are of the view that the key challenges affecting deal activity for the next 12 months will be: (1) the exit environment; (2) asset valuation; (3) rising interest rates; (4) stock market volatility; and (5) the geopolitical landscape.

What was talked about at the inaugural Fund Finance Symposium in Singapore?

After a three-year hiatus, the first in-person APAC Fund Finance Symposium took place in Singapore on 3 November 2022. This was also the first-ever Fund Finance Symposium to be held in the country.

Symposium panellists highlighted that given the challenges of the current market and liquidity crunch, product diversification is key. There is a need to "get creative" in financing structures, and to look beyond the traditional capital call facility to meet the current leverage needs of funds.

Commercially, for financiers, there is talk about looking at the right value proposition when lending, and the need to focus on product diversification for clients.

Enter: "Fund Finance 2.0". This is not a new term, and is one that has been talked about at length in the APAC market as well as overseas in the US and Europe.

For a long time, particularly in the APAC region, there were doubts as to whether there would be any uptake in alternative structures; however, in 2022, panellists were able to confidently say for the first time that such structures are entering the market.

The three most common alternative fund finance structures discussed were: NAV Facilities; Hybrid Facilities; and GP Facilities. There was also mention of private credit and preferred equity structures.

In the face of tightening liquidity, NAV and Hybrid Facilities in particular were identified as potential financing solutions to the increasing levels of fund assets under management. Preqin expects the size to almost double by 2027 compared to current levels.

It was also observed that such structures could require significantly more involvement of the financier on an ongoing basis to assess valuations and key performance indicators.

Most experts agreed that alternative structures have only really started to enter the market in the past 12–18 months and not all transactions make it across the finish line. These alternative structures are expected to become more prevalent as traditional subscription line facilities do not fully address the growing challenges and complexities faced by fund managers.

Singapore's investment fund vehicle – VCC 2.0

The Variable Capital Company (VCC) is a new specialised corporate structure in Singapore that can be used as one or more collective investment schemes (whether open- or closed-ended). The VCC is constituted under the VCC Act, which came into force in 2020, and is touted as a "game-changer".

To encourage industry adoption of the VCC framework in Singapore, the Monetary Authority of Singapore (MAS) launched the Variable Capital Companies Grant Scheme, which will help to defray the costs involved in incorporating or registering a VCC by co-funding up to 70% of eligible expenses paid to Singapore-based service providers.

The grant is capped at S$150,000 for each application, with a maximum of three VCCs per fund manager. An extension to the grant scheme is being reviewed but it is otherwise due to lapse on 15 January 2023.

According to the Alternative Investment Management Association (AIMA), by mid-2022, over 540 VCCs had been established in Singapore. The figures indicate that around one-third of those were closed-ended private equity or venture capital funds, 20% were hedge funds, 28% were multi-family offices or external asset managers, and 14% were traditional long only. In addition, there were 15 redomiciliations, as asset managers in the region explore its potential.

The VCC has found favour with fund managers operating different investment strategies such as hedge funds, venture capital funds and private equity funds. It has also drawn many wealth management players, keen to establish fund platforms for their high-net-worth clients, and family offices.

What makes the VCC attractive as a fund vehicle?

The VCC functions as a corporate structure tailored specifically for investment funds. More specifically, it is incorporated under the VCC Act, instead of the Companies Act, to allow it to function as a fund vehicle instead of as a generic corporate entity. Despite being administered by Singapore's corporate regulator, the Accounting and Corporate Regulatory Authority (ACRA), and unlike other companies registered with ACRA, the VCC's register of shareholders is not made public, although the register must be disclosed to public authorities upon request for regulatory, supervisory and law enforcement purposes.

In addition to the grant mentioned above, there are numerous tax incentives offered to a VCC. These include, in particular, tax incentives under Section 13O (Singapore Resident Fund) and Section 13U (Enhanced Tier Fund) of the Singapore Income Tax Act. In effect, for eligible funds, all income from designated investments will be tax-free, resulting in no tax outcome, similar to that of a Cayman fund.

The Section 13O scheme exempts specified income received by an approved company in Singapore from tax, where such income is derived from designated investments in funds managed in Singapore by a licensed or exempt resident fund manager. It will not be applicable if all of the approved Singapore companies' issued securities are beneficially owned by Singapore persons. The fund must incur at least S$200,000 in global business expenses a year and the fund's administrator must be based in Singapore.

The Section 13U scheme applies to funds with a minimum size of S$50 million that are managed or advised by a Singapore fund manager, which can be an exempted Singapore family office or a licensed multi-family office. The fund manager must employ at least three investment professionals in Singapore who are substantively engaged in an investment management or advisory role, and the fund must incur at least S$200,000 in business spending in Singapore, which typically covers investment management fees payable to the fund manager.

In addition, if its constitution so allows, a VCC will have the flexibility to issue and redeem shares without having to seek shareholders' approval. As a VCC is not subject to the same restrictions on capital reduction as those of a company structure, it allows investors to exit their investments in the investment fund when they so wish, as redemption proceeds can be paid out of profits or capital. A VCC is also not subject to the restriction of only being able to pay dividends out of profits and, accordingly, can pay dividends using its capital as well.

More broadly, the VCC may be established as a standalone fund or as an umbrella fund with multiple sub-funds. The umbrella fund structure creates economies of scale. Sub-funds under the same umbrella fund can share a common board of directors and use the same service providers, including the same fund manager, custodian, auditor and administrative agent. As a safeguard for VCC shareholders and to enhance creditor protection, the VCC Act provides for the statutory ring-fencing of assets and liabilities of each sub-fund from the other sub-funds.

The VCC will allow for a wider scope of accounting standards to be used in preparing financial statements, which helps to serve the needs of global investors. Apart from Singapore accounting standards and recommended accounting principles, International Financial Reporting Standards and US Generally Accepted Accounting Principles can be used by VCCs.

Looking ahead, it has been reported that MAS is in the process of revising its VCC fund structure to expand the pool of fund managers that can use the scheme and to make fund conversions and multiple offshore fund redomiciliation easier. The MAS is keen to expand the reach of the scheme further to attract more asset managers to launch new funds using the new vehicle.

What's next – VCC 2.0

The MAS is revising its VCC structure to attract a wider pool of managers to Singapore. It issued a consultation paper on the VCC in 2019 and responded to the feedback received in 2020. This academic dialogue has been useful to elicit industry views of what is top of the wish list.

The much-anticipated revisions to the VCC fund structure are expected to include an expansion to the pool of fund managers that can use the vehicle, and a process to make fund conversions and multiple offshore fund redomiciliation easier.

At present, only managers who hold capital markets services licences for fund management (or managers who fall within certain exemptions) are permitted to use the VCC. This is limiting as it potentially excludes a wide pool of single-family offices and real estate fund managers who are exempt from licensing under Singapore's Securities and Futures Act.

The concern is that if the licensing requirement is relaxed, it may result in too many VCCs being used for private wealth vehicles. However, there tends to be a stronger desire to encourage more traditional asset classes like private equity, real estate and infrastructure to look at the Singapore VCC as a potential vehicle.

In spite of the competing views, developments in this sphere are always useful as many feel that this is all part of the path to developing the VCC structure into a globally recognised investment vehicle that can compete with the likes of offshore fund structures.

The other key change expected to be made to the VCC is to improve the manner in which existing fund structures may be converted into VCCs. Prior to the VCC, fund managers who wanted to set up a private fund in Singapore typically used the limited partnership, unit trust, or private limited company structures.

If a fund manager wishes to convert its existing fund vehicle to a VCC structure, it is only possible to do so by setting up a new VCC and subsequently transferring the assets from the existing fund to the VCC. This is a tiresome process and also triggers potentially significant tax consequences such as stamp duty.

In addition to fund conversion, the MAS is also looking into allowing the redomiciliation of multiple offshore funds into a single VCC. Currently, managers are only allowed to redomicile one offshore standalone or umbrella fund into one Singapore standalone or umbrella VCC, respectively.

Sustainable Finance

The MAS' vision for Singapore is to be a leading centre for Green and Sustainable Finance both in Asia and globally, and it has spearheaded a number of initiatives in this space to facilitate the championing of this cause. We set out briefly a few key developments in 2022 below.

Disclosure and Reporting Guidelines for Retail ESG Funds

To mitigate the risk of greenwashing for Retail ESG Funds, the MAS published a circular[6] on 28 July 2022, which will take effect on 1 January 2023, to apply to prospectuses of retail environmental, social and governance (ESG) funds (i.e. Retail ESG Funds) that are lodged with the MAS on or after 1 January 2023.

In brief, a fund that is sold to retail investors in Singapore using ESG factors as a key investment focus and strategy, or represents itself as an ESG-focused scheme, will need to justify its ESG labelling. This includes the required details on a scheme's ESG focus, investment strategy, reference benchmark and risks associated with such ESG focus.

Second consultation paper on Green Taxonomy

Singapore's Green Finance Industry Taskforce (GFIT) published a second consultation paper on 12 May 2022, which sets out details of thresholds and criteria for a revised Singapore taxonomy for Singapore-based financial institutions to identify "green" activities or activities transitioning towards green.

This paper follows the publication of the January 2021 paper, which introduced a proposed taxonomy for Singapore-based financial institutions to identify activities that can be considered "green" or transitioning towards green. Similar to the taxonomy being developed in the EU, the paper broadly introduced a "traffic light" system for classifying activities as green (environmentally sustainable), amber (transition), or red (harmful) based on their contributions to a proposed set of environmental objectives.

The second consultation paper sets out threshold criteria for economic activities in three sectors – energy, transport and real estate. The paper also provides more details of the application of a traffic light system by sub-categorising activities in the above sectors and proposes detailed benchmarks and thresholds for these activities.

GFIT is expected to finalise this Green Taxonomy in 2023.

ESG Registry

On 18 May 2022, fintech company Hashstacs (Stacs) launched a blockchain-based platform known as ESGpedia, which powers the new ESG Registry. The objective of having this registry is to make it easier for financial institutions to access companies' sustainability data from multiple certification bodies and verified sources. This platform is one of the four digital utility platforms housed under Project Greenprint, which the MAS is developing in partnership with the industry.

Let's go back to basics – security package 101

In this section, we consider some of the typical security package considerations for a fund finance transaction. The key concepts for the taking and perfection of security common to a fund finance transaction (fortunately) remained unchanged and are consistent with similar concepts in other established common law jurisdictions such as England & Wales.

One of the key aspects of a fund finance transaction is the security package. This will typically be secured by: (1) the unfunded capital commitments of the fund's investors; (2) the right to make capital calls from investors and receive proceeds of such capital calls; (3) the bank accounts into which the capital contributions are funded; and (4) the rights within the underlying fund documentation, in particular the right to enforce against such investors of the fund.

It is important to conduct good and thorough due diligence of the fund documentation to ensure that a financier has as many unfettered rights as possible in respect of the above when its security is enforced. A good lawyer not only advises on what is required under law, but also on best practice in the market or (if unable to adopt best practice) the risks involved.

An assignment of the rights pursuant to the fund documentation and a charge over bank accounts will be standard forms of security taken under a typical financing. Under Singapore law, an assignment is effective if: (1) it is an absolute assignment; (2) it is made in writing under the hand of the assignor; and (3) express notice in writing has been given to the counterparty (i.e. the investor). Strictly speaking, no acknowledgment is required but it is usually taken (or attempts to ask for it will be made) to incorporate additional protections for the financiers.

These protections include, for example: (1) an undertaking by the investor to pay directly to the secured account; (2) representation by the investor that it will not exercise any set-off or counterclaim of the amount it owes to the fund entity; and (3) a confirmation that it received no prior notice of assignment or security.

For charges, registration at ACRA is required if it is granted by a Singapore company or a foreign company registered in Singapore. This will be relevant if, for example, the security is entered into by the general partner of the fund entity, and that general partner is a company incorporated or registered under the Companies Act. The charge must be registered within 30 days of the date of creation of the charge, and an unregistered registrable charge is void against a liquidator and any creditor of the company, such that the creditor would effectively be an unsecured creditor in a liquidation.

One key point to flag is that the charge registration regime has a public notification aspect to it. The nature of the security and the fact that the fund company has obtained financing will become public knowledge. In addition, it is a legal requirement that a copy of the charge document must be kept available at the company's place of business for its creditor's inspection without fee and any person may, upon application to the company and payment of a nominal fee, be furnished with a copy of such instrument.

The year ahead

In October 2022, the MAS reported that the Singapore economy is projected to slow further at a "below-trend pace" in 2023 amid growing challenges in the external environment. It also said that dampened global and regional trade flows will adversely affect many sectors in Singapore even as global supply frictions continue to ease. Many expect that the Singapore economy is in for a bumpy ride in 2023.

* * *

Endnotes

1. Data from DealStreetAsia–Ontra private equity (PE) landscape report analysis 2022; and Preqin's Private Capital Market Update at the 2022 APAC Fund Finance Symposium and the following reports: (1) Insights+, "Preqin 2022 Alternatives in Asia-Pacific"; and (2) Insights+, "ESG in Alternatives 2022: The Transparency Tipping Point Sample Pages".
2. IMF Blog, "Asia Sails Into Headwinds From Rate Hikes, War, and China Slowdown" (https://www.imf.org/en/Blogs/Articles/2022/10/13/asia-sails-into-headwinds-from-rate-hikes-war-and-china-slowdown).

3. Insights+, "Preqin 2022 Alternatives in Asia-Pacific" report.
4. *Private Equity International*, "Apollo to keep Fund X in market longer, citing denominator effect" (https://www.privateequityinternational.com/apollo-to-keep-fund-x-in-market-longer-citing-denominator-effect).
5. *The Straits Times*, "Bill Ackman's Spac returns $5.6b to investors; too early to tell if S'pore Spac market will lose steam" (https://www.straitstimes.com/business/companies-markets/bill-ackmans-spac-returns-56-billion-to-investors-as-interest-wanes-too-early-to-tell-if-spore-spac-market-will-lose-steam).
6. Circular No. CFC 02/2002 on Disclosure and Reporting Guidelines for Retail ESG Funds.

Jean Woo
Tel: +65 6416 3345 / **Email:** jean.woo@ashurst.com

Jean is a partner in the international finance department in Ashurst's Singapore office, specialising in international banking and finance transactions. Jean has nearly 15 years of experience in the financing space and covers a wide range of bank lending areas, including syndicated lending, cross-border leveraged transactions, acquisition finance, funds financing, structured lending and financing the acquisition of non-performing loan portfolios. Jean has broad exposure to a number of jurisdictions in Asia with a particular focus on jurisdictions in South and Southeast Asia.

Danny Tan
Tel: +65 6416 3356 / **Email:** danny.tan@ashurst.com

Danny is widely regarded as one of the top investment funds lawyers in Singapore. With two decades of experience advising on investment funds, capital markets, and mergers and acquisitions, Danny has extensive experience in fund formation and restructuring, fund investments and fund regulatory matters.

His expertise with both onshore and offshore fund vehicles is well regarded in the Singapore fund management industry, whether for private equity funds, hedge funds, fund of funds, real estate, infrastructure or venture capital funds. He frequently acts for governmental bodies and sovereign wealth funds, local and international fund managers, family offices and financial institutions.

Cara Stevens
Tel: +61 3 9679 3376 / **Email:** cara.stevens@ashurst.com

Cara is a counsel based in Ashurst's Melbourne office. Cara has experience in a wide range of banking and finance transactions including fund finance, green and sustainability-linked loans, project finance, corporate finance, construction finance and share-backed loans, in sectors such as real estate, fintech, mining and infrastructure. Cara works with Ashurst's global loans teams in both Australia and Singapore, and has previously worked in Vietnam. Cara has also spent time on secondment at ANZ in Singapore.

Ashurst LLP

12 Marina Boulevard, #24-01 Marina Bay Financial Centre Tower 3, Singapore 018982
Tel: +65 6221 2214 / URL: www.ashurst.com

Spain

Jabier Badiola Bergara
Dentons Europe Abogados, S.L. (Sociedad Unipersonal)

Overview[1]

Despite the uncertainty governing 2021, the venture and private equity market in Spain has shown resilience by reaching the second-best figures in its history in terms of investment. Indeed, during 2021, venture and private equity grew by almost 20% compared to the previous year and provided 90% of the financing granted to small and medium-sized companies for their start-up or growth needs. This performance of the venture and private equity market in Spain during 2021 shows that any potential slowdown resulting from COVID-19 pandemic has already been superseded.

Approximately 1,000 private equity deals were closed during 2021 for a total investment volume of €7,572.7 million while 773 deals were closed by venture capital funds, which is a record and more than twice of the number of deals closed in 2020, and more than 10 large deals represented 54% of the total investment amount.

Fundraising by venture and private equity companies during 2021 also had a record year in Spain with a total amount of €2,961 million.

The figures above and growth of interest in the Spanish venture and private equity companies have not been reflected in structured subscription (capital call) or net asset value (**NAV**) financings. There are different reasons for this hibernation stage of the Spanish market: (i) the size of the funds incorporated in Spain is usually significantly smaller than other European funds, which does not make it particularly attractive for large financial institutions; (ii) the risk profile of investors in funds incorporated in Spain differs to those investing in European funds; and (iii) some financial institutions continue to provide "corporate financing" to Spanish funds.

From a legal standpoint, there have been no significant updates since the enactment of Act 22/2014, dated 12 November 2014, regulating venture capital entities, other closed-ended investment entities and closed-ended investment entities' management companies (**Private Equity Act**), which implemented Directive 2011/61/EU of the European Parliament and of the Council of 8 June 2011 on Alternative Investment Fund Managers (**AIFM Directive**) and amended Directives 2003/41/EC and 2009/65/EC and Regulations (EC) 1060/2009 and (EU) 1095/2010. The Private Equity Act has played, and still plays, an important role in enhancing access to financing in Spain of venture capital and closed-ended investment entities, as explained in more detail below.

Fund finance framework in Spain

The Private Equity Act indirectly created the necessary legal framework to allow funds to accede to fund financing by allowing the assets of a private equity entity to be charged. In this sense, section 93.d) of the Private Equity Act contemplates that funds can pledge their assets provided that this does not result in a breach of their bylaws (*estatutos sociales*) or limited partnership agreements (*reglamentos de gestión*). Article 15.4 of the AIFM Directive (which is implemented by section 62.4 of the Private Equity Act) also sets forth the possibility of charging the assets of private equity entities. The Private Equity Act addresses a point that the previous legislation did not tackle: it formally recognises the possibility of charging the assets not only for private equity companies (*sociedades de capital-riesgo*), but also for private equity funds (*fondos de capital-riesgo*).

During the last few years, as fund financing has emerged in Spain, an increasing number of Spanish private equity houses have expressly included in their bylaws or limited partnership agreements the ability to enter into third-party financings, and charge the assets of their investment vehicles or the undrawn commitments of their investors. This trend could not have arisen without the change to the Private Equity Act, but it probably owes as much to influences from the United States and the United Kingdom, as well as the favourable curve of interest rates. In any case, it is a type of financing that better fits the current needs of managers of private equity funds.

It lowers the cost of capital, enhancing the fund manager's returns and giving the fund manager fast and reliable access to liquidity – typically within a couple of business days. Not having to issue multiple capital call notices to investors facilitates the speed and certainty of deal execution. Indeed, fund financing provides short-term revolving credit to funds, which bridges the gap between making an investment and receiving capital contributions from investors.

The possibility of charging fund assets or the undrawn commitments of investors extends to all investment vehicles promoted by Spanish fund managers, irrespective of the domicile of the investment vehicle.

Financing and collateral structure

As regards the financing structure for fund financing transactions, most of the transactions closed in the Spanish market and by Spanish players are still subscription line (capital call) facilities. Lately, however, Spanish private equity companies have also participated in several NAV and hybrid facility transactions.

Subscription (capital call) facility transactions

A standard subscription (capital call) facility transaction typically consists of a committed revolving credit facility – *subscription facility* – granted by a fund or credit institution directly at fund level.

Subscription (capital call) facility transactions contemplate that repayment will be made from the prospective capital commitments of the investors. Lenders carefully analyse the creditworthiness of the investors and decide whether to include their prospective contributions when calculating the size of the facility.

The security instruments that Spanish investment funds put in place for this kind of transaction consist of: (i) Spanish law pledges over the credit rights of the fund against investors who have committed to make future contributions – *unfunded capital commitments* (**UCC Pledge**); and (ii) Spanish law pledges over the bank accounts in which capital contributions are deposited – *deposit account* (**Bank Account Pledge**).

In addition to this collateral, it is essential for the lenders to obtain from the fund an irrevocable power of attorney that allows them to call and receive the undrawn investors' commitments in the event of a default under the subscription facility (**Power of Attorney**). The Power of Attorney must comply with the requirements of Spanish law, such as the requirement that a duly empowered representative of the fund must grant them in a public deed (*escritura pública*) before a Spanish Notary Public.

NAV and secondary fund facility transactions

Although most of the transactions closed in the Spanish market have been subscription line (capital call) facilities, Spanish private equity companies have also participated in certain NAV and secondary fund facility transactions. These types of transactions provide either for financing of the acquisition of assets on the secondary market or financing of the investment vehicles' current portfolios.

The borrowing base for NAV and secondary fund facilities comprises the reported NAV of the investment vehicles' portfolio, and requires significant due diligence by the lenders on the assets to be financed and the permitted indebtedness of the investment vehicles, considering the structural subordination that may be put in place for the NAV facilities.

Collateral for NAV and secondary fund facilities is based on Spanish law pledges over: (i) share or quotas held by the investment vehicle in the leveraged vehicle or asset; and (ii) proceeds attributable to leverage excess and the credit rights from the bank account to which proceeds will be paid.

In case the investment period of the fund has terminated and no further recourse to the investors of the fund is available, these NAV structures may turn into holdco financings.

Practical issues affecting the collateral – notifying the investors under the UCC Pledge

The investor's notification of the UCC Pledge is one of the hot topics in subscription financing transactions not only due to perfection requirements of the pledge over capital call, but also for reputational risk resulting from this notification.

In addition, as further developed below, due to a case involving the Abraaj Group, giving notice of the security to investors is regarded by lenders as a particularly relevant topic.

(a) *The necessity to notify*: Spanish law does not expressly regulate pledges over credit rights (such as the UCC Pledge). This lack of clear legal regulation has led to debate among legal scholars. The majority of scholars and the case law follow the conservative approach that, in order to create a valid pledge over credit rights, it is necessary to notify the debtor (in the case of the UCC Pledge, the investor who has committed to invest in the fund). For most scholars, serving notice of the creation of the pledge constitutes delivery of possession of the pledged credit rights, which perfects the creation of the pledge. But some scholars[2] do not consider it necessary to notify the debtor, and follow the more commercial approach that notification serves only to enable the investor to discharge the pledge by paying his subscription.

Funds have argued that serving notices on debtors as a perfection requirement of the UCC Pledge is burdensome and uncommercial, triggering a significant reputational risk for the fund manager.

In practice, lenders are reluctant to dispense with notices. Traditionally, notices were sent through the Spanish Notary before whom the UCC Pledge was granted. Sending notices through a Spanish Notary is the safest position for the lenders because, if notices are sent through a Spanish Notary, the risk of the investors claiming that they have not been notified of the creation of the UCC Pledge is, in our opinion, very limited. This is especially relevant further to the *Abraaj* case. Lately, however, the system of serving notices is becoming more creative and in some deals, other options are explored. The most aggressive position would probably be serving notices by mailing systems or web-based notices. Another option would be to include notices in the relevant investor report but, in our view, there is a risk that investors may claim that they were not properly made aware of the creation of the UCC Pledge unless irrefutable evidence of receipt of such notifications may be provided.

(b) *Sensitivity of the notice*: Notices to all the investors of a private equity fund need to be drafted so as not to jeopardise the commercial relationship between the investors and the fund, while meeting the requirements for perfection under the conservative approach; hence the sensitivity of fund managers to the requirement for notices. A standard notice would ideally inform the investor clearly that (i) on a relevant date, the fund has entered into a facility agreement with the lender and that, to secure the obligations of the fund under such financing, a pledge over the commitments of the investor has been granted in favour of the lender, and (ii) as of the date on which the lender (or security agent, if applicable) informs the investor of the occurrence of an event of default according to the financing, the investor must deposit its commitment into the bank account indicated by the lender (or security agent, if applicable) when such commitment is called. Language of this notice should be carefully chosen so that the commercial relationship with the investor is not damaged, while at the same time drafted in a way that would limit the risk of the investor claiming that it was not made aware of the existence of the financing and the pledge over its commitments.

(c) *Transfer of interests*: Investment vehicles often permit the transfer of units or the shares, as the case may be, by their investors, in certain circumstances and subject to certain conditions. Fund financing should not limit this right to transfer. However, the collateral must be drafted in such a way that any future acquirer is notified of the pledge. Otherwise, a good faith payment to an account of the fund that is not pledged would defeat the UCC Pledge. In order to facilitate this: (i) the notification should contain a statement that the existing investor must notify any transferee investor of the existence of the pledge; and (ii) the pledge should allow the lender to update the list of investors and to carry out the steps necessary in order to maintain the pledge (including serving notice on investors acquiring shares or units from existing investors).

(d) *New closings*: Investment vehicles in Spain, as elsewhere in the global private markets, are characterised by sequential closings, such that new investors acquire shares or units at different stages. The security package in a fund financing must include an obligation on the fund manager to update the pledge in order to capture all prospective commitments. This will entail new notices to incoming investors.

Specific documentation issues

Defaulting investor

By and large, limited partnership agreements for Spanish funds contain the same provisions as one would expect to see in limited partnership agreements in more familiar jurisdictions and, in particular, shortfall provisions and remedies in the event of a default by an investor in funding its commitment. Usually, limited partnership agreements first impose a penalty on a defaulting investor, to be paid with its commitment within a period of time (15 days to a month). Then, if the defaulting investor does not pay the penalty and its commitment within that period, the fund manager may sell the units or the shares of the defaulting investor to a third party, or the investment vehicle may acquire the units or shares of the defaulting investor and then redeem them.

Defaulting investors do have an impact on the UCC Pledge. Although the investment vehicle still holds the pledged credit right, in practice, if an investor defaults, the UCC Pledge is weakened because the credit right is unlikely to be paid. In addition, the lender does not have a direct action against the defaulting investor; only the investment vehicle has an action. Given that the fund usually sells or redeems the units or shares, the credit right against the defaulting investor ceases to exist.

If the fund sells the units to a third party (incoming investor), the fund acquires credit rights against the incoming investor over its unfunded capital commitments. The original UCC Pledge can capture these substitute credit rights if the incoming investor is notified of the UCC Pledge. Hence, if the incoming investor is creditworthy, the lenders should not be affected by the sale of the units or shares of the defaulting investor to the incoming investor.

If the fund redeems the units or shares of the defaulting investor, the pledged credit rights diminish. Even though the fund still holds credit rights against the defaulting investor for the non-payment penalty, and even though the UCC Pledge subsists over these credit rights, the amount of the penalty is lower than the amount of the promised investment (and it may be difficult to recover).

Side agreements and non-disclosure agreements

In most jurisdictions, investors may enter into separate agreements with the fund that alter the terms of their subscription agreements to provide, among other things, that they retain sovereign immunity, waive violations of investment policies, or alter their rights to transfer. These side agreements may operate to reduce facility limits.

The existence of such side agreements or letters is also common in funds incorporated in Spain. In that regard, special attention should be taken with respect to non-disclosure agreements that may be entered into by the fund and certain investors (**Anonymous Investors**). These non-disclosure agreements would typically provide that the fund is refrained from disclosing certain information about the Anonymous Investors, which may even extend to disclosing the identity of the Anonymous Investors to any third party (other than employees of the fund). The fund being unable to disclose the identity of the Anonymous Investors may have an impact on (i) charging the commitments of the Anonymous Investors under the UCC Pledge, and (ii) calling and receiving the undrawn Anonymous Investors' commitments by using the Power of Attorney.

Contrary to other jurisdictions, under Spanish law, there is no floating charge or "catch all" security documents. In order to pledge the commitments of the investors under the UCC Pledge, as a matter of Spanish law, it is necessary to clearly identify the credit rights charged under the pledge. In case the fund (as pledgor under the UCC Pledge) cannot disclose the identity of the Anonymous Investors pursuant to the terms of the relevant non-disclosure agreements, then the commitments of the Anonymous Investors may not be pledged under the UCC Pledge as notification to these Anonymous Investors may not happen as explained in point (a) above. The relevance of the fact that the commitments of the Anonymous Investors are not pledged under the UCC Pledge may, however, be considered limited as the amounts to be contributed by the Anonymous Investors will be deposited into a bank account pledged in favour of the lenders by virtue of the Bank Account Pledge.

The impact of not disclosing the identity of the Anonymous Investors is probably more relevant in the ability of the lenders to call and receive the undrawn investors' commitments by using the Power of Attorney. Even if, from an investor point of view, capital calls made by the lenders using the Power of Attorney would in fact be carried out by the fund (represented by the lenders as its attorney), if the attorney (i.e. the lenders) does not know the identity of the Anonymous Investors, it would not be materially possible to make capital calls against such Anonymous Investors.

According to the above, lenders should carefully consider the existence of non-disclosure agreements and Anonymous Investors when structuring a fund finance transaction.

Key developments

As previously mentioned, in accordance with section 93.d) of the Private Equity Act, a private equity fund manager may charge its assets. These entities do not have legal personality according to Spanish law and therefore could not charge their assets before the enactment of the Private Equity Act. This legal development was essential in the emergence and development of fund finance.

It is also worth noting as regards private equity funds (but not private equity companies) that the possibility of these funds being declared bankrupt according to Spanish law continues to be questionable, due to the fact that they lack legal personality. Section 1 of Act 22/2003, dated 9 July 2003 and as amended, sets forth that the declaration of bankruptcy can be ruled only in respect of persons or legal entities with legal personality.

The *Abraaj* case – what would happen in Spain in a similar set of facts?

As mentioned above, hot topics of discussion in the Spanish market are now finding more sophisticated and less burdensome ways to send notices to the pledged debtors in order to perfect the UCC Pledge, and the impact on it, by redeeming the units or shares of the defaulting investor and achieving a satisfactory regulation in relation to side letters that investors and the fund may have entered into. A view should, however, be taken in relation to these hot topics in light of the *Abraaj* case.

It is not our intention in this chapter to analyse the specifics of the *Abraaj* case as much has been written in that regard, especially taking into consideration that there is no Spanish element in that case. However, to the best of our knowledge, the *Abraaj* case is the only precedent of a fund finance going into default; we therefore think it may be useful to analyse what would happen in Spain, in our opinion, further to a set of facts similar to the *Abraaj* case.

Lessons to be learnt from the *Abraaj* case include that (i) notices to the investors of the creation of the pledge of commitments should be given sooner, (ii) provisions should be included in the facility agreements to prevent the fund from amending or releasing investors of their obligations without the prior consent of the lenders, and (iii) events of default related to litigation between the fund and its investors should also be included.

Assuming that a Spanish law-incorporated fund enters into a facility agreement with a lender, grants a UCC Pledge and, on that same date, sends a notice to its investors through a Spanish Notary informing them that (i) the fund has entered into a facility agreement and a UCC Pledge, and (ii) the lender has informed the investor of the occurrence of an event of default, the investor must deposit its commitment into the bank account indicated by the lender.

Based on the assumptions above, at a later stage, the fund may send a notice to its investors releasing them from their commitments or, alternatively, the lender may send a notice to the investors informing them of the occurrence of an event of default and instructing them to deposit their commitment into a certain bank account. Furthermore, would investors be released from their commitments or, on the contrary, would they be bound to follow the lender instructions?

To the best of our knowledge, there is no case law nor scholar opinion in respect of an equivalent set of facts. In our opinion, even if the obligation of the investor to attend capital calls arising from the subscription agreement is an obligation of the investor *vis-à-vis* the fund (and not *vis-à-vis* the lender), once the investor is informed and has acknowledged the existence of the financing and the UCC Pledge, it would be very difficult for an investor to pretend not to attend instructions from the lender; first, because some scholars[3] consider that, once a notice is served to the debtor, the lender has the benefit that the pledgor cannot enter agreements with the debtor for the purposes of releasing the pledged debt; and second, because a debtor who pays the assignor, before being aware of a debt assignment, is released from any responsibility according to article 1527 of the Spanish Civil Code. In our view, the rationale behind article 1527 is to protect debtors who have paid in good faith (*buena fe*). In the case at hand, the debtor (i.e. the investor) would indeed be aware of the assignment (i.e. the UCC Pledge) and could not pretend to be a good faith debtor if it claims to be released from its responsibilities *vis-à-vis* the lender. Lastly, even if ruled for different sets of fact, there is certain Spanish case law[4] that maintains that payments from the debtor after being notified of a debt assignment should be considered as carried out at the debtor's own risk (even if it acts in good faith).

In any event, in order to prevent the above from happening, it would be very advisable to (i) send notice of the creation of the UCC Pledge to the investor promptly (in order to mitigate the risk of the fund releasing the investor of its commitments before it is aware of the existence of the pledge), clearly (in order to avoid the investor claiming that it did not understand that its commitment was pledged) and in a proper manner (ideally through a Spanish Notary) in order to avoid the investor claiming that it did not receive the relevant notice, and (ii) include a provision in the facility agreements preventing the fund from releasing investors from their obligations without the prior consent of the lender.

* * *

Endnotes

1. Information provided by *Asociación Española de Capital, Crecimiento e Inversión* (the Spanish Private Equity and Venture Capital Association – **ASCRI**), 2022 Report for Venture & Private Equity in Spain.
2. Angel Carrasco Perera: *Tratado de los derechos de garantía*, page 252.
3. Angel Carrasco Perera: *Tratado de los derechos de garantía*, page 253.
4. STS 28 November 2013, SAP Castellón, section 3, 24 May 2012 and SAP Valencia, section 10, 30 May 2012.

Jabier Badiola Bergara
Tel: +34 91 43 23 225 / Email: jabier.badiola@dentons.com
Jabier Badiola is a partner in the banking and finance department of Dentons' Madrid office and managing partner of Dentons Spain. He was included in *Iberian Lawyer*'s "40 Under Forty" Awards 2017 and is highly ranked by *Chambers*, *The Legal 500* and *Best Lawyers*.

Jabier has more than 20 years' experience as a finance lawyer. He specialises in cross-border syndicated financing transactions with a particular focus on general lending (acquisition finance, LBOs, MBO, BIMBO, etc.), asset finance, project finance, structured finance, corporate finance and restructuring, acting for large credit institutions, corporates, investment funds and sponsors.

Dentons Europe Abogados, S.L. (Sociedad Unipersonal)

Paseo de la Castellana, 53, 8th floor, 28046 Madrid, Spain
Tel: +34 91 43 63 325 / URL: www.dentons.com

USA

Jan Sysel, Flora Go & Duncan McKay
Fried, Frank, Harris, Shriver & Jacobson LLP

2022 in a nutshell

Keeping the tradition going, it is only right to start off this year's chapter as we have done in the past by observing the activity in the stock market. In 2021, DJIA figures on the first day of trading closed at 30,223.89 points, and throughout the year, dropped to a low of 29,982.62 points (on January 29, 2021), and reached a high of 36,488.63 points (on December 29, 2021). In 2022, DJIA figures on the first day of trading closed at 36,585.06 points, and throughout the year, dropped to a low of 28,725.51 points (on September 30, 2022), and reached a high of 36,799.65 points (on January 4, 2022). Over recent years, the DJIA steadily increased with 22.34% growth in 2019, 7.25% in 2020 (which of course was driven by the initial COVID-19 outbreak), and 18.73% in 2021. However, 2022 brought a different result with stock market value dropping 7.88% (as of December 9, 2022).

A number of industry and global events impacted the broader finance and capital markets in 2022. For example, the cryptocurrency market experienced widespread turmoil in recent months, leading the world's most popular cryptocurrency, Bitcoin, to lose more than 60% of its value, with other notable cryptocurrencies like Terra and Celsius failing outright, ultimately culminating the infamous chapter 11 bankruptcy filing by the industry's second-largest cryptocurrency exchange, FTX, which lost approximately $32 billion in value in a matter of one week.

Global inflation also weighed heavily on financial markets. According to the U.S. Bureau of Labor Statistics, which uses the consumer price index to calculate inflation based on cost of goods, inflation peaked at 9.1% in June 2022 and currently sits at 7.7% in November. Rising crude oil prices (a major economic input) played a significant role, which hiked to their highest point in over a decade as the United States and its allies imposed sanctions on Russia and subsequently banned imports of Russian oil. Another main driver of inflation is the price of energy, including gasoline, diesel fuel, heating oil, natural gas, electricity and coal, which all have increased in cost as the demand for energy rebounded from the COVID-19 pandemic at a pace faster than what the economy was ready to handle. While prices have decreased somewhat from their summer peak, according to the U.S. Energy Information Administration, the national average for gasoline is $3.80 per gallon (as of November 2022), the highest it has been in eight years.

The rise of inflation has also forced the Federal Reserve to grapple with raising interest rates, which rose from 0.25% to 4.5% over the course of the year and are at their highest level in 15 years. Of course, higher interest rates and increased borrowing costs are highly relevant to the financial and fund finance markets, and heavily influence the willingness and appetite to borrow. These conditions may stoke fear of an economic downturn and in turn push down the prices of stocks and other investments further, creating a cycle of negative events triggering each other. While not necessarily unexpected after the recent years of extremely low interest rates, the change in environment was still rather abrupt.

State of the market

Private capital fundraising took a turn in 2022 along with the broader market, as only 1,250 private equity funds closed (as of Q3 2022), compared to the 2,250 in 2021, according to Preqin. Fundraising is becoming increasingly challenging for funds due to fears of recession, inflation, monetary tightening and geopolitical concerns, which all adversely impact investor confidence. Although fundraising is proving more challenging (it is down by over 50.5% in value and by 57.8% by number of funds compared to the same period last year), the 2022 total fundraising as of September still represents the second-highest recorded, surpassing previous January to September records set in 2017 and 2019.

While the beginning of the year may have looked promising, the numbers gradually started reflecting a different story. Deal counts went from 6,404 in 2021 to 3,880 in 2022 (as of September 30, 2022). Q3 deal counts for U.S. venture capital-backed companies were at $43 billion compared to $90 billion in Q3 of 2021. Q3 deal activity from non-traditional investors is still higher than for any quarter before 2021, at $145.1 billion, which includes private equity investors, mutual funds, sovereign wealth funds, hedge funds, corporations and family offices. On the bright side, as of November 2022, there remain historic levels of private equity "dry powder" (committed but unallocated capital a firm has on hand) estimated at $1.92 trillion.

So far this year, only 100 first-time funds successfully launched, compared to 307 last year. In terms of allocation between asset managers, however, already established firms with sizeable fund offerings are continuing to grow. According to Pitchbook, funds sized $1 billion or larger have received three-fifths of the capital so far in 2022, up from 34% in 2021. As limited partners navigate these uncertain waters, their investments seem to be guided by risk-averse motivations.

Leveraged loans, according to Oaktree Capital, recorded a 3.3% loss in the first nine months of 2022. When compared to U.S. investment-grade and high-yield bonds (which suffered losses of 18.1% and 14.2%), however, that figure appears less damaging. According to Debtwire Par, in the broader leveraged lending market, banks and investors are beginning to chip away at the loose, borrower-friendly terms that characterised loan documents in recent years. Analysis by Covenant Review scored loan covenants a 3.39 in May 2022, on a scale with 1 representing highly protective covenant loans and 5 representing less-protective loans. This 3.39 score constitutes the most protective score since August 2020, with a score of 3.93 in March and 4.14 in February.

Lenders are also beginning to push on pricing as a way to mitigate risk. According to Debtwire Par, average margins on first-lien institutional term loans reached 4.31% in Q2 2022, far ahead of the Q1 3.96% average. As interest rates continue climbing, it is likely that higher pricing and stricter terms will become a regular part of credit agreements moving forward.

Market developments: Bank regulatory capital requirements

Over the course of the past several years, there have been mounting liquidity constraints on large systematically important U.S. banks that, in 2022, finally resulted in a material and market-wide pull-back by such institutions in the growth of their corporate loan books, which was and continues to be felt across the fund finance market. This pull-back manifested in such institutions' diminished ability to entertain new mandates, renew existing mandates, and to deploy capital at the historical levels that provided the fuel for the proliferation of subscription financing and other fund finance-related transactions in prior years.

Whilst the reasons for such liquidity constraints are multi-faceted, there are several regulatory and market drivers of primary concern, most notably stemming from the implementation by U.S. regulators of Basel III requirements concerning regulatory capital, and recent turmoil in the financial markets. Whilst a detailed discussion of the regulatory capital treatment of loans made to asset managers under subscription credit facilities is beyond the scope of this chapter, as has been noted at length by both bankers and law firms alike, the historical credit quality of such loans has been high, with no reported credit-originated losses to date.

It is thus unfortunate that U.S. regulators have determined to treat, from a regulatory capital perspective, loans of such high credit quality the same as much riskier corporate loans, and therefore require these institutions to hold significantly more regulatory capital than what might otherwise have been required if those institutions were permitted to assign an internal credit quality rating to such loans that conformed to the actual historical loss histories of such loans. Additionally, U.S. regulators are implementing heightened capital charges by way of capital buffers and surcharges for global systemically important banks, which will further constrain liquidity as such institutions are required to hold even more regulatory capital. Furthermore, the above regulatory capital constraints have not been experienced to the same degree by banks other than large systematically important U.S. banks who are subject to a divergent regulatory capital treatment by U.S. regulators.

Dislocation in the financial markets has also contributed to the liquidity constraints that have been experienced in 2022 and have imposed upon U.S. banks further regulatory capital pressures. For example, in the rising interest rate environment, such institutions have been required to mark-to-market the value of fixed income, which has dropped substantially (given the inverse relationship between bond prices and interest rates), and has in turn required U.S. banks to realise billions of dollars in paper losses.

Despite the regulatory and market pressures described above, indications are that fund finance facilities will continue to be utilised in 2023. Large traditional banks may become more selective as they reassess how best to allocate capital and offset their regulatory constraints, but are still expected to be major players in the market albeit at a decreasing rate.

Additionally, developments of the proposed Basel IV regulations may enhance some of the above-discussed constraints (such as limiting the use of internal risk assessment modelling, and introducing new buffers/surcharges for global systemically important banks), while others may be alleviated (such as adjusting standardised reporting to provide more favourable regulatory treatment for higher-quality bank assets). The exact implications of these Basel IV changes on the fund finance market and banking practices generally, however, remain to be seen.

Lastly, many small and medium-sized alternative credit providers have emerged in the space that are not subject to or are less affected by the regulatory and market pressures discussed. In the event that traditional credit providers try to limit exposure, these alternative financing sources should still remain available to meet the debt needs of sponsors, and we have started to see this occurring in 2022.

Market developments: Rated Note Feeder transactions

A theme in U.S. sponsor-side fund finance that continues to gain steady traction has been the uptick in utilisation by asset managers of transactions that are a clear departure from intermediated bank finance deals. Namely, asset managers are increasingly willing to explore, and where they can, utilise, bespoke structured and capital markets solutions as a tool for fundraising and/or monetising existing pools of assets *in lieu* of a sale, securitisation or bank financing of such assets.

Whilst there continues to be a steady uptick in asset managers utilising so-called "Rated Note Feeders" as part of a broader fundraising strategy, we observed a clear trend towards the adaptation of structured finance technology, similar to a collateralised loan obligation ("CLO"), with such transactions becoming increasingly specialised and tailored to both the objectives of the fund and its structure and of the end-investors.

At its most basic, Rated Note Feeder structures have been utilised over a number of years by asset managers primarily as a fundraising tool targeted towards insurance company investors who achieve favourable regulatory capital treatment when holding funded capital commitments in the form of loans. The terms of such debt, which are incurred by a special purpose feeder fund that in turn holds a limited partnership interest in an applicable investment fund, generally mimic the terms of the underlying fund and, to a large extent, are designed to operate as a pass-through of the equity commitment terms to the end-investors.

The terms of such debt are typically documented under an indenture and/or a note purchase agreement, and drawdowns on the notes are usually required to be made *pro rata* with equity capital called from limited partners. Rated Note Feeder issuances are commonly structured with both a senior tranche and a junior tranche (usually legal form debt and equity for U.S. tax purposes) to provide a sufficient level of subordination to support the investment-grade rating required by insurance company investors for the senior notes.

In the more "typical" structure, each investor holds its *pro rata* portion of both senior notes and junior notes, i.e., in "strips", and, depending on rating agency and regulatory considerations, have been issued together as a single "stapled" investment.

The evolution of Rated Note Feeder structures referenced above has been most pronounced within the last year, with the employment of multiple tranches of senior, mezzanine and junior debt.

In these "evolved" structures, each tranche of debt possesses differing economics, payment subordination, and, consequently, differing credit ratings. The debt can be structured and issued in the form of "loans" under a credit agreement and/or "notes" under a purchase agreement and/or indenture, depending on jurisdictional particulars of the holders, some of whom may prefer to hold "loans". Similar to the earlier forms of Rated Notes, the senior tranche of notes is paid a fixed or floating coupon, which is a payment in kind to the extent that distributions from the underlying fund are not available to be swept periodically to pay cash interest.

Furthermore, we have seen tranches of debt being marketed to and held by different pools of investors, i.e., such notes are not "stapled" and may be assigned freely on a tranche-by-tranche basis. Commonly, these structures (and the rating(s) of the debt) are supported by a liquidity facility provided by one or multiple of the investors.

Another salient feature of these transactions is that the manager of the Rated Feeder has the ability to direct the drawdown of commitments from different tranches of note on a *non-pro rata* basis as between the tranches. To that end, the fund manager can choose to draw down the cheaper tranche in full before borrowing the more expensive junior tranche(s).

Moreover, we have seen transactions where the asset manager and its affiliates are the holders of the junior notes, thus enabling the asset managers to effectively finance its junior note commitment with the senior note proceeds, whilst partaking in the equity returns of the underlying investment fund.

Finally, it is important to note that the National Association of Insurance Commissioners, who coordinate regulatory oversight of the insurance industry, are currently reviewing these structures in light of the increased attention and focus by market participants.

Market developments: The LIBOR endgame is here

Where in the world is LIBOR?

On November 30, 2020, the Board of Governors of the Federal Reserve System, the Office of the Comptroller of the Currency, and the Federal Deposit Insurance Corporation issued a joint statement providing that by December 31, 2021, banks should cease originating new loans that use USD LIBOR. On March 5, 2021, the ICE Benchmark Administration issued a statement confirming its intention to cease the publication of one-week and two-month USD LIBOR after December 31, 2021 and of all other USD LIBOR tenors after June 30, 2023. On the same date, the Financial Conduct Authority announced that as of such dates, LIBOR would either cease to be provided or no longer be representative.

In its March 2021 progress report, the Alternative Reference Rates Committee ("ARRC") wrote that these announcements effectively lay out an "endgame" for USD LIBOR. The cessation dates for LIBOR have now become clear, and the fallback provisions in most existing LIBOR loans will require transition on or before June 30, 2023 (if they do not mature prior to that point). In addition, on July 29, 2021, the ARRC formally recommended CME Group's forward-looking Secured Overnight Financing Rate ("SOFR") term rates ("Term SOFR"). By the end of last year, market participants had generally accepted the "hardwired" fallback provision, and this announcement cemented the Term SOFR as the successor rate for credit agreements using that approach.

Market acceptance and uniformity

By the third quarter of last year, the majority of new loans that we saw in the fund finance space had been negotiated and priced at USD LIBOR. However, by the fourth quarter, banks generally ceased originating new loans that use USD LIBOR. Most of the loans that we saw in the fourth quarter and in the early part of 2022 were priced at Term SOFR, and a significant portion of the loans that we see today provide for both Term SOFR and Daily Simple SOFR.

Spread adjustment

The fallback provisions have historically contemplated a spread adjustment once the transition from USD LIBOR has taken place. This is because, historically, USD LIBOR has been higher than SOFR. LIBOR represents the cost of unsecured funding in a specified currency and specified term in the London interbank market. Since the mid-1980s, a panel of banks submitted to the administrator the rate at which they could borrow funds by asking for, and then accepting, interbank offers in a reasonable market size. Therefore, LIBOR theoretically reflected some measure of bank credit risk and faced concerns (and subsequently criticism) that, because of a relatively small number of underlying transactions, the metric could be subjective or even susceptible to manipulation. SOFR, on the other hand, is a rate derived from the overnight repurchase agreement ("repo") market for Treasury securities. Therefore, SOFR is fully transaction-based and based on a deep market (i.e., the repo market for Treasury securities) underpinned by nearly $800 billion of daily transactions. Importantly, given that repos are effectively fully secured transactions backed by the highest quality collateral, SOFR is considered a nearly risk-free rate. The spread adjustment is intended to counter the inherent difference between the two rates in order to minimise the economic impact of switching from one rate to the other.

The ARRC recommended that "hardwired" fallback provisions also provide a fixed spread adjustment, which is calculated based on the five-year historical median difference between USD LIBOR and SOFR. The March 5, 2021 announcement by the ICE Benchmark Administration fixes the date on which the five-year lookback period ends, and accordingly specifies the recommended spread adjustments for credit agreements using the "hardwired" fallback provisions. Those spread adjustments are (i) 11.448 bps for one-month USD LIBOR, (ii) 26.161 bps for three-month USD LIBOR, and (iii) 42.826 bps for six-month USD LIBOR.

In the last few years with near-zero interest rates, we saw the difference between USD LIBOR and SOFR be much lower than the historical median noted above. This led a number of borrowers to request a lower spread adjustment (for instance, (i) 10 bps for one-month USD LIBOR, (ii) 15 bps for three-month USD LIBOR, and (iii) 25 bps for six-month USD LIBOR) or no adjustment at all. With recent rising interest rates, however, the difference between USD LIBOR and SOFR has been rising closer to the historical median. Nonetheless, we have seen that the prevailing market trend is for borrowers to request a lower spread adjustment. In addition, a significant portion of the borrowers we see now opt to borrow solely one-month Term SOFR (typically with a spread adjustment of 10 bps or 11.448 bps) or Daily Simple SOFR.

<u>Testing SOFR</u>

In a year otherwise marked with uncertainty and surprise developments, the transition away from LIBOR has been smoother for many than expected. While the transitioning of loan agreements before June 30 of next year remains a daunting task, market participants have a clear successor rate, and in many cases, provisions that have recently passed vetting between the parties. It remains to be seen whether the real-life application of SOFR will pose practical and operational challenges or unexpected market consequences. We expect that the discourse on the transition away from LIBOR will continue even as the market has coalesced around SOFR.

Legal developments: Sanctions

Following Russia's invasion of Ukraine in February 2022, the Office of Foreign Assets Control ("OFAC") as well as sanctions authorities in the United Kingdom, European Union, and elsewhere imposed a number of new sanctions and restrictive measures on Russian individuals and entities. Some of these new sanctions include (i) investment prohibitions and restrictions, (ii) limitations on the use of correspondent and payable-through accounts, and (iii) import bans. Others are traditional "blocking" sanctions, which prohibit U.S. persons from dealing with sanctioned persons and any property in which the sanctioned person has an interest. OFAC's 50 Percent Rule extends this prohibition to property and interests in property or entities that are, directly or indirectly, owned 50% or more in the aggregate by one or more blocked persons.

The sanctioned persons that OFAC has designated in connection with Russia's invasion have included high-profile Russian oligarchs and business leaders that have commercial dealings in the West, including investments in private funds managed by U.S. sponsors. In order to ensure their compliance with all applicable sanctions, funds or their administrators should continuously screen the fund's limited partner base against the sanctions list, especially if the fund has non-U.S. investors. In the event that a limited partner becomes sanctioned, funds are required to block that limited partner's interest consistent with OFAC's requirements for blocked property.

In addition to the above requirements, many U.S. sponsors have run into issues with subscription facilities that contain representations and covenants regarding sanctions compliance and sanctioned investors. When revising or negotiating subscription facilities, funds with non-U.S. limited partners should consider including language permitting the borrower to continue drawing from the facility if a limited partner has been sanctioned as long as the fund has taken all required legal measures to address the sanctioned investor. This language may avoid a lender imposing a draw stop and having to address the issue under time constraints and without leverage, should an investor be designated by OFAC or another sanctions authority.

Legal developments: Anti-money laundering

On September 30, 2022, the U.S. Department of the Treasury's Financial Crimes Enforcement Network ("FinCEN") issued a final rule ("Final Rule") implementing the expanded beneficial ownership disclosure requirements of the Corporate Transparency Act ("CTA"), which was signed into law in 2020. The Final Rule specifies which new and existing entities must report beneficial ownership information to FinCEN, what information must be reported, and when reports are due. The Final Rule will take effect on January 1, 2024, although reporting companies in existence at that time will have an additional year to file any required beneficial ownership information.

Under the Final Rule, "reporting companies" must provide certain beneficial ownership information to FinCEN. Reporting companies include (i) a "domestic reporting company" – i.e., any corporation, a limited liability company, or other entity that is created by the filing of a document with a secretary of state or similar office, and (ii) a "foreign reporting company" – i.e., any foreign-organised corporation, limited liability company, or other entity that is registered to do business in any state or tribal jurisdiction by the filing of a document with a secretary of state or similar office.

This broad definition of reporting company is made narrower through 23 exemptions, many of which are for different types of regulated entities, including banks, credit unions, depositary institutions, investment advisors, and securities brokers and dealers, as well as public companies, governmental authorities, and tax-exempt entities. Sole proprietorships, trusts, and general partnerships that are not created through the filing of a document with a secretary of state or similar office would not generally be treated as reporting companies, even when applying or registering for a business licence when the entity is already in existence.

Importantly, the definition of reporting company also contains an exception for any "large operating company", which is defined as any entity that (i) employs more than 20 employees on a full-time basis in the United States, (ii) has an operating presence at a physical office in the United States, and (iii) had at least $5 million in gross receipts or sales in the previous year. Additionally, pooled investment vehicles such as private investment funds are exempt if operated or advised by an exempt regulated entity.

The Final Rule clarifies that, while subsidiaries of pooled investment vehicles are not themselves exempt, reporting companies that are owned by exempt entities shall report the name of the exempt entity *in lieu* of personal data for any beneficial owner that exists by virtue of the exempt entity's ownership. In a practical sense, this means that reporting companies owned by pooled investment vehicles will not be required to provide personal identifying information for any individuals at the pooled investment vehicle that are considered beneficial owners of the reporting company only by virtue of the vehicle's ownership of the reporting company.

This exemption, however, applies only to beneficial owners who have a direct or indirect ownership in the reporting company by virtue of an exempt entity's ownership of the reporting company; it does not apply to beneficial owners who exercise substantial control of a reporting company through an exempt entity.

Foreign pooled investment vehicles are not exempt and, under the Final Rule, are required to provide for the beneficial ownership information for the sole individual who "has the greatest authority over the strategic management of the entity".

The Final Rule requires that all reporting companies disclose a suite of information on all of its "beneficial owners", which is defined to cover any individual who, directly or indirectly, exercises substantial control over the reporting company, or who owns or controls at least 25% of the ownership interest of the reporting company.

The Final Rule broadly defines substantial control, so as to include senior officers, those who can appoint or remove senior officers of a majority of the board of directors, and those who can direct, determine, or have substantial influence over the important decisions made by the reporting company. Similarly, ownership interest is broadly defined and includes ownership by means of equity, stock, any capital or profit interest, and convertible instruments, as well as warrants and rights to purchase, sell, or subscribe to any of the foregoing.

The information that reporting companies must provide for each of their beneficial owners includes (i) full legal name, (ii) date of birth, (iii) complete current address, (iv) a unique identifying number from a non-expired U.S. or foreign passport, or other non-expired government-issued identity document, and (v) an image of the document from which the unique identifying number was taken.

The new beneficial ownership reporting requirements are the culmination of nearly a year of agency rulemaking and mark a shift in responsibility from financial institutions to a wider range of private companies and the federal government to provide and collect beneficial ownership information.

Many entities that did not previously have any reporting companies will be required to comply with the beneficial ownership reporting regulation beginning in 2024 and it is incumbent upon all entities formed or operating in the United States to understand whether they are covered by the Final Rule and what their reporting obligations under the rule are.

What does 2023 hold?

In February 2022, the Fund Finance Association ("FFA") put together its signature event, the Global Fund Finance Symposium in Miami, where hundreds of market participants gathered in person. In contrast to November of 2021, when the European, Asia-Pacific and Global conferences were merged and transformed into a week-long online event, this was a much welcome opportunity to meet again with industry friends and colleagues. Subsequently, the European Fund Finance Symposium was held in London at the end of June and the Asia-Pacific Symposium changed venues from Hong Kong to Singapore at the beginning of November.

The FFA is already in the advanced stages of planning a live conference next year, and there are some exciting developments ahead for 2023, in particular the expanded format of the European Symposium, which will now consist of three separate events. If we could base economic predictions on indication of interest from sponsors and attendees so far, there would be much to look forward to.

As many have noted, our industry is, if nothing else, and above all, collegial. The relationships and mutual support of people involved have no doubt contributed to the resiliency of this market as it has weathered the pandemic. Even as the global economy faces new headwinds and geopolitical challenges, there are some indicators that support growth in our industry. For example, the demand for subscription financings has continued despite a more limited number of new fund entrants, and current volume of previously extended facilities that are outstanding remains robust. Smaller banks and alternative capital providers have stepped in to supplement a more cautious approach by large financial institution providers in many instances. We are cautiously optimistic that 2023 will again see the industry on an upward trajectory.

* * *

Acknowledgments

The authors would like to thank Joseph Vitale (joseph.vitale@friedfrank.com), Michael Gershberg (michael.gershberg@friedfrank.com) and Gregory Bernstein (gregory.bernstein@friedfrank.com) for their contribution to this chapter.

Mark Maciuch – Associate, Finance
Email: mark.maciuch@friedfrank.com

The authors would particularly like to acknowledge the assistance and input provided by Mark Maciuch in preparing this chapter. Mark is a corporate finance associate in Fried Frank's New York office and represents clients on a wide array of corporate matters including fund financings.

Jaklin Guyumjyan – Associate, Finance
Email: jaklin.guyumjyan@friedfrank.com

The authors would particularly like to acknowledge the assistance and input provided by Jaklin Guyumjyan in preparing this chapter. Jaklin is a corporate finance associate in Fried Frank's New York office and represents clients on a wide array of corporate matters including fund financings.

Jan Sysel
Tel: +1 212 859 8713 / Email: jan.sysel@friedfrank.com

Jan Sysel represents sponsors, borrowers, arrangers, and lenders across a range of industries on financing transactions, primarily in connection with fund formation. Clients highly regard Jan's extensive experience in structuring, negotiating, documenting, and executing complex financings, including syndicated senior facilities, mezzanine facilities, and private debt placements. Jan's work includes unsecured and secured first and second lien facilities, both cash-flow-based and asset-based, with a particular focus on fund subscription facilities and other types of investment fund leverage. Clients also seek Jan's advice in leveraged acquisitions, spinoffs, recapitalisations, and restructurings.

Flora Go
Tel: +1 212 859 8152 / Email: flora.go@friedfrank.com

Flora Go represents asset managers, sponsors, corporates, lead arrangers, and private funds in complex leveraged financing transactions. The world's leading asset managers seek Flora's representation in financings for their private equity, senior credit, mezzanine credit, real estate, infrastructure, and other investment funds during all parts of the fund life cycle. Clients benefit from Flora's extensive experience in asset-based facilities, subscription-based facilities, and hybrid facilities, and in other types of investment fund leverage.

Duncan McKay
Tel: +1 212 859 8961 / Email: duncan.mckay@friedfrank.com

Duncan McKay is a partner in the Corporate Department and the Finance Practice, resident in New York. Duncan represents financial sponsors in connection with a wide range of complex and bespoke financial transactions related to their private equity, secondaries, real estate, infrastructure, mezzanine debt, and other investment funds. He has extensive experience in investment fund, asset-based, and leveraged financing transactions. Duncan's "fund finance" practice includes work on: NAV facilities; subscription facilities; management company facilities; employee co-invest and general partner facilities; single and multi-asset back-leveraged financings; and GP stake investments. He is also experienced in financings for managed account vehicles and GP-led secondary transactions.

Fried, Frank, Harris, Shriver & Jacobson LLP

One New York Plaza, New York, NY 10004, USA
Tel: +1 212 859 8000 / Fax: +1 212 859 4000 / URL: www.friedfrank.com

NOTES

NOTES

NOTES

NOTES

NOTES

NOTES